MARRIAGE AND THE FAMILY
IN THE DOCUMENTS OF THE MAGISTERIUM

RAMÓN GARCÍA DE HARO

MARRIAGE AND THE FAMILY IN THE DOCUMENTS OF THE MAGISTERIUM

A Course in the Theology of Marriage

Second Edition, revised with the help of
Carla Rossi Espagnet

Translated by
William E. May

IGNATIUS PRESS   SAN FRANCISCO

Title of the Italian Original:
Matrimonio & Famiglia nei Documenti del Magistero
Corso di telogia matrimoniale
© 1989 Edizioni Ares, Milan

Cover by Riz Boncan Marsella

CONTENTS

Foreword *by Monsignor Carlo Caffarra*   11

Preface   13

Translator's Introduction for the English Edition   15

Chapter One
The Christian Understanding of Marriage and the Magisterium   19

    1. The Present Crisis of the Family and the Magisterium   20
       A. *The mission of the Magisterium*   20
       B. *Principal errors of today on the role and*
          value of the Magisterium   24
       C. *The question of dissent*   29

    2. Theology, the Science of Faith, and the Magisterium   34
       A. *Faith and theology*   35
       B. *The scientific method of theology and the Magisterium*   36

    3. The Magisterium—Guardian of the Truth of Salvation   44

    4. The Obedience Due to the Magisterium, According to
      the Degree of the Obligation Owed to Its Proper Authority,
      in Its Different Teachings   48

    5. The Question of Intrinsically Evil Acts and of Moral Absolutes   54

Chapter Two
The Magisterium on Marriage and Family: An Overview   63

    1. Fifteen Centuries of the Church:
      The Portrait Drawn at the Council of Trent   64
       A. *The doctrine on marriage at the beginning of the Reformation*   64
       B. *Criticisms of the Reformers*   66
       C. *The decrees and canons of Trent on marriage*   69
       D. *The implementation of the Council: open questions*   77

2. New Problems Posed by the "Laicization" of the State
   in Christian Nations: The Magisterium of the Popes
   from Benedict XIV to Pius XI   79
   - A. *The theory of the regalists and the de-Christianization
     of thought during the 17th to 18th centuries*   79
   - B. *The Magisterium and the reaffirmation of
     the divine regimen of marriage*   87
   - C. *The Encyclical* Arcanum divinae sapientiae *of Leo XIII*   93
   - D. *Marriage in the* Code of Canon Law *(1917 Code)*   95

3. The Crisis of Christian Society in the 20th Century
   and the Magisterium of Popes Pius XI and Pius XII   97

4. Vatican Council II and the Renewal of the Church   99

5. The Magisterium of the Pontificates after Vatican Council II   101

Chapter Three
Analysis of the Encyclical *Casti Connubii*   107

1. Its Historical Genesis   107

2. The Contents of the Encyclical   110
   - A. *The principles: the divine institution and sanctity
     of marriage; the necessity of human cooperation
     with the divine plan*   110
   - B. *The goods of marriage: children, fidelity, the sacrament*   118
   - C. *Errors against Catholic doctrine and vices
     that despoil marriage*   129
   - D. *The remedies: the return to
     the divine plan for marriage*   139

3. The Enduring Significance of the Principal Teachings
   of *Casti Connubii*   142

Chapter Four
The Magisterium of Pius XII   147

1. A Summing up of His Pontificate and the Principal Arguments
   of his Magisterium Relating to the Family   147

2. Addresses to New Spouses   149

3. Documents Concerning Themes of Conjugal Morality   152
   - A. *A crucial question: the relationship between
     conjugal love and procreation*   157

    B. *Sex education* — 179
    C. *Other questions of conjugal morality* — 181

4. Teachings on the Role and Rights of the Family in Society — 184

5. The Encyclical *Sacra Virginitas* and Other Teachings — 190

Chapter Five
**The Position of the Magisterium at
the Opening of Vatican Council II** — 195

  1. Continuity of Vatican II with the Previous Magisterium — 195

  2. Firmly Established Points in the Teaching of the Church — 198
    A. *On the nature, goods, and ends of marriage* — 199
    B. *On conjugal morality* — 201
    C. *On the relationship between the family and society* — 205
    D. *On the powers of the Church and
       State in marriage matters* — 206

  3. The Task Assigned to the Council: To Integrate
    Doctrine More Profoundly into Life — 207

Chapter Six
Marriage and Family in Vatican Council II — 211

  1. The Historical Background to *Gaudium et spes* — 211

  2. The Major Lines of the Conciliar Teaching on Marriage — 215
    A. *Marriage as a vocation to holiness* — 215
    B. *The role of conjugal love in the structure of marriage* — 234
    C. *The unbreakable connection between love and procreation* — 256

  3. Systematic Commentary on the Chapter of *Gaudium et Spes*
    Devoted to Marriage and the Family — 262
    A. *The situation of marriage and family
       in the contemporary world* — 262
    B. *The concept and nature of marriage:
       the holiness of marriage and the family* — 264
    C. *Conjugal morality: duties toward the other spouse
       (the development of love) and toward their children* — 269
    D. *The defense and promotion of the family* — 277

  4. Other Teachings of the Council on Marriage and the Family — 278

Chapter Seven
The Teachings of Paul VI on Marriage and Family   283

   1.   A General Overview of His Pontificate   283

   2.   The Encyclical *Humanae Vitae*   286
       A. *Some aspects of the mentality and public opinion*
          at the time of the promulgation of Humanae vitae   286
       B. *A summary of the contents of the encyclical*   291
       C. *The importance and significance of* Humanae vitae   300
       D. *The obligatoriness in conscience of number* 14
          of Humanae vitae   302

   3.   Other Teachings on Marriage and Family   315
       A. *The Declaration* Persona humana *on sexual ethics*   315
       B. *Other teachings on conjugal morality*   322
       C. *Teachings on marriage cases and on*
          the indissolubility of marriage   326
       D. *Mixed marriages*   328

Chapter Eight
**The Magisterium of John Paul II on the Family and
the Apostolic Exhortation *Familiaris Consortio***   333

   1.   The Occasion, Importance, and General Scheme of
       Familiaris Consortio   334

   2.   A Detailed Commentary on the Content of
       Familiaris Consortio   335
       A. *First part: bright spots and shadows for the family today*   335
       B. *Second part: the plan of God for marriage and the family*   341
       C. *Third part: the role of the Christian family*   350
       D. *Fourth part: pastoral care of the family*   375

   3.   Other Teachings of John Paul II on Marriage and Family   381
       A. *Characteristics of and major occasions for these teachings*   382
       B. *Some contents of particular significance*   388

Chapter Nine
**The Postconciliar Episcopal Teaching on Marriage:
General Lines of Thought**   409

   1.   The Unique Characteristics, Modality, and Scope
       of the Obligatory Nature of the Episcopal Magisterium   409

2. Declarations Emerging from the Conferences of Bishops
on the Occasion of *Humanae Vitae*   413
    A.   *A global overview*   414
    B.   *The problem of the faithful who are reluctant*   418

Index   425

FOREWORD

The present volume of Professor Ramón García de Haro marks the first in a collection that will be published by the Pontifical Institute of John Paul II for Studies on Marriage and Family: the publication of the principal courses developed in it. It is happy coincidence that the collection begins with the synthetic presentation of the doctrine of the Magisterium on marriage and family. It is only by always rooting itself more deeply in the Faith of the Church that the theology of marriage and of the family can become a way of building up the Church (in the Pauline sense of that term).

The decision to publish the principal courses is not only motivated by the need, common to every academic institution, to help the students of the institute in their academic work. We also wish to offer them to a wider circle in order to provoke reflection, primarily on the part of married people and those who prepare couples for marriage.

St. Thomas affirms that interpersonal love is born from the contemplation of the spiritual beauty of the person. Thus, on the level of the spirit, that phenomenon of the refraction of light, described in physics, comes to life: the ray of created spiritual beauty reflects in a limited, but real (albeit analogously!) way the Uncreated Beauty that shines forth in the love of Christ. Man and woman live in their conjugal love an experience of a love that dwells in them and transcends them: they reflect the Uncreated Love because their love is rooted in the self-giving of Christ.

The collection now beginning hopes to be a modest contribution for helping spouses live this wonderful and mysterious reflection.

Monsignor Carlo Caffarra, President
Pontifical Institute of John Paul II for
Studies on Marriage and Family
Rome, May 30, 1989

PREFACE

This course began at the John Paul Institute in Rome in 1981: an interdisciplinary institute on marriage and family needs to have a course explicitly devoted to the doctrine of the Magisterium. In 1983, a first draft of material was distributed to the students. This, after successive reworkings, now comes to light in this definitive form.

The term *course* emphasizes its destination for the use of students for the licentiate in theology and for the master's degree in marriage and the family. Without avoiding the necessary depth of analysis of questions, it seeks to be useful for teaching. The desire has been to pursue in this way the academic tradition of developing curricula and institutes of various kinds. Its undeniable usefulness is evident from the practice of many universities both secular and ecclesiastical throughout the world. In conformity with this aim, we have tried to emphasize, even by the typography used, the ideas and principal points in a way we hope will make its study easier. I wish to thank all who have encouraged this initiative.

This is the second Italian edition, which will be at the same time the first English edition and the first Spanish edition (*Matrimonio y Familia en los Documentos del Magisterio. Un Curso de Teologia Matrimonial,* Editiones Internationales Universitarias, Barcelona, 1993). In his "Translator's Introduction", Professor William E. May has noted almost everything concerning the new material found in this second edition, save the fact—which he concealed but which I have a duty to note—that this edition owes much to him: not only the accurate and competent English translation itself but also the correction of some errors in the footnotes that escaped me but were detected by him; above all, this edition is in debt to Professor May for an enrichment of the bibliography with English-language literature and a deepening and clarification of its contents, the fruit of his effort to express the same ideas in another language, and finally the encouragement the English translation gave me to revise the Italian edition and not to rest content with simply reprinting the book. For all this, and for many other reasons not related to the translation, I want to express my heartfelt thanks to Professor May.

I also wish to thank Doctor Carla Rossi Espagnet for her help in preparing the second Italian edition, in particular for gathering together the teachings of Pope John Paul II from 1990 on in the section of chapter 8 devoted to "Other teachings of John Paul II", and, in addition, for adding the references to the *Enchiridion Familiae.*

The Author
Rome, December 25, 1992

TRANSLATOR'S INTRODUCTION

From 1975 through 1990, I taught a graduate course at The Catholic University of America on Christian Marriage and the Family, and currently I annually teach a course on Marriage in the Christian Tradition at the John Paul II Institute for Studies on Marriage and the Family in Washington, D.C. In order to understand properly the Catholic understanding of marriage and family, it is absolutely indispensable to know, as fully as possible and in depth, what the Magisterium of the Church has taught and teaches about these realities.

Of the many books and articles that I have read over the years since 1975 in preparing my courses, Ramón García de Haro's study of marriage and family in the documents of the Magisterium is by far the best available for helping everyone—teachers, students, priests, religious, and ordinary lay people—come to an accurate and profound understanding of and appreciation for the teaching of the Magisterium on marriage and the family. When I first read it upon its publication in Italian in 1989, I resolved to make it available for the English-speaking public. During the summer of 1992, I had the opportunity to devote my energies almost exclusively to its translation. When I sent Don Ramón a copy of the first draft of the translation, he informed me that he and his assistant, Carla Rossi Espagnet, were in the process of preparing the second, revised Italian edition. It was thus possible for me, during the fall of 1992, to incorporate into my translation the new material prepared for the second Italian edition. The new material is found principally in Chapters 1, 2, and 8. In Chapter 1 the issue of theological dissent is taken up in greater depth than in the first edition, and the subject of intrinsically evil acts and absolute moral norms is examined at some length because of its relevance to issues of conjugal morality. In Chapter 2, the thought of the reformers is examined more fully, along with some further details on some medieval positions and on the struggle of the papacy during the 16th and 17th centuries to defend the competence of the Church on marriage questions. In Chapter

8, which is devoted to a study of Pope John Paul II's truly beautiful teaching on marriage and family, the revised edition has been able to integrate themes and ideas developed by Pope John Paul II from 1988, when the first edition was published, through 1992.

In the first Italian edition, the author made use of an Italian collection of the magisterial documents of Pius XI and Pius XII entitled *Insegnamenti pontifici,* vol. 1: *Il matrimonio* (Rome: Ed. Paoline, 1957), referring to documents in this collection by the abbreviation *Ins.* I have retained this reference in the English text. However, in 1992, a six-volume work, entitled *Enchiridion Familiae: Textos del Magisterio Pontificio y Conciliar sobre el Matrimonio y la Familia (Siglos I a XX),* was published jointly by the Instituto de Ciencias para La Familia of the Universidad de Navarra and the Istituto Giovanni Paolo II per Studi su Matrimonio e Famiglia in Rome. This multivolume work, edited by Augusto Sarmiento and Javier Escrivá-Ivars, provides relevant texts on marriage and family found in the papal and conciliar Magisterium from the time of Pope Clement of Rome (97 A.D.) until 1988 (Pope John Paul II). Volume 1 includes material from Clement of Rome up to and including Pius XI; volume 2 from Pius XII and John XXIII; volume 3 from Paul VI, John Paul I, and John Paul II (for the years 1978–1980 of the latter's pontificate). Volumes 4 and 5 are devoted entirely to material from John Paul II, covering the years 1981 to 1982 and 1983 to 1988, respectively. Volume 6 is a masterful index to the previous five volumes. The texts of the Magisterium are given in their original language (Latin, Italian, French, English, etc.) in the bottom half of the page, while a Spanish translation is provided in the first half of the page. I have made use of this masterful source throughout the translation, referring to it in both text and notes so that interested readers can easily find the text of the original documents.

I have used the U.S. Catholic Conference translations for documents from Popes Pius XI and Pius XII where these are available. For Paul VI's *Humanae vitae* I have, except where noted, used the translation of Janet Smith, as found in her *Humanae Vitae: A Generation Later* (Washington, D.C.: The Catholic University of America Press, 1991). For addresses of Paul VI, I have used the U.S. Catholic Conference translations when possible. The translation of *Gaudium et spes* found in the text is my own. I have used the Vatican Polyglot Press English translation of *Familiaris consortio* in the chapter given over to the thought of John Paul II. For the many addresses of John Paul II used in the study, I have made my own translation from the Italian text or else used the English text given in *Enchiridion Familiae* for addresses originally given in English.

The author of this masterful study, Ramón García de Haro, is a Spanish priest of the Prelature of Opus Dei. He has been teaching at the Istituto Giovanni Paolo II per Studi su Matrimonio e Famiglia in Rome since 1981. He writes in both Spanish and Italian. A scholar of first rank, he has authored many articles in theological journals and several outstanding books, among them *Karl Marx: El Capital* (1977), *Cuestiones fundamentales de Teología moral* (with Ignacio Celaya, 1980), *Legge, coscienza e libertá* (1984), *L'agire morale et le virtù* (1988), and, most recently, *La vida cristiana* (1992), his master work, a comprehensive and detailed account of the Christian moral life.

I want to thank Leslie Bridges, secretary of the John Paul II Institute for Studies on Marriage and Family in Washington, D.C., for her courteous and efficient help in printing out various drafts of this translation and the final copy. Without her aid the work would have been much more difficult.

William E. May
Michael J. McGivney Professor
  of Moral Theology
John Paul II Institute for
  Studies on Marriage and Family
Washington, D.C.
November 3, 1992

Chapter One

THE CHRISTIAN UNDERSTANDING
OF MARRIAGE AND THE MAGISTERIUM

In conformity with the divine plan of creation and redemption, man, from the depths of his being, is directed toward the true and the good: toward God—Truth and Goodness, the principle of every good and of every truth there is. Such is man's path. A path to pursue with his own freedom, where difficulties, shadows, and contradictions are not lacking. Perhaps among them the most fundamental is the contrast between man's aspirations for justice, peace, love, generosity, and for the good in all its forms and what man finds, many times, around himself and, even more sadly, within himself.

Like every human reality, marriage and family show this disconcerting character. Indeed, one could say that with them we deal with one of the areas where today the contrast between the desires whereby one disposes oneself (love, joy, fullness) and the sad situations that often result (divorce, abortion, the refusal to hand on life) is most evident and acute. Christ alone, who is the Way, the Truth, and the Life (Jn 14:6), makes man able to overcome this contrast. And Christ and his truth visibly remain in the Church and the Magisterium. Therefore, the service the Magisterium offers ought not to arouse wonder, and it would be absurd to obscure it. Consequently, it seems right to begin our study with a description of the heart of the matter behind the doubts that have arisen concerning conjugal and family morality, in order to occupy ourselves in what follows—briefly, but without foregoing the rigor that ought not to be ignored—with an opportune response. Three ideas seem important for a balanced judgment on the position of "dissent" and for understanding more deeply the mission proper to the Magisterium in helping theology and the whole Christian life: (1) theology is the science of Faith (it pertains to Christian wisdom, which faith alone makes us able to know in a singularly wonderful way); (2) this knowledge has the peculiarity of being the only knowledge that has the full truth about man and, therefore, also about marriage and the family. Therefore, (3) without faithfully adhering to the Magisterium, a true knowledge of the Faith does not endure, nor is the full truth about man possessed: Catholic theology disappears together with the Christian conscience.[1]

1. The Present Crisis of the Family and the Magisterium

Today there is much talk about the crisis of the family. Everywhere solutions are sought, because everyone knows well how important the family is. In practice, there are many aspects and problems involved requiring the collaboration of many forces. But there is, at the root, only one definitive source for a solution: a return to the truth of Christ.

A. *The mission of the Magisterium*

The mission of the Magisterium is to guard and hand on, with divine authority, the truth of salvation brought to us by Christ; the problems facing the family today vividly show the urgency of this mission.

To emphasize the liberating role of truth is a constant feature of the Magisterium of John Paul II: "Don't fear! Therefore, open, open wide the gates to Christ! . . . Christ knows what is within man. Only He knows this. . . . Let Christ speak to man. Only He has the words of life, yes, of life eternal."[2] The mission of the Church is one of service to

---

[1] On this matter, see Servais Pinckaers, *Les sources de la morale chrétienne (Sa méthode, son contenu, son histoire)* (Fribourg: Editions Universitaires Fribourg; Paris: Editions du Cerf, 1985), pp. 59–104; Ramón García de Haro, "Lex Spiritus Sancti, conscienza morale e Magistero", in *Atti del Congresso Internazionale di Pneumatologia, Roma 1982* (Vatican City: Libreria Editrice Vaticana, 1983), pp. 1223–38; García de Haro, *Legge, coscienza e libertà*, 2nd ed. (Milan: Ed. Ares, 1990), pp. 81–140.

[2] John Paul II, Homily at the Solemn Beginning of His Pontificate, October 22, 1978; *Insegnamenti di Giovanni Paolo II*, 1 (Vatican City: Typis Polyglottis Vaticanis, 1979–), pp. 38–39.

the truth, to the Truth that is Christ, the only Truth capable of saving man. Only by serving the truth does she serve man; she continues working as Christ and in Christ:

> Jesus Christ meets the man of every age, including our own, with the same words: "You will know the truth, and the truth will make you free." These words contain a fundamental requirement and a warning: the requirement of an honest regard for the truth as a condition for authentic freedom; and the warning to avoid every kind of illusory freedom, every superficial unilateral freedom, every freedom that fails to enter into the whole truth about man and the world. Today also, even after two thousand years, we see Christ as the One who brings man freedom based on truth, frees man from what curtails, diminishes and, as it were, breaks off this freedom at its root, in man's soul, his heart and his conscience.[3]

The Magisterium not only guards the deposit of faith, but continues the prophetic function of Christ in announcing the Truth.[4] Christ, who is the Truth (Jn 14:16), handed on to the apostles the deposit of revelation not only in order that they might guard it faithfully (1 Tim 6:20), but also that they might proclaim it to all peoples, for all ages (Mt 28:18–20). The apostles were aware of the importance of their mission: "That is why we thank God constantly that in receiving his message from us you took it, not as the word of men, but as it truly is, the word of God at work within you who believe" (1 Th 2:23). They faithfully exercised this mission and, "in order that the full and living Gospel might be always preserved within the Church, left the bishops as their successors, 'handing on to them their own role as teachers'[5]."[6]

The mission proper to the Magisterium, therefore, consists in preserving the deposit of faith and in handing it on in a living way. This is precisely the original meaning of the word "prophecy": not the prediction of future events, but the manifestation of God's word, in his name and with his authority.[7] Our Lord spoke in this way and thus "left

---

[3] John Paul II, encyclical *Redemptor hominis,* March 4, 1979, no. 12.

[4] Cf. Vatican Council II, dogmatic constitution *Dei verbum,* November 18, 1965, nos. 7–10; dogmatic constitution *Lumen gentium,* November 21, 1964, no. 25.

[5] St. Irenaeus, *Adversus Haereses,* III, 3, 1: PG 7.848.

[6] Vatican Council II, *Dei verbum,* no. 7.

[7] Cf. Bruce Vawter, "The Nature of Prophecy", in *The Jerome Biblical Commentary,* 1st ed.

the crowds spellbound at his teaching. The reason was that he taught with authority and not like their scribes" (Mt 7:28–29). The Church could not fulfill this mission without the charism of infallibility, which is the charism of fidelity to the truth:

> The Magisterium of the Church not only implies the handing on of God's word, but also its handing on characterized by a specific duty toward the truth that it contains. And it is here, where the Magisterium coincides with the prophetic mission of the People of God, that its responsibility toward the truth of the word of God becomes evident in a critical way.[8]

■ Like life, faith is preserved among men that it might be handed on from generation to generation: fidelity to the revealed deposit, an ineradicable characteristic of the Church as the "pillar and bulwark of truth" (1 Tim 3:15), cannot be separated from the mission of teaching it by using all the resources of the human mind, in an opportune manner in every age, with absolute faith in the power of the Holy Spirit.[9]

This prophetic mission is today particularly necessary because of the serious ills afflicting the mind of contemporary man. If the mission of the Magisterium has always been that of serving men by authentically interpreting and handing on the word of God, "this mission in the situation of today is particularly grave and urgent, indeed—in some respects—it has never been so grave and urgent", because man finds himself afflicted by the most serious illness that has ever struck his intelligence, the illness of doubt, following the loss of the sense of the transcendent, which leaves man deprived of every orientation.[10]

■ Different perspectives indicate that this condition is the characteristic error of our time. A clear sign of this is the elevation of doubt to the

---

(Englewood Cliffs, N.J.: Prentice-Hall, Inc., 1968), pp. 224ff.; V. Zubizarreta, *Theologia Fundamentalis*, 4th ed. (Bilbao, 1948), p. 142.

[8] Karol Wojtyla, "Bishops as Servants of the Faith", *Irish Theological Quarterly* 43, no. 4 (1976): 267.

[9] Cf. Donald McCarthy, "The Teaching of the Church and Moral Theology", in *Principles of Catholic Moral Life*, ed. William E. May (Chicago: Franciscan Herald Press, 1980), pp. 47–80; Josef Ratzinger, "Le fonti della teologia morale", *Cris Documenti*, no. 4 (Rome, 1985), pp. 13–30, 34–38.

[10] Cf. Carlo Caffarra, "La Chiesa e l'ordine morale", *L'Osservatore Romano*, no. 5, (January 16, 1976): 4. See also Carlos Cardona, "La situazione metafisica dell'uomo", *Divus Thomas* 75 (1972): 30ff.

status of an emblem "of the dignity of intelligence, in such a way that it considers the need of the highest certainties as an interior poverty, the sign of an infantile state, and it ends up by equating the certainty of objective truth with a chain on freedom".[11] The method of doubt—it has also been said—was precisely that adopted by the serpent with our progenitors: "The serpent begins his dialogue with Eve: 'is it true that God told you . . . ?' In like manner, scientistic thought, which was born by putting everything in doubt and arose from the desire for absolute dominion, addresses its questions about man in this way, for the sake of arranging everything for his pleasure."[12] This doubt erodes the difference between good and evil, by considering them equally as moments necessary for human progress, thus inclining people toward indifferentism.

Thus the present importance of the Magisterium:

Because to the bishops is entrusted the task of feeding the flock of Christ, and the *first* pastoral duty is that of announcing the Truth of Christ, by defending it from errors that are the most insidious for the salvation of man. In this respect, the words of St. Irenaeus have incredible significance today: "The apostles, sent to find those who were lost, to enlighten the blind and to heal the sick, certainly did not speak to them in conformity with the opinions of the moment but in conformity with the requirements of the Truth which they announced. . . . " But ignorance, the mother of all these evils, cannot be driven away except by knowledge. Therefore it was knowledge that the Lord gave to His disciples and it is through them that He healed the sick and converted sinners. He did not speak to them by confirming them in their opinions. . . . [13]

Only by firmly keeping the truth that the Magisterium, thanks to the help of the Holy Spirit, enjoys will it be possible to give back to marriage and the family their authentic dignity: this is the first service the Magisterium offers humanity.

[11] Caffarra, "La Chiesa e l'ordine morale", p. 4.

[12] Stanislaw Grygiel, "Reflexiones filosóficas sobre el libro de Juan Pablo II, 'El amor humano en el plan divino' ", paper given at a conference held at the University of Navarra, pp. 3ff. See also on the genesis of this attitude, Carlos Cardona, "R. Descartes: Discurso del metodo", in *Colección Crítica Filosófica,* 2nd ed. (Madrid: Emesa, 1979).

[13] Caffarra, "La Chiesa e l'ordine morale", p. 4, no. 5.

■ This is a service of preaching the truth without fear of becoming a sign of contradiction, as *Humanae vitae* emphasizes: "It is not surprising that the Church finds herself a *'a sign of contradiction'* (Lk 2:34)—just as was [Christ] her Founder. But this is no reason for the Church to abandon the duty entrusted to her of preaching the whole moral law firmly and humbly, both the natural law and the law of the Gospel. Since the Church did not make either of these laws, she cannot change them. She can only be their guardian and interpreter; thus it would never be right for her to declare as morally permissible what is truly not so. For what is immoral is by its very nature always opposed to the true good of Man. By preserving the whole moral law of marriage, the Church knows that she is supporting the growth of a true civilization among Men. . . . The Church shows her sincere and generous love for Men as she strives to help them, even during this earthly pilgrimage 'to share as sons and daughters, the life of the living God, the Father of all Men'."[14,15]

B. *Principal errors of today on the role and value of the Magisterium*

The errors most frequently leveled against the Magisterium today are those concerning its relationship with theology, its competence in moral matters, and its divine authority.

One can say that the present doctrinal crisis appeared in its full virulence and in a very clear way the moment *Humanae vitae* was published.[16] We will, consequently, consider principally the errors

---

[14] Paul VI, encyclical *Populorum progressio*, March 26, 1967, no. 21.

[15] Paul VI, encyclical *Humanae vitae*, July 25, 1968, no. 18. The translation is that of Janet Smith, *Humanae Vitae: A Generation Later* (Washington, D.C.: The Catholic University of America Press, 1991), p. 287.

[16] On the global significance of the "challenge" directed against *Humanae vitae*, see Josef Ratzinger, *The Ratzinger Report* (San Francisco: Ignatius Press, 1985), pp. 83–92; Ermenigeldo Lio, *"Humanae vitae" e coscienza. L'insegnamento di Karol Wojtyla teologo e Papa* (Vatican City: Libreria Editrice Vaticana, 1980); Germain Grisez, *The Way of the Lord Jesus*, vol. 1, *Christian Moral Principles* (Chicago: Franciscan Herald Press, 1983), pp. 871–916. Furthermore, it is good to emphasize how few times a document of the Magisterium has been developed with such care and caution, after consultation with so many different voices: despite everything, the Magisterium has never experienced such serious dissent. Cf. William B. Smith, "The Question of Dissent in Moral Theology", *Persona, Verità e Morale: Atti del Congresso Internazionale di Teologia Morale (Roma, 7–12 aprile 1986)* (Rome: Città Nuova Editrice, 1987), pp. 235–54.

shown in the criticism directed against the Magisterium on that occasion; at their root will be found an obscuring of the faith about the supernatural authority of the Church.

I. For some, *the Magisterium cannot exercise its authority without a substantial consensus of theologians; and in the Church there is a twofold Magisterium: that of the theologians and that of the bishops.* This is an idea that has been sufficiently spread about. In practice, it leads one to behave, with respect to the Magisterium, as if it were a merely human voice, enjoying only the authority proper to a theologian. This kind of mentality explains the strange conduct of those who reject the Magisterium's teachings by appealing to the contrary opinions of some theologian or expert.

■ Thus, for instance, Richard A. McCormick affirms: "It is my judgment that the Holy Father and the college of bishops should not formulate a teaching *against* a broad or even a very significant consensus of theologians."[17] A similar mentality already had been shown during the modernist movement; in fact, the decree *Lamentabili* had condemned the following proposition: "The learning Church (*Ecclesia discens*) and the teaching Church (*Ecclesia docens*) so work together in defining truths, that the only function of the teaching Church is to ratify the generally held opinions of the learning Church."[18] However, today the consequences of this kind of thought are even more serious because of the wide diffusion these ideas receive through the means of social communication and the critical and scientistic mentality to which we have already referred.[19]

Aware of the dangers of a mentality of this kind, *Familiaris consortio* noted that truth does not depend on the consensus of men, but on their fidelity: "Following Christ, the Church seeks the truth, which is not always the same as the majority opinion. She listens to conscience and not to power, and in this way she defends the poor and the downtrodden."[20]

[17] Richard A. McCormick, "Conscience, Theologians, and the Magisterium", *New Catholic World* 220, no. 1320 (December 1977): 271.

[18] H. Denzinger and A. Schoenmetzer, *Enchiridion Symbolorum Definitionum et Declarationum de rebus fidei et morum*, 34th ed. (Barcelona-Rome: Herder, 1967), no. 3406: "In definiendis veritatibus ita collaborant discens et docens Ecclesia, ut docenti Ecclesiae nihil supersit, nisi communes discentis opinationes sancire." Hereinafter this work will be referred to as DS.

[19] Cf. McCarthy, "Teaching of the Church and Moral Theology", pp. 55–56.

[20] John Paul II, apostolic exhortation *Familiaris consortio*, November 22, 1981, no. 5.

In a line of thought more or less similar, others affirm the existence of a *magisterium of theologians,* endowed with "a true authority and competence which are lacking to the Hierarchy as such".[21] Some of the adherents of this view affirm that the Catholic Theological Society of America has "opted for an independent magisterial situation, based on its own authority".[22]

■ There is no doubt that science has its own authority, and that collaboration between theologians and the Magisterium is to be hoped for, as indeed it is today requested by the hierarchy itself.[23] But in theology, as we will see in taking up the scientific method proper to it, that authority is either established and based on that of the Church or it becomes a false science, since, as St. Thomas already noted, "the true teaching of Catholic doctors has its authority from the Church: hence, it is necessary to adhere to the authority of the Church rather than to that of Augustine or Jerome or any other doctor."[24]

2. There are not lacking others for whom *the Magisterium of the Church is infallible in the area of dogma, but not when it is concerned with questions relative to human conduct, and therefore, in the area of morality.* In the field of morality, they affirm, which is subject to the contingencies of history, the teachings of the Magisterium, "although assisted by the Spirit, are nonetheless susceptible to error and therefore fallible."[25] Here we find one of the most widespread arguments against the irreformable and infallible character of the condemnation of contraception, reconfirmed by *Humanae vitae.* On this, they argue that holy Scripture never, or almost never, specifies the moral good or evil of our concrete acts (contraception, premarital relations, masturbation, etc.) and that, if it does so (for instance, Rom 1:26–27, on homosexual

---

[21] McCormick, "Conscience, Theologians, and the Magisterium", p. 271.

[22] Rosemary R. Ruether, in *Christian Century* (August 1977): 682.

[23] Cf. Paul VI, address *Ad Conv. Theologiae Concilii Vaticani II,* October 1, 1966, AAS 58 (1966): 889–96; John Paul II, *Familiaris consortio,* no. 31.

[24] *Summa theologiae,* II–II, q. 10, a. 12. Cf. the suggestive remarks in this matter in the address of Cardinal Ratzinger to more than 250 American bishops in February 1984, at a workshop sponsored by the Pope John XXIII Center. The address, entitled "Moral Theology Today", is found in *Moral Theology Today: Certitudes and Doubts* (St. Louis, Mo.: The Pope John Center, 1984), pp. 3–26. Ratzinger has summed this address up in "Le fonti della teologia morale", pp. 12–18, 34–38.

[25] Timothy E. O'Connell, *Principles for a Catholic Morality,* 1st ed. (New York: Seabury Press, 1978), p. 95.

acts), it only gives historically conditioned norms, valid only for the period in which the Scriptures were written.[26]

■ At the root of this position lies an idea that the last word about man's conduct belongs to the human sciences more than to revelation. Faith cannot be incarnated or handed on in changeable and contingent responses, which are appropriate and suitable only for a determinate period of time—so this idea goes. Faced with an error of this kind, it is worth recalling that the Church has always taught that she has complete competence in matters of *faith and morals,*[27] a competence explicitly reaffirmed in *Humanae vitae:* "When Jesus Christ imparted His divine authority [*potestatis*] to Peter and the other apostles and sent them to all nations to teach His commandments, He established those very men as authentic guardians and interpreters of the whole moral law, that is, not only the law of the Gospel, but also of natural law."[28]

At other times, the competence of the Magisterium in moral matters is acknowledged, but only for teaching general norms, and not specific concrete norms of an absolute character. At the basis of this thesis, one often finds a philosophical error concerning the very possibility of there being moral norms having universal and permanent validity. But the existence of such norms is a revealed truth,[29] and the contrary error is due to a false conception of the relationships between the autonomy of the spirit and the reality of divine norms, between the uniqueness of the person and the universality of moral norms.[30]

3. Finally, not a few theologians *identify in practice the documents of the Magisterium, when they do not define a truth infallibly, with nonbinding opinions which are,* ab initio, *subject to refutation or correction.* To dissent

[26] This, for example, is the argument of Josef Fuchs, "Vocazione e speranza", *Seminarium* 11 (1971): 404ff.; Fuchs, *La Moral y la Teología Moral Postconciliar* (Barcelona: Herder, 1969), pp. 51–52. The distinction between *categorical norms* and *transcendental norms,* worked out by some theologians, seems to have been quite decisive here. On this see Ramón García de Haro and Ignacio de Celaya, *La moral cristiana* (Madrid: Rialp, 1975), pp. 21–27, 80ff.

[27] On this see T. López, " 'Fides et mores' en Trento", *Scripta theologica* 5, no. 1 (1973): 175–221; Jacques Marie Aubert, "Le Magistère Morale de l'Eglise", *La foi et les temps* (July-August 1981): 311–33; Ronald Lawler, "The Magisterium and Catholic Moral Teaching", in *Persona, Verità e Morale,* pp. 217–33.

[28] Paul VI, *Humanae vitae,* no. 4 (Smith trans., pp. 274–75); cf. Grisez, *Christian Moral Principles,* pp. 176ff.; Marcelino Zalba, "Omnis et salutaris veritas et morum disciplina: Sentido de la expresión 'mores' en el Concilio de Trento", *Gregorianum* 54 (1973): 674–715.

[29] Cf. F. Ocáriz, "La nota teologica sull'insegnamento dell'*Humanae vitae* sulla contraccezione", *Anthropotes* 4, no. 1 (1988): 26ff.

[30] Cf. García de Haro, "Magisterio, norma moral y conciencia", *Anthropotes* 4, no. 1 (1988): 46–48.

from them would thus—according to these theologians—be a necessary manifestation of a legitimate pluralism. But they forget what Vatican Council II willed explicitly to note, namely, that when the Church does not desire to bind her infallibility to some document, she at least obliges one to a "religious assent (*religiosum obsequium*) of will and mind".[31] Moreover, we must note that the expression "infallible Magisterium", which is of recent vintage, is reserved for signifying the highest grade of certitude that a teaching can enjoy. Therefore, when there is certitude of this kind for a teaching, it qualifies it in a very positive way. But this does not lead to a devaluing of other teachings, much less does it lead one to make the distinction between infallibly proposed teachings and noninfallibly proposed teachings equivalent to the distinction between *the truth* and *opinion*. The "infallible Magisterium" is not opposed to a *"Magisterium of opinion"*, because every authentic teaching of the Magisterium obliges the faithful at least to a religious submission of mind and will.[32]

Common to all these errors is an obscuring of the way in which Christ promises to his Church his permanent assistance, in the person of the apostles and their successors: "Go, therefore, and make disciples. . . . Teach them to carry out everything I have commanded you. And know that I am with you always, until the end of the world" (Mt 28:19, 20). But today not only the Magisterium but the whole Church and theology itself have lost their authority:

> In fact today nothing is considered to have certitude save the certitude proper to the "human sciences"; but this is the certitude of hypotheses, over which one can argue, but on whose basis no one can learn how to live his life. . . . [But] the proclamation [of the Gospel] is meant to tell man who he is and what he must do to be fully himself, and why he can live and die. No one can die for a myth which can be substituted for another myth; if a myth, for any reason, causes difficulties, one can replace it, one can choose another. Nor can one live by hypothesis, because life itself is not an hypothesis. It is an eternal reality, to which is bound an eternal destiny. But how could the Church teach in a binding way if this teaching must be non-binding for theologians?[33]

[31] Vatican Council II, *Lumen gentium*, no. 25.

[32] On this, see García de Haro, "Magisterio, norma moral y conciencia", pp. 62ff.

[33] Josef Ratzinger, "Teologia e Chiesa", *Communio* [Italian edition] no. 87 (1986): 93, 104–5.

Therefore, "if, for theology, the Church and ecclesial authority are something foreign to science, to the science of theology, the Church and theology are both in danger."[34]

C. *The question of dissent*

We have noted several times the problem of theological dissent. First of all, it is a question of recent origin, principally with respect to the value of the ordinary and universal Magisterium of the Pope.

The dogmatic declaration of the infallibility of the Roman Pontiff when he speaks *ex cathedra,* promulgated by Vatican Council I, was simply a confirmation of a truth always believed within the Church. But the exact delimitation of the acts of the Supreme Pastor endowed of themselves with infallibility inevitably raised the question of the precise obligatoriness of his remaining Magisterium and of the *ordinary Magisterium of the Pope with the bishops,* which had always been the habitual way in which the indefectibility of the Church manifested itself.

Pius XII, in his encyclical *Humani generis,* confronted the first attitudes that minimized the value of the papal Magisterium, emphasizing above all the importance of encyclicals.[35] His intervention put a brake to the currents of thought tending to attribute simply an ad hoc value to the Magisterium of the Pope that was not *ex cathedra* and, in general, to every noninfallible teaching of the Magisterium. Nevertheless, the task of establishing the precise value of the ordinary Magisterium of the Roman Pontiff remained; and, in a certain sense, there remained the task of clearly confirming the infallibility of the ordinary and universal Magisterium, which Vatican Council I had initially determined.

The infallible character of the ordinary and universal Magisterium of the Pope with the bishops even in moral questions, and specifically in their teachings on the obligation to respect absolute moral norms,

---

[34] Ibid., p. 94.

[35] "Neque putandum est, ea quae in Encyclicis Litteris proponuntur, assensum per se non postulare, cum in iis Pontifices supremam sui Magisterii potestatem non exerceant. Magisterio enim ordinario haec docentur, de quo illud etiam valet: 'Qui vos audit, me audit' (Lk 10:16); ac plerumque quae in Encyclicis Litteris proponuntur et inculcantur, iam aliunde ad doctrinam catholicam pertinent. Quodsi Summi Pontifices in actis suis de re hactenus controversa data opera sententiam ferunt, omnibus patet rem illam, secundum mentem ac voluntatem eorumdem Pontificum, quaestionem liberae inter theologos disceptationis iam haberi non posse" (Pius XII, encyclical *Humani generis,* August 12, 1950, DS 2313 [3885]).

was a firm and common conviction among theologians before and after Vatican Council II, a conviction sustained, for example, explicitly by Karl Rahner himself,[36] up to the publication of *Humanae vitae* (1968). This common opinion of authors was based on a long and uninterrupted tradition which, rooted in and derived from the explicit promulgation of the natural law in the Ten Commandments proclaimed on Mount Sinai, continues in the whole catechetical tradition of the Church and is crystalized in the *Roman Catechism* or the *Catechism for Pastors* or *Catechism of the Council of Trent.*[37] This uninterrupted tradi-

---

[36] Karl Rahner, S.J., *Nature and Grace: Dilemmas in the Modern Church* (London: Sheed & Ward, 1963), pp. 51–52: "The Church teaches these commandments [the Ten Commandments] with divine authority exactly as she teaches the other 'truths of the faith,' either through her 'ordinary' magisterium or through an act of her 'extraordinary' magisterium in *ex cathedra* definitions of the Pope or a general council, but also through her ordinary magisterium, that is, in the normal teaching of the faith to the faithful in schools, sermons, and all the other kinds of instruction. In the nature of the case this will be the normal way in which moral norms are taught, and definitions by Pope or general council the exception; but it is binding on the faithful in conscience just as the teaching through the extraordinary magisterium is. . . . It is therefore quite untrue that only those moral norms for which there is a solemn definition . . . are binding in the faith on the Christian as revealed by God. . . . When the whole Church in her everyday teaching does in fact teach a moral rule everywhere in the world as a commandment of God, she is preserved from error by the assistance of the Holy Ghost, and this rule is therefore really the will of God and is binding on the faithful in conscience."

[37] These words of William E. May express the matter clearly: "I believe—and so do other theologians—that the core of Catholic moral teaching, as summarized by the precepts of the Decalogue (the Ten Commandments), precisely *as these precepts have been traditionally understood within the Church,* has been taught infallibly by the magisterium in the day-to-day ordinary exercise of the authority divinely invested in it. We are not deliberately to kill innocent human beings; we are not to fornicate, commit adultery, engage in sodomy; we are not to steal; we are not to perjure ourselves. Note that I say that the core of Catholic moral teaching is summarized in the precepts of the Decalogue *as these have been traditionally understood within the Church.* Thus, for example, the precept 'Thou shalt not commit adultery,' has traditionally been understood unequivocally to exclude not only intercourse with someone other than one's spouse (adultery), but all freely chosen genital activity outside the covenant of marriage. This was precisely the way this precept of the Decalogue was understood by the Fathers of the Church, for example, St. Augustine, by the medieval scholastics, and by all Catholic theologians until the middle of the 1960s. Thus, in discussing the sixth commandment, Peter Lombard, whose *Libri IV Sententiarum* was used as *the* basic text in Catholic theology from the middle of the twelfth century until the middle of the sixteenth century, stressed that this commandment required one to forbear all nonmarital genital activity. Lombard, together with all medieval theologians and, indeed, all Catholic theologians until very recent years, held that any sexual activity fully contrary to the purposes of marriage and of the sexual differentiation of the species into male and female was gravely sinful and a violation of this precept of the Decalogue. This is, in addition, the teaching found in the *Roman Catechism,* and the teaching of this catechism on the precepts of the Decalogue is crucially important. The *Roman Catechism,* popularly known as *The Catechism of the Council of Trent,* was mandated by Trent, was written primarily by St.

tion was integrated by Vatican Council II in number 25 of *Lumen gentium*.[38] Therefore, when the problem of dissent arose with respect to *Humanae vitae*, at the beginning there were no doubts on this matter nor on the existence of moral absolutes, but only on the binding character of the ordinary Magisterium of the Roman Pontiff with

---

Charles Borromeo, was published with the authority of Pope St. Pius V in 1566, and was in use throughout the world until the middle of this century. It was praised by many Popes, who ordered that it be put into the hands of parish priests and used in the catechetical instruction of the faithful. In 1721 Pope Clement XIII published an encyclical, *In Dominico Agro*, devoted to this catechism. In it he said that there was an obligation to use it throughout the universal Church as a means of 'guarding the deposit of faith.' He called it the printed form of 'that teaching which is common doctrine in the Church.' Vatican Council I said that as a result of this catechism 'the moral life of the Christian people was revitalized by the more thorough instruction given to the faithful.' From all this, one can see the significance of the witness of this catechism to truths both of faith and morals. It is a reputable witness to the ordinary, day-to-day teaching of bishops throughout the world in union with the Holy Father" (*An Introduction to Moral Theology* [Huntington, Ind.: Our Sunday Visitor, 1991], pp. 210–12).

[38] "This teaching of the *Roman Catechism* was in no way changed by Vatican Council II. It was, indeed, firmly reasserted. Recall that this Council, after affirming that matters of faith and morals can be taught infallibly in the day-to-day exercise of the magisterial authority by bishops throughout the world in union with the pope, insisted that this is even more the case when the bishops, assembled in an ecumenical council, act as teachers of the universal Church and as judges on matters of faith and morals. In the light of this clear teaching it is most important to examine some key statements made by the Fathers of Vatican Council II about *specific moral norms*. An examination of this kind shows, beyond the shadow of a doubt, that the bishops united at Vatican Council II under the leadership of the pope unambiguously insisted that certain specific norms proposed by the magisterium are to be held definitively by the faithful. In doing so, they fulfilled the conditions set forth in *Lumen Gentium* and noted already under which the bishops can propose matters of faith and *morals* infallibly. For instance, after affirming the dignity of human persons and of human life, they unequivocally brand as infamous numerous crimes against human persons and human life, declaring that 'the varieties of crime [against human life and human persons] are numerous: all offenses against life itself, such as murder, genocide, abortion, euthanasia, and willful self-destruction; all violations of the integrity of the human person such as mutilations, physical and mental torture, undue psychological pressures; all offenses against human dignity, such as subhuman living conditions, arbitrary imprisonment, deportation, slavery, prostitution, the selling of women and children, degrading working conditions where men are treated as mere tools for profit rather than free and responsible persons; all these and their like are criminal; they poison civilization; and they debase their perpetrators more than their victims and militate against the honor of the Creator' (*Gaudium et spes*, n. 22). Some of the actions designated as criminal here are, it is true, described in morally evaluative language, such as 'murder,' 'subhuman,' 'arbitrary' and 'degrading.' But other actions are described factually, without the use of morally evaluative language, e.g., abortion, euthanasia, willful self-destruction (suicide), slavery, the selling of women and children. Specific moral norms proscribing such deeds are absolute, exceptionless" (May, *Introduction to Moral Theology*, pp. 212–13).

respect to the affirmation of the intrinsic wickedness of every form of contraception, including chemical means (an issue then under discussion, as we will see in our treatment of absolute moral norms in chapter 4).

The task of giving a precise meaning to the character of the noninfallible Magisterium was within the competence of Vatican Council II. The Council, in its dogmatic constitution *Lumen gentium,* drawing together the whole preceding tradition, in addition to declaring formally the infallible character of the ordinary and universal Magisterium, taught that *in a very special way the religious submission (obsequium) of will and of mind* is owed to the ordinary Magisterium of the Roman Pontiff, that very religious submission that is owed in general to the teaching of bishops.[39] During the redaction of number 25 of *Lumen gentium,* some Council Fathers asked why the assent of the mind was required for teachings that were not infallible and suggested that only an attitude of respectful obedience be demanded, leaving open the possibility of adhering at least interiorly to it. The Theological Commission of the Council replied that "approved theological expositions ought to be consulted [*consuli debent probatae expositiones theologicae*]" concerning the question of interior assent[40] and kept intact the text emphasizing the need of a religious submission of both will and mind.

We are now in a position to enter into the concrete origins of dissent. As William B. Smith has stressed, dissent, as it has come to be set forth by Curran and his followers, is a problem of recent origin:

A review of standard theological encyclopediae or dictionaries of theology finds no entries under the title of "Dissent" prior to 1972. Standard manuals of theology [in use up to the time of the Council] did raise possible questions about the rare individual who could not give or offer personal assent to formal Church teaching, and such questions were

[39] Vatican Council II, *Lumen gentium,* no. 25: "Hoc vero religiosum voluntatis et intellectus obsequium singulari ratione praestandum est Romani Pontificis authentico magisterio, etiam cum non ex cathedra loquitur; ita nempe ut magisterium eius supremum reverenter agnoscatur, et sententiis ab eo prolatis sincere adhereatur, iuxta mentem et voluntatem manifestatam ipsius, quae se prodit praecipue sive indole documentorum, sive ex frequenti propositione eiusdem doctrinae, sive ex dicendi ratione [This religious submission of will and of mind must be shown in a singular way to the authoritative Magisterium of the Roman Pontiff, even when he does not speak *ex cathedra;* in such wise indeed that his supreme Magisterium is acknowledged reverently, and one sincerely adhere to the decisions rendered by him, in accord with his manifest mind and will, which makes itself known principally either by the nature of the documents, or by the frequent proposal of the same teaching, or by the way in which his decision is rendered]."

[40] *Acta Synodalia,* III, 8, no. 159.

discussed under treatments of the Magisterium or the Teaching of the Church—the status of such teaching and its binding nature and/or extent.[41]

Vatican Council II, contrary to what some have claimed, has in fact not provided any access to change this state of affairs. The only episode at the Council having relationship to this topic is that previously noted in the response of the Theological Commission of the Council to the question formulated by three bishops regarding the meaning of the *religious assent of mind and will*, when a person maintains that *he cannot give internal assent (interne assentire non potest)*. What must he then do? We have seen that the reply was quite clear: consult the works of theology of proven credibility, that is, sound works. As Smith observes: "It should be noted that the question as posed to the Commission concerned the negative inability to give positive assent (*'interne assentire non potest'*) which is not precisely, nor at all the same, as an alleged positive right to dissent."[42] Moreover,

> if these "approved theological treatises" are examined, one discovers, as Germain Grisez has shown in detail, that no approved manual of theology ever authorized dissent from authoritative magisterial teaching. Some of them treated the question of *withholding internal assent* by a competent person who has serious reasons for doing so. The manuals taught that such a person ought to maintain silence and communicate the difficulty he experienced in assenting to the teaching in question to the magisterial teacher (pope or bishop) concerned.... They [the approved treatises] spoke, not of *dissent,* but of *withholding assent,* which is something far different from dissent.[43]

In fact, this is so evident that even Curran himself has recognized it, seeking to sustain the right to dissent not on the grounds of what the Council said or by referring to the traditional manuals to which the Theological Commission referred, but on the grounds of what Cardinal Newman had said in his *Grammar of Assent.*[44] This claim, as May comments, is simply amazing, if we recall what Newman actually

---

[41] W. Smith, "Question of Dissent in Moral Theology", pp. 235–54, at 235. See also, by the same author, "Is Dissent Legitimate?" *Social Justice Review* 77 (1986): 164ff.

[42] W. Smith, "Question of Dissent in Moral Theology", p. 239.

[43] May, *Introduction to Moral Theology,* p. 216. See Grisez, *Christian Moral Principles,* pp. 853, 867–69, nn. 38, 39, 41, and 42; cf. pp. 873–74.

[44] Charles E. Curran et al., *Dissent in and for the Church: Theologians and "Humanae Vitae"* (New York: Sheed and Ward, Inc., 1969), pp. 47–48.

wrote.[45] In conclusion, "the claim made by Curran and others that 'it is common teaching in the Church that Catholics may dissent from authoritative, noninfallible teachings of the magisterium when sufficient reasons for doing so exist' is spurious, supported only by weak and tendentious arguments."[46] All this has been confirmed by the recent *Instruction on the Ecclesial Vocation of the Theologian* of 1990, promulgated by the Congregation for the Doctrine of the Faith, which distinguishes and treats separately the *difficulties* theologians can find when confronted by some teachings of the Magisterium (nos. 23–31) and *dissent* from such teachings (nos. 32–41). The *Instruction*, while recognizing that the raising of doubts and personal difficulties is compatible with the *religious submission* demanded by *Lumen gentium*, clearly repudiates any kind of dissent, for this is of itself directly contrary to the ecclesial vocation of the theologian.

2. Theology, the Science of Faith, and the Magisterium

To understand in depth the relationships between theology and the Magisterium, it is necessary to penetrate into the characteristics of this science, inasmuch as it is knowledge of the Faith, different from and more perfect than any merely human knowledge. It is for this reason that, for centuries, Christians rejected the use of the term "theology" to designate Christian wisdom, in the fear that someone might confuse it with one of the human sciences, with those limited kinds of knowledge the pagans had of God and of man.[47]

Because of its principle of knowing, which is the Faith, and because of the characteristics proper to its method, theology requires a loyal

---

[45] Newman in no way asserted a right of Catholics to dissent from authoritative teachings of the Magisterium. Quite to the contrary, he wrote, in speaking of conscience, that "the sense of right and wrong, which is the first element in religion, is so delicate, so fitful, so easily puzzled, obscured, perverted, so subtle in its argumentative methods, so impressible by education, so biased by pride and passion, so unsteady in its course that, in the struggle for existence amid the various exercises and triumphs of the human intellect, this sense is at once the highest of all teachers, yet the least luminous; and *the Church, the Pope, the hierarchy are, in the divine purpose, the supply of an urgent demand*" (John Henry Cardinal Newman, "Letter to the Duke of Norfolk", in *Certain Difficulties Felt by Anglicans to Catholic Teaching*, vol. 2 [Westminster, Md.: Christian Classics, 1969], p. 240).

[46] May, *Introduction to Moral Theology*, pp. 219–20.

[47] Cf. Pierre Batiffol, "Theologia, theologi", *Ephemerides Louvanienses* 5 (1928): 213–17; José L. Illanes, "Theología", *Gran Enciclopedia Rialp*, vol. 22 (Madrid, 1975), pp. 233ff.

adherence to the Magisterium; otherwise, it disappears as a science and is a mere personal opinion of the theologian; it simply becomes "thought".[48]

A. Faith and theology

Theology is not confused with faith, but it is a knowledge of faith; and, without fidelity to the Magisterium, it cannot remain in the fullness of faith.

Theology is a science, with its own undeniable requirements of rigor, order, and precision distinguishing it from the common knowledge of the Faith proper to all the faithful, made up of those who are endowed with their own gifts of grace. Not all the saints are doctors of the Church. This notwithstanding, theology remains a knowledge of the Faith: it belongs to that knowledge of God, and of creatures in relationship to him, which comes from revelation and which only faith allows one to attain.

Without faith there is no true theology; the vigor of theological science requires that of faith. Where faith is lacking, there is lacking also the very principle of theological knowledge, and a science of revealed truths thus becomes impossible, in the same way that any intellectual theorem is beyond beings who are deprived of reason. The Holy Father has recently emphasized this: theology must "spring from a deep attitude of faith, from an active exercise of faith, which entails communion and colloquy with the very Word of God, the Master who teaches and gives from within [*ab intus*]."[49] And Paul VI said that "faith is more indispensable for the theologian than subtlety of mind."[50]

■ Indeed, theology requires an operative faith, which is reflected in its works. In fact, theology is speculative and practical at the same time.[51] Practical truth, inasmuch as it is the *truth of what is to be done (veritas facienda)*, is in itself inseparable from right action: to know it involves

[48] On the difference between "thinking" and "knowing", see Carlos Cardona, *Metafísica de la opción intelectual,* 2nd ed. (Madrid: Rialp, 1973), pp. 87–125.

[49] John Paul II, Address to the Institutes of Ecclesiastical Studies in Rome, March 4, 1979; *Insegnamenti di Giovanni Paolo II,* 2.1 (1979), p. 790.

[50] Paul VI, *Ad Conv. Theologiae Concilii Vaticani II;* AAS 58 (1966): 895.

[51] St. Thomas, *Summa theologiae,* I, q. 1, a. 4; *In I Sent.,* prol., aa. 2–4.

knowing what we must do; if, therefore, one has not chosen to love ordinately, one cannot discover the science of rectified love.[52] Ethics definitely presupposes the experience of freedom, of good and evil,[53] which in moral theology is done under the light of faith, and of a faith operative of itself.[54]

Therefore, *the first condition for the renewal of theology is to strengthen one's faith.* Certainly, it is important—many note this—to renew biblical and patristic studies, to have increasing rigor in the use of auxiliary disciplines; in a word, there is the obligation to engage in serious scientific work. But one must not forget that, in some way—and radically—the first source of theology is faith itself, understood as a virtue: as the supernatural active principle that makes a man able to understand the content of holy Scripture, Tradition, and the Magisterium in their proper and revealed meaning, one that surpasses human powers. A renewal of theology that is not based on a revival of faith, therefore, is not possible.[55] "A theology which does not deepen the faith, does not lead to prayer, can be a discourse of words on God, but it can never be a true discourse about God, the living God, the God who is both Being and Love."[56]

B. *The scientific method of theology and the Magisterium*

Theology has a proper method, rooted in the uniqueness of its principles, which are the articles of faith. Adhesion to the Magisterium is a condition for its rigor as a science.

[52] Cf. John Finnis, "The Practicality of Ethics", chap. 1 of *Fundamentals of Ethics* (Washington D.C.: Georgetown University Press; Oxford: Clarendon Press, 1983), pp. 1–25.

[53] Cf. Karol Wojtyla, *I fondamenti dell'ordine etico* (Bologna: Cseo, 1980), in particular his analysis of ethical experience as an experience regarding the exercise of one's own freedom on pp. 15–35.

[54] "Moral knowledge is formed by a method of dynamic reflection on human acts. Beginning with the acts themselves, it is forced to go to their source and their cause in the human person. It is not limited to a retrospective observation, but it seeks to recover the interior of the movement which produces the action, for directing it and carrying it out. This method is in harmony with that of philosophy; but it becomes theological when the light of Revelation and the movement of the Spirit penetrate into the active interiority of a believer" (Pinckaers, *Les sources de la morale chrétienne,* p. 69; see also, in general, pp. 59–104).

[55] Cf. Servais Pinckaers, *Le renouveau de la morale (Etudes pour une morale fidèle à ses sources et à sa mission présente),* 2nd ed. (Paris: Téqui, 1978), pp. 59–60.

[56] John Paul II, Address to Priests, Religious, and Missionaries, at St. Patrick's Seminary, Maynooth, October 1, 1979; *Insegnamenti di Giovanni Paolo II,* 2.2 (1979), p. 490.

Among the modern errors about the Magisterium and its relationships with theology, many depend at root on a mistaken notion of science and method. Science is an analogical reality: physics, metaphysics, and theology are not sciences in the same sense. What is essential to every science is that it be a *true and rigorous* knowledge, which goes back to the causes (those with which each of the sciences is concerned), and that it also be *ordered and complete* (within its own field). Only when these conditions are met do we have a science.

■ Therefore, a necessary manifestation of the scientific character of an intellectual work is that it reaches the truth. Error can never be scientific; it could, at the most, have the appearance of science, but it never has its source in true mental rigor. A reasoning, a study, is rigorous because it proceeds rightly, without leaps into the void, toward the truth. No work of theology which distances itself from the rule of divine truth, i.e., from the deposit of faith,[57] can be said properly to be scientific: whatever obscures or separates from the truth is not science. Only what leads one to the truth, which makes knowledge— *scire faciens* —is truly scientific.

The *scientific method,* consequently, is essentially constituted by that *way of working* that leads to a true, rigorous, ordered, and complete knowledge in the field proper to that science. Therefore, the requirements of method are not the same for all the sciences. They depend on the characteristics of the realities studied and of the way in which human intelligence attains them. The notion of method is analogous, as is that of science.[58] Specifically, there are characteristics of the theological method, proper to the science of Faith: the necessity of a solid and docile union with the Magisterium, in order not to break faith with the principles it receives from faith; the absolute need to base it on a sound metaphysics, as an instrument without which it cannot proceed;[59] finally, respect for all the methodological requirements

[57] "Guard what has been committed to you. Stay clear of worldly, idle talk and the contradictions of *what is falsely called knowledge*" (1 Tim 6:20; see also 2 Tim 1:12 and 14). The commentary of St. Vincent of Lerins is well known; see L. F. Mateo Seco, *San Vicente de Lerins. Tratado en defensa de la antigüedad y universalidad de la fe católica. Commonitorio* (Pamplona: Eunsa, 1977); see also Ratzinger, "Le fonti della teologia morale", pp. 38–39.

[58] On this analogical character of the concept of science, with the relative diversity in scientific methods, and in particular on the different methods to be used in human sciences and in theology, see Pinckaers, *Les sources de la morale chrétienne,* pp. 60–98.

[59] "It belongs [to philosophy], which always maintains its own autonomy, to secure the instruments of reason that are indispensable for every theological inquiry. Did not, after all,

proper to the sciences theology uses as auxiliaries, to the extent that it has need of them.

■ It is common to every science to proceed on the foundation of some first principles that guide it and from which it develops as from starting points: a reality that shows how God has ordered human intelligence from within (*ab intrinseco*), directing it to discover truth and to make progress in it. In virtue of his own natural inclination, which is customarily called the habit of first principles, every time a man wants to know he grasps as evident some truth of this kind (the whole is greater than its parts; we must not will for others what we do not will for ourselves)—truths that allow the root constituents of being and of the good to emerge and to show themselves to us, truths that then guide all man's reasonings, whereby he analyzes experiences by knowing their intrinsic truth. It is in this way that man makes progress in his knowledge.[60]

In moral theology, this development of knowledge under the guidance of first principles is realized under the influence of the Spirit,[61] and it relies on the very flourishing of our free action: it is the penetration into the depths of ethical experience under the guidance of faith.[62] Theological knowledge is sustained by the longing for the good nestled in our will and draws nourishment

from the direct, intuitive, global, often instantaneous, and dynamic grasp of all the elements of action in the original whole that unites them,

---

St. Thomas affirm that metaphysics 'is wholly ordered to the knowledge of God as to its last end, whence it is called the divine science' (*Contra Gentiles,* 3.25)?" (John Paul II, Homily at the Mass for the Universities of Rome, October 23, 1981; *Insegnamenti di Giovanni Paolo II* 4.2 [1981], no. 4).

[60] In the so-called "positive sciences" other truths, not evident in themselves, often serve as principles—along with the first principles or self-evident truths—but these are the primary application of these self-evident truths in the field proper and limited to their area of inquiry (thus, for example, the principles of physics, of mathematics, or of economics). At times, "postulates" have the role of principles, i.e., hypotheses held provisionally as true in order to facilitate and delimit a specific kind of research.

[61] "Such is the knowledge or 'originating' (*fontale*) awareness which we all have at the time of acting. . . . One can locate this 'originating' (*fontale*) knowledge at the level of the spirit, in the highest and most secret part of ourselves, according to the words of St. Paul: 'Who knows a man's innermost self but the man's own spirit within him?' (1 Cor. 2:11). Or again: 'The Spirit himself gives witness with our spirit . . .' (Rom. 8:16). Truly, it is at the heart of this active interiority that the Holy Spirit works within us" (Pinckaers, *Les sources de la morale chrétienne,* p. 63).

[62] Let us recall what was said above about this: cf. Wojtyla, *I fondamenti dell'ordine etico,* pp. 15–35.

proper to their originating cause, which we ourselves are. It is to reach the "I" and the reality which surrounds us, the act and its object, in an association always new, where the question of the truth, the good, of happiness, and of the quality of our moral action comes into play.[63]

1. *The first requirement of theological method is to receive adequately the proper principles, which are the articles of faith, and to work in conformity with them.* The decisive role that its own principles play in every science holds true for theology, but only in an analogical way. The other sciences, in truth, posit the principles proper to them; theology, on the other hand, receives them from God, "because the science of theology is an analogous participation in the very knowledge of God, which in its wondrous simplicity and truth embraces all the truths which the theologian, relying on Revelation, discovers and penetrates little by little".[64] Therefore, it does pertain to theology to prove its own principles, but to receive them with the obedience of faith (cf. Heb 11:8); it is therefore one of its characteristics to argue on the basis of the authority of the Church about everything referring to the acceptance of revealed truths; and, without obedience to the Magisterium, it destroys itself.

[a.] *The articles of faith,* through the infused light which this virtue confers, are *per se known* to all who have it, just as the first natural principles are evident to the mind. Theology does not have the power of proving the principles which serve as the starting points from which it proceeds, but only that of defending them from everything which claims to contradict them. . . . The habit of faith is not acquired by means of theology.[65]

This is what "the blessed Apostle Peter teaches us when he says, 'be ever ready,' not to prove, but 'to give a reason for your hope' (1 Pet. 3:15), that is, to show with reason that what the Catholic faith professes cannot be false."[66]

■ The theologian cannot behave as a provisional believer, who first tries to prove his principles in order then to proceed scientifically in his

---

[63] Pinckaers, *Les sources de la morale chrétienne,* p. 62.
[64] Paul VI, Address of October 1, 1966.
[65] St. Thomas, *In I Sent.,* prol., q. 1, a. 3, sol. 2.
[66] St. Thomas, *De rationibus fidei,* c. 2.

work, because in this case he would no longer be doing theology, the science of the Faith.[67] What is proper to theology is not to prove the Faith, but to penetrate into its inexhaustible riches, and also to show how we have concluded that an article or principle belongs to the deposit of faith. It is not, on the other hand, his task to prove the intrinsic truth of these articles or principles, and not even their very belonging to the deposit of revelation, as if faith were not open to receive in its integrity the revealed deposit as this is taught by the Church in virtue of its divine authority and not by the authority of men.

b. Consequently, it is characteristic of and proper to theology

to argue from authority... inasmuch as the principles of this doctrine are held through revelation, and thus it is necessary that the authority of those to whom revelation has been made must be believed. Nor does this in any way derogate from the dignity of this doctrine, for although the argument from authority is the weakest when it is based on human authority, nonetheless the argument from the authority which is based on divine revelation is the most efficacious.[68]

The witnesses of revelation—sacred Scripture, Tradition, and the Magisterium—provide the principal arguments of theology, above any apparent argument of reason, which, if it disagrees with these witnesses, does so only because it has fallen into error.

This does not, however, mean in any way that the work of theology is finished once it has had recourse to authority. It belongs to theology *to open up the whole truth contained in the principles* received with faith by helping men to enter into divine realities: "Theology must teach *how one can understand, as far as possible, what it affirms;* otherwise, it would be limited to repeating what the authorities say; it would certify that *this* is the truth, but it would give neither knowledge nor understanding, and the mind of those who listen would remain empty of knowledge and understanding."[69] On the other hand, this means that human intelligence, in penetrating into divine things, must not rely principally on its own powers but on faith, on prayer, on the authority of the Church:

---

[67] Cf. Cardona, *Metafísica de la opción intelectual,* pp. 261–69.

[68] St. Thomas, *Summa theologiae,* I, q. 1, a. 8, ad 2.

[69] St. Thomas, *Quodlibet.,* IV, c. 9, a. 3 resp. Cf. Alvaro del Portillo, "Magistero della Chiesa e teologia morale", in *Persona, Verità e Morale,* pp. 19ff.

Theology can be authentic only in the Church, the community of faith:... "the faith delivered once for all to the saints" (Jude 3). This is not a limitation for the theologians, but a liberation, because it preserves them from changing fads and keeps them bound securely to the immutable truth of Christ, the truth which sets them free (cf. Jn 7:32).[70]

This is their bond to the truth, which remains solid precisely by means of the effective practice of the virtue of faith.[71]

c. Finally, *the Magisterium is the proximate norm of theology*, since it is the proximate norm of faith: "The proximate and obligatory norm in the teaching of the faith—also concerning family matters—belongs to the hierarchical Magisterium."[72] We will, then, see how theology must collaborate with the Magisterium, and the way in which it guides faith: in the continuity of the 20 centuries of the life of the Church, in the diversity of its documents. Here we are only interested in showing that, without a firm adherence to the totality of what the Church teaches, theology disappears, because faith itself disappears, the "obedience" of faith:

> Whoever does not adhere to the teaching of the Church, which comes from the truth first set forth in Scripture, as to an infallible and divine rule, does not have the habit of faith.... On the other hand, whoever adheres to the teaching of the Church as to an infallible rule assents to everything that the Church teaches. Otherwise, if he holds whats he wants to hold of those things which the Church teaches and does not hold what he does not want to hold, he no longer adheres to the teaching of the Church as to an infallible rule, but to his own will.[73]

2. *Second, one cannot maintain a scientific rigor in theology without the proper scientific use of one's own mind, that is, with a metaphysics of being.* Theology necessarily serves reason, because faith presupposes, heals, and elevates intelligence. One cannot grasp the truths proper to theology

---

[70] John Paul II, Address to Priests, Religious, and Missionaries, St. Patrick's Seminary, Maynooth, October 1, 1979; *Insegnamenti di Giovanni Paolo II* 2.2 (1979), p. 490, no. 5. Cf. on this matter Ratzinger, "Le fonti della teologia morale", pp. 13–18.

[71] Ralph McInerny, *Ethic Thomistica: The Moral Philosophy of Thomas Aquinas* (Washington, D.C.: The Catholic University of America Press, 1982), pp. 92ff.

[72] John Paul II, *Familiaris consortio*, no. 73.

[73] St. Thomas, *Summa theologiae*, II–II, q. 5, a. 3 c.

without the help of analogous concepts drawn from natural reason, which God himself has used in revealing himself. This scientific use of reason is nothing else than metaphysics.[74] A late medieval author said: "The doctor of Catholic truth begins his road there where metaphysics ends; one who is not versed in metaphysics can in no way be called a true theologian. Precisely because the one who mistakes the door, how can he not make errors when he goes inside?"[75]

This is an argument that merits emphasis: "Only the principle of creation and metaphysical transcendence fully saves the historicity of man without falling into contradiction and the heresy (the denial of creation) of identifying being with pure becoming."[76] Without metaphysics, neither the historicity of man nor the Incarnation of God in the history of mankind can be saved: the words of revelation remain perennially present as a guide for men only if the concepts used by God have a universal value; when metaphysical truth is reduced to pure becoming, revealed truth is likewise equally reduced.

■ A metaphysics is valid to the precise extent to which *it opens itself to reality*. The Holy Father emphasizes this in pointing to the services presented to theology by thomistic metaphysics: "The philosophy of St. Thomas merits attentive study and hearty acceptance by the youth of our day, because of its spirit of *openness* and its universalism, characteristics which are difficult to find in many currents of contemporary thought. I mean an *openness* to the whole of reality in all its parts and dimensions, without reductions or particularisms (without absolutizing individual points), just as openness is required of the mind in the name of objective and integral truth about reality."[77]

3. Finally, to the extent to which it serves them, *theology must respect the methods proper to the human sciences it uses in an auxiliary way,*

---

[74] "It is necessary, therefore, that ethical reflection be founded and rooted ever more deeply on a true anthropology, and this, ultimately, on the *metaphysics* of creation which is at the center of all Christian thinking. The crisis of ethics is the most evident proof of the crisis of anthropology, a crisis in turn due to the rejection of *truly metaphysical* thinking" (John Paul II, Address to the Participants in the International Congress of Moral Theology, April 10, 1986; *Insegnamenti di Giovanni Paolo II*, 9.1 [1986], p. 972; reprinted in *Persona, Verità e Morale*, p. 13 [English translation], p. 9 [Italian text]).

[75] Domenico of Flanders, *Quaestiones in XII Met. lib. Arist.*, prol. (Venice, 1499), Inc. V 10 BT 6 (Angelicum).

[76] Caffarra, "La Chiesa e l'ordine morale", p. 2, no. 1.

[77] John Paul II, Address at the Angelicum, November 17, 1979, no. 6; *Insegnamenti di Giovanni Paolo II*, 2.2 (1979), pp. 1183–84.

without, however, forgetting that it can never abandon its own method and that its perspective is different. It uses the sciences of law, history, psychology, hermeneutics, etc., but as external authorities that are only probable; it never forgets that it is not based on human authority, but on God's. In theology, human authorities are such only to the extent that their natural knowledge of the truth is always and inevitably in agreement with faith, since both natural truth and revealed truth equally have God as their author.[78] If they are not in agreement with it, this signifies that they have fallen into the possibility, so human, of error.

■ Matters, in fact, are this way: moral science "considers human acts from the point of view of the dynamic interiority of man, and by way of its manifestation in them; on the other hand, the positive sciences contemplate the same acts, but from outside and according to that method of observation which is proper to each.... The human sciences have need of moral science because of themselves they are not able to go beyond the external and visible aspect of human actions. The richest and most decisive human acts, such as love and hatred, intention and free choice, one's endurance of suffering and evil, truth and duty, escape these sciences, as does faith; that is, all the movements of human interiority without which there can be neither an authentic understanding nor true explanation of our acts is removed from them. And, therefore, never can they reach satisfactory practical conclusions for application in guiding actions. Every day it is more clearly recognized that the positive sciences do not suffice to know man and to reply to the great issues and questions which he poses for himself."[79]

In fact, these sciences generate new and very serious problems, unless they let themselves be guided by ethics: "Scientific truth", the Holy Father has noted, "can be used, precisely in the name of human liberty, for objectives opposed to the good of man himself, or the good which is the proper object of ethics. Therefore, when science is separated from morality, man runs grave risks."[80]

This must not, however, make us forget that "in its turn morality has need of the positive sciences for a better knowledge of many

[78] Cf. Vatican Council I, dogmatic constitution *Dei filius*, 1870, chap. 4 (DS 1795–1800, 3015–20). Also see Pius IX, encyclical *Qui pluribus*, November 9, 1846 (DS 1637, 2778).

[79] Pinckaers, *Les sources de la morale chrétienne*, pp. 69–92; the citation is taken from p. 82.

[80] John Paul II, Address on the Dialogue between Science, Faith, and Theology on the Subject of Procreation, June 7, 1984, no. 2; *Insegnamenti di Giovanni Paolo II*, 7.2 (1984), pp. 1626–28.

factors of the social, psychological, historical, and cultural orders, etc., which are in fact integrated in concrete action and must be taken into account, to the full extent possible, for elaborating an adequate moral judgment."[81]

3. The Magisterium—Guardian of the Truth of Salvation

The Magisterium is the guardian of the unique truth of salvation, which is capable of bringing to fulfillment the good of marriage and the family.

Since theology is the science of Faith, adherence to the Magisterium appears as a *condition of its authenticity.* Moreover, inasmuch as the Magisterium guards the truth of Christ, this adherence is shown in its *transcendent value* for the good of humanity.

Only Christ has the full truth about man and, therefore, about marriage and the family. A theological science that would not express Christ's wisdom regarding human love and family life, even if it should have many other qualities, could not save the family: "Jews demand 'signs' and Greeks look for 'wisdom,' but we preach Christ crucified—a stumbling block to Jews and an absurdity to Gentiles . . . for God's folly is wiser than men, and his weakness more powerful than men" (1 Cor 1:22, 25). Only the wisdom of God, which comes to us through Christ, is powerful and conquers evil (Col 2:3; Eph 1:17, etc.).

■ This is one of the most basic points of Vatican II, which overcomes the impasse of certain school theologies and an apologetic elaborated, as it were, exclusively in the name of reason: "In the light of Christ . . . the Council intends to speak to all men in order to illumine the mystery of man and to cooperate in the search for a solution to the principal problems of our time."[82] This is a truth which the Holy Father has put at the basis of all his teachings, beginning with the homily at the beginning of his pontificate,[83] continuing with his first encyclical *Redemptor hominis,*[84] and through all the great later documents up to

---

[81] Pinckaers, *Les sources de la morale chrétienne,* p. 82. Cf. also Ramón García de Haro and Ignacio de Celaya, *La sabiduria moral cristiana* (*La renovación de la moral a veinte años del Concilio*) (Pamplona: Eunsa, 1985).

[82] Vatican Council II, Pastoral constitution *Gaudium et spes,* December 7, 1965, no. 10.

[83] Homily of October 22, 1978; *Insegnamenti di Giovanni Paolo II,* 1 (1978), pp. 35ff.

[84] Cf. *Redemptor hominis,* no. 8.

Familiaris consortio. [85] This is a truth that needs to be repeated, because men can freely turn themselves away from it.

History "is not simply a fixed progression towards what is better, but rather an event of freedom, and even a struggle between freedoms that are in mutual conflict, that is, according to the well-known expression of St. Augustine, a conflict between two loves: the love of God to the point of disregarding self, and the love of self to the point of disregarding God.[86]"[87] In this struggle, only Christ has "the original truth of marriage, the truth of the 'beginning,'[88] and, freeing man from his hardness of heart, He makes man capable of realizing this truth in its entirety."[89]

The Church has a plan for marriage and the family, at once ambitious and realistic, because she knows both the condition of fallen man and the infinite power of redemption.

What man is and what is fitting for him do not depend on human plans or inventions but on the design of God himself, the Creator and Redeemer. The Bible teaches that man was created in the image and likeness of God (Gen 1:28; 2:16ff.). Yahweh created man and raised him to the state of grace: "God made mankind straight" (Qo 7:29).[90] The sacred text recalls that "man, tempted by the Evil One, from the very beginning of history abused his freedom, raising himself up against God and seeking to attain his end without Him."[91] From then on, he was deprived of grace and wounded in the very forces of his nature, in such a way that it is very difficult for man to live conformably to his own natural dignity. "Man finds himself unable to overcome efficaciously, by himself, the assaults of evil, in such wise that he feels as if bound by chains."[92] But God has not abandoned man, and the "Lord Himself

---

[85] John Paul II, *Familiaris consortio,* nos. 6, 13, 49, 51, etc. See also his *Address to the International Theological Commission,* October 6, 1981, no. 5; *Insegnamenti di Giovanni Paolo II,* 4.2 (1981), pp. 362–63.

[86] Cf. St. Augustine, *The City of God,* 14, 28; *Corpus Scriptorum Ecclesiasticorum Latinorum* 40, II, 56ff.

[87] John Paul II, *Familiaris consortio,* no. 6.

[88] Cf. Gen 2:24; Mt 19:5.

[89] John Paul II, *Familiaris consortio,* no. 13.

[90] Cf. Council of Trent, session V, decree *De peccato originali,* can. 1 (DS 788–1511).

[91] Vatican Council II, *Gaudium et spes,* no. 13.

[92] Ibid., no. 13.

came to free man and to give him strength, renewing him inwardly and casting out the 'prince of this world,'[93] who held him in slavery to sin."[94]

■ Human being and action are not grasped in their full sense if they are not seen within the history of salvation, as this is illumined by faith: in its condition as *created, fallen, and redeemed*.[95] This is the real condition of man and the nucleus of the biblical anthropology which underlies the Christian vision of marriage and the family. Thus one can understand the insistence of the Roman Pontiff for a return in Christ to the pristine dignity of marriage: "Only by acceptance of the Gospel are the hopes that man legitimately places in marriage and in the family capable of being fulfilled."[96]

Although Christian truth about marriage is demanding, and in its integrity inaccesible without faith, nonetheless nonbelievers can see that it is in harmony with their experience and the noblest human aspirations. The courage of the apostles in speaking of Christ to every man, believer or not, is not without its importance. To be heard by the contemporary world one does not have to hide aspects of Christian truth; indeed only by presenting it without mutilations and fears will we be heard or, at least, respected. The desire for the absolute good always remains in every man and, when he seeks it sincerely, he ends by recognizing his own need for God, and, at the same time, his incapacity for restoring by himself a relationship of friendship with him. This is the dialectic of fallen nature, which understands both its own tendency to God and its inability to attain him; this thus disposes man to desire redemption. A condition of our nature whose origin revelation explains to us, but which simultaneously constitutes a datum of experience: "What is made known to us through divine Revelation is in harmony with personal experience. In fact, when man looks within his heart, he finds that he is inclined to evil and sunk in so many miseries which cannot come from his holy Creator."[97]

■ That Christianity has its own charm and powers of transformation must not be confused with a philosophical ethic or with a utopia of a

---

[93] Jn 12:31.

[94] Vatican Council II, *Gaudium et spes*, no. 13.

[95] On this see Philippe Delhaye, *La scienza del bene e del male. La morale del Vaticano II e il "metaconcilio"* (Milan: Ed. Ares, 1981), 25ff., 81ff.

[96] John Paul II, *Familiaris consortio*, no. 3.

[97] Vatican Council II, *Gaudium et spes*, no. 13.

faith in human progress, nor must the requirements with which Christian morality is concerned be abased to the level of common opinion. Neither the Greeks, nor the Romans, nor the philosophy of the Enlightenment, neither Freud nor Marx, neither practical nor speculative materialism know what is within man and what his deepest desires consist in. Only the Christian message, in its integrity, without compromises, satisfies fully the longings of our heart. "In every man's life there comes a time sooner or later when his soul draws the line. He has had enough of the usual explanations. The lies of the false prophets no longer satisfy. Even though they may not admit it at the time, such people are longing to quench their thirst with the teachings of our Lord."[98]

A condition of pastoral theology that must, therefore, be required today is *the practical conviction that no human plan of marriage and family can be more attractive than God's.* The theologian and the pastor must always act with this assurance. A serious equivocation occurs when this is forgotten:

> In our pastoral considerations on marriage and the family we must overcome strictly external perspectives, which at times ignore and obscure in part their deepest and genuine meaning: *the identity of love sanctified by the sacrament.* Perhaps a little superficially, we sometimes are content with consulting statistics and studies—perhaps reached on the basis of prevailing ideologies—which welcome changeable and even manipulable aspects, reflecting in their turn changing situations of a cultural, sociological, political, or economic nature.... Let us not forget that behind so many analyses and statistics lies hidden a great emptiness which surrounds persons, who, acting in this way, in reality confess their own loneliness, their own moral and spiritual emptiness because no one has sufficiently educated them on the *authentic meaning of the marital union* and of family life, as a vocation and fertile experience, unique and irrepeatable, of a communication in harmony with the original and lasting plan of God.[99]

■ For this end, it is necessary to conquer not only prejudices but also the real difficulties in which they find refuge. This demands an

---

[98] Blessed Josemaría Escrivá, homily "That All May Be Saved", in *Friends of God* (New Rochelle, N.Y.: Scepter Press, 1981), no. 260, p. 232.

[99] John Paul II, Address to a Group of Venezuelan Bishops on Their *ad limina* Visit, November 15, 1979; *Enchiridion Familiae; Textos del Magisterio Pontificio y Conciliar sobre el Matrimonio y la Familia (Siglos I a XX),* ed. Augosto Sarmiento and Javier Escrivá-Ivars, vol. 3 (Madrid: Ediciones Rialp, 1992), p. 2450, no. 2.

unshakable confidence in the energies placed by God himself in the bosom of the family, for carrying his plan of love for man to completion: "The role that God calls the family to perform in history derives from what the family is; its role represents the dynamic and existential development of what it is. Each family finds within itself a summons that cannot be ignored, and that specifies both its dignity and its responsibility: family, *become* what you are."[100] Therefore, the work of the Christian moralist cannot be limited to denouncing evil, nor to lamenting and combating opinions opposed to the divine plan. It must activate convictions with *the courage of the Faith:* "The Christian moralist must dare to take the initiative. Only he grasps, by virtue of faith, the deep meaning of human things, their divine meaning; only he can indicate for human actions the movement which will carry them to their fulfillment and perfection."[101]

4. The Obedience Due to the Magisterium, According to the Degree of the Obligation Owed to Its Proper Authority, in Its Different Teachings

In its infallible teachings, the Magisterium binds the believer with the obedience of faith. The remaining teachings of the Magisterium require a "religious submission of will and mind".

In the economy of revelation, the Church, which continues the mission of Christ, acts like him in a way that is at once visible and invisible. The interior action of grace on the soul accompanies the Church's Magisterium, which is visible and external. This means that where adherence to the Magisterium is lacking there is no longer the dynamism of the Christian conscience. The power of the Magisterium, in fact, is directed to faith.[102]

Vatican Council II, following Vatican I, has made the characteristics of this obedience precise,[103] according to the different modalities of the teaching of the Church on faith and morals and the extent to which she intends to bind with her magisterial power. Without entering into a detailed analysis, we will note the essential points.

[100] John Paul II, *Familiaris consortio,* no. 17.
[101] Pinckaers, *Le renouveau de la morale,* p. 23.
[102] Cf. Alvaro del Portillo, *Laici e fedeli nella Chiesa* (Milan: Ed. Ares, 1960), pp. 62ff.
[103] Vatican Council II, *Dei verbum,* no. 5.

1. *A full internal and external adherence must be given to the infallible Magisterium—whether extraordinary or "ordinary and universal".*[104] Our concern here is with the same obedience of faith given to God who reveals, since Christ himself has willed this infallibility for the Church when, speaking in his name (cf. Lk 10:16; Mt 16:19), she defines a doctrine of faith or morals.[105] This infallibility belongs to the Roman Pontiff "when, as supreme pastor and teacher of all the faithful—who confirms his brothers in the faith (cf. Lk. 22:32)—he proclaims a doctrine on faith or morals by a definitive act." It belongs to the college of bishops when, either united in a Council or, "even dispersed throughout the world, but preserving the bond of communion among themselves and with the Successor of Peter, in their authentic teaching on matters of faith and morals, they agree that a particular teaching is to be *held definitively.*"[106]

■ It is fitting to note also that almost all infallible teachings in the field of morality are contained not in solemn definitions but precisely in the teachings of the ordinary and universal Magisterium. This has led some to think that there are no infallible teachings in the field of morality, inasmuch as, in fact, there are no texts in which such infallibility is explicitly claimed.[107] This assertion fails to recognize, however, that the ordinary and universal Magisterium, which by nature does not adopt such solemn expressions, is precisely the normal way in which the infallibility of the Church is exercised: "The *Magisterium* is not above the divine word, but serves it with a special certain *charism of truth* (*Dei Verbum*, n. 8), which includes the charism of infallibility, which is present not only in the solemn definitions of the Roman Pontiff and of Ecumenical Councils but also in the ordinary and universal Magisterium (*Lumen gentium*, n. 25), which can be considered *the usual expression of the infallibility of the Church.*"[108] Practically all

---

[104] Vatican Council II, in fact, makes it clear that the Magisterium is infallible not only when it is exercised in an "extraordinary" way (through *ex cathedra* pronouncements of the Holy Father or through solemn definitions of ecumenical councils) but also when it is exercised in an "ordinary and universal" way through the day-to-day teaching of the bishops throughout the world in proposing that something of faith or morals "be held definitively". On this matter see Lio, *"Humanae vitae" e coscienza,* no. 31, p. 33. See also Grisez, *Christian Moral Principles,* chap. 35.

[105] Vatican Council II, *Lumen gentium,* no. 25.

[106] Ibid., no. 25, pars. 2 and 3.

[107] Cf., for example, Bernard Haering, *Free and Faithful in Christ,* vol. 1 (New York: Seabury Press, 1978), pp. 353–55.

[108] John Paul II, Address of October 15, 1988.

concrete moral norms that are absolute, today under debate (on abortion, contraception, homosexual acts, premarital relations, euthanasia, divorce, masturbation), have been taught by the ordinary and universal Magisterium and are hence infallible.[109]

2. *A "religious submission ('obsequium') of will and mind" is due to the rest of the authoritative teaching of the Roman Pontiff and to the ordinary Magisterium of bishops.*[110] This religious submission means more than the usual obedience required for the legitimate commands of the hierarchical authority of the Church. Specifically, it means the following:

a. The *ordinary response* will be a sincere adherence not only of the will but also of the intelligence. In an exceptional case, a teaching might not be intellectually convincing. Then, the first duty is to doubt oneself, giving credibility to the Magisterium. Almost always, this attitude of faith and common sense will be enough to resolve the doubt and will lead to a full intellectual assent. But it can happen that at times, in an absolutely extraordinary way and for serious reasons, a person thinks that there is a defect in the expression of a specific teaching, which does not allow him to give his full assent. Even then one must give an internal acceptance, which is not mere silence; this does not mean that one must stop working on research and presenting to the authorities, in a private way, one's own reasons and the possible formulations that one might suggest as being better suited for expressing the truth.[111]

b. In any case, religious submission implies the obligation to *avoid every dissent;* the only thing admissible is to suspend or withhold assent.[112] If dissent is made publicly and obstinately opportune, sanctions would be in order (*Code of Canon Law,* cans. 1371, par. 1 and 753).

---

[109] Cf. García de Haro, "Magisterio, norma moral y conciencia", pp. 63ff.

[110] Vatican Council II, *Lumen gentium,* no. 25. On this see U. Betti, "L'ossequio al Magistero Pontificio 'non ex cathedra' nel n. 25 della *Lumen gentium*", *Antonianum* (1987): 423–61.

[111] On the discussion in the sessions of the Council and on the corresponding conclusions concerning the nature and requirements of this submission of the mind, see Betti, "L'ossequio al Magistero Pontificio 'non ex cathedra' ", pp. 436ff.

[112] The so-called theology of dissent acts without scientific rigor in identifying this traditional doctrine on the withholding of assent with a right to dissent, even publicly. On this see W. Smith, "Question of Dissent in Moral Theology", pp. 244ff.

Even in its noninfallible teachings, the Magisterium is directed to the Faith and requires a religious obedience. The teaching of the Magisterium is not like an ecclesiastical law, which emanates from the power of jurisdiction, and about which a respectful public dissent is lawful. The Magisterium is excluded from every public criticism of the faithful, especially of those who have received a *munus docendi*.[113]

3. We have been concerned up to now with the proper attitude of the believer with respect to the teaching of the Magisterium. Let us now pose a further problem: whether one can have an erroneous conscience in good faith regarding matters taught by the Magisterium and whether in such a case one is bound in conscience.

a. We can begin by answering the second question, which is simpler. In fact, the judgment of a right conscience, that is, one based on a will truly desirous of doing God's will, or in good faith, always obliges. St. Thomas is clear:

Some say that conscience can err either in matters that are *per se evil* or in matters that are indifferent. A conscience erring in matters which are *per se evil* does not [they say] bind, but one erring in indifferent matters does bind. But those who say this do not seem to understand what it means to say that conscience binds. For conscience is said to bind because someone incurs sin if he does not do as his conscience bids; but this does not mean that one who does as conscience bids acts rightly.... Therefore, conscience is not said to bind to something because if one acts in accord with conscience one's act becomes good because of one's conscience, but because one incurs sin if one does not do what conscience bids. It does not indeed seem possible that any one can avoid sin if he is disposed to act contrary to what conscience, however much it errs, should declare as a precept of God, whether it be an act indifferent in itself or *per se evil*. For in this case, insofar as it depends on himself, a man shows that he does not have the will to obey God's law; whence he would sin mortally.[114]

b. With respect to the possibility of having an invincibly ignorant or inculpably erroneous conscience on matters already explicitly judged by the Magisterium, we must say that here we deal with a situation

---

[113] Cf. Ratzinger, "Le fonti della teologia morale", pp. 36–37.
[114] St. Thomas, *Quaestiones disputatae de Veritate*, q. 17, a. 4 resp.

that is difficult to find; in fact, with respect to the infallible teachings of the Magisterium, this can only happen if one is inculpably ignorant of the existence or the infallibility of such teaching.[115] In any event, it will not last long, since the desire to know the will of God leads one to know what God really wills, sooner or later, but without too much delay.[116]

■ We want to close this section by noting that the dilemma of an erroneous conscience must not be confused with two similar situations. The first, already known by the apostolic Church (cf. Rom 14; 1 Cor 8), appears when someone, convinced of the *liceity* of an action because he grasps its effective moral goodness, finds himself nonetheless in a situation in which competent authority prohibits this way of behaving. The Christian must then adapt himself to the decision taken by the hierarchy and "cannot appeal, in this case, to the contrary judgment—not erroneous but true—of his conscience. . . . Now while negative moral norms (e.g., 'do not do evil') oblige always and in every case, it is not true that one is obliged to perform an action simply because it is morally good. Indeed, factors may arise that oblige one to abstain from performing it. One of those factors may be precisely the indication, coming from those in the Church charged with the good of the community, that abstention from the action is required for that good."[117]

The second is the case of a simple doubt, in which "it will be necessary for the person to evaluate the foundation for his knowledge through deeper reexamination and dialogue with competent persons and to ascertain the level of authoritativeness with which the Magisterium proposes the norm in question."[118]

Criteria for determining the value of a teaching

The authority of the Church, in proposing the doctrine of Christ opportunely, in addition to infallible teachings, expresses other doctrines that are certain, but not yet definitive or irreformable; or, at times, the Magisterium simply gives counsels to circumstances.

---

[115] Cf. ibid., ad 3 and ad 5.

[116] On this see García de Haro, *Legge, coscienza e libertà*, pp. 98–107.

[117] Carlo Caffarra, *Living in Christ: Fundamental Principles of Catholic Moral Teaching*, trans. Christopher Ruff (San Francisco: Ignatius Press, 1987), p. 122.

[118] Ibid., 123.

To determine the value of each teaching, especially if found in a document of the Roman Pontiff, there will be need to pay heed to his specific desire according to the mind and will shown by him, which "is made known chiefly either by the nature of the documents, or by the frequency with which the same teaching is repeated, or by the way in which it is expressed."[119] Therefore, the *form* of the document is neither the only nor the decisive factor; it is one of the indications of the will of the Roman Pontiff—or of a corresponding authority— about the more or less definitive and obliging character of his teaching, as are the *repetition* of the same teaching, *the language adopted,* etc.

■ With respect to form, the fundamental distinction is that between documents coming directly from the Roman Pontiff or, indirectly, by way of the different organs of the Holy See. Among the first, the most solemn are the encyclicals and apostolic constitutions; then exhortations, apostolic letters, *motu proprios,* etc., and finally radio messages, homilies, addresses, etc. For the second, we need to distinguish between documents explicitly approved by the Pope (*in forma specifica*) and others (which are said to be approved *in forma communi*).

Obviously, in the same document we can find teachings of different authority, which can be evaluated insofar as a teaching is already contained in previous documents (with their own level of obligatoriness) or not, in addition to the very tenor and sense of the expressions used.

■ It goes without saying that we also need to evaluate the teachings of bishops—or of bishops' conferences—with respect to their binding power. Often these are solicited because of contingent events, and they have characteristic forms that differentiate their level of authority. In any case, and except when we are dealing with a teaching that enjoys moral unanimity in the whole Church, we are here dealing with a nonuniversal Magisterium and therefore one that is binding only on those to whom it is addressed.

We can conclude this section with an observation. The direct study of the Magisterium, as one of the essential aspects of theological work, includes different tasks: analyses that assure an exact *interpretation* through a knowledge of the sources, the process of editing, and the relationship each document has with the previous Magisterium, by reason of its continuity and unity, as a work of the same Holy Spirit; the verification

---

[119] Vatican Council II, *Lumen gentium,* no. 25, par. 1.

of the *level of authority* of each document and of the propositions found in it, in order to know whether one is dealing with a "defined" doctrine or not, a reformable or irreformable doctrine, etc. But, intimately linked to these analytical studies—and not as a secondary task—there is the obligation to penetrate into the deepest meaning of each teaching, in order to grasp the power of the divine seed sown in it by the Holy Spirit, with its power to bear fruit in abundance if it falls on ground that is well disposed and fertile (cf. Mt 13:23, 31).

5. The Question of Intrinsically Evil Acts and of Moral Absolutes

We have noted the existence of such acts and such absolutes in discussing dissent. There are some acts that are always evil by reason of their objects, that is, acts which, by reason of the description of the external act the person executes or proposes, already include a necessarily negative relationship to the moral order. These are deeds a person can never will without realizing a moral evil, without sinning. The norms prohibiting these acts have come to be customarily referred to by the expression "moral absolutes". Traditionally, the Church has taught as norms of this kind those prohibiting the direct killing of the innocent, lying or deceit, adultery, abortion, stealing, masturbation, bestiality, contraception, etc.[120] Intrinsically evil acts constitute a small, but significant, part of moral behavior. They are only a small number of those acts governed by negative precepts—not all negative precepts are moral absolutes—while the larger part of the precepts of the divine law are positive. These indicate the development of the virtues and, most definitely, of charity. Nevertheless, moral absolutes have a great importance because respect for the dignity of every person radically depends on their observance. In fact, current theological dissent has always been clearly identified with a discussion of the existence of moral absolutes and of the competence of the Magisterium to teach infallibly that they exist: these theologians do not deny that abortion or contraception are evil for the most part, but rather, they deny that

---

[120] Dissenting theologians deny that there are acts that are always in and of themselves illicit and which, therefore, when done without any defects of knowledge or of freedom, always constitute a sin and, save in the case of lying and of theft that admit parvity of matter, are always grave.

they are *always* immoral and that the Church can teach infallibly that they are *always* immoral.[121]

The denial of moral absolutes by Catholic theologians is of recent origin and is well known. It began with the so-called "Majority Opinion" of the Commission for the Study of Population, the Family, and Natality established during Vatican Council II, prior to the publication of *Humanae vitae*. This Commission was asked to give its opinion whether the "pill", of recent discovery at that time, came under the clear and imperative teachings of the Church on *contraception*.[122]

---

[121] An excellent treatment of this topic is provided by John Finnis, *Moral Absolutes: Tradition, Revision, and the Truth* (Washington, D.C.: The Catholic University of America Press, 1991); see also William E. May, *Moral Absolutes: Catholic Tradition, Current Trends, and the Truth* (Milwaukee: Marquette University Press, 1989).

[122] The topic that Paul VI reserved to himself, excluding it from discussions in the conciliar hall, was exclusively this. The intrinsic wickedness of the means of contraception known up to then (onanism, barriers, etc.) presented no doubts, but pertained from time immemmorable to the teachings of the Church, in its ordinary and universal Magisterium. Thus Pius XI, confronted with the fact that this teaching had been put into doubt by the Anglican Church in its Lambeth Conference, had willed formally to call it to mind: "Since, therefore, openly departing from the uninterrupted Christian tradition some recently have judged it possible solemnly to declare another doctrine regarding this question, the Catholic Church, to whom God has entrusted the defense of the integrity and purity of morals . . . raises her voice in token of her divine ambassadorship and through Our mouth proclaims anew: any use whatsoever of matrimony exercised in such a way that the act is deliberately frustrated in its natural power to generate life is an offence against the law of God and of nature, and those who indulge in such are branded with the guilt of grave sin" (*Casti connubii*, December 31, 1930). Pius XII willed explicitly to sanction anew this teaching in terms no less unequivocal: "Our Predecessor, Pius XI . . . in his Encyclical *Casti connubii*, December 31, 1930, solemnly proclaimed anew the fundamental law governing the marital act and conjugal relations; he said that any attempt on the part of the husband and wife to deprive this act of its inherent force or to impede the procreation of a new life, either in the performance of the act itself, or in the course of the development of its natural consequences, is immoral, and furthermore, no alleged 'indication' or need can convert an intrinsically immoral act into a moral and lawful one. This precept is as valid today as it was yesterday, and it will be the same tomorrow and always, because it does not imply a precept of human law, but it is the expression of a law which is natural and divine" (Address to the Italian Catholic Union of Midwives, October 29, 1951). This teaching had newly been confirmed by Vatican Council II, which, indicating the exclusively legitimate ways of regulating conceptions, expressly referred to both these documents (cf. *Gaudium et spes*, no. 50, n. 14). The element under discussion during the preparation of the Encyclical of Paul VI, on which the Magisterium of Pius XII (cf. his Address to the Seventh International Hematological Congress, September 12, 1958) had provided a precedent, was therefore exclusively the definitive confirming of the contraceptive character of the so-called "pill", that is, of biochemical means understood to deprive the conjugal act of its procreative capacity; because these means do not intervene "either in the performance of the conjugal act itself" nor "in the course of the development of its natural consequences", but rather entail prior acts which affect the biological processes

The documents of that Commission, which ought to have been reserved for the Holy Father alone, were on the other hand made public in an effort to exert pressure on Paul VI. They contained, in defense of the licitness of the use of the "pill", the principal arguments that would then be used by those who claim that there are no specific moral absolutes, although at that time the persons who signed the "Majority Opinion" did not take into account that future development and did not themselves deny completely the existence of moral absolutes.[123]

Specifically, the arguments on which the "Majority Opinion" is based are substantively the following two:

a. First of all, there is the argument based on the "preference principle" or the "principle of proportionate reason". Every act can rightly be done if there is a proportionate reason for doing it. Thus, to take the

---

and not directly the physical performance of the act; means, in other words, which science had only recently made available for human persons and whose spread had suddenly reached a high point during the time of the Council. No theologian, in fact, had seriously doubted, for example, that onanism is an act intrinsically evil by reason of its object. The only theological problem under debate was that concerning these new pharmacological means. The issue was whether they ought to be considered equally evil. What contributed to the disorientation of many was the idea that the Church had at that time cast doubt on what she had taught before on contraception and felt constrained to rethink this issue. If such had been the case, if a matter on which the Magisterium had expressed itself with such firmness allowed for reconsideration, then all its teaching from that time on would have become provisional, beginning with that which might be expressed in the future encyclical. But such was not the case. The only thing that was subject to questioning and on which the Holy Father Paul VI reserved for himself the final judgment, was the issue of the contraceptive character of these chemical means (all this is evident from the *Relatio* to the schema of July 3, 1964, and can also be inferred from the documents cited in note 14 of chap. 2 of *Gaudium et spes*).

[123] In fact, as William E. May has noted: "They insisted, in company with all Catholic moral theologians of the time, that there are moral absolutes, for they vehemently denied the charge, made by theologians on the commission who held that the norm against contraception by married couples was unchangeable, that the reasoning they employed to justify contraception by married couples could also be used to justify such acts as anal and oral sex. The authors of this Majority Report expressed outrage over this charge, and by doing so showed that they did indeed accept as true some moral absolutes. Despite their protests, however, it soon became clear that the reasoning they advanced to support their view that married persons could, under given conditions, rightly practice contraception could also be used to justify exceptions to other norms that had been regarded up to that time as absolute by Catholic moral theologians. This point has been conceded by revisionist theologians such as Charles E. Curran [cf. Charles E. Curran, "Divorce from the Perspective of a Revised Moral Theology", in his *Ongoing Revision* (Notre Dame, Ind.: University of Notre Dame Press, 1976), p. 121]" (*Introduction to Moral Theology*, p. 101).

life of another would be morally bad "not because life is under the exclusive dominion of God, but because it is contrary to reason *unless there is question of a good of a higher order*".[124]

b. Second, and in a way complementing the principle of proportionate reason, is the argument from the so-called "principle of totality". According to this argument, conjugal acts ought not to be examined in isolation but within the *whole* or *totality* of the marital life. If they are examined in this way, one will realize that, although there is a "material privation" (or what will later be called an "ontic" or "premoral" or "nonmoral" evil) inasmuch as the act is deprived of its procreative capacity, nonetheless this act receives its moral species from the total or entire behavior of the spouses, justifiable by reason of the previous or future execution of acts open to new life as well as by reason of the act's ordering to the fostering of love between the spouses or their mutual aid.[125]

---

[124] Papal Commission, Majority Opinion, *Documentum Syntheticum de Moralitate Nativitatum*, translated as "The Question Is Not Closed", in *The Birth Control Debate*, ed. Robert Hoyt (Kansas City, Mo.: The National Catholic Reporter, 1969), p. 69.

[125] William E. May, whom we follow in this exposition, writes: "Revisionist theologians — among them Franz Boeckle, Charles E. Curran, Josef Fuchs, Bernard Haering, Louis Janssens, Richard McCormick, Timothy E. O'Connell, Richard Gula, Franz Scholz, and Bruno Schueller — while denying the existence of moral absolutes in the sense previously described [i.e., as negative norms, universally valid, proscribing sorts or kinds of human actions describable in nonmorally evaluative terms], acknowledge that there are other kinds of moral absolutes. They admit, first of all, that there are absolutes in the sense of 'transcendent principles' that direct us to those elements of our existence whereby we transcend or surpass the rest of material creation. Thus they acknowledge the absoluteness of such principles as 'One ought always act in conformity with love of God and neighbor' and 'One must always act in accordance with right reason.' Similarly, they regard as absolute the norms they call 'formal.' These norms articulate what our inner dispositions and attitudes ought to be. It is thus always true that we should act justly, bravely, chastely and so on. Such formal norms express the qualities that ought to characterize the morally good person. They are *not* concerned with specific human acts and choices but rather with the moral *being* of the agent. In a way they are, as Josef Fuchs has said, 'exhortations rather than norms in the strict sense' (*Christian Ethics in a Secular Arena* [Washington: Georgetown University Press, 1984], p. 72), and, as Louis Janssens has noted, they 'constitute the absolute element in morals' ("Norms and Priorities in a Love Ethic," *Louvain Studies* 6 [1977]: 208). Finally, these theologians admit that norms using morally evaluative language to refer to actions that human persons ought never freely choose to do are absolute. Thus, we ought never to *murder*, because to murder is by definition to kill a person *unjustly*. Likewise, we ought never to have sex with the *wrong* person, because such sex is also wrong by definition. Yet norms of this kind are tautological and do not help us know which specific acts of killing are unjust or which specific kind of sex is sex with the wrong person, etc. As Fuchs observes, these 'absolute' norms are 'parenetic,' not instructive, and simply serve to remind us of what we already know and exhort us to avoid morally wrong actions and to engage in morally right ones (*Christian Ethics in a Secular Arena*, p. 72). While acknowledging 'absolutes' of the foregoing kind,

In addition to the two arguments of the "Majority Report" just noted—the "principle of proportionate reason" and the "principle of totality"—the authors who have come to deny openly and as a general thesis the existence of moral absolutes have recourse to a third new argument to support their position. Persons come to know particular or concrete norms—they say—by reasoning in common with other persons with whom they live in specific communities and reflecting on shared human experiences.[126] Given that concrete or "material" norms are discovered in this way, it follows, in the judgment of these authors, that such norms are affected by the historicity of human nature. Given the historical character of our human nature, they affirm, "we can never exclude the possibility that future experience, hitherto unimagined, might put a moral problem into a new frame of reference which would call for a revision of a norm that, when formulated, could not have taken such new experience into account."[127]

Following May, we can summarize the critique of this view in four points:

a. First of all, *the claims made by revisionist theologians about the Catholic tradition are incorrect:* the teaching that some acts are morally bad by reason of their *objects* has nothing to do with the reduction of morality to physical or ontic evils, nor were such actions judged morally bad without *any reference* to the intentions of the agent, since the objects of the acts in question are precisely and first of all *what* the person *wills.*[128]

---

revisionist theologians deny that there are moral absolutes in the sense of norms universally proscribing specifiable sorts of human action described in morally neutral language. They call such norms 'material' or 'behavioral/material' norms. According to them, such norms identify 'physical acts' or 'material acts' or 'behavior,' including, in some cases, the 'direct' or immediate effects of such acts, described independently of *any* of the acting subject's purposes (Fuchs, *Personal Responsibility and Christian Morality* [Washington, D.C.: Georgetown University Press, 1983], p. 74; Janssens, "Norms and Priorities in a Love Ethic," 210, 216; Richard Gula, *Reason Informed by Faith* [New York: Paulist Press, 1989], pp. 288–289). As one revisionist theologian, Richard Gula, puts it, such 'material norms,' 'when stated negatively, point out the kind of conduct which ought to be avoided *as far as possible,*' but all such norms 'ought to be interpreted as containing the implied qualifiers, "if there were no further intervening factors," or "unless there is a proportionate reason," or "all things being equal" ' (*Reason Informed by Faith,* p. 291)" (*Introduction to Moral Theology,* pp. 103–4, notes 12–18).

[126] Francis Sullivan, S.J., *Magisterium: Teaching Authority in the Catholic Church* (New York: Paulist Press, 1983), pp. 150–51. Sullivan lists Curran, Fuchs, Boeckle, Schueller, Haering, and other revisionists as agreeing with this way of putting the matter.

[127] Ibid., pp. 151–52. See Fuchs, *Personal Responsibility and Christian Morality,* p. 140.

[128] "Revisionist theologians . . . uniformly refer to moral absolutes as 'material' or 'concrete

b. Second, *the "principle of proportionate good" is not an evident truth,* contrary to what these authors seem to think. The comparing or commensurating of the various goods in conflict, on which this principle claims to be based, cannot be seriously proposed: since they are concerned with goods of the person, and not with mere material goods, there is no unambiguous standard according to which they can be measured, as material goods can be measured by a quantitative standard.[129]

c. Third, *the argument from totality,* as these authors use it, *is inexact.* It is true that an act must be judged by taking into account all of its elements, inasmuch as an act is morally good only if good in its totality: *bonum ex integra causa.* On the other hand, it is not true that it is impossible to judge that an act is bad if we do not take into account *all* the elements, since if only *one* of its substantial elements (the end

---

behavioral' norms. They say that these norms identify 'physical acts' or 'material acts,' including, in some instances, the direct effects of these acts. They maintain that such 'material' acts are physical or material events considered in abstraction of *any* purpose or intention of their agents. But Catholic theologians who today defend the truth of moral absolutes and those who did so in the past, including St. Thomas Aquinas . . . offer a much different account of these 'material' or 'behavioral' norms, which they *never* call 'material' or 'behavioral' norms. According to these theologians, the human acts identified and morally excluded by such norms are not specified independently of the agent's will. Rather, they are specified 'by the object' (*ex obiecto*) and by 'object' they mean exactly *what the agent chooses,* i.e., the act to be done or omitted and the proximate result sought in carrying out the choice to do this act. Thus, for example, Pope John Paul II, in *Reconciliatio et Poenitentia,* referred to 'a doctrine, based on the Decalogue and on the preaching of the Old Testament, and assimilated into the *kerygma* of the Apostles and belonging to the earliest teaching of the Church, and constantly reaffirmed by her up to this day.' What doctrine? The doctrine that 'there exist acts which *per se* and in themselves, independently of circumstances, are always seriously wrong *by reason of their object (propter obiectum)'* (n. 17). The Catholic tradition affirming these moral absolutes held that these norms do not bear upon acts 'in their *natural* species' but rather upon them 'in their *moral* species (or genus)' (cf. *Summa theologiae,* 1–2, 20, 2; *In II Sent.,* d. 40, q. un., a. 2)" (May, *Introduction to Moral Theology,* pp. 110–11).

[129] A comparison or commensurating of the human goods at issue would be possible only "if they could be reduced to some common denominator . . . such as centimeters, inches, or feet, scales adopted not by discovering a truth about these realities but by an arbitrary act of the will. But the goods involved in moral choice are not reducible to some common denominator. They are simply different and incomparable goods of human persons. Thus the presupposition upon which the alleged 'preference principle' rests is false: one cannot determine, prior to choice, which alternative unambiguously promises the 'greater' good. One cannot determine, in a nonarbitrary way, which human goods are greater or lesser. They are all incomparably good, irreducible aspects of human flourishing and well-being. And the same is true of individual instances of these basic goods of human persons. Who could judge whether Jane Smith's life is a 'greater good' than the life of John Jones?" (May, *Introduction to Moral Theology,* p. 113).

intended or the object chosen) is bad, we can then already affirm that the *whole* act is morally vitiated. For analogous reasons, no immoral act can be justified on the grounds of the generality of the person's behavior, as if individual personal dishonest acts only generate ontic evils and do not degrade the one who chooses to do them, so that these individual bad acts of the person could be evaluated on the basis of a general calculus of their effects. The recourse on the part of revisionist theologians to the principle of totality forgets that the totality also includes the immoral act that is of itself incapable of being justified.[130]

d. Finally, with respect to the *argument from the historicity of human existence,* revisionist theologians do not explain how and for what reasons basic human goods, such as life itself, knowledge of the truth, friendship, etc., can cease being goods and perfective of the person, nor how such a kind of radical changes in the valuation of the goods proper to human nature can be compatible with the unity of the human race and with its solidarity with Christ. In short, these theologians do not succeed in showing in what way their claim can be harmonized with the fundamental truth of Catholic Faith that "all human beings... have the same nature and the same origin",[131] "a common human nature",[132] and are "called to the same destiny" and so, having essentially the same human and supernatural destiny, can be citizens of the one People of God, regardless of race or place or time.[133]

---

[130] This argument, moreover, was explicitly taken up by *Humanae vitae* in connection with contraception, in a way that allows no doubts about its inadmissibility as a way of justifying conjugal acts intentionally rendered infertile: "Nor is it possible to justify deliberately depriving conjugal acts of their fertility by claiming that one is choosing the lesser evil. It cannot be claimed that these acts deprived of fertility should be considered together as a whole with past and future fertile acts and thus that they [should be judged to] share in one and the same moral goodness of the fertile acts [of marriage]. Certainly, it is sometimes permissible to tolerate moral evil—when it is the lesser evil and when one does so in order that one might avoid a greater evil, or so that one might promote a greater good. It is never permissible, however, to do evil so that good might result, not even for the most serious reasons. That is, one should never willingly choose to do an act that by its very nature violates the moral order [*ex propria natura moralem ordinem transgrediatur*] for *such acts are unworthy of Man for this very reason.* This is so even if one has acted with the intent to defend and advance some good either for individuals or for families or for society. Thus, it is a serious error to think that a conjugal act, deprived deliberately [*ex industria*] of its fertility, and which consequently is intrinsically wrong [*intrinsice inhonestum*], can be justified by being grouped together with the fertile acts of the whole of the marriage" (*Humanae vitae,* no. 14; Smith trans., pp. 283–84).

[131] Vatican Council II, *Gaudium et spes,* no. 29; *Lumen gentium,* no. 19.

[132] Vatican Council II, *Lumen gentium,* no. 13.

[133] Vatican Council II, *Gaudium et spes,* no. 29; *Lumen gentium,* no. 13.

The denial of moral absolutes "on the alleged claim that there is a radical change in concrete human nature because of 'historicity' simply cannot be sustained".[134]

The teaching of the Church on moral absolutes, constant within the Tradition, becomes clarified if one keeps in mind the distinction between affirmative demands and negative injunctions in the Christian vocation:

Because the human person's vocation is to love, even as he or she has been and is loved by God in Christ, it is not possible to say, affirmatively, precisely what love requires, for its affirmative obligations must be discovered by us in our creative endeavor to grow daily in love of God and neighbor. But moral absolutes show us what love *cannot* mean: it cannot mean that we deliberately set our wills *against* the good gifts that God wills to flourish in his children and close our hearts to our neighbors. Each true specific moral absolute summons each person to revere the goods intrinsic to human persons. Human persons, each in his or her corporeal and spiritual unity (*Gaudium et spes,* no. 14), are the only earthly creatures God has willed for themselves (*Gaudium et spes,* no. 24). Respect for human persons, each for his or her own sake, is therefore required by the Creator's design, and is a primary element in love of God and of one's neighbor as oneself. Such a respect and reverence is, moreover, a primary demand of that divine dignity to which Christ has raised human nature by assuming it (*Gaudium et spes,* no. 22).[135]

[134] May, *Introduction to Moral Theology,* p. 118.

[135] Ibid., p. 123. In an appendix to this chapter of his book, May explains the debate concerning the thought of St. Thomas concerning moral absolutes, which some have interpreted erroneously. May concludes: "His thought can be summarized as follows: 1. He teaches that there are acts that are 'evil in themselves in their kind' (*secundum se mala ex genere*), which may never be done 'for any good' (*pro nulla utilitate*), 'in no way' (*nullo modo*), 'in no event' (*in nullo casu*)—and gives examples of such acts in morally neutral terms: killing the innocent (*Summa theologiae,* 2-2, 64, 6), committing adultery in order to overthrow tyranny (*De malo,* q. 15, a. 1 ad 5), 'putting forth falsehood' (*Summa theologiae,* 2-2, 69, 2). 2. He teaches that besides affirmative precepts (which bind generally, *semper,* but not universally, *ad semper*), there are negative precepts which are valid and binding always and universally (*semper et ad semper*), e.g., 'at no time is one to steal or commit adultery' (*In Ep. ad Romanos,* c. 13, lect. 2; cf. *In III Sent.,* d. 25, q. 2, a. 1b, ad 3; *In IV Sent.,* d. 17, q. 3, a. 1d, ad 3; *De malo,* q. 7, a. 1, ad 8; *Summa theologiae,* 2-2, 33, 2; 79, 3, ad 3). 3. He everywhere rejects arguments attempting to solve 'conflict' cases by identifying a state of affairs or effects which could seem to be a lesser evil (*minus malum*) than doing an act that is wicked in itself or of its kind (*secundum se malum ex genere*) (*In IV Sent.,* d. 6, q. 1, qua 1, a. 1, ad 4; *Summa theologiae,* 2-2, 110, 3, ad 4; 3, 68, ad 3; 80, 6, ad 2). 4. He teaches that it is a revealed truth that evil may not be done for the sake of good, even the highest and greatest good such as salvation (*Summa theologiae,* 3, 68, 11, ad 3). 5. He teaches . . . that the precepts of the Decalogue, most of which are negative and binding always and universally (*semper et ad semper*) are, when properly understood, subject to no exceptions whatsoever, even by divine dispensation (*Summa*

The position of the Magisterium regarding both the existence of moral absolutes and the possibility of proposing them infallibly is and has always been unequivocal. Thus the *Instruction on the Ecclesial Vocation of the Theologian* has reminded us:

> The Magisterium has the task of discerning, by means of judgments normative for the consciences of believers, those acts which in themselves conform to the demands of faith and foster their expression in life and those which, on the contrary, because intrinsically evil, are incompatible with such demands. By reason of the connection between the orders of creation and redemption, and by reason of the necessity, in view of salvation, of knowing and observing the whole moral law, the competence of the Magisterium also extends to that which concerns the natural law.[136] Revelation also contains moral teachings which *per se* could be known by natural reason. Access to them, however, is made difficult by man's sinful condition. It is a doctrine of faith that these moral norms can be infallibly taught by the Magisterium.[137,138]

---

theologiae, 1-2, 100, 8; *In III Sent.,* d. 37, q. 1, a. 4). The conclusion is evident: St. Thomas affirmed the truth of moral absolutes" (ibid., pp. 135–36).

[136] Cf. Paul VI, *Humanae vitae,* no. 4, AAS 60 (1968): 483.

[137] Cf. Vatican Council I, *Dei filius,* chap. 2: DS 1786, 3005.

[138] Congregation for the Doctrine of the Faith, instruction *Donum veritatis* (*Instruction on the Ecclesial Vocation of the Theologian*), May 24, 1990, no. 16.

Chapter Two

THE MAGISTERIUM ON MARRIAGE
AND FAMILY: AN OVERVIEW

We will begin our account with the Council of Trent. The reason for doing so is simple. The mission of the Magisterium, as we have seen, is "to proclaim the Word of God, in his name and with his authority, and to define the proper meaning of this Word every time that this becomes necessary."[1] The Church has not ceased teaching the Word of God in every age. But the appearance of documents of the Magisterium, where a specific question is determined or defined, is usually linked to historical moments of confusion or doctrinal discussion that have required a clarifying intervention on the part of the hierarchy. With respect to marriage, one can say that the first moment of this kind, or at any rate the most significant one, was the Council of Trent, when the deposit of revelation was threatened by the Protestant Reformation.

■ In reality, there is a somewhat prior synthesis of Catholic doctrine on marriage: the *Decree pro Armenis* of the Council of Florence (1439). In enumerating the sacraments, with a view toward union with the Armenians, the document summarized Catholic doctrine on matrimony as follows: "The seventh is the sacrament of matrimony, sign of the union of Christ with the Church, as the Apostle says: 'this is a great mystery: I mean in reference to Christ and to the Church' (Eph 5.32). The efficient cause of matrimony is mutual consent, ordinarily expressed through words and having reference to the present. Three blessings are assigned to matrimony. The first is the procreation and education of children for the worship of God. The second is the fidelity that each of the spouses must observe towards the other. The third is the indissolubility of matrimony, indissoluble because it signifies the indivisible union between Christ and the Church. Although a

---

[1] Louis Bouyer, *Dictionary of Theology* (New York: Desclee, 1965), p. 288.

63

separation from bed may be permitted by reason of marital infidelity, nevertheless it is not permitted to contract another matrimony since the bond of marriage lawfully contracted is perpetual."[2] It seems, however, preferable to begin with Trent, since Trent offers a more extensive and detailed analysis, providing a nucleus of the Tradition of the Church, solemnly proposed by the Church.

We should add that—as we will have occasion to verify—the principal issues treated by the Magisterium are: (a) the nature, goods, and ends of marriage; (b) marital morality; (c) the competence of the Church with respect to marriage; (d) the urgency, for the well-being of both Church and society, that the divine plan for marriage and the family be respected.[3]

1. Fifteen Centuries of the Church: The Portrait Drawn at the Council of Trent

We will divide our presentation of the teaching of Trent into four major areas: the establishment of the deposit of faith regarding marriage up to Trent; the attacks on this by the Reformers; the fundamental content of the teachings of the Council on marriage; and the implementation of the Council and open questions.

A. *The doctrine on marriage at the beginning of the Reformation*

Its character as a sacrament, as well as the properties of the marriage bond, had already been irreformably formulated prior to Trent. On the other hand, other issues, such as the nature of sacramental grace, the minister of the sacrament, the relation-

[2] Council of Florence, bull *Exultate*, November 22, 1439, H. Denzinger and A. Schoenmetzer, *Enchiridion Symbolorum Definitionum et Declarationum de rebus fidei et morum*, 34th ed. (Barcelona-Rome: Herder, 1967), (DS) no. 1327; trans. John F. Clarkson, S.J., John H. Edwards, S.J., William J. Kelly, S.J., John J. Welch, S.J., in *The Church Teaches: Documents of the Church in English Translation* (St. Louis, Mo.: B. Herder, 1955; reprinted, Rockford, Ill.: Tan Books, 1973), p. 335. In *Enchiridion Familiae: Textos del Magisterio Pontificio y Conciliar Sobre el Matrimonio y la Familia (Siglos I a XX)*, ed. A. Sarmiento and J. Escrivá-Ivars, vol. 1 (Madrid: Ediciones Rialp, 1992), p. 139.

[3] Indeed, man himself is at stake, precisely because of the "familial character of human life". See Pope John Paul II, encyclical *Laborem exercens*, September 14, 1981, no. 9.

ships between contract and sacrament, etc., had not been formulated in this way.

From her very beginning, the Church has lived in virtue of the power of the seven sacraments instituted by Christ. This is so even if the doctrine of her sacraments had not yet been elaborated as we know them today.[4] Concretely, thanks to the witness of the Fathers, it is clear that marriage has always been regarded as a source of the grace needed by spouses in order to live a holy life, that it is the symbol of the union between Christ and the Church. That truth was so deeply rooted and experienced that the Faith, at least two times—once in the Roman society and later with the Germanic tribes—succeeded in changing social customs, making them abandon their habits with respect to divorce.[5]

Nonetheless, the detailed development of the doctrine on marriage as a sacrament took place over many centuries. So much time was required because of the peculiarity of this sacrament. Although its sacramental nature was not in doubt, a precise determination of the specific content of the sacramental grace of marriage[6] and of its proper sign had not been successfully worked out: however, prior to the Reformation, it had already been established—at the Council of Florence—that the sign of the sacrament of marriage was the very act of consent of the spouses.[7] Trent, as we will see, will solemnly proclaim the dogmatic character of the principal teachings of the Church, already firmly proposed before, but not always defined as truths of Faith.

---

[4] Still, it was earlier and more extensively than some think today. See the interesting study of G. Baldanza, "Il rito del matrimonio nell'Eucologio Barberini 336. Analisi della sua visione teologica", *Ephemerides Liturgicae* 93 (1979): 316–51.

[5] On this see the important study of F. Delpini, *Indissolubilità matrimoniale e divorzio dal I al XII secolo* (Milan: Ned, 1979).

[6] On this see the accurate study of G. Baldanza, "La grazia sacramentale matrimoniale al Concilio di Trento. Contributo per uno studio storico-critico", *Ephemerides Liturgicae* 98 (1983): 89–140. See also Edward Schillebeeckx, *Marriage: Human Reality and Saving Mystery*, trans. N. D. Smith (New York: Sheed & Ward, 1965), pp. 244–60.

[7] Consent, however, understood—as we will have occasion to repeat—as a covenant of conjugal love, similar to and a sign of the covenants of the Old and New Testaments. Only later was the understanding of consent reduced to being like that of exchange contracts; on the problems raised by this reduction see G. Baldanza, "L'approfondimento del segno sacramentale per il rinnovamento e lo sviluppo della teologia matrimoniale: alcune nuove prospettive", *La Scuola Cattolica*, 102 (1974): 1–48.

Nor had it been fully clear, prior to Trent, who was the *minister* of marriage. Certainly, the recognition that the sign of the sacrament was the very consent of the spouses led to considering them as its ministers. But some difficulties remained: in a marriage with a non-Catholic, how could the non-Catholic spouse be minister? What, too, was the role in the sacramental sign played by the priest's blessing and, therefore, by the priest himself? Nor was there agreement about the moment of the *institution* of the sacrament of marriage; indeed, even today this has not been specified by the Magisterium.

The Council was principally concerned to respond to the errors of Luther and, in addition, to resolve the problem of the canonical form required for the *validity* of marriage—the latter so that an end could be brought to the abuses of clandestine marriages.

B. *Criticisms of the reformers*

At the heart of the crisis of the Reformation, even with respect to matrimony, is an error about the relationships between nature and grace: thus the holiness and the reality of the sacrament were rendered obscure.

Luther and Calvin rejected the teachings of the Church on marriage. Here it is opportune to stress that the root of their errors is anchored in the very heart of Lutheran thought: the idea of the corruption of nature and of justification as a merely extrinsic reality.[8]

> ■ If human nature is totally corrupt, if grace does not intrinsically reorder it, marriage can aim only at the satisfaction of concupiscence, with the characteristics proper to corrupt nature. Concupiscence itself, therefore, would be the law of marriage, and grace would be limited to excusing sin. Christian marriage is not understood nor are its laws understood if one forgets the real situation of man: *natura condita, lapsa et redempta.* Then one can also understand how the present crisis has developed, having as its basis another historical moment in which the relationships between nature and grace are also found at the center of

---

[8] Cf. L. F. Mateo Seco, "Bondad del hombre y santidad del matrimonio", in *Cuestiones fundamentales sobre matrimonio y familia (Actas del II Simposio Internacional de Teología),* ed. A. Sarmiento et al. (Pamplona: Eunsa, 1980), pp. 211–29.

theological debate.[9] In modern errors regarding the holiness of marriage, one can notice, as at the time of Luther, an antecedent incomprehension either of original sin or of the nature of justification or of the efficacy of the sacrament.

For the reformers, *marriage was not a sacrament.* Luther expresses himself this way:

> In every sacrament we find the word of a divine promise, which he who receives the sign must believe: of itself the sign cannot constitute the sacrament. But in no place is it known that a man who takes a wife will receive the grace of God. Moreover, no sign has been given by God to marriage. One can nowhere read that marriage has been instituted by God to signify what it is, although every visible thing can be understood as a figure and an allegory of invisible things. But figure and allegory are not sacraments in the precise sense that Christianity attributes to that word.[10]

In like manner, Calvin denies the sacramental character of marriage, which, according to him, would have begun to have been acknowledged only at the time of Pope Gregory the Great. The text of St. Paul in his Epistle to the Ephesians did not give any foundation to the doctrine of the sacrament, because in it the word *sacrament* simply designates in a general way the idea of a mystery. Making marriage a sacrament, according to Calvin, was purely an attempt by the Church to take over the power of legislating and judging in the area of marriage.[11]

■ The Church has never defined, even today, the moment of the institution of marriage, because it does not seem able to determine this either from Scripture or from Tradition. On the other hand, the Church has defined the institution itself, which is clear from revelation; because Christ restored marriage to its original dignity (Mt 19:4–6), something that would not have been possible without a specific help of grace. Moreover, this is shown through the presence of Christ at the wedding in Cana (Jn 2:1ff.), a presence the Tradition has always understood as a manifestation of his will "to sanctify the principle of

---

[9] Carlo Caffarra, "Le lien entre mariage-réalité de la création et mariage-sacrement", *Esprit et Vie* 24 (1978): 375.

[10] Martin Luther, *De Captivitate Babylonica Ecclesiae praeludium* (1510), ed. Weimar, *Schriften* 4.527.

[11] John Calvin, *Institution de la Religion Chrétienne*, in *Corpus Ref.*, 32, 1121–25.

human generation ... and to prepare grace for those who are to be born through marriage", as St. Cyril of Alexandria explicitly affirms.[12] Finally, the rich Pauline doctrine on marriage as a participation and sign of the union between Christ and the Church (Eph 5:32), which only grace can bring about, requires this.

In practice, the denial of the sacramental character of marriage is linked to the Lutheran thesis that holds that *marriage is nothing else than the institution destined to satisfy concupiscence,* which has its own rights in man. Luther affirms: "The conjugal debt is a sin, a raging sin. It differs in no way from adultery and fornication as regards the ardor and pleasure found in it. It would be fitting not to fall into such sin, but spouses cannot avoid it. Thus God, because of His mercy, does not impute this sin to them."[13] "The marital debt can never be fulfilled without sin, but mercifully God pardons this sin, because marriage is His work; and by way of this sin He preserves all the good which He had included and blessed in marriage."[14] Marriage surely provides an an external cover of dignity to the intrinsically perverse act of satisfying

[12] St. Cyril of Alexandria, *In Ion. Comm.,* II, 1–4; PG 73.224–25.

[13] Martin Luther, *De votis monasticis Martini Lutheri judicium,* ed. Weimar, *Schriften,* 8.654, 19–22.

[14] Martin Luther, *Vom ehelichen Leben,* ed. Weimar, *Schriften,* X-1, p. 304. These assertions can seem almost incredible to contemporary men. But it is necessary to have a sense of history—precisely to overcome the limits of a historicist mentality. Although the Church has always taught fully the goodness of marriage and of the marital act which is proper to spouses, as this is reflected in Tradition and in the Magisterium, theologians have not always been able to attain the heights of the full richness found in revealed truth. Although the Fathers of the Church fought it, manicheanism left its traces: even Peter Lombard, the master of the *Sentences,* thought that after the fall of man marriage, which prior to the fall was an office of nature (*officium naturae*), became rather a *remedy for concupiscence,* a support for nature and a brake on vice. For the master of the *Sentences,* the bodily union of the spouses, in the state of fallen nature, would be in itself evil—because of the law of sin existing in our members—if it was not excused by the goods of marriage (*fides, proles, sacramentum*). It was only with St. Albert and St. Thomas that a full recovery of the biblical teaching on the goodness of marriage and of the marital act was achieved. In his *Scriptum super IV Libros Sententiarum (In IV Sent.,* dist. 41, a. 3), St. Thomas affirmed that since the marital act comes from a nature created by God it is impossible that this act not be done in a virtuous way, and he characterized the opposing view as manichean. Indeed, he did not fail to add (dist. 41, a. 4) that the marital act is not only good but also meritorious if it is done according to the norms established by virtue. On this point see Servais Pinckaers, "Ce que le Moyen Age pensait du mariage", in *L'Evangile et la morale* (Fribourg: Editions Université Fribourg Suisse; Paris: Editions du Cerf, 1990), pp. 142–65. See also Germain Grisez, "Marriage: Reflections Based on St. Thomas Aquinas and Vatican Council II", *The Catholic Mind* 64 (June 1966): 4–19; Fabian Parmisano, "Love and Marriage in the Middle Ages I and II", *New Blackfriars* 50 (1969): 599–606, 649–60.

concupiscence; from the vantage point of a corrupt nature it is not possible to consider marriage as a holy and sanctifiable reality. Logically, along with the sacred and sacramental character of marriage the whole Christian morality of marriage also falls: *marriage would not be indissoluble, nor would it even be directed any longer to the procreation and education of children, nor would it have unity as its necessary property.* If the conjugal act is not the expression of a spiritual love, but the satisfaction of a physical need, it would evidently be contrary to nature to keep bound together in marriage spouses who could no longer mutually procure this satisfaction for themselves,[15] just as the celibacy of the clergy is also contrary to nature.[16] Luther finally allows polygamy, through analogous reasons regarding the need to satisfy concupiscence.[17] He ends up by seeing in marriage merely a civil matter about which the Church has no competence.[18]

■ These doctrines have a dangerous echo for two reasons: first, there is a connaturality between them and certain ideas of some humanists: for example, Erasmus said that the Fathers never thought of making marriage a sacrament, although he personally did not repudiate the discipline of the Church.[19] The second is that for various reasons—not always equally valid—secular princes wanted to get more control over marriage. To reduce it simply to a civil contract made this easier to do. Here one can think of the battle between the emperor and the Pope regarding the dissolution of the marriage of Louis of Bavaria, in which Ockham—in his *Tractatus de jurisdictione imperatoris in causis matrimonialibus*—affirmed his acceptance of the thesis that marriage is simply a civil contract.

C. *The decrees and canons of Trent on marriage*

As we have said, the Fathers of the Council of Trent were concerned with two issues: reaffirming, finally in a dogmatic proclamation, the perennial teaching of the Church, put into doubt by the Reformers, and solving the serious pastoral questions that had arisen regarding

---

[15] Martin Luther, *An dem christlichen Adel deutscher Nation von des christlichen standes Besserung*, ed. Weimar, *Schriften*, 6.558.

[16] Martin Luther, *Schmalkaldische Artikel*, ed. Weimar, *Schriften*, 50.248–49.

[17] G. Le Bras, "Mariage", *Dictionnaire de Théologie Catholique* (hereinafter referred to as DTC), 9.2226.

[18] Ibid.

[19] Desiderius Erasmus, *Opera*, ed. Clericus, 6.692ff.

clandestine marriages. Four schemas were examined before there was success in reaching a definitive text, which was divided into two decrees: one on the sacrament itself (*De doctrina sacramenti matrimonii*) and the other on its canonical form (*Super reformatione circa matrimonium*). The first canon of the second decree began with the word *Tametsi*, and it is by this name that this decree is usually designated.

■ Among the lengthy discussions of the various schemas we would like to emphasize, in an apparently capricious way, one fact. When they were discussing the canonical form of marriage and had reached a stalemate in their debates, one of the conciliar Fathers—Cardinal di Lorena—broke the impasse with a thought worth noting: we are not, he said, debating "theories", but the actual state of many families, of uncertain marriages, of abortions, etc.[20] Even today we must note that in the morality of the family the happiness and, indeed, the existence of many human lives are at stake, each one of which—as the Holy Father is pleased to repeat—is unique, unrepeatable, and worthy of love.

A recent study in a famous medical journal in the United States provided data regarding the terrible number of psychical illnesses found in the children of divorced parents.[21] When one opts for the dissolubility of the bond, in practice one is choosing to torment these lives. A great many sufferings, often unjust, of many persons is dependent on whether or not one respects God's plan for marriage and the family.

The teaching of Trent on marriage can be summarized in the following way.

1. *The divine institution of marriage and its later elevation by Christ to the level of a sacrament.* The decree *De doctrina sacramenti matrimonii* began precisely by calling to mind the divine institution of marriage, at the very beginnings of the human race, established as a unique and indissoluble bond between two persons:

The first parent of the human race, under the inspiration of the Divine Spirit, proclaimed the perpetual and indissoluble bond of matrimony

[20] S. Ehses, *Concilii Tridentini Actorum pars sexta* (Fribourg, 1924), p. 642.

[21] M. S. Jellinek and L. S. Slovik, "Divorce: Impact on Children", *New England Journal of Medicine* 305, no. 10 (September 1981): 557–60, with an ample bibliography. See also *Beyond Rhetoric: A New American Agenda for Children and Families*, Final Report of the National Commission on Children (Washington, D.C.: National Commission on Children, 1991), part I.

when he said, "This now is bone of my bones, and flesh of my flesh. . . . Wherefore a man shall leave father and mother and cleave to his wife: and they shall be two in one flesh" (Gen. 2:23f; see Eph. 5:31) (Int., par. 1).

Marriage is, therefore, a good explicitly willed by God. In the face of every kind of manicheanism, the Church has always defended the natural goodness proper to marriage, which remains even after original sin. However, with his faculties wounded, man is not able to succeed in living this rightly, in its fullness. To give spouses the help necessary and to turn marriage into a road to holiness, Christ made of it a sacrament, which produces grace:

> Christ Himself, who instituted the holy sacraments and brought them to perfection, merited for us by his passion the grace that brings natural love to perfection, and strengthens the indissoluble unity, and sanctifies the spouses. The Apostle Paul intimates this when he says: "Husbands, love your wives, just as Christ also loved the Church, and delivered himself up for her" (Eph. 5:25); and he immediately adds: "This is a great mystery—I mean in reference to Christ and to the Church" (Eph. 5:32) (ibid., par. 3).[22]

> ■ The reasoning of the Magisterium does not enter into disputes over the meaning of the word "sacrament" in the Epistle to the Ephesians,[23] nor is it concerned with the "moment" of institution; it simply emphasizes that, if marriage could not give grace, what Christ and the Church have always demanded of it would not have been possible, nor would it ever have been experienced in the way it has always been in the Christian community.

The Council not only proclaims anew the teaching that marriage is a sacrament, but it also explicitly defends this character as a *dogma of the Faith*: "If anyone says that marriage is not truly and properly one of the seven sacraments of the law of the Gospel, and says that it was not instituted by Christ, but introduced into the Church by men, and that it does not confer grace, let him be anathema" (can. 1). In order to speak out in these terms, the Council of Trent appealed to the constant

---

[22] On the doctrinal importance and the history of the text of the decree *De doctrina sacramenti matrimonii*, cf. Baldanza, "La grazia sacramentale matrimoniale al Concilio di Trento", pp. 121–29.

[23] But it holds as sufficient the texts of Eph 5:25 and 5:32 to "show that marriage is a sacrament". Cf. ibid., p. 125.

teaching of "the holy Fathers, the councils, and the Tradition of the universal Church" (Int., par. 4).

2. *The unity and indissolubility of marriage and its character as sanctifying the spouses.* The Council explicitly sanctioned the unity of marriage in the face of all Luther's errors: "If anyone says that Christians are permitted to have several wives simultaneously, and that such a practice is not forbidden by any divine law (see Matt. 19:4–9): let him be anathema" (can. 2). Unity and indissolubility are explicit teachings of Christ, which he himself presented as intrinsic to the original institution:

> Christ our Lord taught more clearly that only two persons are joined and united by this marriage bond. He referred to the words of Genesis spoken by God ["they shall be two in one flesh"] and said: "Therefore now they are no longer two, but one flesh" (Matt. 19:6); and immediately after this, with the words, "What therefore God has joined together, let no man put asunder" (Matt. 19:6; Mk. 10:9), he confirmed the stability of that same bond which had been declared by Adam so long before (Int., par. 2).

Even this is a teaching of dogmatic value, as two canons confirm: "If anyone says that the Church is in error when it has taught and does teach according to the doctrine of the Gospels and apostles (see Mk. 10; 1 Cor. 7) that the marriage bond cannot be dissolved because of adultery on the part of either the husband or the wife . . . let him be anathema" (can. 7; see also can. 5).

> ■ The indissoluble character of marriage was always stressed by the Church, even in evangelizing peoples who practice divorce. Thus the witness of St. Ambrose: "Dismiss your wife, as if you had the right to do so and as if by doing so you committed no crime; you judge in this way because human law does not forbid it; but the divine law does forbid it."[24] This firmness of the Church had, as we have seen, the salutary effect of changing not only the mentality but also the civil laws of the people to whom the Church brought the Faith: first the Romans, then the barbarians.[25] By doing this, the Church surely remains faithful to God; but moreover, she shows her great love for men, by helping them cease a practice that harms them, even if they think the opposite.[26] Therefore, like a mother, the Church has never

[24] St. Ambrose, *Expositio Ev. sec. Lucam,* 8.5; PL 15.1767.
[25] Cf. Delpini, *Indissolubilità matrimoniale e divorzio.*
[26] John Paul II, *Familiaris consortio,* nos. 82–84.

admitted to the Eucharist those who have remarried after divorce—according to civil law—a mother never stops fighting what brings harm to the health of her children.[27]

Twice the Council affirmed that marriage *confers grace and sanctifies the spouses:* "Marriage, in the new law . . . by means of Christ confers grace" (Int., par. 3); Christ merited "the grace that brings natural love to perfection . . . and sanctifies the spouses" (Int., par. 2).[28] But this was not, nevertheless, a matter particularly examined in depth by the Council; perhaps because it had other basic concerns: for instance, that of emphasizing, in the face of all the contrary affirmations of the Reformers, the value and superiority of virginity. In fact, it devoted one canon to this: "If anyone says that the married state is to be preferred to the state of virginity or of celibacy and that it is not better and holier to remain in virginity or celibacy than to be joined in marriage (see Matt. 19:11f; I Cor. 7:25f, 38, 40): let him be anathema" (can. 10).

■ To affirm the doctrine—revealed—on the superiority of virginal love for God, does not require any diminishing of the grandeur of marital love. To the contrary, it is the same pessimism that denies the possibility of celibacy that denies the holiness of marriage and its sublime demands, reducing it to a selfish satisfaction of instinct.[29] The understanding of the holiness of human love and of the exclusive gift of self to the Lord grow together: "Only among those who understand the value of human love in all its depth . . . can there arise that other ineffable understanding of which Jesus spoke (Matt. 19:11). It is a pure gift of God which moves one to surrender body and soul to our Lord, offering him an undivided heart, without the mediation of earthly love."[30]

3. *The power of the Church over the sacrament.* In elevating marriage to the level of a sacrament, Christ gave to the Church the corresponding power of guarding its holiness. In fact, the Church has always done this. And this is another of the truths explicitly defined by Trent and

[27] As *Familiaris consortio* has newly confirmed; cf. no. 84. On this matter also see F. Sancho, "Situaciones matrimoniales irregulares y recepción de la Eucaristia", *Cuestiones fundamentales sobre matrimonio y familia,* pp. 201–10.

[28] On this see Baldanza, "La grazia sacramentale matrimoniale al Concilio di Trento", pp. 110–14 and 135–38.

[29] Cf. Mateo Seco, "Bondad del hombre y santidad del matrimonio", pp. 214–15.

[30] Blessed Josemaría Escrivá, *Conversations with Monsignor Escriva* (Manila: Sinag-Talag, 1974), no. 122, p. 143. On this see F. Festorazzi, "Matrimonio e verginità nella Bibbia", in *Matrimonio e verginità* (Venegono Inferiore, 1963), pp. 51–158.

with a fullness that demands attention: six canons. This insistence is explained by the fact that at stake was the principle—even if it was not defined—of the unity between the conjugal covenant and the sacrament, the basis for the whole teaching of the Church on marriage. Specifically, the *competence* proper to the Church is affirmed explicitly with respect to the regimen of impediments (canons 3, 4, and 9), to the Church's vicarious power of dissolving a ratified but not consummated marriage (canon 6), and of decreeing separation without dissolution of the bond (canon 7); finally, this competence is affirmed for the Church's jurisdiction over marriage cases: "If anyone says that marriage cases are not under the jurisdiction of ecclesiastical judges: let him be anathema" (canon 12).

In the authentic interpretation of this last canon, made by Pius VI in 1788, it is affirmed that the *reason* for this competence is found in the fact that the contract is the same as the sacrament:

> The words of the canon are so general that they comprise and embrace all cases: the spirit or mind of the law is of such amplitude that it does not allow exceptions or limitations. In fact, these cases belong to the jurisdiction proper to the Church for no other reason than that the marriage contract is truly and properly one of the seven sacraments of the Law of the Gospel; since the meaning of a sacrament is common to every marriage case, all ought to pertain exclusively to ecclesiastical judges.[31]

■ The Magisterium did not exclude by this canon—and afterward the Magisterium has clarified the matter many times—the competence of civil tribunals regarding the "civil effects" of marriage. The power of the Church over the contract derives from the fact that it is one of the seven sacraments: this power extends to whatever affects the marriage bond and to its inseparable effects (but not to separable or civil effects such as the economic arrangements of the household, hereditary rights, etc.). As on so many other occasions, therefore, progress took place more rapidly in the practice and life of the Church than in theological formulations. Theologians had not yet come to express precisely the doctrine of the inseparability of marriage and the sacrament, but the Magisterium took as guide in its judgments the implicit truth of faith, without doubts or hesitations, in this matter as in that regarding the canonical form of marriage. Nonetheless, there were some Council Fathers opposed to this canon. They said that this teaching

---

[31] Pius VI, letter *Deessemus nobis,* September 16, 1788; DS 2598; *Enchiridion Familiae,* 1.312.

would annoy temporal rulers as an abuse of power on the part of the Church, because the Church has competence only for "cases concerning the sacrament and not the contract".[32] But the Magisterium, under the guidance of the Holy Spirit, did not vacillate; behind the lack of precision existing at that time in doctrinal formulations, it seized the very reality of sacramental life, the inseparable unity—in baptized persons—which linked marriage, as an institution of nature, to the sacrament.

4. *The requirement of canonical form: doctrinal implications of a disciplinary solution.* The second of the Tridentine decrees on marriage—the decree *Tametsi*—is concerned with a disciplinary question: to establish a canonical form required for *the validity of marriage (ad validitatem)*, in order to resolve the serious pastoral problem of clandestine marriages. Up to the time of Trent, the Church had forbidden them with severe penalties, though always acknowledging their validity. Nonetheless, taking into account the fact that "these penalties were not efficacious because of the disobedience of men and that clandestine marriages were the occasion of serious sins", the Council judged it necessary to establish a canonical form for validity itself. Specifically, it required the celebration of marriage in the presence of the parish priest and two or three witnesses (chap. 1, pars. 2 and 3). In the event that these conditions are not respected, the contracting parties become *ipso iure*, incapable of marriage, and, therefore, their marriage contract is void (ibid., par. 3).

In the course of discussions, the conciliar Fathers raised for themselves the problem of providing a foundation for this nullity by reason of the lack of a proper "canonical form". This provided an occasion for reproposing the thesis that there is a separation between the marriage contract and the sacrament. As a matter of fact, there were no precedents in the life of the Church for establishing the invalidity of the sacrament simply because certain forms prescribed only by ecclesiastical law were not observed. Nullity had always been limited to flaws in the essential form of the sacrament, that is, consent; the formalities established through ecclesiastical law only made the marriage illicit, not invalid. On the other hand, to impose a juridical form for the validity, not of the sacrament, but only of the contract, would not

[32] Ehses, *Concilii Tridentini Actorum*, pp. 662, 672, 717.

have posed any difficulty.[33] Despite this, the majority of the Fathers was definitely opposed to this, because the separability of the contract from the sacrament was contrary to the traditional practice, always opposed to this separation, which served as the basis for canon 12, and whose great importance had been shown throughout history.[34] A just solution was thus arrived at: the Church could establish, as she had in fact done many times in the past, diriment impediments of human positive law. Thus from now on [i.e., after Trent]—the Council decided—the failure to have recourse to the canonical form would entail a canonical irregularity, rendering the contracting parties incapable of marrying and, therefore, nullifying the marital covenant, the sign of the sacrament. For this reason, clandestine marriages prior to the new Tridentine norm were considered by the Council as true sacramental marriages, even if they were celebrated in the absence of a priest (chap. 1, par. 1). Thus the lack of canonical form would render the sacrament null precisely because it rendered the contract null; it did not modify the form of the sacrament, but the irregularity resulting from a canonical impediment regarding the contracting parties. At the base of the solution adopted was, in truth, the conviction of the *inseparability between contract and sacrament.*[35]

■ It has thus been said that, although "the *explicit* condemnation of the separability [between contract and sacrament] is relatively recent, the thesis of such inseparability is a constant teaching of the Church, implicitly contained in the ecclesiastical Tradition from the first centuries, recognized in the formulations (some with true dogmatic character) of the solemn and ordinary Magisterium and in the common opinion of the overwhelming majority of authors."[36]

On the other hand, the thesis of the separability appears as a novelty, introduced by some theologians, for the purpose of resolving the difficulties brought up by them for providing—from the perspective of their own schema for understanding matters—an adequate explanation of certain realities. Scotus acted in this way, in order to justify the marriages of deaf persons and marriages by proxy, because he thought—in conformity with his own "system"—that the sacramen-

[33] Ibid., pp. 645, 650–51, 661–65, 667–69, 673–75.
[34] Ibid., pp. 671 and 677.
[35] Cf. Javier Hervada, "La inseparabilidad entre contracto y sacramento en el matrimonio", *Cuestiones fundamentales sobre matrimonio y familia*, pp. 259–72.
[36] Ibid., p. 261.

tal sign could not be efficacious without words (something that is not true). Or, likewise, Billuart, who hoped to clarify the situation of baptized persons who want to contract a valid marriage without intending to receive the sacrament, perhaps even with the explicit intention of not receiving it. Melchior Cano was another author of this mind, with his proposal to show that the blessing of the priest—in his opinion—conferred the sacrament: his blessing would be the form of the sacrament, while the consent of the spouses would only be its matter. Finally, some of the Tridentine Fathers allowed themselves to be carried away by this error in their desire to provide an explanation for establishing the canonical form *ad validitatem.*

Despite this, the Church always holds the inseparability between marriage and the sacrament. This conviction is at the root not only of the Tridentine solution for requiring the canonical form but of the uninterrupted tradition, constant from the apostolic age, of not requiring any marriage rite of spouses who convert, precisely because Tradition held that the administration of baptism implied the elevation of the existing conjugal pact to the level of a true sacrament. Sacrament and contract are, among the baptized, inseparable, because Christ made the institution of marriage—*institutum naturae*—itself, i.e., the contract or conjugal covenant, to be a sacrament. St. Leo the Great had already said: "Where among Christians there is not a sacrament, there is not even marriage."[37]

D. *The implementation of the Council: open questions*

In 1564, the Holy Father Pius V created the *Sacra Congregatio Cardinalium Concilii Tridentini interpretum,* or simply the Congregation of the Council, which had the duty to watch over its faithful implementation. Its faculties were augmented by St. Pius V; and Pius VI also gave it the power to interpret authoritatively all the decrees of the Tridentine reform. Relative to the decree *De reformatione matrimonii,* the new

[37] St. Leo the Great, *Epistula 167, ad Rusticum Narbonense,* resp. ad inquis. 4 (Mansi 4.401ff). Cf. Hervada, "La inseparabilidad", pp. 270–71, n. 22. On this matter see also Carlo Caffarra, "Marriage as a Reality in the Order of Creation and Marriage as a Sacrament", in *Contemporary Perspectives on Christian Marriage,* ed. Richard Malone and John R. Connery, S.J. (Chicago: Loyola University Press, 1984), pp. 117–80.

congregation clarified, among other matters, the following questions: (a) that the priest assisting at marriage does not carry out any act of jurisdiction, but is simply a qualified witness, a *testis spectabilis;*[38] (b) that the mere physical presence of witnesses does not suffice, but they must assure their own certitude that the contracting parties actually give true marital consent;[39] and (c) that the thesis of a *presumed marriage* can in no way be admitted,[40] etc.

We can conclude that the Council of Trent teaches in a solemn way, in a succinct but complete way, the nucleus of the Christian Tradition—fifteen centuries of fidelity to Christ—on marriage: its divine institution and elevation to a sacrament of the New Law, the grace it gives to the spouses, its unity and indissolubility, and finally the power Christ attributed to the Church for protecting marriage and bringing it to its fulfillment. On the other hand, the inseparability between the conjugal pact and the sacrament, which will be the object of the Magisterium of the 17th to 18th centuries, was not explicitly made. Nonetheless, the question that perhaps most needed development—and which had behind it an enormously rich tradition—was that of the holiness of married life.[41] One author, a half-century ago, wrote as follows: "The most attractive chapter of the doctrine of marriage in modern times will not, probably, be found in dogmatic or exegetical theology, but in moralists and in the directors of souls who succeed in teaching their own contemporaries, in a more lively language than that of the scholastics, the richness of the Christian tradition."[42] As we shall see, this will be the work begun with *Casti connubii,* developed as a dogmatic and pastoral teaching by Vatican II, emphasized and completed by *Familiaris consortio.*

---

[38] Schulte and Richter, *Canones et decreta Concilii Tridentini* (Lipsia, 1953), no. 49, p. 229.

[39] Ibid., no. 65, p. 235.

[40] Ibid., no. 32, p. 226.

[41] On the biblical and patristic basis of this, known to the Fathers and theologians at Trent, cf. Baldanza, "La grazia sacramentale matrimoniale", 98–100 and 135–38.

[42] Le Bras, "Mariage", 9.2254.

2. New Problems Posed by the "Laicization" of the State in Christian Nations: The Magisterium of the Popes from Benedict XIV to Pius XI

We will briefly detail the process of the "secularization" of marriage that developed in the 17th to 18th centuries, in order to take up in the following sections the teachings of the Magisterium on this issue. The encyclical of Leo XIII, *Arcanum divinae sapientiae,* truly a summing up of this Magisterium, and the *Codex Iuris Canonici,* which set forth ecclesiastical law on marriage, merit particular attention.

■ By "secularization" or "laicization", terms ordinarily employed by the Magisterium of the period, we mean the process of de-Christianization of society, at that time under way.

A. *The theory of the regalists and the de-Christianization of thought during the 17th to 18th centuries*

Solemnly reaffirmed by Trent, Catholic doctrine on marriage was at this time subjected to the criticisms made by the advocates of regalism and of rationalism.

After Trent, the teaching of the Church on marriage for a while enjoyed a period of tranquility, during which such important studies as Robert Bellarmine's *De matrimonii sacramento* appeared,[43] along with the Dominican P. de Ledesma's *De magno matrimonii sacramento* (Salamanca, 1592) and the famous *De sancti matrimonii sacramento disputationum libri X* of the Jesuit Thomas Sanchez (Genova, 1592). Doctrinal difficulties appearing in these centuries came from events external to the Church: the de-Christianization of thought and, little by little, of social customs.

■ In the development of the secularizing process, the so-called "School of Natural Law" and the philosophers of the French Revolution had a decisive impact. Le Bras describes matters in this way: "The School of Natural Law studies the needs of man more than the law of Christ, although it does not exclude God from its thought. Further removed

---

[43] In vol. 3 of *De controversiis* (Coloniae Agrippinae, 1615).

from Christianity, the French philosophers of the period will carry to extremes a critique of the traditional concept [of man vis-à-vis God], not stridently, but in a way that is very corrosive because of their method: looking upon faith and religion as mere social facts, which they analyze from a political point of view; with their allegories and examples they destroy in the mind of many readers respect for the teachings of the Church. Like the regalists, but much more audaciously, they sever the human and legal aspect of marriage from its condition as a sacrament. . . . The philosophers of the 17th century laicize the concept of marriage, habituating persons to repudiate the rules of religion as if they imposed arbitrary and cruel limitations concerning the needs and rights of man.[44]

Gallicanism, like regalism, claimed for the state a competence which, in truth, surpassed its just powers. One cannot deny, in modern society, the need of an intervention of state authority in the marriage of its own subjects, because of their manifest consequences in the temporal order. But together with this, not rarely, we find mingled desires for a radical independence not only from ecclesiastical but also from divine laws. Thus emerged the gallican and regalist theses. Originally, these were different from later secularizing movements because they continued to recognize marriage as a sacrament (under which title the Church can and ought to intervene in the regulation of marriage). Initially, those favoring these currents of thought only demanded a separation of competencies, guided and ruled by the separation between the contract and the sacrament; they ended, however, by repudiating the divine power of the Church, seeking to put it totally under the power of the state.

■ The work of the apostate archbishop of Spalato, M. A. de Dominis' *De republica ecclesiastica,* is an example of this. In the first part, he admits, as a hypothesis, that marriage is a sacrament; but at the same time, he denies any power whatsoever of the Church over the contract, which is absolutely autonomous. At the beginning of humanity, God would have instituted marriage merely as a natural contract. Jesus Christ, for his part, will be concerned to reestablish the primitive monogamy and to make marriage indissoluble, save in the case of adultery which—he affirmed—would make divorce legitimate. But Christ, he adds, was in no way interested in the contract, nor did he

[44] Le Bras, "Mariage", 9.2267ff.

change its nature: it continues to be a merely civil, natural contract, fully under the power of the state. And he concludes: What is the Church looking for by getting involved in a contract "completely human and corporal, if not power? The natural things that the Church uses in the sacraments—bread, wine, water—are not formed by her, nor do they fall under her control: they are under her power *quoad usum* but not *quoad esse.* The same can be said of the natural contract of marriage."[45]

In the second part of his work, the archbishop goes even further. He denies the sacramental character of marriage, ending up by adhering, to the letter, to many of the Protestant theses: there is no sacrament, or one must admit that all signs are such; the Church had badly understood the Pauline expression *sacramentum magnum,* which does not mean sacrament but mystery. Jesus Christ did not institute a sacrament for marriage, nor did he promise that this can give grace. All the arguments that the Church uses in this matter are contrary to reason and to Tradition.[46]

"Laicist" thought, diffused by the French Revolution, is not limited to denying the Church power over marriage; it affirms that the Church has denatured the natural regimen of marriage, for which "laicist" thought proposes a new morality. The process was, in broad lines, the following. The School of Natural Law, founded by Grotius and systematized and diffused by Pufendorf, affirmed the existence of a natural law that is valid *even if God does not exist (etsi Deus non daretur).* This natural law finds its foundation in man, as reason can recognize even prescinding from God and from revelation.[47] Once the break with transcendence was made and the guidance of faith lost, almost everything was progressively abandoned, although initially many Christian truths were preserved, which were imagined as conquests of pure reason. The first divergence immediately appeared with respect to the indissolubility of marriage: the love that is at the root of marriage—they will affirm—cannot be

---

[45] M. A. de Dominis, *De republica ecclesiastica,* nos. 1–23. The answer to his argument is clear: the conjugal agreement is a natural reality, but not material (as bread or water), but rather spiritual and free; therefore the Church teaches what it truly is, by recognizing it and living it freely.

[46] Ibid., nos. 24–29.

[47] The idea had already appeared in some scholastic authors (Suarez, Vasquez, Gregory of Rimini), a fact that reveals the existence of the deepest roots of the crisis of the 18th century: cf. Ramón García de Haro, "Persona, libertad y destino", *Etica y Teología ante la crisis contemporanea (Actas del I Simposio Internacional de Teología)* (Pamplona: Eunsa, 1975), pp. 115–19.

subject to laws; if this is lacking, and experience shows that this does not happen rarely, it is unjust to continue to oblige the spouses to live together. Little by little, the divergence will spread to other fields: polygamy will be considered less progressive, but not a matter for reproach; Thomasius will reach the point where he doubts that sodomy and bestiality are contrary to natural law, etc.[48]

■ The indissolubility of marriage, Voltaire said, is a "barbaric and cruel" imposition; equity, history, and the example of all people, "save the Roman Catholic people", stand in favor of divorce.[49] Nothing, argues Montaigne, so assures the duration of marriage than the possibility of divorce: "What saved marriage at Rome, for so long a time the height of honors and of strength, was the freedom to break it. Men loved their wives better when they had fear of losing them."[50] Finally, Kant was among the first to deny that procreation is the proper and intrinsic end of marriage, affirming that this can be excluded by the will of the spouses.[51]

The progressive expansion of like ideas will lead to the establishment of "civil marriage" in many states in which Catholics were the majority. In the two final decades of the 18th century, beginning with France, different countries of the West issued laws making civil marriage valid for Catholics and indeed the only valid form of marriage. At the same time, they usually allowed for divorce. This is not surprising, since divorce is a logical consequence when marriage is considered the "creation" of human will: what the will creates of itself it can destroy of itself. Although many were not aware of it at the time, the whole Christian and human way of life of the West was at stake: prior to Christ, no society had come to respect fully the natural dignity of man. If Christ and his teachings are taken from social life, a decadent ethic inevitably returns.

■ The problem thus posed was in reality most difficult. In fact, from the time of the Protestant Reformation and the wars of religion and continuing with the diffusion of the ideas of the rationalistic Enlighten-

---

[48] Le Bras noted this. Cf. his article "Mariage", in particular, col. 2268.

[49] F.-M. Voltaire, "Adultère (Memoire d'un Magistrat ecrit vers l'an 1764)", in *Dictionnaire Philosophique* (Paris: P. et J. Didot, 1816), p. 108.

[50] Michel E. de Montaigne, *Les Essais* (Ed. Armagnaud, 1926), t. IV, p. 148.

[51] Cf. Immanuel Kant, *Foundations for the Metaphysics of Morals,* trans. L. W. Beck (New York: Liberal Arts Press, 1945), pp. 65–88.

ment, a historical situation that had prevailed for centuries in western Europe collapsed: namely, Christendom, or the society confessionally Catholic, where state and Church were the two authorities recognized by all as supreme. Although these authorities were at odds on particular questions, they were in substantive accord with regard to the principles of human and social life. The consciousness of the depth of the change that had been wrought will be obscured for a time, and the remnant of the medieval idea of the two powers will be proposed once more by means of concordats regulating the relationships between state and Church—a new formula adopted for stitching together an accord—already fragile and of uncertain foundation—between these powers, because, in reality, the whole conception of the state and of its relationship with the Church had been radically changed. An adequate reformulation of their relationship became indispensable, particularly after the state, in some European countries, returned to persecute Christians in ways even harsher than those used in the first centuries of the life of the Church in the Roman Empire.

Thus one can well understand that, in this area, the Magisterium of the 18th to 20th centuries assumed at times the characteristics contemplated by number 24 of the Instruction *Donum veritatis (Vatican Instruction on the Ecclesial Mission of the Theologian).* [52] Consequently, in our subsequent exposition of its teachings, we will limit ourselves *to set forth what in its teaching has been essential and permanent.* One has to wait for the documents of Vatican Council II, in particular *Gaudium et spes* [53] and *Dignitatis*

---

[52] "When it comes to the question of interventions in the prudential order, it could happen that some Magisterial documents might not be free from all deficiencies. Bishops and their advisors have not always taken into immediate consideration every aspect or the entire complexity of a question. But it would be contrary to the truth, if, proceeding from some particular cases, one were to conclude that the Church's Magisterium can be habitually mistaken in prudential judgments, or that it does not enjoy divine assistance in the integral exercise of its mission. In fact, the theologian, who cannot pursue his discipline well without a certain competence in history, is aware of the filtering which occurs with the passage of time. This is not to be understood in the sense of relativization of the tenets of the faith. The theologian knows that some judgments of the Magisterium could be justified at the time in which they were made, because while the pronouncements contained true assertions and others which were not certain, both types were inextricably connected. Only time has permitted discernment and, after deeper study, the attainment of true doctrinal progress" (Congregation for the Doctrine of the Faith, instruction *Donum veritatis,* May 24, 1990, no. 24).

[53] "Many of our contemporaries seem to fear that, if the associations between human activity and religion are strengthened, the autonomy of men, of society, and of science will be endangered. If by the autonomy of earthly realities we mean that created things and societies themselves have their own proper laws and values, which man gradually discovers, uses, and orders, then we are dealing with a legitimate demand which is not only postulated

humanae,[54] for a reproposing in depth of this matter. We believe that
the most profound presentation of the matter is found in the address of
John Paul II to the European Parliament in Strasbourg, October 11,
1988. In it he said: "The Church's message concerns God and the
ultimate fate of humanity, questions which are closely woven into
every aspect of European culture. How could we, in all truth, conceive
of a Europe stripped of this transcending dimension? On European soil
in this modern era, fresh currents of thought have developed which
have gradually distanced God from the understanding of the world
and of humanity. Two opposing points of view fuel a constant state of
tension between the faithful and agnostic, and at times atheistic,
humanists.

"The former believe that obedience to God is the source of all true
freedom, which is never arbitrary or aimless, but aspires to truth and
goodness since these two supreme qualities are always beyond humanity's
capacity to grasp them entirely. From the moral point of view, this
basic attitude is put into practice by the acceptance of principles or

---

by the men of our day but is also in accord with the will of the Creator. Indeed, it is by
reason of their very condition as creatures that all things receive their proper stability, truth,
goodness, their proper laws and order. . . . If, on the other hand, the expression 'the autonomy of earthly realities' means that created things do not depend on God, that man can use
them without referring them to the Creator, then everyone who believes in God will see
how false is such a claim. Without a Creator, there can be no creature" (Vatican Council II,
pastoral constitution *Gaudium et spes,* December 7, 1965, no. 36; see also nos. 40–43).

[54] This document is titled precisely *Declaration on Religious Liberty: On the Right of the
Person and Communities to Social and Civil Liberty in Religious Matters.* In its first paragraph, it affirms: "The Sacred Council begins by affirming that God Himself has made
known to the human race how men by serving Him can come in Christ to be saved and made
holy. We believe that this one true religion subsists in the Catholic and Apostolic Church, to
which the Lord Jesus has entrusted the task of communicating it to all men. . . . All men are
bound to search for the truth, especially in what regards God and His Church, and to
embrace it and hold fast to it once they come to know it. The Sacred Council also professes
that these duties touch and bind the conscience of every man, but *truth can impose itself only
with the power of truth,* which wins over the mind of man with both gentleness and power.
And since *religious liberty,* which men demand in fulfilling their obligation to honor God,
concerns the immunity from coercion in civil society, it leaves intact the traditional Catholic
doctrine on the moral obligation of individuals and society toward the true religion and the
one Church of Christ" (Vatican Council II, declaration *Dignitatis humanae,* December 7,
1965, no. 1). This important document, which undeniably advances Church-state relations,
nonetheless does not escape the conditionings and limits indicated by the difficulties of the
question and of the intermingling of acquired truths and problems not yet resolved (see
Donum veritatis, no. 24). On this subject see Ramón García de Haro, *La vida cristiana (Curso de
Teología Moral Fundamental)* (Pamplona: Eunsa, 1992), pp. 532–34; F. Ocáriz, "Sulla libertà
religiosa (Continuità del Vaticano II con Il Magistero precedente)", in *Annales Theologici* 3
(1989): 71–97.

modes of behavior conforming to reason or deriving from the authority of the word of God, which people, either individually or collectively, cannot interpret as they wish to suit fashion or changing interests.

"The latter attitude is that, having dispensed with all submission to God on the part of His creatures or to a transcending order of truth and goodness, humanity itself is the beginning and the end of all things, and society, with its laws, its standards and its aims, is humanity's supreme achievement. Thus morality is only based on social consensus, and individual freedom is only bounded by the limits imposed by society to protect the freedom of others.

"Some people believe that civil and political freedom, which in the past was achieved by overturning the old order based on religious faith, goes hand in hand with shouldering aside or even suppressing religion, which they fear may be a force of alienation. The opposite is true for some of the faithful: the only way to live according to the faith would be to go back to the old way of things, which is often viewed with nostalgia. Neither of these two opposing viewpoints holds a solution compatible with the Christian message and the spirit of Europe. Because, so long as civil liberty reigns and religious freedom is guaranteed, faith can only grow stronger by accepting the challenge levelled at it by unbelief, and atheism can only display its limited nature when challenged by faith.

"Given this difference of opinion, the highest function of the law is to guarantee equally to all citizens the right to live according to their consciences, and *not go against those standards of the moral order recognized by reason.*

"At this point, I feel that it is important to stress that modern Europe planted the principle which essentially governs its public life—so often lost to view during the centuries of 'Christianity'—in the rich *humus* of the Christian Creed. This principle is the one, first uttered by Christ, whereby a distinction is made between 'what belongs to Caesar' and 'what belongs to God' (cf. Mt 22:21). This fundamental distinction between the sphere of administrating the external aspects of an earthly city and that of the autonomy of the person, becomes clear given the repective natures of the political community that all citizens belong to by definition, and of the religious community that the faithful join of their own free will.

"After the advent of Christ, it is no longer possible to venerate society as a collective supremacy which swallows up human beings and their irreducible destiny. Society, the state and political power all belong to the shifting and always perfectable framework of this world. No amount of planning on the part of society could ever create the kingdom of God, which implies eschatological perfection, here on earth. Frequently, political messianisms spring from the worst tyrannies. The structures that societies set up for themselves never last forever; neither can they, of themselves, take the place of the human conscience nor replace humanity's quest for the ultimate truth.

"Public life and the orderly functioning of the state depend on the virtue of its citizens, which leads them to subordinate their individual interests to the common good and only to accept as law that which is objectively just and good. Already the Greeks had discovered that no democracy can survive unless all submit to the law, and no law can prevail which is not based on a transcendent standard of what is true and just.

"Saying that it is up to the religious community and not to the state to administer 'what belongs to God' places a healthy restriction on human power, and this restriction is governed by conscience, by final aims, by the ultimate meaning of existence, by a vision of the Absolute, by striving toward something unattainable, which encourages greater effort and is an inspiration in making the right choices. All the schools of thought in this old continent of ours should reflect on the bleak prospects before us were God to be excluded from public affairs or from His role as the ultimate arbiter of morality and the last defense against all human abuses of power."[55]

No doubt this laying of a new foundation for the relationship between Church and state implies the need for a more creative attitude on the part of the faithful in regard to the defense of the family, along the lines already set forth by Vatican Council II on the responsibility of the laity,[56] and which has been beautifully synthesized by the *Instruction on Respect for Human Life in Its Origin and on the Dignity of Procreation* (*Donum vitae*): "It is part of the duty of the public authority to ensure that the civil law is regulated according to the fundamental norms of the moral law in matters concerning human rights, human life and *the institution of the family.* Politicians must commit themselves, through their interventions upon public opinion, to securing in society the widest possible consensus on such essential points and to consolidating this consensus wherever it risks being weakened or is in

[55] John Paul II, Address to the European Parliament, October 11, 1988, nos. 7–9 (emphasis added); *Insegnamenti di Giovanni Paolo II,* 11.3 (1988) (Vatican City: Typis Polyglottis Vaticanis, 1988); also in *Origins: NC Documentary Service,* October 27, 1988, 18, no. 20 (1988): 331–32.

[56] See Vatican Council II, dogmatic constitution *Lumen gentium,* November 21, 1964, nos. 30–38; *Gaudium et spes,* nos. 23ff., 43; decree *Apostolicam actuositatem,* November 18, 1965, nos. 7ff., 13ff.

danger of collapse. . . . The civil legislation of many states confers an undue legitimation upon certain practices in the eyes of many today; it is seen to be incapable of guaranteeing that morality which is in conformity with the natural exigencies of the human person and with the 'unwritten laws' etched by the Creator upon the human heart. *All men of good will must commit themselves, particularly within their professional field and in the exercise of their civil rights, to ensuring the reform of morally unacceptable civil laws and the correction of illicit practices.* In addition, 'conscientious objection' vis-à-vis such laws must be supported and recognized."[57]

B. *The Magisterium and the reaffirmation of the divine regimen of marriage*

The popes of the second half of the 18th century and the beginning of the 19th developed the doctrine of the inseparability between the marriage contract and the sacrament; and they confirmed the competence that, by God's will, the Church has over marriage.

One of the signs of the divine nature of the Church is the imperturbable courage with which the Magisterium defends the truth received from Christ, even when worldly powers contest it. Both doctrines opposed to her teachings and the establishment of legal ordinances that ignore her serve as an occasion for the Church to investigate more deeply the sacred character of marriage (even as an institution of nature) and the unbreakable unity, willed by God for the baptized, between the conjugal pact and the sacrament. We will give a synthesis of the principal documents of this time.

■ Specifically, we take up the teachings of the following popes on this matter: Benedict XIV (1740–1758), Clement XIII (1758–1769), Pius VI (1775–1799), Pius VII (1800–1823), Gregory XVI (1831–1846), Pius IX (1846–1878), Leo XIII (1878–1903), and St. Pius X (1903–1914).[58]

[57] Congregation for the Doctrine of the Faith, instruction *Donum vitae (Instruction on Respect for Human Life in Its Origin and on the Dignity of Procreation)*, February 22, 1987, part III; *Enchiridion Familiae* 5.4649–50 (in the original, the entire text was emphasized; here, the selection of material emphasized is ours).

[58] There are two collections of these documents. The first, which includes the teaching of Pius XI and Pius XII, has been published under the title: *Insegnamenti pontifici*, vol. 1: *Il matrimonio* (Rome: Edizione Paoline, 1957), which will be referred to as *Ins.* The second,

I. *The development of the doctrine of the inseparability between the marriage contract and the sacrament.* As we have seen, this had been the traditional thesis and practice of the Church. If it was at times denied by theologians, for the purpose of resolving specific practical or theoretical problems, the response of the Magisterium was always that of finding a solution conformable to the doctrine of inseparability. After the discussions at Trent, St. Robert Bellarmine was able to write: "The common and true opinion ignores absolutely such a separation and establishes no difference between the marriage contract between Christians, its matter, its form, and its minister and the sacrament of marriage, its matter, its form, and its minister."[59] The Magisterium afterward will formulate this doctrine in a solemn way. We provide the principal texts:

The "marriage contract itself is truly and properly one of the seven sacraments of the law of the Gospel";[60] the sacrament *is not therefore an adjunct to the contract,* but the fruit of its transformation into a sacrament by Christ.[61] Therefore,

> it is a *dogmatic error many times condemned* by the Church . . . to reduce the sacrament to a merely extrinsic ceremony and to a condition of a mere rite. An affirmation of this kind subverts the essential concept of Christian marriage, in which the conjugal bond, sanctified by faith, is identified with the sacrament and is inseparably with it one only subject, one only reality.[62]

Therefore, *there is no marriage between baptized persons which is not at the same time a sacrament:*

---

published in 1992, is entitled *Enchiridion Familiae: Textos del Magisterio Pontificio y Conciliar sobre el Matrimonio y la Familia (Siglos I a XX)* (Madrid: Ediciones Rialp, 1992). This work, edited by Augusto Sarmiento and Javier Escrivá-Ivars and sponsored by the Instituto de Ciencias Para La Familia of the University of Navarra and the Istituto Giovanni Paolo II per Studi su Matrimonio e Famiglia of the Lateran University in Rome, contains six volumes. Volumes 1 to 5 contain all texts of the papal and conciliar Magisterium from the time of Clement of Rome in 89 A.D. up to 1988 (John Paul II) dealing with marriage and the family. This will be referred to as *Enchiridion Familiae*.

[59] *Controversiarum de Sacramento Matrimonio liber unicus,* ed. Vives, t. V, p. 57.

[60] Pius VI, *Deesemus nobis; Ins.* no. 44; *Enchiridion Familiae*, 1.312.

[61] Cf. Pius IX, apostolic letter *Ad Apostolicae Sedis,* August 28, 1851; *Ins.* no. 91; *Enchiridion Familiae,* vol. 1, pp. 390–92; cf. also Pius IX, *La Lettera,* September 9, 1852; *Ins.* no. 94; *Enchiridion Familiae,* 1.394–97; Pius IX, *Syllabus,* December 8, 1864; *Ins.* no. 107; *Enchiridion Familiae,* 1.437, no. 73.

[62] Leo XIII, letter *Ci siamo,* June 1, 1879; *Ins.* no. 132; *Enchiridion Familiae,* 1.475–76, no. 4.

No Catholic is ignorant, nor can he be ignorant, of the fact that marriage is truly and properly one of the seven sacraments of the law of the Gospel established by Christ our Lord. And therefore, among the faithful there can be no marriage without it being at one and the same time a sacrament. Every union among Christian men and women outside the sacrament is nothing else than a base and deadly concubinage, repeatedly condemned by the Church. The sacrament can never be separated from the conjugal covenant [coniugali foedere]. [63]

The contrary thesis, numbered among the errors listed in the Syllabus, [64] was also repudiated by Leo XIII: "The distinction between the contract and the sacrament is of no avail for those who want to infer from it that among Christians there could be a valid marriage contract which is not a sacrament." [65]

The doctrine of the inseparability must be regarded, after the teachings of Pius IX and Leo XIII—and confirmed by Pius XI—as *outside discussion among theologians*. [66] Leo XIII also revealed the importance of respecting, or not respecting, this truth for the common good. [67]

■ The insistence of the popes, always made with respect for the laws of the state, *that marriage be celebrated canonically before it is registered in civil law*, is a practical application of this teaching: the sacramental nature of the marital contract itself is thus made clearer. [68]

2. *The reaffirmation of the competence of the Church over marriage, as pertaining to her proper power over the sacraments.* Since every marriage between baptized persons is a sacrament, the Church has by divine institution a direct and immediate power over the marriage of Christians. Pius VI affirmed:

It is a dogma of faith that marriage, which even prior to the coming of Christ was nothing other than an indissoluble contract, has become

---

[63] Pius IX, allocution *Acerbissimum vobiscum*, September 27, 1852; *Ins.* no. 101; *Enchiridion Familiae*, 1.398–99, no. 3.

[64] *Ins.* no. 107.

[65] Leo XIII, letter *Il divisamento*, February 8, 1893; *Ins.* no. 218; *Enchiridion Familiae*, 1.555, no. 2.

[66] This is the argument of Hervada, "La inseparabilidad entre contrato y sacramento en el matrimonio", p. 272.

[67] Cf. his *Ci Siamo: Ins.* no. 129ff.; *Enchiridion Familiae*, 1.474–81.

[68] Therefore, there is *no confusion* between the contract or conjugal covenant and the sacrament, but *only their inseparability*, because the covenant of conjugal love between Christians is the sign of the sacrament.

after the Incarnation one of the seven sacraments of the Law of the Gospel. . . . It follows from this that to the Church alone, the depository of all that regards the sacraments, pertains every right and power of determining the value of this pact elevated to the most high dignity of a sacrament; and, consequently, it belongs to the Church alone to judge the validity or invalidity of marriage.[69]

This power belongs to the Church "not by the delegation of the State or by the assent of the Princes, but by the command of the divine Founder of Christianity and the Author of the sacraments."[70]

■ The commitment of the popes in reminding us of this truth is noteworthy, as it is a guarantee of respect for the divine plan for marriage.[71] The different documents are not only concerned with setting forth Catholic teaching but with showing how groundless are the criticisms leveled against it: for example, the hypothesis that there was no awareness of such a power at the time of the apostles.[72] Moreover, they provide detailed limits to the extent of their power: as far as the sacrament is concerned, this is the substance of the conjugal contract inseparable from it and its religious and moral effects;[73] from this derives the competence of the Church over *impediments to marriage*,[74] over the meaning of the indissolubility of the bond—even among non-Christians[75]—over espousals,[76] etc.

In no way was the reaffirmation of the Magisterium's own competence made to the detriment of the *legitimate powers of civil authority*: in fact the Church "admonishes all to follow the customs of the region in respecting the dispositions of earthly rulers".[77] In this way, the teaching of our Lord was reproposed: give to Caesar what is

[69] Pius VI, *Deesemus nobis; Ins.* no. 43.

[70] Leo XIII, *Ci siamo; Ins.* no. 130; *Enchiridion Familiae,* 1.474, no. 2.

[71] Cf. Benedict XIV, apostolic constitution *Dei miseratione,* November 3, 1741; *Ins.* no. 2; *Enchiridion Familiae,* 1.227–28.

[72] Cf. Pius VI, letter *Post factum tibi,* February 2, 1782; *Ins.* nos. 37–40; *Enchiridion Familiae,* 1.297–300.

[73] Cf. Pius VI, *Deessemus nobis, Ins.* no. 45; *Enchiridion Familiae,* 1.312.

[74] Cf. Pius VI, *Post factum tibi; Ins.* no. 38; *Enchiridion Familiae,* 1.297–300.

[75] Cf. Pius IX, letter *Verbis exprimere,* August 15, 1859; *Ins.* nos. 102ff.; *Enchiridion Familiae,* 1.427–29.

[76] Cf. Pius VI, apostolic letter *Auctorem fidei,* August 28, 1794; *Ins.* no. 52; *Enchiridion Familiae,* 1.323–25; Pius IX, *Syllabus, Ins.* no. 115; *Enchiridion Familiae,* 1.437, no. 74.

[77] Benedict XIV, letter *Redditae sunt nobis,* September 17, 1746; *Ins.* no. 19; *Enchiridion Familiae,* 1.254, no. 4.

his, and leave to the Church what pertains to her (Mt 22:21; Mk 12:17; Lk 20:25):

> The civil power disposes of the civil effects which derive from the wedding, but leaves to the Church the regulation of its validity among Christians. Civil law takes as its point of departure the validity or nonvalidity of marriage as determined by the Church. And, starting with this fact, which is outside its sphere of competence, it then disposes of the civil effects.[78]

3. *In addition, marriage between non-Christians is no mere civil contract.* Faced with the practice of some Christian states of the Western world, which allow divorce at least for civil marriage, the popes teach that this way of acting is contrary not only to revelation but also to the order inscribed by the Creator in human nature: "Whoever thinks that marriage, on condition that it is not a sacrament, becomes a merely civil contract which can be dissolved by human authority deceives himself. . . . Marriage is not a civil contract, but a natural contract instituted and ratified by divine law prior to every civil society."[79] Therefore, its indissolubility belongs to the natural law[80] and is applicable to all persons, including the Jewish people, because Christ abolished the law of repudiation,[81] reestablishing the primitive unity taught by Scripture: "Let not man separate what God has joined" (Mt 19:6).[82]

The question of mixed marriages and other pastoral issues

Although the practice of the Church concerning mixed marriages today has changed in not a few accidental aspects because of changed historical circumstances, it is worth noting the large number of

---

[78] Pius IX, *La Lettera; Ins.* no. 98; *Enchiridion Familiae,* 1.396–97, no. 6.

[79] Pius VI, letter *Litteris tuis,* July 11, 1789; *Ins.* no. 50; *Enchiridion Familiae,* 1.313–14.

[80] Cf. Pius IX, *Syllabus, Ins.* no. 108; *Enchiridion Familiae,* vol. 1, p. 436, no. 67. This theme had been already clarified in a definite way by Trent, where the Fathers confirmed that this has been the perennial doctrine of the Church and the authentic interpretation of Mt 19:6; cf. Baldanza, "La grazia sacramentale matrimoniale al Concilio di Trento", pp. 125 and 134–35.

[81] Cf. Benedict XIV, apostolic constitution *Apostolici ministerii,* September 16, 1747; *Ins.* nos. 21–23; *Enchiridion Familiae,* 1.256–59.

[82] Cf. Benedict XIV, encyclical *Matrimonii,* April 11, 1741; *Ins.* no. 1; *Enchiridion Familiae,* 1.225–27; Leo XIII, allocution *Afferre incundiora,* December 16, 1901; *Ins.,* no. 244; *Enchiridion Familiae,* 1.582–84.

documents concerned with this matter during this period.[83] Leo XIII summed up the difficulties these unions present in three points that are still equally valid: risks for the faith of the Catholic spouse; difficulties in educating the children; and the danger of indifferentism.[84] These are difficulties that can be overcome by using the opportune means of prudence and by giving persons a sound foundation; but they must never be underestimated.

Two other questions, again of concern today, can be noted. The *pastoral care of divorced persons* who have entered a new marriage and are now penitent. To a question from the bishop of Magonza on the possibility of admitting them to the sacraments, this response was given: "There can be no doubt of this, so long as they have done works worthy of penance; among which the first will be separation from the second spouse if the first is still alive."[85] The second concerns the validity of *a marriage celebrated under conditions contrary to its substance.* The solution depends on the fact whether such a condition is explicitly formulated in the contract or whether one is dealing with a simple error on the part of those who are contracting marriage. Only in the first case is marriage invalid, because a marriage between non-Catholics, celebrated in a confession which allows divorce, where however this possibility is not explicitly made, is presumed to be valid and indissoluble.[86]

---

[83] Cf. Benedict XIV, encyclical *Inter omnigenas,* February 2, 1744; *Ins.* nos. 11–13; *Enchiridion Familiae,* 1.247–50; Benedict XIV, encyclical *Magnae nobis,* June 29, 1748; *Ins.* nos. 25–30; *Enchiridion Familiae,* 1.261–66; Clement XIII, apostolic letter *Quantopere,* November 16, 1763; *Ins.* nos. 31–36; *Enchiridion Familiae,* 1.284–88; Pius VI, letter *Exequendo nunc,* July 13, 1782; *Ins.* nos. 41–42; *Enchiridion Familiae,* 1.300–304; Pius VII, letter *Etsi fraternitatis,* October 8, 1803; *Ins.* no. 56; *Enchiridion Familiae,* 1.327–31; Pius VII, letter *Que Votre Majesté,* June 26, 1805; *Ins.* no. 60; Pius VII, encyclical *Vix nova a nobis,* February 17, 1809; *Ins.* no. 63; *Enchiridion Familiae,* 1.334–35; Pius VIII, apostolic letter *Litteris altero,* March 25, 1830; *Ins.* nos. 66–68; *Enchiridion Familiae,* 1.356–59; Gregory XVI, *Summo jugiter,* May 27, 1832; *Ins.* nos. 69–80; *Enchiridion Familiae,* 1.359–67; Gregory XVI, apostolic letter *Quas vestro,* April 30, 1841; *Ins.* no. 87; *Enchiridion Familiae,* 1.379–82; Gregory XVI, breve *Non sine gravi,* May 23, 1846; *Ins.* no. 90; *Enchiridion Familiae,* 1.385–87.

[84] Leo XIII, encyclical *Arcanum divinae sapientiae,* February 10, 1880; *Ins.* no. 196; *Enchiridion Familiae,* 1.514–15, no. 26.

[85] Pius VII, *Etsi fraternitatis; Ins.* no. 58; *Enchiridion Familiae,* 1.330, no. 7.

[86] Pius VI, letter *Gravissimam,* July 11, 1789; *Ins.* nos. 46–47; *Enchiridion Familiae,* 1.315–16.

C. *The encyclical* Arcanum divinae sapientiae *of Leo XIII*

From the very beginning of his pontificate, Leo XIII gave much attention to make known and loved the truth about marriage, in order to overcome the moral crisis of society.[87] The encyclical *Arcanum divinae sapientiae* of February 10, 1880, was the fruit of this concern. In effect, this summarized and completed the Magisterium of the past few centuries on the subject of marriage and family. We will present its major points.

In Christ, God restored humanity, and therefore marriage and the family, in such a way that spouses can attain their own holiness. "Jesus Christ, the restorer of human dignity . . . did not make the subject of matrimony His least or last care. He ennobled the nuptials of Cana of Galilee by His presence (cf. Jn. 2) . . . [and abolished] the privilege of repudiation (cf. Matt. 19:9). . . . [He] raised matrimony to the dignity of a sacrament" so that "married people, guarded and protected by the celestial grace provided by His merits, should derive holiness from marriage itself", a union symbolizing that between Christ and the Church (cf. Eph 5:25) (nos. 6–7; *Ins.* nos. 152–53; *Enchiridion Familiae,* 1.487–88). Moreover, the Lord sanctioned once again the "unity and perpetual constancy" of marriage (cf. 1 Cor 7:10, 11; 5:39; Eph 5:32; Heb 13:4; no. 7; *Ins.* no. 154; *Enchiridion Familiae,* 1.489). He rendered the end of marriage more noble by ordering it for the generation not only of human life but for the generation of children of God in the Church (cf. Eph 1:19), and he strengthened and elevated conjugal and family love by means of divine charity, which the sacrament infuses into the spouses (cf. Eph 5:23–24; 6:4) (no. 8; *Ins.* nos. 156–57; *Enchiridion Familiae,* 1.489–90).

■ The text of the encyclical is particularly clear in affirming that Christ is the only restorer of *human dignity* and—in a way never before so explicit—in stressing that *marriage is the place where the spouses are sanctified.* These are two truths that will be the object of particular development in Vatican Council II.

Marriage, thus elevated to the dignity of a sacrament by Christ, was entrusted to the care of the Church, "which has exercised authority over the

---

[87] Encyclical *Inscrutabili,* April 21, 1878; *Ins.* nos. 123–24; *Enchiridion Familiae,* 1.463–65, nos. 14–15. See also encyclical *Quod apostolici,* December 28, 1878; *Ins.* nos. 126–27; *Enchiridion Familiae,* 1.471–72, nos. 1, 8.

marriages of Christians at every time and in every place, and has so
exercised it as to show that it was her own inherent right, not obtained
by the concession of men, but divinely bestowed by the will of her
Author" (no. 9; *Ins.* no. 158; *Enchiridion Familiae,* 1.491). The encyclical
then lists the benefits that are the result of this care: for example, abuses
of marriage were promptly corrected (cf. Acts 15:29; 1 Cor 5:5); the
dignity of women and the equality among the spouses were restored,
as St. Jerome bears witness: "Among us what is not lawful for women
is equally unlawful for men, and the condition of both is the same"[88]
(no. 9; *Ins.* no. 158; *Enchiridion Familiae,* 1.491–92).

> ■ History, as Leo notes, bears witness to the truth that the Church
> constantly and efficaciously used the means to protect the dignity of
> marriage, transforming the laws of the emperor; such councils as those
> of Elvira, Chalcedon, Arles, and others bear witness to this (cf. no. 11;
> *Ins.* nos. 166–69; *Enchiridion Familiae,* 1.497–98). To forget this would
> be grave folly, it would be to squander centuries of experience. And,
> in practice, it would be to misconceive a truth of Faith: "For when the
> salutary fear of God is removed, and when that alleviation of troubles
> which is to be found nowhere more effectual than in the Christian
> religion is taken away, it often and naturally happens that the duties
> and obligations of marriage appear almost intolerable" (no. 15; *Ins.*
> no. 177; *Enchiridion Familiae,* 1.503). A confirmation of this is the
> spread of divorce and abortion wherever the work of the Church is
> impeded or disturbed; inevitably, since men, of themselves, do not
> have the divine remedies the Lord has granted to his Church, such
> evils will take root and spread (nos. 17–20; *Ins.* nos. 178–81; *Enchiridion
> Familiae,* 1.505–9).

To assure the dignity of marriage and to avoid the evils that threaten
it, the Pope wishes for good relationships between Church and state: a
collaboration responding to the teachings of our Lord on the proper
task of each of the two powers (nos. 20–24; *Ins.* nos. 185–89; *Enchiridion
Familiae,* 1.509–12). But—and here we have an interesting clarification—
the only guarantee of such an accord will be the success of pastors in
keeping alive in the hearts of the faithful the deposit of Christ: the
faithful must know and as citizens struggle to defend the truth that
marriage, instituted by God and not by men, has been restored by
Christ and that only through the personal commitment of the faithful

---

[88] St. Jerome, Letter 77, to Oceanus; PL 22.691.

will marriage acquire once more the fullness that belongs to it according to God's plan and will (nos. 25–27; *Ins.* nos. 190–95; *Enchiridion Familiae,* 1.512–16).[89]

D. *Marriage in the* Code of Canon Law (1917 *Code*)

Within this historical period, the publication of the *Code of Canon Law* also merits consideration. The Code collected into an organic whole, with detailed and precise norms, the juridical aspects of the teaching of the Church on marriage.

During Vatican Council I, the practical difficulties stemming from the condition of the sources of canon law became quite clear. These sources were dispersed in a multitude of bulls, briefs, and constitutions completing the decrees of the Council of Trent. Thus, the opportunity of providing an organic codification of these norms was quite auspicious. The work was finally undertaken by St. Pius X with his motu proprio *Arduum sane munus* of 1904, which named a commission for this purpose. The task was completed during the pontificate of Benedict XV, with the publication of the Code with the bull *Providentissima Mater* on May 27, 1917.[90]

With respect to the teaching on marriage—the object of title VII of book 3 (cans. 1012–1141)—it is important to stress the ratification of the *unity between the contract and the sacrament:* "Christ our Lord raised to the dignity of a sacrament the contract of marriage itself between the baptized" (can. 1012, par. 1), from which it follows that "among the baptized there can be no valid contract of marriage without its being a sacrament" (can. 1012, par. 2). It is also important to note how the Code formulated the doctrine of the *ends of marriage:* "The primary

---

[89] This teaching has been particularly developed in broad outline for the whole life of the Christian by John Paul II in his apostolic exhortation *Reconciliatio et poenitentia* of December 1, 1984, nos. 16, 18, and 24–27, and in his encyclical *Sollicitudo rei socialis,* December 30, 1987, nos. 27ff., 31ff., and 45ff.

[90] On this see A. Knecht, *Das neue kirchliche Gesetzbuch* (Strasburg, 1918); M. Falco, *Introduzione allo studio del "Codex Iuris Canonici"* (Turin, 1925); S. Kuttner, "El Código de Derecho Canónico en la Historia", in *Revista Espanola de Derecho Canónico* 24 (1968): 131ff.; J. Hervada and P. Lombardía, *El Derecho del Pueblo de Dios* (Pamplona: Eunsa, 1970), pp. 131–37; Lombardía, "Código de Derecho Canónico", *Gran Enciclopedia Rialp,* vol. 5, pp. 820ff.

end of marriage is the procreation and education of children; the secondary end is mutual help and a remedy for concupiscence" (can. 1013, par. 1) and the properties of marriage: *unity and indissolubility* (can. 1013, par. 2). These affirmations, together with the consecration of the principle in favor of the law (*favor iuris*) with reference to marriage (can. 1014) and the reiteration of the competence of the Church, save for the civil effects of marriage (can. 1016), are the basic content of the introductory articles, or of those that are most doctrinal, within the title devoted to marriage.

The remainder of the canons are concerned with the celebration of marriage and marriage banns (chap. I), with impediments (chaps. II–IV), with marital consent (chap. V), with the form and time of celebrating marriage and with the "marriage of conscience" (chaps. VI–VIII), with the effects of marriage (chap. IX), with the separation of the spouses (chap. X), and with the convalidation of defective marriages (chap. XI).

■ As we will have occasion to note again, in the period in which the Code was promulgated, the majority of canonists conceived marriage as a contract of yielding rights (principally the *right to the body* — the *ius ad corpus*) on the part of the spouses.[91] The Code, nonetheless, did not accept this theory explicitly, although it used it with regard to the object of consent (can. 1081). However, it did not give a definition of marriage, perhaps in the desire to avoid a formulation — like that in use among canonists — less responsive to the theological moral tradition (which tended to emphasize in marriage the community of persons, husband and wife, for the end of procreating and educating children). With respect to the ends of marriage, it followed the traditional thesis: it did not include conjugal love among these ends; it placed as the primary end the procreation and education of children, and as secondary ends the "remedy of concupiscence" and "mutual help".[92]

A more precise definition of marriage was contemplated in the first draft of the new (1982) code: "Marriage which is made by mutual consent . . . is the (intimate) union of the whole life between a man and a woman, which, of its own nature, is ordered to the procreation and

[91] Cf. Serrano Ruiz, "El 'Ius in corpus' como objecto del consenso matrimonio", in *El consentimiento matrimonial hoy* (Salamanca, 1976), pp. 63–90.

[92] On this see S. D. Kozul, *Evoluzione della dottrina circa l'essenza del matrimonio dal C.I.C. al Vaticano II* (Vicenza: Ed. Lief, 1980), pp. 137–255.

education of children" (can. 243, par. 1).[93] In the definitive redaction, the formula was made more complete: "The covenant of marriage, by which a man and a woman establish between themselves a partnership of the whole of life, is by its nature ordered to the good of the spouses and the procreation and education of offspring; this covenant between baptized persons has been raised by Christ the Lord to the dignity of a sacrament" (can. 1055, par. 1).[94] As we will see, here the doctrine of the goods of marriage, under the inspiration of Vatican Council II, is welcomed.

3. The Crisis of Christian Society in the 20th Century and the Magisterium of Popes Pius XI and Pius XII

Faced with the crisis of social morals, Popes Pius XI and Pius XII set forth anew the moral teaching of the Church on marriage and seek to prevent very widespread theoretical and practical errors.

The doctrinal and legal crisis about marriage, which broke open in the 17th to 18th centuries, led to a decay in morals. Materialism, the propaganda of the neomalthusians (which obscured the end of marriage), the increasing number of divorces, etc., ended up by shaking the Christian convictions of not a few persons. Nevertheless, the serious difficulties of the time coincided with an apogee in the moral prestige of the Church, which led to an intense magisterial activity in these years.

■ In this chapter, we will give only a brief description of this period and of the two remaining ones, namely, those of Vatican II and of the

[93] Pontifical Commission for the Code of Canon Law, *Schema documenti pontificii quo disciplina canonica de sacramentis recognoscitur* (Vatican City: Typis Polyglottis Vaticanis, 1975). The Latin text reads: "Matrimonium quod fit mutuo consensu . . . est (intima) totius vitae coniunctio inter virum et mulierem, quae, indole sua naturali, ad prolis procreationem et educationem ordinatur." The schema was studied at the meeting of February 21, 1977, and on May 24, 1977, there was a plenary session that considered, among other matters, the notion of marriage. See *Communicationes* 9 (1977): 79–80.

[94] English translation is from *The Code of Canon Law: Text and Commentary,* commissioned by the Canon Law Society of America (New York: Paulist Press, 1985), p. 740. The Latin text reads: "Matrimoniale foedus, quo vir et mulier inter se totius vitae consortium constituunt, indole sua naturali ad bonum coniugum atque prolis generationem et educationem ordinatum, a Christo Domino ad sacramenti dignitatem inter baptizatos evectum est."—Trans.

pontificates that have sought its implementation in order to complete our overview of the development of the Magisterium on marriage and the family. The detailed analysis of the Magisterium of Popes Pius XI and Pius XII, of Vatican Council II, and of Popes Paul VI and John Paul II will be taken up in succeeding chapters.

The principal documents of the Magisterium in this period are Pope Pius XI's encyclical *Casti connubii* of December 31, 1930 (found in *Enchiridion Familiae*, 1.709–94), and the following documents from the pontificate of Pius XII: 1) Address to the Italian Catholic Union of Midwives, October 29, 1951 (*Ins.* nos. 593–652; *Enchiridion Familiae*, 2.1424–62), on contraception and natural methods of regulating conception; 2) Address to Large Families, November 26, 1951 (*Enchiridion Familiae*, 2.1463–74), on generosity in transmitting life and on respect for human life; 3) Address to the 26th Congress of the Italian Society of Urology, October 8, 1953 (*Ins.* nos. 693–703; *Enchiridion Familiae*, 2.1495–1503), on sterility and impotence; 4) encyclical *Sacra virginitas,* March 25, 1954 (*Ins.* nos. 707–20; *Enchiridion Familiae*, 2.1509–58), which is concerned with virginity and marriage; 5) Address to the Second World Congress on Fertility and Sterility, May 19, 1956 (*Ins.* nos. 732–46; *Enchiridion Familiae*, 2.1595–1607), which takes up anew the question of births and of contraception; and finally 6) Allocution to the Seventh International Hematological Congress, September 12, 1958 (*Ins.* nos. 777–800; *Enchiridion Familiae*, 2.1695–1710), on artificial insemination and on sterilization for eugenic reasons.

With respect to the *content* of these teachings, one can say that, after overcoming theological controversies, the Magisterium is concerned with the following: to teach with constancy the major truths about marriage and the family; to defend these truths in the face of new errors; to respond to problems that social changes and scientific progress pose to mankind. In fact, no question proper to the age escaped the attention of the Magisterium. The whole corpus of Catholic doctrine is thus confirmed and illumined by its application to modern needs. Such is the fruit of the Magisterium of this period, relatively brief but intense, of Popes Pius XI (1922–1939) and Pius XII (1939–1958).

4. Vatican Council II and the Renewal of the Church

Vatican Council II undertook the task of evangelizing the modern world in a way more adapted to its needs. Two truths, intimately interrelated, emerge with respect to marriage: the dignity of conjugal love and the call of the spouses to holiness.

Aware of her treasure, the Church reacts when faced with the growing crisis of humanity by preaching Christ courageously to all men: it is he alone who possesses the whole truth about man (*Gaudium et spes,* no. 22). In this way, the Church fulfills that "plan of divine love: 'to unite all things in him, things in heaven and things on earth' (Eph. 1:10)" (ibid., no. 45). Included within this purpose, and indeed as one of its most urgent tasks, the Council is concerned with teaching the truths necessary to reestablish the "dignity of marriage and the family" (ibid., no. 47). Specifically, the Council devoted the following documents to marriage and the family: chapter 1 of the second part of the pastoral constitution *Gaudium et spes* (nos. 47–52); numbers 11, 34–35, and 41 of the dogmatic constitution *Lumen gentium,* with reference to the exercise of the common priesthood of the faithful, to the mission of laypersons in the Church and to the universal call to holiness; number 11 of the decree *Apostolicam actuositatem,* on the apostolate in and of the family; finally, numbers 3 and 6 of the declaration *Gravissimum educationis,* concerning the rights and duties of parents in the education of their children.

With respect to its teachings, in addition to reconfirming the whole doctrine that had already been proclaimed by Trent (the divine institution of marriage and its elevation to a sacrament by Christ; its properties of unity and indissolubility; the goods and ends of marriage, etc.), the Council emphasized the following:

a. *The grandeur of conjugal love.* With marriage, a divine mission is put into operation: the spouses receive the task of transmitting and educating human life: their love makes them "cooperators with the love of God the Creator" (*Gaudium et spes,* no. 50). Indeed, they find themselves faced with an authentic participation in the creative power of God: "Willing to communicate to man a special participation in His creative work, He blessed the man and the woman, saying to them, 'Increase and multiply' (Gen. 1:28)" (ibid., no. 50). Moreover, "the

Lord has deigned to heal and elevate this love by His special gift of grace and charity" (ibid., no. 49), thereby making it possible for the spouses "to cooperate courageously with the love of the Creator and Savior, who through their love continually increases and enriches His own family" (ibid., no. 50).

Conjugal love, therefore, must not be confused with the desire for satisfying concupiscence, with mere physical pleasure. As *Casti connubii* had already said, conjugal love is a reality that is born from the Spirit and is meant to be the formal and life-giving principle of the whole of marriage.[95] There can thus be no true contradiction between love and procreation:[96]

> By their own inner nature, the institution of marriage itself and conjugal love are ordered to the procreation and education of children, and in them find their crowning glory. Thus the man and the woman, who through the conjugal covenant are "no longer two but one flesh" (Matt. 19:6), help and serve each other by their marriage partnership; they become conscious of their unity and experience it more intensely day by day (*Gaudium et spes*, no. 48).

> ■ This doctrine, as we will see more precisely when we take up the teaching of Vatican II in detail, corrects the frequent, but inexact, perception of conjugal love as one of the secondary ends, or even the primary end, of marriage, but one contraposed to the procreation and education of children. Years ago the then Cardinal Wojtyla called attention to this: "It seems clearly indicated that the *mutuum adiutorium* mentioned in the teaching of the Church on the purposes of marriage as second in importance after procreation must not be interpreted—as it often is—to mean 'mutual love.' Those who do this may mistakenly come to believe that procreation as the primary end is something distinct from 'love,' as is also the tertiary end, *remedium concupiscentiae*, whereas both procreation and *remedium concupiscentiae* as purposes of marriage must result from love as a virtue.... There

---

[95] "Conjugal love permeates all the duties of conjugal life and holds pride of place in Christian marriage." Pius XI, encyclical *Casti connubii*, December 31, 1930, no. 23; *Ins.* no. 285; *Enchiridion Familiae*, 1.723.

[96] Cf. F. Gil Hellín, "El matrimonio: amor e institucion", *Cuestiones fundamentales sobre matrimonio y familia*, pp. 231ff.; Antonio Miralles, "Naturaleza y sacramento en la doctrina del Concilio Vaticano II sobre el matrimonio", *Cuestiones fundamentales sobre matrimonio y familia*, pp. 155ff.; P. J. Viladrich, "Amor conyugal y esencia del matrimonio", *Ius Canonicum* 12 (1972): 311ff.

are no grounds for interpreting the phrase *mutuum adiutorium* to mean 'love'."[97] Thus, the Council returned to the classic doctrine of love as the form of marriage, which is found, for instance, in St. Thomas.[98]

b. *Marriage, a road to holiness.* This teaching is intimately linked to the previous one. The requirement of conjugal love, in the fullness in which the Church proposes it, is a source of joy and happiness; but it passes by way of the cross, of suffering, of the generous gift of self. This is a goal that is not accessible to fallen man, without the help of grace, that is, of the interior action of the Holy Spirit. The Council expresses this nicely: "A virtue above and beyond the ordinary is required for the faithful fulfillment of this Christian vocation (marriage); therefore the spouses, made strong by grace for leading a holy life, must assiduously cultivate strength of love, magnanimity, the spirit of sacrifice, begging these with their prayers" (*Gaudium et spes*, no. 49).

Spouses, like all the faithful, "are called and obliged to pursue holiness and the perfection proper to their state of life" (*Lumen gentium*, no. 42), in such a way that "according to their own state of life, they must support each other with constant love all through life, and instruct their children, whom they have lovingly received from God, in Christian doctrine and in the evangelical virtues" (ibid., no. 41).

5. The Magisterium of the Pontificates after Vatican Council II

The Magisterium of the popes after the Council is chiefly concerned with promoting the faithful implementation of the Council, as a way of assuring that once more the truth about marriage will be made secure and that marriages will grow in holiness.

The implementation of Vatican Council II, both in general and, in particular, with regard to its teaching on marriage, did not take place

[97] Karol Wojtyla, *Love and Responsibility*, trans. H. Willetts (New York: Farrar, Straus, Giroux, 1981), p. 68.

[98] *Summa theologiae*, III, q. 29, a. 2. On the meaning in which it is affirmed that love is the form (formal principle) of marriage, see below, chapter 3, "Matrimonial consent is an act of conjugal love", pp. 114–18.

easily. Ordinarily, as we have seen in our examination of the Council of Trent, the implementation of a council is always difficult. But in the case of Vatican II, this has been made particularly difficult because of the revolt, doctrinal and practical, experienced after Vatican II and expressively called the "metacouncil".[99]

> ■ Knowledge of history helps one not to be surprised by this and similar facts. Every council is a great grace of God to men, but its implementation usually entails difficulties: time is needed to let new aspects of the perennial truth, emphasized according to new needs, penetrate into the minds of people and become known in their perfect continuity and unity with the whole prior life of the Church. To secure the fruits of the Council of Trent, as we have seen, a congregation, having as its purpose the authentic interpretation of the Council's decrees, was created; moreover, many universities inaugurated chairs for facilitating the understanding and diffusion of the conciliar teachings, etc. If it took more than a century after Trent to prepare the seminaries wished for by the Council Fathers, can we be surprised that today many do not understand the proclamation of the universal call to holiness? Without doubt, we are dealing with a truth endowed with a very great number of demands and practical consequences that are difficult to carry out.[100]

Confronted with these problems, the popes have insisted, constantly and unanimously, on the need of an integral implementation, without distinctions, of the conciliar Magisterium.[101] In particular, concerning the teaching of the Council on marriage and family, they have emphasized the following points:

---

[99] Cf. Philippe Delhaye, "Metaconcilio: la mancanza di discernimento", *Cris Documenti* no. 43 (Milan: Ed. 1981), pp. 6–8; Delhaye, *La scienza del bene e del male. La morale del Vaticano II e il "metaconcilio"* (Milan: Ed. Ares, 1981), pp. 37ff. and 97ff.

[100] On this see Ramón García de Haro, "Discernere il bene dal male", *Studi cattolici* 25, no. 224 (June 1981): 389ff.

[101] On this see Paul VI, Homily in the Mass for the Tenth Anniversary of the Closing of Vatican Council II, December 8, 1975, in *Insegnamenti di Paolo VI*, vol. 13 (Vatican City: Typis Polyglottis Vaticanis, 1975), pp. 1492–97; John Paul II, Homily to the Cardinals after His Election, October 17, 1978, in *Insegnamenti di Giovanni Paolo II*, 1 (1978), pp. 5ff. This is a theme on which John Paul II insisted in the plenary meeting of the Sacred College of Cardinals in succeeding years: Addresses of November 7, 1979, November 4, 1980, November 30, 1981, November 26, 1982, December 21, 1984: *Insegnamenti di Giovanni Paolo II*, 2.2 (1979), pp. 1049ff.; 3.2 (1980), pp. 1057–59; 4.23 (1981), pp. 536–39; 5.3 (1982), p. 1448; 7.2 (1984), pp. 1623–24.

a. *The true nature of conjugal love,* which is the basic principle for understanding the requirements it entails: thus *Humanae vitae* (nos. 8ff.) insisted on its condition as a fully human love—therefore rooted in the mind and will—total, faithful and exclusive, fertile; and, as a result, on the inseparability between the unitive and procreative meanings of conjugal love (nos. 9–12);

b. *The perfection of the divine laws on marriage,* which assure the good of the spouses, of the family, and of society:

> The teaching of the Church about the proper spacing of children is a promulgation of the divine law itself. No doubt many will think this teaching difficult, if not impossible, to keep. And truly, just as with all good things outstanding for their nobility and utility [keeping] this law requires strong motivation and much effort from individual Men, from families, and from society. Indeed, this law is not able to be kept without the abundant grace of God, *on which good moral choices [bona voluntas]* of Men depend and from which they get their strength. Moreover, those who consider this matter thoroughly will see that [their] efforts to keep God's law *increase human dignity and confer benefits on human society.*[102]

> Moral norms do not militate against the freedom of the person or the couple; on the contrary they exist precisely for that freedom, since they are given to ensure the right use of freedom. Whoever refuses to accept these norms and to act accordingly, whoever seeks to liberate himself or herself from these norms, is not truly free. Free indeed is the person who models his or her behavior in a responsible way according to the exigencies of the common good. What I have said here regards the whole of conjugal morality.[103]

c. *The urgency of renewing faith in the grace of the sacrament.* John Paul said in Ireland:

> Above all, hold high the esteem for the wonderful dignity and grace of the Sacrament of marriage. Prepare earnestly for it. Believe in the spiritual power which this Sacrament of Jesus Christ gives to strengthen the marriage union, and to overcome all the crises and problems of life together. Married people must believe in the power of the Sacrament to

102 Paul VI, encyclical *Humanae vitae,* July 25, 1968, no. 20; translation of Janet Smith, *Humanae Vitae: A Generation Later* (Washington, D.C.: The Catholic University of America Press, 1991), p. 288.

103 John Paul II, Homily at the Mass celebrated in Logan Circle, Philadelphia, October 3, 1979; *Insegnamenti di Giovanni Paolo II,* 2.2 (1979), pp. 583–84; *Enchiridion Familiae,* 3.2374.

make them holy; they must believe in their vocation to witness through their marriage to the power of Christ's love.[104]

They must be aware that "in the sacrament of marriage a man and a woman—who at Baptism became members of Christ and hence have the duty of manifesting Christ's attitudes in their lives—are assured of the help they need to develop their love in a faithful and indissoluble union and to respond with generosity to the gift of parenthood."[105] Only in this way will they experience all its immense efficacy: "What riches, what requirements, what dynamism derives from this sacrament if it is lived each day with a strong faith, as the image of the mutual gift of Christ and His Church!"[106]

d. *The necessity of appropriate pastoral help.* Paul VI noted: "A great majority of couples have need today of being helped. They are prey, above all, to distrust and doubt, then to fear and discouragement, and finally to abandoning the most noble values of marriage. They often find themselves in this state because those who ought to have been their teachers have instilled doubt into them."[107] He stressed this urgency incisively on another occasion: "Are not pastors in debt to the People of God? Because when they have the courage to speak vigorously, showing thereby their faith in the sacrament of marriage, they find an echo of the deepest sentiments in the human heart, even in ways least suspected."[108] John Paul II aroused in spouses trust in Christ by saying: "As the Vicar of Christ, the Incarnate Word of God, I say to you: have faith in God, the Creator and Father of every human being; have faith in man, created to the image and likeness of God, and called to be a son in the Son!"[109]

[104] John Paul II, Homily at the Mass for Laypeople and Families, Limerick, October 1, 1979; *Insegnamenti di Giovanni Paolo II,* 2.2 (1979), p. 500; *Enchiridion Familiae,* 3.2366. Also see his Address to the Participants in the European Congress of the Pro-Life Movement, February 26, 1979; *Insegnamenti di Giovanni Paolo II,* 2.1 (1979), pp. 467ff.; *Enchiridion Familiae,* 3.2280–82. Paul VI wrote to the same effect in *Humanae vitae,* nos. 19 and 25.

[105] John Paul II, Homily at the Mass on the Capitol Mall of Washington, D.C., October 7, 1979; *Insegnamenti di Giovanni Paolo II,* 2.2 (1979), p. 701; *Enchiridion Familiae,* 3.2382.

[106] John Paul II, Address to the International Congress of the Teams of Our Lady, September 17, 1979; *Insegnamenti di Giovanni Paolo II,* 2.2 (1979), p. 321; *Enchiridion Familiae,* 3.1344.

[107] Paul VI, Address of September 22, 1976; *Insegnamenti di Paolo VI,* 14 (1976), p. 735.

[108] Paul VI, Address to the General Council of the Pontifical Commission for Latin America, October 20, 1975; *Insegnamenti di Paolo VI,* 13 (1975), p. 1155.

[109] John Paul II, Address to the Participants in the European Congress of the Pro-Life Movement, *Insegnamenti di Giovanni Paolo II,* 2.1 (1979), p. 469; *Enchiridion Familiae,* 3.2282.

The Apostolic Exhortation *Familiaris consortio*

We cannot conclude our general overview without mentioning this document. It is, without doubt, the most complete teaching of the Magisterium on marriage and the family: a veritable *Summa* of doctrine.

A half century ago, the famous *Dictionnaire de théologie catholique* concluded the article on "Marriage" and the analysis of 20 centuries of the history of the Church with these words: "The dogma has been defined in precise terms. It is possible that the great work which remains to be done is that of showing to all Christians the enormous moral richness of marriage, and to all other men its great benefits, its incomparable dignity."[110] *Familiaris consortio* has rightly carried out this role: on the foundations established by Vatican Council II, it makes us see that "marriage and the family constitute one of the most precious of human values."[111] The Pope addresses himself to humanity and especially to youth, in order to help them discover the beauty and grandeur of marriage, described vigorously as a "vocation to the love and service of life".[112]

■ In addition, as we will see later, *Familiaris consortio* contains a detailed exposition of the fundamental points of the conjugal morality of the Church, in the fullness of their requirements, made in an attractive and moving way, with replies to the principal modern problems and difficulties, both of spouses and of future spouses. All that, in the light of a conception of marriage as an authentic "path to holiness": and not as a pretty poetic expression but as a reality to be lived.[113]

Moreover, *Familiaris consortio* develops the personalistic doctrine of marriage characteristic of *Gaudium et spes*, bringing its consequences with respect to procreation to fruit: "Conjugal love . . . does not end with the couple, because it makes them capable of the greatest possible gift, the gift by which they become cooperators with God for giving life to a new human person" (no. 14); "In the family the human person is not only brought into being and progressively introduced by means of education into the human community, but by means of the rebirth of baptism and education in the faith the child is also introduced into God's family, which is the Church" (no. 15); "Concern for the child,

[110] G. Le Bras, "Mariage", 9.2316.
[111] John Paul II, apostolic exhortation *Familiaris consortio*, November 22, 1981, no. 1.
[112] Ibid.
[113] Cf. *Familiaris consortio*, nos. 34, 56ff.

even before birth, from the first moment of conception and then throughout the years of infancy and youth, is the primary and fundamental test of the relationship of one human being to another" (no. 26). Taking its point of departure from this affirmation—already given in *Humanae vitae*—namely, that spouses are not only parents but the ministers and servants of life (no. 13), the instruction *Donum vitae* will then appear in all its continuity with the personalism of the Council.[114]

---

[114] Cf. A. Chapelle, "Continuité et progrès dans les enseignements de *Humanae vitae* et de *Donum vitae*", in *"Humanae Vitae": 20 anni dopo (Atti del II Congresso Internazionale di Teologia Morale: Roma 9–12 novembre 1988)* (Milan: Ed. Ares, 1989). The contrast claimed by some to exist between the personalism of *Gaudium et spes* and *Humanae vitae*, and successively between it and *Familiaris consortio*, has no foundation: *Donum vitae* is a clear sign of this.

Chapter Three

ANALYSIS OF THE ENCYCLICAL
CASTI CONNUBII

After having presented in the preceding chapter a panoramic view of the development of the Magisterium on marriage and the family, now we begin the more detailed analysis of the most significant documents that appeared after the Council of Trent. The first to merit this attention is the encyclical of Pope Pius XI, *Casti connubii.* In this chapter, we will be occupied with the genesis, content, and enduring significance of this encyclical.

1. Its Historical Genesis

Pius XI governed the Church from 1922 to 1939. Toward the middle of his pontificate, on December 31, 1930, there appeared the encyclical *Casti connubii:* one of the fundamental works of his Magisterium. It can be said that the entire work of this successor of Peter was a response to his desire to restore to the world a Christian concept of man and of society in the face of the manifestations of a distorted humanism—a laicism, it was then called—that sought to vindicate a radical autonomy and self-sufficiency. In fact,

> Pius XI, as the Roman Pontiff, had to confront the growing predominance of humanisms that repudiated God. This is the background of the last two centuries of contemporary history. It claimed to exalt—from the different perspectives of various ideologies—a concept of man and of the world radically deprived of every transcendent feeling. Thus one can explain the animosity toward the Church which unceasingly bears witness that man is not an end in himself. It is of little importance that, at times, these ideologies—each one with a different project of

humanism — can collide with each other. On the contrary, it could be said that, despite their own confrontations, there is always among them a fundamental — and negative — agreement: the Church is an affront to all these contemporary ideologies. . . . The laicism that spurs on men and the instruments created by them — their States — denies the transcendence of the person, forgetting the intrinsic limits of the authority proper to the person. Everything must be sacrificed to the State: to the violent State of communism and of fascism, or to the State — whose external face is more tranquil but whose interior is radical in its violence — of an indiscriminate democracy, submissive to the omnipotent and blind tyranny of public opinion, so easily manipulable.[1]

In light of this historical background, the entire program of the teachings of Pius XI's pontificate can easily be comprehended, as well as the place that *Casti connubii* held in these teachings. In his first encyclical, *Ubi arcano* (December 23, 1922), Pius XI lodged a complaint against the origin of the troubles facing the world: neither peace nor order reign when men put a distance between themselves and God. A little later, through his encyclical *Quas primas* (December 11, 1925), he established the Feast of Christ the King, proclaiming that the only way to resolve the grave moral crises of humanity is to allow Christ to rule in the mind of every man and of all peoples. Previously, in *Studiorum ducem* (June 29, 1923), he had illustrated the importance of a return to the principles of St. Thomas Aquinas for the reestablishment of the Christian intelligence. This rich nucleus of doctrine would then be developed, throughout his pontificate, in relationship to the different areas of human life: above all, through the family and marriage, the object of two encyclicals, *Divini illius Magistri* (December 31, 1929), which treats of the Christian education of youth, and *Casti connubii*, dedicated completely to the theme of marriage, and in an almost exhaustive manner. Two other encyclicals were concerned with guiding the realization of these principles in the field of social life: *Quadragesimo anno* (May 15, 1931) and *Caritate Christi* (May 3, 1932). In addition, two more documents treat of the priesthood, vocations to which take root in the field provided by the "truly and profoundly Christian family": the constitution *Deus scientiarum Dominus*

[1] G. Redondo, *La iglesia en el mundo contemporáneo*, vol. II, *De León XIII a Pío XI (1878–1939)* (Pamplona: Eunsa, 1979), pp. 179–80. Cf., for our time, M. Schooyans, *La derive totalitaire du liberalisme* (Paris: Editions Universitaires, 1991); V. Possenti, *Le società liberali al bivio* (Perugia: Marietti, 1991).

(May 24, 1931) and the encyclical *Ad catholici sacerdotii* (December 20, 1935).

It is worth noting the importance attributed by his pontificate to the reevaluation of the family, as the basis for the re-Christianization of the world. Already in his encyclical *Ubi arcano*, he had noted that the gravity of laicism had penetrated into the very roots of society, namely, into the family itself;[2] since "in practice society constitutes a reflection of the family", only if God reigns in it can the well-being and peace of society be realized.[3] In an allocution to the Sacred College of Cardinals (December 24, 1930), he thus announced a new document: "An Encyclical on a most important subject", on an "argument of perennial actuality", that "has demanded a long meditation and preparation".[4] The encyclical itself observes that marriage is ordained by God "as the principle and foundation of domestic society and therefore of all human intercourse".[5]

■ Some contingent events favored the appearance of the encyclical: the scandalous incident of the marriage of a princess of Savoy with the king of Bulgaria, celebrated in an irregular way (to avoid the dilemma whether it ought to be celebrated in the Catholic Church or in the Orthodox); the Lambeth Conference (1930), in which 307 Anglican prelates joined together there admitted, with a majority of 193 votes as opposed to 67, with restrained but clear language, the possibility of impeding procreation with means other than continence (total or periodic), always for grave reasons. For the first time, an authority of religious character yielded to the pressures of "eugenic" and "neomalthusian" currents that at the time influenced family life, giving rise to moral abuses. It was a grave scandal.

Nonetheless, these events did not constitute the true cause of the encyclical; indeed—as the Pope himself noted—its cause was his anxiety regarding the decadence of morals and the spread of errors about

---

[2] *Insegnamenti pontifici*, vol. I: *Il matrimonio* (Rome: Edizione Paoline, 1957), cit., no. 257. As we have noted already, we will cite this work by the abbreviation *Ins.*, followed by the reference number. At times the translation will be ours in order to render the language more accurate.

[3] Pius XI, letter *Quod novas*, April 25, 1923; *Ins.* no. 260; *Enchiridion Familiae: Textos del Magisterio Pontificio y Conciliar Sobre el Matrimonio y la Familia (Siglos I a XX)*, ed. A. Sarmiento and J. Escrivá-Ivars, vol. 1 (Madrid: Ediciones Rialp, 1992), p. 680.

[4] Ibid., *Ins.* no. 262; *Enchiridion Familiae*, vol. 1, pp. 708–9.

[5] Pius XI, encyclical *Casti connubii*, December 31, 1930; *Ins.* no. 263 (English translation, no. 1); *Enchiridion Familiae*, 1.710.

the well-known role of the family regarding the salvation of man and of temporal society.[6]

2. The Contents of the Encyclical

The encyclical takes notice of the necessity of *"illuminating the minds* of men with the true doctrine of Christ on marriage", and of *strengthening "their wills with divine grace",*[7] in order that they might be conformed to the law of the Lord and attain all the good promised by him. It appears, as it were, as a repromulgation of the whole Catholic doctrine on marriage, in confrontation both with theoretical streams of thought and practical ways of acting that tend to obscure it toward the end of the second millennium after Christ. The encyclical itself clearly sets forth the plan that it proposes: namely, to treat of "the nature and dignity of Christian marriage, the advantages and benefits which accrue from it to the family and to human society itself, the errors contrary to this most important point of the Gospel teaching, the vices opposed to proper conjugal life, and finally the principal remedies to be applied".[8] Behold, therefore, the three parts into which the encyclical is divided: *the principles and goods* of marriage (which will concern us in two of the sections below); *the errors and vices* opposed to it; and *the principal remedies to be applied.*

A. *The principles: the divine institution and sanctity of marriage; the necessity of human cooperation with the divine plan*

The grandeur of marriage springs from its divine institution; but, as with every human good, it is entrusted, for its realization, to the liberty of men and women.

It can be said that this is the first fundamental doctrine of the encyclical. There is a radical perfection at the origin of marriage,

---

[6] Cf. ibid., *Ins.* nos. 263–65 (E.T., nos. 3–4); *Enchiridion Familiae,* 2.710–12.

[7] On the importance of this encyclical with respect to the doctrine of sacramental grace, cf. G. Baldanza, "La grazia sacramentale matrimoniale nell'enciclica *Casti connubii:* l'influsso del rinnovamento liturgico", *Ephemerides Liturgicae* 99 (1985): 47–59.

[8] Pius XI, *Casti connubii; Ins.* nos. 264–66 (E.T., no. 4); *Enchiridion Familiae,* 1.711.

deriving from the wisdom of the divine plan, but the cooperation of creatures is required in order that every marriage might attain the fullness of which it is capable. This provides us with the twofold aspect that must be considered: the plan of God and the response of men and women.

■ Both these aspects are indispensable to understand what marriage truly is and to avoid evacuating it of its dignity. Faith, certainly, gives us the greatest certainty regarding the awesome wonderfulness and perfection of the divine plan in a matter so fundamental for men; but it is also necessary to remember that, with our freedom, we can either bring this plan to completion or contradict it: true incarnations of the divine plan are then quite distinct from those social forms of marriage deriving from a bad use of freedom. Only in this way can we truly discern "the signs of the times", that are "the historical expression" of the exercise of freedom according to its twofold possibility: to obey the love of God or to close itself off in an egoism of self-love.[9]

Those publications are clearly absurd that—in the name of sociology or of human sciences—judge the diffusion of so-called unions of fact, or of trial unions, of abortion, and of divorce simply as signs of a historical evolution toward a freer type of relationship between man and woman. In fact, these models of behavior degrade human dignity through a bad use of freedom. Not to take this into account signifies that one has lost the capacity to distinguish between good and evil: "They promise them freedom, though they themselves are slaves of corruption" (2 Pet 2:19).

Let it be repeated as an immutable and inviolable fundamental doctrine that marriage was not instituted or restored by man but by God; not by man were the laws made to strengthen and confirm and elevate it but by God, the Author of nature, and by Christ our Lord by whom nature was redeemed, and hence these laws cannot be subject to any human decrees or to any contrary pact even of the spouses themselves. This is the doctrine of Holy Scripture (Gen. 1:27–28; 2:22–23, Matt. 19:3ff.; Eph. 5:23ff), this is the constant tradition of the Universal Church, this the solemn definition of the sacred Council of Trent, which declares and establishes from the words of Holy Writ itself that God is the Author of the perpetuity and indissolubility of marriage, its unity and stability.[10]

[9] Cf. Pope John Paul II, apostolic exhortation *Familiaris consortio,* November 22, 1981, no. 6.

[10] Pius XI, *Casti connubii; Ins.* no. 267 (E.T., no. 5); *Enchiridion Familiae,* vol. 1, p. 712. The formula of the Council of Trent comes to mind: after having affirmed that Adam, "inspired

▪ Therefore, it was God himself who willed marriage to be and who restored it after the fall. It is not an invention of men. He conceived and established the community of persons who constitute the family as the place in which human life can develop properly, the human life that possesses a "family structure",[11] and that can neither grow nor develop rightly and happily outside the family. Precisely because of its importance for the life of every human person, *God protects marriage with laws* that do not restrict the freedom of the spouses but rather guarantee the realization of their love. Let us recall the intrinsic character of the divine law—whether natural or supernatural—since every man receives it as a radical inclination of his own nature to its own proper fullness and perfection, confirmed and amplified by grace that heals and elevates natural energies. Precisely because of this, God alone could restore marriage with its laws of life (cf. Rom 8:2) inasmuch as he alone has the power to recompose the nature wounded by sin; and he did this in Christ—God incarnate—in whom man finds, in addition to a guide, the capacity of living in its integrity the original design of marriage. From this it follows that, far from limiting the freedom of the spouses, the divine laws render them capable of attaining their true happiness. Man can refuse to obey them, but he cannot arrange matters so that this disobedience will render him happy. Denying them does not remove them from his own nature, but rather leads it to ruin and in this way damages society also. It is as if an engineer did not take into account the laws of gravity: he does not bring about the annulment of his own needs but rather risks the collapse of the work he is constructing.[12]

Marriage, thus, is instituted by God, as a reality of creation and redemption, and this great good of marriage has been intimately related by God himself to the free cooperation of the spouses, through whose will marriage is born and

---

by the Holy Spirit", said "there will be two in one flesh" (Gen 2:24), it added that Christ himself confirmed these words as pronounced by God himself when, after having repeated them, he affirmed: "What therefore God has joined, let man not separate" (Mt 19:6) (session 24, Intr., H. Denzinger and A. Schoenmetzer, *Enchiridion Symbolorum Definitionum et Declarationum de rebus fidel et morum,* 34th ed. [Barcelona-Rome: Herder, 1967], hereinafter as DS, no. 969 [1797–98].

[11] Cf. Pope John Paul II, encyclical *Laborem exercens,* September 14, 1981, no. 10.

[12] On the positive character of these indications of the divine laws as a guide to the true good and the happiness of the person, cf. Ramón García de Haro, *Cuestiones fundamentales de teología moral* (Pamplona: Eunsa, 1980), chap. 3, pp. 93ff., and *Legge, coscienza e libertà,* 2nd ed. (Milan: Ed. Ares, 1990).

develops. Marriage depends for it realization on the divine will and on the human will.

> From God comes the very institution of marriage, the ends for which it was instituted, the laws that govern it, the blessings that flow from it; while man, through generous surrender of his own person made to another for the whole span of life, becomes, with the help and cooperation of God, the author of each particular marriage, with the duties and blessings annexed thereto from divine institution.[13]

There are, therefore, two aspects left by God to the free will of man: the *birth* or origin of marriage and the *conservation and development* of the goods proper to marriage.

1. *The origin or birth of each concrete marriage is entrusted to the freedom of the spouses:* "Each individual marriage, inasmuch as it is a conjugal union of a particular man and woman, arises only from the free consent of each of the spouses; and this free act of the will, by which each party hands over and accepts those rights proper to the state of marriage, is so necessary to constitute true marriage that 'it cannot be supplied by any human power.'[14]"[15] Marriage is not a reality solely of the physical order, the fruit of a de facto union or living together, but is a reality that, comprising physical and corporeal elements, comes to birth in and through the spirit *in virtue of the free will of the spouses:* "By matrimony, therefore, the souls of the contracting parties are joined and knit together more directly and more intimately than are their bodies, and that not by any passing affection of sense or spirit, but by a deliberate and firm act of the will; and from this union of souls by God's decree, a sacred and inviolable bond arises."[16]

> ■ This argument will be taken up again in *Familiaris consortio:* the union "by means of which man and woman give themselves to one another through the acts proper and exclusive to spouses is by no means something purely biological, but concerns the innermost being of the human person as such. It is realized in a truly human way only if it is an integral part of the love by which a man and a woman commit

---

[13] Pope Pius XI, *Casti connubii; Ins.* no. 272 (E.T., no. 10); *Enchiridion Familiae,* 1.715.

[14] *Codex Iuris Canonici* (1917), can. 1081, par. 1.

[15] Pius XI, *Casti connubii; Ins.* no. 268 (E.T., no. 6); *Enchiridion Familiae,* 1.713.

[16] Ibid., *Ins.,* no. 270 (E.T., no. 7); *Enchiridion Familiae,* 1.714.

themselves totally to one another until death."[17] Marriage is not the product of a "blind natural instinct", as happens in the unions between beings who lack intelligence and will; only consent, which establishes the community of life and love willed by God, gives rise to a human way of living out one's sexuality.[18] All other forms of union between man and woman are nothing else than the results of a voluntary renunciation of their own proper dignity, something that degrades them to the level of what Scripture calls the "animal man" (cf. 1 Cor 2:14; Jude 19). It is for this reason that the encyclical insists on the fact that "legitimately constituted authority has the right and therefore the duty to restrict, to prevent, and to punish those base unions which are opposed to reason and to human nature".[19] Here we must not forget that the healing of bad social customs is not possible with merely human means but demands recourse to the word and grace of God.

2. *The preservation and development of the goods proper to marriage is, in the second place, entrusted to the freedom of the spouses.* Certainly, "the nature of marriage is entirely independent of the free will of man, so that if one has once contracted marriage he is thereby subject to its divinely made laws and its essential properties."[20] The essential goods of marriage are willed by God himself and are inscribed into the very humanity of man and of woman, insofar as they are intimately inclined toward them, have the capacity to attain them, and the obligation to develop them. Thus, if any one of these goods is excluded from the consent of the spouses, this makes their marriage to be invalid.[21] But the actual realization of these goods—both fidelity in love and the procreation and education of children—demands the constant and courageous effort of the spouses to put into actuality the energies they have received from God and which have been renewed with his Providence—ordinary and extraordinary—and in particular through the sacraments.

---

[17] Pope John Paul II, *Familiaris consortio*, no. 11.
[18] Cf. Pope Pius XI, *Casti connubii; Ins.* no. 270 (E.T., no. 7); *Enchiridion Familiae*, 1.714.
[19] Ibid., *Ins.* no. 271 (E.T., no. 9); *Enchiridion Familiae*, 1.714.
[20] Ibid., *Ins.* no. 269 (E.T., no. 6); *Enchiridion Familiae*, 1.713.
[21] Cf. St. Thomas, *Summa theologiae*, supplement to III, q. 49, a. 3.

Matrimonial consent is an act of conjugal love.

Here it is opportune to put in relief the way in which the encyclical emphasizes both the mission of conjugal love and the precise form in which it is related to the consent of the spouses that serves as the foundation for the marital community.

■ We have already pointed out the difficulties that arise in this matter: some have confused *mutual help*—one of the secondary ends of marriage— with conjugal love. Others, on the other hand, wishing to make evident the importance of conjugal love in marriage, have not known how to make precise the relationships between conjugal love and consent; and thus, not seeing clearly the role of the will—love as an exclusive and indissoluble self-donation—and that of sentiments in the free act of willing of the spouses, have weakened the traditional doctrine according to which *consent makes marriage*. It is precisely here that we find the merit of this encyclical, a clear precedent for the developments that took place at Vatican Council II and in *Familiaris consortio*—and in perfect continuity with Tradition—with respect to the role of love in marriage. It avoided the errors and resolved the objections that have, unfortunately, been proposed once more by some authors in the postconciliar period.[22]

Marriage—*Casti connubii* teaches—comes to be through the consent of the spouses, from the firm and deliberate act of the will that "joins and knits together the souls of the contracting parties more directly and more intimately than their bodies" and involves a "generous surrender of one's own person to another for the whole span of life", giving rise to a "sacred and inviolable bond".[23] This act of the will, so permeated by a generous disposition of the gift of oneself, which implies sentiment without being confused with it, is properly an act of *conjugal love*. It constitutes the love that establishes the matrimonial community, being the principle bringing life to the duty of fidelity between the spouses:

This conjugal faith, however, which is most aptly called by St. Augustine the "faith of chastity," blooms more freely, more beautifully and more

[22] See the argument given by Ramón García de Haro, "El matrimonio, comunidad de amor, al servicio de la vida. Estudio sobre la noción de matrimonio en la Exhortación Apostolica 'Familiaris consortio' ", *Divinitas* 26, no. 3 (1982): 332–49.

[23] Pope Pius XI, *Casti connubii; Ins.* nos. 270–72 (E.T., nos. 7–9); *Enchiridion Familiae*, 1.714. Note the profound personalistic thrust of these passages.

nobly, when it is rooted in that more excellent soil, the love of husband and wife *which pervades all the duties of married life and holds pride of place in Christian marriage.* For matrimonial faith demands that husband and wife be joined in an especially holy and pure love, not as adulterers love each other, but as Christ loves the Church. This precept the Apostle laid down when he said: "Husbands, love your wives as Christ also loved the Church" (Eph. 5:25; Col. 3:19), that Church which of a truth He embraced with a boundless love not for the sake of His own advantage, but seeking only the good of His Spouse.[24] The love, then, of which We are speaking is not that based on the passing lust of the moment nor does it consist in pleasing words only, but in the deep attachment of the heart which is expressed in action, since "love is proved by deeds and not by good arguments."[25,26]

Therefore, without entering into polemics with authors, the encyclical emphasizes what is the constant teaching of Tradition about the nature, importance, and role of conjugal love in marriage.

■ The Church has always assigned to conjugal love, that is, to the union of the souls that establishes the communion of the spouses, a preeminent place in marriage. St. Augustine affirmed, for example, that the perfection of marriage derives from a twofold good: not only that of the generation and education of human life but also that of establishing through that end the intimate community of persons that is the conjugal society.[27] This (conjugal life) comes about in such a way that the exclusion from the conjugal covenant of any one of these two goods implies that the union in question is not a marriage.[28] St. Thomas expresses himself analogously: "In creatures we observe a twofold perfection: the first is constituted by their formal principle, from which they derive their proper nature or species; the second is the activity whereby they tend toward their end. In marriage, the formal principle is constituted by that indivisible union of souls through which each spouse promises faithful love to the other. The end of marriage is the generation and education of children."[29]

---

[24] *Catechism of the Council of Trent,* II, c. 8, 42.

[25] St. Gregory the Great, *Hom. XXX in Evang.* (Jn 14:23–31), no. 1.

[26] Pius XI, *Casti connubii; Ins.* no. 258 (E.T., no. 23); *Enchiridion Familiae,* 1.723–24.

[27] St. Augustine, *De bono coniugali,* c. 3, no. 3; PL 40,375; see the argument of Francisco Gil Hellín, "Los 'bona matrimonii' en la Constitución pastoral *Gaudium et spes*", *Scripta Theologica* 11 (1971): 131–37.

[28] St. Augustine, *De bono coniugali,* c. 5, no. 3.

[29] St. Thomas, *Summa theologiae,* 3, q. 29, a. 2.

The opposition between love and procreation—present in polemics over the ends of marriage—is foreign to Tradition. Tradition has rightly emphasized the opposite: their complementarity as the form and, respectively, the end of marriage.

We can summarize the teaching of the encyclical: marriage *is born of the consent of the parties;* and this consent must embrace, as essential elements, *the exclusive and permanent self-giving* of the spouses and *the orientation to progeny.* "In fact, the Angelic Doctor, discussing conjugal fidelity and children, says: 'these are caused by the conjugal pact itself, so that if anything is expressed in the consent of the parties, which establishes marriage, that is contrary to them, a marriage would not, in truth, exist.'[30]"[31] Therefore, the exclusion of children is not the only thing that vitiates consent; the exclusion of conjugal love (that is, of the gift of self given exclusively and for the whole of one's life) also vitiates it. The conjugal community requires that it be brought to life and informed by love, "which must be present in the different concrete aspects of marriage. In effect, such a love must inwardly shape or inform the procreation and education of children and the mutual help between the spouses, in order that these might be truly human ends. In the same way, the unity and indissolubility of marriage must be animated by love."[32]

But let us emphasize that conjugal love and the ordination toward procreation pertain to the essence of the matrimonial pact not as fully existing "de facto", but—as St. Thomas said[33]—"in their principles". *Consent* — or the conjugal agreement—appears as the *first act of conjugal love,* as the act of the love that establishes marriage, that embraces the promise of exclusivity and of permanance and of orientation to children.

■ If the role of conjugal love in the essence of marriage and the relationship that it has with consent are thus understood, we will avoid the danger of obscuring the truth of its ordination to the service of life and the risk of multiplying causes for the nullity of marriage. Consent indissolubly concerns both love and the procreation of children: from

[30] Ibid., 3, supplement, q. 49, a. 3.

[31] Pius XI, *Casti connubii; Ins.* no. 269 (E.T., no. 6); *Enchiridion Familiae,* 1.713.

[32] Francisco Gil Hellín, "El matrimonio: amor e institución", in *Cuestiones fundamentales sobre matrimonio y familia (Actas del II Simposio Internacional de Teología),* ed. A. Sarmiento et al. (Pamplona: Eunsa, 1980), pp. 239–40.

[33] St. Thomas, *Summa theologiae,* 3, supplement, q. 40, a. 3 c and ad 4.

the moment of consent both are "due", morally and juridically, even if in fact they can be lacking because of the will of the spouses, inasmuch as they are goods entrusted to human freedom and, as such, exist only if the spouses loyally maintain the commitment they have assumed. It is possible that they may not exist because of disorder, fault, or injustice on the part of the spouses; but they do not cease to be owed. Therefore, the factual absence of them—either of love or of progeny—does not annul the marriage, but such absence illegitimately deprives marriage of its own goods in a sinful way: this is the risk of freedom. To recognize that love is an essential good of marriage, and therefore a necessary object of matrimonial consent, does not imply new titles of nullity in addition to those that are manifested in vices affecting consent:[34] that is, the lack of the essential (not accidental) fullness of that act of the will.

This lack can never be presumed, because it is unnatural, deformed, contrary to the most intimate inclinations of the spouses; how is it possible to desire, in the very moment of giving oneself in marriage, the positive exclusion of children or of the unity and indissolubility of one's own union? We would no longer be present before a marriage but before one of the forms of a degraded and degrading union—a union of fact, a marriage of convenience or of experiment—between a man and a woman that always carries with it the awareness that one is not willing to contract marriage.

B. *The goods of marriage: children, fidelity, the sacrament*

The encyclical sets forth the content of marriage within the perspective—rooted in a long tradition—of the "bona matrimonii": proles, fides, sacramentum.

As a rule, the manuals of the period followed the scheme of the ends, properties, and laws of marriage. *Casti connubii,* on the other hand, prefers to follow that of the *bona matrimonii* (the goods of marriage) which, elaborated by St. Augustine, had been widely diffused as a particularly fitting way of giving a catechetical exposition of marriage; moreover, this scheme had shown itself to be very suitable for the dynamics of Christian action, wherein the divine promises—

---

[34] Cf. Javier Hervada, "Cuestiones varias sobre el matrimonio", *Ius Canonicum* 13 (1973): 51ff.

the goods—encompass and lay the foundation for the precepts. In fact, the ends established by God are, precisely, the goods promised by him; and he has established his laws in their service, as the active intimate principle and external guide for the successful attainment of those very ends.

> ■ Traced out by St. Augustine, principally to combat the residues of manicheanism present among his contemporaries, the doctrine of the *goods of marriage* was, for very profound reasons, incorporated into the common tradition of the medieval theologians. Both *Casti connubii* and, later, Vatican Council II appealed to this doctrine: "In acknowledging and employing the schema of the goods, the Council certainly transcended the presentation of the school authors and joined itself to the sources of the great masters, St. Augustine and St. Thomas. The goods appear ... as those fundamental coordinates within which the ends, the properties, and the levels—natural and Christian—of the existence of marriage are integrated."[35]

The good of children

The encyclical emphasizes that this good occupies the "first place",[36] precisely because it is the "primary end" of marriage;[37] and it is always the end that determines the characteristics of any plan. The grandeur of the objective—the transmission of human life and care for its development—is the first cause of the properties and excellences of the conjugal community. Unless it were a community of love, one and indissoluble, it could not carry out such a precious task of generating human life and helping it develop. The centrality of service to life both deepens and expands the other goods of marriage.

For this reason, *Casti connubii* sets forth with particular detail what this good consists in[38] and the laws with which God has protected it.[39] The orientation of marriage to the good of children is a truth taught by holy Scripture; it confers on the spouses the honor of becoming cooperators with God and embraces a twofold aspect: the procreation and education of children.

---

[35] Gil Hellín, "Los 'bona matrimonii' ", p. 176.

[36] Cf. Pius XI, *Casti connubii; Ins.* no. 274 (E.T., no. 12); *Enchiridion Familiae*, 1.716.

[37] Cf. ibid., *Ins.,* no. 279 (E.T., no. 17); *Enchiridion Familiae*, 1.720.

[38] Cf. ibid., *Ins.,* nos. 274–79 (E.T., nos. 12–17); *Enchiridion Familiae*, 1.716–20.

[39] Cf. ibid., *Ins.,* nos. 280 and 314–15 (E.T., nos. 18 and 54–55); *Enchiridion Familiae*, 1.721, 741–42.

1. In affirming that the primary end of marriage is the *transmission of life,* the Church does no more than act as the faithful voice of Scripture and Tradition:

> Indeed the Creator of the human race Himself, who in His goodness wished to use men as His helpers in the propagation of life, taught this when, instituting marriage in Paradise, He said to our first parents, and through them to all future spouses: "Increase and multiply, and fill the earth" (Gen. 1:28). St. Augustine admirably deduces this same truth from the words of the holy Apostle Saint Paul to Timothy (1 Tim 5:14) when he says: "The Apostle himself is therefore a witness that marriage is for the sake of generation. 'I wish,' he says, 'young girls to marry.' And, as if someone said to him, 'Why?,' he immediately adds: 'To bear children, to be mothers of families.'[40]"[41]

The *grandeur of this good* is related to the grandeur of the person, to the "dignity and to the most noble end of man". God, in fact, not only created man reasonable and free, at the summit of all the other beings of the visible universe, but he created him because he could know and love God himself, and in virtue of grace could live in familiarity and intimacy with God, so that he could succeed in attaining to God as he is in himself in heaven. This was the design of his generosity that surpasses all desires and thoughts: "For eye has not seen, nor ear heard, nor has it entered into the heart of man" (1 Cor 2:9). From this "it is easily seen how great a gift of divine goodness and how remarkable a fruit of marriage are children born by the omnipotent power of God through the cooperation of those bound in wedlock."[42]

> ■ It is important to insist on this. The *better known* a good is, the more easily does love for it arise. Every time that parents say yes to life, God cooperates with them in creating an immortal soul: a new existence that is intelligent and free, that will remain for all eternity; they give life to a person who will be flesh of their flesh and who will owe to its parents the eternal capacity to know and to love. Thus is to be understood the saying of our Lord, reported also in the encyclical, that bears witness to the logical reaction when confronted with the gift of life: "When a woman . . . has borne her child, she no longer remembers her pain for joy that a man has been born into the world" (Jn 16:21).

---

[40] St. Augustine, *De bono coniugali,* c. 24, no. 32.

[41] Pius XI, *Casti connubii; Ins.* no. 274 (E.T., no. 12); *Enchiridion Familiae,* 1.716–17.

[42] Ibid., *Ins.* no. 275 (E.T., no. 13); *Enchiridion Familiae,* 1.717–18.

2. Christian parents know that their mission is even more ample because, in cooperating with God in giving life to their children, they also furnish *"new members of the Church of Christ . . .* fellow citizens of the Saints, and members of God's household" (cf. Eph. 2:19), children who may be regenerated through the laver of Baptism whereby the Church transforms them into "living members of Christ, partakers of immortal life, and heirs of that eternal glory to which we all aspire from our inmost heart".[43]

■ With this, the encyclical recalls that, while original sin is an evil of nature that is transmitted through generation,[44] the regeneration is, in its turn, a personal good: it presupposes the encounter of each soul with Christ that is accomplished in baptism (or in a way known only by God for those who, possessing good will, are now in ignorance of revelation).[45] This condition of carrying out redemption makes one understand the grave obligation of parents not to delay the baptism of their children.

3. In addition, the mission of parents is not ended with the generation of life but is prolonged in the care given to the *education of life,* since "the primary end of marriage is the procreation and education of children."[46] As we have already said, the transmission of human life, in a way adequate to its dignity, demands the prolonged love and protection of the family: "The most wise God would have failed to make sufficient provision for children that had been born, and so for the whole human race, if He had not given to those to whom He had entrusted the power and right to beget them, the power also and the right to educate them."[47] Children have need of their parents for many years, not only in the area of material goods but also and even more in that of the spiritual: the family constitutes the first and most important school of humanity and sociality, as well as of education in the Faith.

Three precepts of divine law protect the good of children: only marriage provides the human ambit in which it is legitimate to generate life; conjugal

---

[43] Ibid., *Ins.* no. 276 (E.T., no. 14); *Enchiridion Familiae,* 1.718.

[44] Cf. ibid., *Ins.* no. 277 (E.T., no. 14); *Enchiridion Familiae,* 1.718.

[45] Cf. Vatican Council II, pastoral constitution *Gaudium et spes,* December 7, 1965, no. 22.

[46] Pius XI, *Casti connubii; Ins.* no. 279 (E.T., no. 17); *Enchiridion Familiae,* 1.720.

[47] Ibid., *Ins.* no. 278 (E.T., no. 16); *Enchiridion Familiae,* 1.719.

love and procreation are inseparable; the parents are, by the will of God, the first educators of their children. In fact, the encyclical affirms: "Since the duty entrusted to parents for the good of their children is of such high dignity and of such great importance, every use of the faculty given by God for the procreation of new life is the right and the privilege of the married state alone, by the law of God and of nature, and must be confined absolutely within the sacred limits of that state."[48] Further on, the encyclical states: "Since, therefore, the conjugal act is destined primarily by nature for the begetting of children, those who in exercising it deliberately frustrate its natural power and purpose sin against nature and commit a deed which is shameful and intrinsically vicious."[49] And finally: "Now it is certain that both by the law of nature and of God this right and duty of educating their children belongs in the first place to those who began the work of nature by giving them birth"; marriage not only constitutes the fitting place for procreating life; "in marriage provision has been made in the best possible way for the education of children that is so necessary, for, since the parents are bound together by an indissoluble bond, the care and mutual help of each is always at hand."[50]

■ Only conjugal love—that is, the love between a man and a woman united in the totality, exclusivity, and perpetual fidelity proper to marriage—offers the fitting ambience for the generation and growth of human life. The person has need to be born and to be supported by true love, not by an impulse of passion; nor can marital life be lived well if it is regarded as a painful duty to the egoism-a-deux of the spouses. Love and life, repeats the Holy Father—must go together: "The vocation to love is linked in an unbreakable way with the vocation to *the gift of life*. The Church has always taught this unbreakable connection: conjugal love is the fountain of human life, and the gift of human life requires conjugal love at its origin. . . . The familial community . . . is the place where love generates life and life springs from love. Neither of these realities, that is, *love* and *life*, can be authentic if they are severed from each other."[51]

[48] Ibid., *Ins.* no. 280 (E.T., no. 18); *Enchiridion Familiae*, 1.721.
[49] Ibid., *Ins.* no. 315 (E.T., no. 55); *Enchiridion Familiae*, 1.742.
[50] Ibid., *Ins.* no. 278 (E.T., no. 16); *Enchiridion Familiae*, 1.720.
[51] John Paul II, Discourse of December 7, 1981, to the Participants at Two Meetings on the Family, *Insegnamenti di Giovanni Paolo II*, 4.2 (Vatican City: Typis Polyglottis Vaticanis, 1981), no. 2.

The good of conjugal fidelity

This is the second of the goods of marriage with which the encyclical is concerned. In reality, it is dealing with nothing else than *conjugal love*, designated by the name of its first essential property: fidelity. Conjugal love—which establishes and must inform the entire community of life between the spouses and whose end is the work of generating and educating children—can not be other than a *faithful love*: the spouses must be joined in "an especially holy and pure love".[52] It is put in the second place, not because it is to be considered secondary, but in accordance with a traditional custom that finds its explanation in the fact that, metaphysically, the end determines the form: the ordination to the generation and education of human life defines the requirements and unique characteristics of conjugal love. The encyclical wishes to emphasize that conjugal love must "inform and pervade all the duties of married life", including the fulfillment of the primary end, which is the good of children.[53] In this way, the encyclical links itself to the line of the Augustinian-Thomistic tradition, which gave to love the role of being the vital principle of marriage, informing it, giving it its dynamic.

■ With respect to the good of fidelity, the most original contribution of the encyclical is the way in which it develops the perfecting of the love between the spouses through conjugal charity, recognizing in matrimonial grace a dynamic principle that involves and increases all the energies of the spouses.[54] The properties of the good of fidelity are equally unity and indissolubility.[55] *Casti connubii,* less precise in this respect, treats of indissolubility in connection with the good of the sacrament, according to a manner customary at that time; in discussing the good of fidelity it treats only of unity, of conjugal charity, and of the order of love that this generates.

Conjugal love, which must inform the entire married life and the mutual obligations of the spouses, cannot be but one; and it is perfected by conjugal

[52] Pius XI, *Casti connubii; Ins.* no. 285 (E.T., no. 23); *Enchiridion Familiae,* 1.723.

[53] Ibid., *Ins.* no. 285 (E.T., no. 23); *Enchiridion Familiae,* 1.723.

[54] On this see Baldanza, "La grazia sacramentale matrimoniale nell'enciclica *Casti connubii*", pp. 50ff.

[55] Thus, in fact, the *Code of Canon Law* puts the matter this way: "The essential properties of marriage are unity and indissolubility, which in Christian marriage by reason of the sacrament obtain a special firmness" (can. 1056).

charity, which leads the spouses to imitate the holiness of Christ. Conjugal love—the encyclical affirms—

> demands in the first place the complete unity of matrimony which the Creator Himself laid down in the beginning when He wished it to be not otherwise than between one man and one woman. And although afterwards this primeval law was relaxed to some extent by God, the Supreme Legislator, there is no doubt that the law of the Gospel fully restored that original and perfect unity . . . as the words of Christ and the constant teaching and action of the Church show plainly.[56]

Thus did the Council of Trent solemnly declare. Therefore, the reestablishment of the unity of marriage was so perfect and complete that our Lord not only prohibited every kind of polygamy, whether simultaneous or successive, but "in order that the sacred bonds of marriage may be guarded absolutely inviolate, He forbade even wilful thoughts and desires of such like things: 'But I say to you, that whosoever shall look on a woman to lust after her has already committed adultery with her in his heart' (Matt. 5:28)."[57]

This love, which must be chaste—that is, conformed to the law of God and not to egoism[58]—is perfected and elevated by *charity,* which impels the spouses always to grow more in the "true love toward God and their neighbor, on which indeed 'depends the whole Law and the Prophets' (Matt. 22:40)". In this way, the spouses are also called to "imitate that most perfect example of holiness placed before man by God, namely Christ Our Lord, and by God's grace to arrive at the summit of perfection, as is proved by the example set us of many saints."[59]

> ■ The expressions of *Casti connubii* anticipate, also on this matter, the doctrine that Vatican Council II will proclaim about the universal call to holiness: everyone, of whatever condition they may be and whatever honest way of living they may have chosen, can and ought "to imitate Christ, the exemplar of all holiness and in this way attain to the very heights of perfection".[60] A capital point, because the Church acts principally through her saints, and by the laws of life, the majority of the faithful pertain to the state of matrimony.

[56] Pius XII, *Casti connubii; Ins.* no. 282 (E.T., no. 20); *Enchiridion Familiae,* 1.721–22.
[57] Ibid., *Ins.* no. 283 (E.T., no. 21); *Enchiridion Familiae,* 1.722.
[58] Cf. ibid., *Ins.* no. 284 (E.T., no. 22); *Enchiridion Familiae,* 1.723.
[59] Ibid., *Ins.* no. 286 (E.T., no. 23); *Enchiridion Familiae,* 1.724.
[60] Cf. ibid., *Ins.* no. 286; *Enchiridion Familiae,* 1.724.

Conjugal love or charity thus supports the order of the domestic society which, according to the Augustinian expression, is an "order of love". Following the teachings of Scripture, the encyclical sets forth the principal lines: "Let women be subject to their husbands as to the Lord, because the husband is the head of the wife, as Christ is the head of the Church" (Eph 5:22–23; cf. Eph 5:25; Col 3:19; 1 Pet 3:1–7); in a parallel manner, children ought to be submissive to their parents, and these should take care to govern them with love (Col 3:20; Eph 6:1–4). With respect to the role of the father and the mother within the familial community, the encyclical confirms that to the man corresponds the "chief place in ruling", and to the woman, on the other hand, the "chief place in love".[61] In addition, it emphasizes that the way of living this *ordo* —a requirement of the "family structure" and a "fundamental law established and confirmed by God"—varies with times and places, but must be always respected in its essence, considering that "the husband represents Christ and the wife represents the Church, and that divine charity ought to be the perpetual moderator of the relations and obligations of the spouses."[62]

The good of the sacrament

This is the third of the goods of marriage. It designates both the indissolubility of the bond that the "sacrament" names in the narrow sense and the raising and hallowing of the marriage by Christ himself.[63]

■ As we have said, indissolubility pertains of itself to the good of fidelity. Notwithstanding this, it is customarily included in the sacrament, because in fact it has been reestablished by Christ, along with the elevation of marriage to a sacrament. St. Augustine himself many times makes this transposition. In fact, he often affirms all three of the goods of marriage indistinctly of every marriage,[64] although at other times, with greater precision, he limits the *bonum sacramenti* to Christian marriage: "The good of marriage for the sake of generating life and of maintaining chaste fidelity is found in all nations; but what

[61] Ibid., *Ins.* no. 289 (E.T., nos. 26–27); *Enchiridion Familiae*, 1.725–26.
[62] Ibid., *Ins.* no. 291 (E.T., nos. 28–29); *Enchiridion Familiae*, 1.726–27.
[63] Cf. ibid., *Ins.* no. 293 (E.T., no. 31); *Enchiridion Familiae*, 1.727.
[64] Cf. *De sancta virginitate*, c. 12, no. 12; PL 40,401; *De genesi ad litteram*, IX, c. 7, no. 12; PL 34,397.

pertains to the People of God is the sanctity of the sacrament."[65] In the strict sense, indissolubility pertains to the *bonum fidei,* but both this good and the *bonum prolis* are perfected by the *sacramentum.*[66] Because of this, already from the time of St. Augustine, indissolubility is often treated as part of the *bonum sacramenti* insofar as from it it takes its fullness.[67]

1. *After the renewal worked by Christ, indissolubility becomes a property of every marriage, as it was in the first institution: and this is made even fuller through the "consummation" and the sacrament.* The encyclical repeats what the Council of Trent solemnly had taught, how this has been revealed by our Lord himself, when he said: "Let not man separate what God has joined" (Mt 19:6), referring these words to the marriage of the progenitors, the prototype of every future marriage. Although, prior to Christ, this law of indissolubility had been in a way mitigated when Moses permitted the chosen people, "on account of the hardness of their hearts", to give for specific reasons a bill of repudiation to their wives, Christ "restored the primeval law in its integrity".[68] Therefore, even when "the sacramental element may be absent from a marriage as is the case among unbelievers, still in such a marriage, inasmuch as it is a true marriage there must remain and indeed there does remain that perpetual bond which by divine right is so bound up with matrimony from its first institution that it is not subject to any human power", and, therefore, if those contracting marriage positively exclude "that perpetual bond, in that case there is no marriage but an illicit union opposed of its very nature to the divine law."[69]

■ In what follows, the encyclical clarifies that indissolubility is perfected by the "consummation" of marriage and by the sacrament. This explains how it is possible, in exceptional cases, to dissolve the marriage bond between the nonbaptized, when one of the spouses receives baptism and the other does not wish to continue peacefully conjugal life (the

---

[65] *De bono coniugali,* c. 24, no. 32; PL 40,394: "Bonum igitur nuptiarum per omnes gentes atque omnes homines in causa generandi est, et in fide castitatis; quod autem ad Populum Dei pertinet, etiam in sanctitate sacramenti."

[66] Thus St. Augustine, *De nuptiis et concupiscentia,* c. 17, no. 19; PL 44, 424.

[67] On the development of this doctrine of the *bona matrimonii* cf. Gil Hellín, "Los 'bona matrimonii' ", pp. 131–37.

[68] Pius XI, *Casti connubii; Ins.* no. 295 (E.T., no. 34); *Enchiridion Familiae,* 1.728–29.

[69] Ibid., *Ins.* no. 296 (E.T., no. 34); *Enchiridion Familiae,* 1.729. In this passage, Pius XI is citing from his predecessor Pius VI, *Rescript. ad Episc. Agriens.,* July 11, 1789.

Pauline privilege) and to dissolve a marriage that is ratified but not consummated, even among the baptized (for example, by entrance into religious life). On the other hand, it is never possible to dissolve a marriage ratified and consummated among the baptized.[70] The encyclical gives the reason of this divine will: marriage is the sign of the union between Christ and his Church, "If we wish with all reverence to inquire into the intimate reason of this divine decree ... we shall easily see it in the mystical signification of Christian marriage which is fully and perfectly verified only in consummated marriage between Christians."[71]

This part of *Casti connubii* ends with an enumeration of the *fruits of indissolubility* both for the spouses and their children and society itself. The stable character of the bond, in fact, protects conjugal love, since it stimulates the spouses to the generous and unconditioned gift of their own person in the exclusive and permanent union of their hearts; and it is a bulwark of a faithful chastity because it closes the door to fear or anxiety about its permanence in times of adversity and drives jealousy away; in addition, it assures the dignity of the mutual love, because its perpetuity reminds the spouses that their union is contracted rather for eternal goods than for transient interests. On the other hand, indissolubility is a condition and guarantee of the education of the children, since only a full and enduring union of the powers of both spouses can assure this. Finally, it constitutes a splendid good for society, as the fountain of an honesty of life and integrity of morals.[72]

2. The *bonum sacramenti* designates, in the second place, the fact that Christ, "by raising the marriage of His faithful to the dignity of a true sacrament of the New Law, made it *a sign and source of a peculiar internal grace*."[73] On this subject, the encyclical reaffirms the Magisterium of the recent pontiffs who, basing themselves on the constant Tradition of the Church, had proclaimed the inseparability between the contract and the sacrament. Christ, in fact, constituted *the valid consent itself*

---

[70] Cf. *Casti connubii, Ins.* no. 297 (E.T. no. 35); *Enchiridion Familiae,* 1.730.

[71] Ibid., *Ins.* no. 298 (E.T., no. 36); *Enchiridion Familiae,* 1.730. On the importance of the signification of marriage as a sign of the union between Christ and his Church, on the elaboration of the doctrine of its character as a sacrament, see T. Rincon, *Matrimonio, misterio y signo. Siglos IX–XIII* (Pamplona: Eunsa, 1971).

[72] Cf. Pius XI, *Casti connubii; Ins.* nos. 299–300 (E.T. no. 37); *Enchiridion Familiae,* 1.731–32.

[73] Ibid., *Ins.* no. 301 (E.T., no. 38); *Enchiridion Familiae,* 1.733.

between the faithful into a *sign of grace:* "The sacramental nature is so intimately bound up with Christian wedlock that there can be no true marriage between baptized persons 'without it being by that very fact a sacrament'[74]."[75]

From this it follows that the *ministers* of marriage are *the spouses themselves,* for in the very moment in which "with a sincere mind they give such consent, they open up for themselves a treasure of sacramental grace from which they draw supernatural power for the fulfilling of their rights and duties faithfully, holily, perseveringly even unto death."[76]

We must note the width and depth with which *Casti connubii* deals with *sacramental grace:* above all, it affirms that the sacrament of marriage increases sanctifying grace, adding to it "particular gifts, dispositions, seeds of grace" that perfect the forces (intelligence, will, sentiment) of the spouses in order that they may be assisted "not only in understanding, but in knowing intimately, in adhering to firmly, in willing effectively, and in successfully putting into practice, those things which pertain to the married state, its aims and duties, giving them in fine right to the actual assistance of grace, whensoever they need it for fulfilling the duties of their state".[77] If the married state is permanent, permanent too is the action of grace. "St. Augustine teaches, just as by Baptism and Holy Orders a man is set aside and assisted either for the duties of Christian life or for the priestly office and is never deprived of their sacramental aid, almost in the same way (although not by a sacramental character) the faithful once joined by marriage ties can never be deprived of the help and binding force of the sacrament."[78] This is valid even in cases in which spouses have received the sacrament in a state of sin or commit grave sins after having received it: when through the sacrament of reconciliation they return to the state of friendship with God, they acquire once more the sacramental grace of marriage; at least as a treasure offered to them, it always remains with them. The capacity to give fruit requires, however,

---

[74] The *Codex Iuris Canonici* (1917 ed.) thus taught, can. 1012, par. 1.

[75] Pius XI, *Casti connubii; Ins.* no. 302 (E.T., no. 39); *Enchiridion Familiae,* 1.733–34.

[76] Ibid., *Ins.* no. 303 (E.T., no. 40); *Enchiridion Familiae,* 1.734.

[77] Ibid., *Ins.,* no. 303 (E.T., no. 40); *Enchiridion Familiae,* 1.734.

[78] Ibid., *Ins.* no. 304 (E.T., no. 42); *Enchiridion Familiae,* 1.735. On the progress that this doctrine sets forth see Baldanza, "La grazia sacramentale matrimoniale nell'enciclica *Casti connubii*", pp. 50ff.

the personal cooperation of the spouses:[79] only then will their union be "the living image of that most fruitful union of Christ with the Church", which is the model of conjugal charity.[80]

■ The universality of redemption must not obscure the need of personal cooperation on the part of everyone. Christ restored the original divine plan for all, inasmuch as through his work of redemption he united himself in some way to every man,[81] offering to him his own grace; but not all receive it. The divine salvific initiative passes through our liberty: man can refuse it, abandoning it to submit himself to the disordered inclinations of his fallen nature. If, along with the universal character of redemption, one does not also emphasize the necessity for personal correspondence to grace, one prepares the way for a progressive depreciation of the sacraments and, with the absence of the grace that follows this, the increasing degradation of morals, in a way that ends up in claiming that the sweet yoke of the Lord is insupportable (cf. Mt 11:30).

C. *Errors against Catholic doctrine and vices that spoil marriage*

The encyclical locates the root of contemporary errors about marriage in a false desire of human autonomy. It distinguishes between general errors and errors against each of the three goods of marriage.

Like the last Synod of Bishops on the Family (1980),[82] *Casti connubii* had already revealed, as the root of the contemporary errors about marriage, the forgetting of its true nature: the idea that "marriage is not instituted by the Author of nature nor raised by Christ our Lord to the dignity of a true sacrament, but invented by man",[83] in such a way that "the laws, institutions, and customs by which wedlock is governed, since they take their origin solely from the will of man, are subject entirely to him, hence can and must be founded, changed and

---

[79] Pius XI, *Casti connubii; Ins.* no. 304 (E.T. no. 43); *Enchiridion Familiae,* 1.736.

[80] Ibid., *Ins.* no. 305 (E.T., no. 43); *Enchiridion Familiae,* 1.736.

[81] Cf. Vatican Council II, dogmatic constitution *Lumen gentium,* November 21, 1964, no. 16; *Gaudium et spes,* no. 22.

[82] Cf. Synod of Bishops on the Family (1980), *Lineamenta,* p. 12.

[83] Pius XI, *Casti connubii; Ins.* no. 310 (E.T., no. 50); *Enchiridion Familiae,* 1.739.

abrogated according to human caprice."[84] Marriage would thus be a creation of man, that he can use at his pleasure. The most varied ideas about marriage would become legitimate, as are the various concepts regarding the organization of the state or the city. Thus, it would become necessary "to emancipate it from ancient prejudices", among which is Christian doctrine,[85] whose overcoming qualifies as a conquest of modern culture.[86]

■ The encyclical notes that not all accept such extreme consequences; some think that it would be enough to recognize, without renouncing the general doctrine about marriage, the need to make concessions "as regards certain precepts of the divine and natural law".[87] But this apparent moderation—*Casti connubii* insists—makes these teachings even more dangerous: because, by explicitly repudiating only some specific points, it abandons in reality the founding principle of the divine origin of marriage and of the supreme authority of the Creator. We need to keep in mind that in denouncing the errors of "modern culture", the encyclical—as other documents of that period—was not, obviously, struggling against realizations of humanity or the historical characteristics of that time. Loving the world of every age, the Church nonetheless rejects the spirit of a false autonomy of the creature, a spirit that permeates the thought of the last centuries and prevents men from becoming aware of the central truth of the divine paternity, renouncing in this way the most profound basis of their own dignity: "The supreme reason for the dignity of man consists in his vocation to communion with God."[88] In this way, in the name of a false autonomy and grandeur, men abandon themselves solely to their own powers, with the risk of generating a massive return "in truly cultured nations to the barbarous standards of savage peoples".[89]

Before analyzing the different errors attacking each one of the goods of marriage that flow from this mentality, the encyclical condemns the pretense of legitimating some forms of union between man and woman that, in reality, are the very negation of the whole institution of matrimony: concretely "*temporary* marriage, *experimental* marriage, and a third that they call *companionate,* which offer all the indulgence

---

[84] Ibid., *Ins.* no. 311 (E.T., no. 51); *Enchiridion Familiae,* 1.740.
[85] Ibid., *Ins.* no. 307 (E.T., no. 46); *Enchiridion Familiae,* 1.737.
[86] Cf. ibid., *Ins.* no. 313 (E.T., no. 53); *Enchiridion Familiae,* 1.741.
[87] Ibid., *Ins.,* no. 308 (E.T., no. 48); *Enchiridion Familiae,* 1.738.
[88] Vatican Council II, *Gaudium et spes,* no. 19.
[89] Pius XI, *Casti connubii; Ins.* no. 313 (E.T., no. 53); *Enchiridion Familiae,* 1.741.

of marriage and its rights without, however, the indissoluble bond and without offspring",[90] that is, the two essential goods of every marriage. These are errors that in our own day, unfortunately, are newly proposed.[91]

Errors opposed to the good of children

The encyclical takes this matter up in detail. It begins by noting, with a just intuition, that at root all these errors derive from a *hedonistic mentality that regards children as a burden and not as a good and leads to crimes against the life of the child to be born.* We can summarize its exposition in the following points:

1. *Contraception is an intrinsically immoral act,* which by reason of its object is a *grave sin.*

No reason, however grave, may be put forward by which anything intrinsically against nature may become conformable to nature and morally good. Since, therefore, the conjugal act is destined primarily by nature for the begetting of children, those who in exercising it deliberately render it inapt for this purpose sin against nature and commit a deed which is shameful and intrinsically vicious. Holy Scripture itself bears witness that the Divine Majesty regards with greatest detestation this horrible crime and at times has punished it with death. As St. Augustine notes, "Intercourse even with one's legitimate wife is unlawful and wicked where the conception of the offspring is prevented. Onan, the son of Judah, did this and the Lord killed him for it."[92,93]

■ The intrinsically immoral character of contraception had already been declared by a response of the Holy Office, April 19, 1853 (DS 2795), in which, in response to the question whether, in extreme cases, one could licitly practice onanism, it answered: "Negatively; for it is intrinsically wicked." A response of the Sacred Penitentiary of November 13, 1901, confirmed this, adding that it has the character of a *grave sin* and setting down as obligatory the refusal of absolution to one who would not be disposed to abandon such conduct. Moreover, the *Catechism of the Council of Trent* had already taught this: "It happens

[90] Ibid., *Ins.* no. 312 (E.T., no. 52); *Enchiridion Familiae,* 1.740–41.
[91] Cf. *Lineamenta,* pp. 8ff.; John Paul II, *Familiaris consortio,* nos. 80–82.
[92] St. Augustine, *De coniugiis adulterinis,* 1.2, no. 12.
[93] Pius XII, *Casti connubii; Ins.* no. 315 (E.T., no. 56); *Enchiridion Familiae,* 1.742.

that the crime of those who, joined in marriage, either impede conception by medicines or expel the life conceived, is most grave; for this must be considered the impious conspiracy of murderers."[94]

2. This doctrine, the encyclical insists, pertains to the deposit of revelation and is to be maintained definitively and irreformably:

> Since, therefore, openly departing from the uninterrupted Christian tradition some recently have judged it possible solemnly to declare another doctrine regarding this question, the Catholic Church, to whom God has entrusted the defense of the integrity and purity of morals . . . in order that she may preserve the chastity of the nuptial union from being defiled by this foul stain, raises her voice in token of her divine ambassadorship and through Our mouth proclaims anew: any use whatsoever of marriage exercised in such a way that the act is deliberately deprived of its natural power to generate life is an offense against the law of God and of nature, and those who indulge in such are branded with the guilt of a grave sin.[95]

The terms used leave no doubt: we are dealing here with a definitive teaching of the *ordinary and universal* Magisterium and, therefore, one that is infallible.[96]

> ■ In one of the most authoritative commentaries that appeared shortly after the publication of the encyclical, we read, in fact: "In the presence of this language of the supreme Pastor, we cannot doubt that we find ourselves in one of those cases, not very rare, in which *the Pope teaches*

---

[94] *Catechism of the Council of Trent,* part II, c. 7, no. 13: "Fit ut illorum sit scelus gravissimum qui, Matrimonio iuncti, medicamentis vel conceptum impediunt, vel partum abigunt; haec enim homicidarum impia conspiratio existimanda est."

[95] Pius XI, *Casti connubii; Ins.* no. 316 (E.T., no. 57); *Enchiridion Familiae,* 1.743.

[96] Here there is need to point out a detail that, as we will see in our analysis of *Humanae vitae,* is found at the origin of not a few confusions. The doubts raised during the Council regarding the regulation of births turned on the contraceptive or noncontraceptive character of biochemical means—the "pill"—but they did not tolerate the putting into question of the intrinsic immorality of contraception. Therefore, *Gaudium et spes,* in repudiating the "illicit means" of regulating births—no. 51 and n. 14—made reference to all the preceding condemnations of contraception, except the document of Pius XII of September 12, 1958, in which he considered contraceptive the use of progestin substances; a document that, in turn, was explicitly called to mind by *Humanae vitae,* in no. 14, n. 16. The general controversy over the wickedness of contraception emerged in later theological circles, as the fruit of their fallacious claims, born of their desire to justify biochemical contraceptives. Previously, no Catholic author had doubted the intrinsic malice of onanism and of other physical means of contraception. In fact, it belonged to the constant teaching of the Church, to her ordinary and universal Magisterium, as the encyclical *Casti connubii* insists.

infallibly a truth already defined and believed by the Church. This is so because the Supreme Pontiff can present himself as the infallible interpreter of the primitive Church."[97]

As a matter of fact, one of the arguments often advanced today in favor of the irreformable character of this truth in the teaching of *Humanae vitae* is that this character had already been emphasized in *Casti connubii* and that both documents bear witness to a constant Tradition, as Pius XI explicitly claimed in his encyclical.[98]

3. The Church knows that at times there are *grave reasons* — danger to the life of the mother, harsh conditions of poverty, etc. — *that lead the spouses to think that it would not be prudent to have more children.* A situation of this kind must be considered as a burden, for which there exists no other way than "a noble continence, practiced when both spouses consent to it".[99] A little later on, the encyclical makes it clear that there is nothing to oppose the proper use of marriage by couples "although on account of natural reasons either of time or of certain defects, new life cannot be brought forth".[100] The Church takes into account the exigent character of this doctrine, but she knows that the sufferings that result from the commitment to fulfill the divine will, even if painful, do not destroy conjugal love, but on the contrary purify it and render it more noble and strong. God is always our Father, and he never abandons those who seek to do his will:

> There is no possible circumstance in which husband and wife cannot, strengthened by the grace of God, fulfill faithfully their duties and preserve in wedlock their chastity unspotted. This truth of Christian Faith is expressed by the teaching of the Council of Trent. "Let no one

[97] A. Vermeersch, *Catechismo del matrimonio cristiano secondo l'Enciclica "Casti connubii"* (Turin-Rome: Marietti, 1931), 57; cf. also J. Ryan, "The Moral Teaching of the Encyclical *Casti connubii*", *The Ecclesiastical Review* (1931): 265ff. Although their argument may not be precise, these authors clearly saw that they were faced with a definitive teaching of the ordinary and universal Magisterium, a form of teaching that the Church has always believed is a way of exercising the infallibility proper to it; thus *Lumen gentium*, no. 25, recognized this — and made it more precise — not as its own invention but, precisely, as a testimony verified and confirmed by the fact that certitude of this kind has always existed.

[98] Cf. J. Bökmann, *Nicht Unfehlbar? Zum misslungenen Angriff auf die untruegliche Wahrheit und dem verbindlichen Anspruch von Humanae vitae* (Abensberg, 1981), pp. 23ff., 26ff., etc.; cf. also J. C. Ford and G. Grisez, "Contraception and the Infallibility of the Ordinary Magisterium", *Theological Studies* 39 (1978): 258–312; E. Lio, "Contracepción conyugal e irreformabilidad de la moral", in *Cuestiones fundamentales sobre matrimonio y familia*, pp. 601ff., in particular, 607–8.

[99] Pius XI, *Casti connubii; Ins.* no. 314 (E.T., no. 54); *Enchiridion Familiae*, 1.741–42.

[100] Ibid., *Ins.* no. 319 (E.T., no. 60); *Enchiridion Familiae*, 1.745.

be so rash as to assert that which the Fathers of the Council have placed under anathema, namely, that there are precepts of God impossible for the just to observe. God does not ask the impossible, but by His commands instructs you to do what you are able, to pray for what you are not able that He may help you."[101,102]

■ *Casti connubii*, therefore, is concerned with situations in which there exists an objective difficulty in desiring more children; it insists that in each case *contraception* is intrinsically immoral and can not be allowed for any reason; one can only have recourse to a noble continence. It explicitly does not take any position on the use of periodic continence, recently discovered and not yet subjected to a sufficient moral reflection. That is why it speaks only of continence (according to the teaching of the apostle in 1 Cor 7:15), adding separately that there is nothing opposed to the use of marriage when—for natural causes—conception is not possible. Thus, without closing the argument, it avoids precipitously making a pronouncement on a question so delicate.

In addition, the encyclical is not unaware that "not rarely one of the spouses" can find himself or herself forced to tolerate an improper use of marriage "when for grave reasons he or she permits the perversion of the right order but to this he or she does not consent." But one must always remember that, according to the law of charity, one cannot neglect "to seek to dissuade and to deter the other spouse from sin".[103]

4. It is necessary *to adopt all the means for forming the consciences of the faithful adequately in this matter,* with confessors and pastors being obliged to remove them from error: "We admonish, therefore, priests who hear confessions and others who have the care of souls . . . not to allow the faithful entrusted to them to err regarding this most grave law of God." And, Pope Pius continues, with a severe and solemn formula,

If any confessor or pastor of souls, which God may forbid, lead the faithful entrusted to him into these errors or should at least confirm them by approval or by guilty silence, let him be mindful of the fact that he must render a strict account to God, the Supreme Judge, for the betrayal of his sacred trust, and let him take to himself the words of

[101] Council of Trent, session VI, c. 11.
[102] Pius XI, *Casti connubii; Ins.* no. 320 (E.T., no. 62); *Enchiridion Familiae,* 1.746.
[103] Ibid., *Ins.* no. 319 (E.T., no. 60); *Enchiridion Familiae,* 1.744–45.

Christ: "They are blind and leaders of the blind; and if the blind lead the blind, both fall into the pit" (Mt 15:14).[104]

■ The encyclical responds in this way, in a public manner, to an argument that had twice faced the Sacred Penitentiary. In a response of December 14, 1776, during the pontificate of Benedict XIV, on the occasion of a question of a pastor in Angers, it declared that, because of the gravity of onanism, it is not licit to leave the penitent in error—even if the error is not culpable—and it is much less licit to lead the penitent into this error; moreover, if this error is suspected there is need to make a prudent interrogation of the penitent. A second response of March 10, 1886, under Leo XIII, specified this issue even more clearly: always, when there exists a "founded suspicion", the confessor must carry out a "prudent and discreet interrogation", and he cannot absolve the penitent unless there is a clear proposal of amendment.[105]

These teachings are inspired by an attitude of concern: children are a gift of God and a precious good for the family; they strengthen the love and unity between the spouses and are for them a source of indissoluble joy and at the same time a marvelous way for them to make a generous gift of themselves. When children are refused because of egoism, the family destroys itself; we ought not forget that the divine laws regarding marriage are a protection and guide for attaining the goods God wills for the spouses. Under Pius XI, the Church began a long and difficult battle, still under way, to unmask the contraceptive mentality contrary to life, inspired by a materialistic hedonism, that dominates in so many circles; faced with this mentality, *Familiaris consortio* has proclaimed anew: "The teaching of the Church is ever old and ever new: the Church stands on the side of life."[106]

5. Finally, the encyclical *once again condemns abortion*, not only when this is done because of the arbitrary will of the father or mother, but when it is done *for any reason, and in particular because of any "medical, social or eugenic indications"*.[107] The encyclical laments the fact that "there are not lacking those who ask that the public authorities provide aid for these death-dealing operations", and it

[104] Ibid., *Ins.* no. 317 (E.T., no. 58); *Enchiridion Familiae,* 1.743–44.
[105] DS 3185–87.
[106] John Paul II, *Familiaris consortio,* nos. 6, 14, 28, 30, and 50.
[107] Pius XI, *Casti connubii; Ins.* no. 322 (E.T., no. 63); *Enchiridion Familiae,* 1.746–47.

reaffirms that "no cause can ever render excusable the direct killing of the innocent."[108]

■ Finally, the Magisterium confronts the false argument—that many today repeat—of considering the fetus as an unjust aggressor: "Who would call an innocent child an unjust aggressor?"[109] It adopts the expression "direct killing" to exclude those cases in which the death of the child is an unintended consequence, even if foreseen, of a therapy necessary to save the mother, according to the rule of the indirectly voluntary. However, on this matter, the encyclical exhorts doctors to find ways "to guard and preserve the lives of both mother and child".[110]

With reference to the then nascent science of "eugenics", while encouraging progress, the encyclical stresses that it can never furnish a reason for killing the fetus or for preventing human persons from entering marriage, even if at times one can counsel individuals not to contract it: to will otherwise would be to forget that "men are begotten not for the earth and for time, but for Heaven and eternity."[111]

Errors against the good of conjugal fidelity

The encyclical points out as the first error, among those widely diffused at that time, the *banalization of adultery*. On this view, the attitude that confines sexual expression "within the narrow limits of monogamous marriage" must be repudiated as too rigid, and according to it a "greater freedom of feeling and action in such external relations should be allowed to a man and wife". Such a pretentious view is directly opposed to the teachings of Christ: "Whoever looks at a woman to lust after her has already committed adultery with her in his heart" (Mt 5:28); and, in addition, it directly damages the personal dignity of the spouses.[112]

---

[108] Ibid., *Ins.* no. 324 (E.T., no. 64); *Enchiridion Familiae,* 1.747.

[109] Ibid., *Ins.* no. 324 (E.T., no. 64); *Enchiridion Familiae,* 1.748.

[110] Ibid., *Ins.* no. 324 (E.T., no. 64); *Enchiridion Familiae,* 1.748. The encyclical alludes, with reference to this, to a country where a number of abortions is scandalous (cf. *Ins.* no. 322; E.T., no. 63). As Vermeersch observes (*Catechismo del matrimonio,* p. 79), this is a reference to Russia, where the number of abortions at that time was around 30,000 annually. This is a matter for reflection, for today this number is greatly surpassed in so-called Christian countries. Concerning the risks of not properly understanding the principle of double effect in this matter, cf. Ramón García de Haro, "Nota critica a F. Boeckle, *I concetti fondamentali della morale*", *Anthropos: Rivista di studi sulla persona e sulla famiglia* (1985): 105ff.

[111] Pius XI, *Casti connubii; Ins.* nos. 326–31 (E.T., nos. 68–70); *Enchiridion Familiae,* 1.750–51.

[112] Cf. ibid., *Ins.* no. 334 (E.T., nos. 73–74); *Enchiridion Familiae,* 1.752–53.

Another error, spread by some feminist currents of thought, insists on *taking the wife away from her place in the domestic hearth,* by means of a false aggrandizement of her dignity that, in reality, deprives her of the "values inherent in her noble office as a wife and mother".[113] The Church has always defended—and no serious history can deny it—the equality in personal dignity between man and woman; but precisely because of this, she at the same time guards the characteristic properties of femininity, willed by the divine wisdom—much higher than that of mankind—that confer on women the capacity of making their own contribution, diverse from that made by men, with a specific role within the family, and a guarantee of their own perfection and of the good progress of society. No doubt, different times and cultures allow for diversifications and modifications in the exercise of this mission, but they cannot misconceive the essential lines of woman's role without damaging women themselves and, with them, the life of the family and the social order.[114]

Finally, the Holy Father deplores the progressive diffusion of a *base notion of conjugal love,* one which reduces it to passion: some want to substitute for a sincere and solid love—which is the foundation of an intimate and strong conjugal happiness—a fragile compatibility of temperaments and a kind of a sympathetic justice, which on ceasing would lead to the dissolution of the marital bond. But this is to build marriage upon the sand, while our Lord directed that it be built on rock (cf. Mt 7:27). True conjugal love sustains itself and bases itself on a "deliberate and constant union of spirit", irrevocable and deriving from marital consent.[115]

Errors against the good of the sacrament

The encyclical mentions two of these: the first error consists in *attacks against the indissolubility and the sacred character* of marriage, while the second is *the increasing facility of divorce.*

Some would have marriage to be a *profane reality,* ruled by power and civil laws and not subject to any religious power of the Church. In the case of Christians, the sacrament is an extrinsic addition, fully distinct from and separate from the civil contract; it is a religious rite

[113] Cf. ibid., *Ins.* nos. 335–36 (E.T., nos. 74–75); *Enchiridion Familiae,* 1.754–55.
[114] Cf. ibid., *Ins.* nos. 337–38 (E.T., nos. 76–77); *Enchiridion Familiae,* 1.755–56.
[115] Ibid., *Ins.* no. 339 (E.T., no. 79); *Enchiridion Familiae,* 1.756–57.

adventitiously added to marriage.[116] Faced with these repeated assertions, *Casti connubii* reminds us that *every marriage is a sacred reality, not subject to manipulation by the arbitrary judgment of men:*

> Even by the light of reason alone and particularly if the ancient records of history are investigated, if the unwavering popular conscience is interrogated and the manners and institutions of all races examined, it is sufficiently obvious that there is a certain sacredness and religious character attaching even to the purely natural union of man and woman, "not something added by chance but innate, not imposed by men but involved in the nature of things", since it has "God for its author and has been even from the beginning a foreshadowing of the Incarnation of the Word of God."[117]

Its end, the transmission of life, corroborates this,[118] for this makes spouses become cooperators with God in the unrepeatable creation of an immortal soul. This religious character of marriage, already proper within the order of creation, receives an even stronger emphasis among Christians by reason of the sacrament, which is always an action of Christ himself.[119]

> ■ The Pope refers to the religious character of marriage in order to explain Church discipline with respect to *mixed marriages.* Therefore, although this discipline can vary with times and circumstances—and in fact it has been changed more than one time—it always has to do with respect for the requirements of what is due to God: that is, by avoiding the dangers for the faith of the Catholic spouse and guaranteeing that of future children.[120]

The second error attacking the good of the sacrament is the *increasing facility for divorce;* and, in particular, the zeal of neopaganism for introducing divorce laws even into Christian countries.[121] The arguments are more or less the same, refuted many times by the Magisterium: the good of the innocent spouse; to help the children escape suffering by witnessing the discord among their parents; society would profit by the dissolution of marriages incapable of producing their fruits, etc.

---

[116] Ibid., *Ins.* nos. 340–41 (E.T., no. 80); *Enchiridion Familiae,* 1.757–58.

[117] Ibid., *Ins.* no. 342 (E.T., no. 83); *Enchiridion Familiae,* 1.758–59; internal citation from Leo XIII, encyclical *Arcanum divinae sapientiae,* February 10, 1880, *Ins.* nos. 143ff.

[118] Pius XI, *Casti connubii; Ins.* no. 343 (E.T., no. 83); *Enchiridion Familiae,* 1.759.

[119] Cf. ibid., *Ins.* no. 344 (E.T., no. 84); *Enchiridion Familiae,* 1.759–60.

[120] Cf. ibid., *Ins.* no. 345 (E.T., no. 85); *Enchiridion Familiae,* 1.760.

[121] Cf. ibid., *Ins.* no. 345 (E.T., no. 88); *Enchiridion Familiae,* 1.762.

Faced with the repetition of these arguments, the Holy Father first of all recalls the teaching of Scripture, constantly confirmed by the Church that did not "err nor does err when it taught and teaches" the absolute indissolubility of marriage.[122]

Then, having recourse to reason and experience, he compares the advantages of fidelity with the pretended goods of divorce:

It is hardly necessary to point out what an amount of good is involved in the absolute indissolubility of wedlock and what a train of evils follows upon divorce. Whenever the marriage bond remains intact, then we find marriages contracted with a sense of safety and security, while, when separations are considered and the dangers of divorce are present, the marriage contract itself becomes insecure, or at least gives ground for anxiety and surprises. On the one hand we see a wonderful strengthening of good will and co-operation in the daily life of husband and wife, while, on the other hand, both of these are miserably weakened by the presence of a facility for divorce. Here we have at a very opportune moment a source of help by which both parties are enabled to preserve their purity and loyalty; there we find harmful inducements to unfaithfulness. On this side we find the birth of children and their education and upbringing effectively promoted, many avenues of discord closed amongst families and relations, and the beginnings of rivalry and jealousy easily suppressed; on that, very great obstacles to the birth and rearing of children and their education, and many occasions of quarrels, and seeds of jealousy sown everywhere. Finally, but especially, the dignity and position of women in civil and domestic society is reinstated by the former; while by the latter it is shamefully lowered and in danger of being abandoned.[123]

The matter is very grave, he concludes, and notes that—as facts have confirmed—once the plague of divorce has become rooted it becomes much more difficult to recover the moral strength of society.[124]

D. *The remedies: the return to the divine plan for marriage*

If the evil that afflicts the family proceeds from having abandoned God's plan—in the deceitful illusion of constructing another one—the

---

[122] Ibid., *Ins.* nos. 351–53 (E.T., nos. 90–92); *Enchiridion Familiae*, 1.763–65.
[123] Ibid., *Ins.* no. 356 (E.T., no. 96); *Enchiridion Familiae*, 1.767–68.
[124] Cf. ibid., *Ins.* nos. 357–58 (E.T., nos. 97–98); *Enchiridion Familiae*, 1.768.

remedy will be in returning to God's plan. For reaching this end, the encyclical insists on the following matters.

1. First of all, *recourse to prayer and to the sacraments,* for without them the spouses will lack the power to live out the requirements of Christian marriage. Spouses have the need of grace that heals the weakness inflicted on them by original sin and their own sins and that gives to them the capacity of acting in a supernatural way. It is necessary that "the spouses be imbued with a profound piety toward God, one that will inform their whole life, and fill their minds and wills",[125] through which they must be encouraged at every opportunity "to exercise their religion so that they should give themselves to God, continually ask for His divine assistance, frequent the sacraments, and always nourish and preserve a loyal and thoroughly sincere filial devotion to God".[126] Certainly, in order to facilitate the accomplishment of their duties, they must also have recourse to all the human means possible, including those drawn from the positive sciences, but these would serve for little without the help of divine grace.[127]

> ■ In this way, *"family life itself,* in all its varying circumstances, is seen as a call from God and lived as a filial response to His call. Joys and sorrows, hopes and disappointments, births and birthday celebrations, wedding anniversaries of the parents, departures, separations and homecomings, important and far-reaching decisions, the death of those who are dear, etc.—all of these mark God's loving intervention in the family's history. They should be seen as suitable moments for thanksgiving, for petition, for trusting abandonment of the family into the hands of their common Father in heaven."[128] Not only the sacrament of marriage, but the frequent reception of the Eucharist and of penance are indispensable for the spouses to live in a way conformable to that holiness to which they have been called.[129]

2. At the same time, it is necessary that there be *docility to the Magisterium.* The difficulties that beset the mind of the faithful in a secularized world make the external guidance of the Magisterium

[125] Ibid., *Ins.* no. 364 (E.T., no. 104); *Enchiridion Familiae,* 1.772–73.

[126] Ibid., *Ins.* no. 365 (E.T., no. 105); *Enchiridion Familiae,* 1.773.

[127] Cf. ibid., *Ins.* no. 366 (E.T., no. 106); *Enchiridion Familiae,* 1.773–74.

[128] John Paul II, *Familiaris consortio,* no. 59.

[129] Cf. ibid., nos. 56–62.

particularly urgent. "It is necessary that a filial and humble obedience toward the Church should be combined with devotedness to God and the desire of submitting to Him. For Christ Himself made the Church the teacher of truth in those things also which concern the right regulation of moral conduct."[130]

■ The encyclical notes that this obedience is due not only to solemn definitions but also to all the documents in which the Magisterium teaches a moral doctrine or refutes a contrary opinion.[131] In particular, he calls attention to the dangers of a "false autonomy of reason",[132] and of the intention—which will develop, on a vast scale, the "theology of dissent"—of judging the Magisterium as if it were no more than a human authority, at least in its noninfallible declarations; as if its power did not proceed from a divine investiture, with the special assistance of the Holy Spirit. One cannot reasonably think that the Church, instituted and destined by the Lord to teach all the peoples, is not "conversant with present affairs and circumstances", or conclude that Catholics "must obey only in those matters which she has decreed by solemn definition, as though her other decisions might be presumed to be false or putting forward insufficient motive for truth and honesty."[133]

3. On the other hand, the *personal cooperation of spouses with grace* is absolutely required. Already within the order of nature, the existing energies in creation are developed with the concurrence of human action. "So also men must diligently and unceasingly use the powers given them by the grace which is laid up in the soul by this sacrament [of marriage]."[134] Therefore the spouses, once aware of the goods that God has conceded to marriage and of the generosity of his divine plan, must become impregnated "with a firm will of observing the holy divine laws" by which they are protected.[135]

4. Finally, it is necessary to have an *adequate preparation, proximate and remote, to receive the sacrament.* When there is an education to generosity and to purity, it will become easy to satisfy the requirements proper to the truly Christian marital communion. Moreover, it

---

[130] Pius XI, *Casti connubii; Ins.* nos. 367–68 (E.T., nos. 108–9); *Enchiridion Familiae,* 1.775–76.
[131] Cf. ibid., *Ins.* no. 369 (E.T., no. 109); *Enchiridion Familiae,* 1.776.
[132] Ibid., *Ins.* no. 370 (E.T., no. 109); *Enchiridion Familiae,* 1.776.
[133] Ibid., *Ins.* no. 371 (E.T., no. 109); *Enchiridion Familiae,* 1.776.
[134] Ibid., *Ins.* no. 379 (E.T., no. 116); *Enchiridion Familiae,* 1.780.
[135] Ibid., *Ins.* no. 377 (E.T., no. 115); *Enchiridion Familiae,* 1.779.

is necessary to encourage future spouses to make a prudent choice, taking into account not only human reasons but above all their own spiritual good and that of the children, seeking divine help, that is, letting themselves be guided by "a true and noble love and by a sincere affection for the future partner; and let them strive in their married life for those ends for which the State was constituted by God", never forgetting to ask their parents for opportune advice.[136]

The duties of pastors and civil authorities

Pastors are obliged to offer to spouses the fitting doctrinal formation, moral and ascetic, so necessary for the well-being of marriage, concretely: on the very great importance of the goods that God has confided to them; on the fatherly guidance contained in the divine precepts that liberate them from the dangers of egoism and help them to establish and develop a family full of a human and Christian sense, where happiness is never wanting, not even in the midst of sorrow; finally, to help them to put their trust in the power of grace, that renders them capable of overcoming all possible difficulties. In a word, to make sure that no one lacks the conviction of the paternal wisdom and goodness of God in the institution of marriage and in its elevation to a sacrament.[137]

On the other hand, it is necessary to insist on the obligation of every man, and especially of those constituted in authority, to secure respect for the moral order and to secure the promotion of the material goods necessary for the proper development of the family. It is a field in which human laws can do much.[138] There is hope here for noble cooperation between Church and state.[139]

3. The Enduring Significance of the Principal Teachings of *Casti Connubii*

Up to now we have see how much there is to convince us of this significance, which at bottom is nothing other than a consequence of

[136] Ibid., *Ins.* nos. 381–85 (E.T., nos. 117–19); *Enchiridion Familiae,* 1.781–83.
[137] Cf. ibid., *Ins.* nos. 372–74 (E.T., nos. 121–22); *Enchiridion Familiae,* 1.784–85.
[138] Cf. ibid., *Ins.* nos. 390–93 (E.T., nos. 123–24); *Enchiridion Familiae,* 1.786.
[139] Cf. ibid., *Ins.* no. 394 (E.T., no. 127); *Enchiridion Familiae,* 1.788–89.

the perennial validity of Catholic doctrine along with the continuance of the roots of the crisis with which *Casti connubii* was confronted. We will emphasize in particular three points:

1. The central idea of *Casti connubii,* as of *Familiaris consortio* later on, is that of recalling the attention of men to the *perfection of the divine plan for marriage and family.* Christianity has always been a religion founded on the positive, on the attractiveness of the good, of affirmations, not negations. The Church knows the weakness of fallen man, but she also knows his greatness and his noble aspirations: her mission is to propose to all the faithful, and in particular to all married couples, the whole plan of God for their marriage, in order that they may become enthusiastic over the grandeur of this plan and that there might arise in their hearts the sincere desire to make it fruitful, with a spirit of sacrifice, under the impulse of divine grace.

▎ *Familiaris consortio* expresses this with these words: "Illuminated by the faith that gives her an understanding of all the truth concerning the great value of marriage and the family and the deepest meaning, the Church once again feels the pressing need to proclaim the Gospel, that is the 'good news', to all those who are called to marriage and are preparing for it, to all married couples and parents in the world."[140] Faith permits spouses "to discover and admire with joyful gratitude the dignity to which God has deigned to raise marriage and the family, making them a sign and meeting place of the loving covenant between God and man, between Jesus Christ and his bride, the Church."[141] In sum, it is necessary to remind spouses, so that they never lose hope, that "the family possesses and continues still to release formidable energies capable of taking man out of his anonymity, keeping him conscious of his personal dignity, enriching him with deep humanity and actively placing him, in his uniqueness and unrepeatability, within the fabric of society."[142]

2. It is also worthwhile to recall the conception of *conjugal love as an essential good of marriage, its vital principle.* With this, the encyclical prepares for the teaching of Vatican Council II and of *Familiaris consortio* and attaches itself to an ancient tradition on the complementarity

[140] John Paul II, *Familiaris consortio,* no. 3.
[141] Ibid., no. 51.
[142] Ibid., no. 43.

of love and procreation, as form and end, respectively, of the conjugal community. That is a decisive truth for confronting with correctness the problems posed within conjugal morality in the contemporary period. Conjugal love must inform all the duties of the spouses, being as it were the soul of their familial community. Without love, *Familiaris consortio* will say, the family cannot grow and live as a community of persons;[143] a love, precisely because of this, that is at the service of the life that is the end of that community.[144]

3. Finally, the trust that the Church nourishes regarding the *feasibility of the Christian restoration of marriage,* if one has recourse to the means willed by God. This is a truth that today—as then—has great importance. Perhaps one of the most dangerous temptations—in periods of generalized crisis—is in fact the tendency to imagine that the Christian ideal, while remaining sublime and worthy of admiration, remains unattainable for ordinary mortals. The announcing of the Christian doctrine on marriage, as that of the beatitudes in the Sermon on the Mount, would be an unattainable ideal, really a sublime madness. We cannot exhaust this argument; we only desire to emphasize two points: first of all, that one can and must often do much more in order to resolve the human aspects of the problem. Second, that in every case it is necessary to insist—as does the Church—that Christian morality, and even more so natural morality in its fullness, can not be lived only with human means. Its attractiveness and its actuality are fully verified only with the help of grace: "My yoke is sweet and my burden light", says our Lord (Mt 11:31); *"all things are possible to the one who believes"* (Mk 9:22). For the man who has confidence only in himself, Christianity asks too much; but the madness consists in forgetting that the Church asks this of him relying on the infinite power of grace.

> ■ This will also be a central teaching of *Familiaris consortio*. This document, while proclaiming the necessity of *a return to the beginning,* to the divine idea of marriage, does not cease repeating that this will be possible only by means of faith and the grace of Christ. "Willed by God in the very act of creation,[145] marriage and the family are interiorly ordered to fulfillment in Christ[146] and have need of his graces in

---

[143] Cf. ibid., no. 18.
[144] Ibid., nos. 28ff. On the meaning in which love is the form of marriage, see pp. 144–19 ff.
[145] Cf. Gen 1:2.
[146] Cf. Eph 5.

order to be healed from the wounds of sin[147] and restored to their 'beginning',[148] that is, to full understanding and the full realization of God's plan."[149] From this follows the insistence of the exhortation on the need to have recourse to the means of the supernatural order: prayer and the sacraments;[150] and the need for the courage that, without becoming frightened when faced with the difficulties of this historical moment, stimulates the family, relying on its own proper riches of nature and grace, to fulfill "its mission of proclaiming to all the plan of God for marriage".[151]

[147] Cf. Vatican Council II, *Gaudium et spes,* no. 47; John Paul II, letter *Appropinquat iam Synodus,* 1 (August 15, 1980); AAS 72 (1980): 791.

[148] Cf. Mt 19:4.

[149] John Paul II, *Familiaris consortio,* no. 3.

[150] Cf. ibid., nos. 56–62.

[151] Ibid., no. 3.

Chapter Four

THE MAGISTERIUM OF PIUS XII

Since *Casti connubii* had already set forth a very complete picture of Catholic doctrine on marriage, the new Pope will not devote any new encyclical to it. Instead, he will be repeatedly concerned with concrete problems, especially regarding conjugal morality and the protection of the family. Therefore, the proper way to present his teaching will be to group together the contents of different documents on these matters.

1. A Summing up of His Pontificate and the Principal Arguments of His Magisterium Relating to the Family

The pontificate of Pius XII began under a twofold sign: the grave moral crisis of the human race, whose profound tensions exploded in the Second World War, and the great doctrinal prestige of the papacy, the fruit of the substantive magisterial work of the last several pontiffs. The name he selected showed that the new Pope desired to continue the work of his predecessors, St. Pius X and Pius XI: to proclaim unceasingly—in face of the different mirages that deceived mankind—that only Christ has the true and full answer to human questions.

One could thus write, analyzing this pontificate full of activity in favor of peace, marked by numerous canonizations, etc., that,

> above all its other merits, it excelled in the history of the Church by reason of its doctrinal Magisterium.... One could say, and this is no exaggeration, that no question of genuine interest for mankind, large or small, escaped his study and teaching. His Allocutions fill many volumes.

... Similarly, his Messages, among which are included his Christmas Messages. But above all his numerous Encyclicals, which contain the thought of the Church on fundamental themes of religion and human life. . . . Vatican Council II made continuous reference to these, finding in them a fountain of first rank for setting forth the teaching of the Magisterium; his influence on contemporary Catholic thought and life was, therefore, decisive.[1]

■ Without pretending to be exhaustive, we can provide the outlines of a synthesis of his principal encyclicals. The encyclical *Summi pontificatus* (October 20, 1939) was the first of his teachings. This encyclical, after having set forth a panoramic view of the situation of the world, exhorts men to return to the order of the divine precepts. But this return is not possible without Christ and, therefore, not without the Church that he founded and through means of which he continues to be present among men; in order the better to help men know her — and to combat the errors of those who wanted an invisible Church without laws — he published *Mystici corporis* on June 29, 1943. Two other encyclicals were concerned with theological studies in relationship to the progress made in the sciences and in contemporary thought: *Divino afflante Spiritu* (September 30, 1943) and *Humani generis* (August 12, 1950). Like Pius XI, his predecessor, the new Pope repeated the constant recommendations of the previous Magisterium to base oneself, in one's theological work, on the rich Christian experience of the previous ages, masterfully gathered together in the work of St. Thomas; at the same time he urged theologians to remain firm in the conviction that there can be no contradiction between faith and any true progress of science, inasmuch as God is the author of the order of creation and its laws no less than of that of grace and revelation. Also worthy of note are the encyclicals *Mediator Dei* (November 20, 1947), on the liturgical renewal, and *Sacramentum ordinis* (November 30, 1947). In addition, we note encyclicals devoted to promoting devotion to the Madonna — *Ad Coeli Reginam* (October 11, 1954), in some ways preceded by *Munificentissimus Deus* (September 1, 1950), which proclaimed the dogma of the Assumption of Mary, and devotion to the Sacred Heart, *Haurietis aquas* (May 15, 1956). Finally, more closely related to the family and marriage, is *Sacra virginitas* (March 25, 1954), which

---

[1] A. de la Hera, "Pío XII", in *Gran Enciclopedia Rialp* (Madrid, 1975), vol. 28, p. 538. See also A. Alcala, *Medicina y moral en los discursos de Pío XII* (Madrid, 1959); C. Mueller, *L'Encyclique "Humani generis" et les problèmes scientifiques* (Louvain, 1951).

exalts the value of chastity—also matrimonial chastity—in face of the sensualism so dominant in the world.

From the very first of his encyclicals, *Summi pontificatus,* Pius XII stresses—as did his predecessors—the decisive role of the family for the well-being and progress of society. He does not hesitate to affirm that one of the most serious dangers for the new generations derives "from the misconception and progressive abolition of the rights proper to the family",[2] since this "essentially influences the spirit of young people".[3] The protection of the family and conjugal morality will be precisely the focal points of the doctrinal work of this Pope, in his constant catechesis on the family. In fact, the then Monsignor Montini, in a letter to the 27th Social Week of Pisa (September 19, 1954), could affirm that Pius XII "has made family questions the preferred theme of his apostolate".[4]

We have divided the abundant material of his Magisterium on marriage and the family into the following sections: (1) addresses to new spouses, in practice a gloss on the previous Magisterium; (2) documents relating to *conjugal morality,* without doubt the most important of his Magisterium; (3) teachings with reference to *the rights of the family;* (4) teachings, finally, on *virginity and conjugal chastity* and instructions regarding *matrimonial procedures,* whether civil or ecclesiastical.

2. Addresses to New Spouses

For many years, from the very beginning of his pontificate, the Holy Father had the habit of presenting a full catechesis on marriage in the audiences given to new spouses. In their entirety, the addresses given at these audiences repropose, as it were, the entire doctrine of the Church on this subject. Particularly extensive are those of March 5 and 19,

[2] Pius XII, encyclical *Summi pontificatus,* October 20, 1939, no. 50; *Insegnamenti pontifici,* vol. 1 of *Il matrimonio* (Rome: Ed. Paoline, 1957), (*Ins.*) no. 419; *Enchiridion Familiae: Textos del Magisterio Pontificio y Conciliar Sobre el Matrimonio y la Familia (Siglos I a XX),* ed. A. Sarmiento and J. Escrivá-Ivars, vol. 2 (Madrid: Ediciones Rialp, 1992), pp. 847–48. This will also be a fundamental point made in *Familiaris consortio,* in particular with its recommendation that there be a "charter of the rights of the family" (no. 46).

[3] Pius XII, *Summi pontificatus,* no. 52; *Ins.* no. 421; *Enchiridion Familiae,* 2.849.

[4] Letter of Monsignor Montini to His Eminence Cardinal Siri on the occasion of the 27th Social Week of Pisa, September 19, 1954, *Ins.* no. 715.

1941,[5] and of April 22 and 29, 1942.[6] Let us review some of the aspects emphasized by the Pope, paying heed to the new conditions providing their context:

1. Spouses ought to be secure in the *power of grace, which allows them to attain even to heroism.* The Church does not hide the difficulties of the ideal Christian, who walks in the way of the Cross; on the contrary, she teaches that this is inaccessible to purely human powers. But it would be a very grave error to judge it impossible:

> You have heard it said that Christian marriage imposes on the spouses excessive burdens, impossible to fulfill. Impossible, yes, for only human powers; but for this the sacrament has placed and keeps in you, with the state of grace, divine powers. Nothing that God prescribes is beyond these supernatural powers, present and operating in you. "In him who is the source of my strength I have strength for everything" (Phil 4:13), exclaimed the Apostle to the Gentiles. "Not I, but the grace of God that is with me" (1 Cor 15:10).[7]

> ■ He will return to this line of thought on many occasions during his pontificate. Christians must be convinced that the *sacraments are the power of the Church:* "The true secret of the moral power of the Church is found in the sources of the grace that she dispenses, above all in the principal source of grace, namely, the sacraments."[8] Even if doctrine is most important and the revealed word has in itself the divine power to move men, the sacraments are absolutely indispensable, because "Christ acts in the souls of men through the infusion of grace, even more so than through His teachings, His exhortations, His promises;

[5] Pius XII, Address to New Spouses, March 5, 1941; *Ins.* nos. 445–53; *Enchiridion Familiae,* 2.964–71; Address to New Spouses, March 19, 1941; *Ins.* nos. 454–61; *Enchiridion Familiae,* 2.972–78.

[6] Pius XII, Address to New Spouses, April 22, 1942; *Ins.* nos. 480–88; *Enchiridion Familiae,* 2.1111–20; Address to New Spouses, April 29, 1942; *Ins.* nos. 489–99; *Enchiridion Familiae,* 2.1120–27.

[7] Pius XII, Address to New Spouses, January 17, 1940; *Ins.* no. 429; *Enchiridion Familiae,* 2.877. See also Address to New Spouses, July 12, 1939; *Ins.* no. 417; *Enchiridion Familiae,* 2.838–40; Address to New Spouses, March 5, 1941; *Ins.* no. 466; *Enchiridion Familiae,* 2.964–71; and Address to New Spouses, August 20, 1941; *Ins.* no. 466; *Enchiridion Familiae,* 2.996–1002.

[8] Pius XII, Radio message to the Faithful of Haiti, December 8, 1949; *Ins.* no. 564; *Enchiridion Familiae,* 1400–1401.

above all, He is, by virtue of the Eucharist, the fountain of life and of holiness."[9]

2. One must always keep present in one's mind *the sublimity of the work of parents in transmitting life, both natural and supernatural.* This is a constant doctrine of the Church, but it was set forth with particular emphasis in an Address of March 5, 1941.[10] God awaits the "yes" of the spouses in order to exercise his omnipotence and create an immortal soul:

God alone can create souls; God alone can produce grace; but He has deigned to submit Himself to your ministry in drawing from nothing the souls of your children, as He has likewise made use of your consent in order to bestow His sacramental grace. In the one and in the other of these collaborations, God will await, in order to exercise His omnipotence, your own "yes"; . . . He does not will to treat you as inert instruments without reason . . . but wills that you freely place the act that He waits for in order to complete His creative and sanctifying work.[11]

On the spouses depends the coming "to the threshold of life of 'those simple souls (anime semplicette), who know nothing'[12] whom Infinite Love desires to call to life, in order one day to make them His elect in Heaven".[13]

■ In this way, the Pope emphasizes *the enormous dimension of freedom:* "The incomparable grandeur of that very great gift, which is the freedom of choice, and the terrible responsibility given to intelligent men to be masters of themselves and of life, their own and others, of that life that rises toward eternity, and the power—with rebellion from God—to stop its course."[14] "You have", he insists, "at your disposition the powers of life, not only in the natural order but also in the spiritual and supernatural order, with the awesome power of impeding its course."[15]

[9] Pius XII, Radio Message to the Families of France, June 17, 1945; *Ins.* no. 514; *Enchiridion Familiae,* 2.1316–17.

[10] Pius XII, Address to New Spouses, March 5, 1941; *Ins.* nos. 445–53; *Enchiridion Familiae,* 2.964–71.

[11] Ibid., *Ins.* nos. 447–48; *Enchiridion Familiae,* 2.965–67.

[12] Dante, *Purgatorio,* 16, 87.

[13] Pius XII, Address to New Spouses, March 5, 1941; *Ins.* no. 449; *Enchiridion Familiae,* 2.968.

[14] Ibid., *Ins.* no. 451; *Enchiridion Familiae,* 2.969.

[15] Ibid., *Ins.* no. 452; *Enchiridion Familiae,* 2.970.

3. In his Address of April 29, 1942,[16] he shows how *the unity and indissolubility of marriage flow from the very essence of true conjugal love.* After having recalled that revelation teaches, as the most profound root of the indissoluble unity of the bond, the fact that marriage constitutes a sign of the most perfect union of Christ and his Church, he asks what nature has to say when faced with such demands of grace; he answers that there is no contradiction because grace does not destroy but perfects nature: the perpetual indissolubility established by Christ "is willed also by nature. Grace fulfills the longings of nature and gives it the power to be what it is led to desire to be by its best wisdom and willing."[17] It is enough to ask one's own heart to know that such is truly the voice of nature, when one lets one's heart speak without darkening it by egoism:

> You attribute to your nuptial love, without actually being aware of it, a holy jealousy, that characteristic sign that the Apostle Paul ascribed to charity when, exalting it, he said: *"caritas numquam excidit"* (1 Cor 13:8), "love never fails". . . . The indissolubility of marriage is therefore the satisfaction of a pure and uncorrupted impulse of the heart, of the soul that is *naturally Christian.*[18]

Unity and indissolubility are not rules externally imposed on the spouses and restrictive of conjugal love, but are the manifestation of its most intimate requirements, which assure its truth and dignity as

> the simultaneous spiritual and disinterested devotion of the spouses to each other, with the consciousness, alive and rooted in each, of willing to belong completely to each other, of willing to remain faithful to each other in all the events and circumstances of life, in good days and in bad, in health and in sickness, in youth and in old age, without limits or conditions so that at last God will be pleased to call them to eternity.[19]

3. Documents Concerning Themes of Conjugal Morality

During this pontificate, social movements and scientific discoveries that for some time had been raising moral questions for the Church

[16] Pius XII, Address to New Spouses, April 29, 1942; *Ins.* nos. 489–99; *Enchiridion Familiae,* 2.1120–27.

[17] Ibid., *Ins.* no. 490; *Enchiridion Familiae,* 2.1121.

[18] Ibid., *Ins.* no. 491; *Enchiridion Familiae,* 2.1122.

[19] Ibid., *Ins.* no. 493; *Enchiridion Familiae,* 2.1123.

posed these issues with particular urgency, under the impulse of hedonism and of a growing de-Christianization. Numerous are the documents in which Pius XII responds to new problems: among them the famous Address to the Italian Catholic Union of Midwives of October 29, 1951,[20] and his Addresses to the Associations of Large Families of November 26, 1951, and of January 20, 1958.[21] It is also important to note his Addresses to the Fourth International Congress of Catholic Medical Doctors of September 29, 1949,[22] to the 26th Congress of Urology of October 8, 1953,[23] to the Members of the Second World Congress on Fertility and Sterility of May 19, 1956,[24] and to the Seventh International Hematological Congress of September 12, 1958.[25]

These addresses, naturally, contain repetitions and, on some points, are simply developments of what had been said previously. We will gather their content together by summing up the lines of argumentation, offering, first of all, a short synthesis of the principles that guide the search for moral solutions. These principles are of great relevance today.

1. *Both temporal happiness and eternal happiness cannot be attained save by the fulfillment of the divine laws.* In the Address to the Cardinals, Archbishops, and Bishops of November 2, 1950, the Holy Father insisted that in their mission as pastors they must teach "men, who yearn for temporal and eternal happiness, that both the one and the other can be found only by fidelity to the bond linking them to their obligations and to the law of God."[26] The obligation of the Church

[20] Address to the Italian Catholic Union of Midwives, October 29, 1951; *Ins.* nos. 593–652 (E.T. in *Official Catholic Teachings: Love and Sexuality,* ed. Odile M. Liebard [Wilmington, N.C.: McGrath, 1978], nos. 259–338); *Enchiridion Familiae,* 2.1424–62.

[21] Address to the Associations of Large Families, November 26, 1951; *Ins.* nos. 654–68 (E.T., in Liebard, nos. 340–55); *Enchiridion Familiae,* 2.1463–74; Address to the Italian Association of Large Families, January 20, 1958; *Ins.* nos. 763–66 (E.T., in Liebard, nos. 677–721); *Enchiridion Familiae,* 2.1668–82.

[22] Address to the Fourth International Congress of Catholic Medical Doctors, September 29, 1949; *Ins.* nos. 553–57 (E.T., in Liebard, nos. 238–57); *Enchiridion Familiae,* 2.1390–94.

[23] Address to the 26th Congress of Urology, October 8, 1953; *Ins.* nos. 693–702 (E.T., in Liebard, nos. 357–70); *Enchiridion Familiae,* 2.1495–1503.

[24] Address to the Members of the Second World Congress on Fertility and Sterility, May 19, 1956; *Ins.* nos. 732–47 (E.T., in Liebard, nos. 493–512); *Enchiridion Familiae,* 2.1595–1607.

[25] Address to the Seventh International Hematological Congress, September 12, 1958; *Ins.* nos. 777–800 (E.T., in Liebard, nos. 769–825); *Enchiridion Familiae,* 2.1695–1710.

[26] Pius XII, Address to the Cardinals, Archbishops, and Bishops, November 2, 1950; *Ins.* no. 572; *Enchiridion Familiae,* 2.1407.

to see that the divine laws be observed is a maternal solicitude for the well-being of mankind. Created and redeemed by God, man can attain his own perfection and fullness of being only by conforming himself to the plan of God's wisdom and love. To help us understand this, the Magisterium appeals to that original and primordial inclination in the human heart, that is, *the natural desire for happiness,* a longing that cannot be satiated outside a personal encounter with God, that is, in the love of God and neighbor. This desire constitutes the driving force and compass inscribed by the Creator in the depths of the heart of every man in order that each one feels impelled to search for it. The moral ideal cannot ever be opposed to this ineradicable desire without rendering it utopian and causing men to lose heart; it is also inhuman to reduce it to a simple desire for pleasure, for one or another form of hedonism.[27]

■ Therefore, it is a mistake "to wish to separate man from the bond to the divine order by appealing to the freedom given him by God",[28] because this would be to leave him without a guide and to render distressful his most profound aspirations, vainly endeavoring to fill him up with temporal and finite goods. Pastors of souls are in error who "in their teaching and in their practice . . . are silent when in married life spouses violate the laws established by God, laws that are valid always and in every case".[29] Hedonism arouses the human desire for happiness in a sterile way, for it lacks the power to satisfy it. Only God satisfies our desire for the infinite; every created good whatsoever leaves man restless, discontented. Permissivism—every yielding—is never a sign of true love in human affairs but, to the contrary, is cowardice.

2. In conformity with the plan of God, who created marriage to protect the transmission and growth of human life, *one must place at the very heart of conjugal morality the principle that marriage is an institution at the service of life:*

In the course of the last few years, We have taken every opportunity to expound one or another of the essential points of that [conjugal]

---

[27] Cf. on this matter S. Pinckaers, *La quête du bonheur* (Paris: Téqui, 1979); Ramón García de Haro, "Las Bienaventuranzas y la moral cristiana", *Doctor Communis* 34, no. 2 (1981): 209ff.

[28] Pius XI, Address to the Cardinals, Archbishops, and Bishops; *Ins.* no. 573; *Enchiridion Familiae,* 2.1407.

[29] Ibid.

morality, and more recently to indicate it in its entirety, not only by confuting the errors which corrupt it, but also by showing positively its meaning, duty, and importance, its values for the happiness of the married couple, the children, and the whole family, for stability and greater social benefits from the domestic hearth even to the State and to the Church herself. At the center of this doctrine marriage appeared as an institution at the service of life.[30]

■ Describing the contemporary crisis, it has been affirmed that "the most evident sign" of the actual "moral devaluation is the refusal to transmit life. This implies at the same time a pessimistic judgment on existence and a marked preference for immediate pleasures, menaced—it is thought—by the responsibilities and obligations of fatherhood and motherhood. In fact, right here we find the nucleus of the hurricane of immorality and permissiveness that has swarmed over us, as on the other hand there is the awareness that the family is in truth the microcosm of lived morality."[31]

In the service of life—so these authors insist—the whole of conjugal and social morality is put into play. Thus, in the face of contemporary crises, the Magisterium returns to insist on this very point: "Against the pessimism and the selfishness which cast a shadow over the world, the Church stands for life: in each human life she sees the splendor of that 'Yes,' of that 'Amen,' who is Christ Himself. To the 'No' which assails and afflicts the world, she replies with this living 'Yes,' thus defending the human person and the world from all who plot against and harm life."[32]

3. The discoveries of science, as all temporal goods, are at the service of man: they must help him to reach his perfection, under the guidance of the moral law. They are instruments at the service of man and are used well when that is not forgotten. *Only morality possesses a complete vision of man:* when science contradicts the teachings of morality, this occurs because it errs about the true nature of man and the way in which he attains his happiness and perfection. The Church loves science, as all true progress, because it is a gift of God: "We do not ignore or undervalue the progress that medicine, psychology, and sociology have made; we desire, on the contrary, that

[30] Pius XII, Address to the Associations of Large Families; *Ins.* nos. 659–60 (E.T., nos. 346–47); *Enchiridion Familiae,* 2.1466–67.

[31] Philippe Delhaye, *La scienza del bene e del male. La morale del Vaticano II e il "metaconcilio"* (Milan: Ed. Ares, 1981), p. 40.

[32] John Paul II, apostolic exhortation *Familiaris consortio,* November 22, 1981, no. 30.

the results of these sciences contribute to ethics and moral theology and to the procedures used in the care of souls."[33] But when we are dealing with man, scientific knowledge must recognize its limits: (a) *it is never right to experiment* with human life, which is sacred, and it is wrong to apply and spread abroad those things that are only hypotheses and that carry risks for human life;[34] (b) in every case, science *does not have the last word* wherever freedom comes in, because the free act has a grandeur that surpasses science, and the latter can only illegitimately pretend to take to itself full control of human life. Science is limited to the finite directly capable of being experimented on by sensible means, and "the importance of a human act consists precisely in going beyond the moment itself at which the act is posited to consider the entire orientation of a life, and to bring it into relation with the absolute."[35]

4. It would be an error to relativize the demands of Christian morality to any judgment about their practical feasibility, since *God himself confers the powers needed to live according to his law,* with gifts of nature and of grace: "It is therefore before God that the family responds with its own existence, dignity and social function, because from God Himself the family has received them and before Him is responsible for them."[36] Certainly, conjugal chastity, as all other aspects of the Christian life of the family, does not succeed in keeping constantly alive "without the help of God's grace".[37] But from the very conjugal contract, which is a religious act raised by Christ to the dignity of a sacrament, there flow "all those graces, all those divine helps that are necessary and opportune for sanctifying married life, for fulfilling the duties of the conjugal state, for overcoming difficulties, for keeping its promises".[38]

---

[33] Pius XII, Address to the Cardinals, Archbishops, and Bishops; *Ins.* no. 568; *Enchiridion Familiae,* 2.1404.

[34] Ibid., *Ins.* no. 569; *Enchiridion Familiae,* 2.1404-5.

[35] Pius XII, Address to the Members of the Second World Congress of Fertility and Sterility; *Ins.* no. 738 (E.T., no. 505); *Enchiridion Familiae,* 2.1599-1600.

[36] Pius XII, Address to Fathers of Families, September 18, 1951; *Ins.* no. 578; *Enchiridion Familiae,* 2.1414.

[37] Pius XII, Address to the Discalced Carmelites, September 23, 1951; *Ins.* no. 592; *Enchiridion Familiae,* 2.1423.

[38] Pius XII, Address to New Spouses, July 12, 1939; *Ins.* no. 417; *Enchiridion Familiae,* 2.838.

A. *A crucial question: the relationship between conjugal love and procreation*

A great part of the difficulties springing up regarding conjugal morality, both during the past century and in the present, has to do with this issue. Contraception and sterilization and abortion, as well as the recourse to infertile periods, all have at their base the relationship between conjugal love and procreation, even if, logically, they are problems that are also raised in the use of sexuality outside of marriage. If it is admitted that the generative act is licit only within marriage, some ask whether it is possible to separate this act from procreation, in certain cases, for certain reasons, and with certain methods. The problem is complex because, in reality, different questions are here intertwined. On the one hand, the pretenses of an *anticonceptive mentality*, that denatures marriage; on the other, the question whether it is licit to have recourse to the exclusive use of the infertile periods—according to the discoveries of science—when there are grave reasons that seem to counsel a spacing of births; finally, the doubt whether for the most serious reasons it is possible to place an obstacle at all costs to the conception of a child or to the continuation of a pregnancy. Pius XII is particularly concerned with this issue in his Address to the Italian Catholic Union of Midwives of October 29, 1951, returning to it more succinctly in his addresses of September 14, 1952, and of September 12, 1958. His doctrine can be summarized as follows:

The Church can never cease proclaiming, as the explicit will of the Creator, that the first good and end of marriage is the procreation and education of children, repudiating the contraceptive mentality. Never licit are abortion, contraception, or sterilization. For "serious reasons" one can licitly restrict the use of marriage to the infertile periods.

In practice, therefore, Pius XII reaffirms the perennial doctrine of the Church in the face of a growing contraceptive mentality; then, drawing inspiration from the principles that have always informed it, he studies the new problem of the use of marriage during the infertile periods. We can articulate his teaching (which will be at the base of the teachings of *Gaudium et spes* and, later on, *Humanae vitae* and *Familiaris consortio*) in the following way.

1. As a fundamental principle, there is *the inseparability between conjugal love and procreation, because this love finds itself at the service of life according to the explicit divine will.*[39] Holy Scripture, Tradition, all the Fathers and Doctors present as a constant and essential teaching — faithfully guarded by the Magisterium, as the authoritative interpreter of divine revelation — that *children are a great gift from God, the first end and good of marriage;* every intent to *sever conjugal love from procreation is directly opposed to the divine will* and overturns the plan of the Creator for marriage.

Holy Scripture, in fact, repeatedly emphasizes the grandeur of fatherhood and motherhood, exalting the *admirable collaboration* of the parents with God in the raising up of new life; there come to mind the inspired words in which the book of Maccabees speaks of that heroic mother: "I know not how you were formed in my womb; for I neither gave you breath, nor soul, nor life, neither did I frame the limbs of every one of you. But the Creator of the world formed the nativity of man" (2 Macc 7:22).[40] In the same way, it affirms that children *are a blessing of God to the just:* "Your wife will be like a fruitful vine on the sides of your house, and your children as olive plants round your table. Behold, thus shall the man be blessed who fears the Lord" (Ps 128:4).[41] Motherhood is a *grace and a way of salvation* (cf. 1 Tim 2:15). The good sense of people, the Pope reminds us, has always recognized and appreciated this — today, unfortunately, no longer — seeing in a large family "the guarantee of the physical and moral health of peoples".[42]

> ■ Therefore, nothing can be more opposed "to the thought of God, to the language of Scripture, and to sound reason itself", than the contraceptive mentality that considers children not as a blessing from God but as an evil from which spouses are to be liberated. Therefore, if there can be extraordinary circumstances in which it is legitimate for the spouses to have recourse to periodic continence — in order to space conceptions — it will always be for serious reasons that compel them to a kind of painful decision to forego conception; but if the use of

[39] "Never is it permitted to separate these two aspects to the positive exclusion either of the procreative intention or of the conjugal relationship" (Address to the Second World Congress on Fertility and Sterility; *Ins.* no. 737 [E.T., no. 503]; *Enchiridion Familiae,* 2.1598-99).

[40] Pius XII, Address to the Italian Catholic Union of Midwives; *Ins.* no. 593 (E.T., no. 259); *Enchiridion Familiae,* 2.1424.

[41] Ibid., *Ins.* no. 600 (E.T., no. 274); *Enchiridion Familiae,* 2.1432.

[42] Pius XII, Address to the Italian Association of Large Families; *Ins.* no. 766 (E.T., no. 681); *Enchiridion Familiae,* 2.1670.

periodic continence were permitted because of the arbitrary will of the parents, this would denote an attitude of rejection of life and a lacking of respect of its sacred value.[43] *The Church has always condemned this contraceptive mentality.* In 1974, the Congregation for the Doctrine of the Faith took note of it and said: "It is not permitted to spread that way of thinking and, even more, that way of feeling, which regards fertility as an evil, without repudiating it thoroughly."[44] In the same way, *Familiaris consortio* criticizes the attitudes that are the products of "excessive prosperity and the consumer mentality, paradoxically joined to a certain anguish and uncertainty about the future", which "deprive married couples of the generosity and courage needed for raising up new human life".[45] And John Paul II puts us on guard against the grave harms that flow from this mentality: "How burdensome is the whole force of this refusal of children, progressively emphasized, on the psychology of parents, who bear inscribed in their being the desire for children, and how will it affect the future of society? And what are we to think of an education of the young in sexuality that does not put them on guard against the search for immediate and selfish pleasure, dissociated from the responsibilities of conjugal love and of procreation?"[46]

2. *In teaching that marriage and conjugal love find themselves at the service of life, the Church does not ignore the grandeur of conjugal love but defends it against every degradation.* The Church proclaims the inseparability between the conjugal act and procreation precisely because she does not see this act as the mere satisfaction of an instinct, but as the free cooperation of the spouses in a spiritual work: the transmission and education of human life. Therefore, the Church will be opposed to every conjugal union that excludes procreation, just as she will be opposed to artificial fecundation that takes place without the personal union of the spouses. "The marital act, in its natural structure, is a personal act. It is the simultaneous and direct cooperation of the

---

[43] Pius XII, Address to the Italian Catholic Union of Midwives; *Ins.* no. 605 (E.T., no. 300); *Enchiridion Familiae,* 2.1445.

[44] Congregation for the Doctrine of the Faith, *Declaration on Procured Abortion,* November 18, 1974, no. 27; AAS 66 (1974): 734; *Enchiridion Familiae,* 3.2093.

[45] John Paul II, *Familiaris consortio,* no. 6; *Enchiridion Familiae,* 4.3210–11; cf. also no. 30; *Enchiridion Familiae,* 4.3254–56.

[46] John Paul II, Address to CLER (Centre de Liasion des Equipes de Recherche) and to FIDAF (Federation International d'Action Familiale), November 3, 1979, no. 7; *Enchiridion Familiae,* 3.2428.

spouses which, by the very nature of the agents and the propriety of the act, is the expression of the mutual giving which, in the words of Scripture, results in the union 'in one flesh' (Gen 2:24)."[47] Here, we are, therefore, dealing with a personal and free act pertaining to the moral dimension and transcending man, which cannot be governed by "physical or biological laws which are automatically obeyed by agents not endowed with reason, but . . . by laws, the execution and effects of which are confided to the voluntary and free cooperation of man."[48]

An ensemble of impulses and natural tendencies—willed by God—enters into play and disposes the bodily union of husband and wife, a union destined to transmit life: the spouses act as persons and children of God if they act in conformity to the will of the Creator. From this it follows that the spouses do not really love each other if they do not put their love to the service of life:

> Not only the exterior common life, but also all the personal wealth, the qualities of mind and spirit, and finally all that there is of the more truly spiritual and profound in married love as such, has been placed by the will of nature and the Creator at the service of the offspring. Of its nature perfect married love means also the complete self-sacrifice of the parents on behalf of their children, and love of husband and wife in its strength and tenderness is an essential need for the most earnest care of the child and the guarantee that this will be taken.[49]

■ One can understand, after reading these paragraphs, how superficial are the accusations of physicalism and of a neglecting of the personalist aspects of marriage that are leveled by some against the Magisterium. The Church, confronting every form of manicheanism, has always defended *the holiness of conjugal love,* understanding it in both its bodily and its spiritual integrity. If the Church does not will to separate love and procreation, if she always repudiates contraception, if she grants only under specific conditions recourse to infertile periods, she does this in order to safeguard personal love. She does not ignore the importance of the marital union in its physical aspects: "The same Creator has arranged that the husband and wife find pleasure and happiness of mind and body in the performance of that function [the conjugal act]. Consequently, the husband and wife do no wrong in seeking out and enjoying this pleasure. They are accepting what the

---

[47] Pius XII, Address to the Italian Catholic Union of Midwives; *Ins.* no. 637 (E.T., no. 317); *Enchiridion Familiae,* 2.1454.

[48] Ibid., *Ins.* no. 594 (E.T., no. 260); *Enchiridion Familiae,* 2.1424–25.

[49] Ibid., *Ins.* no. 636 (E.T., no. 316); *Enchiridion Familiae,* 2.1453–54.

Creator intended for them."[50] But she sees this union within the spiritual dimension of man, in the integrity of his personal being; for this reason she notes that they ought not to seek this pleasure "as an end in itself, but rather in its destiny in serving life".[51] It is precisely the dignity of the person and of conjugal love that requires the freely willed ordination of their acts to the service of life. Confronted by all the pretenses of materialism, according to which "happiness in married life is in direct ratio to the mutual enjoyment of married relations", the Church maintains that happiness in marriage, on the contrary, "is in direct ratio to the unconquerable respect the husband and wife have for each other, even in the intimate act of marriage . . . because the respect and mutual esteem which arise from it are one of the strongest elements of a love which is all the more pure because it is the more tender."[52] The most profound source of a tender, true, and disinterested love is precisely the service of life, which attacks selfishness in its very root, preventing it from giving rise to a search for pleasure, deeming it the ultimate end or primary end of marital union.[53]

This doctrine has been freshly set forth by *Familiaris consortio:*

The fundamental task of the family is to serve life, to actualize in history the original blessing of the Creator—that of transmitting by procreation the divine image from person to person. Fecundity is the fruit and sign of conjugal love, the living testimony of the full reciprocal self-giving of the spouses: "While not making the other purposes of matrimony of less account, the true practice of conjugal love, and the whole meaning of the family life which results from it, have this aim: that the couple be ready with stout hearts to cooperate with the love of the Creator and the Savior, who through them will enlarge and enrich His family day by day."[54,55]

Therefore, the polemical view that opposes love to procreation is foreign to the Tradition of the Church, which has, on the contrary, always emphasized their complementarity, the intimate unity that naturally exists, as we have already seen, between the life-giving and formal principle—conjugal love—and the end of the conjugal

---

[50] Ibid., *Ins.* no. 643 (E.T., no. 325); *Enchiridion Familiae,* 2.1457.

[51] Ibid. *Ins.* no. 651 (E.T., no. 333); *Enchiridion Familiae,* 2.1460.

[52] Ibid., *Ins.* no. 650 (E.T., no. 332); *Enchiridion Familiae,* 2.1460–61.

[53] On this matter see K. Wojtyla, *Love and Responsibility,* trans. H. Willetts (New York: Farrar, Straus, Giroux, 1981), pp. 119ff.; Pius XII, Address to the Italian Catholic Union of Midwives, *Ins.* no. 651 (E.T., no. 333); *Enchiridion Familiae,* 2.1461.

[54] Vatican Council II, pastoral constitution *Gaudium et spes,* December 7, 1965, no. 50.

[55] John Paul II, *Familaris consortio,* no. 28; *Enchiridion Familiae,* 4.3253.

community—the procreation and education of children. As *Familiaris consortio* affirms, repeating almost verbatim the words of Vatican Council II, "The Church . . . is convinced that there can be no true contradiction between the divine law on transmitting life and that of fostering authentic conjugal love."[56]

Moreover, and definitively, "according to traditional language, love, that superior *power*, coordinates the actions of the persons, of the husband and of the wife, *within the sphere of the ends of marriage.* Although neither the Conciliar Constitution *Gaudium et spes* nor the Encyclical *Humanae vitae,* in confronting this matter, use the language customary at one time, they nonetheless treat of the reality to which these traditional expressions refer." One must therefore affirm that in the renewal worked out in *Gaudium et spes,* as also in *Humanae vitae,* "the traditional teaching on the ends of marriage (and on their hierarchy) is confirmed and wholly deepened from the perspective of the interior life of the spouses, that is, of conjugal and familial spirituality."[57]

3. In addition, Pius XII insists, *as a truth pertaining to the ordinary and universal, and therefore infallible, Magisterium, that every voluntary deprivation from the marital act of its ordination to procreation is gravely immoral.* The words of the Pope are solemn, as had been those used in *Casti connubii,* to which he appeals: Pius XI, his predecessor, he says,

solemnly proclaimed anew the fundamental law governing the marital act and conjugal relations; he said that any attempt on the part of husband and wife to deprive this act of its inherent force or to impede the procreation of a new life, either in the performance of the act itself, or in the course of the development of its natural consequences, is immoral, and furthermore, no alleged "indication" or need can convert an intrinsically immoral act into a moral and lawful one. This precept is as valid *today as it was yesterday, and it will be the same tomorrow and always,* because it does not imply a precept of human law, but it is the expression of a law which is natural and divine.[58]

■ It is necessary to emphasize that the disorder consists in the *freely willed deprivation* of the proper ordering of the marital act to procreation

---

[56] Ibid., no. 33; *Enchiridion Familiae,* 4.3263; cf. Vatican Council II, *Gaudium et spes,* no. 51.

[57] John Paul II, *Uomo e donna lo creò* (*Catechesi sull'amore umano*) (Rome: Città Nuova Editrice Libreria-Editrice Vaticana, 1985), pp. 478–79.

[58] Pius XII, Address to the Italian Catholic Union of Midwives; *Ins.* no. 613 (E.T., nos. 288–89); *Enchiridion Familiae,* 2.1439–40.

inscribed in the conjugal act. This helps us understand why recourse to infertile periods can be licit, inasmuch as the Church has never opposed the use of marriage when—for reasons outside the will of the spouses—conception is not possible. And the reason is that marriage and the conjugal act have other ends—legitimate and holy. These ends, while not capable of justifying the willed deprivation of the principal end, allow spouses to engage in the marital act despite the fact that this end cannot be naturally attained.[59] At the same time it must be understood that the moral problem with respect to the practice of periodic continence arises not from "the use of their marital right even on days of natural sterility", but from the fact that this continence means limiting "the conjugal act exclusively to these days", a practice which "seems to be the clear expression of a will opposed to that fundamental readiness" to serve life. Therefore, "the conduct of the married couple must be examined more attentively", to make sure that it in no way includes a contraceptive intention.[60]

4. Abortion, sterilization, and contraception are opposed to this doctrine of the Church—based on the explicit will of God about marriage and its service to life: *therefore every action that directly intends the procuring of abortion, sterilization, or the impeding of procreation is gravely immoral,* no matter what the reason (eugenic, medical, social, etc.). "There is no man, no human authority, no science, no medical, eugenic, social, economic, or moral 'indication' that can offer or produce a valid juridical title to a direct deliberate disposal of an innocent human life", as is that of the child who has been conceived.[61] With different levels of perversion, and always gravely immoral, as opposed to the divine and natural law, are "direct sterilization, whether permanent or temporary, of the man or of the woman".[62] In short, the deprivation of any marital act of its procreative power is intrinsically and gravely immoral.[63]

---

[59] Ibid., *Ins.* no. 633 (E.T., no. 296); *Enchiridion Familiae,* 2.1442–43.

[60] Ibid., *Ins.* nos. 615–17 (E.T., nos. 293–96); *Enchiridion Familiae,* 2.1442–45.

[61] Ibid., *Ins.* no. 598 (E.T., no. 272); *Enchiridion Familiae,* 2.1429–30.

[62] Ibid., *Ins.* no. 614 (E.T., no. 291); *Enchiridion Familiae,* 2.1440–41.

[63] Ibid., *Ins.* nos. 613 (E.T., nos. 288–89); *Enchiridion Familiae,* 2.1439–40. Pius speaks in the same sense, using like expressions, in his Address to the Seventh International Hematological Congress; *Ins.* nos. 779–90 (E.T., nos. 780–92); *Enchiridion Familiae,* 2.1695–1710; and in his Address to the Associations of Large Families; *Ins.* nos. 659–68 (E.T., nos. 347–55); *Enchiridion Familiae,* 2.1463–74.

■ The Pope speaks of *direct action* in order to distinguish this from actions having a twofold effect. For example, when "the safety of the life of the future mother, independently of her state of pregnancy, might call for an urgent surgical operation, or any other therapeutic application, which would have as an accessory consequence, in no way desired nor intended, but *inevitable,* the death of the foetus, such an act could not be called a *direct* attempt on the innocent life."[64]

Here we cannot treat of the controversies over the requirements necessary if there is to be properly an action having two effects.[65] Here it suffices to say that to avoid a laxist interpretation, the document had previously insisted that "neither the life of the mother nor that of the child may be submitted to an act of direct suppression. Both for the one and the other the demand cannot be but this: to use every means to save the life of both the mother and the child."[66]

In like manner, with respect to sterilization (temporary, with the use of drugs), he affirms: "If a woman takes such a medicine [a drug that causes temporary sterility], not to prevent conception, but only on the advice of a doctor as a necessary remedy because of the condition of the uterus or the organism, she produces *indirect* sterilization, which is permitted according to the general principles governing acts with a double effect."[67] However, one must be truly dealing with an indirect sterilization—one not willed—and for a serious reason that truly demands the use of a drug, that is, one is absolutely obliged not to attempt a remedy for a pregnancy, as if it were an evil, but to cure a disease by use of a drug that every prudent person would take even if he or she had not need to make use of marriage; moreover, it is necessary that there not be another remedy for curing the disease; and, in particular, it can never become licit to use drugs in order to impede the conception of a child whom one fears may be handicapped, under the pretense of correcting, as it were, a "natural defect".[68]

[64] Pius XII, Address to the Associations of Large Families; *Ins.* no. 665 (E.T., no. 352); *Enchiridion Familiae,* 2.1471–72.

[65] On this issue see Servais Pinckaers, "La question des actes intrinsequement mauvais et le 'proportionalisme' ", *Revue Thomiste* (1982): 181–212 and (1984): 618–24; see also William E. May, "Double Effect, Principle of", in *Encyclopedia of Bioethics,* ed. Warren T. Reich, 1st ed., vol. 1 (New York: Free Press, 1978), pp. 168–75.

[66] Pius XII, Address to the Associations of Large Families; *Ins.* no. 662 (E.T., no. 349); *Enchiridion Familiae,* 2.1468.

[67] Pius XII, Address to the Members of the Seventh International Hematological Congress; *Ins.* no. 785 (E.T., no. 786); *Enchiridion Familiae,* 2.1699–1700. This Address, given on September 12, 1958, was the first to condemn, in connection with the notion of temporary sterilization, the use of the chemical contraceptives that gave rise to the "pill".

[68] Ibid., *Ins.* nos. 785–86 (E.T., no. 787); *Enchiridion Familiae,* 2.1700–1701.

5. Finally, the Pope is also concerned with the theme of periodic continence, which up to that time had not been explicitly resolved by the Magisterium. He teaches that *the use of marriage limited to infertile periods can be morally legitimate, but only for "serious" reasons.*[69] The doctrine can be summed up in the following words:

> The moral lawfulness of such conduct would be affirmed or denied according as to whether or not the intention to keep constantly to these periods is based on sufficient and reliable moral grounds. The sole fact that a couple do not offend against the nature of the act and that they are willing to accept and bring up the child that is born notwithstanding the precautions they have taken, would not of itself alone be a sufficient guarantee of a right intention and of the unquestionable morality of the motives themselves.[70]

This teaching thus includes a twofold aspect: a) in the first place, *it establishes an objective difference between contraception and the use of marriage exclusively in infertile periods:* the former always supposes an intrinsic contradiction to the moral law; the latter, on the other hand, does not; the act by reason of its object — prescinding from the subjective intention of the end for the sake of which one chooses to limit conjugal acts to infertile periods — is not immoral inasmuch as the spouses do not offend its nature and are disposed to accept the child who might come to be; otherwise the act would become contraceptive in itself; b) but, he adds, the fact itself *is not alone sufficient to guarantee the rectitude of the conduct: also required is the presence of just reasons or motives,* which assure the rectitude of the intention of excluding any and every contraceptive intent. The determination of *serious reasons* must be made "in the light of reasonable and fair judgment".[71]

■ There is here, in essence, an attempt to avoid every contraceptive attitude. In order that the use of marriage limited to infertile periods not constitute a refusal of the orientation of the conjugal act to procreation, there must be present sufficiently serious reasons for not desiring, reasoanbly, a new conception.

On the other hand, "the intention . . . to restrict the marital right

---

[69] Pius XII, Address to the Italian Catholic Union of Midwives; *Ins.* nos. 617–22 (E.T., nos. 293–301); *Enchiridion Familiae,* 2.1442–48.

[70] Ibid., *Ins.* no. 619 (E.T., no. 298); *Enchiridion Familiae,* 2.1443–44.

[71] Cf. ibid., *Ins.* no. 622 (E.T., no. 301); *Enchiridion Familiae,* 2.1445.

itself to the periods of sterility, and not merely the use of that right, in such a way that the other partner would not even have the right to demand the act at any other time . . . would imply an essential defect in the matrimonial consent", inasmuch as it would be a manifestation of a will directly opposed to the inseparability between conjugal love and procreation.[72] Likewise, the actual limitation of the use of marriage to infertile periods for reasons that are not serious is always immoral: "To embrace the married state, to make frequent use of the faculty proper to it and lawful only in that state, while on the other hand, always and deliberately to seek to evade the primary duty without serious reasons, would be to sin against the very meaning of married life."[73]

In order to grasp the implications of this doctrine and the importance of understanding it rightly — never as a brake on marital generosity, we will here occupy ourselves briefly with its theological foundation, with its development by the Magisterium, and with the principal pastoral guidelines useful for applying it correctly. The Holy Father John Paul II, with great pastoral insight, has put us on guard of the danger of introducing a contraceptive mentality into the practice of the so-called natural methods,[74] because when this mentality develops all its consequences in the unconditioned and selfish search for pleasure, it runs the risk of leading to the practice of abortion. In truth, the dissociation between genital pleasure and procreation imperceptively draws us to put ourselves in danger of wanting to legitimate any conduct in order that pleasure might be secured: masturbation, homosexual acts, premarital relations, contraception, and ultimately abortion. In the final analysis, abortion and contraception "place us, while surely on different levels, in the same line of fear of the child, of a refusal of life, of a lack of respect for the act and fruit of the union of husband and wife in the way in which this has been willed by the Creator. Those who study these problems in depth know this well, despite what certain currents of opinion would have us believe."[75]

---

[72] Ibid., *Ins.* no. 618 (E.T., no. 297); *Enchiridion Familiae*, 2.1443.

[73] Ibid., *Ins.* no. 621 (E.T., no. 300); *Enchiridion Familiae*, 2.1445.

[74] See his General Audience of October 8, 1980, no. 3; *Enchiridion Familiae*, 3.2832–33; and his Address to CLER and FIDAF, no. 7; *Enchiridion Familiae*, 3.2427–28.

[75] John Paul II, Address to CLER and FIDAF, no. 8; *Enchiridion Familiae*, 3.2428–29.

The doctrine of periodic continence in the light of the structure of free or moral action

Our Lord taught his apostles that the goodness of their actions depended on two essential and complementary elements. First, it depends on *the intention in the depths of the human heart* ("ab intus, a corde hominum": Mk 7:20–21; Mt 15:19), since from the heart flow good or evil acts; indeed, with such radicality that the one who desires the wife of another has already committed adultery with her in his heart (cf. Mt 5:27–28).[76] But, precisely because they are the roots of human action, the intimate intentions of the heart are manifested in *external works* as in their proper fruit, and the latter are equally an essential element of our moral conduct: "By their works you will know them" (Mt 7:16–20; Lk 6:44). The apostles understood this well: in contrast to what some claim today, they clearly taught that a true concern for the interior life is attentively on watch in order that one's works might be good, inasmuch as "it is not those who hear the law who are just in the sight of God; it is those who keep it who will be declared just" (Rom 2:13); or, as St. John says, "let us love in deed and in truth and not merely talk about it" (1 Jn 3:18).[77]

The first condition for the rectitude of conduct is that the deeds, the *external acts* —prescinding from [further] intentions of the agent—be *morally licit,* that is, ordainable to God. And this is fulfilled in the use of marriage in the infertile periods: "The natural method, unlike artificial methods, seeks to regulate conception by taking advantage of circumstances in which conception cannot occur for biological reasons. Because of this the 'naturalness' of sexual intercourse is not affected—whereas artificial methods do destroy the naturalness of intercourse."[78]

But this is not enough, because the morality of a human act also requires the goodness of both the external act and the interior act of the will, that is, of the *intention;* moreover, the latter is always the root of the former.[79] From this it follows that if the intention of the spouses

---

[76] On the importance of the *interiority* of Christian morality, see John Paul II, General Audiences commenting on Genesis of September 24, October 8, and November 10, 1980, and elsewhere; *Enchiridion Familiae,* 3.2809–15, 2830–38, and 2929–32.

[77] On this see Ramón García de Haro, "Los elementos del acto moral en su especificidad cristiana", *Scripta Theologica* 15, no. 1 (1983): 524–62; R. Yannuzzi, *La diferencia moral entre contracepción y continencia periódica* (Rome: Pontificià Universita Lateranense, 1988).

[78] Wojtyla, *Love and Responsibility,* pp. 240–41.

[79] St. Thomas, *Summa theologiae,* 1-2, q. 18, aa. 2 and 6; q. 20, aa. 2 and 3; *In II Sent.,* d. 38, q. 1, a. 5; d. 40, q. 1, a. 2.

in using the infertile periods exclusively is that of seeking pleasure by excluding procreation, then, although the act is good by reason of its object, it is changed into an act of contraception by reason of its end—by reason of its intention—and therefore immoral: "We tend to approach 'the natural method' and 'artificial methods' from the same point of view, to derive them from the same utilitarian premises. Looked at like this, the natural method is just another means to ensure the maximum pleasure, differing from artificial methods only in the direction it takes."[80] In sum, periodic continence can be licit only when it is an act of the virtue of chastity, and not the fruit of carnal selfishness:

> *Continence as a virtue cannot be regarded as a "contraceptive measure".* The spouses who practice it are prepared to renounce sexual intercourse for other reasons (religious reasons for instance) and not only to avoid having children. Self-interested, calculating continence awakens doubts. Continence must, like all other virtues, be disinterested, and wholly concerned with "justice", not merely with "expediency".... Only then is the "natural method" congruent with the nature of the person; its secret lies in the practice of virtue—technique alone is no solution here.[81]

■ There is need, in short, always to take into account both the object of the act and the intention. If the object is immoral, the intention on its part cannot make the act good. The object of the human act is not the physical object, but what is usually called the *moral object,* or the content of the action in its relationship to the order of creation and to the destiny of the human person. Thus, "it is the intentionality and the thrust of the act in itself that confer upon it its meaning and intelligibility, which cannot be eliminated or changed by our motivations."[82] The moral object of the act is good or evil by reason of the ordering or not ordering of the human person to God that the object contains (for this reason some call it the *finis operis*). If the object is intrinsically evil (contraception, for example), the subjective intention cannot render the object good, cannot change its objective "intention".

Likewise, if the intention is disordered the rectitude of the object cannot take its wickedness away from the act. If the physical union of the spouses in infertile periods springs from a contraceptive intention,

---

[80] Wojtyla, *Love and Responsibility,* p. 240.
[81] Ibid., 241–42.
[82] William E. May, "Contraception, Abstinence, and Responsible Parenthood", *Faith & Reason* 3, no. 1 (Spring 1977): 34–52.

this cannot be periodic continence, because the intention distorts the object, keeping it from being an act of chastity and changing it into an act of contraception, which "can only arise from a false appreciation of life and from motives that run counter to true standards of moral conduct".[83]

The Pope descends to the particular conditions within which there is the danger, more or less, of a contraceptive intent: (a) for example, the lack of the *disposition to accept the child* in the event that one comes to be,[84] since the will "of avoiding conception at any cost" always manifests a contraceptive intention;[85] (b) the absence of *serious reasons* that counsel against a new pregnancy (a serious threat to the life of the mother, the moral impossibility of bringing up new children). In truth, only when the intention can be right (not merely the refusal of the burdens of parenthood, which is always selfish and immoral) can periodic abstention be an act of chastity (and not merely a way of inordinately seeking pleasure). Only for serious reasons can the desire to avoid temporarily (or even for an indefinite period) a new child correspond to the value of responsible parenthood, as this has been defined by *Humanae vitae*: the search for the will of God, manifested through the seriousness of the reasons that counsel against a new conception, reasons that can be regarded as the basis of a true moral impossibility or, at least, of a level of habitual heroism that God ordinarily does not demand. This is the reason why the Magisterium has always required the concurrence of serious reasons for the use of natural methods: "It suffices to recall the adjectives that Pius XII himself adopted (AAS 43 [1951]: 845); 'grave reasons, serious reasons, serious personal reasons or reasons stemming from external causes' (ibid., 867); 'serious reasons' (ibid., 846); 'proportionately serious reasons (and indications of a eugenic nature can have this character)' (AAS 50 [1958]: 736); 'notable inconvenience' (ibid., 737). We reach the same conclusion in the light of *Humanae vitae*: on the two occasions on which Paul VI makes mention of reasons, in referring to the regulation of births, he speaks of 'serious reasons, deriving from the physical or psychological conditions of the spouses, or from external circumstances,' or else he speaks of 'just reasons' (n. 16)."[86]

---

[83] Pius XII, Address to the Italian Catholic Union of Midwives; *Ins.* no. 622 (E.T., no. 301); *Enchiridion Familiae*, 2.1445.

[84] Ibid., *Ins.* no. 619 (E.T., no. 300); *Enchiridion Familiae*, 2.1443–44.

[85] Wojtyla, *Love and Responsibility*, pp. 242–43.

[86] J. L. Soria, *Paternità responsabile* (L'Aquila: Japadre, 1969), pp. 53–54; see also John Paul II, *Familiaris consortio*, nos. 30 and 32; *Enchiridion Familiae*, 4.3254–56, 3259–62.

In other words, *the intention and the deed must both be good.* It is not right to have recourse to contraception even when there are serious reasons counseling against a new conception.

> When it is a question of harmonizing marital love with the responsible transmission of life, it is not enough to take only the good intention and the evaluation of motives into account; objective criteria must be used, criteria drawn from the nature of the human person and human action, criteria which respect the total meaning of mutual self-giving and human procreation in the context of true love.[87]

The seriousness of the reasons can never justify the use of contraceptives. Likewise, the use of natural methods, carried out with a contraceptive mentality or intention, can never be legitimate, because the act, in its totality, would be nothing else than a form of contraception. The Church condemns the use of natural methods when these are employed with a contraceptive mentality.

The progressive development of the Magisterium on this matter

The Church, from the time that medical science discovered the existence of the naturally infertile periods of the woman, has acted with great prudence: and this was logical inasmuch as at stake was a fundamental principle of conjugal morality, and therefore the happiness and sanctity of marriage: its essential destination in the service of life.

> ■ This attitude does not reflect a lack of confidence in conjugal love nor an animus against pleasure, united by God himself to the use of marriage; in fact, the Church has never doubted the liceity of the use of marriage even in periods that are not fertile, or between couples who are naturally sterile.[88] The Church, on the contrary, has been concerned with the voluntary limitation of the use of marital relations *exclusively* to infertile periods, because a limitation of this kind could signify a disordered and selfish search for pleasure, opposed to the other goods of marriage and regarded as an ultimate end. The Church *does not consider pleasure as an evil;* in itself it rather constitutes a good, and as such can be legitimately sought even as the proximate end of an action. In truth, there are not a few acts in a fully Christian life that do not rarely have as their proximate end a legitimate pleasure—the

---

[87] Vatican Council II, *Gaudium et spes,* no. 51; *Enchiridion Familiae,* 3.1839.

[88] The doubts that some theologians—even St. Augustine—have nourished on this matter have never been accepted by the Magisterium.

exercise of the arts, experimentations with different foods, the use of refreshing drinks, etc. What the Church *rejects is the disordered search for pleasure,* as happens when it is desired as the ultimate end of life or when it is sought in opposition to the order established by the Creator.

1. The first document that spoke of the recourse to the infertile periods is a *response of the Sacred Penitentiary* of June 16, 1880, in the time of Leo XIII. It was limited to affirming that spouses who adopted the natural methods "are not to be disturbed"; and that these methods can also be cautiously counseled for spouses who practice onanism, as a way to be followed in freeing themselves from this sin. Therefore, this first response was prudent and moderate.

■ As we have seen, Pius XI in *Casti connubii* did not explicitly treat of this question. He limited himself to affirm once more the intrinsic wickedness of contraception and the licitness of the use of marriage *even* in infertile periods, but without pronouncing himself on its *exclusive* use (whether this might be legitimate, when, and for what reasons).

2. Pius XII was later to occupy himself, in his Address to the Italian Catholic Union of Midwives, more fully with the discussion, studying the theological foundation of its solution. The Pope presented the principal lines of reasoning: it can be legitimate, but it is not always so. In the concrete, he required a right and honest intention; in judging this, he principally emphasized the existence of just and serious reasons.

■ The reasons or motives are not concomitant or accidental "subjective intentions", which are also customarily called "motives" or "reasons", but in the context must be understood as those proportionate *causes* or *reasons* for holding that it is not, objectively, reasonable to have other children in such a way that the proximate end of choice cannot be contraceptive. Therefore, they are not subjective "ideas", more or less arbitrary in character, for judging matters, but external circumstances determining a truly moral impossibility.[89]

The motives or reasons must have a serious character, because they must be proportionate to the good that, on the basis of these reasons, is excluded: the transmission of life, which is a most important good and

---

[89] For this reason *Gaudium et spes* speaks of the "evaluation of motives", i.e., of the causes, behind such conduct (cf. no. 51, par. 3; *Enchiridion Familiae,* 3.1838–39); and Pius XII says that *intention* must be "based on sufficient and reliable moral grounds" (Address to the Italian Catholic Union of Midwives, *Ins.* no. 619 [E.T., no. 298]; *Enchiridion Familiae,* 2.1444).

to which are ordered, by their very nature, both spousal love and the conjugal union.[90]

3. Paul VI's *Humanae vitae* brings out a new point. Most importantly of all, this affirms with the greatest solemnity that the Church can never allow contraception, because it is contrary to the personal dignity of the spouses and to the holiness of marriage. It clarifies that this is also true with respect to biochemical means, whose contraceptive character was then under discussion. Moreover, basing itself on the words and ideas of the Second Vatican Council, it elaborates the concept of *responsible parenthood,* the point of departure for a deepening of the study on the recourse to the infertile periods. Concretely, periodic continence can not be practiced as an "arbitrary" plan of life, but only as a way of living the value of "responsible parenthood". It is this that explains its radical difference from contraception.

■ *Humanae vitae* was decisively important, not only by reason of the firmness with which it condemned artificial contraception—faced with the doubts of so many theologians and pastors—but also by reason of the precisions it made with reference to the concept of responsible parenthood: (a) in paragraphs 2 to 4 of number 10, it lists in a complete way the different elements—external and internal, biological and spiritual—required for the virtuous recourse to infertile periods, emphasizing the importance of the virtue of chastity; (b) in paragraphs 5 to 6, it sets forth the criterion for judging the conduct of spouses, unconditionally seeking a more profound relationship to the objective moral order willed by God and refusing every claim to constitute themselves the "arbiters" of life; (c) finally, in a decisive manner and in order to avoid practical deviations, it clarifies that responsible parenthood is presented, in reality, under this alternative: "responsible parenthood is exercised, either by the deliberate and generous decision to raise a numerous family, or by the decision, made for grave motives and with due respect for the moral law, to avoid for the time being, or even for an indeterminate period, a new birth" (no. 10, par. 4).

4. *Familiaris consortio* continues and deepens the previous Magisterium. It reconfirms *Humanae vitae* in its integrity (nos. 19, 31, 34). Among the points in which it advances previous teaching, we will single out the

---

[90] Cf. Vatican Council II, *Gaudium et spes,* nos. 48 and 50; *Enchiridion Familiae,* 3.1830, 1836; John Paul II, *Familiaris consortio,* no. 26; *Enchiridion Familiae,* 4.3249–50.

following: (a) the urgency to restore a mentality in favor of life (nos. 14, 30), as the best corrective to the dominant selfishness that is wearing out the family; (b) the personalistic significance not only of conjugal love but also of procreation, preparing in this way for the teachings to be found in *Donum vitae*, the *Instruction on Respect for Human Life in Its Origin and on the Dignity of Procreation;*[91] (c) reaffirming the condemnation of contraception, it is able to point out better and more clearly the radical difference that separates recourse to the rhythms of fertility from contraceptive means, since these imply two radically different and irreconcilable concepts of the human person (no. 32); (d) it exhorts men and women to continue studying the matter, using all the discoveries of science, in the certainty that there can never be any contradiction between the law of handing life on and that of fostering conjugal love (nos. 33 and 34).

■ In the following chapters, we will see more fully these doctrines. But it was fitting here to give at least a general outline of the development of the Magisterium, in order to understand better the teachings of Pius XII. Pope Pacelli set forth the bases for understanding the difference between contraception and periodic continence, but in determining its use he considered the question almost exclusively from the perspective of the *motives or reasons for its liceity. Humanae vitae* makes a more global analysis, developing the theme of "responsible parenthood", already emphasized by Vatican Council II. In this context, periodic continence—along with total continence—appears as one of the ways of living out responsible parenthood in cases in which the search for God's will—and not the arbitrary judgment of the spouses, and far less that of one of them—leads to the decision of avoiding a conception, for a determinate or indeterminate period, for serious motives, and always with a complete respect for the moral law. *Familiaris consortio* pursues this analysis, showing the radical difference between contraception and responsible parenthood. *Responsible parenthood* is the attitude proper to those who seek to fulfill completely the will of God; it takes as its inspiration service to life and presupposes the practice of virtue; it is not reconcilable with a selfish calculus; it demands respect for the other spouse, counting on his or her consent, and it requires that one avoid every danger of incontinence (cf. 1 Cor 7:5). It sees in the openness to children the logical requirement of a

---

[91] Cf. A. Chapelle, "Continuité et progrès dans les enseignements de *Humanae vitae* et de *Donum vitae*", in *"Humanae vitae: 20 anni dopo" (Atti del II Congresso Internazionale di Teologia Morale: Roma, 9–12 novembre 1988),* (Milan: Ed. Ares, 1989), pp. 291ff.

truly personalist vision of conjugal love that of its nature issues in a personalist doctrine of procreation: "In its most profound reality, love is essentially a gift; and conjugal love, while leading the spouses to the reciprocal 'knowledge' which makes them 'one flesh',[92] does not end with the couple, because it makes them capable of the greatest possible gift, the gift by which they become cooperators with God for giving life to a new human person."[93]

Contraception, on the other hand, whether practiced by artificial means or by natural means, springs from the fact that the spouses— urged on by a materialistic and selfish mentality—want to make themselves the arbiters of life. At issue, then, are two diverse conceptions of man, radically opposed to each other.

In short, John Paul II, in *Familiaris consortio*, restates the perennial doctrine of the Church, according to the needs of the times. He never affirms, as he has sometimes erroneously been interpreted as affirming, that periodic continence is legitimate without taking into account the circumstances that justify it; to the contrary, citing number 51 of *Gaudium et spes*, he explicitly calls to mind the need for a right intention and of serious reasons as elements in the morality of the conduct of the spouses (cf. no. 32). But, confronted by a campaign of public opinion and of not a few theologians who claim to identify contraception and periodic continence, he undertakes a courageous defense of the latter (cf. also no. 32). Moreover—taking into account the difficulties in evaluating the different external circumstances usually brought forth as just motives—he prefers to put into relief the profoundly felt attitude of the spouses for an openness to life, for generosity, for struggling against selfishness, which ultimately ends up being the only guarantee for the proper evaluation of these motives. Therefore, always affirming the indications already established by *Humanae vitae* with respect to the serious reasons or motives,[94] he insists above all on the dispositions that lead one to evaluate these motives with an attitude of full openness to life; he insists on repudiating every contraceptive mentality,[95] by means of a constant struggle

[92] Cf. Gen 2:24.

[93] John Paul II, *Familiaris consortio*, no. 14; *Enchiridion Familiae*, 4.3225–26.

[94] Ibid., no. 32; *Enchiridion Familiae*, 4.3259–61; cf. nos. 29 and 31; *Enchiridion Familiae*, 4.3253–54, 3257–58.

[95] Cf. ibid., nos. 28–30; *Enchiridion Familiae*, 4.3252–57; no. 14; *Enchiridion Familiae*, 4.3225–26; etc.

against selfishness, and on the practice of conjugal chastity, which makes love even richer and more generous.[96]

Some pastoral directions

All that we have seen leads us to emphasize some practical/pastoral directions, already outlined by Pius XII in his Address to the Italian Catholic Union of Midwives, then confirmed by the later Magisterium, in particular, by *Familiaris consortio,* which point out a concrete and viable way for helping spouses in this matter, so very important for marital holiness and the temporal happiness of families.[97] We will make a summary of these pastoral/practical directions.

1. First and foremost, it is necessary to remind spouses of the doctrine of the Church, in all its depth, regarding *the wonderful mission of cooperating with God in the raising up of new lives and in educating their children to live as true children of God.* One cannot forget that knowledge and love of the good are what make easy the sacrifice inseparable from every noble human task. This is the way the address of Pius XII to the midwives began (cf. *Ins.* no. 593; E.T., no. 259; *Enchiridion Familiae,* 2.1424): if one succeeds in keeping this principle clearly before one's mind, the enormous majority of problems vanish from sight: "When spouses appreciate the honor of producing a new life, and await its coming with a holy impatience, your part [i.e., that of the midwives] is a very easy one" (ibid., *Ins.* no. 611; E.T., no. 287; *Enchiridion Familiae,* 2.1438).

■ As we have seen, *Familiaris consortio* vigorously addresses this issue: "Children, the most precious gift of marriage", are for the spouses "the living reflection of their love" (no. 14); to give them birth is to cooperate with "the love of God the Creator", and "fecundity is the

---

[96] Cf. ibid., no. 33; *Enchiridion Familiae,* 4.3262–66; see also no. 32; *Enchiridion Familiae,* 4.3259–61; etc.

[97] On this issue see the interesting study of A. Orózco, "Paternidad responsable y castidad conyugal", *Cuestiones fundamentales sobre matrimonio y familia (Actas del II Simposio Internacional de Teología),* ed. A. Sarmiento et al. (Pamplona: Eunsa, 1980), 584–99; Ramón García de Haro, "Orientamenti teologici per l'insegnamento della dottrina cattolica sulla procreazione responsabile", *Studi cattolici* 336 (1989): 101ff.; García de Haro, *The Formation of the Priest in Pastoral Assistance to the Family* (Rome: Pontifical Council for Pastoral Assistance to the Family, 1991).

fruit and sign of conjugal love, the living witness of the full reciprocal self-giving of the spouses" (no. 28; see also no. 30).

2. As a corollary, it is necessary *to combat the prejudices opposed to the natural appreciation of fatherhood and motherhood,* because truth is made evident only when the errors that seem to render it doubtful or unacceptable are known and clarified in their very roots. Pius XII also noted this in his address to the midwives, pointing out as an objective of their work not only abstention from every cooperation with evil but also the positive duty to unmask the errors at the basis of these evils: "Deftly apply yourselves to the removal of preconceived ideas, various fears or fainthearted excuses, and as far as possible to the removal also of the external obstacles which may cause distress where the acceptance of motherhood is concerned."[98]

■ Pius XII put the faithful on guard against the danger of a *false pre-occupation with demography,* flowing from the erroneous idea "that the number of men ought to be regulated according to the economy, something that is equivalent to overturning the order of nature and the entire moral and psychological order linked to it."[99] *Familiaris consortio* also insists on this matter, inviting mankind to rethink the meaning of the demographic danger, that creates in some a "certain panic" deriving from exaggerated claims of futurologists and ecologists.[100] Another error that frequently has a negative influence on the mind of spouses and that equally needs to be combated is a *disordered preoccupation for the better education of children,* one that forgets that "it is certainly less serious to deny children certain comforts or material advantages than to deprive them of the presence of brothers and sisters who could help them grow in humanity and to realize the beauty of life at all its ages and in all its variety."[101] Finally, it is necessary to encourage Christian couples to *struggle against selfishness, enlivening their trust in God,* because—according to the happy formula of Pius XII—"as long as there is no sincere determination to let the Creator carry on His work as He chooses, then

[98] Pius XII, Address to the Italian Catholic Union Midwives; *Ins.* no. 611 (E.T., no. 287); *Enchiridion Familiae,* 2.1438–39.

[99] Pius XII, Radio message to the World, December 24, 1952; *Ins.* no. 677; *Enchiridion Familiae,* 2.1482–84.

[100] John Paul II, *Familiaris consortio,* no. 30; *Enchiridion Familiae,* 4.3255–56.

[101] John Paul II, Homily at the Mass on the Capitol Mall of Washington, D.C., " 'Stand Up' for Human Life", October 7, 1979; in *Origins: NC Documentary Service* 9, no. 18 (October 18, 1979), no. 5, 279; *Enchiridion Familiae,* 3.2383.

human selfishness will always find new sophistries and excuses to still the voice of conscience (to the extent it can) and to carry on abuses."[102]

3. It is necessary also *to promote among spouses the certainty that it is always possible to live Christian doctrine,* indeed to live it is the best thing for them to do for themselves and for their children,[103] and that, if grave difficulties arise unexpectedly, they will succeed in conquering them with heroism:

> To overcome the many trials of conjugal life there is above all the most powerful aids of a lively Faith and a frequenting of the Sacraments, whence emerge torrents of strength whose efficacy is hardly clearly known by those who are outside the Church.... Be trustful! Nature's energies and, above all, those of grace with which God has enriched your souls by the means of the Sacrament of matrimony are like a solid rock, against which the waves of a stormy sea break up powerless.[104]

> ■ This argument is taken up again in *Familiaris consortio:* "Just as husbands and wives receive from the sacrament the gift and responsibility of translating into daily living the sanctification bestowed on them, so the same sacrament confers on them the grace and the moral obligation of transforming their whole lives into a 'spiritual sacrifice.' "[105] "It is an eminent form of love to give it [the Christian family] back its reasons for confidence in itself, in the riches that it possesses by nature and grace, and in the mission that God has entrusted to it."[106] The advantage consists in the fact that living with this confidence leads to verifying the truth of it all, while trusting only in human promises leads many times to betrayal, because men often promise more than they can give; while with God the opposite is the case, because he gives more than he promises.

4. In couples who find themselves in situations when they must have recourse to periodic continence in order to postpone a conception, one must *inspire the conviction that "ways of determining fertility" have a*

[102] Pius XII, Address to the Italian Association of Large Families; *Ins.* no. 764 (E.T., no. 687); *Enchiridion Familiae,* 2.1671.
[103] Pius XII, Address to the Italian Catholic Union of Midwives; *Ins.* nos. 625–26 (E.T., nos. 305–6); *Enchiridion Familiae,* 2.1447–48.
[104] Pius XII, Address to the Associations of Large Families; *Ins.* no. 668 (E.T., no. 355); *Enchiridion Familiae,* 2.1473.
[105] John Paul II, *Familiaris consortio,* no. 56, par. 5; *Enchiridion Familiae,* 4.3308.
[106] Ibid., no. 86, par. 9; *Enchiridion Familiae,* 4.3369.

sound scientific basis and security and are accessible, and that *periodic continence for just reasons,* precisely because it constitutes a way of living the virtue of conjugal chastity, *not only is practicable but strengthens their mutual love,* whereas contraceptives destroy it. Certainly, this demands an asceticism that is not easy, but

> thanks to its beneficent influence, husband and wife fully develop their personalities, being enriched with spiritual values. Such discipline bestows upon family life fruits of serenity and peace, and facilitates the solution of other problems; it favors attention for one's partner, helps both parties to drive out selfishness, the enemy of true love, and deepens their sense of responsibility.[107]

As a result, a serious pastoral help also embraces giving to spouses having need of it opportune directions so that they may more easily be able to take advantage of medical services where the use of natural methods is taught.

5. Finally, it is necessary to clarify, without delay and without fears, *the conditions in which periodic continence is morally licit,* because responsible parenthood is not a pretext for selfishness,[108] but the just and right way of living generously the virtue of conjugal chastity. When there are no serious reasons for having recourse to periodic continence, spouses will find themselves frustrated in practicing it: then they either decide to accept children generously or with ease fall into contraception. There are realities too serious to resolve with a play of words: if just reasons for postponing conception are lacking, recourse to the infertile periods is never "responsible" parenthood. Pius XII noted: "The sole fact that the couples ... are willing to accept and bring up the child that is born notwithstanding the precautions they have taken, would not of itself alone be a sufficient guarantee of a right intention or of the unquestionable morality of the motives themselves."[109] There must be just causes for such behavior, even more so when it is a question not of a brief period of time but for an indefinite period; they must make their decision with respect for the divine order, not arbitrarily, taking

---

[107] Paul VI, encyclical *Humanae vitae,* July 25, 1968, no. 21; *Enchiridion Familiae,* 3.1928–29; cf. also John Paul II, *Familiaris consortio,* nos. 32–34; *Enchiridion Familiae,* 4.3259–69.

[108] Cf. T. López, "Paternidad responsable", in *Cuestiones fundamentales sobre matrimonio y familia,* 577ff.

[109] Pius XII, Address to the Italian Catholic Union of Midwives; *Ins.* no. 619 (E.T., no. 298); *Enchiridion Familiae,* 2.1444.

into account the requirements of the virtue of chastity, etc. Moreover, it is fitting for the spouses to request opportune counsel—not to remove their own personal responsibility before God—but precisely because this is a matter in which one can too easily be deceived by one's own inclination toward selfishness.

■ John Paul II has summarized the proper attitude in these words: "Direct unceasingly your prow toward the idea of chaste conjugal relations that respect the nature and finality of the conjugal act; never let yourselves be carried away by a concession, more or less full, more or less acknowledged, to the principle and to the practices of contraceptive attitudes. God calls spouses to holiness in marriage, for their own good and for the quality of their witness."[110]

B. *Sex education*

The Church conceives sex education as timely education in the virtue of chastity: she cannot allow this meaning of sex education to be emptied out and corrupted.

At the time of Pius XII, many were spreading, often under the excuse of sex education, "writings, books and articles regarding the initiation of sexuality that often attain enormous success and flood the entire world", disturbing, with their morbid descriptions, both spouses and future spouses. The Pope terms this a "baneful propaganda" and particularly laments the fact that not infrequently such writings have their origin in "Catholic circles", without sufficiently marking out the "boundary between this initiation into sexuality, which they call 'Catholic,' and erotic and obscene publications and illustrations".[111]

The Pope reacts to this abuse by calling to mind the constant attitude of the Church: the respect with which one must discuss this matter and the context that makes sense out of it: *education in the virtue of chastity.*[112] In fact, it is true of human sexuality that it must be ordained to its proper end by the free will of man himself; but this is

---

[110] John Paul II, Address to CLER and FIDAF, no. 6; *Enchiridion Familiae*, 3.2426–27.

[111] Pius XII, Address to the Fathers of Families; *Ins.* nos. 585–87; *Enchiridion Familiae*, 2.1419–20.

[112] Pius XII, Address to the Parish Priests and Lenten Preachers of Rome, February 23, 1944; *Ins.* nos. 506–7; *Enchiridion Familiae*, 2.1282–85.

the function that develops the virtue of chastity, assuring that order and rectitude which is, on the contrary, purely instinctive in lower beings. It is precisely *moral education* in virtue that enables this result, proper and specific to man, to occur, in such wise that every other knowledge of human sexuality must be framed within "the absolute necessity for the virtue of chastity and for permanent education in it".[113] In his address to the midwives, Pius XII had summarized this matter, affirming that, in general, "common sense, natural instinct, and a short instruction on the clear and simple maxims of the Christian moral law, will suffice";[114] and this, not because of any manicheanism or jansenism, but because the Church, in her profound respect "for the holiness of marriage, has in theory and in practice left the spouses free in what that impulse of a sound and noble nature grants".[115]

■ The principle that sex education is above all education in chastity is also valid, one can easily understand, for the teaching to be given in the questions of fertility awareness. *Familiaris consortio,* in exhorting that "every effort must be made to render such knowledge accessible to all married people and also to young adults before marriage, through clear, timely, and serious instruction and education given by married couples, doctors and experts", emphasized that this knowledge must lead to education in chastity, which "by no means signifies rejection of human sexuality or lack of esteem for it; rather it signifies spiritual energy capable of defending love from the perils of selfishness and aggressiveness, and able to advance it towards its full realization."[116]

Pius XII then emphasized that, under the regnant conditions—which today are even more serious—Catholic spouses, as in general all Christians, have a grave obligation to try to avert the situation in which, under the pretense of sex education, there would take place a gradual perversion of young people and of conjugal morality. In this matter, as in many others, those who choose not to struggle against the current often end up being dragged under by it because, as the Pope sadly affirmed, the deformation and pressure of public opinion can

[113] John Paul II, *Familiaris consortio,* no. 33; *Enchiridion Familiae,* 4.3262–64.

[114] Pius XII, Address to the Italian Catholic Union of Midwives; *Ins.* no. 651 (E.T., no. 333); *Enchiridion Familiae,* 2.1461.

[115] Pius XII, Address to Fathers of Families; *Ins.* no. 586; *Enchiridion Familiae,* 2.1419.

[116] John Paul II, *Familiaris consortio,* no. 33; *Enchiridion Familiae,* 4.3265. On this issue see U. Poletti, "Continenza periodica e 'metodi naturali' nel Magistero della chiesa", Address to the International Congress on the Family, Rome, March 18, 1988.

become so great that "although paganism itself seems to maintain respect when faced with the secret of marital intimacy, one must recognize nonetheless that it violates this mystery by presenting both to the public at large, and particularly to youth, the vision—sensual and experienced—of its inmost intimacy."[117]

C. Other questions of conjugal morality

The Church does not admit artificial fecundation and does not permit anyone to prohibit marriage for eugenic reasons.

The discoveries of medical science posed a twofold problem on which the Holy Father was consulted: 1) the liceity of recourse to artificial fecundation in case of the natural infecundity of the spouses for which the former seemed to be able to provide a remedy;[118] 2) the action to be taken when science offers the prognosis, more or less probable, that the child will be handicapped. Pius XII treated both these questions in his addresses of May 19, 1956, to the Second World Congress on Fertility and Sterility[119] and of September 12, 1958, to the Seventh International Hematological Congress.[120]

The Pope teaches that *"artificial fecundation violates the natural law and is contrary to justice and morality."*[121] Moreover, "experiments in artificial fecundation *in vitro* ... must be rejected as immoral and absolutely illicit."[122] One must never forget that "human fecundity, beyond the physical factors, takes on essential moral aspects", and therefore is not ruled solely by the data of science.[123] Human life must never become

---

[117] Pius XII, Address to Fathers of Families; *Ins.* no. 587; *Enchiridion Familiae,* 2.1419–20.

[118] On this matter see Ramón García de Haro, "La fecondazione artificiale", *Studi cattolici* 28 (1984): 269–74; A. Rodriguez Luño and R. Lopez Mondejar, *La fecondación in vitro,* 2nd ed. (Madrid: Epalsa, 1968); William E. May, "Catholic Teaching on the Laboratory Generation of Human Life", in *Trust the Truth: A Symposium on the Twentieth Anniversary of Humanae Vitae,* ed. Russell E. Smith (Braintree, Mass.: Pope John XXIII Center, 1991), pp. 175–89.

[119] Pius XII, Address to the Members of the Second World Congress on Fertility and Sterility; *Ins.* nos. 732–47 (E.T., nos. 493–512); *Enchiridion Familiae,* 2.1595–1607.

[120] Pius XII, Address to the Members of the Seventh International Hematological Congress; *Ins.* nos. 777–800 (E.T., nos. 769–825); *Enchiridion Familiae,* 2.1695–1710.

[121] Pius XII, Address to the Members of the Second World Congress on Fertility and Sterility; *Ins.* no. 740 (E.T., no. 508); *Enchiridion Familiae,* 2.1600–1601.

[122] Ibid., *Ins.* no. 739 (E.T., no. 507); *Enchiridion Familiae,* 2.1600.

[123] Ibid., *Ins.* nos. 737–38 (E.T., nos. 505–6); *Enchiridion Familiae,* 2.1598–1600.

the object of scientific experimentation, because both its transmission and its eternal destiny are radically placed under the plans of the Creator: human life is not the fruit of a merely biological process, but presupposes the collaboration of the spouses with God, who generates an immortal life.[124] Just as it is not morally licit to exclude the procreative meaning from the conjugal act, so one cannot claim to generate life outside the bodily union of the spouses, precisely because the generation of human life, including its more biological aspects, is always a deeply personal act.[125] Moreover, fecundation of this kind of demands the prior obtaining sperm in an illicit manner (i.e., by masturbation).[126]

■ Let us note that the Church considers artificial fecundation not only immoral but also contrary to natural justice itself, i.e., that ethical *minimum,* within the natural law, whose violation directly imperils the common good.[127] But it does not regard as artificial fecundation an intervention giving assistance for a marital act to attain its own proper end.

In addition, Pius XII teaches that *the medical prognosis of an irregularity in the child does not authorize either the state to prohibit marriage or the spouses to make use of contraceptives.* In effect, the Holy Father does no more here than to apply to this hypothesis the general doctrine on the

---

[124] Ibid., *Ins.* nos. 738–40 (E.T., nos. 506–7); *Enchiridion Familiae,* 2.1599–1600.

[125] Ibid., *Ins.* no. 737 (E.T., no. 503); *Enchiridion Familiae,* 2.1598: "The Church has rejected . . . the attitude which would pretend to separate, in generation, the biological activity from the personal relation of the married couple. The child is the fruit of the conjugal union when that union finds full expression by bringing into play the organic functions, the associated sensible emotions, and the spiritual and disinterested love which animates the union. It is in the unity of this human act that we should consider the biological conditions of generation. Never is it permitted to separate these various aspects to the positive exclusion either of the procreative intention or of the conjugal relationship." This teaching has been confirmed and deepened in its reasons, relating them to more recent discoveries of science, by the instruction of the Congregation for the Doctrine of the Faith of February 22, 1987, *Donum vitae (Instruction on Respect for Human Life in Its Origin and on the Dignity of Human Procreation).*

[126] Ibid., *Ins.* nos. 741–44 (E.T., no. 509); *Enchiridion Familiae,* 2.1601–2. On this see also Address to the Seventh International Hematological Congress; *Ins.* no. 777; *Enchiridion Familiae,* 2.1696; and the Address to the Fourth International Congress of Catholic Medical Doctors; *Ins.* nos. 553–56; *Enchiridion Familiae,* 2.1390–94.

[127] On this see Ramón García de Haro, *Cuestiones fundamentales de teología moral* (Pamplona: Eunsa, 1980), pp. 135ff.; García de Haro, *La vida cristiana (Curso de Teología Moral Fundamental* [Pamplona: Eunsa, 1992]), pp. 487ff.

regulation of births, developed in his address of 1951.[128] He repeated as the teaching of *Casti connubii:* "Pius XI also stated . . . that, even if a couple is, in spite of everything, incapable of having healthy children, no one has the right to prevent them from marrying or from implementing their legitimately contracted marriage",[129] because marriage is a natural right for every person.

This does not mean that one cannot—indeed might be obliged to—counsel against marriage or its use in a case in which there is a real danger for the child.[130] On the responsibility involved in giving counsel of this kind, one must pay heed to the gravity of the risks, judged according to

> the general obligation to avoid all more or less serious danger or damage to the interested party, his spouse and his descendants. This obligation is proportionate to the seriousness of the possible damage, to its greater or less probability, to the intensity and proximity of the harmful influence exercised, to the seriousness of the reasons that one has for performing the dangerous acts and for permitting their pernicious consequences. These questions are for the most part questions of fact to which only the interested party, the doctor, and the specialists they consult can give an answer. From the moral point of view it can be said in general that a person has no right to disregard real risks of which one is aware.[131]

> ■ The reason at the heart of the doctrine of the Pope is that one cannot forget the difference between physical and moral evil: the illness of the child, taking into account the truth the men are not generated only for time but principally for eternity, is not an absolute evil, as, on the other hand, sin is. In every case, spouses must be aware of their obligations toward their child who can be born handicapped; this will demand a sacrifice often heroic, both on the part of the spouses and on that of their other children. But life—even burdened by suffering—is a great good that is enjoyed principally in eternity; they ought not to have excessive fears of temporal sufferings, but rather to accept them with courage and trust in God.

---

[128] Pius XII, Address to the Members of the Seventh International Hematological Congress; *Ins.* nos. 779–90 (E.T., nos. 780–95); *Enchiridion Familiae,* 2.1695–1700, wherein Pius XII refers repeatedly to his Address to the Italian Catholic Union of Midwives.

[129] Ibid., *Ins.* no. 795 (E.T., no. 809); *Enchiridion Familiae,* 2.1706.

[130] Ibid., *Ins.* nos. 794–95 (E.T., nos. 806–12); *Enchiridion Familiae,* 2.1705–7.

[131] Ibid., *Ins.* no. 793 (E.T., nos. 801–2); *Enchiridion Familiae,* 2.1704–5.

The so-called "premarital medical visit"

Scientific progress, to the extent that it allows us to foresee future difficulties in the health of children, even prior to the contracting of marriage, raises the question of the fittingness of a premarital visit to the doctor. The criterion set forth by Pius XII is that a visit of this kind can be counseled; indeed, one ought to visit the doctor if the risks foreseen are grave. However, here the issue is more that of medical science than of morality, because the gravity of the obligation depends on scientific factual data; from this it follows that confessors and moralists "ought to avoid a categorical yes or no in individual cases, since only a study of all the facts in a given case, which surpasses the competence of moralists and confessors, will permit one to decide whether he is faced with a serious obligation or not."[132]

4. Teachings on the Role and Rights of the Family in Society

Through the will of God, the family is the foundation and the first vital cell of society. From the ends proper to it flow its obligations and rights, which the state must respect.

This was another important aspect of the teachings of Pius XII. He often said so explicitly: "From the time that We were elevated to the See of Peter, in Our first encyclical *Summi pontificatus,* We affirmed that We regarded it as a pressing duty of conscience, imposed by Our apostlic ministry, to provide a firm defense of the rights of the family."[133]

Numerous documents in his pontificate will be devoted to this issue. Among them, we can note the following: first of all his encyclical *Summi pontificatus* of October 20, 1939,[134] the addresses of September 20, 1949, to the International Union of Family Organizations,[135] and of September 18, 1951, to the Fathers of Families;[136] in addition, the letter on the 27th Social Week of Pisa of September 19, 1954,[137]

---

[132] Ibid., *Ins.* no. 794 (E.T., no. 805); *Enchiridion Familiae,* 2.1705.

[133] Pius XII, Address to the International Union of Family Organizations, September 20, 1949; *Ins.* no. 544; *Enchiridion Familiae,* 2.1383.

[134] *Ins.* nos. 418–21; *Enchiridion Familiae,* 2.844–50.

[135] *Ins.* nos. 544–52; *Enchiridion Familiae,* 2.1383–90.

[136] *Ins.* nos. 578–90; *Enchiridion Familiae,* 2.1414–22.

[137] Letter of Mons. Montini to His Eminence Cardinal Siri; *Ins.* nos. 721–30.

and the Message to the World Congress of the Family of June 10, 1958.[138]

"The Family does not exist for society, but society exists for the family."[139] It is in the family that human life develops and is educated for society. According to the very order of creation, the family is the first vital cell of the human community: a society depends upon the families that compose it as a body depends upon its members. Therefore, society and the state must consider it their prime interest, as by an instinct for their self-preservation, to protect families. "They must guarantee absolutely the values that secure the order of families, their human dignity, their health, their happiness. These values, which are likewise elements of the common good, can never be allowed to be sacrificed to what can appear to be a common advantage."[140]

■ One must recognize that the common good is not reduced to material aspects only, even if these are very important, but that it embraces spiritual elements. One of the fundamental errors of materialism, whether liberal or Marxist, is the illogical claim according to which the state must not procure anything other than the increase of material goods, as if those of the spirit were not, in truth, the most profound source of the human energies that are capable of establishing the social order. Precisely because these goods are cultivated particularly within the family, the common good depends upon their good progress: "The life of the family itself, its health, its energy, its activity secure the life, health, energy, and activity of the whole society."[141]

Linked to the obligation on the part of the state is that of the family itself to defend itself *in its proper rights.* "Since the family receives from God its existence, its dignity, its social function, it is responsible before Him for all these. Its rights and its privileges are inalienable, intangible; it has the duty, above all before God and secondarily before society, to defend, vindicate and promote efficaciously these rights and these privileges, not only for its own proper advantage but for the glory of God and the well-being of the collectivity."[142] Unfortunately, the family often forgets this because of an odd paternalism that would want everything to take

[138] *Ins.* nos. 769–71; *Enchiridion Familiae,* 2.1683–86.
[139] Pius XII, Address to Fathers of Families; *Ins.* no. 581; *Enchiridion Familiae,* 2.1416.
[140] Ibid., *Ins.* no. 581; *Enchiridion Familiae,* 2.1416.
[141] Ibid.
[142] Ibid., *Ins.* no. 578; *Enchiridion Familiae,* 2.1414; see also the Address to the International Union of Family Organizations; *Ins.* no. 545; *Enchiridion Familiae,* 2.1383–84.

its origin from the state and from public organisms. Thus are neglected the bases and the energies given directly to the family by God himself.

The rights of the family and the duties that protect them are therefore prior to and independent of the state; the latter does not create these rights and duties, which, to the contrary, flow from the very being of the family; but it has the obligation to protect them. "The dignity and the rights of the family are, in fact, as old as humanity and are independent of the power of the state; but when they are in any way menaced, the state has the duty to protect and defend them." They are "sacred in every period of history and in every climate", and "every attack harming them is an attack against humanity."[143] The state must watch over *the moral health* and the *good economic conditions* of the family, seeing to it that a climate and laws exist that favor the development of the family and help to overcome difficulties facing it.[144]

■ There must absolutely be avoided the situation in which, on the excuse of protecting and defending the rights of the family, the state interjects itself into it and claims to change its finality and its characteristics, or in any way whatsoever to suffocate its vitality.[145] Among the dangers of this interjection, the Pope denounces a badly understood "social security", which seeks to substitute itself for the family and injures its rights and goods: " 'Social security' cannot mean anything else than, in society and by means of society, the favoring of the life of man, with his birth and natural development within marriage and the family, the foundation of society, which must favor the exercise and fulfillment of the duties and obligations proper to the family itself."[146]

All Catholics are obliged to devote themselves to seeing to it that the rights of the family are recognized and protected: on this matter unity is necessary, whatever might be one's own positions on economic, political, and other questions. Pius XII says: "On other economic and political

---

[143] Pius XII, Address to the International Union of Family Organizations; *Ins.* no. 545; *Enchiridion Familiae,* 2.1383.

[144] Letter of Mons. Montini to His Eminence Cardinal Siri, *Ins.* nos. 726–27; Pius XII, Message to the World Congress of the Family, June 10, 1958, *Ins.* no. 771; *Enchiridion Familiae,* 2.1686.

[145] Pius XII, Address to the International Union of Family Organizations; *Ins.* no. 546; *Enchiridion Familiae,* 2.1383.

[146] Pius XII, Address to the Cardinals, Archbishops, and Bishops; *Ins.* no. 574; *Enchiridion Familiae,* 2.1407–8.

questions there can be" legitimate disagreement, but "with respect to what concerns the essential rights of the family, the true faithful of the Church are obliged to sustain them from first to last."[147] By means of this unanimity, they must make heard clearly and forcefully the voice of Christian truth, without allowing, by their culpable silence, any materialistic mentality and attitudes contrary to the divine design to gain the upper hand.[148]

> ■ This advice was surely illuminating; if it had been heard, it would have avoided in good part the evils of the de-Christianization that has taken place. It has frequently been the case that Catholics, because of pressures, have been united in accidental matters and on political opinions while, on the other hand, they have neglected their obligation in conscience to defend the rights of God in society. When Vatican Council II proclaimed the rightful autonomy of temporal matters, it was thinking precisely of combating a deformation of this kind: it desired to prevent ecclesiastics from injecting themselves into strictly political issues. It could not imagine that some would have claimed, in the name of such a legitimate autonomy, to proclaim the renunciation of the Church to teach to all the doctrine of Christ. On the contrary, it saw the need to remind Catholics that they cannot yield on essential points of the divine law, among them, the rights of the family.[149]

The principal rights of the family set forth by Pius XII

In his address of September 18, 1951, given to fathers of families, the Pope enumerated, with a straightforward formula, the principal rights of the family, menaced at that time:

> The *indissolubility* of marriage, the *protection of life* from conception onward; *decent housing* for the family, not only for childless families or for those with only one or two children, but also for larger families; the availability of *work*, because unemployment of the father is a bitter anxiety for the family; the rights of the parents of children before the state, and specifically *their full right to educate their children* in the true faith and, consequently, the right of Catholic parents to schools that

[147] Pius XII, Address to Fathers of Families; *Ins.* no. 583; *Enchiridion Familiae*, 2.1417.

[148] Pius XII, Address to the International Union of Family Organizations; *Ins.* no. 547; *Enchiridion Familiae*, 2.1384.

[149] On this issue see Philippe Delhaye, *La scienza del bene e del male*, pp. 97–112 and 155ff.

correspond faithfully to their beliefs; a condition of public life and, above all, a *public morality* such that families, and particularly the young, are not enticed to corruption.[150]

In other documents, Pius XII completes the enumeration of these rights and the description of their content. It is worth noting the insistence with which he promoted private initiative—with appropriate public support—for solving the problem of housing. Without the help of society and of the state, spouses cannot solve this problem; and here we are dealing with a question of decisive influence on the morality of the family: "How heavy does it weigh on the consciences of Christians when future spouses, or growing families, are not able to find any home or only a dwelling that is inadequate and frequently much too costly. Only the Lord knows in how many cases human weakness has led to the shipwreck of Christian conduct and perhaps even the faith!"[151] Moreover, the diffusion of private property and, in particular, the family patrimony is pointed out as a necessary guarantee of the freedom fitting for families. "Must not, perhaps, private property secure for the father of the family that healthy freedom, of which he has need, of being able to fulfill the duties assigned to him by the Creator, with respect to the physical, spiritual, and religious well-being of the family?"[152] Finally, the protection of *large families* is a rigorous requirement of justice: to take care of them, there is need for "dues—tax relief, subsidies, indemnities, etc.—not regarding these as gratuitous handouts but rather as a modest retribution for the service of high social value that they render."[153]

---

[150] Pius XII, Address to Fathers of Families; *Ins.* no. 581; *Enchiridion Familiae,* 2.1416–17.

[151] Pius XII, Address to the Institute for Popular Homes, November 21, 1953; *Ins.* no. 705; *Enchiridion Familiae,* 2.1505–6; see also Radio message to the World, June 1, 1941; *Ins.* no. 461; *Enchiridion Familiae,* 2.984–87; Address to the Delegates of the International Bureau of Work, March 25, 1949; *Ins.* nos. 540–41; *Enchiridion Familiae,* 2.1371–72; Address to the Women of Catholic Action, July 24, 1949; *Ins.* no. 543; *Enchiridion Familiae,* 2.1373–81; Address to the International Union of Family Organizations; *Ins.* no. 550; *Enchiridion Familiae,* 2.1384; letter *Testes obsequii,* October 18, 1949; *Ins.* no. 558; *Enchiridion Familiae,* 2.1394–95.

[152] Pius XII, Radio message to the World, June 1, 1941; *Ins.* no. 462; *Enchiridion Familiae,* 2.984.

[153] Pius XII, Address to the International Union of Family Organizations; *Ins.* no. 551; *Enchiridion Familiae,* 2.1388; see also Address to the Italian Association of Large Families; *Ins.* nos. 763–67 (E.T., nos. 677–721); *Enchiridion Familiae,* 2.1668–82.

■ *Familiaris consortio* has recently insisted on these rights, reminding us—together with the synod—of the urgency of putting an end to the abuses of the state in this field: "Institutions and laws unjustly ignore the inviolable rights of the family and of the human person; and society, far from putting itself at the service of the family, attacks it violently in its values and fundamental requirements. Thus the family, which in God's plan is the basic cell of society and a subject of rights and duties before the State or any other community, finds itself the victim of society, of the delays and slowness with which it acts, and even of its blatant injustice."[154]

Catholics, who in many countries are still an important part of the population, cannot continue to tolerate, in a matter so decisive, the imposition by others, and against their deepest feelings, of anti-Christian solutions. As Pius XII said to the faithful of Austria, "It is necessary to insist that public legislation take due account of the will that animates the enormous majority of the people."[155] In sum, Catholics of every state ought to make their convictions known and to inform public opinion clearly "about the nature and extent of the inviolably sacred rights of the human person and of the family."[156] Toward this end, first the Synod of Bishops of 1980 and then *Familiaris consortio* promised the publication of a "Charter of the Rights of the Family".[157]

Here we deal definitively with a few well-known requirements: (a) respect for the indissolubility of marriage and of public morality; (b) the recognition of the rights of parents to educate their children and to promote opportune centers for study; (c) on the economic plane, the protection of the right to work, to family housing, to private property, and, often concretely, to a just family wage; and of the rights of a large family.[158]

[154] John Paul II, *Familiaris consortio*, no. 46; *Enchiridion Familiae*, 4.3289.

[155] Pius XII, Radio message to the Faithful of Austria, September 14, 1952; *Ins.* no. 669; *Enchiridion Familiae*, 2.1479–80.

[156] Pius XII, Address to French Journalists, March 17, 1946; *Ins.* no. 529; *Enchiridion Familiae*, 2.1344.

[157] John Paul II, *Familiaris consortio*, no. 46; *Enchiridion Familiae*, 4.3288–91. This "Charter" was published on October 22, 1983.

[158] On this see J. Orlandis, "La familia en la sociedad urbana e industrial", *Cuestiones fundamentales sobre matrimonio y familia*, pp. 553ff.

5. The Encyclical *Sacra Virginitas* and Other Teachings

Finally, among the teachings of Pius XII meriting attention are his solemn reconfirmation of the doctrine on the holiness of marriage and the excellence of virginal chastity, along with his directives regarding marriage cases.

The superiority of virginity and of celibacy over marriage was taught by the Lord himself, and "was solemnly defined as a dogma of divine faith by the holy council of Trent, and explained in the same way by all the holy Fathers and Doctors of the Church".[159] However, the Pope continues, since today this doctrine is once more attacked, it is necessary to reaffirm it, unmasking the false reasons used to deny it. Virginity — some say — is prejudicial to health; they thus forget the dominion of the spirit over the flesh and the energies that derive from grace. Others claim that it is easier to sanctify oneself in marriage than in virginity, "because marriage is a sacrament and virginity is not", and because solitude is an obstacle to personal perfection: but these are affirmations that experience does not corroborate and that are directly opposed to the words of our Lord and of the apostle.[160] Finally, they affirm that marriage plunges into society and thus renders the apostolate more efficacious and easier to carry out; they forget that, as experience teaches, souls dedicated totally to the Lord are the most firm support of all the apostolic work of the people of God, and that virginity and celibacy can live in the midst of the world, as did the first Christians and as many do today.

This uninterrupted teaching of the Church, faithful to Christ, on the value of virginity does not in any way mean the obscuring or placing into doubt of the holiness of marriage, which is also a *way of holiness:*[161] "Witness to this are the many holy men and women, who are publicly honored by the Church, and who were faithful spouses and stood out as an example of excellent fathers and mothers; indeed it is not rare to find married people who are very earnest in their efforts

---

[159] Pius XII, encyclical *Sacra virginitas*, March 25, 1954; *Ins.* no. 712 (E.T., no. 32); *Enchiridion Familiae*, 2.1531.

[160] Ibid., *Ins.* nos. 716–17 (E.T., nos. 37–39); *Enchiridion Familiae*, 2.1533–35.

[161] "The marital union of Christians is also a *way of holiness*", Pius XII, Address to New Spouses, August 13, 1941; *Ins.* no. 465; *Enchiridion Familiae*, 2.994–95. It is worth noting here that this expression was explicitly adopted by the Magisterium here for the first time.

for Christian perfection."[162] However, it will be necessary to wait for Vatican Council II, in its deepening of this constant reality in the life of the Church, for the Magisterium to declare not only the possibility but also the obligation of all spouses to strive for holiness.

Directives regarding marriage cases

The Magisterium, in its prophetic function of proclaiming with divine authority the truth taught by Christ, is concerned with combating the errors that are most widely disseminated at the time. The increasing mentality in favor of divorce thus gave rise to different interventions of the Pope intended to remind all of the perennial doctrine of the Church: whether in facing the danger of a penetration by osmosis of this mentality even among ecclesiastical judges themselves, by means of a laxist interpretation of the doctrine on the nullity of marriage, or by responding to problems of conscience that, with greater and greater frequency, civil laws openly contrary to the order of creation were posing for every honest magistrate. Specifically, *ecclesiastical tribunals, in their sentences on matrimonial cases, must faithfully interpret the norms of canon law according to the "mind" of the Supreme Pontiff;*[163] and his mind is this: "No other practice and norm can be valid within the Church save that established by God, the author of nature and of grace."[164] To this end, one must always respect with care the canon law in force; and one must be mindful of the principle that marriage enjoys the "favor of the law"; one cannot declare a marriage null unless there exists *true moral certainty* that such is the case.[165] Finally, as far as the dissolution of the bond in virtue of the Pauline privilege goes, or in the case of nonconsummated marriages, the criterion is to apply the vicarious power of the Supreme Pontiff according to the constant practice of the Church—and fidelity to Tradition bears witness to this—keeping present within one's mind the end of canon law, namely the "salvation of souls".[166]

With respect to matrimonial cases *in civil tribunals, the judges must*

---

[162] Pius XII, *Sacra virginitas; Ins.* no. 720 (E.T., no. 46); *Enchiridion Familiae*, 2.1539.

[163] Pius XII, Address to the Tribunal of the Rota, October 3, 1941; *Ins.* no. 467; *Enchiridion Familiae*, 2.1024–25.

[164] Ibid., Ins. no. 475; *Enchiridion Familiae*, 2.1031.

[165] Ibid., *Ins.* no. 472; *Enchiridion Familiae*, 2.1028–29.

[166] Ibid., *Ins.* nos. 473–76; *Enchiridion Familiae*, 2.1029–31; see also Pius XII, Address to the Tribunal of the Rota, October 6, 1946; *Ins.* nos. 531–36; *Enchiridion Familiae*, 2.1353–57.

remember that human laws directly contrary to the divine, such as those that establish divorce, can never oblige in conscience; they can be applied, if necessary, according to the moral principles that regulate material cooperation in evil. No judge can rightly abdicate his proper responsibility, turning it over entirely to an unjust law; the author of the law is, surely, the one principally responsible; but the one who applies it becomes "a concomitant cause, and therefore really responsible for its effects". Therefore, in order that the action of a judge who applies such a law can be licit, the following conditions are required: (a) that one is *never* involved in *formal cooperation*, i.e., the judge "cannot by his decision oblige anyone to an act that is intrinsically immoral, because this is against the laws of God and of the Church", but is only tolerating such an act, always avoiding scandal—and to do this it is necessary to make it clear that he "in no way condones or approves the unjust law" (he can do this, for example, by saying explicitly to the spouses that their marriage remains wholly valid in the eyes of God, even though the state considers it dissolved); (b) moreover, all the conditions of the indirectly voluntary must concur, in particular, because of the gravity of the case, it must be such that the solution provides "the *only means* of avoiding an even greater evil".[167]

The judgment of the Roman Rota on the ends of marriage, January 22, 1944

Here we are dealing with a vote, made for a particular case regarding the nullity of marriage, which contains the official summary of rotal jurisprudence on the subject; although it does not properly constitute the Magisterium, it enjoys a certain authority—as an authorized opinion—both by having been inserted into the *Acta Apostolicae Sedis* and by the use that it has received in the documents of the Magisterium.

In substance, it repeats with greater particularity the doctrine received in the 1917 Code of Canon Law. The *primary* end of marriage is the procreation and education of children (nos. 11–16); the secondary end, or, better, *secondary ends,* are "the mutual help" between the spouses and "the remedy for concupiscence" (nos. 17–20). That which delimits

---

[167] Pius XII, Address to Catholic Jurists, November 6, 1949; *Ins.* nos. 559–63; *Enchiridion Familiae*, 2.1395–98.

and defines the matrimonial union is its primary end: not every union between a man and a woman is a marriage, but only that union which unites them indissolubly for the whole of their life and has as its end the procreation and education of children; therefore, this "end distinguishes the conjugal union from every other human association" (no. 21). This does not mean, in contrast to what some have claimed, to attribute to the traditional doctrine a reduction of conjugal love to a secondary end: conjugal love is *not* a secondary end of marriage; the secondary end of marriage is constituted by the remedy for concupiscence and the mutual help of the spouses. Moreover, we must never think that, in the thought of the Church, the characterization of procreation and education of children as the primary end tends to obscure or devalue the importance of mutual help between the spouses, as if the Church understood the secondary end in the sense of a good of only secondary importance; to the contrary, she wishes to express that it is a second end proper to marriage and inseparable from the first. Therefore, she considers that both ends will be realized only as a unity in which the primary end necessarily includes in itself the promotion of mutual help and indeed constitutes the best way through which this can be realized.[168]

■ As we have already emphasized, all this is connected with the problem—more properly that of canon law than of classical theology—of the juridical structure of marriage. After Vatican Council II, there were not lacking authors according to whom the canonical placing of "the essence of marriage in the right to the body or in the bond alone implies a reduction of its essence",[169] and for whom there is, hopefully,

---

[168] This is a thought which is found in St. Thomas: "For St. Thomas the primary end (the procreation and education of children) and the secondary end (mutual help) are both of a purely human order (i.e., not common to lower animals . . .) and they are united and interpenetrating. St. Thomas also could write that the secondary end is contained in the primary, for the communication between the spouses—the *communicatio operum* —is ordered to the education and well-being of the children (*Supplement*, q. 49, a. 2, ad 1); and one can add, without fear of being unfaithful to him, that the successful completion of the work of educating the children simultaneously procures for the conjugal community, for the spouses themselves, their full completion, in such manner that the primary end contributes to the attaining of the secondary end: these finalities are intimately united and coordinated": Servais Pinckaers, "Ce que le Moyen Age pensait du mariage", in *L'Evangile et la morale* (Fribourg: Editions Université, Fribourg Suisse; Paris: Editions du Cerf, 1990), p. 154; see, in general, pp. 152ff.

[169] J. Hervada and P. Lombardía, "Derecho matrimonial", pt. 3, chap. 1, *El Derecho del Pueblo de Dios* (Pamplona: Eunsa, 1970), p. 197.

a juridical formula more adequate to the existential reality of marriage. "We must ask ourselves whether there exists a concept that is, on the one hand, juridical, and in which, on the other hand, the subjects have—by definition—greater relevance; in other words, we are concerned with a notion, applicable to marriage, whose primary note is a union between persons. And in fact this notion exists, namely, the idea of *community*."[170]

Undoubtedly, the juridical notion of community—a perpetual community between a man and a woman, in which they unite their souls and their bodies in order to procreate and educate children—allows us to make more precise in a better way the place of love in marriage, in a way perfectly in accord with its primary finality. However, we must not forget that the experience and wisdom of many authors and pastors, learned and prudent, in the course of many centuries, contributed to the previous [canonical] construction of marriage as the granting of the "ius ad corpus". The Council has defined marriage as a community of life and love, and the New Code of Canon Law (1983) has given juridical formulation of this: "the community of the whole of life, by its nature ordered to the good of the spouses and to the procreation and education of children". This formulation (can. 1055 in the 1983 Code) is more precise and fitting for our times. But there is need, acting prudently, to integrate into this the wisdom already acquired in order to avoid losing a patrimony that, since we are not its authors or fathers, we are obliged to hand on.[171]

[170] Ibid., p. 199.
[171] See, on the dangers of a superficial attitude in this matter, the interesting study of L. Del Amo, "El amor conyugal y la nulidad del matrimonio en la jurisprudencia", *Ius Canonicum* 17, no. 34 (July–December 1977): 75–104.

Chapter Five

THE POSITION OF THE MAGISTERIUM AT THE OPENING OF VATICAN COUNCIL II

Christian doctrine is a living treasure: "The words I have spoken to you are Spirit and life" (Jn 6:64). Because it is a living reality, the deposit of revelation, while remaining identical with itself, offers new fruits in every age that, born of the same seed, manifest themselves in a constant and indefectible continuity: *in the same sense and the same meaning (in eodem sensu et eadem sententia).* [1]

Before beginning our study of Vatican Council II, by means of which the Holy Spirit has spoken to men and women of our age, it seems useful to present a summary of the situation of the deposit of revelation, as it had been already fixed by the Magisterium, because this will be the seed that in the Council will produce new fruits.

Another reason, this time historical, counsels this. There are not lacking those who want to present Vatican Council II as if it were "an absolutely new point of departure", forgetting its roots in Tradition.[2]

1. Continuity of Vatican Council II with the Previous Magisterium

The correct and proper application of the Council is of capital importance for the renewal of the Church. Among other things, this requires that it be interpreted in the light of Tradition and in continuity with the entire previous Magisterium.

---

[1] St. Vincent of Lerins, *Commonitorium*, no. 23.

[2] Cf. Philippe Delhaye, *La scienza del bene e del male. La morale del Vaticano II e il "metaconcilio"* (Milan: Ed. Ares, 1981), p. 176; also E. Lio, *"Morale perenne" e "Morale nuova" nella formazione ed educazione nella coscienza* (Rome: Città Nuova Editrice, 1979), pp. 60–85.

Pope John Paul II has underscored the importance and urgency of this faithful application for the unity and strengthening of the Church: today obedience to the Holy Spirit

> is expressed in the authentic realization of the duties indicated by the Council, in full accord with the teaching proposed in it . . . ; its "integral" teaching, that is, its teaching understood in the light of all the holy Tradition and rooted in the steadfast Magisterium of the Church herself. . . . The Church, the living community of the children of God united in truth and love, must make a great effort, at this time, to enter on the way of realizing Vatican II. . . . Only this way, that of an honest and sincere obedience to the Spirit of truth, can serve the unity, and at the same time, the spiritual power of the Church.[3]

With these words, the Holy Father forestalls possible misunderstandings and misconceptions whether on the part of those unwilling to change or on the part of that sector of theology that, as we have just said, wanted to present Vatican Council II as a phenomenon of breaking with Tradition.

> ■ The difficulties in applying the Council did not surprise those who were well-informed. On the contrary, matters have often been this way. We remember that the Council of Trent was compelled to create a congregation to assure its proper interpretation and that, despite the attention of the popes, it took more than a century to prepare the seminaries called for by that Council. But the phenomenon that occurred in the wake of Vatican Council II can be said to be, in truth, novel, because — precisely in the name of the "spirit" of the Council — its true content has been radically misinterpreted and misunderstood, so much so that one can even speak of a true metamorphosis of the Council: the "metacouncil" that "not only leaves the Council in the past but wishes to go beyond it, to surpass it, and to change it".[4] An attitude of this kind, in addition to generating useless polemics, has provoked misunderstandings, throwing obstacles in the way of applying the conciliar teachings and of bringing to maturation not a few of its fruits. Because of this, it is useful to emphasize this insistence on the part of Pope John Paul II: only in the light of Tradition and of the entire previous

---

[3] John Paul II, Address at the Plenary Meeting of the Sacred College, November 6, 1979, nos. 5–6.

[4] Philippe Delhaye, "Metaconcilio: la mancanza di discernimento", *Cris Documenti*, no. 43 (Milan: Ed. Ares, 1981), p. 8.

Magisterium can the last Council be understood in its richness; otherwise it will be deformed.[5]

Continuity is a characteristic of every act of the Magisterium, but Vatican Council II has willed to emphasize this explicitly in order to avoid badly misinterpreting its pastoral language. In particular, the Council has insisted on its own continuity with all the elements of the biblical conception of man that stand at the root of Christian morality, such as the dogma of original sin, the relationships between nature and grace, the radical gratuity of the latter, etc., even if at times it uses a more pastoral terminology:

> From its very beginning Vatican Council II linked itself to the whole of Tradition and, even more explicitly, to the Councils of Trent and of Vatican I (see, for example, *Dei verbum*, no. 1). It wants to continue these and to present them in a clearer way, more accessible to men of the twentieth century. It often seeks to translate technical language into more pastoral terms. In *Lumen gentium* (no. 59) and elsewhere it will speak of "original blemish" (*originalis labes*) rather than of "original sin" (*peccatum originale*), because the word "sin" comes to be used always to designate only the taking of a position, directly and knowingly, willed by the person himself. It will speak only a few times of the "supernatural" (17 times), but it will insist on the divinization of man, on the fact that salvation history not be confused with human history. Christ will be constantly pointed out as the only Savior of mankind. The conciliar Fathers were not able to foresee that the metacouncil would look on Vatican Council II as an absolute beginning, to the point that it could regard as abolished everything that happened before that the Council did not take care to reaffirm explicitly.[6]

Moreover, Vatican Council II has confirmed in an express way the objectivity of the moral order in all its content and, specifically, that of conjugal morality: the inseparability between love and procreation; the condemnation of abortion and of contraception, the indissolubility of marriage, etc. It is

---

[5] Cf. on this matter the decisive work of Josef Cardinal Ratzinger, *The Ratzinger Report* (San Francisco: Ignatius Press, 1985); see also Ramón García de Haro, "La sabiduría moral cristiana", *Actas del III Simposio Internacional de Teología de la Universidad de Navarra* (Pamplona: Eunsa, 1982), pp. 177ff.

[6] Delhaye, *La scienza del bene e del male*, pp. 63–64; cf. also Antonio Miralles, "Naturaleza y sacramento en la doctrina del Concilio Vaticano II sobre el matrimonio", *Cuestiones fundamentales sobre matrimonio y familia: Actas del II Simposio Internacional de Teología* (Pamplona: Eunsa, 1980), pp. 151ff.

unjust to attribute to Vatican Council II the claim of leaving conscience without the guidance of Tradition and the Magisterium. How
could one imagine that such would be the fruit of the long work of
bishops and their periti, united under the action of the Holy Spirit?
The Council, in fact, reaffirmed the objectivity of Christian morality,
warning that it does not belong to conscience to create values (cf.
Gaudium et spes, no. 16; *Dignitatis humanae,* no. 3); at the same time it
never stopped calling to mind that only in Christ can these values be
fully known (cf. *Gaudium et spes,* nos. 22, 28, etc.).[7]

■ Thus, the first chapter of the second part of *Gaudium et spes,* devoted
to marriage and the family, explicitly refers to the principal previous
writings of the Magisterium; in particular, *Casti connubii* is cited five
times; likewise the two basic documents of Pius XII on conjugal morality
are noted: his Address to the Italian Catholic Union of Midwives of
October 29, 1951, and that of January 20, 1958, to the Italian Association
of Large Families. The other principal sources for this chapter are, in
addition to sacred Scripture, St. Augustine and St. Thomas, as the most
representative authorities of the theological tradition of the Church.[8]

2. Firmly Established Points in the Teaching of the Church

**When Vatican Council II began, the ensemble of revealed doc-
trine on marriage and the family had already in large measure
been explicitly established by the Magisterium.**

We refer here to irreformable doctrines or to those, at least, that can
be considered beyond discussion by theologians, taking into account
the insistence with which they have been proclaimed. As the Council
reminds us, in addition to that truth "regarding faith and morals" that
the Magisterium "sanctions with a definitive act",[9] those truths also

---

[7] Cf. García de Haro, "La sabiduría moral cristiana", pp. 177ff.; William E. May, "The
Moral Methodology of Vatican Council II and the Teaching of *Humanae Vitae* and *Persona
Humana*", *Anthropotes* 5, no. 1 (May 1989): 29–45.

[8] Cf. John Finnis, "The Natural Law, Objective Morality, and Vatican II", in *Principles of
Catholic Moral Life,* ed. William E. May (Chicago: Franciscan Herald Press, 1980), pp. 113–49.

[9] Vatican Council II, dogmatic constitution *Lumen gentium,* November 21, 1964, no. 25;
Vatican Council I, dogmatic constitution *Pastor aeternus,* H. Denzinger and A. Schoenmetzer,
Enchiridion Symbolorum Definitionum et Declarationum de rebus fidei et morum, 34th ed. (Barcelona-
Rome: Herder, 1967), (DS), no. 1839.

are beyond discussion to which the popes show they want given a firm adhesion of will and mind: this will be made known "principally either by the character of the documents in question, or by the frequency with which a certain doctrine is proposed, or by the manner in which the doctrine is formulated".[10]

■ Precisely because of this, Vatican Council II in many of its documents—particularly in *Gaudium et spes*—is concerned not so much with offering a detailed exposition of the ensemble of Catholic truth, "but rather with showing and inculcating its applications to the conditions of our age and to pastoral needs of the day".[11]

A. On the nature, goods, and ends of marriage

1. *Marriage has been instituted by God and not by man; after the original fall, it has been restored to its original dignity and raised to the level of a sacrament by Christ:* Council of Florence, decree *Pro Armenis* (DS 1327);[12] Council of Trent, session 24, decree *De doctrina sacramenti matrimonii* (DS 1800; EF, 1.142–43) and canon 1 (DS 1801; EF, 1.144–46); Pius VI, letter *Deessemus nobis*, September 16, 1788 (EF, 1.312);[13] Leo XIII, *Inscrutabili*, April 21, 1878 (*Ins.* no. 123; EF, 1.463–64); encyclical *Arcanum divinae sapientiae*, February 10, 1880 (*Ins.* nos. 147–53; EF, 1.481–84); Pius XI, encyclical *Casti connubii*, December 31, 1930 (*Ins.* nos. 267–68; EF, 1.712–13).

2. *Every marriage comes to be through the consent of the spouses, but with a divinely established content: endowed with unity and indissolubility, and ordained to the procreation and education of children:* Council of Florence, decree *Pro Armenis* (DS 1327; EF, 1.137–38); Council of Trent, decree *De doctrina sacramenti matrimonii*, session 24 (DS 1797–98; EF, 1.142–43) and canons 2, 5, and 7 (DS 1802, 1805, and 1807; EF, 1.144–46); Benedict XIV, encyclical *Matrimonii*, April 11, 1741 (*Ins.* no. 1; EF, 1.225–26); apostolic constitution *Dei miseratione*, November 3, 1741 (*Ins.* no. 3; EF,

---

[10] *Lumen gentium*, no. 25.

[11] The introductory *Relatio* to the schema of May 28, 1965, of *Gaudium et spes*: *Acta Synodalia Sacrosancti Concilii Oecumenici Vaticani II* (Vatican City: Typis Polyglottis Vaticanis), vol. IV, pars I, p. 521; see also vol. III, pars VI, p. 5; vol. IV, pars VII, pp. 471–72.

[12] *Enchiridion Familiae: Textos del Magisterio Pontificio y Conciliar sobre el Matrimonio y la Familia (Siglos I a XX)*, ed. A. Sarmiento and J. Escrivà-Ivars, vol. 1 (Madrid: Ediciones Rialp, 1992), pp. 847–48 (henceforth in this chapter abbreviated EF).

[13] *Insegnamenti pontifici*, vol. 1 of *Il matrimonio* (Rome: Ed. Paoline, 1957), (*Ins.*), no. 43.

1.227–28); Leo XIII, encyclical *Quod apostolici,* December 28, 1878 (*Ins.* no. 127; EF, 1.471–73); encyclical *Arcanum divinae sapientiae* (*Ins.* nos. 147–48; EF, 1.483–85); Pius XI, encyclical *Casti connubii* (*Ins.* nos. 267–84, 294–97; EF, 1.712–15, 721–25); Pius XII, encyclical *Sertum laetitia,* November 1, 1939 (*Ins.* no. 423; EF, 2.855–56).

■ Before the Council, the Magisterium had not clearly and unequivocally pronounced on the nature of the marriage contract. In the most constant theological tradition, it appeared as a consent to the union, exclusive and indissoluble, between a man and a woman, with the end of procreating and educating children; on the other hand, in the canonical doctrine of the last few centuries, it was regarded more as a contract of yielding rights (principally, the *ius ad corpus*). Not rarely, the Magisterium adopted the expression, consonant with the theological tradition, of "a conjugal society": thus Leo XIII, encyclical *Rerum novarum,* May 15, 1891 (*Ins.* no. 210); encyclical *Arcanum divinae sapientiae* (*Ins.* no. 153); the Magisterium also used the language of "a spiritual and moral union": Pius XII, Address of November 1, 1953 (*Ins.* no. 705); and others of similar nature. However, sometimes—at least in the *Codex Iuris Canonici* (of 1917)—it adopted simply the idea of consent to the yielding of the mutual right to the body (can. 1081, par. 2).

3. *Marriage has, in addition, as secondary ends the mutual help of the spouses and the remedy for concupiscence:* 1917 *Codex Iuris Canonici* (can. 1013, par. 1); Pius XI, encyclical *Casti connubii* (*Ins.* no. 319; EF, 1.745); Pius XII, Address to the Tribunal of the Rota, October 3, 1941 (*Ins.* no. 470; EF, 2.1027); Decree of the Holy Office, March 29, 1944 (DS 3838); Address to the Italian Catholic Union of Midwives, October 29, 1951 (*Ins.* nos. 633–34; EF, 2.1451); Address of March 19, 1956 (*Ins.* nos. 736–37).

■ Let us repeat—as we have already had occasion to notice several times—the Magisterium had never understood conjugal love as a secondary end of marriage. Therefore, Vatican Council II will be able to locate it—without disturbing but rather developing the Tradition—as the formal, life-giving principle of the conjugal community: a community of life and of love, whose end is the procreation and education of children.

4. *The consent of the spouses, or the conjugal contract, is the sign of the sacrament; therefore, among Christians, there cannot be a marriage contract*

without its being at the same time a sacrament: Pius IX, Address of September 27, 1852 (*Ins.* no. 101; EF, 1.398–99); *Syllabus of Errors,* December 8, 1864 (*Ins.* no. 114; EF, 1.436); Leo XIII, letter *Ci siamo,* June 1, 1879 (*Ins.* no. 132; EF, 1.475–76); encyclical *Arcanum divinae sapientiae* (*Ins.* no. 169; EF, 1.499); letter *Il divisamento,* February 8, 1893 (*Ins.* no. 218; EF, 1.556–57); St. Pius X, letter *Afflictum proprioribus,* November 24, 1906 (*Ins.* no. 252; EF, 1.612–13); Pius XI, encyclical *Casti connubii* (*Ins.* no. 270; EF, 1.733–34); Pius XII, Address to New Spouses, March 5, 1941 (*Ins.* no. 446ff.; EF, 2.964ff.).

5. *The sacrament of marriage confers on those who have the right dispositions habitual grace and the title to actual graces necessary to live holily the duties of their state of life:* Council of Trent, session 24, decree *De doctrina sacramenti matrimonii* (DS 1799; EF, 1.142–43); 1917 *Codex Iuris Canonici,* canon 1110; Leo XIII, encyclical *Arcanum divinae sapientiae* (*Ins.* no. 174; EF, 1.488); Pius XI, encyclical *Casti connubii* (*Ins.* nos. 301–5; EF, 1.734–36); Pius XII, Address to New Spouses, July 12, 1939 (*Ins.* no. 417; EF, 2.838–40); Address to New Spouses, January 17, 1940 (*Ins.* no. 429; EF, 2.877–78); Address of February 17, 1945 (*Ins.* no. 513; EF, 2.1310–12); Address to the Italian Catholic Union of Midwives (*Ins.* nos. 625–26; EF, 2.1447–48); encyclical *Sacra virginitas,* March 25, 1954 (*Ins.* nos. 716–17; EF, 2.1533–34).

6. *The ensemble of the perfections that God gave to marriage can be summed up in three goods: children, fidelity, and the sacrament:* Council of Florence, decree *Pro Armenis* (DS 1327; EF, 1.137–38); Pius XI, encyclical *Casti connubii* (*Ins.* nos. 273–305; EF, 1.715–36).

B. *On conjugal morality*

1. *Marriage is a good and holy reality: in it the spouses can seek holiness; but the charism of celibacy is higher:* First Council of Toledo, October 400, canon 236 (DS 206; EF, 1.16); Council of Braga, May 1, 563, canons 11 to 13 (DS 461–63; EF, 1.41); Lateran Council II, March 4, 1139, canon 23 (DS 718; EF, 1.104); Innocent III, epistula *Eius exemplo,* December 18, 1208 (DS 794; EF, 1.124); Lateran Council IV, February 4, 1215 (DS 802; EF, 1.125); Council of Florence, decree *Pro Jacobitis,* February 4, 1442 (DS 1353; EF, 1.139–40); Council of Trent, session 24, decree *De doctrina sacramenti matrimonii,* canon 10 (DS 1810; EF, 1.146); Leo XIII, letter *Il divisamento* (*Ins.* no. 222; EF, 1.558); Pius XII, Address to the Discalced

Carmelites, September 23, 1951 (*Ins.* no. 591; EF, 2.1453); encyclical *Sacra virginitas* (*Ins.* nos. 707–20; EF, 2.1530–34).

■ Note that before Vatican Council II the possibility, but not the *duty, of all* Christian spouses to seek this holiness had been explicitly formulated. This truth is clear in Scripture and in the life of the early Christians, but in time it was forgotten, and it was the work of Vatican Council II to repropose it vigorously.

2. *Marriage is ruled, in the development of its ends and goods, by divine laws that men cannot change:* to fulfill these laws is the only way to the perfection and happiness of the spouses and the good of society: Council of Trent, session 24, decree *De doctrina sacramenti matrimonii* (DS 1800; EF, 1.142); Pius VIII, encyclical *Traditi humilitati,* May 24, 1829 (*Ins.* no. 64; EF, 1.354–55); Leo XIII, encyclical *Arcanum divinae sapientiae* (*Ins.* no. 152; EF, 1.483–84); Pius XI, encyclical *Casti connubii* (*Ins.* no. 267; EF, 1.712–13); Pius XII, Address to the International Union of Family Organizations, September 20, 1949 (*Ins.* nos. 545–46; EF, 2.1383–84); Address to the Cardinals, Archbishops and Bishops, November 2, 1950 (*Ins.* nos. 571–72; EF, 2.1406–7).

3. *Through the divine will, marriage is at the service of life, which is sacred from the moment of conception: for no reason whatsoever can abortion be licit,* nor any attack upon life already conceived: Stephen V, letter *Consuluisti de infantibus,* September 14, 891 (DS 670; EF, 1.87); Innocent XI, decree *Sancti Officii,* March 2, 1679, *Errores doctrinae moralis laxioris,* no. 34 (DS 2134; EF, 1.216); Leo XIII, *Responsa Sancti Officii,* August 14, 1889 (DS 3258); *Responsa Sancti Officii,* July 24, 1895 (DS 3298); *Responsa Sancti Officii,* May 4, 1898 (DS 3336–38); Pius XI, encyclical *Casti connubii* (*Ins.* nos. 323–27; EF, 1.746–47); Pius XII, Address to the Italian Catholic Union of Midwives (*Ins.* nos. 597–98; EF, 2.1429–30); Address to the Associations of Large Families, November 26, 1951 (*Ins.* nos. 660–65; EF, 2.1467–69).

4. *It is never right for the spouses to break, by their own free will, the bond between conjugal love and procreation. Every kind of contraception and steril- ization is intrinsically immoral.* In particular, on the *intrinsically* immoral character, of itself contrary to the divine law, of every perversion of the conjugal act, see: St. Pius V, *Catechism of the Council of Trent,* part II, chapter 7, no. 13 (EF, 1.162–63); Pius VII, *Responsa S. Paenitentiariae,* April 23, 1822 (DS 2715; EF, 1.349); Gregory XVI, *Responsa S. Paeni-*

tentiariae, June 1, 1842 (DS 2758–60; EF, 1.382–83); Leo XIII, *Responsa S. Paenitentiariae*, March 10, 1886 (DS 3185–87; EF, 1.527–28); Benedict XV, *Responsa S. Paenitentiariae*, June 3, 1916 (DS 3638–40; EF, 1.623–24); Pius XI, encyclical *Casti connubii* (*Ins.* nos. 314–15, 320; EF, 1.742–43, 745–46); apostolic letter *Con singolare compiacenza*, January 18, 1939 (*Ins.* no. 413; EF, 1.819–20); Pius XII, Address to New Spouses, March 5, 1941 (*Ins.* nos. 451–53; EF, 2.970–71); Address to the Italian Catholic Union of Midwives (*Ins.* no. 613; EF, 2.1439–41); Address to the Members of the Second World Congress on Fertility and Sterility, May 19, 1956 (*Ins.* nos. 740–45; EF, 2.1600). On the illicitness of direct sterilization, whether temporary or permanent, for any reason whatsoever, see: Pius XI, encyclical *Casti connubii* (*Ins.* nos. 328–31; EF, 1.751–52); Address of December 23, 1933 (*Ins.* nos. 406–7); Pius XII, Address of September 7, 1953 (*Ins.* nos. 684–89; EF, 2.1489–94); Address to the 26th Congress of Urology, October 8, 1953 (*Ins.* nos. 693–96; EF, 2.1495–1503); Address to the Seventh International Hematological Congress, September 12, 1958 (*Ins.* nos. 779–785; EF, 2.1697–1701).

5. *On the other hand, the use of marriage limited to infertile periods is licit, when there exist serious reasons or motives:* Leo XIII, *Responsa S. Paenitentiariae*, June 16, 1880 (DS 3148; EF, 1.517); Pius XII, Address to the Italian Catholic Union of Midwives (*Ins.* nos. 617–22; EF, 2.1441–45); Address to the Associations of Large Families (*Ins.* no. 667; EF, 2.1472–73); Address to the Seventh International Hematological Congress (*Ins.* nos. 787–90; EF, 2.1702–3).

■ The Church has always taught that it is licit to abstain from the use of marriage, for a set time and for religious motives, when both spouses consent to it and there is no reason to fear incontinence (cf. 1 Cor 7:5); moreover, at times she counseled it (see *Catechism of the Council of Trent*, part II, chapter 7, no. 34; EF, 1.182–83). Moreover, she has never condemned the use of marriage when, for natural causes, the spouses have not been able to generate life (cf. Pius XI, encyclical *Casti connubii, Ins.* nos. 319 and 366; EF, 1.745).

The problem arose after the discovery of infertile periods, because to make use of marriage only in these periods seems to carry with it the willingness of excluding procreation. Although the question was discussed from the time of Leo XIII to Pius XII, there nonetheless remained some particular points to determine more precisely at the time of the opening of the Council. Thus, it fell to *Humanae vitae* to deepen the thought on this matter and to clarify definitively—and in this way to originate a teaching of the ordinary and universal Magisterium—that biochemical methods are a form of contraception.

6. *Every attack on conjugal fidelity, even if only in desire, is intrinsically and gravely sinful. Catechism of the Council of Trent,* part II, chapter 7, no. 24 (EF, 1.174–75); Pius XI, encyclical *Casti connubii* (*Ins.* nos. 332–34; EF, 1.721–22); Pius XII, Address to the Parish Priests and Lenten Preachers of Rome, February 23, 1944 (*Ins.* no. 507; EF, 2.1282–84); Radio message to the Families of France, June 17, 1945 (*Ins.* no. 515; EF, 2.1315–18).

■ *Artificial fecundation* is also an attack on conjugal fidelity: Pius XII, Address to the Fourth International Congress of Catholic Medical Doctors, September 29, 1949 (*Ins.* nos. 553–57; EF, 2.1390–94); Address to the Italian Catholic Union of Midwives (*Ins.* nos. 637–39; EF, 2.1454); Address to the Members of the Second World Congress on Fertility and Sterility (*Ins.* nos. 739–45; EF, 2.1598–1600). The same is true of everything that is contrary to *mutual love* and *the order of the familial society:* Pius XI, encyclical *Casti connubii* (*Ins.* nos. 335ff.; EF, 1.722ff.; Pius XII, Address to the Cardinals, Archbishops, and Bishops (*Ins.* no. 571; EF, 2.1406–7); Radio message of December 24, 1953 (*Ins.* no. 706; EF, 2.1506–7). The formulation of a complete and definitive doctrine on artificial fecundation had, however, to wait for the *Donum Vitae* (*Instruction on Respect for Human Life in Its Origin and on the Dignity of Procreation*) of February 22, 1987.

7. *Christian morality* demands that none of the so-called "negative" precepts—those that mark off the limits beyond which the order of the divine law is ruptured—be violated; but Christian morality is not limited to this: *it requires, above all, the fulfillment of all the "positive" duties that actively lead to the attainment of the three "goods of marriage", i.e., children, fidelity, and the sacrament, synthesized, in practice, in the precept of conjugal and familial charity:* that love between the spouses, and between parents and children which, since it is one of the most profound inclinations of nature, comes to be elevated and strengthened by the bond of charity, whose foundation is the love of charity toward God (and includes, in practice, the recognition and fulfillment as a "sweet yoke" of the "negative" precepts): *Catechism of the Council of Trent,* part II, chapter 7, nos. 25–27, 33; EF, 1.176–78; 181–82; Pius XI, encyclical *Casti connubii* (*Ins.* nos. 273–80, 285–93, 304–5; EF, 1.714–15, 718–20, 723–25); Pius XII, Address to New Spouses, March 5, 1941 (*Ins.* nos.

445ff.; EF, 2.967); Address of March 22, 1942 (*Ins.* nos. 480ff.); Radio message of June 17, 1945 (*Ins.* nos. 514ff.; EF, 2.1315ff.); Letter of September 19, 1954 (*Ins.* nos. 724ff.); Address to the Italian Association of Large Families, January 20, 1958 (*Ins.* nos. 763ff.; EF, 2.1668ff.).

C. *On the relationship between the family and society*

1. *The family is, by God's will, the institution destined for the handing on and development of human life; as such it is prior to society, of which it is the principle and foundation:* Leo XIII, encyclical *Quod apostolici* (*Ins.* nos. 126–27; EF, 1.471–73); encyclical *Arcanum divinae sapientiae* (*Ins.* nos. 174–75; EF, 1.501–2); encyclical *Sapientiae christianae,* January 10, 1890 (*Ins.* nos. 206–7; EF, 1.541–42); Pius XI, encyclical *Ubi arcano,* December 23, 1922 (*Ins.* nos. 257–59; EF, 1.675); encyclical *Lux veritatis,* December 25, 1931 (*Ins.* no. 404); Pius XII, letter *Czestochoviensis Beatae Mariae,* January 17, 1946 (*Ins.* no. 524; EF, 2.1345); Address to the International Union of Family Organizations (*Ins.* nos. 544ff.; EF, 2.1383ff.); radio message to the World, December 24, 1952 (*Ins.* no. 673; EF, 2.1482).

2. *The rights of the family, which protect the fulfillment of its duties and obligations, are sacred; the state cannot fail to recognize them or stamp them underfoot; rather it must protect them:* Leo XIII, encyclical *Quod apostolici* (*Ins.* no. 126; EF, 1.471); encyclical *Rerum novarum,* May 15, 1891 (*Ins.* nos. 210–13); Pius XI, encyclical *Divini Redemptoris,* March 19, 1937 (*Ins.* nos. 409–10; EF, 1.812–14); Pius XII, radio message of April 1, 1941 (*Ins.* nos. 462–64); radio message of June 13, 1942 (*Ins.* nos. 500–501); Address to French Journalists, March 17, 1946 (*Ins.* no. 529; EF, 2.1349); Address to the International Union of Family Organizations (*Ins.* nos. 545–46; EF, 2.1383–89); Address to Fathers of Families, November 18, 1951 (*Ins.* nos. 578–83).

■ The Council will bring a deepening to this matter, proclaiming that the proper mission of lay people in the Church is to sanctify from within the structures of society: with absolute freedom in all that God has left to the choice of men. Moreover, *Familiaris consortio* will go even further, making precise the prior responsibility of the family in its own defense: without entrusting itself too much to the powers either of the state or of any other structure.

D. *On the powers of Church and state in marriage matters*

1. *The authority of the Church over the marriage of the baptized is of divine institution. It is founded on its proper and exclusive power over the sacraments:* Council of Trent, session 24, canons 4, 7, 8, and 12 (DS 1804, 1807, 1808, and 1812; EF, 1.144–46); Pius VI, letter *Post factum tibi,* February 2, 1782 (*Ins.* no. 37; EF, 1.299–300); letter, *Deessemus nobis,* September 16, 1788 (*Ins.* nos. 43–44; EF, 1.312); Gregory XVI, encyclical *Commissum divinitus,* May 17, 1835 (*Ins.* nos. 82–83; EF, 1.369–70); Pius IX, apostolic letter *Ad Apostolicae Sedis,* August 28, 1851 (*Ins.* nos. 91–93; EF, 1.390–91); *Syllabus* (*Ins.* nos. 68–70, 109–11; EF, 1.436–437); Leo XIII, letter *Ci siamo* (*Ins.* no. 130; EF, 1.476); encyclical *Arcanum divinae sapientiae* (*Ins.* nos. 153ff., 165ff.; EF, 1.496, 512–13); letter *Il divisamento* (*Ins.* no. 218; EF, 1.553f.); St. Pius X, letter *Afflictum proprioribus* (*Ins.* nos. 250–52; EF, 1.612–14); Pius XI, encyclical *Casti connubii* (*Ins.* nos. 340–44; EF, 1.730ff.); Pius XII, Address of October 3, 1941 (*Ins.* nos. 471ff.; EF, 2.1022ff.); Message of June 10, 1958 (*Ins.* nos. 769ff.; EF, 2.1683ff.).

2. *This power of the Church extends to whatever bears upon the existence and nature of the conjugal bond and its religious effects:* it extends, therefore, to all the conditions required for the validity of the conjugal contract (impediments and juridical form) and to the relevant judicial processes; moreover, it includes the *vicarious* power of the Roman Pontiff to dissolve marriages between non-Christians, by virtue of the Pauline privilege, and also the nonconsummated marriages of the faithful: Second Council of Lyon, June 2, 1274 (DS 860); Council of Trent, session 24, canons 4, 6, 7, 9, 11, and 12 (DS 1804ff.; EF, 1.144–46); Benedict XIV, constitution *Ad Apostolicae servitutis,* February 25, 1742 (*Ins.* no. 9); apostolic constitution *Apostolici ministerii,* September 16, 1747 (*Ins.* no. 24; EF, 1.256–59); Pius VI, *Post factum tibi* (*Ins.* nos. 37–38; EF, 1.299–300); letter *Deessemus nobis* (*Ins.* nos. 43–46; EF, 1.312); Pius IX, *Syllabus* (*Ins.* nos. 109–15; EF, 1.436–37); Leo XIII, encyclical *Arcanum divinae sapientiae* (*Ins.* nos. 160–68; EF 1.512–13); letter *Quam religiosa,* August 10, 1898 (*Ins.* no. 241; EF, 1.578–79); Pius XI, encyclical *Casti connubii* (*Ins.* no. 354; EF, 1.756ff.); Pius XII, Address to New Spouses, April 22, 1942 (*Ins.* no. 484; EF, 2.1111–19); Address to the 26th Congress of Urology (*Ins.* no. 703; EF, 2.1502).

■ Since the natural institution of marriage itself proceeds from God, the competence of the Church to defend the essential properties, goods, ends, and laws of every marriage follows therefrom, even among the nonbaptized; these properties derive from human nature itself, conformably to the will of the Creator: thus, Leo XIII, encyclical *Arcanum divinae sapientiae* (*Ins.* nos. 143–44; EF, 1.482–83); letter *Il divisamento* (*Ins.* no. 221; EF, 1.557ff.); Pius XI, encyclical *Casti connubii* (*Ins.* nos. 316 and 368; EF, 1.742–43).

3. *The power of the state, in turn, extends to sanctioning and protecting the fulfillment of the natural law and of regulating the civil effects of marriage:* it cannot, however, touch the substance of marriage or put limits to the natural rights of the spouses, nor the rights of any person to contract marriage or to achieve its principal end, procreation, under any eugenic, economic, social, or other kind of pretext: Pius VII, letter *Que Votre Majesté*, June 26, 1805 (*Ins.* no. 61); Pius IX, letter *La Lettera*, September 9, 1852 (*Ins.* no. 98; EF, 1.394–97); Leo XIII, letter *Ci siamo* (*Ins.* no. 135; EF, 1.467f.); encyclical *Arcanum divinae sapientiae* (*Ins.* nos. 186–87, 193); letter *Il divisamento* (*Ins.* no. 218; EF, 1.555f.); letter *Quam religiosa*, August 10, 1898 (*Ins.* no. 241; EF, 1.577f.); letter *Dum multa*, December 24, 1902 (*Ins.* no. 247; EF, 1.597); St. Pius X, letter *Afflictum proprioribus* (*Ins.* no. 252; EF, 1.612f.); Pius XI, encyclical *Casti connubii* (*Ins.* no. 394ff.); Pius XII, Message of June 10, 1958 (*Ins.* nos. 769–71; EF, 2.1683f.).

3. The Task Assigned to the Council: To Integrate Doctrine More Profoundly into Life

The doctrinal questions then open—even if not negligible—did not have the same significance and urgency that the task assigned to the Council had: to find, in a world that was progressively becoming de-Christianized, appropriate ways for bringing to life the rich doctrine of the Church in the midst of the new conditions of men and women and of society.

This was in fact the prime preoccupation of the Council, as the very first paragraph of the pastoral constitution *Gaudium et spes,* devoted to the family, indicates: "The Council intends to present certain key points of the Church's teaching in a clearer light; and it hopes to guide and encourage Christians and all men who are trying to preserve and to foster the dignity and supremely sacred value of the married state."[14] We have seen how, already in the *Relatio* that accompanied the schema of June 28, 1965, this predominant intention, practical and pastoral in nature, was affirmed.[15]

> ■ This does not mean that the Council did not pay attention to doctrinal questions not yet fully resolved: to express more precisely the nature of the conjugal covenant in a way that would foster a better understanding of the place of conjugal love within marriage; to shed light on the relationships between love and procreation, which needed clarification in the face of the growing anticonceptive mentality, the discovery of the "pill", etc. (cf. nos. 48–51 of *Gaudium et spes*).

However, the principal problem facing the Council was pastoral and practical. The Church possessed and possesses a rich and solid doctrine on *conjugal morality*, whose power of humanization could not but attract men of good will. Nonetheless, a widespread and dominating selfishness was keeping many from understanding the true significance of this morality, and not a few were beginning to consider it a beautiful but utopian ideal; and this was occurring even among the faithful themselves. The Church, moreover, had proclaimed forcefully the *rights of the family*, as essential for the well-being of society, but in practice these were becoming more and more stamped out by civil legislation: public morality was in a state of clear decadence; and education was more and more being taken from the parents and given over to the state, which was often disdainful of the truth of Christ, or more irenically, less interested in distinguishing between the true and the false, between good and evil. Moreover, social changes, the abnormal development of urban centers, made the solution of certain basic human problems—of work, of housing, etc.—more difficult, at least on the part of private persons, and the "socialistic" solutions often showed themselves less consonant with the Christian ideal (housing that was inadequate for a large family, etc.).

> ■ Humanly speaking, the problems were overwhelming the capacity of every pastor of souls, taken individually, to solve them, or at least to fight against an environment hostile to some Christian truths; this made it all the more heroic to fulfill the demands of Christian morality, which had previously been practiced with a certain facility thanks to

[14] Vatican Council II, pastoral constitution *Gaudium et spes*, no. 47.
[15] *Acta Synodalia*, vol. IV, pars I, p. 521.

the general environment and to the formation that had been received. For example, how was one to combat the almost universal incomprehension of modesty and chastity or of large families? Or, entering into the field of the protection of the rights of the family, how efficacious could the proclamation of such rights be when no one seemed disposed to take on the obligations involved with them, since the majority believe neither in the indissoluble character of the marital bond nor in the necessity of giving parents the real opportunity to choose a school in conformity with their ideals?[16]

Under the action of the Holy Spirit, the conciliar Fathers proposed for this problematic the only solution really efficacious: *to awaken once more the energies planted by God in the family, promoting as a phenomenon of universal character holiness in marriage and in the family, in the midst of the world, and in this way to lead the world back to God.*

By reason of their special vocation, it belongs to the laity to seek the kingdom of God by engaging in temporal affairs and directing them according to God's will. They live in the world, that is, they are engaged in each and every work and business of the earth and in the ordinary circumstances of social and family life which, as it were, constitute their very existence. There they are called by God that, being led by the Spirit to the Gospel, they may contribute to the sanctification of the world, as from within like leaven, by fulfilling their own particular duties. Thus, especially by the witness of their life, resplendent in faith, hope, and charity, they must manifest Christ to others. It pertains to them in a special way so as to illuminate and order all temporal things with which they are so closely associated that these may be effected and grow according to Christ and may be to the glory of the Creator and Redeemer.[17]

■ A most ambitious task! The world was sinking because it had turned from God, and it was always withdrawing further from him because men were not searching with the necessary drive the truth and the grace of Christ. Society could not recover itself save by a return to God; this meant that every man must personally draw himself anew to him. In truth, the problem was piercing to the very roots of human life: in the dehumanization of man who was forgetting his Creator and Savior. Therefore, the solution must also begin with a personal return of each individual to God.

[16] On this see A. Rodriguez, "La Carta dei diritti della famiglia", *Divus Thomas* 84 (1981): 330–41.
[17] Vatican Council II, *Lumen gentium*, no. 31.

The events that took place after the Council have shown that its task was not only enormous, but difficult. From a certain point of view, one might think that the doctrine of the Council has not been heard; or rather, it seems that it has, as it were, become lost in a void. In reality, matters are not precisely this way: in addition to considering how individuals conform themselves to the Council's teaching, there is need to take into account the temporal and historical dimension of every human event. And thus we can find in the teachings of *Familiaris consortio* the ideal set forth by the Council, developed more fully and clearly, better explained in its practical manifestations, more accessible. The apostolic exhortation of John Paul II repeats vigorously and precisely the call to holiness directed to spouses by the Council, confirms and deepens its concept of the person, and indicates in detail everything that an appropriate pastoral approach can today demand of the family.

Chapter Six

MARRIAGE AND FAMILY IN VATICAN COUNCIL II

Taking into account everything said thus far, let us now pass to the study of the conciliar texts. Yet it seems useful to us to introduce the texts with a brief historical analysis of *Gaudium et spes*. In the following, the major lines of its teaching, which, one can say, mark a deepening of the perennial doctrine of the Church, will be set forth. In the light of this introduction, we will then recapitulate the whole of the conciliar doctrine on marriage.

1. The Historical Background to *Gaudium et Spes*

If a historical approach is useful for the knowledge of every document of the Magisterium, in this case it is almost necessary, given the peculiar vicissitudes of its redaction and the pastoral language adopted by the constitution. For, although *Gaudium et spes,* by its very way of expressing itself, allows an immediate and accessible ascetical doctrinal reading, at the strictly theological level, it requires a more attentive reading, frequently necessitating recourse to the *modi* and *emendamenti* of the Council Fathers, something that makes a knowledge of its history necessary.[1] The *Acta Synodalia* include four "schemes" of the constitution, the last of which contains the definitive redaction, and

---

[1] Thus A. Miralles, "Naturaleza y sacramento en la doctrina del Concilio Vaticano II sobre el matrimonio", *Cuestiones fundamentales sobre matrimonio y familia (Actas del II Simposio Internacional de Teología)*, ed. A. Sarmiento et al. (Pamplona: Eunsa, 1980), pp. 151–52; Philippe Delhaye, "La dignità della persona umana", in *La Chiesa nel mondo di oggi (Studi e commenti intorno alla Costituzione pastorale "Gaudium et spes")* (Florence: Vallecchi, 1966), pp. 264–66.

they make mention of a fifth, even older one, that was not considered fit for study by the Fathers. We can therefore speak of the following redactions: (a) the *text of 1963*, which was never examined in the Council; (b) the first *Schema de Ecclesia in mundo huius temporis*, also called the *Zurich text*, which, in its definitive redaction of July 3, 1964, was discussed at the third session of the Council;[2] (c) the schema of February 1965 or the *text of Ariccia*, which underwent different reelaborations before being presented to the Fathers as the *Schema receptum*, with the date of May 28, 1965;[3] this schema was then reworked twice, giving rise to (d) the *textus recognitus* of November 13, 1965,[4] and to (e) the *textus denuo recognitus*, distributed on December 2, 1965,[5] both of which were discussed during the fourth session of the Council.

We will make in the following a brief summary of the entire process that developed up to the time of definitive approval.[6] In fact, the constitution *Gaudium et spes* was not foreseen as such in the preparatory phase of the Council. It rather came to birth as the fruit of the needs precipitated during the development of the Council and of the growth of the conciliar spirit, with all the advantages that this implies, but also with the limitation that it was not able to enjoy the benefit, as did other documents, of a true preparatory work. The advisability for a constitution of this kind became clear at the end of the first session (1962), in the desire to see reflected, in the various sectors of life, the great dogmatic contents of *Lumen gentium*, whose teachings on the universal call to holiness and on the role of the laity in the Church seemed destined to have great practical impact. To this end, and in response to the desire of a significant number of the Fathers, Pope John XXIII, shortly after the closing of the first session, established a commission to coordinate the work of the Council. This commission

---

[2] It is found in the *Acta Synodalia*, vol. III, pars V, pp. 116–42. Cf. also the introductory or general *Relatio* (ibid., pp. 142ff.) and the *Adnexa* (ibid., pp. 147ff.).

[3] The text is found in the *Acta Synodalia*, vol. IV, pars I, pp. 435–516; the *Relatio*, pp. 517ff.

[4] *Acta Synodalia*, vol. IV, pars VI, pp. 421–99; the corresponding *Relationes* are found on pp. 500–568.

[5] *Acta Synodalia*, vol. IV, pars VII, pp. 234–314, with the *Relatio generalis* on pp. 646ff., and the *modi* on pp. 347–464, and the *corrections admitted* on pp. 315–46.

[6] On this see M. G. McGrath, "Note storiche sulla Constituzione", in *La Chiesa nel mondo di oggi*, pp. 141–56; S. D. Kozul, *Evoluzione della dottrina circa l'essenza del matrimonio dal C.I.C. al Vaticano II* (Vicenza: Ed. Lief, 1980), pp. 213–55.

reduced to 17 the number of council schemata (originally there had been more than 70). The first of these was called *De Ecclesia* and the last was called *De Praesentia activa Ecclesiae in mundo*, and this schema stood at the origin of *Gaudium et spes*. John XXIII entrusted the work on these schemata to a mixed commission, made up of members of the doctrinal commission and of the commission for the apostolate of the laity. The new Schema 17 foresaw six chapters: on the "wonderful vocation of man", in his human and Christian significance; on the human person and his rights; marriage and the family; culture, the social order and economics; the community of the people and peace. A first draft was ready in May 1963, the so-called *text of '63*. But in May, John XXIII died, before there could be an examination of this project.

Subsequently, under Paul VI, the Council, now in its second session, was reconvened, but only at the end of November did the *plenum* of the mixed commission come together to study the document, which was judged by the Council of the Presidency as not yet ready for discussion in the conciliar hall. At the conclusion of the plenary session of the mixed commission, a small committee was elected and charged with the task of drawing up a new general schema; as a result, the *text of '63* never reached the point where it was studied by the Fathers.

The small committee, reunited in Zurich, began its labors and sent to the mixed commission a new schema in January 1964, the so-called *Zurich text*, which, after having been studied and modified by the mixed commission, was finished in June 1964 and approved by the commission for coordinating the Council for presentation during the third session of the Council. It is the first of the texts of Schema 17, which had now become Schema 13, which figures in the *Acta Synodalia* (the Schema of July 3, 1964). At the conclusion of the debates in the council hall, the conciliar Fathers introduced 830 pages of observations and gave directions for a reworking of the schema. This took place between January and November 1965, in the interval between the third and fourth sessions of the Council.

From January 31 to February 6, 1965, a new redaction was prepared at Ariccia (the *text of Ariccia*), which was approved by the mixed commission in a meeting of February 8 to 13, with directions, nonetheless, for new revisions. Discussed again from March 29 to April 6, the schema was finally approved and sent to the Fathers on May 28, 1965. There then took place the second discussion in the Council, at the fourth session, beginning on September 24 and continuing for two weeks. The observations and addresses were very numerous, giving rise to the *textus recognitus*, which was distributed to the Fathers on November 13, 1965. This last text was not discussed but voted on, in every part and number, and the Council Fathers approved it, adding, however, more than 20,000 modi or *emendamenti*. Thus, we come to the *textus denuo recognitus*, distributed to the Fathers on December 2, 1965, together with the relations explaining the corrections accepted and the responses of the commission to each one of the 20,000 modi that had been submitted; all this material constitutes without doubt the most important source for interpreting *Gaudium et spes*.[7] With this new redaction, the text was definitively approved in the ninth public session, on December 7, 1965.[8]

■ In referring to the four schemas contained in the *Acta*, we will speak of them respectively as the first schema or the schema of 1964 (which is based on the *Zurich text*), the *Schema receptum* of May 1965 (which is based on the *text of Arricia*), the *textus recognitus* (that of November 1965), and the *textus denuo recognitus* (that of December 1965). There is a detailed study of the history of the text of *Gaudium et spes* given over to the chapter on marriage and the family, examining it paragraph by paragraph. This work greatly facilitates the use of the material gathered together in the *Acta Synodalia*.[9]

In the approved text of the constitution, marriage and the family are the object of the first chapter of the second part, devoted to "some more urgent questions". This has the title *The dignity of marriage and the family*, and it comprises numbers 47 to 52 of the document. The plan is the following: (a) first of all, it gives a brief introduction to *Marriage and the family in the world today*, describing the factual situation in its positive and negative aspects and reaffirming the need for promoting adequately the dignity of marriage and the family (no. 47); (b) it then treats of the *Holiness of marriage and of the family* (no. 48), according to human and Christian principles; (c) then in two successive numbers it

---

[7] As has been said, the *textus denuo recognitus* and the responses to the *modi* are found in the *Acta Synodalia*, vol. IV, pars VII, on pp. 234–314 and 347–464, respectively.

[8] Gathered together in the *Acta Synodalia*, vol. IV, pars VII, pp. 739–804.

[9] Francisco Gil Hellín, *Constitutionis Pastoralis "Gaudium et spes," Synopsis historica. De dignitate matrimonii et familiae fovenda* (Pamplona: Eunsa, 1982). There is also the *Synopsis historica* of part I: *"De Ecclesia et vocatione hominis"*, under the editorship of Francisco Gil Hellín, A. Sarmiento, J. Ferrer, and J. M. Yanguas (Pamplona: Eunsa, 1985).

singles out the essential goods of marriage: *Conjugal love* (no. 49) and *The fruitfulness of marriage* (no. 50); (d) in the following section, it emphasizes the great unity between these two elements, seen as *The harmony of conjugal love and respect for human life* (no. 51); and (e) finally, it takes up *The duty of all to foster the good of marriage and the family* (no. 52).

■ This plan corresponds substantially with the *text of Ariccia* which, in conformity with the directions received from the Fathers, set out to treat of the salient points, moral and spiritual, of marriage and the family, in order to bring back to light other truths already set forth in the Council.

2. The Major Lines of the Conciliar Teaching on Marriage

Three central truths provide the context for the force and novelty of the teaching of *Gaudium et spes* on marriage and the family. First of all, the *presentation of marriage as a specific vocation to holiness,* in a way never previously done in a document of the Magisterium. Second, its precisions on *the role of conjugal love in the structure of marriage,* a necessary aspect for understanding its dynamism and at that time the subject of no little polemics, due both to an inexact understanding of the data of Tradition and to the influence of ideas nourished by the growing selfishness of the environment. The final point, intimately related to the previous ones and a matter of fierce discussion in the past few years, regards the clarification of the *relationships between love and procreation,* in the context of a powerful "antilife" mentality and of the problems posed by the diffusion of contraceptives, by demographic growth, and by the regulation of conception.

A. *Marriage as a vocation to holiness*

Christian marriage is an authentic supernatural "vocation"; therefore, spouses can and must seek holiness in the fulfillment of their duties; moreover, precisely within their family life, they are called to carry out an intense apostolic work in the midst of the world.

Let us recall that *Gaudium et spes* sprang up spontaneously within the Council as it developed, as a deeply felt need to give a practical and opportune opening to the truths set forth in *Lumen gentium*. This was noted immediately after the Council:

> We find—in chapter I of the second part of the [Pastoral] Constitution —a basic scheme of the doctrine on marriage and the family, a doctrine that in other conciliar documents, e.g., the Dogmatic Constitution on the Church (nn. 35 and 41), the Decree on the Apostolate of Lay People (n. 11), the Declaration on Christian Education (nn. 3, 6, 8) had not been emphasized.[10]

Gaudium et spes, therefore, develops *Lumen gentium,* the first and most elaborately developed document of the Council, to which, in one way or another, all the rest refer. Its nucleus is the universal call to holiness, an element that characterizes the entire conciliar Magisterium and constitutes its ultimate end.[11] One cannot be surprised, therefore, that this is the mother truth that guides the treatment of marriage. After having presented an overview of the world, noting its bright spots and its dark ones, the first number of *Gaudium et spes* devoted to marriage concludes by affirming that "it hopes to guide and encourage Christians and all men who are trying to preserve and to foster the dignity and supremely sacred value of the married state" (no. 47, par. 3). The following number is devoted to the *holiness of marriage* and of the family (no. 48), describing the "vocation to marriage", an expression repeatedly adopted in the following numbers (49 to 52).

■ We will set forth this doctrine of the Council by analyzing the following: the texts in which it is contained; its novelty and importance; the need for deepening our understanding of it; the concept of vocation; the characteristics of the vocation to marriage; the vocation to marriage and the vocation to virginity; pastoral implications.

This breadth of treatment is advisable both because of the importance of this theme in itself and because of the fact that it has not yet received, with some notable exceptions,[12] the attention it merits from

[10] V. Heylen, "La promozione della dignità del matrimonio e della famiglia", in *La Chiesa nel mondo di oggi,* p. 535.

[11] Cf. Paul VI, motu proprio *Sanctitas clarior,* March 19, 1969, preface.

[12] Cf., for instance, K. Majdanski, *Communione di vita e d'amore. Teologia del matrimonio e della famiglia* (Milan: Vita e Pensiero, 1980). The author bases his entire treatment on the meaning of vocation ("Matrimonio e famiglia. Una vocazione", pp. 13ff.; cf. also pp. 43ff.)

students, too often conditioned by the noise of polemics, of less doctrinal and practical import, arising in the wake of the Council. As in other cases and other times, here too is verified—for the field of doctrine—the adage: "often the tree hides the forest", or, as is more common in English, "one can't see the forest for the trees."

1. *The principal conciliar texts on the vocation to marriage as a vocation to holiness.* Number 48 of the pastoral constitution *Gaudium et spes,* in sketching the image of marriage as God has willed it, and after having noted its holy structure in the plan of creation, adds that Christian

spouses, therefore, are fortified and, as it were, consecrated for the duties and dignity of their state by a special sacrament;[13] fulfilling their conjugal and family role by virtue of this sacrament, spouses are penetrated with the spirit of Christ and their whole life is suffused by faith, hope, and charity; thus they increasingly further *their own perfection and their mutual sanctification,* and together they render glory to God (no. 48, par. 2).[14]

Therefore, spouses are called to the perfection of Christian life, that is, to holiness, precisely in the fulfillment of their duties of state.

■ By affirming this, GS does nothing else than to place the very meaning of marriage in harmony with what had been proclaimed by *Lumen gentium* regarding the universal call to holiness: "In virtue of the sacrament of Matrimony by which they signify and share (cf. Eph. 5:32) the mystery of the unity and faithful love between Christ and the Church, *Christian married couples help one another to attain holiness in their married life and in the rearing of their children.* Hence by reason of their state in life and of their position they have their own gifts in the People of God (cf. 1 Cor 7:7)" (*Lumen gentium,* no. 11, par. 2).

This is so because "*all in the Church,* whether they belong to the hierarchy or are cared for by it, *are called to holiness,* according to the apostle's saying: 'For this is the will of God, your sanitification' (1 Thes 4:3, cf. Eph 1:4). This holiness of the Church is constantly

precisely as a demand of the Council. Also see D. Tettamanzi, *Matrimonio cristiano oggi* (Milan: Ancora, 1975), particularly pp. 101ff.

[13] Cf. Pius XI, encyclical *Casti connubii,* AAS 22 (1930): 538 (E.T., no. 110).

[14] In this chapter, the citations from the Council will be noted in the text, within parentheses, with the usual signs, keeping other citations for the footnotes. Throughout the rest of this chapter, we will indicate *Gaudium et spes* by GS. In this chapter, precise references to the pages in *Enchiridion Familiae* where the text of *Gaudium et spes* is found are not given.

shown forth in the fruits of grace which the Spirit produces in the faithful, and so it must be; it is expressed in many ways by the individuals who, each in his own state of life, *tend to the perfection of love,* thus edifying others" (*Lumen gentium,* no. 39, par. 1). And it continues a little later: "It is therefore quite clear that *all Christians in any state or walk of life are called to the fullness of Christian life and to the perfection of love,*[15] and by this holiness a more human manner of life is also fostered in earthly society" (*Lumen gentium,* no. 40, par. 2).

The Council calls everyone to seek, each in his or her own position in life, the one and common holiness: "*The forms and tasks of life are many but holiness is one* — that sanctity which is cultivated by all who act under God's Spirit and, obeying the Father's voice and adoring God the Father in spirit and in truth, follow Christ, poor, humble, and cross-bearing, that they may deserve to be partakers of his glory" (*Lumen gentium,* no. 41, par. 1). And thus "Christian married couples and parents, following their own way, should support one another in grace all through life with a faithful love.... They stand as witnesses and cooperators of the fruitfulness of mother Church, as a sign of, and a share in that love with which Christ loves his bride and gave himself for her"[16] (*Lumen gentium,* no. 41, par. 5) because "*strengthened by so many and such great means of salvation, all the faithful, whatever their condition or state—though each in his own way—are called by the Lord to that perfection of sanctity by which the Father himself is perfect*" (*Lumen gentium,* no. 11, par. 3).

Vatican Council II, therefore, sees Christian marriage as a *supernatural vocation to holiness* that, precisely for this reason, is also the *principle of a specific apostolic mission,* particularly important for the world:

> Let married couples themselves, who are created in the image of the living God and constituted in an authentic personal dignity, be *united* together in equal affection, agreement of mind, and mutual *holiness.*[17] Thus, in the footsteps of Christ, *the principle of life,*[18] they will bear

---

Here it should be noted that the complete text of *Gaudium et spes* is found in the third volume of this reference work, pp. 1825–43, or 3.1825–43.

[15] Cf. Pius XI, encyclical *Rerum omnium,* January 26, 1923, AAS 15 (1923): 50.

[16] Pius XI, *Casti connubii,* AAS 22 (1930): 548ff.; cf. St. John Chrysostom, *In Eph. Hom.,* 20, 2; PG 62,136ff.

[17] Cf. *Sacramentarium Gregorianum;* PL 78,262.

[18] Cf. Rom 5:15 and 18; 6:5–11; Gal 2:20.

witness by their faithful love in the joys and sacrifice of their calling to that *mystery of love which the Lord revealed to the world* by his death and resurrection[19] (GS, no. 52, par. 7).

This vocation, therefore, *illumines their whole behavior,* revealing its true meaning and strengthening it with the means given by Christ and guarded by the Church. It is a call to live heroically in the practice of the virtues, under the action of the Holy Spirit: "*Outstanding courage is required for the constant fulfillment of the duties of this Christian calling:* spouses, therefore, will need grace for leading a holy life; they will eagerly practice a love that is firm, generous, and prompt to sacrifice, and will ask for it in their prayers" (GS, no. 49, par. 2). More specifically, heroic virtue is required for the fulfillment of the primordial end of marriage, by means of which in particular the spouses tend toward their perfection: "Whenever Christian spouses in a spirit of sacrifice and trust in divine Providence[20] carry out their duties of procreation with generous human and Christian responsibility, they glorify the Creator and perfect themselves in Christ" (GS, no. 50, par. 2). A perspective of this kind is to characterize the entire pastoral effort of the Church to married people; the mission of priests, in this field, is "to nurture the vocation of married people in their married and family life by different pastoral means, by the preaching of the Word of God, by liturgy, and other spiritual assistance" (GS, no. 52, par. 5).

2. *The novelty and importance of this conciliar doctrine.* Although now no one would question the vocational character of marriage, understood as a call to the fullness of Christian life and to holiness, before the Council this was not so. Holiness was seen by many as a path reserved for a small portion of the people of God. Not only were those who felt themselves called to marriage judged to have, as it were, renounced Christian perfection, but so too were secular priests; the call to perfection was seen as a privilege of the religious state.

■ Because it may be difficult today to imagine a mentality such as this, by way of illustrating it, we here cite some words of Cardinal Mercier who, as is known, was very courageous in promoting the quest for holiness among the secular clergy: "*You belong to the first*

---

[19] Cf. Eph 5:25–27.
[20] Cf. 1 Cor 7:5.

religious order established in the Church; your founder is Jesus Christ Himself; the first religious of His order were the Apostles; their successors are the bishops and, in communion with them, the priests, the ministers of the sacred order."[21] Even in 1941, there were not lacking those who considered it to be "criminal and matter of the most grave sin" not to counsel all, to the extent possible, to the religious state rather than the secular priesthood.[22] Surely, there was a failure to grasp the true richness of the Church, evident in the very diversity and multiplicity of vocations, not opposed but complementary (cf. Rom 12:4ff.; 1 Cor 12:12–31 etc.), without forgetting the superiority of the virginal charism, affirmed by the Lord himself (cf. Mt 19:12) and repeatedly called to mind by the Magisterium.[23]

The Council, therefore, confirms that Christ has established marriage as a divine vocation in the full sense. "For a Christian marriage is not just a social institution, much less a mere remedy for human weakness. It is a real supernatural calling."[24] Before the Council, an affirmation of this kind caused scandal in some circles, but today it is an acquired and fundamental truth for the moral renewal of society. In fact, not only is holiness the only efficacious remedy for the present crisis of the world, but the majority of the faithful must seek it, by the law of life, in marriage. And as long as the character of the supernatural vocation to marriage is not recognized, its enormous apostolic power and, therefore, that of the majority of the faithful within the Church, will remain obscure.

■ This is a teaching particularly dear to *Familiaris consortio.* It is necessary that the family discover "the riches that it possesses by nature and by grace",[25] that it become what it ought to be, and that it be what it already is by creation and the work of redemption.[26] Only in the light of this divine call can one understand the moral power of the family; as

---

[21] Cardinal Mercier, *La vida interior* (Barcelona, n.d.), p. 186.

[22] P. Guerrero, "Un interesante problema de teología y ascética, sacerdote secular o religioso?" *Razon y Fe 123* (May–August 1941): 201ff.; the citation is taken from p. 222.

[23] On this matter cf. E. Ancilli, article "Santità", in *Dizionario di Spiritualità* (Milan: Ed. OR, 1981); J. L. Illanes, *La santificazione del lavoro* (Milan: Ed. Ares, 1980), pp. 38ff.

[24] Blessed Josemaría Escrivá, "Marriage: A Christian Vocation", in *Christ Is Passing By* (New Rochelle, N.Y.: Scepter Press, 1974), no. 23, p. 44. The author had already written in *The Way,* in its first edition, in 1939: "Do you laugh because I tell you that you have a vocation to marriage? Well, you have just that—a vocation", no. 27. The idea was constantly present in his preaching, oral and written.

[25] John Paul II, apostolic exhortation *Familiaris consortio,* November 22, 1981, no. 86.

[26] Ibid., no. 17.

the Holy Father reminds us, speaking of the need of spouses to fulfill in their integrity the divine laws, even when this does not seem easy.[27]

3. *The need to deepen our understanding of the meaning of marriage as a divine vocation.* We have already said this: the implementation of a Council is not, ordinarily, an easy task. History teaches us this: as happened with Trent, so today. The cause of this is the very nature of man: ideas progress slowly, and only with time is the opportune perspective acquired. It was only a quarter century ago that Vatican Council II advanced its bold affirmation of marriage as a vocation to holiness: people, both the faithful and their pastors, need, even from a psychological point of view, a little time in order to evaluate the significance of the novelty of this teaching, drawn from the perennial seed of the Gospel and in perfect continuity with Tradition.[28] In particular, it is important to emphasize the following points:

a. The first, which we have already stressed, is the *light that the call to holiness throws on the whole of conjugal morality,* in the integrity with which the Church teaches it, in the trust in the dignity of man — the image and child of God — which it inspires, in the generosity that characterizes it. In fact, is not the cause of the fears that some experience in demanding from spouses that heroism in daily life that is a characteristic trait of holiness a result of having forgotten this truth? On the other hand, if one recognizes that this call to holiness is addressed to spouses, one will not lack the audacity to ask that they listen to the

command of Christ the Lord to overcome difficulties with constancy. "And so what is known as the 'law of gradualness' or step-by-step advance cannot be identified with 'gradualness of the law', as if there were different degrees or forms of precept in God's law for different individuals and situations. In God's plan, all husbands and wives are called in marriage to holiness, and this lofty vocation is fulfilled to the extent that the human person is able to respond to God's command with serene confidence in God's grace and in his or her own will."[29,30]

---

[27] Ibid., no. 34.

[28] Cf. Philippe Delhaye, "Metaconcilio: la mancanza di discernimento", *Cris Documenti* (Milan: Ed. Ares, 1981), p. 7.

[29] John Paul II, Homily at the Conclusion of the Sixth Synod of Bishops, October 25, 1980, no. 8.

[30] John Paul II, *Familiaris consortio,* no. 34.

■ Finally, those theologians—so characteristic of the new morality—who set out to soften or diminish the stringent requirements of the Gospel show that they fail to grasp the meaning of the Council. It is a paradox that this is done in the name of Vatican Council II! The one who inspired the Council is the Holy Spirit; and one of the truths that he has willed to emphasize through it is the universal call to holiness. Proclaiming this call, the Council obviously could not claim at the same time that we should become defenders of (or at least accomplices in) divorce, abortion, materialism in all its forms, permissivism, social hatred, denying the existence of objective and transcendent norms. "That some moralists work against morality by exalting selfishness and subjectivism does not completely surprise anyone who knows the history of morality. But that they take as their starting point for this work of demolition Vatican Council II is indeed something mind-boggling."[31]

b. The second point is the need to avoid a more subtle danger: *to confuse,* because of a residue of clericalism, which always continues to insinuate itself, *the teaching of the Council on the apostolic dynamism of the family,* inscribed into the universal vocation to holiness, with a simple revival of the participation of the lay married in ecclesiastical activities. Certainly, the Council wills such collaboration, but it would be an impoverishment of its teaching to reduce its more substantive doctrine to this. To understand that new yet ancient truth that the Council wishes to say, one must recognize and support the great power of marriage and the family in themselves, independent of every superimposed structure, as was done in the early ages of the Church. This is a matter that had already been taken up, some years ago, in discussions on the general mission of the laity:

> Today, after the solemn teachings of Vatican II, it is unlikely that anyone in the Church would question the orthodoxy of this teaching. But how many people have really abandoned the narrow conception of the apostolate of the laity as a pastoral work *organized from the top down?* How many people have got beyond the previous "monolithic" conception of the lay apostolate and understand that it can and indeed should exist without the necessity of rigid centralized structures, canonical missions and hierarchical mandates? How many people who consider the laity as the "long arm of the Church," do not at the same time

[31] Philippe Delhaye, *La scienza del bene e del male. La morale del Vaticano II e il "metaconcilio"* (Milan: Ed. Ares, 1981), p. 97.

confuse in their minds the concept of Church-People of God with the more limited concept of hierarchy? How many laymen understand that unless they act in tactful communion with the hierarchy they have no right to claim the legitimate sphere of apostolic autonomy?[32]

■ To awaken the apostolic power of the family, it is necessary to overcome the restricted view of the past few centuries, in order to recover the special and rich dynamism of the family within the bosom of the Church. In sum, we are not dealing here with the "hierarchical" organization of families, but with the recognition of the value that families have as organizations of their own. A little realism suffices to grasp this. What organization constituted by man, in fact, shows itself able to develop the energies that flow spontaneously and superabundantly from the family? A father, a mother, especially when they are completely united in themselves and work strengthened by grace, make sacrifices that human laws and organizations cannot impose and that no one even dreams of. The family contains in itself a natural inclination to heroism, generated by love and strengthened by charity, that is absolutely unrepeatable.

Basically, it is this that the Council wants to reintroduce into the world, saving families with the power of Christian doctrine and of the sacraments. Because it is only in a climate of love that man gives the most of himself: in understanding, in love, in sacrifice, in joy, in work, in relationships with others, in virtue . . . in everything. Man has been made in the image of God, who is love, and "man cannot live without love. He remains a being that is incomprehensible for himself, for his life is senseless, if love is not revealed to him."[33] And since the family is the place where this climate of love spontaneously arises, it is also the seat for the transmission and the increase of human life, of its happiness and its power. It is, at the same time, the true school for inserting man into society and into the Church.[34]

4. *Some basic comments on the theological notion of vocation.* The notion of vocation is typically biblical. It already appears in the Old Testament as an initiative of God, either toward a person—Abraham, Isaac, etc.—or toward an entire people such as Israel (cf. for example Dt 7:6ff; Ezek 16:1–4, etc.). It is an initiative consistent with the call to a

---

[32] Blessed Josemaría Escrivá, *Conversations with Monsignor Escrivá* (Manila: Sinag-Tala Publishers, 1974), no. 21, p. 34.

[33] John Paul II, *Familiaris consortio,* no. 19; encyclical *Redemptor hominis,* March 4, 1979, no. 10.

[34] Cf. John Paul II, *Familiaris consortio,* no. 15.

mission (cf. Is 43:9; 49:6), which confers a peculiar dignity and impels one to a determinate kind of behavior (cf. Lev 11:45; Ex 19:6; Dt 7:3–6; 26:18). In the New Testament, this call is addressed by Christ himself, who reveals to men the plan for their divinization through his redemptive work. The Christian vocation is, therefore, a call to unite oneself to Christ and to take him as one's model, to follow and imitate him, thanks to the gift of his own life:

> Christ's life is our life, just as he promised his Apostles at the last supper: "If anyone love me, he will keep my word, and my Father will love him, and we will come to him and make our home with him" (Jn 14:23). That is why a Christian should live as Christ lived, making the affections of Christ his own, so that he can exclaim with St. Paul: "It is now no longer I that live, but Christ lives in me" (Gal 2:20).[35]

If we penetrate to the theological and moral significance of the notion of vocation—frequently elaborated only a little—we can emphasize that it is the way of expressing *the relationship of the spiritual creature with God in its foundation and integrity;* that is: it is the ontological situation resulting from the gift of a spiritual principle of life. When a being is rendered capable of participating with God according to an intelligent and free nature, in a way that the creature is able to recognize and to love the "gift" received, one can say that God calls: the very "gift" granted implies a vocation.

Therefore, vocation is not something that is added to the gift of life, of being, and of grace, but rather represents the way of possessing these realities in a way fitting for the person or the subject of a spiritual nature; that is, *the liberty and responsibility with which this creature must develop its own proper energies, according to the intrinsic ordination written by God in nature itself:*

> The people of our time are more and more convinced that the human person's dignity and vocation demand that they should discover, by the light of their own intelligence, the values innate in their nature, that they should ceaselessly develop these values and realize them in their lives in order to achieve an ever greater development. In moral matters man cannot make value judgments according to his personal whim: "In the depths of his conscience man detects a law which he does not impose on himself, but which holds him to obedience. . . . For man

[35] Escrivá, "Christ's Presence in Christians", in *Christ Is Passing By*, no. 103, p. 146.

has in his heart a law written by God. To obey it is the very dignity of man; according to it he will be judged."[36,37]

■ In this way, one sees the depth of the notion of vocation and what this means for human existence and human conduct: "Man is a reality ontologically finalized inasmuch as he is freely created by God and carries inscribed in his being a vocation" through which "the essential elements of every human person become, by reason of human freedom, values that impose themselves on the very freedom of the person as values to be realized and developed (*facienda*). There are many values inasmuch as man is a complex reality. Here once more is an example of the wonderful equilibrium of Christian discourse which rejects both a physicist-cosmicist vision of the natural law and a conception of freedom as the possibility of all possibilities. It is not human nature as such that imposes itself on man (the notion of a natural moral law 'even if God did not exist' is miserably bankrupt), but human nature insofar as it is an expression of the creative project of God (and the classic concept of natural law is precisely this, a *formal,* that is, consciously aware, participation in the eternal law of God) and, on the other hand, human freedom is not as such an ontological priority,[38] but its own choices proceed from an absolute distinction that precedes them and judges between the true and the false, the good and the bad."[39]

The supernatural vocation moreover entails the transformation of man into a child of God by the work of grace. Since the creative act determines the being and the operative capacity of man as the image of God, *his supernatural vocation intrinsically determines his new condition as a child of God, a condition that stands at the origin of a new kind of behavior.* It is a transformation that divinizes the person and his operative capacities by means of the infused virtues and the gifts of the Holy Spirit, enabling him to live already in this world in familiarity with the three Divine Persons and to participate in their very own life. After original sin, the gift of grace—in which the Christian vocation consists—has the double effect of restoring the natural dynamism of man and of elevating him so that he is now capable of a life that is truly divine and

---

[36] *Gaudium et Spes,* no. 16.

[37] Congregation for the Doctrine of the Faith, declaration *Persona humana (Declaration on Certain Questions of Sexual Ethics),* December 29, 1975, no. 3, AAS 68 (1976): 78–79.

[38] Cf. F. Schelling, *Philosophische Untersuchungenueber das Wessen der menschlichen Freiheit,* Werke, Ab. I, Bd. 7, p. 370.

[39] Carlo Caffarra, "La Chiesa e l'ordine morale", *L'Osservatore Romano* (January 16, 1976): pp. 3–4, no. 5.

therefore holy: "Our faith teaches us that man, in the state of grace, is *divinized*. We are men and women, not angels. We are flesh and blood, people with sentiments and passions, with sorrows and joys. And this divinization affects everything human; it is a sort of fore-taste of the final resurrection."[40] The doctrine of the universal call to holiness reminds us that, if the whole man lives the divine life, his entire conduct must be holy, because God is holy: "Be holy as I am holy" (Lev 11:44); "this is the will of God: your sanctification" (1 Th 4:3).

> ■ Because of this, it is within the perspective of vocation that the true and full meaning of human life can be perceived: "Our calling discloses to us the meaning of our existence. It means being convinced, through faith, of the reason for our life on earth. Our life, the present, past and future, acquires a new dimension, a depth we did not perceive before. All happenings and events now fall within their true perspective: we understand where God is leading us, and we feel ourselves borne along by this task entrusted to us. God draws us from the shadows of our ignorance, our groping through history, and, no matter what our occupation in the world, he calls us with a strong voice, as he once called Peter and Andrew, 'Follow me and I will make you fishers of men' (Mt 4:19)."[41]

Here we need to make two observations. First of all, together with the vocation to holiness common to all the faithful that flows from the gift of baptismal grace, there also exist *specific vocations*, corresponding to the particular gifts of grace (personal) or to foundational charisms (common to a group of faithful). In the second place, one must keep in mind that the loss of sanctifying grace does not entail the loss either of the general vocation to holiness or of one's specific vocation; it implies, on the other hand, the incapacity to live this vocation with the help of its operative principle, while the divine call yet remains. Precisely because of this arises the dissatisfaction of the soul by reason of its failure to respond; yet there perdure the helps that God, in his faithfulness, does not fail to give to his elect so that they might recover their lost dignity. It is, therefore, analogous to the situation of man after the original fall.

[40] Escrivá, "Christ's Presence in Christians", no. 103, p. 146.
[41] Escrivá, "In Joseph's Workshop", *Christ Is Passing By*, no. 45, p. 73.

5. *Characteristics of the vocation to marriage as a call to holiness.* Every Christian vocation, as a gift of grace made to a human person already existing, implies a concrete singularity: a personal encounter with Christ, individual, unique, and unrepeatable for each man and woman, although it demands the same holiness of all. St. Paul said to all: "I plead with you . . . to live worthily the vocation you have been called to" (Eph 4:1). Whence arises the diversity of vocations, a diversity "which corresponds to the specification of the gifts (of grace), while preserving the most perfect unity: 'there are different works but the same God who accomplishes all of them in everyone' (1 Cor 12:6; cf. ibid. 8:11 and 28, 30; Gal 4:7)."[42]

Specifically, *the vocation to marriage presents itself as a call to holiness in the daily realities of married life,* precisely because the supernatural vocation divinizes human realities and begins with them. Therefore, the holiness of spouses and their most important ecclesial mission are not foreign and accessory to their daily tasks. Indeed, they are intertwined with them, divinizing their apparent "vulgarity"; and it is in them that the sacramental grace of marriage operates in practice. The Council, particularly GS, emphasizes this many times: "Fulfilling their conjugal and family role . . . they thus increasingly further their own perfection and their mutual sanctification" (GS, no. 48, par. 4). Specifically, as GS stresses, "they perfect themselves in Christ" by fulfilling "their proper mission to transmit human life", fulfilling "their role with a sense of human and Christian responsibility" (GS, no. 50, par. 2).

■ While in the specific case of the vocation of the religious for whose witness a certain distance from the world is proper (cf. *Lumen gentium,* no. 44, par. 3), the Christian vocation does not take anyone from his proper place in life and in society. St. Paul already made this clear: "The general rule is that each one should lead the life the Lord has assigned to him, continuing as he was when the Lord called him. . . . Everyone ought to continue as he was when he was called" (1 Cor 7:17 and 20). It is a characteristic of the secular vocation not to change one's own proper human condition but to divinize it, without destroying or deforming it: God penetrates the interior of human life and makes it a way of holiness. Thus in marriage, by means of the sacrament, Jesus "fills the soul of husband and wife and invites them to follow him. He transforms their whole married life into an occasion for God's presence

---

[42] Majdanski, *Communione di vita e d'amore,* pp. 44–45.

on earth. Husband and wife are called to sanctify their married life and to sanctify themselves in it."[43]

It is precisely this awareness that *fully enhances marriage,* as GS wishes, *showing that through Christian spouses "human love and marriage duties are part of their divine vocation."*[44] Not only does human love, as the other duties of marriage, not have anything blamable about it, but it is an *essential element of the divine call* of the spouses: it is by loving one another that the spouses become holy; their love leads them to God. It is not just that they are allowed to love one another; on the contrary, their very love has become a road to holiness. So long as one does not grasp this, one imperfectly understands the conciliar doctrine on the vocation to marriage. Thus, spouses would commit

a serious mistake if they were to exclude family life from their spiritual development. The marriage union, the care and education of children, the effort to provide for the needs of the family as well as for its security and development, the relationships with other persons who make up the community, all these are among the ordinary human situations that Christian couples are called upon to sanctify. They will achieve this aim by exercising the virtues of faith and hope, facing serenely all the great and small problems which confront any family, and persevering in the love and enthusiasm with which they fulfill their duties. In this way they practice the virtue of charity in all things.[45]

■ The Holy Father has stressed this in *Familiaris consortio:* "*Family life itself...* in all its varying circumstances is seen as a call from God and lived as a filial response to His call. Joys and sorrows, hopes and disappointments, births and birthday celebrations, wedding anniversaries of the parents, departures, separations and homecomings, important and far-reaching decisions, the death of those who are dear, etc.—all of these mark God's loving intervention in the family's history. They should be seen as suitable moments for thanksgiving, for petition, for trusting abandonment of the family into the hands of their common Father in heaven."[46]

Finally, we need to stress that it is *a vocation of great import for the building up of the community of the Church and for the formation in it of all*

[43] Escrivá, "Marriage: A Christian Vocation", no. 43, p. 44.
[44] Escrivá, *Conversations with Monsignor Escrivá,* no. 91, p. 107.
[45] Escrivá, "Marriage: A Christian Vocation", no. 43, pp. 44–45.
[46] *Familiaris consortio,* no. 59.

vocations: "Christian married couples and parents, following their own way . . . build up the brotherhood of charity, and they stand as witnesses to and cooperators with the fruitfulness of mother Church, as a sign of, and a share in that love with which Christ loved his bride and gave himself up for her" (*Lumen gentium,* no. 41, par. 5). They form their children "to a Christian and apostolic life; they offer them wise guidance in the choice of vocation, and if they discover in them a sacred vocation they encourage it with all care" (*Apostolicam actuositatem,* November 18, 1965, no. 11, par. 2).

■ One can thus understand that the Council has willed, following an expression of some of the Fathers of the Church, to speak of the family as the "domestic Church" (*Lumen gentium,* no. 11, par. 2). That is, it is that focal point of Christian community that expands itself into society with a charm at once divine and human. We can say this in the words of our Holy Father, John Paul II, *"The future of humanity passes by way of the family."*[47]

6. *The vocation to marriage and the vocation to virginity.* The Church has always taught that the priestly vocation, and in general *the vocation to virginity, is a superior gift to that of the vocation to marriage.*[48] In its turn, Vatican Council II repeated this teaching: among the different charisms of the people of God:

Towering among the counsels [which the Lord proposes to his disciples] is that precious gift of divine grace given to some by the Father (cf. Mt 19:11; 1 Cor 7:7) to devote themselves to God alone more easily with an undivided heart (cf. 1 Cor 7:32–34) in virginity or celibacy.[49] This perfect continence for love of the kingdom of heaven has always been held in high esteem by the Church as a sign and stimulus of love and as a singular source of spiritual fertility in the world (*Lumen gentium,* no. 42, par. 3).

The Church has not hesitated to proclaim that "the duty of fostering vocations to the priesthood[50] falls on the whole Christian community,

---

[47] Ibid., no. 86.

[48] Cf. F. Festorazzi, "Matrimonio e verginità nella Bibbia", in *Matrimonio e verginità* (Venegono Inferiore, 1963), pp. 51–158; S. Maggiolini, *Il matrimonio, la verginità,* 3rd ed. (Milan: Ed. Ares, 1984).

[49] On the excellence of sacred virginity see Tertullian, *Exhort. Cast.,* 10; PL 2, 925; St. Cyprian, *Hab. Virg.,* 3 and 22; PL 4, 443 B and 461 A; St. Athanasius, *De Virg.;* PG 28, 252.

[50] Almost everywhere, one of the chief anxieties of the Church today is the dearth of

and they should discharge it principally by living full Christian lives"
(*Optatam totius,* October 28, 1965, no. 2, par. 1).

This doctrine *must not, however, be misunderstood in such wise that the superiority of virginity should throw into darkness the grandeur of the vocation to marriage or that the latter should imperil vocations to celibacy.* Every opposition between them is an error, because together these vocations are complementary.

> In the Church which, notwithstanding the variety of gifts, is one body in Christ (cf. 1 Cor 12:12–13), all vocations form a unity and are necessary for the Church (cf. 1 Cor 12:29–30). "Everyone ought to remain as he was when he was called" (1 Cor 7:20). "We, though many, are one body in Christ and individually members one of the other. We have gifts that differ according to the favor bestowed on each of us" (Rom 12:5–6). Therefore, here we are dealing not only with the harmony of integration but also of a mutual existential conditioning.[51]

History bears witness to this reality: esteem for marriage and esteem for virginity increase together, whereas the same pessimism that denies the possibility of celibacy leads to a rejection of the demands of marital holiness. Therefore, the more there is esteem for marriage, the more do vocations to apostolic celibacy flourish.

> ■ This is a point frequently stressed by the Magisterium. Thus, at the opening of the Council, John XXIII said to spouses: "Continue your efforts to reach Christian perfection in the conditions of your daily conjugal and family life. If it is true that the state of virginity is, of its own nature, superior to the state of marriage, it is equally true that this affirmation is in no way opposed, as you know, to the call given to all the faithful that 'they be holy, as the heavenly Father is holy' (Mt 5:48). The very honor that has been accorded by the Church to Christian virginity is precious for spouses, because the perfect chastity of consecrated persons is a constant reminder of the love of

---

vocations. Cf. Pius XII, apostolic exhortation *Menti Nostrae,* September 23, 1950: "Both in Catholic countries and in mission territories, the number of priests is insufficient to cope with the increasing demands" (AAS 42 [1950]: 682); John XXIII: "The problem of ecclesiastical and religious vocations is a daily preoccupation with the Pope.... Vocations are the object of his prayer, the ardent longing of his soul" (from the Allocution to the First International Congress on Religious Vocations, December 16, 1961, *L'Osservatore Romano,* [December 17, 1961]; AAS 54 [1962]: 33).

[51] Majdanski, *Communione di vita e d'amore,* pp. 58–59.

God; in marriage this love must also enliven and support the esteem for chastity proper to this state of life."[52]

The proper understanding of this complementarity implies that *wherever the holiness of marriage is fostered, there also vocations to celibacy flourish.* This is a fruit that must be expected from the Council, and it is surely not among the least. Always, in authentically Christian families, above all in large ones—which Vatican Council II praises in a special way (GS, no. 50, par. 6) and in which responsible parenthood flourishes in a way singled out by the Magisterium[53]—vocations to virginity are abundant. The Council insists, moreover, on reminding spouses of their obligation to promote such vocations: "The greatest contribution [to the fostering of priestly and religious vocations] is made by families which are animated by a spirit of faith, charity and piety and which provide, as it were, a first seminary" of vocations to the priesthood and to virginity (*Optatam totius,* no. 2, par. 1; cf. *Presbyterorum ordinis,* December 7, 1965, no. 11).

■ One expression of this complementarity is the fact that fidelity to celibacy is a condition for assuring and confirming the spouses in their search for holiness. The Holy Father John Paul II sets this forth in strong language: "Christian couples have the right to expect from celibate persons a good example and a witness of fidelity to their vocation until death."[54]

7. *Some pastoral implications.* The essential points that need to be cared for in the realization of this doctrine on the vocation of spouses to holiness can be synthesized as follows:

a. To consider as a duty of first rank, in the pastoral care of the family, the *reestablishment of the awareness of the dignity of marriage as a vocation to holiness.* The Council wished to emphasize this especially, pointing to it as one of the aspects for concern in the formation of candidates to the priesthood: "Students should have a proper knowledge of the duties and dignity of Christian marriage" (*Optatam totius,* no. 10, par. 2). Not only before, but also after, the Council—something

[52] John XXIII, *Discorsi, Messaggi, Colloqui,* vol. I, p. 297.
[53] Cf. Paul VI, encyclical *Humanae vitae,* July 25, 1968, no. 10, and *Familiaris consortio,* nos. 6, 14, 29, 30–32.
[54] *Familiaris consortio,* no. 16.

somewhat more inexplicable—this point was and has been forgotten to such an extent that one writer could say:

> Neglect of the doctrine about marriage as a vocation—and therefore God's plan for man as realized in the marriage of two persons—is at the same time both a symptom and a cause of the loss of its religious meaning. To me it seems that . . . here there is a specific *sin of omission* of pastoral theology today. It is necessary to safeguard and foster not only "the natural dignity of the state of matrimony" but also "its most high sacred value" (cf. GS, no. 47).[55]

> ■ On the other hand, when this teaching is set forth properly, the results have been indescribably fertile. "For almost forty years I have been preaching the vocational meaning of marriage. How many times have I seen the faces of so many, both men and women, light up, who, thinking that in their life devotion to God and a noble and pure love were incompatible, heard me say that marriage is a divine path on earth! . . . The person who is called to wedlock finds in it, with the grace of God, all the necessary means for being holy, for identifying himself more each day with Jesus and for leading to the Lord the persons with whom he lives."[56]

b. Moreover, it is necessary to know how *to shed on all the questions and difficulties that spouses can meet along their path the light of their call to holiness.* In truth, all aspects of the exigency of Christian doctrine on marriage and the family can be understood only in this light. At times— and today this will not be rare—it will be necessary, because of the confusion that dominates, to proceed with particular delicacy and comprehension in order to open human hearts and minds to the integrity of the divine demands; but always without obscuring the grandeur of this vocation. This is the meaning of the *law of graduality* spoken of in *Familiaris consortio:* far from yielding on any truth, the issue is to teach the truth with a love that is based on faith and hope in the help of God. It is, therefore, in no way a moral permissiveness, but rather the awareness that grace works in time and in men wounded by sin. Man would be betrayed were there not presented to him, because of a false indulgence,

> the full measure of what he can and must demand of himself. It would be to lie to the human spirit, to betray God's wisdom, and to

[55] Majdanski, *Communione di vita e d'amore*, pp. 62–63.
[56] Escrivá, *Conversations with Monsignor Escriva*, no. 91, p. 107.

enter into agreement with "the silence of shame," to denigrate the power of love and to devalue the freedom of the life to which man finds himself in fact called. What needs to be done is the precise contrary to all this. The Church, because it shares in the passion of Christ, knows better than anyone else the depth of that wound by which man has been harmed, how serious is his loss, with what love he must be loved even in his most extreme falls, in his ultimate misery, in the abyss of perdition. Reminding man of the demands of God's love, the Church itself lives this love, by sharing in the mercy of the shepherd who goes in search for his lost sheep, of the doctor who heals the sick, of the just one who carries the sins of those who offend him.

Refusing "concessions on the problems of the family and on the mystery of human love, the Church, far from taking an inhuman position, places herself—responding to her vocation—in the condition of Christ who is full of mercy and of goodness: she proclaims the salvation of man, reminding him of his deepest needs."[57]

> ■ Hiding the perspective of fidelity in love, or of generosity with respect to the transmission of life does not save man; this will take place, on the other hand, only by helping him to discover that with the grace of God he can live fully that way of life which perfectly corresponds to the call to holiness he has received.

c. Finally, it is necessary *to help spouses see that a clear manifestation of the holiness of their marriage is the joy with which they welcome vocations for their children and beg the Lord for them.* In truth, the family, the school of every vocation (cf. GS, no. 52), must be this school in a special way for vocations to celibacy and to virginity (GS, nos. 49 and 52; *Lumen gentium*, no. 11; *Apostolicam actuositatem*, no. 11). Not a small influence on this is exercised by the generosity with which they live their love and open themselves to the gift of life, because those who limit the number of their children for selfish reasons accept with more difficulty— and desire even less—the exclusive dedication of their children to God: the family "that fulfills its duties with generous fidelity, and is aware of its daily sharing in the mystery of the glorious Cross of Christ, becomes

---

[57] Jean-Marie Cardinal Lustiger, "Gradualité et conversion. En marge de l'Exhortation Apostolique *Familiaris consortio*", *L'Osservatore Romano* (February 16, 1982): 18. Cf. also A. Guenthor, "Das Gesetz der Gradualitaet oder das Wachsen und Reifen im christlichen Leben", in *Befreiung vom objektiv Guten? Vom verleugneten der Antikonzeption zum befreienden Ethos* (Vall-Schönstatt: Patris Verlag, 1982), pp. 139–55.

the primary and most excellent seedbed of vocations to a life of consecration to the Kingdom of God."[58]

B. *The role of conjugal love in the structure of marriage*

If the texts of the Council on marriage and the family are compared with those of the previous Magisterium, the novelty of its teaching on the vocational character of marriage is clearly recognized. But from a reading of the papers that came out during the Council and from the first comments, often heatedly made, one could think that the salient theme of the Council was another: to establish the role of conjugal love in marriage and its relationship to procreation.[59]

On this question, as a matter of fact, in the Council there were two tendencies that generated not a few polemics.

> The first of these feared that an excessive value had been given to conjugal love, in a way that imperiled the primordial importance of procreation as an end of marriage. The second, on its part, wishing to emphasize the capital value of conjugal love for the good of marriage, in practice ended up by reducing the importance of procreation as an essential end of marriage, fearing, as it were, that this would obscure conjugal love.[60]

In truth, GS did not accept either of these two tendencies; indeed, it overcame them in a deepening of doctrine, following its own proper line of argumentation in a way consistent with its teaching on the dignity and holiness of marriage. There is neither opposition nor any mutual hindering between conjugal love and procreation, but rather a comple-

---

[58] John Paul II, *Familiaris consortio*, no. 53.

[59] See for example Heylen, "La promozione della dignità del matrimonio e della famiglia", pp. 351ff.; Philippe Delhaye, "Impressions conciliaires. Esquisse d'une axiologie chrétienne", *L'Ami du clerge*, an. 75 no. 42 (1966): pp. 594ff.; F. Gil Delgado, *El matrimonio, problemas y horizontes nuevos* (Madrid: Alameda, 1967), pp. 129ff.; S. Lener, "Matrimonio e amore coniugale nella *Gaudium et spes* e nella *Humanae vitae*", in *La civiltà cattolica*, no. 2851 (1969): 26ff.

[60] Francisco Gil Hellín, "El lugar propio del amor conyugal en la estructura del matrimonio segun la *Gaudium et spes*", in *Annales Valentinos* 6, no. 11 (1980): 1–35; the citation is from p. 1. At the base of this polemic is the well-known study of H. Doms, *On the Meaning of Marriage* (New York: Sheed & Ward, 1940), a translation of his *Vom Sinn und Zweck der Ehe* (Breslau, 1935). On this see P. J. Viladrich, "Amor conyugal y esencia del matrimonio", *Ius Canonicum* 12 (1972): 342–49; Viladrich, *El amor y el matrimonio* (Madrid: Rialp, 1977); E. Molano, *Contribución al estudio sobre la esencia del matrimonio* (Pamplona: Eunsa, 1977).

mentarity. In fact, the texts of GS never speak of conjugal love as an end of marriage; they do not even conceive of it as a property of marriage; on the contrary, they predicate of love the same ends and the same properties that they predicate of the whole institution of marriage.[61]

Marriage is the institution of conjugal love: conjugal love, as marriage itself, is ordained to the "bonum prolis" and is the life-giving principle of the entire institution of marriage.

This is the second of the great lines of argument in the conciliar teaching. We will begin with the texts of GS that express the role of love in marriage; then we will discuss the nature of this love, its ends, and its properties; afterward, we will seek to specify how its role is differentiated in the matrimonial community, in the conjugal pact or "covenant". We will thus be able to conclude that GS, in effect, retrieves the classical doctrines of the *goods of marriage* and of conjugal love as the formal element of the community of persons that is marriage and makes them more explicit.

1. *The principal texts of the Council that establish the role of conjugal love in marriage: the relationship between love-institution and the end of marriage.* Right after the Council, the idea was widely diffused that GS had defined conjugal love as one of the ends of marriage, indeed its essential one: "It is undeniable that conjugal love, raised to the level of an objective end of marriage, has attained a place of first rank, by beginning to be considered as the primary reason of the matrimonial union."[62]

Since this mentality is widely disseminated, in order to avoid the equivocations it supports, it will be necessary to give an attentive reading to the conciliar texts: in them, love and the institution are shown as the two aspects of the unitive principle of a community of persons, marriage, which is ordained to the procreation and education of children.

GS teaches that marriage is a personal communion — *communitas coniugalis* — which springs from the conjugal pact or covenant (*foedus*). Thus, in order to designate marriage, it often uses indiscriminately the

---

[61] Gil Hellín, "El lugar propio del amor conyugal", p. 2.
[62] Heylen, "La promozione della dignità del matrimonio e della famiglia", p. 358.

terms *marriage* (*matrimonium*), the *conjugal community* (*communitas coniugalis*), and the *conjugal covenant* (*foedus coniugale*). It is to be noted that the constitution uses the term "marriage" (*matrimonium*) only a few times (no. 48, pars. 1, 2, and 4; no. 49, par. 2; no. 50, pars. 1 and 3; no. 52, pars. 1, 2, and 4). This is explained by recalling that from the very beginning of the chapter marriage is designated also by the expression "*communitas coniugalis*". "The well-being (*salus*) of the individual person and of both human and Christian society is closely bound up with the healthy state of the conjugal and family community [*communitatis coniugalis et familiaris*]" (GS, no. 47, par. 1). The will of the Fathers to present marriage as a community is evident, because the following number (no. 48)—which more amply describes marriage in its entirety—begins with the same expression: "The intimate *community of life and conjugal love* [*intima communitas vitae et amoris coniugalis*], established by God and endowed with its own proper laws, is rooted in [*instauratur*] the conjugal covenant [*foedere coniugii*]" (GS, no. 48). Therefore, marriage or the conjugal community is a reality that comes to be by reason of the contract or *conjugal covenant,* as the same number of the constitution reminds us a little later: "Thus the man and the woman, who by reason of their conjugal covenant [*foedere coniugali*] 'are no longer two but one flesh' (Matt. 19:6) . . . " (no. 48, par. 1).

a. The formal or unitive principle of this community is integrated by a *twofold element: conjugal love and the institution.* Such, in fact, is the meaning of the expression: "the intimate community of life and conjugal love established by God and endowed with its own proper laws" (no. 48, par. 1). The words "of life and love" (*vitae et amoris*) did not appear in the first redaction presented in the Council hall, which spoke only of the "conjugal community" (*communitas coniugalis*):[63] these words were introduced at the request of a good number of the Fathers, who wanted to make it clear, from the very beginning, that marriage is not only "an institution", but also a "*communitas vitae et amoris*".[64] The *Relatio* corroborates this interpretation, affirming that, as often as it

---

[63] "Communitas coniugalis a Creatore condita suisque legibus instructura, foedere coniugii seu irrevocabili consensu personali instauratur", *Schema receptum,* 61, p. 41, lines 6–7 (*Acta Synodalia,* vol. IV, pars I, p. 478).

[64] "Multi Patres inde ab initio non tantum institutum sed communionem vitae in instituto sublineare intendunt: quare aditio in texto proponitur: 'Intima communitas vitae et amoris' ", *Relatio ad Textum recognitum,* 52, A, p. 14 (*Acta Synodalia,* vol. VI, pars IV, p. 483).

speaks, in the continuation of paragraph 1 of number 48 of the stability of marriage, it seeks to emphasize that, even if love is an essential element for the existence of marriage, its later absence does not invalidate it.[65] Marriage, therefore, has two elements: love and the institution.[66] Thus the following paragraph can express matters in this way: "By their own nature [*indole autem sua naturali*] the very institution of marriage and conjugal love [*ipsum institutum matrimonii amorque coniugalis*] are ordained to the procreation and education of children [*ad procreationem et educationem prolis ordinantur*]" (GS, no. 48, par. 2).

The desire of the Fathers to emphasize this twofold dimension of the elements in marriage is also evident in the modifications introduced, or not admitted, in the definitive redaction, for the purpose of reestablishing or preserving the equilibrium between the two elements: "When the text explicitly mentions one with the absence—at least apparent—of the other, there immediately follows the proposal that the former be omitted or, on the other hand, that the missing element be introduced."[67] Thus in number 48, paragraph 1, the expression "covenant of love" (*foedere dilectionis*) will be changed into "conjugal covenant" (*foedere coniugalis*).[68] For this reason the constitution often adopts a double subject, i.e., "institution" and "conjugal love" in different expository passages: "The very institution of marriage and conjugal love are ordained to the procreation and education of children [*ipsum institutum matrimonii amorque coniugalis ad procreationem et educationem prolis ordinantur*]" (GS, no. 48, par. 1); "marriage and conjugal love . . . are ordained [*matrimonium et amor coniugalis . . . ordinantur*]" (GS, no. 50, par. 1). In short,

> it is not rare to find throughout the chapter passages in which there is attributed to conjugal love what had elsewhere been affirmed of the

---

[65] Cf. *Relatio ad Schema receptum*, 61, A, p. 103 (*Acta Synodalia*, vol. IV, pars I, p. 536).

[66] Thus Philippe Delhaye affirms: "The definitive text wished to take into account these two points of view (the institution and the personalist aspect of love). On the one hand, it affirmed that marriage is a human institution confirmed by the divine law and having its own goods and ends, thus removing it from human fantasies (GS, n. 48, par. 1). But on the other hand, from the very first words, marriage is presented as a community." "Dignité du mariage et de la famille", in *L'Eglise dans le monde de ce temps* (Paris: Editions du Cerf, 1966) II, p. 423.

[67] Gil Hellín, "El lugar propio del amor conyugal", pp. 21–22.

[68] *Textus Recognitus:* Responsum ad modum 24, I pars (*Acta Synodalia*, vol. IV, pars VII, p. 480).

institution or of marriage itself in general. . . . Thus, for example, there is affirmed of *amor coniugalis*[69] what had previously been said in a global way of the *communitas coniugalis*,[70] that is, the esteem in which it is held by so many people. Again, the one and the other, taken individually, that is, the institution [*institutum*][71] and conjugal love [*amor coniugalis*],[72] are noted as the targets of serious attacks against their nature and dignity. Thus, again, conjugal fidelity, with its intrinsic laws of unity and indissolubility, is seen as something proper to *amor coniugalis*,[73] being already a natural requirement of the *communitas coniugalis*[74,75]

These examples can be multiplied: it suffices, in fact, to examine number 49, paragraph 1, and number 48, paragraph 2, with respect to the elevation to the supernatural order of both the one (the institution) and the other (conjugal love), and number 48, paragraph 2, on the sacramental efficacy on them both, etc.[76]

---

[69] "Plures quoque nostrae aetatis homines verum amorem inter maritum et uxorem variis rationibus secundum honestos populorum et temporum mores manifestatum, magni faciunt [Many men of our time also have a high regard for true love between husband and wife as manifested in the noble customs of various times and peoples]" (GS, no. 49, par. 1).

[70] "Ideo christiani, una cum omnibus qui eandem communitatem [communitatis coniugalis et familiaris] magni aestimant, sincere gaudent de variis subsidiis quibus homines, in hac communitate amoris fovenda et in vita colenda, hodie progrediuntur [Thus Christians, along with all who highly esteem this same community (of conjugal and family life), today rejoice over the various helps whereby men make progress in this community for fostering love and for reverencing life]" (GS, no. 47, par. 1).

[71] "Non ubique vero huius institutionis dignitas eadem claritate illucescit, siquidem polygamia, divortii lue, amore sic dicto libero, aliisve deformationibus obscuratur [But not everywhere does the dignity of this institution shine forth with the same clarity, for it is obscured by polygamy, the plague of divorce, so-called free love, and other deformations]" (GS, no. 47, par. 2).

[72] "Insuper amor nuptialis saepius egoismo, hedonismo et illicite usibus contra generationem profanatur" [Moreover, married love is too often profaned by selfishness, hedonism, and illicit acts against the generation of life]" (GS, no. 47, par. 2).

[73] "Amor ille mutua fide ratus . . . inter prospera et adversa corpore ac mente indissolubiliter fidelis est, proinde ab omni adulterio et divortio alienus remanet [Endorsed by mutual fidelity, this love . . . is faithful amidst prosperities and adversities of both body and mind, and hence remains a stranger to every adultery and divorce]" (GS, no. 49, par. 2).

[74] "Quae intima unio, utpote mutua duarum personarum donatio, sicut et bonum liberorum, plenam coniugum fidem exigunt atque indissolubilem eorum unitatem urgent [This intimate union, as the mutual giving of two persons, just as the good of the children, demand the full fidelity of the spouses and require their indissoluble unity]" (GS, no. 48, par. 1).

[75] Gil Hellín, "El lugar propio del amor conyugal", p. 28.

[76] Cf. no. 48, par. 2, and no. 49, par. 2; etc. See Gil Hellín, "El lugar propio del amor conyugal", pp. 29–30.

■ Something that reveals this difference and, at the same time, the complementarity between the institution and conjugal love, above all if one keeps in mind the history of the redaction of the text, is the second paragraph of number 47, where the evils and deformations of marriage are described. Leaving to one side socioeconomic difficulties, the text distinguishes two kinds of errors: the first kind—polygamy, divorce, and free love—obscure the dignity of the institution of marriage itself; among the others that are then enumerated, on the other hand—selfishness, hedonism, and illicit practices against conception—none directly attacks the essential properties of marriage and hence can coexist with the institution; but they are opposed to conjugal love, which is protected by the institution, and destroy it, ending up, as it were, by corrupting the institution of marriage. This subdivision is the fruit of not a few proposals and modifications made by the Fathers, and their admission into the text served to guide the aforesaid differentiation between the institution of marriage and conjugal love and the evils attacking each.[77]

b. Conjugal love and the institution of marriage have *the same ends and properties;* that is, respectively, the procreation and education of children and mutual help, and unity and indissolubility. As we have seen, number 48, paragraph 1, speaks in this way with respect to the principal end: "Indole autem sua naturali, ipsum institutum matrimonii amorque coniugalis ad procreationem et educationem prolis ordinantur [By their very nature the institution itself of marriage and conjugal love are ordained to the procreation and education of children]" (cf. also no. 50, par. 1). With respect to the properties of marriage, there are several texts indicating unity and indissolubility as the properties of both the institution and of conjugal love (GS, nos. 48, par. 1, and 49, par. 2). Moreover, of both—love and the institution—is it affirmed that they are perfected and elevated by the grace of the sacrament (GS, nos. 48, par. 1, and 49, par. 2).

■ Here also the history of the text confirms that this was the desire of the Fathers. For example, with respect to the redaction of number 50, where the matter under discussion is the end of marriage and of conjugal love, the *Relatio* insists that the word *matrimonium,* which at first was not used, was added for this reason: "Mention of the *institution*

---

[77] See *Textus Recognitus. Responsum ad Modum 5 et 6 (Acta Synodalia,* vol. IV, pars VII, pp. 473–74). Cf. Gil Hellín, "El lugar propio del amor conyugal", pp. 10–13.

of marriage was added, so that a juridical element might be joined to the life of personal love."[78] At the same time the *Relatio* justified the inclusion of the words *"eo tendunt ut"* precisely because the "finality of the institution and the finality of love [*finalitas instituti et amoris*]" is in this way more clearly expressed.[79]

c. What distinguishes and, at the same time, inseparably unites love and the institution, as elements of the marital community, is that *love constitutes the personal reality that the institution confirms, protects, and sanctions before God and men.* In particular, GS affirms that

> from the conjugal covenant ... that is, from the human act by which the spouses mutually give and receive each other, there arises in society an institution [marriage], confirmed by divine ordination [*institutum ordinatione divina firmum oritur etiam coram societate*]; this holy bond [*hoc vinculum sacrum*], for the good of the spouses themselves, for the good of their children, and for the good of society [*intuitu boni, tum coniugum et prolis tum societatis*], does not depend on human choice [*non ex humano arbitrio pendet*]. God himself is the author of marriage, endowed with various goods and ends [*Ipse vero Deus est auctor matrimonii, variis bonis ac finibus praediti*] (GS, no. 48, par. 1).

Therefore, the institution of marriage arises from an act of love, and the institution protects love, for true conjugal love is not limited or impeded by it, but rather both these elements mutually require and complete each other, as integrative elements of the one same reality: marriage or the conjugal community.[80]

> ■ Love and the institution "come to be in a mutual and essential dependence, and they constantly require each other: *love* has need of the institution in order to be conjugal, and the institution of marriage always implies a radical exigency to be enlivened by love. From this it follows that conjugal love must be present in the different concrete aspects of marriage, such as procreation, the education of children, and the mutual help the spouses give to each other, because they are truly

[78] *Relatio ad Schema receptum*, 63, B, p. 105 (*Acta Synodalia*, vol. IV, pars I, p. 538): "Mentio de *matrimonii instituto* addita est, ut elementum iuridicum cum vita personalis amoris coniungatur."

[79] "Loco: 'eo proditur ut' dicitur: 'eo tendunt ut', ut tollatur ambiguitas vocabuli usurpati et melius indicetur finalitas instituti et amoris" (*Relatio ad Schema receptum*, 63, C, p. 105 [*Acta Synodalia*, vol. IV, pars I, p. 539]).

[80] Cf. P. Bonnet, *L'essenza del matrimonio canonico. Contributo allo studio dell'amore coniugale* (Padua: Cedam, 1976), pp. 130ff.

human ends. In the same way, the unity and indissolubility of marriage demand to be enlivened by conjugal love.... If it is necessary that conjugal love be present in the whole reality of marriage this is so because the institution and conjugal love are the two formalities that adequately define it; that is, marriage is the institution of conjugal love."[81]

This is a matter on which *Familiaris consortio* will be especially explicit; specifically, speaking of the gift proper to conjugal love, and of its totality, it affirms: "The only 'place' in which this self-giving in its whole truth is made possible is marriage, the covenant of conjugal love freely and consciously chosen, whereby man and woman accept the intimate community of life and love willed by God himself.[82] ... The institution of marriage is not an undue interference by society or authority.... Rather it is an interior requirement of the covenant of conjugal love."[83]

2. *The nature, properties, and ends of conjugal love according to "Gaudium et spes".* Love, to which the constitution attributes such an important role in marriage, is not a passion or mere sentiment, but that *"eminently human"* affection that proceeds from free will and assumes into itself, ennobling them, all the natural tendencies of the person:

> That love, as eminently human, since it is directed from one person to another person by an affection rooted in the will [*cum a persona in personam voluntatis affectu dirigatur*], embraces the good of the whole person and therefore is capable of enriching with a peculiar dignity the manifestations of both mind and body and to ennoble them as elements and special signs of conjugal friendship (GS, no. 49, par. 1).[84]

It is therefore a *love of friendship,* that is, that kind of love that exists only in God and in the spiritual creature, and that in man, while sinking its roots principally in the spirit, also embraces the integrity of body and soul. Therefore, being an act of the person and not a more or less blind instinctive impulse, this love can stand at the origin of the stable community of life that is marriage, by means of the conjugal covenant of love (cf. GS, no. 48, par. 1).

[81] Gil Hellín, "El lugar propio del amor conyugal", p. 35.

[82] GS, no. 48.

[83] John Paul II, *Familiaris consortio,* no. 11.

[84] On this see Antonio Miralles, "Amor y matrimonio en la *Gaudium et spes*", *Lateranum* 48.2 (1982): 295–354.

■ Thus is refuted the Platonism that has at times infiltrated into the minds of those who study marriage, a Platonism that looked on conjugal love with a kind of diffidence, at times as a kind of permission— one thinks of the exasperation this idea of love aroused in Luther— rather than as a noble reality of man and therefore good and sanctifiable. "The pure and noble love of spouses is a sacred thing. As a priest, I bless it with all my heart. . . . Marriage is a sacrament that makes one flesh of two bodies. Theology expresses this fact in a striking way when it teaches us that the matter of the sacrament is the bodies of husband and wife. Our Lord sanctifies and blesses the mutual love of husband and wife. He foresees, not only a union of souls, but a union of bodies as well."[85] One can thus write that, "after so many centuries, we have begun to think that Thomistic hylemorphism must be applied also to sexual life. One then sees that bodily union can be—must be—the expression of that of souls. A human being communicates with other human beings by means of the body: by word, by gesture. Therefore, conjugal acts are an expression" proper to conjugal friendship.[86]

"Our Lord", GS continues, "has deigned to *heal, perfect, and elevate this love with a special gift of grace and of charity* [Hunc amorem Dominus, speciali gratiae et caritatis dono, sanare, perficere et elevare dignatus est]" (GS, no. 49, par. 2). The Church knows that conjugal love is realized in men wounded by original sin and that they many times tend toward selfishness. Therefore, even if this love, being a love of friendship, is already inclined to the generous gift of self, in order for it to develop fully, it has need of the healing action of grace. With this, it becomes fully human and then divine:

A love like this, bringing together the human and the divine, leads the spouses to the free and mutual gift of themselves, experienced in tender affection and action, and permeates the whole of their lives;[87] moreover, this love is perfected and grows by its generous exercise [Talis amor, humana simul et divina consocians, coniuges ad liberum et mutuum sui ipsius donum, tenero affectu et opere probatum, conducit totamque vitam eorum pervadit; immo ipse generosa sua operositate perficitur et crescit]" (GS, no. 49, par. 2).

[85] Escrivá, "Marriage: A Christian Vocation", no. 24, p. 45.
[86] Delhaye, "Impressions conciliaires", p. 597.
[87] Cf. Pius XI, *Casti connubii;* AAS 22 (1930): 547–48.

Grace, therefore, heals and perfects the nature of conjugal love, establishing marriage as a sacrament and the state of marriage as a divine vocation (GS, no. 49, par. 3).

Conjugal love, then, is characterized by GS as having the following properties: *unity and indissolubility.* Already, on the natural plane of creation, it has this requirement: "This intimate union, as the mutual giving of two persons, as well as the good of the children, demand the full fidelity of the spouses and require their indissoluble unity" (GS, no. 48, par. 1). Both properties are confirmed and ratified by grace: in virtue of the sacrament, "Christ remains with them [the spouses], so that just as he loved the Church and gave himself up for her,[88] so too the spouses, by their mutual self-giving, may love each other with perpetual fidelity [*se invicem perpetua fidelitate diligant*]" (GS, no. 48, par. 2). And later on, it is said:

> This love, endorsed by mutual fidelity, and above all consecrated by Christ's sacrament, is indissolubly faithful amidst prosperity and adversity both of the body and of the spirit, and consequently remains foreign to every kind of adultery and divorce. The unity of marriage, confirmed by the Lord, shines forth brilliantly in the equal personal dignity which must be given to man and wife in mutual and unreserved love (GS, no. 49, par. 2).

Finally, GS teaches that *conjugal love has as its intrinsic end the procreation and education of children.* This is the end both of the institution of marriage and of conjugal love: "By their own nature, both the institution of marriage itself and conjugal love are ordained to the procreation and education of children [Indole autem sua naturali, ipsum institutum matrimonii amorque coniugalis ad procreationem et educationem prolis ordinantur]" (GS, no. 48, par. 1); this is almost literally repeated in number 50: "Marriage and conjugal love by their own nature are ordained to procreating and educating children [Matrimonium et amor coniugalis indole sua ad prolem procreandam et educandam ordinantur]" (par. 1). Later on, the document furnishes the biblical foundation for this teaching: "God himself said: 'it is not good that man should be alone' (Gen. 2:18), and 'from the beginning [he] made them male and female' (Matt. 19:4), wishing to communicate to them a

---

[88] Cf. Eph 5:25.

special participation in his own creative work, he blessed the man and woman, saying, 'Increase and multiply' (Gen. 1:28)." And the passage then concludes:

> As a result, *the true cultivation of conjugal love* and the whole structure (*ratio*) of the family arising therefrom, without neglecting [*posthabitis*] the other ends of marriage, *tend to this* [*eo tendunt*], that the spouses are disposed by a courageous spirit [*forti animo dispositi sint*] *to cooperate with the love of the Creator and Redeemer,* who through them will day by day increase and enrich his family (GS, no. 50, par. 1).[89]

> ■ It is difficult to understand how some could have attributed to GS the making of conjugal love as an end—indeed, the first end—of marriage. The constitution says, many times, that the primordial end of marriage is children.[90] And when it speaks of the other ends, conformably to the Tradition cited, it refers to mutual aid and the remedy of concupiscence. It does not list them in detail, however, perhaps in order not to exclude other ends, such as the apostolic and social tasks of the family (cf. GS, no. 52), and because of the more technical character of an enumeration of this kind.

Therefore, the most novel affirmation of GS, and that which signals true theological advance on the issue, is that conjugal love— and not only marriage—has as its end the procreation and education of children.

What distinguishes this text, in relationship to the previous Magisterium on the ends of marriage, is that it distinguishes between two formally diverse elements contained in the conjugal community [the institution of marriage and conjugal love]. It thus makes explicit "the significance of conjugal love even for the procreating and educating of children" [*momentum amoris coniugalis etiam ad ipsam prolem procreandam et educandam*].[91] While up to now the Magisterium of the Church affirmed that marriage "tends toward [the procreation and education of children]," Vatican Council II tells us that both the

[89] On this see R. Schnackenburg and H. Greeven, "Die Ehe nach dem Neuen Testament", in *Theologie der Ehe* (Regensburg: Pustet, 1969), pp. 9–79.

[90] And this is shown, in a radical way, in the works cited in the notes of the document, including the first note of no. 48 of GS. On this see E. Lio, *"Humanae vitae" e coscienza. L'insegnamento di Karol Wojtyla teologo e Papa* (Vatican City: Libreria Editrice Vaticana, 1980), pp. 99–100.

[91] "Mentio fit duo, uti multi patres petierunt, de matrimonio simul et amore. Momentum etiam amoris coniugalis etiam ad ipsam procreandam educandamque sublineatur" (*Relatio ad Schema receptum,* 61, C, p. 103 [Acta Synodalia, vol. IV, pars I, p. 536]).

institutional aspect and conjugal love "tend toward [the procreation and education of children]."[92]

So runs the history of the text.[93]

3. *Conjugal love, always maintaining its essentiality to marriage, has a different role in the marital covenant and in the marital community.* Here we reach a central point for understanding GS. Conjugal love appeared there in its fundamental importance, along with the institution, in the structure of the community of marriage with the same ends and properties of the institution and of the whole community. Therefore, it is neither an end nor a property of marriage and is not to be confused either with the institution. But then, what is its specific role in marriage and in the covenant that stands at the origin of marriage? We will proceed as follows:

a. Marriage is a community of persons, a man and a woman, destined to develop itself in the more complete community of the family, and is specified as such by *two essential elements.* On the one hand, its intrinsic and proper *end* is the procreation and education of children. On the other hand, its *unitive or formal principle* is precisely conjugal love: that natural attraction between a man and a woman that leads them to the most intimate and indissoluble union, ordained for the procreation and education of children; a natural inclination that is assumed and ratified by the spouses by means of their conjugal "covenant", their mutual faith in each other (*"Amor ille mutua fide ratus"*, GS no. 49, par. 2, tells us).

■ The greatest rigor appears here. Every community of persons, if freely chosen, arises from an agreement and is characterized by two elements: the end proposed and the relationships of the union that are established along with that end. It is this way also that the twofold aspect of marriage is explained: the formal or unitive element of the conjugal community is love; and the institution that helps and protects it. In this case, we are concerned with an institution directly willed and structured by God. ("From the human act, whereby the spouses mutually give and receive each other, arises an institution confirmed by

[92] Gil Hellín, "El lugar propio del amor conyugal", p. 16.

[93] Cf. *Schema receptum, Textus recognitus* and *Modi (Acta Synodalia,* vol. IV, pars VII, pp. 347–464). On the line of argumentation see Gil Hellín, "El lugar propio del amor conyugal", pp. 14–21.

divine ordination [Actu humano, quo coniuges sese mutuo tradunt atque accipiunt, institutum ordinatione divina firmum oritur]", of which "God himself is the author . . . endowed with various goods and ends [Ipse vero Deus est auctor . . . variis bonis ac finibus praediti]" [GS, no. 48, par. 1]).

Recognizing conjugal love as the unitive or formal element of marriage is in harmony with the traditional doctrine; at the same time, doing so avoids the danger of making matters ambiguous by assigning to an institution two essential ends that could become opposed to each other. To do this, however, i.e., to assign to marriage two essential ends, is nothing but an error, spread abroad after the Council; it is the source of not a few of the present-day confusions about the concept of responsible parenthood.[94] The Council was very clear on this matter, as is evident from the *Acta,* since the matter was discussed during the conciliar sessions. Conjugal love *was never conceived* by the Fathers as an end juxtaposed to or in contraposition to procreation; indeed, GS emphasizes many times that conjugal love *is ordained* to procreation (GS, no. 48, par. 1; no. 50, par. 1).

The constitution speaks of conjugal love and of children as *two great goods* of marriage and insists on the unity between them.[95] But it recognized one *primordial end,* to which are ordained, by their very inner nature, both marriage and conjugal love: this end is the procreation and education of children.[96] Moreover, the conciliar commission, responding to the modi presented by the Fathers, explicitly made it clear that, although it did not adopt the terminology of primary and secondary ends, this was due to the technical character of these terms and because it was already abundantly clear in the text of the docu-

[94] Cf. the Secretary of State of the Holy See, Letter to the Second Congress for the Family of the Americas, August 11, 1982.

[95] The *Relatio* of the *Schema* of May 28, 1985, makes this quite clear: "Introductio huius ideae duorum principalium bonorum matrimonii (procreationis nempe et amoris) uniendorum, semper fortius expetita fuit et in duobus supplementis scriptis fere unanimiter expostulatur [The introduction of this idea of two principal goods of marriage (procreation, namely, and love) that must be kept united was desired more strongly more and more and was asked for almost unanimously in two written supplements]" (*Acta Synodalia,* vol. IV, pars I, p. 536).

[96] In particular, the expressions *indole sua naturali* and *ordinantur* of no. 48 of GS (repeated in no. 50) were introduced in the final scheme in order to accept a proposal of 179 Fathers, who demanded that procreation be emphasized as constituting the *intrinsic* end of marriage, and another, of 16 Fathers, on the *primary* character of this end; see *Acta Synodalia,* vol. IV, pars VI, p. 475.

ment that the primordial end of marriage is the procreation and education of children.[97]

b. The community of life and love proper to marriage arises from the *"foedus"* or covenant of conjugal love, as we have seen. However, the role of love differs in the community and in the conjugal covenant, although it is essential for both.

In the conjugal covenant, love is one of the essential goods on which consent bears; that is, that "intimate conjoining of persons and of activities [*intima personarum atque operum coniunctione*]" by which the man and the woman "by reason of their conjugal covenant *are no longer two but one flesh* (Matt. 19:6) [*foedere coniugali iam non sunt duo sed una caro*]" (GS, no. 48, par. 1). Certainly, the cause of marriage is the mutual consent manifested by the spouses [*"foedere coniugii seu irrevocabili consensu personali instauratur"*], i.e., the human act "whereby the spouses mutually give and receive one another [*quo coniuges sese mutuo tradunt atque accipiunt*]" (GS, no. 48, par. 1);[98] but conjugal love is the object of this consent, inasmuch as it is one of its essential contents (the intimate "community of life and love" it establishes: GS, no. 48, par. 1). This has always been taught by Christian Tradition, and in an especially explicit way in the Augustinian-Thomistic formulation. In fact, St. Augustine said: "The perfection of marriage derives not only from procreation, but from the natural communion which it establishes between the man and the woman",[99] in such a way that, "if the one or the other is excluded, I do not see how we can continue to call it a marriage."[100] And, on his part, St. Thomas affirms that faithful love until death and the ordination to children are essential elements of marital consent in such a way that, if one or the other is wanting, "marriage cannot exist, because these are caused in marriage by the very consent of the spouses; so that, if anything contrary to them is expressed in the consent that makes marriage, it would not be a true marriage."[101] The consent constitutive of marriage, constitutive of the *foedus* or covenant, therefore

---

[97] Cf. *Acta Synodalia*, vol. IV, pars VII, p. 478. On this subject see Miralles, "Naturaleza y sacramento", pp. 155–58.

[98] "Causa efficiens matrimonii . . . est mutuus consensus" (Council of Florence, *Decretum pro Armenis* [H. Denzinger and A. Schoenmetzer, *Enchiridion Symbolorum Definitionum et Declarationum de rebus fidei et morum*, 34th ed. (Barcelona-Rome: Herder, 1967), (DS), no. 1327]).

[99] *De bono coniugali*, cap. 3, no. 3; PL 40,375.

[100] Ibid., cap. 5, no. 5.

[101] *Summa theologiae*, III, supplement, q. 49, a. 3.

bears on both conjugal love and on the end of marriage, that is, on the good of procreation.

■ Because of this, one can say: "Conjugal consent is nothing else than the mutual decision to get married, that is, the irrevocable choice of a total openness to the other, the communication and self-giving to the 'thou' of the other of all one's maleness or femaleness respectively. In this sense, conjugal consent is the foundational act of the marriage."[102] Consent itself is, therefore, an act of love; independently of their prior love as fiancés, the spouses bind themselves with mutual love, which from then on will be owed: a *love ratified by an obligation,* which is *destined to grow precisely through its generous exercise* (cf. GS, no. 49, pars. 1–2).

The Council preferred, for these reasons, the term conjugal *covenant* (*foedus coniugale*), rich in biblical resonances, to that of *contract. Foedus* better expresses the idea of the mutual gift of love, being the word with which is designated, in holy Scripture, the relationship of predilection between God and the people Israel, of which the sacrament of matrimony is the sign: "Just as of old God encountered his people with a covenant of love and fidelity,[103] so now the Savior of men and the Spouse of the Church[104] encounters Christian spouses by means of the sacrament of matrimony . . . so that spouses, by their mutual gift of self, might love one another with perpetual fidelity" (GS, no. 48, par. 2).

The term *contract,* although it serves to express similar realities, is too generic and vague; in fact, ordinarily it is adopted in modern languages to designate those agreements that bear on things and are usually capable of being rescinded by the mutual agreement of the parties.[105]

In the conjugal community, love is the life-giving principle, owed by virtue of the very consent that has generated it, but whose actual absence does not destroy it. Born from the human act with which the spouses give themselves to one another and receive one another, destined to be and to grow as a community of life and of love, the community of marriage does not depend on the arbitrary will of the spouses; and this

[102] Viladrich, "Amor conyugal y esencia del matrimonio", 311; see also P. Bonnet, *L'essenza del matrimonio canonico,* p. 40.

[103] Cf. Hos 2; Jer 3:6–13; Ezek 16 and 23; Is 54.

[104] Mt 19:15; Mk 2:19–20; Lk 5:34–35; Jn 3:29; cf. also 2 Cor 11:2; Eph 5:27; Rev 19:7–8, 21:2, and 9.

[105] "Mentio non fit 'de contractu matrimoniali,' sed verbis clarioribus sermo est 'de irrevocabili consensu personali,' secundum vota Patrum. Additur terminus biblicus 'foedus,' intuitu etiam orientalium, pro quibus 'contractus' quasdam difficultates facit" (*Relatio ad Schema receptum,* 61, A, pp. 102ff. [*Acta Synodalia,* vol. IV, pars I, p. 536]). See also Marcelino Zalba, "Dignidad del matrimonio y la familia", *Comentarios a la Constitución "Gaudium et spes" sobre la Iglesia en el mundo actual* (Madrid: Bac, 1968), p. 411.

is so because their consent is the origin of an "institution ratified by divine ordination" (GS, no. 48, par. 1). Therefore, the unjust and unlawful violation later on of the requirements of love cannot annul either the consent of the community, as the Fathers willed explicitly to emphasize (cf. GS, no. 48, par. 1).[106] Therefore, in the conjugal community, love is also an *essential good,* existing at least *as a requirement,* although it can actually be lacking. In fact, "the intimate union [of the spouses], as the mutual gift of two persons, as well as the good of the children . . . *require* the full fidelity of the spouses and demand their indissoluble unity" (GS, no. 48, par. 1). The "love ratified by mutual faith" must be "indissolubly faithful amidst the prosperities and adversities of both body and spirit" (GS, no. 49, par. 2).

■ Therefore, those ways of interpreting the Council are inadmissible that claim to multiply the causes of nullity, to the point that they hold that the absence of love, often reduced to sentiment, is a reason for dissolving marriage.[107] This is a false interpretation, which was pointedly and directly repudiated by Paul VI as corruptive of the meaning of conjugal love as formulated by the Council: "There cannot be admitted, in any way, a notion of conjugal love which leads to abandoning or diminishing the force and the meaning of the well-known principle: *matrimonium facit partium consensus.* . . . Such consent is an *act of the will* having the character of a covenant (the *conjugal covenant,* as we are accustomed to say)", which generates a relationship or stable bond that can not be revoked. "This is the doctrine that the Constitution *Gaudium et spes,* notwithstanding its pastoral character, openly taught with the words: 'the intimate community of life and love, founded by the Creator, and endowed with its own laws, is established by the conjugal covenant, that is to say, by their irrevocable personal consent'.[108]"[109]

Thus, acknowledging, in conformity with the Council, the essential role of love in marriage does not mean making marriage dependent

---

[106] "Notio instituti matrimonii sequenti phrasi firmatur, ne ullus censeat sese illud arbitrio suo postea dissolvere posse; aut, deficiente amore etiam requisito, matrimonium suum nullum fieri" (*Relatio ad Schema receptum,* A, p. 103 [*Acta Synodalia,* vol. IV, pars I, p. 536]).

[107] Cf. V. Fagiolo, "Essenza e fini del matrimonio secondo la Costituzione pastorale *Gaudium et spes*", *Ephemerides Iuris Canonici* 23 (1967): 179ff.

[108] GS, no. 48.

[109] Paul VI, Address of February 9, 1976 (*Ad Praelatos Auditores, Advocatos et Officiales Sacrae Romanae Rotae*); AAS 68 (1976): 206–7; *Enchiridion Familiae: Textos del Magisterio Pontificio y Conciliar sobre el Matrimonio y la Familia (Siglos I a XX),* ed. A. Sarmiento and Javier Escrivá-Ivars, vol. 3 (Madrid: Ediciones Rialp, 1992), pp. 2158–59. Cf. G. Baldanza, "In che senso ed

upon the contingent presence of this love in fact, nor does it imply that other causes of nullity other than the absence of consent or factors that vitiate it.[110] Rather, it makes manifest the true nature of marriage as an institution born of love, which is the origin of marriage and must permeate it, and whose institutional requirements are not an extrinsic adjunct to love but the expression of its very being. In the conjugal covenant, the spouses, as Paul VI says, "express the decision of belonging to one another for all of their life and of contracting with that end an objective bond whose laws and requirements, far from being a slavery, are a guarantee and a protection."[111]

■ Love is an essential good of marriage, but at the same time, it is a fruit of freedom. Therefore, it can not exist other than in this way. First, in marriage *in its becoming (in fieri)*, it exists as the object of the covenant: *"in suis principiis"*, as St. Thomas says.[112] Afterward, in the community of life and love already established, in marriage *in its having become (in facto esse)*, it exists as a fundamental good through its development, which is moreover a stringent obligation of the spouses, but it can be lacking in fact, being a good entrusted to human freedom. The same thing is true of the good of children, because both are essentially the object of matrimonial consent (in such wise that, should they be excluded, there is no marriage); but once the covenant has been established, both become obligations, moral and juridical; but they can, in fact, be missing because of the will of man. In such case, they are absent, essentially, as disordinations, as faults, as injustices, while remaining in their condition as duties. They are missing not from the essence but from the life of the marriage, without annulling it: this is the risk inseparable from every good that is to be preserved through the work of human freedom.

4. *The Council substantively adopted for itself the doctrine of the "goods of marriage" and that of love as the form or life-giving principle of marriage,* which enjoyed wide acceptance and welcome in Tradition, developing these doctrines in conformity with the needs of the modern mind.

---

entro quali limiti si puo parlare di rilevanza giuridica dell'amore coniugale dopo la Costituzione pastorale *Gaudium et spes"*, *La Scuola Cattolica* 96 (1968): 43–66; A. de la Hera, "Sobre la significación del amor en la regulación jurídica del matrimonio", *Ius Canonicum* (1966): 569–82.

[110] On this see Javier Hervada, "Cuestiones varias sobre el matrimonio", *Ius Canonicum* 13 (1973): 51. See also Miralles, "Amor y matrimonio en la *Gaudium et spes"*, 319–21.

[111] Paul VI, "Il matrimonio: perfezione umana, sacramento cristiano", in *Insegnamenti di Paolo VI* (Vatican City: Typis Polyglottis Vaticanis, 1970), vol. 8, p. 303.

[112] *Summa theologiae*, III, supplement, q. 49, a. 3, corpus and ad 4.

In fact, rereading, in the light of everything said thus far, number 48 of GS, one can easily recognize the scheme of the *goods*. In the first paragraph, after a global and implicit reference to the "three goods" ("endowed with various goods and ends [*variis bonis ac finibus praediti*]"), these are examined one after the other according to the traditional order: *proles* (children) and *fides* (faithful love) (in the successive points of paragraph 1) and the *sacramentum* (the sacrament) (in par. 2). Then, numbers 49 and 50 are devoted to the study, respectively, of conjugal love and of children, or of the two goods, essential to every marriage, that in Christians are perfected by the sacrament. Therefore, the schema of the goods, if not formally present, is found in fact at the basis of the conciliar doctrine on marriage.[113] And this is so because this schema is also more apt for the pastoral purpose of the constitution.[114]

■ Certainly, the term *good* is adopted many times in the Constitution also in a more general sense. But the reference to the "three intrinsic goods" in number 48, paragraph 1, is made clear by the footnote accompanying the words *"variis bonis ac finibus praediti"*, in which reference is made to the classic texts on the doctrine of the goods,[115] distinguishing them from other goods derived from them.[116] Moreover, responding to the "modus" of a Father who wanted explicit mention of the three goods,[117] the commission itself refuted its opportuneness precisely because "the primordial importance of *procreation and education* is

[113] Thus one author affirms: "In redactione numeri 48 textus conciliaris schema bonorum sublatet ac notabilem influxum procul dubio in ea exercuit.... Expositio doctrinae de matrimonio et familia quae in constitutione habetur, potius accedit ad schema bonorum quam ad quodlibet ex aliis duobus schematibus conceptualibus (de finibus vel de essentia et proprietatibus), quibus doctrina de matrimonio traditionaliter proponitur [The schema of the goods lies underneath the redaction of number 48 of the conciliar text, and no doubt exercised a notable influence on it.... The exposition of the doctrine on marriage and the family which is found in the Constitution is in greater harmony with the schema of the goods than any of the other two conceptual schemes (of the ends of marriage or of its essence and properties) whereby the doctrine on marriage was traditionally proposed]" (U. Navarrette, "Structura iuridica matrimonii secundum Concilium Vaticanum II", *Periodica de re morali, canonica, liturgica* 56 (1967): 577 and 564.

[114] Gil Hellín, "Los 'bona matrimonii' en la Constitución pastoral *Gaudium et spes*", *Scripta Theologica* 11 (1971), particularly pp. 32ff.

[115] In fact, this note, the first of no. 48, says: "Cf. St. Augustine, *De bono coniugali*: PL 40,375–376 and 394; St. Thomas, *Summa Theologiae*, Supplement, Quaest. 49, art. 3 ad 1; *Decretum pro Armenis*: Denz. 702 (1327); Pius XI, Encyclical *Casti connubii*: AAS 22 (1930): 543–555: Denz. 2227–2238 (3703–3714)."

[116] Cf. Gil Hellín, "Los 'bona matrimonii' ", no. 49, p. 34.

[117] "Unus denique Pater petit ut *explicite* memorentur *bona* matrimonii: 'de hisce bonis revera agitur, attamen ...'" Modus 15, F (*Acta Synodalia*, vol. IV, pars VII, p. 477).

mentioned at least 10 times in the text, the *sacrament* is mentioned many times, and *fidelity and indissolubility* are emphasized at least seven times in the text."[118]

Thus, we can say that the constitution not only welcomed in its substance the schema of the goods, but did this with greater precision than any other document of the Magisterium. In the first paragraph of number 48, it speaks of the two goods of marriage as an institution of creation. It begins with the good of children (*bonum prolis*), the intrinsic and natural end of marriage: "By their own nature the institution of marriage and conjugal love are ordered to the procreation and education of children" (GS, no. 48, par. 1; cf. no. 52, par. 1). And it regards this as an end precisely in its formality as a good: "Children are the most outstanding good of marriage and greatly contribute to the good of the parents themselves [Filii sunt praestantissimum matrimonii bonum et ad ipsorum parentum bonum maxime conferunt]" (GS, no. 50, par. 1). In what follows, the constitution is concerned with the *bonum fidei,* which implies the need of unity and indissoluble fidelity: "This intimate union, as the mutual gift of two persons, and the good of the children demand the full fidelity of the spouses and require their indissoluble unity [Quae intima unio, utpote mutua duarum personarum donatio, sicut et bonum liberorum, plenam coniugum fidem exigunt atque indissolubilem eorum unitatem urgent]" (GS, no. 48, par. 1). Therefore, the "good of fidelity" appears in its integrity: in its aspect of a good, of a mutual self-giving and union, of help joined to service, which implies, as a negative duty, the obligation of breaking neither the unity nor the indissolubility of marriage.[119] It avoided, as *Casti connubii* had not, linking indissolubility to the *bonum sacramenti;* and it emphasized fidelity in the biblical sense of a communion between the spouses: their "one flesh". The sacrament not only establishes but perfects this indissolubility, already pertaining to the order of creation, just as it also perfects the unity or the way of tending toward the good of children: that is, all the goods that by nature are proper to marriage.

■ The relationship between these two goods, *proles et fides,* which integrate the essence of every marriage, even among the nonbaptized —

---

[118] *Responsum ad Modum* 15, F (*Acta Synodalia,* vol. IV, pars VII, p. 477).

[119] This is clearly brought out in a footnote to no. 48, par. 1, when it speaks of the "intimate union", that is, note 2, which refers to the numbers of *Casti connubii* treating of the *bonum fidei.* It was understood in this way by the Fathers who asked for this inclusion and by the commission that accepted their suggestion; cf. *Modum* 25b and *Responsum ad Modum* 25b (*Acta Synodalia,* vol. IV, pars VII, pp. 481–82).

that is, when there is no sacrament—was not explicitly formulated by the Council. It says that the *good of children* (*bonum prolis*) is the primordial and intrinsic good of marriage, and to it is ordered not only the institution of marriage but also conjugal love itself. Consequently, "there can be no true contradiction between the divine laws of handing on life and of fostering authentic conjugal love" (GS, no. 51, par. 2). With respect to love, GS takes its inspiration from the classic doctrine that sees in it the *form of marriage,* particularly in the thomistic tradition, as was set forth in the analysis of *Casti connubii.*[120] This tradition was accepted by the Council of Trent[121] and was taken up again by *Casti Connubii.*[122]

The complementarity *Gaudium et spes* emphasizes between love and procreation does not at all suggest the idea of two finalities, which are capable of coming into conflict with each other, but that unbreakable presence and mutual interrelationship that St. Thomas defined as characteristic of the relationship between end and form (or the operative principle of the being). Moreover, the reference to the biblical foundations of this doctrine confirms this interpretation. After having recalled that the end of conjugal love, as of marriage as such, is procreation, GS prominently draws attention to its relationship with the unitive or formal element: "God who said, 'it is not good for man to be alone' (Gen 2:18) and 'who from the beginning created man male and female' (Matt. 19:4), willing to communicate to him a special kind of participation in his own creative work, blessed the man and the woman, saying, 'Increase and multiply' (Gen 1:23)" (GS, no. 50, par. 1).

The good of children (*bonum prolis*) and the good of faithful love (*bonum fidei*) are the object of the first paragraph of number 48; the second paragraph, in turn, is devoted to the good of the sacrament

[120] For example, in the celebrated text of *Summa theologiae,* III, q. 29, a. 2 corpus, where St. Thomas writes: "A marriage is said to be true from the fact that it attains its perfection. Now there is a twofold perfection of anything: the first and the second. The first perfection is found in the form of the thing, from which it receives its species; the second perfection consists in its operation, through which a thing in some way attains its end. The form of marriage is found in a certain indivisible conjoining of souls, through which one of the spouses is indivisibly held to be faithful to the other. The end of marriage is the procreation and education of children; it attains the first through the conjugal act and the second through the various deeds of the husband and wife, whereby they serve one another in nourishing their children." On this matter, see Ramón García de Haro, "El matrimonio, comunidad de amor, al servicio de la vida. Estudio sobre la noción de matrimonio en la Exhortación Apostólica, 'Familiaris consortio' ", *Divinitas* 26, no. 3 (1982): 332–49.

[121] Cf. *Catechism of the Council of Trent,* pars II, chap. VI, no. 13.

[122] Cf. *Insegnamenti pontifici,* vol. 1 of *Il matrimonio* (Rome: Ed. Paoline, 1957), no. 285.

(*bonum sacramenti*).[123] It (par. 2) thus begins: "Christ our Lord has abundantly blessed this love. . . . For just as God of old encountered his people in a covenant of love and fidelity,[124] so now the Savior of men and the Spouse of the Church[125] encounters Christian spouses by means of the sacrament of matrimony" (GS, no. 48, par. 2). The *sacrament* is a *good* proper to *Christian spouses:* on this the Council is very precise. Although the primeval law of indissolubility has been restored for all men along with the elevation of the marriage of the faithful to a sacrament, nonetheless, the one and the other are different things. In fact, while indissolubility pertains to the *bonum fidei,* the sacrament, as such, exists only in the conjugal covenant between the baptized. Therefore, the Council, while affirming of marriage in general that it is a sign of the union of God with the people Israel and through means of this of the union of Christ with the Church (*"ad exemplar suae cum Ecclesia unionis"*), attributes to marriage among Christians not only the image but also an authentic *participation* in Christ's covenant of love with the Church (*"imago et participatio foederis dilectionis Christi et Ecclesiae"* [GS, no. 48, par. 4]). The love of Christian spouses "is ruled and enriched by the redemptive power of Christ and by the saving action of the Church", and the spouses are "strengthened and, as it were, consecrated[126] by a special sacrament for the duties and the dignity of their state" (GS, no. 48, par. 2).

■ The difference between Christian marriage and that of non-Christians (whose marriage is an *image* but not a *participation* in Christ's union with the Church) is the reason adopted by the conciliar commission when it treats of natural marriage,[127] adding that

---

[123] This separation between the goods of nature and of grace followed the express will of the Fathers. For example, an allusion to the good of the sacrament was rejected in paragraph 1 by the commission, saying: "Cum in hoc loco de matrimonio in ordine naturali agatur, bona christiana (uti sacramentum) hic enumerari nequeunt" (*Responsum ad Modum* 15, F [*Acta Synodalia,* vol. IV, pars VII, p. 447]).

[124] Cf. Hos 2; Jer 3:6–13; Ezek 16 and 23; Is 54.

[125] Cf. Mt 9:15; Mk 2:19–20; Lk 5:34–35; Jn 3:29; 2 Cor 11:2; Eph 5:27; Rev 19:7–8, 21:2, and 9.

[126] Cf. Pius XI, *Casti connubii;* AAS 22 (1930): 538.

[127] "25 Patres rogant ut quaedam addantur: 'ad exemplar (unus Pater addit 'et participationem') suae unionis cum Ecclesia" (*Modus* 26, F [*Acta Synodalia,* vol. IV, pars VII, p. 482]).

the opportune place for this inclusion is found, rather, where the document speaks of Christian marriage in a specific sense.[128]

The sacrament is not a simple adjunct to natural marriage, but implies its true transformation: grace, by assuming nature without destroying it, heals it and elevates it. It is not limited to confirming the requirements of nature but demands more, because it makes the spouses conform to Christ and to his mystery of love for the Church. By means of the sacrament, "Christ encounters Christian spouses" and "remains with them because, as he himself has loved the Church and given himself up for her, so the spouses, by their mutual gift of themselves, may love each other with a perpetual fidelity" (GS, no. 48, par. 2). Therefore, first of all, the sacrament works in nature that healing proper to grace upon which follows its natural fullness. But in addition, it has its own effects, which are truly quite different from the healing of nature:

> Fulfilling by virtue of this [the sacrament] their conjugal and family duties [*cuius virtute munus suum coniugale et familiare explentes*], imbued with the spirit of Christ, by means of which their whole life is permeated by faith, hope, and charity, Christian spouses more and more come to their own perfection and mutual sanctification [*spiritu Christi imbuti, quo tota eorum vita fide, spe et caritate pervaditur, magis ac magis ad propriam suam perfectionem mutuamque sanctificationem*] (GS, no. 48, par. 2).

Here we are dealing with the elevating action that leads to supernatural action rooted in the theological virtues. Finally, as a fruit of their transformation and participation in Christ, Christian spouses, "following Christ, the principle of their life,[129] in the joys and sacrifices of their vocation, by means of their faithful love, become witnesses of that mystery of love which the Lord has revealed to the world by his death and resurrection"[130] (GS, no. 52, par. 7).

■ GS explicitly emphasizes that the *bonum sacramenti* perfects—heals and elevates—the other two goods: *proles et fides*. The perfection of the *bonum fidei* implies, we have seen, the transformation of conjugal love into the participation in the love of Christ and the capacity of fulfilling completely the requirements of fidelity (see no. 48, par. 2; no. 49, par.

---

[128] " . . . De 'participatione' cf. p. 7, lin. 9", that is, the text previously cited from par. 4 of no. 48.

[129] Cf. Rom 5:15 and 18; Gal 2:20.

[130] Cf. Eph 5:25–27.

2, etc.). With respect to the *bonum prolis*, Christian spouses receive the help of the Magisterium in guiding their consciences and a new sense of generosity and trust in Providence in order to fulfill their mission of procreating and educating children (see no. 50, par. 2; no. 48, pars. 2 and 4).

C. *The unbreakable connection between love and procreation*

Behind the theme, apparently rather technical, of the role of love in marriage, in reality a practical question was at issue. A whole complex of doctrines, ideologies, factual situations, and position-takings were immersed within the so-called "regulation of births": the possibility of rendering the marital act infertile with artificial means (the "pill", etc.), as well as the use of natural methods. And all of this was against the background, real or imagined, of demographic problems and of various and opposed concepts regarding life. As is known, polemics entered into the matter to such an extent that the Holy Father Paul VI had to intervene. He reserved to himself the decision on some very delicate questions. A footnote of GS records this. We will linger for a moment on this matter, because forgetting the precise significance of the facts has frequently been the cause here, as in the case of the teaching of *Casti connubii* on contraception—as we have noted—of not a few confusions on the judgment of the conciliar Magisterium with regard to this question. The footnote in question is inserted as a commentary on the Council affirmation that "it is not lawful for children of the Church . . . in the regulation of procreation, to enter into ways which have been disapproved by the Magisterium in its explanation of the divine law [Filiis Ecclesiae . . . in procreatione regulanda, vias inire non licet, quae a Magisterio, in lege divina explicanda, improbantur]" (GS, no. 51, par. 3). The note begins by citing all the basic documents of the Magisterium that condemn contraception, except for the Address of Pius XII of September 12, 1958, in which the Pope declared contraceptive the use of chemical means for impeding ovulation. And it was precisely to this that the note refers—and not to contraception in general—when it adds in what follows:

> Some questions in need of further and more diligent investigation, have, by command of the Supreme Pontiff, been handed over to a Commission for the study of population, the family, and birth, so that after this Commission has carried out its task, the Supreme Pontiff can

render judgment. With the teaching of the Magisterium standing in this way, the Sacred Synod does not intend immediately to propose specific solutions [Quaedam quaestiones quae aliis ac diligentioribus investigationibus indigent, iussu Summi Pontificis, Commissioni pro studio populationis, familiae et natalitatis traditae sunt, ut postquam illa munus suum expleverit, Summus Pontifex iudicium ferat. Sic stante doctrina Magisterii, S. Synodus solutiones concretas immediate proponere non intendit].[131]

The Council, therefore, by confirming the doctrine of the Magisterium that had never been changed, did not, in its turn, give an answer regarding the contraceptive character of the "pill", whose precise nature was still a matter of discussion insofar as it had been mentioned only one time by the Magisterium, in formulations not to be considered definitive, and on which not only had science furnished new data, but about which not a few practical problems had also been raised. Moreover, the Council reaffirmed and deepened the doctrine already established on the relationship between love and procreation, adding the important concept of responsible parenthood, with which we will be concerned in the next section. Its doctrine can be summed up in the following way.

The Church reminds us that "there can be no true contradiction between the divine laws of transmitting life and of fostering authentic conjugal love" (GS, no. 51, par. 2). To resolve practical problems, one must consider both the intention of the spouses and the object of their acts (cf. no. 51, par. 3).

These affirmations are the heart of number 51 of GS. We will discuss them separately because of their great significance.

■ It is worth noting that, even if the labors of council Fathers are so important and necessary, councils are not their work alone but that of the Holy Spirit. The Fathers of Vatican Council II were preoccupied with and divided over ways of confronting concretely the regulation of births. But this matter was taken from their judgment by the intervention of the Pope. All the preparatory texts, beginning with that of October 1964, emphasized the difficulties that were perceived

---

[131] Vatican Council II, *Gaudium et spes*, no. 51, par. 3, n. 14.

in the attempt to harmonize in practice conjugal love and procreation. In the definitive text, these are described in this way:[132] "The Council knows that spouses, in harmoniously ordering their conjugal life, are often hindered by certain conditions of contemporary life and can find themselves in circumstances in which the number of children, at least for a time, cannot be increased, and the faithful practice of love and the full intimacy of their life can be maintained not without difficulty" [Concilium novit coniuges, in vita coniugali harmonice ordinanda, saepe quibusdam hodiernis vitae condicionibus praepediri atque in circumstantiis versari posse in quibus numerus prolis, saltem ad tempus, augeri nequit, et fidelis amoris cultus atque plena vitae consuetudo non sine difficultate conservantur] (GS, no. 51, par. 1).

The important principle cited above was added to the discussions, but for some it was, as it were, a mere verbal concession, of little importance. Thus Monsignor Delhaye, one of the most prestigious of the periti who participated in the discussions, has this comment to make: "At the subcommission, Bishop Colombo had expressed the opinion that it would have been opportune to reaffirm also the principle of compatibility between all the moral laws. This appeal from the 'real' to the 'ideal' was in conformity with the methods always employed in moral theology. On this level, the concession was easy, and in order to please the Lombard prelate the following phrase was added: 'The Church reminds us that there can be no true contradiction between the divine laws of transmitting life and of fostering authentic conjugal love'" (GS, no. 51, par. 1).[133] These words were written in 1966, at a time when the memory of the discussions that had taken place in the conciliar hall was fresh in mind. It seems to me appropriate to note here that, 15 years later, Monsignor Delhaye himself said that the absence of this immediate influence is what places our generation in better circumstances to understand the Council than the circumstances in place at the time. In the course of time, a perspective has been acquired; moreover, we do not know at all what polemical details contributed to make matters obscure in the heat of the debates. Before us remains only the final result, namely, what the Holy Spirit willed to be said, surely in the service of men.

There is no doubt that a few questions are left that must be resolved. But the principle solemnly proposed by the Council is clear: *there cannot be true contradictions between love and procreation.* This is so precisely because, since they concern the end and the life-giving principle

---

[132] Cf. Delhaye, "Impressions conciliaires", p. 604.
[133] Ibid.

of the conjugal community established by the same creative act, there can arise no conflicts among them, save as a consequence of the creature's infidelity. Therefore, we do not find ourselves faced with a vague affirmation, but we are rather in the presence of a great and concrete light on reality. In fact, this principle implies that, in harmonizing conjugal love with procreation, the one cannot be harmed without its resulting in harm for the other; experience confirms that false solutions, in which the true and proper principles of the moral law are not recognized, can never save anything. Reality itself is at the basis of this radical harmony, a fruit of the creative act disturbed only by sin, and it does not tolerate merely verbal and theoretical efforts of reconciliation. For this reason, the Council rejects every immoral solution, every claim of those who would like "to propose shameful solutions to these problems, even not rejecting the killing [of new life] [Sunt qui his problematibus solutiones inhonestas afferre praesumunt, immo ab occisione non abhorrent]" (GS, no. 51, par. 2). And it insists that "it is not lawful for children of the Church to enter into ways that have been disapproved of by the Magisterium" (GS, no. 51, par. 3).

■ *Familiaris consortio* has confirmed the central importance of this principle. The Church, it says, is Mother and Teacher. As Teacher, she never tires of proclaiming the truth or the moral norm that must guide us in the transmission of life. As a Mother, she draws near to couples who find themselves in difficulties. Not only when these are objective, but also when they are not—often the fruit of an environment that simply does not comprehend the values intrinsic to these norms. And thus, as Mother and Teacher, the Church "never ceases to exhort and encourage all to resolve whatever conjugal difficulties may arise without ever falsifying or compromising the truth: she is convinced that there can be no true contradiction between the divine law on transmitting life and on fostering authentic conjugal love."[134]

Accordingly, the concrete pedagogy of the Church must always remain linked with her doctrine and never be separated from it. With the same conviction as my predecessor, I therefore repeat: "To diminish in no way the saving teaching of Christ consitutes an eminent form of charity for souls."[135,136]

---

[134] Vatican Council II, *Gaudium et spes*, no. 51.
[135] Paul VI, *Humanae vitae*, no. 29.
[136] John Paul II, *Familiaris consortio*, no. 33.

After having established the principle of harmony between love and procreation, the constitution takes up the way in which individual acts must be morally judged so that this harmony can be respected. It does this by calling attention to the twofold element of the human act that must be evaluated, that is, *the internal element of the intention, evaluated by just reasons ("ab intus, a corde hominis":* Mt 15:18; Mk 7:21), and *the external element of the objective structure of the acts* (the "works" of which Scripture speaks: Jn 3:20; Gal 5:19ff., etc.). Both are essential. The Council affirms:

> When it is a question of harmonizing conjugal love with the responsible transmission of life, the moral character of the conduct does not depend only on a sincere intention and an evaluation of the motives, but must be determined by *objective criteria, drawn from the nature of the person and his actions,* which preserve the full meaning of mutual self-giving and of human procreation in the context of true love [Moralis igitur indoles rationis agendi, ubi de componendo amore coniugali cum responsabili vitae transmissione agitur, non a sola sincera intentione et aestimatione motivorum pendet, sed obiectivis criteriis, ex personae eiusdemque actuum natura desumptis, determinari debet, quae integrum sensum mutuae donationis ac humanae procreationis in contextu veri amoris observant] (GS, no. 51, par. 3).

And it adds, and this is most important, that to have a right judgment in this matter is not easy; it requires (a) the cultivation "with a sincere mind of the virtue of conjugal chastity", otherwise such rectitude "will not be possible"; (b) if we are speaking of a child of the Church, the cultivation of obedience to the Magisterium, a necessary condition if one's own conscience is not to be confused; and finally (c) no one must forget that the life of man and the duty to transmit it cannot be measured and understood only by criteria taken from this life, but must be referred to the eternal destiny of man (GS, no. 51, pars. 3 and 4).

■ It is worth noting several nuances in this important conciliar text. On them we cannot linger, but it is at least fitting to note them:

First, GS relies on the traditional teaching concerning the elements of the moral act, in a very straightforward version and one closely related to Scripture. It does so in a context in which the presentation of the objectivity of the moral order is rooted in the dignity of the person, that is, his relationship with God according to the plan of creation. In truth, it recognizes the two essential elements of the moral act, in conformity with Scripture: that is, the *intention* and the *deed*, or the objective structure of the act. This structure is measured in relationship to the dignity of the person, therefore, according to the requirements of the proper condition of the image and child of God, precisely because this results from the order inscribed by God in creation and from the work of redemption.[137] When the Council insists on the moral criteria of the dignity of the human person or on the sublimity of the Christian vocation, it in no way promotes subjectivism, nor does it abandon the concept of *nature* or that of *grace*. It simply desires to make evident that the true and full meaning of the notion of *human nature* itself can not be gained if one does not take into account its relationship to God and to Christ, precisely because man has been created by God in his image and then elevated by grace to the condition of a son or daughter. But, after Adam, only in Christ does man receive grace, and the image of God, already corrupted and wounded by sin, comes to be regenerated.[138]

Second, GS explicitly reminds us that if one is to have right judgment of conscience, one must practice virtue, and—since it is concerned with the use of the sexual faculty—the virtue of chastity in particular. One who does not seek to practice this virtue, as St. Thomas has noted, judges only with difficulty his own needs: "Only a virtuous man judges rightly on the end of virtue, in a connatural way, since every man tends to judge things according to his own dispositions."[139] Only the virtuous person, who comports himself rightly in all things, rightly judges in individual cases. Whoever lacks interior rectitude, also lacks rightness in judging; the one who is awake rightly judges both his own affairs and those of the one who sleeps; the one who sleeps, on the other hand, can have right judgment neither of what is his own nor what belongs to the one who is awake. And the same can be said of the healthy and sick . . . of the virtuous and the vicious.[140]

---

[137] On this see Delhaye, *La scienza del bene e del male,* pp. 66ff. Cf. also Ramón García de Haro, "Los elementos del acto moral en su especificidad cristiana", *Scripta Theologica* 15, no. 1 (1983): 524–62.

[138] Delhaye, *La scienza del bene e del male,* pp. 73–79.

[139] *Summa theologiae,* I–II, q. 58, a. 5, c.

[140] *In Ep. I ad Cor.,* c. 2, lect. 3.

Third, the Christian conscience is guided by the Magisterium. Nonbaptized persons indeed have a kind of light from the Magisterium of the Church, but not its full light since they lack the interior principle of faith. Christians, on the other hand, have this interior principle, which orients them to adhere to the Magisterium.[141] Therefore, one who persists in holding a conscience contradictory to the solemn Magisterium cannot have a correct conscience.[142]

Fourth, no one, whether Christian or not, *can rightly judge on this matter with only human and temporal criteria* (demographic, etc.). The truth about man—the Council insists—cannot be understood unless one is aware of the proper relationship of man to God and, therefore, of his own eternal destiny.

3. Systematic Commentary on the Chapter of *Gaudium et Spes* Devoted to Marriage and the Family

Having seen the great lines of thought and the freshness set forth by the Council, our interest now is an examination of the whole teaching of the Council. We will do this by following the conciliar text and its principal divisions. After a presentation of the factual situation of marriage and family in the contemporary world (no. 47), GS is concerned with the notion and nature of marriage (no. 48) and then with its moral requirements, devoting particular attention to the growth of conjugal love and to the obligations of parenthood (nos. 49–51); it concludes by reminding all of their obligation to promote the well-being of marriage as the basis of social life (no. 52).

A. *The situation of marriage and family in the contemporary world*

GS emphasizes, as a positive element, the greater awareness of the goods of conjugal love and the defense of human life. As negative elements, it singles out: polygamy, the plague of divorce and of so-called free love, selfishness, hedonism, and unlawful

---

[141] Paul VI, *Humanae vitae,* no. 29, par. 3.

[142] On this see the exhaustive study of Lio, *"Humanae vitae" e conscienza,* pp. 95ff. On this see also Germain Grisez, *The Way of the Lord,* vol. 1, *Christian Moral Principles* (Chicago: Franciscan Herald Press, 1983), pp. 84–86, 831–71, and William E. May, *An Introduction to Moral Theology* (Huntington, Ind.: Our Sunday Visitor, 1991), pp. 203–27.

practices against conception. Finally, it notes the worsening of some social circumstances and the problems raised by the increase in population.

The constitution begins by reminding us how much the good of the person and that of society depend on the well-being of the conjugal community, in order to encourage and support it, and by describing the different factors, positive and negative, that affect it today.

As *positive factors,* it mentions the various conditions favoring the "fostering of this community of love and of respecting life" (GS, no. 47, par. 1). We need to take into account here that we are not dealing with merely vague sentiments, but with definite currents of opinion in the appreciation of these values—love and life—even though, not rarely, these values are violated in practice. And perhaps these goods are violated today more than in other periods of history; here there comes to mind the tragedy of widespread abortion and the alarming increase of so-called "free love" unions.

■ One can therefore justly say: "The background to the dialogue between the Church and the world found in *Gaudium et spes* perhaps expresses an excessive optimism regarding secular (profane) societies. Re-reading those pages today, one thinks of a later French film called *Tout le monde, il est beau; tout le monde il est gentil.* It is enough to compare that description with the obscurity that from then on became more and more intense. The metacouncil nonetheless maintains this optimistic mentality, impelled by an antitriumphalism that has been transformed into a systematic denigration of the Church and in the abandonment of the Council entrusted to her. *Gaudium et spes* itself, in the course of the work of the revisions made in the fourth session, tempered its own enthusiasm for the encouragement of the institution of marriage that the document attributed to the world (no. 47). Thus the Constitution insisted on including within the text a condemnation of polygamy, divorce, and free love (par. 2), whose existence and wholesale diffusion obviously did not move in the direction of the alliance between Church and the world that had been hoped for."[143]

In presenting *negative factors,* GS divides them into three groups. The first concern *the institution of marriage itself;* they deny its true

[143] Delhaye, *La scienza del bene e del male,* pp. 149–50.

nature and, in practice, destroy it: they are polygamy, which is opposed to the unity of marriage and which is still widespread among some peoples, although there seems to be maturing, even among them, the knowledge of the value of monogamy; the "plague of divorce", explicitly mentioned as such by the constitution because of its uninterrupted growth in our days; and "free love", which was beginning to be spread abroad much more intensely during and after the Council and which constitutes another plague. The second group of negative factors, on the other hand, are those that upset, not so much the institution itself, as its very life, in particular, the *development of the community of love.* The constitution enumerates, as the principal instances of this group, selfishness, hedonism, and unlawful contraceptive practices. The last two are simply external effects of the first, and perhaps the third is the most widespread and dangerous manifestation of an egoism-a-deux, which degrades love and corrupts the mutual respect that should exist between the spouses, who in practice become accomplices in evil.[144] Finally, the third group refers to external circumstances that can, despite the good dispositions of the spouses, pose obstacles to the perfect fulfillment of their duties: on the one hand, social and economic changes (one thinks of the problems of housing, or of wives' having to work outside the home, whether by reason of necessity or for their personal fulfillment); on the other hand, the demographic problem, which can be real or not depending on the locality, but which often causes difficulties, at times legal, to a generous openness to life (no. 47, par. 2).

Aware of these lights and shadows that today surround the family, the Council proposes—by putting into relief some central points of the doctrine of the Church—to "illumine and support Christians and all men who struggle to safeguard and promote the dignity and most excellent and sacred value of the married state" (GS, no. 47, par. 3).

B. *The concept and nature of marriage: the holiness of marriage and the family*

Marriage is the intimate community of life and love, willed by the Creator and structured for the transmission and develop-

---

[144] B. Honings clearly points out the destructive effect that these unlawful practices have on love in his "Procreazione responsabile nella luce conciliare", *Apolinaris* 39 (1966): 61.

ment of human life, which arises by virtue of the consent of the parties. As the author of marriage, God has endowed it with various goods and ends that demand its unity and indissolubility. Christ, moreover, has elevated marriage to the dignity of a sacrament, making of it a vocation to holiness.

As we have already noted, number 48 of GS—although very brief and in pastoral language—is of great density of thought and integrates within itself a deepening of the concept of marriage (principally by means of its teachings relative to its vocational character and the place of conjugal love within it).[145] The text is divided into four paragraphs: the first treats of marriage on the plane of nature;[146] the second is concerned with marriage as a sacrament; the third and the fourth speak of the family in a wider sense. We will comment on the different points, relating all in their essence to the constant Tradition of the Church, and emphasizing their nuances.

1. *Already in the natural order,* marriage is fully understood only in the light of its relationship to God: *it is a sacred institution: the community of life and love, founded by the Creator and structured by its own laws, which determine and protect the goods and ends with which God has endowed it.* It is most important to observe the constant reference to God made by GS, particularly in examining marriage on the plane of nature and in the desire to initiate a dialogue with all men who strive to safeguard the intrinsic natural dignity and the high value of the state of marriage. The paragraph begins by saying that marriage is a community "established by the Creator and structured with its own laws", and it adds that "God himself is the author of marriage, and has endowed it with various goods and ends" and that it is an institution confirmed by the divine law (*institutum divina ordinatione firmum*). It does not hesitate to affirm that the bond marriage establishes between the spouses is sacred: "This sacred bond, in view both of the good of the spouses and of the good of their children and of the good of society, does not depend on the will of man." And all this is said in paragraph 1 of number 48,

---

[145] "A text in which almost every word has its own little history and carries a precise thought, rich and at the same time new" (Heylen, "La promozione della dignità del matrimonio e della famiglia", p. 352).

[146] The Fathers insisted on this repeatedly, as is evident from the *modi* and the responses given to them: see *Acta Synodalia,* vol. IV, par VII, p. 483.

where GS is speaking exclusively of marriage on the plane of nature, according to which every marriage comes to be through a creative act, and is not speaking of marriage as a sacrament.

■ This constant reference to God is repeated throughout the document. Speaking of the love of spouses in its ordination toward procreation, precisely on the plane of nature, the constitution says that it is a participation in the creative power of God ("wishing to communicate to man a special participation in his creative work" [no. 50, par. 1]) and that by means of their love the spouses cooperate "with the love of God the Creator" (ibid.). It is thus possible to note that "if one prescinds from referring to God, the institution of marriage is as it were suspended in the air, without firm foundations, exposed to attacks that tend to depreciate its nature and ends. The defense of marriage, and therefore of the family, considered within the ambit of civil life, can and must begin with reasons that look to the common good of society, in order to unite the forces of all those who desire this good; but, in expounding these reasons one can not neglect to refer to God, as if doing so constituted an unjust imposition of religious convictions. To the contrary, the Council, in its dialogue with the world... did not hesitate to affirm vigorously that marriage has a divine mission to fulfill."[147]

2. Therefore, *even if marriage comes to be from the personal consent of the spouses, the determination of its content is not subject to their will:* "By that human act, whereby the spouses mutually give and receive one another, an institution confirmed by divine ordination arises even in the eyes of society" (GS, no. 48, par. 1). The content of marriage, therefore, does not depend "on the will" either of the spouses or of society (*hoc sacrum vinculum... non ex humano arbitrio pendet*) (no. 48, par. 1). GS reminds us then of the two fundamental elements pertaining to this content. First of all, there is the *ordination of marriage toward children and the consequent unity between love and procreation rather than any kind of contradiction.* "Of their own inner nature, the very institution of marriage and conjugal love... are ordained toward the procreation and education of children", something that entails "the intimate union of the persons and of their acts" (no. 48, par. 1). Second, we find *unity and indissolubility* as properties of marriage: "This intimate union, as the mutual gift of two persons, as well as the good of the children, require

147 Miralles, "Naturaleza y sacramento", p. 153.

the complete fidelity of the spouses and demand their indissoluble unity" (no. 48, par. 1).

■ In describing the two essential *goods* of marriage on the plane of creation (i.e., conjugal love and fecundity), GS is forceful in emphasizing their unity. In fact, in the *Relatio* to the *Schema receptum,* with respect to this matter, we find the following: "The introduction of this idea of two principal goods of marriage (namely, procreation and love) that must be kept united was always very strongly expressed and was asked for almost unanimously in two written supplements."[148] But to point out this unity in no way signifies a change in the classic doctrine on the hierarchy of the ends: not only because the history of the text excludes this explicitly,[149] but also above all because love is not conceived as one of the ends of marriage but rather as its informing principle. Since conjugal love is conceived in this way, any contradiction between it and procreation, as we have said, is not possible.

GS, moreover, teaches that these two natural goods demand that marriage be indissoluble (and one). The mutual personal self-giving of the two spouses demands this, as do the procreation and education of the children. In fact, human beings have need, in their development, of the help of parents who are completely united in this task—one of the reasons why the Creator made marriage indissoluble. The generation and education of children belong simultaneously to the father and the mother, in such a way that they cannot break their bond without unjustly harming their children. Rooted in the reality of their mutual self-giving and on the good of their children,[150] indissolubility does not, therefore, depend on the actual enduring of conjugal love but rather demand sit; this in fact is what the *Acta* make quite explicit.[151]

[148] "Introductio huius ideae duorum principalium bonorum matrimonii (procreationis nempe et amoris) uniendorum, semper fortius expetita fuit et in duobus supplementis scriptis fere unanimiter expostulatur" (*Acta Synodalia,* vol. IV, pars I, p. 536).

[149] In the *Relatio* to the *textus recognitus* (November 13, 1965), it is said that the theme of the hierarchy of the ends was excluded simply because it is too technical: "Commissio ceteroquin iam antea statuit quaestiones technicas de finibus non esse tractandas" (*Acta Synodalia,* vol. IV, pars VI, p. 487). And, in the response to a *modus* of 190 Fathers asking that the hierarchy of ends be better expressed, the conciliar Commission affirmed: "In textu *pastorali* qui dialogo cum mundo instituere intendit elementa illa iuridica non requiruntur. . . . Insuper in textu, qui stylo directo et pastorali mundum alloquitur, verba nimis technica (hierarchia) vitanda apparent" (*Acta Synodalia,* vol. IV, pars VII, p. 478).

[150] The final redaction (*textus denuo recognitus*) that emphasizes this comes from a *modus* made precisely in this sense to the *Schema receptum;* see *Acta Synodalia,* vol. IV, pars VI, pp. 475 and 484.

[151] "*De indissolubilitate matrimonii* inconcusse constat in textu. . . . Textus ipse nullo modo

3. *This conjugal community was sanctified by Christ, who made the very conjugal covenant between baptized persons a sacrament. By doing so, he healed and perfected the spouses both in their mutual love and in their mission as fathers and mothers,* transforming their whole conjugal and family existence into a *path to holiness.* The Savior, GS affirms, "encounters Christian spouses by means of the sacrament of marriage", in such wise that "Christian spouses are strengthened and, as it were, consecrated by a special sacrament for the duties and dignity of their state" (GS, no. 48, par. 2). In keeping with its pastoral character, GS endeavors mightily to show how Christian marriage is in continuity (Christ "assumes and perfects it") with everything that it had been by reason of creation, in all its aspects, and above all in its essential goods, love, i.e., and procreation: "Authentic conjugal love is assumed into divine love and is ruled and enriched by the saving action of the Church, so that spouses might be led efficaciously to God and be helped and supported in their sublime task as father and mother" (no. 48, par. 2).

■ This idea will be developed successively in numbers 49 and 50, showing how the sacrament perfects both conjugal love and the mission of the spouses with respect to children: "The Savior has deigned to *heal* and *elevate* this love with a special gift of grace and charity" (no. 49, par. 2). Just as in this way, love, through the working of the sacrament, becomes inserted into the mystery of Christ's union with his Church ("so that, just as He Himself has loved the Church and has given Himself up for her, the spouses might also love one another with a perpetual fidelity" [no. 48, par. 2]), so too is the transmission of life inserted into this mystery. The spouses "cooperate with the love of the Creator and the Savior, who through them day by day increases and enriches His own family" (no. 50, par. 1). Both love and the transmission of life enter fully not only in the design of the Creator but also in that of the redemption and sanctification of souls.

This healing and elevation imply a true vocation to holiness, as the footnote to the text confirms, for it refers to the principal texts of

---

insinuat matrimonium deficiente amore dissolvi posse" (*Acta Synodalia,* vol. IV, pars VII, p. 472).

Lumen gentium that speak of this call to holiness.[152] In what follows, GS insists that *the spouses are called to holiness precisely in the fulfilling of their conjugal duties:* "Fulfilling by means of this [the sacrament] their conjugal and family office (*munus*), imbued with the spirit of Christ, with which their whole life is permeated by faith, hope and charity, the spouses more and more attain to their own *proper perfection and mutual sanctification,* and thus give glory to God" (no. 48, par. 2).

4. Finally, *marriage is the sanctifying nucleus of the Christian family in its entirety, and, through the family, it spends itself in the evangelization of the whole human family.* The holiness of the spouses radiates through their home and spontaneously affects "the children and indeed all who live with the family", for they will "more easily find the way of a truly human training (*humanitatis*), of salvation, and of holiness" (no. 48, par. 3). This entails definite duties both of the parents (among which GS emphasizes the religious education of their children) and of the children (affection, devotion, faithfulness). The Christian family, sprung from the conjugal *covenant* or *foedus,* which images and participates in the covenant of love between Christ and the Church, thus witnesses to the world the presence of the Savior, by means both of "the love of the spouses, their generous fecundity, their unity and fidelity, and the loving cooperation of all its members" (no. 48, par. 4).

C. *Conjugal morality: duties toward the other spouse (the development of love) and toward their children*

With respect to the theme of conjugal morality, GS is concerned only with some questions that must be given prominent attention in the world today. Number 49 is devoted to conjugal love, and numbers 50 and 51, to the moral requirements with respect to procreation. We will sum up its teachings in three points, which correspond substantively to the aforementioned numbers of the constitution.

I. God wills that in their marriage the spouses nourish and foster their conjugal love, which must become more and more

[152] Note 6 of the chapter reads: "Cf. Conc. Vat. II, Const. dogm. *Lumen gentium:* AAS 57 (1965), pp. 15–16; 40–41; 47."

perfect and grow by means of its generous exercise. Grace sanctifies this love and leads them to live with truly heroic virtue (beyond what is common).

What makes GS special, what gives it its novelty, is that it puts such emphasis on the positive aspect of this duty to love, without forgetting its negative requirements (i.e., never to violate either its unity or its indissolubility). The spouses, it says, "are invited many times by the word of God to nourish and foster their marital union [*coniugium*] with a chaste and undivided love [*casto amore... et indivisa dilectione*]" (no. 49, par. 1). They are to do so in such a way that that love, "which springs from the fountain of divine charity", healed and elevated "by a special gift of grace and charity", must increase continually "by means of its generous exercise". A love, GS adds, that by reason of being eminently human, "embraces the good of the whole person, and therefore can enrich the sentiments of the mind and their physical expressions with a special dignity and can ennoble them as elements and signs of conjugal friendship." Love thus becomes, as *Casti connubii* had already said,[153] the exercise and duty of conjugal charity. Conjugal love is, therefore, a good that is, at the same time, a *duty, because it is confided to human freedom* (GS, no. 49, par. 1).

> ■ In reminding us of this duty to nourish conjugal love, GS bases itself on many texts of Scripture that warrant this (Gen 2:22-24; Prov 5:18-20; 31:10-11; Tob 8:4-8; Song 1:1-3; 2:16; 4:16; 5:1; 7:8-11; 1 Cor 7:3-6; Eph 5:24-33).[154] "Following the Bible, the Fathers have given to love a prominent place in Christian sexual anthropology. In Scripture conjugal love is realistic and human, a matter of body and soul."[155] Therefore, GS stresses the importance, in developing love, of the acts proper to conjugal life. But it demands that they be chaste ("the acts whereby the spouses unite themselves in *chaste* intimacy": no. 48, par. 2), i.e., rectified by the virtue of conjugal chastity, which entails their ordination both to fertility and to mutual self-giving (cf. no. 51, par. 3). "Human love—pure, sincere and joyful—cannot subsist in marriage without the virtue of chastity, which leads a couple to respect the mystery of sex and ordain it to faithfulness and personal dedication. . . . When there is chastity in the love of married persons, their marital life is

---

[153] Pius XI, *Casti connubii; Ins.* no. 287; E.T., no. 23; *Enchiridion Familiae*, 1.723.
[154] See n. 10 of the text of GS, no. 49.
[155] Heylen, "La promozione della dignità del matrimonio e della famiglia", p. 361.

authentic; husband and wife are true to themselves, they understand each other and develop the union between them. When the divine gift of sex is perverted, their intimacy is destroyed, and they can no longer look openly at each other."[156] The positive duty of fostering love does not entail forgetting the negative duty of respecting its existence, that is, indissoluble fidelity; it thus shows how much indissolubility is demanded by love: "This love ... is indissolubly faithful in times both of prosperity and adversity, of both mind and body, and is thus opposed to adultery and divorce (cf. no. 49, par. 2). Indissolubility is presented, therefore, not as the fruit of social imperatives but as the fruit of the requirements of love itself."[157]

Grace, then, *heals and perfects* conjugal love and tends to nourish it under the impulse of the theological virtues, to the end that the spouses exercise "a virtue beyond the ordinary". For Christians, marriage is a call to holiness. Specifically, they must practice the spirit of sacrifice, magnanimity, and steadfastness in love, seeking these virtues in their prayers (no. 49, pars. 1 and 2).

■ Grace is said to heal conjugal love not because it includes in itself anything ignoble ("the acts whereby the spouses unite themselves in chaste intimacy are noble and worthy" [no. 49, par. 2]), but because man is fallen and carries the wounds of original sin. The conciliar commission clarified this matter in response to a *modus* in which it was said that the healing had to do with concupiscence and not love: the commission said: "All nature (therefore, also love) is healed by the grace of Christ."[158] Finally, GS (no. 49, par. 3) considers the importance of the conduct of Christian spouses; they are to develop their love through conjugal chastity and the duties they have toward their children in this matter: it is the obligation of the parents to instruct their children in the delicate and intimate subject of human sexuality, helping to develop in them the virtue of chastity.

II. God indeed wills that this love be ordered to the transmission and education of human life, in such a way that "the true cultivation of conjugal love ... without underestimating the other ends of marriage", tends to bring it about that "the

[156] Escrivá, "Marriage: A Christian Vocation", *Christ Is Passing By,* no. 25, pp. 47, 48.

[157] Delhaye, "Impressions conciliares", p. 598.

[158] *Acta Synodalia,* vol. IV, pars VII, p. 498.

spouses are disposed with courage of mind to cooperate with the love of the Creator and the Savior." Hence their obligation to fulfill this "duty with human and Christian responsibility" (GS, no. 51, pars. 1 and 2).

We have referred repeatedly to the fact that there is no contradiction, but rather a unity, between love and procreation. Now we will develop the moral consequences of this doctrine according to the teachings of the Council, which can be globally designated by the expression *responsible parenthood.* First, we will note that the Council, in conformity with Tradition, reminds us that, while *proles* (i.e., the transmission and education of life) is the primordial end of conjugal love—as it is of marriage itself—the other ends of love are not to be forgotten and that they justify and can demand different manifestations of that love, "even if children, often earnestly longed for, are lacking" (no. 50, par. 3).

■ Contrary to what some have thought,[159] here there is no change in the hierarchy of ends, which, we must stress, the Council did not expressly take up, considering this question too technical.[160] To attribute a change of this kind to GS is to misunderstand its doctrine on conjugal love, seen as the unitive or formal principle of marriage and not as one of its ends, and which, in common with the whole institution of marriage, is essentially ordered, by its own nature, to procreation. The polemic over the ends of marriage was clarified by a decree of the Holy Office of March 29, 1944,[161] and, its most practical aspect—the possibility of using progestines—was excluded from the Council's deliberations and reserved for the Pope. In *Humanae vitae,* in repudiating once more every form of contraception, Pope Paul confirmed the condemnation of these chemical methods, already given by Pius XII in his Address to the Seventh International Hematological Congress.[162] This does not mean that the teaching on the ends of marriage, as set forth in the decree of the Holy Office referred to above, had been completed and fully developed in such wise that it would not be

---

[159] Cf. for example Heylen, "La promozione della dignità del matrimonio e della famiglia", pp. 355–59. See also Theodore Mackin, *What Is Marriage?* (New York: Paulist Press, 1992), pp. 259–73.

[160] Cf. *Acta Synodalia,* vol. IV, pars VI, p. 487 and pars VII, pp. 472 and 478.

[161] DS 2295 (3838); *Enchiridion Familiae,* 2.1285–86.

[162] Pius XII, Address to the Seventh International Hematological Congress, September 12, 1958; *Enchiridion Familiae,* 2.1695–1710, at 1699–1700. Cf. Chapter 4 above, pp. 16ff.

possible to enrich this doctrine in the future. As a matter of fact, the Council's own way of setting forth its teaching on marriage demanded an enrichment of this kind, one that has been a major task of the later Magisterium.[163]

The concept of responsible parenthood, insofar as it takes its origin in the Council, means the free and responsible way in which spouses must fulfill their duty of cooperating with God in the transmission of life. While such transmission is entrusted to instinct in lower beings, in man it demands knowledge and free obedience to the divine law, which is inscribed in human nature and is externally made manifest through divine revelation. For the "divine law makes evident the full meaning of conjugal love, protects it, and impels it to its truly human perfection" (no. 50, par. 2). Consequently, *responsible parenthood* is not synonymous with the *limitation of births,* but rather with the *will to fulfill, consciously and responsibly, the law of God:* "Christian spouses are aware that they cannot proceed according to their own arbitrary judgment [*arbitrium suum*], but must be ruled by their conscience, which must be in conformity with the divine law itself, docile to the Magisterium of the Church, which interprets this law authoritatively [*authentice*] in the light of the Gospel" (ibid.). GS does not encourage selfishness on the part of the parents; thus *having a large family is the way of exercising responsible parenthood most praised by the Council:* generosity is always a condition of human and Christian responsibility ("[spouses] fulfill their obligation with human and Christian responsibility by trusting in divine providence and cultivating a spirit of sacrifice"); and among spouses "those are to be especially kept in mind who, after a prudent and commonly undertaken decision, accept with magnanimity *a more numerous progeny* [*prolem . . . numerosiorem*] to educate properly" (ibid.).

■ Here we are dealing with an issue that, in the conciliar documents, is quite clear: "The Church", so wrote an author shortly afterward, commenting on GS, "appreciates in a special way a [conjugal] life that gives itself and multiplies; therefore, only with regret does the Church accept certain limitations imposed by the difficulties of existence. The

---

[163] Cf. in particular John Paul II's development of the doctrine in his *The Original Unity of Man and Woman* (Boston: St. Paul Editions, 1981); *Blessed Are the Pure of Heart* (Boston: St. Paul Editions, 1983); *Reflections on "Humanae vitae"* (Boston: St. Paul Editions, 1984); and *The Theology of Marriage and Celibacy* (Boston: St. Paul Editions, 1986).

problem of responsible parenthood is introduced by a meaningful consideration of fertility. Marriage and love tend toward fertility by their nature. Children are a precious gift of God for their parents, for the whole family, for society, and for the Church. Their birth corresponds to the ardent desire of the spouses. . . . The biblical texts cited on this matter, which note that the creative love of God gives birth to children, lead to an evident conclusion: authentic conjugal love, one that seeks to attain its fullness, must feel itself obliged to cooperate with the Creator and Christ, the founder of the Church, so that the family itself, in its turn, becomes a little church."[164]

However, progressively, not a few confused responsible parenthood with limiting births, even without just causes or by unlawful means. Some seem to think that the Council had proscribed large families instead of praising them. As a result, the cardinal secretary of state recently lamented this fact in a letter to the Second Congress for the Family of the Americas: "To exercise love in a fully human and generous way leads to the full *valorization of life,* because in the act of generating a child a man, in intimate union with God, gives life, something that is attributed to God Himself. Thus Vatican Council II spoke of *responsible parenthood,* synonymous with a Christian attitude with respect to the transmission of life, as a conscious and free act, made in intimate union with the creative plan of God, and in this way a source of deep spirituality. Yet the expression 'responsible parenthood' has been distorted to make it appear to be precisely the synonym of non-parenthood, of a 'no' to life! It is thus necessary to struggle to restore its true meaning."[165]

When responsible parenthood is properly understood as a human way of obeying the divine laws regulating love and life, its different elements, as set forth by GS, are evident: (a) *the spouses have the duty to determine the number of their children,* and nothing can take the place of the judgment the spouses themselves are obliged to make "in the presence of God"; (b) this judgment must conform to the *divine law,* i.e., to the *objective criteria* that derive from the very order of creation and of grace; in making it, spouses should do so by "taking into account their own good and that of their children, whether already born or foreseen to come, evaluating the conditions, both material and spiritual, of their life at that time and in that state; and, finally, keeping

[164] Heylen, "La promozione della dignità del matrimonio e della famiglia", pp. 363–64.
[165] Letter of August 11, 1982, in *L'Osservatore Romano* (August 23–24, 1982).

in mind the good of the familial society, of the temporal society, and of the Church herself"; (c) in applying this divine law the spouses must act with a conscience that seeks to conform to it, "docile to the Magisterium of the Church, which authoritatively intreprets this law in the light of the Gospel"; otherwise, they would not act conscientiously because, as Paul VI said, "conscience can command insofar as it is itself obedient";[166] and finally, (d) in order to make this judgment without deceiving oneself, there is need for *rectitude in their own dispositions;* GS characterizes these dispositions above all in the following aspects, which form the nucleus of the "human and Christian responsibility": trust in divine Providence, the exercise of the spirit of sacrifice, the practice of the virtues of chastity and of generosity (no. 50, par. 1; no. 51, par. 3).[167]

■ Thus does the Church protect freedom as well as life and love, "because the divine law, of which the Magisterium is the interpreter, safeguards the full meaning of conjugal love, protects it against weakness and guides it in attaining its perfection. The courageous love of Christians must therefore preserve its constant openness to the plans of God and not refuse any reasonable sacrifice necessary for their attainment."[168]

It is *in the presence of God* that the spouses must make their decision: therefore, "when they receive advice and recommendations on this matter, [they must remember] that what they have to do is to discover what God wants of them. With sincerity, a right intention, and a minimum of Christian formation, our conscience knows how to discover God's will in this sphere as in others. . . . God will give his grace to those who act with an upright intention. He will inspire them as to what to do and, when necessary, he will enable them to find a priest who knows how to lead their souls along pure and right paths even though at times they may be difficult ones."[169]

Let us not forget that GS belongs to the Council that issued the universal call to holiness and that it itself reminds us in detail of the vocation of spouses to attain that goal, convinced that "in order to fulfill constantly the duties of this Christian vocation outstanding

[166] General Audience, July 24, 1974, in *Insegnamenti di Paolo VI*, 12 (1974), p. 674.

[167] On this matter see the very precise observations of Miralles, "Amor y matrimonio en la *Gaudium et spes*", 330–44.

[168] Heylen, "La promozione della dignità del matrimonio e della famiglia", p. 365.

[169] Escrivá, *Conversations with Monsignor Escrivá*, no. 93, p. 111.

virtue [*virtus insignis*] is required", that is, a virtue beyond what is common (no. 49, par. 2).

III. In the situations in which spouses are prevented, at least for a time, from increasing the number of their children, the moral character of their way of acting depends not only on the right intention but on objective criteria regarding the nature of the acts themselves: one can never have recourse to base solutions.

Although the previous number (no. 50) of GS treated in general the ordering of conjugal love to procreation, number 51 is concerned with *extraordinary situations* in themselves, although they can be more or less generalized in some times and places: "The Council knows that spouses can often be hindered in harmoniously ordering their conjugal life by certain conditions of modern life, and that they can be put in circumstances in which the number of children, at least for a time, can not be increased", with the resulting difficulties that all this can bring to married love itself (no. 51, par. 1).

■ Here, therefore, we are concerned with exceptional cases in which there is a practical impossibility of increasing "without limits the number of children".[170] The Council does not conceal the fact that, at times, it can be difficult and even heroic to harmonize the law of fostering conjugal love with that of transmitting life. And it is on these difficulties that it seeks to shed light.

As is known, the Church has always recognized the liceity, and indeed the fittingness, of having recourse in such cases to total abstinence; Pius XII also gave some criteria with respect to periodic continence. In the conciliar hall, a debate began whether recourse to chemical means (which some claimed had been excluded from the traditional condemnation of contraception) might be licit, means whose dispersal had produced at that time a "boom". The Holy Father Paul VI, as we have seen, excluded this subject from conciliar discussions. The *Relatio* to the first schema presented to the Council (that of July 3, 1964) took note of this,[171] and this accounts for a footnote to the conciliar text.[172]

---

[170] Heylen, "La promozione della dignità del matrimonio", p. 365.

[171] "De consulto schema necnon adnexum evitarunt omnem allusionem ad problemas pillularum progenesticarum, de qua quaestione Summus Pontifex sapientissime sibi iudicium reservavit" (*Acta Synodalia*, vol. III, pars VI, p. 51).

[172] N. 14 of chap. I, part II, no. 51.

As has been said already, the Council reaffirmed the position of the Church (cf. above, section 2, C, p. 256) in two points: (a) there is no possibility of any true contradiction between love and procreation and (b) to judge the morality of the actions one must take into account both their object and the intention of the spouses, keeping in mind the reasons or motives existing for delaying the conception of a new child. The condemnation of physical contraception remained firm, insofar as it belongs to the definitive teachings of the ordinary and universal Magisterium. The Council abstained from pronouncing in a definitive way on the condemnation (given by Pius XII) of the so-called contraceptive chemical methods.

D. *The defense and promotion of the family*

The family is the most fertile school of humanity and of life together; it is the authentic foundation of society. All must consider it their own obligation to protect the true nature of marriage and the family, the necessary public morality, fitting domestic prosperity, and the right of parents to generate and educate their children. Scientists, public authority, pastors, and spouses themselves have obligations in this regard.

The final number of GS devoted to marriage and the family (no. 52) is concerned with this classic point of the doctrine of the Church, particularly developed by the Magisterium of the last several popes.

Specifically, the constitution presents the obligations of the family in society with the new and stimulating vision of the family as "the most complete and richest school of humanity". It emphasizes clearly that, in order to attain this goal in its fullness, "continual collaboration between the parents in the education of their children" is indispensable, prominently focusing on the role of both mother and of father (no. 52, par. 1). It reminds us, with a brief but precise listing, of the principal rights and obligations of the family, all of which must be promoted and protected. It speaks in a special way of the obligations of *public authorities*. These must "consider it a sacred duty to respect, protect and foster the true nature of marriage, public morality, and domestic prosperity . . . and the right of the parents to generate children and to educate them in the bosom of the family" (no. 52, par. 2).

The remaining paragraphs of number 52, after a general introduction (par. 3), examine accurately the duties of those, together with public authority, who are responsible for promoting and fostering the well-being of the family. *Scientists* are called upon to contribute to the discovery of successful ways of using natural methods of birth regulation: "Certainly, morality is not based on technical progress, but the Church is not unaware that a better knowledge of these methods will be able to combat effectively the grave evils of contraception, abortion, and sterilization."[173] *Priests,* having taken care to acquire the necessary competence, should encourage spouses in their "vocation to holiness", with different pastoral means, principally by preaching the word of God and administering the sacraments; since the vocation to marriage is a following of Christ, spouses meet him especially in the intimacy of the sacraments (par. 5).[174] Then, GS encourages the various *institutions* that are dedicated to the family, noting that it is specially incumbent upon the spouses themselves to promote institutions of this kind (par. 6); it ends by reminding us that the *spouses themselves,* by living and acting rightly, are the ones who can best contribute to making the Christian family loved, testifying to the love that our Lord has for the world (par. 7).

4. Other Teachings of the Council on Marriage and the Family

We will take note of these: a) *Lumen gentium,* **on the family as the domestic Church and on the education of children (no. 11); b) the decree** *Apostolicam actuositatem,* **on the apostolate of the family (no. 11); and c) the declaration** *Gravissimum educationis,* **on the right/duty of parents to educate their children (nos. 3, 6, 8).**

We will not discuss these matters at length; moreover, they are not developed much by the Council. We will sum them up briefly, beginning with *Lumen gentium,* excluding its teachings on the vocation to marriage (nos. 11, 34, 41), which have already been studied (see above, section 2, A, 1, beginning on p. 215).

---

[173] Heylen, "La promozione della dignità del matrimonio e della famiglia", p. 370. Cf. GS, no. 52, par. 4.
[174] Ibid.

In *Lumen gentium,* the Council notes and describes *the important work of the family in the spreading of the Faith, which makes it like a "domestic Church".*

> Christian spouses, by virtue of the sacrament of marriage, by which they are the sign of the mystery of the unity and fruitful love between Christ and the Church and participate in this mystery (cf. Eph. 5:32), help one another to attain holiness in their conjugal life and in the acceptance and education of children. Hence by reason of their own state in life and their own mission, they have their own proper gift within the People of God (cf. 1 Cor 7:7). From this marriage, in fact, comes the family, in which new citizens of human society are born, who by the grace of God received with baptism become children of God and perpetuate through the ages his own people. In this, which can be called the domestic Church, the parents must be for their children the first teachers of the faith, and foster the vocation proper to each, and that to religion (*vocationem . . . sacram*) with special care (no. 11, par. 2).

Therefore, parents are the first *educators in the Faith.* They understand that, just as they have given natural life to their children, so they must be concerned with their participation in that life which makes them "sharers of the divine nature" (2 Pet 1:4). By means of marriage, the Council of Florence taught, the Church grows: "The Church is increased bodily through the family [*Ecclesia per matrimonium corporaliter augetur*]."[175]

Parents are responsible to have their children come to the fonts of grace; they are not to delay baptism or the other sacraments. This is an obligation that springs from their own condition as baptized and Christian spouses: "In the same way in which there is a continuity between baptism and marriage, when marriage is begun, so equally there is a continuity between marriage and baptism when marriage prolongs itself into the new life of a child. . . . One can thus understand the profound contradiction implied in delaying the baptism of children in a Christian marriage."[176] The parents are obliged to guide their children in the Faith by their own behavior, their friendship, their counsels. Because of all this, the family is called the *domestic Church.*

■ The Council takes this expression, "the domestic Church", from the Tradition of the Fathers of the Church. Among the testimonies adopted with respect to the schema of July 19, 1963, the following

[175] Bull *Exultate,* November 22, 1439 (DS 695); *Enchiridion Familiae,* 1.137-39.
[176] Miralles, "Naturaleza y sacramento", p. 166.

incisive words of St. John Chrysostom figured prominently: "When yesterday I said, 'each one of you must see to it that your home becomes a Church,' you responded in loud voices and were pleased at what like words had produced in you."[177] In the domestic Church constituted by the family, it is justly noted, children can and "must learn that the Church is neither the temple to which one goes on occasions, nor the place where only clerics are formed, but the Church is present in one's own home, for all in it belong to Christ."[178]

In the decree *Apostolicam actuositatem,* the Council points out that, since the Creator of all things established marriage as the principle and foundation of human society, *"the apostolate of the spouses and of families acquires a singular importance both for the Church and for civil society"* (no. II, par. 1), and it sets forth in detail the nature of this apostolate: a) first, the parents must be cooperators with grace and witnesses of the Faith in their relationships with their children and with all who belong to the family (par. 2) and b) second, spouses have the obligation to give a Christian formation to society, in particular by the example of their own life and holiness, affirming courageously the right/obligation that they have in the education of their children and defending the dignity, autonomy, and prosperity of the family (par. 3). This, the Council adds, is a mission that the family has received directly from God, and it makes it the first and vital cell of civil society and of the Church (par. 4). It then notes the different activities of the apostolate in which spouses can cooperate, insisting on the fundamental importance of their witness by means of the life of the family (pars. 4 and 5); finally, it points out the possibility of forming associations of parents in order to afford mutual help in carrying out their obligations (par. 6).[179]

On its part, the declaration *Gravissimum educationis* discusses the *rights and duties of parents in the education of their own children.* First of all, it takes up the right and duty of educating them in the Faith and in the human and social virtues, since the family is the first and most important school of humanity and of the Faith. Consequently, parents have a right owed to them to educate their children (no. 3, pars. 1 and 2) with the help of society and especially of the Church, in view of their

---

[177] *In Gen. serm.,* 7, 1: PG 54, 607 (*Acta Synodalia,* vol. II, pars I, p. 264).

[178] Miralles, "Naturaleza y sacramento", p. 166.

[179] On this see L. Moreira Neves, "El dinamismo apostolico de la familia", in *Cuestiones fundamentales sobre matrimonio y familia,* pp. 943ff.

special competence and capacity to form their children in social and Christian virtues (no. 3, pars. 2 and 3).

This right and obligation of the parents, the Council affirms, requires, if it is to be exercised in practice, the following: a) the *free choice of a school;* therefore, "public authorities, who have the duty of protecting and defending the liberties of citizens, are bound according to the principles of distributive justice to ensure that public subsidies to schools are so allocated that parents are truly free to select schools for their children in accordance with their conscience" (no. 6, par. 1);[180] and b) this freedom presupposes the necessary *freedom in the creation of study centers and their management,* with respect for "the principle of subsidiarity" and excluding "every form of monopoly of schools which would be prejudicial to the natural rights of the human person" (no. 6, par. 2). The state must be vigilant about the quality of schools and teachers because all students are to have an appropriate formation, etc., but the state cannot monopolize schools, programs of study, textbooks, etc.

■ These are criteria that serve to secure the existence of a real power of choice for the parents; they are demanded by respect for the dignity of the human person and not because of any particular religious persuasion. But this freedom remains solely theoretical for many if the state does not subsidize private schools in a way similar to its subsidization of public schools, whatever the specific system might be. An example of a fair system is the so-called *scholastic allowance* (or voucher program), which consists in the allocation to each child the cost of one place at a public school; in this way, the parents will not find themselves, in practice, obliged to have recourse to the public school as the only school economically accessible.[181] In short, the Council exhorts the faithful to collaborate with the school, especially by means of parents' associations (no. 6, par. 3); and it notes the duty of Catholic spouses to help schools promoted by the Church (no. 8).

---

[180] Cf. Provincial Council of Cincinnati III, 1861, Collectio Lacensis III, col. 1240, c/d; Pius XI, encyclical *Divini illius Magistri,* December 31, 1929; AAS 22 (1930): 60, 63ff.

[181] On this see J. M. Zumaquero, "Familia, educación y autoridad", in *Cuestiones fundamentales sobre matrimonio y familia,* pp. 853ff. See also Robert A. Destro, "Parental Choice and Educational Equality", in *In Search of a National Morality,* ed. William B. Ball (Grand Rapids: Baker; San Francisco: Ignatius Press, 1992), pp. 157–71; and James W. Skillen, "Parental Freedom of Education Choice", in ibid., pp. 172–84.

Chapter Seven

THE TEACHINGS OF PAUL VI ON MARRIAGE AND FAMILY

1. A General Overview of His Pontificate

Giovanni Battista Montini, born on September 26, 1897, was elected Pope on June 21, 1963, and crowned as Supreme Pontiff on June 30, 1963, taking as his name Paul VI.[1] It was his task to bring Vatican Council II, begun under his predecessor Pope John XXIII, to completion. Quickly, in fact, he had the Council, already in its second session, resume its work on September 29, 1963. The Council ended on December 7, 1965. Continuing the Council was an important enterprise, not only because of the amount of work and of problems that remained, but also because of the existential conditions then prevailing. In fact, a very restless and frequently disoriented climate of public opinion had been created, which was the source of not a few polemics and errors, that made the prompt conclusion of the Council's work imperative. That in the fourth and final session of the Council the documents presented were approved by an almost unanimous majority and that these clearly reaffirmed the supernatural mission of the Church, while at the same time presenting this mission in a way that was responsive to the pastoral needs of the time, contributed much to reassure the minds of people and to prepare the way for the Council's implementation.

However, the difficulties surrounding the Council continued, and it can be said that the entire pontificate of Paul VI seems to be dominated, as it were, by a twofold objective: on the one hand, the constant commitment to bring to fruition the work of the Council, and on the other, the need to combat the errors and disorders of the period after the Council. Paul quickly realized the necessity of these two actions. In his trip to Fatima on May 23, 1967, he said: "The Council has stirred up enormous energies in the bosom of the Church and has opened wide

[1] Cf. J. Ordoñez Marquez, "Paul VI, Pope", *Gran Enciclopedia Rialp*, vol. 18 (Madrid, 1975), pp. 94ff.; J. M. Javierre, *Pablo VI, Pontifice Romano* (Madrid: Ed. Alameda, 1963); J. Guitton, *Dialoghi con Paolo VI* (Milan: Rusconi, 1986).

horizons in the field of doctrine. . . . But what harm there would be if an arbitrary interpretation, not authorized by the Magisterium of the Church, should transform this awakening into a restlessness that would corrupt the Church's traditional and constitutional configuration!"[2] His concern for all this would have a notable influence on his magisterial work.

■ Among the principal documents issued to implement the Council are the following: the motu proprio *Pastorale munus* (November 30, 1964), on the ordinary faculties of bishops; the motu proprio *Apostolica sollicitudo* (November 15, 1965), which established the synod of bishops; the motu proprio *Ecclesiae sanctae* (August 6, 1966), applying various teachings of the Council (on the clergy, etc.); the apostolic constitution *Indulgentiarum doctrina* (August 6, 1966); the apostolic constitution *Missale Romanum* (April 3, 1969); and the motu proprio *Mysterii Paschalis* (February 14, 1969) on liturgical reform; the two motu proprios *Matrimonia mixta* (March 31, 1970) and *Causas matrimoniales* (March 28, 1971) on marriage cases; the motu proprio *Sanctitas clarior* (March 19, 1969), on the new norms for the procedures involved in beatification and canonization, and the apostolic constitution *Regimini Ecclesiae universae* (August 15, 1967), on the norms for reforming the Roman Curia.

Among the more directly doctrinal documents of Paul VI must be noted, first of all, those issued before the end of the Council, namely, the encyclical *Ecclesiam suam* (August 6, 1964), on the dialogue with men, and the encyclical *Mense maio* (April 19, 1965), on the need of the mediation of Mary, the Mother of the Church, both for the personal holiness of individuals and for peace among peoples. After the Council was ended, a large portion of the documents of the new Pope was devoted to dissipating the confusions that had arisen in the highly agitated postconciliar period. The encyclical *Mysterium fidei* (November 3, 1965) had to combat, shortly after the end of the Assembly, errors about the Eucharist; the encyclical *Sacerdotalis caelibatus* (June 24, 1967) was concerned with various issues concerning the doctrine of the priesthood; the encyclical *Humanae vitae* (July 25, 1968) was concerned with reaffirming the condemnation of contraception and with developing some themes of family morality. Shortly before *Humanae vitae,* the publication, although not in the form of an encyclical, of the *Credo of*

---

[2] Paul VI, Homily at Fatima, May 13, 1967.

the People of God (June 30, 1968) had wide influence. Finally, mention must be made of the apostolic exhortation *Evangelii nuntiandi* (December 8, 1975), on the faithful transmission of revealed truth. It is also necessary to add the various and important doctrinal declarations issued by the Sacred Congregation for the Doctrine of the Faith: the declaration *Mysterium Ecclesiae* (June 24, 1973), which rejected the most notable contemporary errors on dogmatic matters; the declaration *De abortu procurato* (November 18, 1974), which emphasized the intrinsic wickedness of abortion; the declaration *Mysterium Filii Dei* (February 21, 1972), on the doctrine of the Trinity and the Incarnation; the declaration *Persona humana* (December 29, 1975), on sexual ethics; the declaration *Inter insigniores, circa questionem admissionis mulierum ad sacerdotium ministralem* (October 15, 1976), on the question of women's ordination, etc.

Another constant theme of Paul VI's Magisterium was his call for peace, for justice, and charity in the social order. This theme is sounded in the following documents: the encyclical *Christi Matri* (September 15, 1966), which established the annual Day of Peace; the encyclical *Populorum progressio* (March 26, 1967), completed by the apostolic letter *Octogesima adveniens* (June 14, 1971), on the eightieth anniversary of *Rerum novarum*. In this area, the Pope shows the same constancy and courage that characterize his teachings on conjugal morality. He thus frequently points out that service to life is frequently hampered by social injustices; it is necessary, both by reason of justice and of charity, that everything possible be done to remove these obstacles.

■ With respect to marriage and the family, in addition to *Humanae vitae*, other very important documents are the two motu proprios *Matrimonia mixta* and *Causas matrimoniales,* as well as the observations about the apostolate of the family found in the apostolic exhortation *Evangelii nuntiandi.* Among more minor addresses and documents we can point out the following: the Addresses to the Teams of Our Lady (May 4, 1970, and September 22, 1976),[3] the Address to the Committee for the Family (November 4, 1977),[4] the two addresses to the Roman Rota of January 28, 1971, and of February 9, 1976,[5] and

---

[3] *Insegnamenti di Paolo VI* 8 (Vatican City: Typis Polyglottis Vaticanis, 1970), pp. 424ff. and 14 (1976), pp. 773ff.; *Enchiridion Familiae: Textos del Magisterio Pontificio y Conciliar sobre el Matrimonio y la Familia (Siglos I a XX),* ed. Augusto Sarmiento and Javier Escrivá-Ivars, vol. 3 (Madrid: Ediciones Rialp, 1992), pp. 1991–2009.

[4] Ibid., 15 (1977), pp. 1011ff.; *Enchiridion Familiae,* 3.2191–94.

[5] Ibid., 9 (1971), pp. 59ff. and 14 (1976), pp. 96ff.; *Enchiridion Familiae,* 3.2155–60.

various addresses and allocutions concerning *Humanae vitae,* in particular those of July 31, 1968; August 11, 1968; and December 23, 1968.[6]

2. The Encyclical *Humanae Vitae*

First of all, we will briefly summarize the situation in which this encyclical came to light and its content; we will then treat of its significance for the value of the moral Magisterium, taking into account the conditions under which Paul VI took this initiative.

A. *Some aspects of the mentality and public opinion at the time of the promulgation of* Humanae vitae

A contraceptive mentality was widespread. There was need to distinguish between genuine problems and ideological positions.

When, during the Council, the Holy Father reserved for himself consideration of the question of regulating births, he had in mind both the gravity of the problem and the enormous ideological pressures that could have weighed on the Council Fathers. It is worth being aware of this in order to grasp more surely the prophetic value of this document of Paul VI.[7]

The majority of those on the commission that John XXIII had established for the study of the problems of population, the family, and natality, and to which Paul VI entrusted, after having increased its numbers, the task of studying this matter more deeply, pronounced itself favorably on controlling births artificially by contraceptive means.[8] This shows how widely diffused was *a contraceptive mentality, which derived from two powerful factors: (a) a highly ideological presentation of the demographic problem and (b) the real difficulties of some couples who, however, sought to resolve their difficulties only by using scientific criteria, forgetting the primacy of ethics.*

---

[6] Ibid., 6 (1968), pp. 1098ff. (*Enchiridion Familiae,* 3.1940–48); pp. 1100ff. (*Enchiridion Familiae,* 3.1949–50); and pp. 680ff. (*Enchiridion Familiae,* 3.1960–61).

[7] Cf. D. Tettamanzi, *Un'enciclica profetica (L'Humanae vitae vent'anni dopo)* (Milan: Ancora, 1988).

[8] The Pope delicately notes this in the encyclical; cf. *Humanae vitae,* July 25, 1968, no. 6.

■ The most serious consequences of this mentality are shown in the drastic interventions made by the state in several countries of the Third World to control births. Thus, allegedly in the name of science and of progress, men had retrogressed and had fallen into a pre-Christian mentality, which permitted slavery and did not recognize the primacy of man over society. In truth, "in the mind of the ancients the individual existed for the city; in the ideal city of Aristotle (cf. *Pol.* VII, 16), as before in Plato, the State regulated married life, which was not a private matter, and regulated births, chiefly by abandoning or killing newborns. But Christianity brought to men an awareness of the person and of his transcendence over political society. To take from the spouses decisions on regulating birth in order to entrust it to public authorities is to sacrifice the person to the totalitarian State and to deny personal freedom."[9]

In *Humanae vitae,* the Holy Father wanted to show that such abuses by the state would be almost fatally increased if unlawful ways of regulating births were allowed, even if one wished to limit their use to spouses who would freely choose them: "Would anyone blame those in the highest offices of the state for employing a solution [contraception] considered morally permissible for spouses seeking to solve a family difficulty, when they strive to solve certain difficulties affecting the whole nation? Who will prevent public authorities from favoring what they believe to be the most effective contraceptive methods and from mandating that everyone must use them, whenever they consider it necessary? And clearly it will come about that men who desire to avoid the difficulties that are part of the divine law, difficulties that individuals, families, or society may experience, will hand over to the will of the public authorities the power of interfering in the most exclusive and intimate mission [*munus*] of spouses."[10]

We will now seek to analyze the principal elements of this contraceptive mentality. With respect to the *demographic problem,* it is necessary to recognize that a *new fact* influences judgments on it: man has conquered many obstacles that threaten life—infant mortality, illnesses,

[9] G. Cottier, *Regulación de la natalidad (Problemas sociológicos y morales)* (Madrid: Rialp, 1971), p. 68.

[10] Paul VI, *Humanae vitae,* no. 17, par. 2. In this chapter, the English translation of *Humanae vitae,* unless otherwise noted, will be that provided by Janet Smith in her *Humanae vitae: A Generation Later* (Washington, D.C.: The Catholic University of America Press, 1991). The passage cited here is found in English translation on p. 286 of Smith's book. The Latin text of *Humanae vitae,* along with a Spanish translation, is found in *Enchiridion Familiae,* 3.1907-39.

famine—so that it is possible to foresee a growth in population. But to affirm that this growth is in itself something negative is an *a priori* judgment, shaped by notable ideological factors, often rooted in selfish interests. In short, the growth of population in poor countries poses a threat in the future—and in the present a reproach—to the power of the richer countries.

> The "pill" performed a symbolic task; it represented the generous gift that *western* science offers for alleviating the misery of starving people. But this ostensible meaning of the pill concealed a hidden one, because in reality matters are quite contrary; it is without doubt an efficacious brake fit to maintain the existing relationship of dominance [of the West over the poor countries] and a protective shield for the interests of the rich. A theory that is limited to concealing facts in defense of social and political interests is, properly speaking, an ideology.[11]

The famous law of Malthus, according to which the population of the world would increase geometrically while the means of subsistence would increase only arithmetically, is, as is the Marxist notion of added value, a suggestive and simple idea; it therefore has the capacity of stimulating feelings and passions. But it does not correspond to scientific truth[12] and shows a pessimistic attitude and little confidence in man; it is the fruit of forgetting God and his way of completing his creative work. The biblical revelation of creation, which springs from the goodness and wisdom and omnipotence of God, on the other hand, bears witness to the generosity of being; Genesis contains a vision of life where fertility and children are a blessing from God. Therefore, to the maledictions of Malthus ("a man who is born in a world already filled does not find a place at the grand banquet of nature. But nature herself orders him to change himself, and she is not slow in putting her threats into effect"), Paul responds in his Address to the United Nations: "You must make bread to abound sufficiently for the table of humanity; and not, on the contrary, foster the artificial

---

[11] Cottier, *Regulación de la natalidad*, p. 53.

[12] Cf. C. Clark, *Population Growth and Land Use* (New York: Macmillan, 1967); J. L. Soria, *Paternità responsabile* (L'Aquila: Japadre, 1969), pp. 19–36; Jacqueline Kasun, *The War Against Population (The Economics and Ideology of Population Control)* (New York: Green Hill Publishers, 1986); idem, *The War against Population: The Economic Ideology of Population Control* (San Francisco: Ignatius Press, 1990); Eamonn Keane, *Popuation Control?* (Sydney: Foundation for Human Development, 1993).

control of births—something irrational—in order to diminish the number of those who share in the banquet of life."[13]

■ One can not, therefore, deny that the increase in population exists and poses problems for men; but it is necessary to trust in human capacities, without pessimism. This is a question that is to be resolved with the help of science. But in any case, it is necessary to provide a new perspective for public opinion and to combat ideological exaggerations. Let us quote a significant comment critical of certain alarmists: "If we wanted to have a conference of all the inhabitants of the world gathered together, and assign each one a square meter of space for hearing it with a measure of comfort, three thousand million square meters would be enough: one meter for each of the three thousand million individuals who today (1969) populate the earth. But then, to have at one's disposal space for all these people, a surface of three thousand square kilometers would suffice, and this would be a surface equal to that of the province of Palermo or the Island of Zanzibar. Another example? Let us place the entire population of the world in the United States of America; if we did so, the density of population would equal that which Holland has right now!"[14]

In addition to the "population explosion"—which is often more a pretext than a real condition, there are the *difficulties, at times grave, experienced by spouses,* due to specific problems of population or to the measures regarding them adopted by public officials. *Humanae vitae* does not ignore the existence of such problems: "Contemporary conditions of work and housing, as well as increased expenses involved in providing for, raising, and educating children, often make it burdensome to support a large family adequately."[15] However, while recognizing these problems, the Church never stops reminding us that in order to solve them we must search for truly ethical solutions. There is, in fact, the danger that

in the eyes of many, the regulation of births is simply a concrete application of the rationalizations which man has used in his progressive acquisition of dominion over nature. Hence there is a propensity to consider procreation simply as one "object," among others, for natural

[13] Address of October 4, 1965, in *Insegnamenti di Paolo VI,* 3 (1965), p. 521.

[14] Soria, *Paternità responsabile,* p. 22.

[15] Paul VI, *Humanae vitae,* no. 2 (Smith trans., p. 273). From now on in this chapter, reference to *Humanae vitae* will be given in parentheses in the text, leaving other citations for the footnotes.

science. This tendency, which looks on man as an "object" of nature, is reflected on many planes. But to adopt it is to oppose oneself to an awareness of the "person".[16]

Human problems *cannot be solved without taking into account the primacy of the ethical.* In truth, this is the only way to provide technology with a just and personalist dimension. It is "necessary, on the part of all, to recover an awareness of the primacy of moral values, which are the values of the human person as such. . . . Science is called to ally itself with wisdom."[17]

In practice, this means working on two fronts: first, in making clear once more the value of sacrifice and of the cross: otherwise we will not be able any longer to be called Christians. Paul VI says:

> It is necessary to maintain the ideal in its sublimity even when it may be difficult to attain these heights, even when the ordinary man feels himself incapable of doing so and therefore sinful. The prophets of Israel and the Apostles of the Church never consented to reduce this ideal; never did they shortchange the measure of perfection or shorten the distance between the ideal and the ordinary; they never watered down the meaning of sin, but rather did everything to the contrary.[18]

Second, and simultaneously, it is necessary to use opportune means for combating the difficulties that have their origin not in the will of God but in the injustices of men. *Humanae vitae* will insist on this:

> Truly it would be a grave injustice to attribute to Divine Providence what seems, on the contrary, to be the result of unwise government policies, or of a rather weak sense of social justice, or of a hoarding of goods for one's selfish use, or finally of a careless negligence in undertaking the labors and tasks by which every people and all their offspring achieve a better standard of living (no. 23, par. 2; Smith trans., p. 290).

> ■ Nor must the grave consequences of forgetting this necessary subordination of the technical to the ethical be ignored. *Humanae vitae* makes this point quite vividly: admitting unlawful ways of regulating births would open the way to conjugal infidelity and to the general corruption of morals; it would furnish a pretext for abusive interventions by the state and would foster all kinds of selfishness and cause

---

[16] Cottier, *Regulación de la natalidad,* p. 105.

[17] John Paul II, apostolic exhortation *Familiaris consortio,* November 22, 1981, no. 8, par. 3.

[18] Paul VI, cited by J. Guitton, *Diálogos con Pablo VI* (Madrid: Cristiandad, 1967), p. 428.

disturbances of all kinds, etc. (no. 17). The warning given here is also valid for natural methods, which ought never be reduced to the level of a mere technique. "For instance, one thinks of what happened after Pius XII spoke of them: the technical aspects of the question displaced its fundamental aspects, which are moral in character, and everywhere one could find a great many tables and calendars that seemed to reduce what was a very delicate problem of morality and one, therefore, that ought to be solved by a prudent and Christian process of reasoning to a problem of perfecting the method technically and scientifically."[19]

Actually, "we tend to approach 'the natural method' and 'artificial methods' from the same point of view, to derive them from the same utilitarian premises. Looked at like this, the natural method is just another means to ensure the maximum pleasure, differing from artificial methods only in the direction it takes.... The 'natural method' is congruent only with the nature of the person [when it is an act of virtue]. Its secret lies in the practice of virtue—technique alone is no solution here."[20] The problems of the transmission of human life, like all other problems proper to the human person as such, are ethical in nature, and technique alone cannot resolve them: but there is no human problem that does not have its ethical solution.

B. *A summary of the contents of the encyclical*

The encyclical can be summed up in five points: (1) the competence of the Magisterium; (2) moral principles for the transmission of life; (3) the reaffirmation of the immorality of contraception; (4) the legitimacy of recourse to periods of infertility, so long as they are ordered to realizing the value of responsible parenthood; and (5) pastoral directives.

The task of handing on life is a source of great joy for spouses, but it frequently entails difficulties. The changes brought about by the passing of time have introduced some new ones, but the Church is not ignorant of them and wishes to shed light on them. This is the purpose

---

[19] Soria, *Paternità responsabile,* p. 52.

[20] Karol Wojtyla, *Love and Responsibility,* trans. H. Willetts (New York: Farrar, Straus, Giroux, 1981), pp. 240, 241–42.

of the encyclical, which is divided into three parts: new aspects and the competence of the Magisterium; doctrinal principles (which embrace points 2 to 4 above); and pastoral directives.

1. *It pertains to the Magisterium to interpret the divine law, both evangelical and natural.* After having described major contemporary changes—the increase in population, the tenor of life, the place of women in society, technical progress—the encyclical takes note of the widespread mentality claiming that now is the time for modern man to entrust the task of regulating births to his own reason and will and no longer to the biological rhythms of his own organism (nos. 2 and 3). This claim demanded a response from the Magisterium of the Church, as the divinely established interpreter of the natural moral law:

> It is indisputable—as Our predecessors have often declared[21]—that when Jesus Christ imparted His divine authority [*potestatis*] to Peter and the other apostles and sent them to all nations to teach His Commandments,[22] He established those very men as authentic guardians and interpreters of the whole moral law, that is, not only of the law of the Gospel but also of natural law. For natural law [as well as revealed law] declares the will of God; [thus] faithful compliance [*fidelis obtemperatio*] with natural law is necessary for eternal salvation[23] (no. 4, par. 2; Smith trans., pp. 274–75).

> ■ As the authoritative interpreter of the natural law, the Church directs herself to all men, even if they have not received the gift of faith. She teaches them what they must do in order not to contradict their own human dignity, although after the original fall they are not able to do this integrally without the help of grace.[24] Hence the importance and

---

[21] Cf. Pius IX, encyclical *Qui pluribus,* November 9, 1846; *Pii IX P.M. Acta,* vol. I, pp. 9–10; St. Pius X, encyclical *Singulari quadam,* September 24, 1912: AAS 4 (1912): 658; Pius XI, encyclical *Casti connubii,* December 31, 1930; AAS 22 (1930): 579–81; Pius XII, Address to the Episcopate of the Catholic World, *Magnificate Domino,* November 2, 1954; AAS 46 (1954): 671–72; John XXIII, encyclical *Mater et Magistra,* May 15, 1961: AAS 53 (1961): 457.

[22] Cf. Mt 28:18–19.

[23] Cf. Mt 7:21.

[24] Cf. Gregory XVI, *Theses de fide et ratione,* September 8, 1840; H. Denzinger and A. Schoenmetzer, *Enchiridion Symbolorum Definitionum et Declarationum de rebus fidei et morum,* 34th ed. (Barcelona-Rome: Herder, 1967), (DS), no. 1627 (2756); Pius IX, letter *Gravissimas inter,* December 11, 1862, DS 1670 (2853); Pius XII, encyclical *Humani generis,* August 12, 1950, DS 2305 (3975); Council of Trent, session VI, cap. I; Concilium Valentinum, January 8, 855, DS 325 (633).

the necessity of the Magisterium's guidance, and the supremacy of its teaching over every human authority. Consequently, the Supreme Pontiff, after having been informed, but with complete freedom, gives the answer of the Church in virtue of the mandate entrusted by Christ to him (cf. nos. 5–6).

Throughout the document, there is an insistence on other characteristics of the mission entrusted to the Magisterium. The Church has the duty to teach the divine law, even if she foresees that this will not be easily heard: "Since the Church did not make either of these laws [the natural and the evangelical], she cannot change them. She can only be their guardian and interpreter; thus it would never be right for her to declare as morally permissible that which is truly not so" (no. 18, par. 1; Smith trans., p. 287). Acting in this way, the Church helps men not to abdicate their own dignity and responsibility (no. 18, par. 2); and she leads them to that happiness to which man aspires with all his being, but which he can attain only by respecting "prudently and lovingly . . . the laws inscribed on their nature by the Most High God" (no. 31; Smith trans., p. 294).

2. *The problem of births,* as any other pertaining to human life, *cannot be resolved save within an integral vision of man, that is, in conformity with the moral law and the principles of morality.* Since, in attempting to justify artificial means of controlling births, an appeal had been made by many to the requirements of conjugal love and of "responsible parenthood", it is necessary to be precise about the meaning of these two great realities of marital life (no. 7). *Conjugal love* is especially illumined when it is considered in its supreme source: God, who is Love (1 Jn 4:8). As a participation in his love, it has its own proper characteristics: it is love surely human (at once of the senses and of the spirit), but which, in its likeness to God's love, must be total (without any reservations or selfish calculations), faithful and exclusive, and, finally, *"fruitful,* since the whole of the love is not exhausted in the communion of the spouses; it also looks beyond itself and seeks to raise up new lives" (no. 9; Smith trans., p. 279: Smith has "contained" for "exhausted").

■ At times the richness of *Humanae vitae*'s teaching on conjugal love (nos. 8 and 9) is not sufficiently emphasized. It marks a deepening of the personalist conception of marriage. Conjugal love is destined not only to give life to the personal communion of the spouses, but it is the way in which they cooperate with God in giving life to a new human person. By their mutual self-donation, the spouses not only "seek a communion of persons" in order to "perfect each other", they also, through this communion, "share with God the task [*operam socient*] of procreating and educating new living beings" (no. 8, par. 2; Smith trans., p. 278). Conjugal love is fruitful because it is "not exhausted in the communion of the spouses", but "looks beyond itself and seeks to raise up new lives". This formula of *Humanae vitae* is a prelude, as it were, to those given in *Familiaris consortio* (no. 14) and in *Donum vitae* (*Vatican Instruction on Respect for Human Life in Its Origin and on the Dignity of Procreation*), in which the personalism of conjugal love is extended to a personalist conception of human procreation: "The generation of a child must be the fruit of that mutual giving which is realized in the conjugal act wherein the spouses cooperate as servants and not as masters in the work of the Creator who is Love. In reality, the origin of a human person is the result of an act of giving. The one conceived must be the fruit of his parents' love. He cannot be desired or conceived as the product of an intervention of medical or biological techniques; that would be equivalent to reducing him to an object of scientific technology" (*Donum vitae*, no. II, B, 4, c, pars. 1 and 2).

These anthropological presuppositions are at the root of the unbreakable bond between the unitive and procreative meanings of the conjugal act, on which the encyclical insists so greatly (no. 12). From this it is also evident that every effort to oppose *Gaudium et spes* and *Humanae vitae*, claiming that the latter has betrayed the personalism of the Council, is superficial.

The parenthood to which conjugal love is ordered must also be free and responsible if it is to be human. This is the meaning of the expression *responsible parenthood*. As a matter of fact, responsible parenthood—as the Pope stresses—means *that the spouses fully recognize their duties to God, to themselves, and to others, inasmuch as these flow from the objective moral order established by God, and of which a correct conscience is the faithful interpreter.* This naturally excludes every attempt to proceed merely on one's personal whim, because the spouses must act in conformity with the creative intention of God, imprinted on their own nature and constantly manifested by the teaching of the Church (no. 10, pars. 5 and 6). Together with this fundamental principle, Paul VI enumerates the different concrete factors to keep in mind in order to foster this free and responsible way of acting: a knowledge of the biological processes, insofar as their laws pertain to the being of the person (no. 10, par. 2); dominion of reason and of will over instinctive drives (no. 10, par. 3); and a consideration of the physical, economic, psychological, and social circumstances that need to be taken into account in order to make a right choice (no. 10, par. 4).

■ Among its presuppositions, the encyclical, therefore, includes the affirmation that the "biological laws" which regulate the transmission of life "pertain to the human person" (no. 10, par. 2). This is a very coherent and rigorous affirmation of personalism, which does not consider the human body, precisely as such, merely as a "thing," but—in the same way as everything that is in man—as a *personal* reality. It does not confuse moral laws with biological laws, but rather knows how to judge the limits that man has in his dominion over biological laws when dealing with his own body, precisely because this is not a thing but an integral part of his person: "In fact, man does not have unlimited power over his own body in general. So, too, for good reason, he clearly does not have power over his generative faculties as such, for they by their very nature are directed to bringing forth human life, and God is the source of human life. Indeed, 'human life must be recognized as sacred by all men,' as Our Predecessor John XXIII declared; 'Indeed, from its very beginning it requires the creative action of God'" (*Mater et Magistra,* AAS [1961] 447) (no. 13; Smith trans., p. 282).

The frequent objection that *Humanae vitae* equivocates at the crucial step on the word "law" is without foundation, an importation of an alien philosophy of law and morals into the reading of the text. Moral laws depend upon how man is, i.e., his nature; they *are* how he is, giving the description of his nature, just as the laws of physics describe perishable nature and, here, the laws of human reproduction describe its nature. But *this* nature is part of man's nature and hence these laws also prescribe part of the rational behavior owed by man. . . . In recognizing that contraception is contrary to nature reason recognizes not only that it is contrary to reason but that it is, more immediately, contrary to our humanity as (rational) animals.[25] *Humanae vitae* does not appeal in vain first of all to the notion of creation and to the laws inscribed in the being of man and of woman, horizons which, with reference to sexuality, concern their participation in the creative power of God.

[25] S. Theron, "Natural Law in *Humanae Vitae*", in *"Humanae Vitae": 20 anni dopo (Atti del II Congresso Internazionale di Teologia Morale: Roma, 9–12 novembre 1988)* (Milan: Edizioni Ares, 1989), pp. 490, 491. The author also shows very precisely the equivocations existing in opposing biological laws, as *descriptive* laws of who man is, and reason, as the *prescriptive* law of moral life. His argument, however, is very complex, and we cannot treat of it here.

It ought also to be noted, with respect to responsible parenthood, that the encyclical, just as it foresaw that it would be subjected to bad interpretations, did not limit itself to noting the factors or elements to be taken into account in making choices, but specified the content of responsible parenthood by clearly stating two alternative ways of exercising it: "Responsible parenthood is exercised by those who, guided by prudent consideration and generosity, elect to accept many children. Those also are to be considered responsible who, for serious reasons [*seriis causis*] and with due respect for moral precepts, decide not to have another child for either a definite or an indefinite amount of time" (no. 10, par. 4; Smith trans., pp. 279–80).

By clarifying what conjugal love is and what the expression "responsible parenthood" means, as well as the relationship that binds the two, one can understand that the principle for judging the lawfulness of a means—objectively and taking for granted the existence of a right intention—is *respect for the nature and finality of the conjugal act* (no. 11), *which requires us never to separate deliberately the two aspects inseparably united in it, namely, the conjugal union and procreation* (no. 12). Only in this way will spouses be faithful to God's plan, precisely because "the one who uses the gift of conjugal love in accord with the laws of generation acknowledges that he is not the lord of the sources of life but rather the minister [*ministerium*] of a plan initiated by the Creator" (no. 13, par. 2; Smith trans., p. 282).

3. The encyclical then treats of the consequences: *every action intended to interrupt the generative process or to abort is always absolutely immoral; likewise, every act of deliberate sterilization, whether perpetual or temporary, or of contraception is always absolutely immoral.* That is, "every action, which, either in anticipation of the conjugal act, or in its accomplishment, or in the development of its natural consequences, proposes [*intendat*], either as its end or as a means, to impede procreation [*ut procreatio impediatur*]" is intrinsically immoral (no. 14, pars. 1–3; here the Smith translation has not been used). Nor is it possible here to invoke the principle of lesser evil, nor that of totality, because although it is at times licit to *tolerate* a lesser moral evil in order to avoid a greater moral evil, it is never morally right—not even for the most serious of reasons—to *do* evil in order that good might come about (no. 14, par. 3).

■ The similarities and the differences between the formulation of *Humanae vitae* and that of Pius XII's Address to the Italian Catholic Union of Midwives of October 29, 1951, need to be noted. Pius XII had said: "Any attempt on the part of the husband and wife to deprive this act of its inherent force or to impede the procreation of a new life, either in the performance of the act itself, or in the course of the development of its natural consequences, is immoral" (E.T., no. 288 in Liebard, *Official Catholic Teachings: Love and Sexuality*, pp. 109–10; *Ins.* no. 613; *Enchiridion Familiae*, 2.1439–40). Paul VI affirms that "every action which, either *in anticipation of the conjugal act,* or in its accomplishment, or in the development of its natural consequences" is absolutely excluded. Pius XII, therefore, analyzes contraception thinking of it as a perversion of the conjugal act (also in the development of its natural consequences); Paul VI, on the other hand, speaks of any action made either in anticipation of the act or in its accomplishment or in the development of its natural consequences: he is thinking not only of the act, but also of the behaviors of the spouses that can precede and accompany the marital act. The reason for this difference hangs on the fact that Paul wants to embrace within the concept of contraception chemical contraceptives such as the "pill". In using the pill, as a matter of fact, there is no perversion of the conjugal act as such, but of the biological laws of the person by means of a previous act. This also explains the doubts that arose during the Council concerning the contraceptive character of the "pill", which led the Pope to reserve this question personally to himself. But the identity of the moral disorder existing in the two types of conduct became evident when attention focused not on the *physical object* — in the first instance, this was directly deformed by the spouses, but not in the second — but rather on the *moral object:* in both instances, this is behavior on the part of the spouses whereby they seek to deprive the conjugal act of its procreative potential. This was the solution of Paul VI in *Humanae vitae.*

When it speaks of abortion and of sterilization, the encyclical speaks in a general way (no. 14, par. 2), making no distinction between these actions outside or within marriage. On the other hand, in considering contraception, it refers specifically to the conjugal act (no. 14, par. 3). This is so because contraception is a specific moral disorder when it is committed within marriage; outside marriage, in adultery for example and, to a lesser extent, in fornication, these acts are already abuses and actions opposed to love and to life, and the use of contraceptive means does not substantially change their wickedness. Whether it is licit to use contraceptives in adultery, not to mention in homosexual acts, in order to prevent AIDS is not truly an ethical question inasmuch as homosexual acts and adultery ought never to be done. When someone has decided to engage in homosexual acts or in adultery, he can not raise this as an authentic moral problem. Whether contraception can add some wickedness to acts of this kind consists in the extent to which, by lessening the risks and responsibilities involved, it makes it easier to engage in them. Finally, it makes no sense to ask whether periodic continence is permitted in nonconjugal relations, because outside of marriage no sexual act can be either lawful or chaste. In this way, we can see more clearly that the Church, in her teaching on the intrinsically wicked character of contraception, does not exaggerate or confuse its wickedness with the more grave malice of adultery, of fornication, etc.[26]

4. *Recourse to periods of infertility is licit if there are serious reasons for spacing births,* i.e., when doing so has as its object the realization of responsible parenthood (no. 16, pars. 1 and 2; no. 10). There is an *essential difference* between this and the use of means opposed to pro-creation by reason of the object of the act (no. 16, par. 3). In the first case, "conjugal acts do not cease being legitimate if the spouses are aware that they are infertile for reasons not voluntarily caused by them; these acts remain ordained [*destinatio*] to expressing and strengthening the union of the spouses" (no. 11, par. 1; Smith trans., p. 280). The spouses "legitimately use a faculty that is given by nature". In the second case, however, "the spouses impede the order of generation from complet-ing its own natural processes" (no. 16, par. 3; Smith trans., p. 285). In addition, natural means require an effort to live conjugal chastity, inasmuch as they entail the sacrifice of engaging in in the conjugal act only during fertile periods (no. 16, par. 3).

---

[26] On this see Ramón García de Haro, "Fondamenti antropologici ed etici della procreazione umana", *Rivista Rosminiana di filosofia e di cultura* 83 (1989). [Translator's note: I disagree with the author on this question, since I believe, with others, that contraception always adds to the malice of fornication and adultery. With Germain Grisez and others, I believe that contracep-tion is not, as such, a *sexual* sin, opposed to the sixth commandment, but a sin *against life* and opposed to the fifth commandment. On this, see Germain Grisez, Joseph Boyle, Jr., John Finnis, and William E. May, " 'Every Marital Act Ought to Be Open to New Life': Toward a Clearer Understanding", *Thomist* 52, no. 3 (1988): 365–426.]

■ Consequently, from the perspective of the moral object of the act, there is an evident and radical difference between these ways of acting. Contraception always entails engaging in a conjugal act intentionally deprived—or in an act that seeks so to deprive a conjugal act—of its procreative capacity, i.e., a *distorted, counterfeit* act. On the other hand, to have recourse to the rhythms of the spouses in order not to procreate is precisely not to engage in the conjugal act. In the first case, one makes use of one's procreative power by debasing it; in the second, one simply does not make use of it. There remains, however, as we have insisted many times, the order of the intention. Recourse to infertile periods can be made with a contraceptive intention. But as long as one takes into account the object of the act, one can not understand the reason for the difficulty that some have in distinguishing between contraception and periodic abstinence. They are obviously quite different in their objects: to engage or not to engage in the conjugal act.

Therefore, the terminology of "natural methods" and "artificial methods" ultimately remains equivocal, because the true ethical difference is found between *contraception* and *conjugal chastity,* one of whose manifestations can be *periodic continence for just causes.* The so-called natural methods are really nothing but *ways of determining fertility:* by being continent one does nothing to impede procreation, but avoids engaging in the procreative act.[27] Such comportment, although not enough to determine the lawfulness of the motives, nonetheless helps to verify them. In fact, if selfishness predominates, there is a tendency to abandon periodic continence by choosing an easier method. On the other hand, if there is the right attitude, the possible insufficiency of the reasons alleged for having recourse to the infertile periods tends to arise within one's conscience. The encyclical, in order to make the disorder of artificial methods clearer, enumerates their bad consequences, both for the couple and for society (no. 17).

5. It ends with a gathering of *pastoral directives.* As Mother and Teacher, the Church does not wish to abandon spouses in their difficulties. First of all, Paul VI reminds us that *it is always possible to observe the divine law* if we are committed to do so, for the help of God's grace can always be counted on (no. 20). It is important and necessary

[27] Cf. Ramón García de Haro, *La actualidad de la "Humanae vitae"* (Madrid: Epalsa, 1984); Garciá de Haro, "Fondamenti antropologici ed etici della procreazione umana". Cf. William E. May, "Contraception, Abstinence, and Responsible Parenthood", *Faith & Reason* 3, no. 1 (Spring 1977): 39–52.

for the spouses to have *solid convictions of the value* of their family life and for them to practice conjugal chastity (no. 21). It is also necessary *to create an atmosphere favorable to chastity* (no. 22); here, as also in promoting a *sound family policy* and a *wise education for respecting the moral law,* public authorities have a grave responsibility (no. 23).

The Pope, moreover, begs *men of science* to make their contribution to a morally upright way of regulating births. They should be convinced that there can never be a true contradiction between the laws that regulate the transmission of life and those that foster authentic conjugal love (no. 24). He asks *Christian spouses* to be faithful to their vocation, thus giving witness to the sweetness of the law that unites the unconquerable love of the spouses and their cooperation with the love of God, the author of human life (nos. 25–26). He asks *doctors and health personnel* to promote in their environment a climate of respect for morality and for right reason (no. 27). Finally, he exhorts *priests* to "promote clearly and completely the teaching of the Church concerning marriage", giving first of all "an example of sincere obedience [*obsequii*] . . . both inwardly and outwardly to the Magisterium of the Church", convinced of the necessity of their own witness for the unity of the Christian people and peace of conscience, aware that "the Holy Spirit of God, who guides the Magisterium in its teaching, will illumine the hearts of the faithful and invite them to give their assent" (nos. 28–29; Smith trans., pp. 293–94). He encourages *bishops* to work arduously, with the help of their priests, in safeguarding the holiness of marriage (no. 30).

C. *The importance and significance of* Humanae vitae

In addition to its specific conclusions, *Humanae vitae* is a fundamental document because of its strong reconfirmation of perennial morality and its repudiation of the "new morality", whose theses are at the root of the disputes that took place both before and after the encyclical.

The teaching of *Humanae vitae* is contained, although not in as explicit and deepened way, in the teaching of the previous Magisterium, to which the encyclical repeatedly refers as a basis of its own authority.

Acting as he did, the Holy Father also confronted another serious problem: the position of the Church with respect to the "new morality", a doctrine as active and diffuse as dangerous. This fact has not passed unnoticed.[28]

The encyclical *Humanae vitae reconfirms the principles of the perennial morality*. The dissent and challenging to which this document has been subjected have in fact arisen because of its repudiation of the claims of the new morality. The encyclical does not only provide a clarification "of a particular point of doctrine, but indeed gives an authoritative response which defends, as an unshakable bulwark, and promotes *true conjugal love* (cf. HV, n. 9)".[29] The encyclical brings to light perennial questions and puts them in the context of the modern world: "Many facts and circumstances persuade us that this light is given at the most propitious time for minds and consciences today."[30]

■ The problems highlighted at the beginning of this chapter, both real and proceeding from a materialistic mentality, have raised the temptation of compromising moral principles, in a way similar to, and indeed in continuity with, the temptation that provoked the modernist movement. Some theologians began to defend ideas that were more and more deviant. Faced with the equivocations of a so-called "horizontal theology", the encyclical takes its point of departure in a methodology that is "theocentric, Christocentric, and ecclesiocentric, rooted in the grand and universal principle of the 'sublimity of the vocation of the faithful in Christ,' which the ecumenical Council itself, in its decree *Optatam totius*, no. 16, gave as the mother idea for perfecting moral theology, in harmony with the doctrine of chapter V of *Lumen gentium*."[31] With respect to its sources, the encyclical constantly sends us back to Holy Scripture (more than a third of its notes contain biblical texts), to Tradition, and to the Magisterium. With respect to the value of the teaching of the Church on the natural moral law—contested by the new morality—"in accord with the previous Magisterium, to which it refers,[32] the encyclical *Humanae vitae* (no. 4) vindicates once

[28] See, for instance, the exhaustive study of E. Lio, *"Humanae vitae" e coscienza* (*L'insegnamento di Karol Wojtyla teologo e Papa*) (Vatican City: Libreria Editrice Vaticana, 1980), especially pp. 25–55. See also Tettamanzi, *Un'enciclica profetica*, pp. 31–43.

[29] Lio, *"Humanae vitae" e coscienza*, p. 6.

[30] Karol Wojtyla, "Proemio" to the *Introduzione all' enciclica Humanae Vitae*, in *Notificaciones e Curia Cracoviense* (Vatican City: Typis Polyglottis Vaticanis, 1969), p. 8.

[31] Lio, *"Humanae vitae" e coscienza*, p. 28.

[32] Paul VI, *Humanae vitae*, no. 1.

again in a clear and categorical manner the competence of the Magisterium, in virtue of the text of Matthew 28:20."[33] Moreover, the encyclical ratifies the subordination of conscience to the objective moral order, in terms constantly taught by the Magisterium (no. 19); it stresses the relationships between conjugal love and procreation, understood in its traditional sense (nos. 7–13); and it notes that a correct pastoral attitude can not imply " 'any compromise concerning the saving doctrine of Christ' (cf. no. 29), but must show that the priest, the father and doctor of souls, in addition to being a judge in the sacrament of penance, is called to use all the good means that do not alienate souls, who must never be abandoned— precisely because the doctor never abandons the sick, even when conditions seem desperate."[34]

This reaffirmation has particular importance because *it was made on the basis of the Christian personalism of Vatican II and in conscious repudiation of the pseudo-personalism of the new morality.* In an article written in 1969, the then Cardinal Wojtyla, in addition to insisting on the fact that "the truth of *Humanae vitae* is, above all, *a normative truth*", reaffirmed its profound personalist character:

> The Encyclical *Humanae vitae* is addressed to man and requires a sense of the dignity of the person. . . . According to the doctrine of the Church *responsible parenthood* is not and cannot be only the result of a "technique" in the cooperation of the spouses. There is a real and fundamental danger for which the Encyclical is a providential remedy: the danger of falling into the temptation of considering this problem outside the realm of ethics, of forcing things so as to exempt man from responsibility for his own acts.[35]

Humanae vitae, in short, rises to the defense of the dignity of the human person.

D. *The obligatoriness in conscience of number 14 of* Humanae vitae

Although a massive campaign of public opinion has claimed the opposite, the teaching of the encyclical is directly binding

[33] Lio, *"Humanae vitae" e coscienza,* p. 31.

[34] Ibid., p. 52.

[35] Karol Wojtyla, "La verità dell'enciclica *Humanae vitae* di Paolo VI", in *L'Osservatore Romano* (January 1, 1969); cf. also Ramón García de Haro, "Magisterio, norma moral y conciencia", *Anthropotes* 1 (1988): 45–71.

in conscience, as the encyclical itself teaches and as sound theology recognizes.

Its vigorous disqualification of the claims of the new morality drew upon the encyclical one of the most fierce campaigns of public opinion that a document of the papal Magisterium of the Church has ever suffered. In particular, an attack was launched against its key point, i.e., the confirmation, despite all claims to the contrary, of the absolute and intrinsic malice of every use of contraceptives, including chemical ones: it was precisely on this matter that the doctrine of the Church and the new morality came into conflict. The attacks on the encyclical's teaching were formulated either directly or by the subterfuge of accepting the doctrine in a general way but adding a way of conceiving respect for the sanctuary of conscience which, in reality, articulated the right of an individual to disobey the norm proposed by the Magisterium, if one personally, in one's own case, does not judge this norm to be convincing.

■ Thus, for instance, Karl Rahner declared: "When a Catholic Christian, after a mature examination of his conscience and with all possible self-criticism, thinks he can adopt a judgment that diverges from the papal norm and then follow this judgment in his own conjugal practice, always respecting the principles already repeatedly mentioned by us as a common patrimony, then a Catholic is not obliged to consider this a subjective sin nor is he to be regarded formally as one who is disobedient to ecclesial authority."[36] Note the expression "not *formally* disobedient"; this is equivalent to affirming that a conscience of this kind must be regarded inculpably erroneous, notwithstanding the explicit knowledge that the Magisterium has clearly taken a position.[37]

On the other hand, *the text of* Humanae vitae *(in particular nos. 14 and 28) clearly shows the binding character of its teaching on conscience, something expressly willed by the Supreme Pontiff.* In fact, number 14, already cited, affirms: "Thus, in relying on these first principles of human and Christian doctrine [*primariis hisce principiis humanae et christianae doctrinae*] concerning marriage, we must again insist [*edicere*] that there must be a

---

[36] Karl Rahner, *Riflessioni sull'enciclica Humanae vitae* (Rome: Edizione Paoline, 1968), p. 52.

[37] A detailed response to this error is found in M. Zalba, "Papel de la conciencia en la calificación de los actos morales", *Gregorianum* 62.1 (1981): 135–57.

rejection of every action which . . . either in anticipation of the conjugal act, or in its accomplishment, or in the development of its natural consequences, proposes, whether as an end or as a means, to impede procreation" (no. 14, pars. 1 and 3; not the Smith translation). And, to support this affirmation, the Pope refers us, in a footnote,[38] to the text of the *Roman Catechism* that speaks of the "most serious crime" of contraception; it then cites *Casti connubii,* which formulated the same teaching in an equally imperative way ("Christian doctrine, taught from the very beginnings, and never modified"; "in sign of her divine mission . . . "; "the Catholic Church, to whom God Himself has entrusted the mandate of teaching and defending . . . ") and which admonishes all priests—who have the care of souls—to obey the authority of the Magisterium because otherwise they will be "blind guides leading the blind" (Mt 15:14). In addition, the encyclical refers to the address of Pius XII to the midwives in which he repeats, one more time, the same doctrine as "a norm certain for all", and likewise to his address to the congress of the hematologists. Finally, it cites John XXIII's *Mater et Magistra* in the precise place in which Pope John affirms that "the transmission of human life has been entrusted . . . to a personal and conscious act . . . subject to the most wise laws of God: laws that are inviolable and immutable and which must be recognized and observed."[39]

The binding character of this teaching on conscience is again emphasized by the Holy Father, in a very insistent way, in his appeal to priests:

> For it is your great and manifest mission [*munere*]—and We address especially those of you who are moral theologians—to promote completely and clearly [*integre aperteque proponere*] the teaching of the Church concerning marriage. In performing your ministry you must be an example of the sincere obedience [*obsequii*] that must be given both inwardly and outwardly to the Magisterium of the Church (no. 28; Smith trans., p. 293).

[38] N. 16, which says: "Cf. *Catechismus Romanus Concilii Tridentini,* pt. 2, chap. 8; Pius XI, Encyclical *Casti connubii* AAS 22 (1930): 562–564; Pius XII, Address to the Italian Medical-Biological Union of St. Luke, Nov. 12, 1944, in *Discorsi e Radiomessaggi di S.S. Pio XII* 6 (1944): 191–192; Pius XII, Address to the Italian Catholic Union of Midwives, Oct. 29, 1951, AAS 43 (1951): 842–43; Pius XII, Address to the Seventh Congress of Hematology, AAS 50 (1958): 734–35; John XXIII, Encyclical *Mater et Magistra* AAS 53 (1961): 447."

[39] For a very full commentary see Lio, *"Humanae vitae" e coscienza,* pp. 81–86.

The Pope reminds his readers that this assent obliges not only because of the reasons used to support the doctrine but above all because of the assistance of the Holy Spirit that the pastors of the Church enjoy. Finally, he adds: "It is of the utmost importance for safeguarding the peace of souls and the unity of the Christian people, that in moral as in dogmatic matters, *all should obey the Magisterium of the Church* and should speak with one voice." And he appeals to the authority of St. Paul: " 'I beg . . . you brothers through the name of our Lord Jesus Christ: that you might all speak as one and that there might be no division among you; that you may be united in the same mind and the same judgment' (1 Cor. 1:10)" (no. 28; Smith trans., p. 293).

■ The encyclical, therefore, stresses the obligation of obedience to the Magisterium even in *moral* matters; an obligation that extends to everyone, both pastors and the faithful (none of them can rightly dissent, even if they do not comprehend the reasons for the teaching). Moreover, to obey the Magisterium is a condition for the peace of consciences: to act otherwise is not to have a right conscience, but one culpably erroneous; and this never confers interior peace.[40]

Despite the criticisms made by some, *sound theology has recognized the binding character of the teaching of number 14 of* Humanae vitae *on conscience* and has given abundant testimony to it.[41] The study published

[40] For a development of this idea see Ramón García de Haro, *La conciencia moral,* 2nd ed. (Madrid: Ediciones Rialp, 1978), pp. 130–39.

[41] Thus, in the German language, see the collective work edited by J. Bökmann, *Befreiung vom objektiv Guten? Vom verleugneten der Antikonzeption zum befreienden Ethos* (Vall-Schoenstatt: Patris Verlag, 1982) (with the collaboration of Professors G. Ermecke, A. Guenthor, G. Martelet, W. Poltawska, J. Stoehr, D. Tettamanzi, and others). In the United States, see the collective work edited by William E. May, *Principles of Catholic Moral Life* (Chicago: Franciscan Herald Press, 1980), in particular, the studies of Donald McCarthy, "The Teaching of the Church and Moral Theology", pp. 113–49, and William B. Smith, "The Meaning of Conscience", pp. 361–82. In addition, other works deserve to be mentioned: Germain Grisez, vol. 1 of *The Way of the Lord Jesus, Christian Moral Principles* (Chicago: Franciscan Herald Press, 1983), chap. 36, "A Critical Examination of Radical Theological Dissent", pp. 871–916; John C. Ford and Germain Grisez, "Contraception and the Infallibility of the Ordinary Magisterium", *Theological Studies* 39 (1978): 258–312. In Italian, see the study, already cited many times, of Lio, *"Humanae vitae" e coscienza;* L. Ciappi, "L'enciclica *Humanae vitae:* valutazione teologica", *Lateranum* 54 (1978): 105–24. In Spanish, see M. Zalba, *Las conferencias episcopales ante la "Humanae vitae" (Presentación y comentario)* (Madrid: Ed. Cio, 1971), particularly pp. 5ff., 63–65, 93, 124–26, 130–32; and Zalba, *La regulación de la natalidad* (Madrid: Bac, 1968), pp. 133–40; and García de Haro, *La actualidad de la "Humanae vitae".* In French, see G. Cottier, *Regulation des naissances et développement démographique* (Brussels:

in 1969, as an introduction to the Polish edition of *Humanae vitae*, under the care of Cardinal Wojtyla and the moral theologians of Crakow, merits special attention.[42] We will transcribe some of the more significant paragraphs of this work: spouses must "discern the specific duties of their vocation in the voice of a well formed conscience. Conscience, however, does not establish moral norms, but it interprets them and applies them to concrete conditions of life. Behind the voice of conscience stands the authority of God Himself and the laws established by Him."[43] Consequently, the norms and moral principles relative to the "supernatural vocation of the children of God are based on divine Revelation and can be known only by means of faith", in such a manner that these norms are transmitted, "together with the whole of the deposit of Revelation, by means of the Magisterium of the Church (HV, no. 10)".[44] And a little later it is added:

> This law of God, therefore, with respect to the ethics of the marital life, has been defined in greater detail and has been transmitted by the authority of the Magisterium of the Church in the Encyclical *Humanae vitae*. Therefore, *after the promulgation of this document, it is difficult to speak, with respect to Catholics, of inculpable ignorance or of error in good faith.*[45]

■ We cannot linger over this interesting document.[46] We will only note that it repeatedly insists on the fundamental importance of recognizing this obligation of conscience toward the Magisterium, as a condition for remaining faithful to the Church. For example, it affirms: "The thesis which claims to legalize the decisions of subjective conscience,

---

Desclee, 1969); Philippe Delhaye, *Discerner le bien du mal dans la vie morale et sociale. Etude sur la morale de Vatican II* (Chambray-les-Tours: Ed. CLD, 1979), pp. 120ff. See also Dietrich von Hildebrand, *The Encyclical "Humanae Vitae": A Sign of Contradiction* (Chicago: Franciscan Herald Press, 1968); Joseph Costanzo, "Papal Magisterium and *Humanae vitae*", *Thought* 44 (1969): 377–412; J. Bökmann, *Nicht Unfehlbar? Zum misslungen Angriff auf die untruegliche Wahrheit und dem verbindlichen Anspruch von Humanae vitae* (Abensberg, 1981); D. Tettamanzi, "L'Humanae vitae nel decennio 1968–1978. Continuità del Magistero e riflessione teologica", *La Scuola Cattolica* (Jan.–Apr. 1979): 3–61; F. Ocáriz, "La nota teologica sull'insegnamento dell'Humanae vitae sulla contraccezione", *Anthropotes* 1 (1988): 25–43.

[42] K. Wojtyla, *Komentarz teologigiczno. Duszpaterski do Humanae vitae* (Rzym: C.O.D.E., 1969); a Vatican translation was sent to the Italian bishops: *Introduzione all'enciclica Humanae vitae*, in *Notificationes e Curia Cracoviense* (Vatican City: Typis Polyglottis Vaticanis, 1969), nos. 1–4.

[43] Wojtyla, *Introduzione*, p. 96.

[44] Ibid., p. 97.

[45] Ibid., p. 97.

[46] For a detailed study of it, see Lio, *"Humanae vitae" e coscienza*, pp. 287–317.

independently of the Magisterium of the Church, is contrary both to the whole of revealed doctrine and to the nature of conscience itself, whose function consists in truth in interpreting the absolutely binding divine law and not in determining which among its principles can be considered as binding, and which not. . . . The Christian conscience cannot ignore the authority of ecclesiastical teaching, under the pain of infidelity to the very foundations of Christian morality."[47] In the Church, as we have already said in the introduction, authority is entrusted to the hierarchy—with the assistance of the Holy Spirit—and not to theologians. It is important to read the following words of Cardinal Wojtyla at the Synod of Bishops of 1977: "The theme of the family has been constantly proposed by the Synod: a most vast theme that cannot be treated without reference to *Humanae vitae. I am in agreement with those who deem it necessary to emphasize the authority of the Magisterium over theologians and their publications."*[48]

We must add that, if sound theology had already known how to recognize at the time of its publication the *definitive* character of number 14 of *Humanae vitae,* it must now, after the repeated ratifications of this teaching by Paul VI, by the Synod of Bishops of 1980, by the teaching of John Paul II—in *Familiaris consortio,* in his catecheses in his Wednesday talks on *Humanae vitae,* and on many other occasions—be concluded that *this teaching can be said to be without doubt not only outside discussion by theologians but clearly something that pertains to the ordinary and universal Magisterium and that it is, therefore, infallible* (cf. *Lumen gentium,* no. 25).

■ In fact, in face of some who continue to put the truth of *Humanae vitae* into doubt, the Holy Father has explicitly affirmed that "its teaching on contraception does not belong to matter that can be freely disputed among theologians. To teach the contrary is equivalent to leading the moral conscience of spouses into error."[49]

More recently, the Holy Father has once more emphasized the grave responsibility of dissent on this subject:

Spouses can be seriously hindered in their obligation to live conjugal love correctly by a certain current selfish mentality, diffused by the mass

---

[47] Wojtyla, *Introduzione,* p. 115.

[48] G. Caprile, *Karol Wojtyla e il Sinodo dei vescovi* (Vatican City: Libreria Editrice Vaticana, 1980), p. 142.

[49] John Paul II, Address of June 5, 1987; *Enchiridion Familiae,* 5.4684.

media, by ideologies and practices contrary to the Gospel; but that can also happen, and with consequences truly grave and disgraceful, when the doctrine taught by the Encyclical is put into question, as it often is, by some theologians and pastors of souls.[50]

As we have many times noted, the teaching on the intrinsic wickedness of contraception belonged to the ordinary and universal Magisterium before the beginning of Vatican Council II; the only matter of discussion at the Council was whether the chemical means recently discovered must also be included within this condemnation. Certainly, this latter question had also been confronted by the Magisterium in the Address of Pius XII of September 12, 1958, to the Seventh International Hematological Congress. The judgment of Pius XII, however, because of the circumstances in which it was given, the terms in which it was expressed, etc., could not be considered a *definitive* teaching of the Magisterium. With the doctrine of the Magisterium in such condition (*Sic stante doctrina Magisterii*), the Council did not resolve the issue, inasmuch as the theme was reserved by the Supreme Pontiff for him to give personally a solution. *Humanae vitae* addressed this point, reproposing the teaching of Pius XII on progestines, but this time *in a definitive manner:* thus were fulfilled the conditions that this doctrine could become a definite teaching of the ordinary and universal Magisterium, and therefore, infallible. This step can be considered effectively completed after the conclusions the Synod of Bishops of 1980 reached and the successive teachings of John Paul II. If this is certain, the condemnation of contraception, even with respect to chemical means, is actually an *infallible teaching of the ordinary and universal Magisterium.*[51] John Paul II affirmed that, after the testimony given by the bishops in the synod of 1980 — "in unity with the faith of the successor of Peter" — on the truth of *Humanae vitae* (a testimony recalled and confirmed by *Familiaris consortio*), one can certainly conclude that this teaching is not

a doctrine invented by men: it has been *inscribed by the creative hand of God into the very nature of the human person* and has been confirmed by Him in Revelation. To question it, therefore, is equivalent *to denying to God Himself the obedience of our intelligence.* It is equivalent to preferring

[50] John Paul II, Address of February 14, 1988, no. 3; *Enchiridion Familiae,* 5.4757.

[51] On this see Ford and Grisez, "Contraception and the Infallibility of the Ordinary Magisterium", 264ff., and Ocáriz, "La nota teologica", 38ff.

the light of our own reason to that of God's Wisdom, thereby falling into the obscurity of error and ending up by damaging other fundamental principles of Christian doctrine.[52]

It does not seem possible any longer to continue to doubt about the obligatoriness in conscience of *Humanae vitae,* number 14. Thus there are, even in those sectors of the Catholic world that have contested the document, some signs of rethinking. Moreover, the years that have passed since the encyclical have shown that "hesitation or doubt over the norm taught in *Humanae vitae* has also involved other fundamental truths of reason or of faith": on conscience, on the Magisterium, and the existence of absolute moral norms. Therefore, the Pope, on the occasion of the 20th anniversary of the encyclical, invited theologians to acknowledge that, at the root of the opposition to *Humanae vitae* is an erroneous understanding of the very foundations on which Christian morality rests.[53] This was also the conclusion reached by more than 300 professors and experts of moral theology during the Second International Congress of Moral Theology, held in Rome in November 1988.

■ In his Address of November 12, 1988, to the Second International Congress of Moral Theology, referred to above, the Holy Father wanted to "acknowledge the encouraging results already achieved by many researchers" during the past years, thanks to whom it has been possible "to throw light on the wealth of truth, and indeed on the illuminating and almost prophetic value of Pope Paul's Encyclical, towards which people of many different cultural origins are now turning their ever increasing attention". And, he continued, as we have noted already, "one can also find signs of a rethinking even in those sectors of the Catholic world that were initially somewhat critical of this important Document."[54] Since this is so, it seems therefore indeed that the time has come to overcome doubts and uncertainties, no longer scientifically tenable by serious theology. It can therefore be of service to give an account of some facts that have taken place since 1968. We have already noted these, but here it is useful to examine them more integrally and in greater detail. The new theological

---

[52] John Paul II, "Address of the Holy Father John Paul II to the Second International Congress of Moral Theology", November 12, 1988, no. 3, in *"Humanae vitae": 20 anni dopo* (*Atti del II Congresso Internazionale di Teologia Morale: Roma, 9–12 novembre 1988*) (Milan: Ed. Ares, 1989), p. 14; *Enchiridion Familiae,* 5.4922.

[53] Ibid., nos. 3–6, pp. 14–16; *Enchiridion Familiae,* 5.4922–28.

[54] Ibid., no. 2, p. 14; *Enchiridion Familiae,* 5.4922–28.

perspective of *Humanae vitae* was not its vigorous affirmation of the malice of contraception: that was immemorably contained in the teaching of the Church and pertained to its ordinary and universal Magisterium. Pius XI had already said: "*Since, therefore, openly departing from the uninterrupted Christian tradition, some recently have judged it possible solemnly to declare another doctrine regarding this question, the Catholic Church, to whom God has entrusted the defense of the integrity and purity of morals . . . raises her voice in token of her divine ambassadorship and through Our mouth proclaims anew:* any use whatsoever of matrimony exercised in such a way that the act *is deliberately deprived of its natural power to generate life* is an offense against the law of God and nature, and those who indulge in such are branded with the guilt of grave sin."[55]

And Pius XII confirmed this teaching with no less solemnity: "Our Predecessor, Pius XI, in his Encyclical *Casti connubii,* December 31, 1930, solemnly proclaimed anew the fundamental law governing the marital act and conjugal relations; he said that any attempt on the part of the husband and the wife to deprive this act of its inherent force or to impede the procreation of a new life, either in the performance of the act itself, or in the course of the development of its natural consequences, is immoral, and furthermore, no alleged 'indication' or need can convert an intrinsically immoral act into a moral and lawful one. *This precept is as valid today as it was yesterday, and it will be the same tomorrow and always,* because it does not imply a precept of human law, but it is the expression of a law which is natural and divine."[56]

Moreover, this teaching was reaffirmed even more recently, and vigorously so, by Vatican Council II.[57] The new element of Paul VI's encyclical, one with what had previously been taught by the Magisterium of Pius XII,[58] is the formal declaration of the contraceptive nature of the "pill", i.e., of those biochemical means of depriving the

---

[55] Pius XI, *Casti connubii*, no. 57 (emphasis added); *Enchiridion Familiae*, 1.743.

[56] Pius XII, address *Vegliare con sollecitudine* to the Italian Catholic Union of Midwives, October 29, 1951, no. 24; *Enchiridion Familiae*, 2.1439–40.

[57] See Vatican Council II, pastoral constitution *Gaudium et spes,* December 7, 1965, no. 51, which, in pointing out ways of regulating births that are to be entirely excluded, in a footnote explicitly referred to both these documents. In fact, n. 14 begins as follows: "See Pius XI, Encyclical *Casti connubii:* AAS 22 (1930): pp. 559–561; Denz. 2239–2241 (3716–3718); Pius XII, *Allocutio Conventui Unionis Italicae inter Obstetrices,* 29 Oct. 1951: AAS 43 (1951): pp. 835–854", and adds another citation from Paul VI; *Enchiridion Familiae*, 3.1839.

[58] In discussing the argument about sterilization for eugenic reasons and repudiating it, Pius XII said: "Sterilization, either of the person or of the act alone, has also been advanced as a solution. On biological and eugenic grounds these two methods now have many proponents;

conjugal act of its procreative power; they were means that science had only recently placed at the disposal of men and the widespread use of them was enjoying a "boom" at the time of the Council. But no serious theologian, in fact, at that time doubted that onanism, for instance, was an intrinsically evil act by reason of its object. The theological problem that had not yet been definitively resolved, and whose resolution Paul VI had reserved for himself, was that of chemical contraception.[59] Without doubt, one of the major causes of the progressive disorientation introduced in regard to this matter within the Church has been the erroneous idea—promoted by some theologians —that the Church, by deciding to study the problem of the "pill", had put into doubt what she had previously taught concerning physical contraception, considering herself constrained—in confrontation with new social circumstances—to reconsider her position. If such had been the case, if such a turnabout regarding a subject on which the Church had expressed herself with such firmness were possible, then every definitive teaching of the ordinary and universal Magisterium would become in practice merely provisional (in fact, this is what the theology of dissent and the theory of the so-called merely pastoral Magisterium of the Church with respect to specific moral questions claimed). But the facts simply were not like that. The only point on which there remained a doubt and on which the Holy Father Paul VI reserved for himself the judgment—during the Council—was the definitive judgment on the question of progestins or whether chemical contraception merited the same judgment as did the barrier methods of contraception.

Here, in fact, we are dealing with a subject in some ways new: with the use of the "pill" the conjugal act apparently remains intact; there is no direct perversion of its physical reality, in contrast to what happens when mechanical or barrier methods are used. There is only an intervention into the biological laws of the fertility of the woman by means of an act preceding the physical union of the spouses. Some theologians

---

they are growing in favor because of new drugs which are more effective and convenient to use [here he is alluding to the progestins]. The reaction of some groups of theologians to this state of affairs is symptomatic and quite alarming. It reveals a deviation of moral judgment, along with an exaggerated haste to revise commonly accepted positions in favor of new techniques" (Pius XII, Address to the Members of the Seventh International Hematological Congress, September 12, 1958; *Enchiridion Familiae,* 2.1696–97).

[59] This is the reason for n. 14 of chap. 2 of part II of *Gaudium et spes,* and this is made explicit in the *Relatio* to the July 3, 1964, schema of that document: "The schema deliberately avoids any allusion to the problems of the progestin pills, concerning which the Supreme Pontiff has most wisely reserved judgment to himself" (*Acta Synodalia,* vol. III, pars VI, p. 51).

argued thus: the spouses have the right to the physical expression of their conjugal love even when there are serious reasons counseling a delay in a new conception. The "pill", which does not vitiate their act (and in fact does not change it if it is considered from a physical point of view) is the solution offered to us by scientific progress. Paul VI realized that such an imposition was against the spirit of Tradition and against the personalistic foundation of the moral life that the Council itself had proposed in a new way with new vigor. It ignores, in fact, the personal character of every exercise of human sexuality through which the spouses are called to cooperate with God in giving life to a new human person. The personalist demands of the conjugal union, therefore, include both the expression of mutual love and the openness to the procreation and education of children. From this point of view, he reminded us that the "biological laws" by which the transmission of life is ruled "pertain to the human person" (no. 10). This is a proper affirmation of a very coherent and thoroughgoing personalism, which never considers the human body as a thing but as a reality inseparable from the substantial wholeness—body and soul—constitutive of the person. He in no way confuses moral laws with biological laws, but rather has the wisdom to judge what are the limits imposed upon man in his dominion over physical laws when his own body is concerned, precisely because the body is an integral part of the person and is not the body of an animal, a body that is subject to man's dominion.[60] From this follows the new formula for defining contraception: "every act which, *either in anticipation of the conjugal act,* or in its fulfillment, or in the development of its natural consequences, proposes, either as end or as means, to impede procreation" (no. 10). Here the clause, "in anticipation", is introduced to include, in addition to the direct mockery of the conjugal act through mechanical or barrier means, its denaturing through means of manipulating biological laws, so characteristic of chemical contraceptive methods. Thus the encyclical ratified the fact that chemical contraception, as well as physical contraception, leads to the destruction of the dignity of conjugal love in its ordination toward life.

"Conjugal love most clearly reveals its true nature and nobility when we recognize that it has its origin in the highest source, as it were, in God, Who is Love and Who is the Father 'from whom all

---

[60] On this see Ramón García de Haro, *La vida cristiana* (*Curso de Teología Moral Fundamental*) (Pamplona: Eunsa, 1992), pp. 119ff. See also Germain Grisez, "Dualism and the New Morality", in *Atti del Congresso Internazionale (Roma–Napoli, 17–24 aprile 1974): Tomasso d'Aquino nel suo Settimo Centenario,* vol. 5, *L'agire morale,* ed. Marcelino Zalba, S.J. (Naples: Ed. Dominicane Italiane, 1977).

parenthood [*paternitas*] in heaven and earth receives its name' (see Eph. 3.15). . . . God the Creator wisely and providently established marriage with the intent that He might achieve His own design of love through Men. Therefore, through mutual self-giving, which is unique [*proprium*] and exclusive to them, spouses seek a communion of persons [*personarum communionem*]. Through this communion, the spouses perfect each other so that they might share with God the task [*operam socient*] of procreating and educating new living beings" (*Humanae vitae,* no. 8; Smith trans., pp. 277–78).

This doctrine, repeatedly reproposed by Paul VI himself and then by John Paul II, has become—as before the condemnation of physical contraception had become—a teaching of the ordinary and universal Magisterium. The affirmations of the Synod of Bishops of 1980 clarify this matter, affirmations represented and confirmed by *Familiaris consortio:* "In continuity with the living tradition of the ecclesial community throughout history, the recent Second Vatican Council and the magisterium of my predecessor Paul VI, expressed above all in the Encyclical *Humanae vitae,* have handed on to our times a truly prophetic proclamation, which reaffirms and reproposes with clarity the Church's teaching and norm, always old yet always new, regarding marriage and regarding the transmission of human life. For this reason the Synod Fathers made the following declaration at their last assembly: 'This Sacred Synod, gathered together with the Successor of Peter in the unity of faith, firmly holds what has been set forth in the Second Vatican Council (cf. *Gaudium et spes,* 50) and afterwards in the Encyclical *Humanae vitae,* particularly that love between husband and wife must be fully human, exclusive, and open to new life (*Humanae vitae,* 11; cf. 9, 12).' "[61]

Can one perhaps demand a more formal declaration on the existence of the presuppositions required in order that a teaching pertain to the ordinary and universal Magisterium? Therefore, this is an irreformable Magisterium and beyond discussion, because "although the individual bishops do not enjoy the prerogative of infallibility, nonetheless they do proclaim infallibly the doctrine of Christ on the following conditions: namely, when, although dispersed throughout the whole world but for all that preserving among themselves and with the successor of Peter the bond of communion, in their authoritative teaching on matters of faith and of morals they are in agreement that a particular teaching is to be held definitively and absolutely."[62]

[61] John Paul II, *Familiaris consortio,* no. 29; *Enchiridion Familiae,* 4.3253–54.
[62] Vatican Council II, dogmatic constitution *Lumen gentium,* November 21, 1964, no. 25. There-

In reiterating the norm of *Humanae vitae,* the Magisterium afterward has explained and deepened the reasons in its support. Here it suffices to consider some affirmations of *Familiaris consortio,* which we will analyze in the next chapter. But *Gaudium et spes* had already said that the ordination to life is not only a characteristic of marriage as an institution—as had always been affirmed—but is indeed a characteristic of marital love. *Familiaris consortio* not only confirmed this (no. 14) but indicated that the opening to the gift of life constitutes the sign of authentic conjugal love, its essential truth: "In its most profound reality, love is essentially a gift; and conjugal love, while leading the spouses to the reciprocal 'knowledge' which makes them 'one flesh,' does not end with the couple, because it makes them capable of the greatest possible gift, the gift by which they become cooperators with God for giving life to a new human person. Thus the couple, while giving themselves to one another, give not just themselves but also the reality of children, who are a living reflection of their love, a permanent sign of conjugal unity and a living and inseparable synthesis of their being a father and a mother."[63]

Familiaris consortio puts into a personalist context not only conjugal love but also procreation—and in this way develops Vatican Council II. It is now evident that contraception constitutes the very negation of the truth of conjugal love, insofar as this is a personal reality: "The innate language that expresses the total reciprocal self-giving of husband and wife is overlaid, through contraception, by an objectively contradictory language, namely, that of not giving oneself totally to the other. This leads not only to a positive refusal to be open to life but also to a falsification of the inner truth of conjugal love, which is called upon to give itself in personal totality."[64]

---

fore, the ordinary and universal Magisterium can "be considered", as the Holy Father reminds us, "as the habitual expression of the infallibility of the Church". John Paul II, Address of October 15, 1988; *Insegnamenti di Giovanni Paolo II* 11.3 (Vatican City: Typis Polyglottis Vaticanis, 1988).

[63] John Paul II, *Familiaris consortio,* no. 14; *Enchiridion Familiae,* 4.3225.

[64] Ibid., no. 32; *Enchiridion Familiae,* 4.3260–61. On this see Ramón García de Haro, "La verità dell'Humanae vitae, ormai fuori discussione", in *L'Osservatore Romano* (March 23, 1990); García de Haro, "Principios doctrinales del Magisterio y conviccines fundamentales en la formación del sacerdote para la pastoral familiar", in *La formazione del sacerdote e la pastorale della famiglia, Atti della VIII Assemblea plenaria del Pontificio Consiglio per la Famiglia,* ed. Elle Di Ci Leumann (Turin, 1991), pp. 27–43 (this article was translated into English, French, and Italian by the Pontificio Consiglio della pastorale per gli Operatori sanitari under the title *The Formation of the Priest in the Pastoral Assistance to the Family* [Vatican City: Polyglota Vaticana, 1991]). For a more complete and definitive study of this doctrine of *Humanae vitae* regarding chemical contraception in the teachings of the ordinary and universal Magisterium, see Carla Rossi, *Il Magistero ordinario del Romano Pontifice in moribus e il suo ruolo nella vita della Chiesa* (Rome: Pontificia Università Lateranense, 1993).

3. Other Teachings on Marriage and Family

First of all, we will be concerned with the declaration *Persona humana* *(Vatican Declaration on Certain Questions of Sexual Ethics)*, an important document of Paul VI's pontificate worthy of treatment in itself. His remaining teachings can be considered under the following headings: (1) questions of conjugal morality (particularly, his addresses to the "Teams of Our Lady" concerning *Humanae vitae* and to other family associations); (2) his teachings relative to *marriage cases* and to the indissolubility of marriage; and (3) his teachings on the theme of *mixed marriages*. We will end with a brief mention of the *Declaration on Procured Abortion*.

A. *The declaration* Persona humana *on sexual ethics*

This document, published by mandate of the Supreme Pontiff, illustrates the importance of chastity within and outside marriage; it clarifies some errors that are widespread today: premarital relations, the gravity of matter in the sixth commandment, etc.

Faced with "erroneous opinions and deviations that continue to be dispersed everywhere" on a matter of "the utmost importance both for the personal lives of Christians and for the social life of our time", the Holy Father wished explicitly that this declaration be published (cf. no. 2).[65] Its object is not the entire field of sexual ethics; it is rather a response to certain particular aspects that are of more urgent consideration (no. 6). Teachings that had been faithfully observed for 20 centuries, the declaration laments, "have been very much unsettled, even among Christians. There are many people today who, being confronted with so many widespread opinions opposed to the teaching

[65] Sacred Congregation for the Doctrine of the Faith, declaration *Persona humana, de quibusdam quaestionibus ad sexualitatem ethicam spectantibus,* December 29, 1975, AAS 68 (1975): 77–96; English translation, *Declaration on Certain Questions Concerning Sexual Ethics* (Washington, D.C.: United States Catholic Conference Publications Office, 1976). The text of this document is found in *Enchiridion Familiae,* 3.2123–50.

which they received from the Church, have come to wonder what they must still hold as true" (no. 1). It is, in fact, surprising that some points have been put in doubt: the evil of homosexuality, the existence and even the concept of grave sin, etc. The declaration is important also for the way in which it presents principles—and anchors its responses in them—regarding the traditional doctrine of the Church.[66] From the perspective of our study, we will focus on the following affirmations:

"*There can be no true promotion of man's dignity unless the essential order of his nature is respected*" (no. 3, par. 4). In order to sound the depths of the meaning of moral conduct, the point of departure is the Christian truth of creation: "God is God and man is the creature." From this, it follows that man is ordered to an end and that this ordering is rooted in his very being; he bears within his own being an intrinsic order to his own proper end, which is God; and therefore, it follows that "freedom must not be conceived as a *freedom of indifference,* or the possibility of all possibilities, but as a freedom called to realize a meaning which is not its own to give but which it receives in obedience." Only thus can the dignity of man, created in the image of God, be saved, as is demonstrated by the fact that "the Hegelian and then the Marxist attempt to think of history independently of the principle of creation ends up in denying history itself and human freedom."[67] This metaphysical situation of the person is, then, illustrated and deepened by God through revelation, which "has made known to us Christians His plan of salvation; and He has held up to us Christ, the Savior and Sanctifier, in His teaching and in His example, as the supreme and immutable Law of life" (no. 3, par. 3). Therefore, both in man's very nature and in the life and words of the God-made-man, we have a clear and secure norm for our moral conduct.

"Hence, those many people are in error who today assert that one can find neither in human nature nor in the revealed law any absolute and immutable norm to serve for particular actions other than the one which expresses itself in the general law of charity and respect for human dignity" (no. 4, par. 1). According to this erroneous view,

---

[66] On the importance of this document, the best study is Carlo Caffarra, "La Chiesa e l'ordine morale", *L'Osservatore Romano* (January 16, 1976): pp. 3–4, no. 5. See by the same author, *Etica generale della sessualità* (Milan: Ed. Ares, 1992).

[67] Caffarra, "La Chiesa e l'ordine morale", no. 1.

every other command, even of Scripture, must be a mere expression of a particular form of culture. But this is equivalent to denying that man is a creature, intrinsically ordered to and governed by God: creation and redemption as well become, in practice, merely myths. And the concept of moral obligation disappears, because, if the imperative of the Absolute is lacking, man does not find himself truly obligated: "As Soren Kierkegaard had already noted, in such a context to continue to speak of such things as moral obligation is no more serious than the blows struck by a Sancho Panza."[68] Reason itself, therefore, bears witness to us of the existence of a natural order willed by God, which can be known in some way. Moreover, we know that the Church was instituted by Christ as the *pillar and ground of truth,*[69] in such wise that, with the help of the Holy Spirit, "she ceaselessly preserves and transmits without error the truths of the moral order, and she authentically interprets not only the revealed positive law but *'also . . . those principles of the moral order which have their origin in human nature itself',*[70] and which concern man's full development and sanctification" (no. 4, par. 3).

■ The Council, as we have already emphasized, in stressing the criteria of the dignity of the person and of man's divinization[71] as principles for understanding the objectivity and transcendence of the moral order, did not at all seek to reject the concepts and the reality of nature, of grace, or of the written law.[72] To the contrary, it refused to conceive them in the flawed manner that results in denying them; that is, it repudiated the idea of a human nature that would be valid *even if God does not exist (etsi Deus non daretur),* because man is the image of God and without a reference to God and to his creative wisdom we cannot know well who man is. Likewise, it opposed a conception of the new law as a code imposed from without, as it were, on the periphery of the divine work of divinizing mankind, because it knew

---

[68] Ibid., no. 1.

[69] 1 Tim 3:15.

[70] Vatican Council II, declaration *Dignitatis humanae,* no. 14; AAS 58 (1966): 940; cf. Pius XI, *Casti connubii,* AAS 22 (1930): 579–80; Pius XII, Address of December 2, 1954; AAS 46 (1954): 671–72; John XXIII, *Mater et Magistra,* AAS 53 (1961): 457; Paul VI, *Humanae vitae,* no. 4; AAS 60 (1968): 483.

[71] Philippe Delhaye, *La scienza del bene e del male. La morale del Vaticano II e il "metaconcilio"* (Milan: Edizioni Ares, 1981), pp. 66–87.

[72] Ibid., pp. 63ff. and 174ff.

that grace, which acts from within, is the principal element of the new law.

Therefore, in order to safeguard the human and Christian dignity of the person, *Vatican Council II taught that "the principles and criteria which concern human sexuality in marriage ... are based upon the finality of the specific function of sexuality"* (no. 5, par. 3). In truth, after having noted that human sexuality is situated within the framework of the superior dignity of the human person, and therefore within the framework of the spouses' collaboration with the creative power of God, the Council concludes by noting the necessity of evaluating not only the intention of the spouses but also the "objective criteria [which], based on the nature of the human person and his acts, preserve the full sense of mutual self-giving and human procreation in the context of true love"[73] (no. 5, par. 4). And the declaration adds, "These final words briefly sum up the Council's teaching—more fully expounded in an earlier part of the same Constitution[74]—on the finality of the sexual act and on the principal criterion of its morality: *It is respect for its finality that ensures the moral goodness of this act*" (no. 5, par. 5).

■ There is no clearer or simpler guarantee of overcoming selfishness in the use of one's sexuality than the fullness of the gift of self in openness to life, when one assumes with joy the role of father or of mother. Therefore, openness to life will always be the prime criterion for judging the morality of sexual activity. That, adds the declaration, is also the principle at the root of the "traditional doctrine, which states that the use of the sexual function has its true meaning and moral rectitude only in true marriage" (no. 5, par. 6); that is, in the indissoluble communion of love between a husband and a wife ordered to the procreation and education of children.

So-called premarital relations are not lawful, even if many today claim that they have a right to them, at least when there is a firm intention to marry and external circumstances make the celebration of marriage difficult. This opinion, the declaration affirms, "is contrary to Christian doctrine, which states that every genital act must be within the framework of marriage." And it indicates the reasons, including biblical ones: outside of marriage there is not that indissoluble union

---

[73] Vatican Council II, *Gaudium et spes*, no. 51; AAS 58 (1966): 1072.
[74] Ibid., nos. 49 and 50; AAS 58 (1966): 1069–70.

demanded by the Lord (cf. Mt 19:4–6); moreover, there is the explicit teaching of St. Paul, when he affirms that, "if unmarried people or widows cannot live chastely they have no other alternative than the stable union of marriage: '. . . it is better to marry than to be aflame with passion'[75]" (no. 7, par. 2). In a note, the declaration adds that "sexual intercourse outside marriage is formally condemned: 1 Cor 5:1; 6:9; 7:2; 10:8; Eph 5:5; 1 Tim 1:10; Heb 13:4; and with explicit reasons: 1 Cor 6:12–20."[76] This, it continues, is "what the Church has always understood and taught,[77] and she finds a profound agreement with her doctrine in men's reflection and the lessons of history" (no. 7, par. 3).

■ Experience confirms that sexual union, in order to fulfill its own requirements of a total and generous gift, demands that the stability of marriage be safeguarded. This is important not only for the couple but even more so for the children (no. 7, pars. 4 and 5). In the following numbers, the declaration considers homosexuality and autoeroticism (nos. 8–9). Some say, speaking of the latter, that the fact that it is so common proves that it is a normal thing; an argument that others use with respect to premarital relations. But this fact justifies nothing. "Sociological surveys are able to show the frequency of this disorder according to the places, populations or circumstances studied. In this way facts are discovered, but facts do not constitute a criterion for judging the moral value of human acts"[78] (no. 9, par. 3). This frequency is only an indication of the weakness of human nature after the fall and of the actual conditions of permissiveness and the loss of the sense of shame (ibid.).

Every act incompatible with the preservation of charity is a mortal sin, and therefore, "every deliberate transgression, in serious matter, of each of the moral laws" is mortally sinful (no. 10, par. 4). The declaration confronts the tendency, quite widespread, of diminishing or, indeed, of denying in practice, the existence of mortal sin, particularly in sexual matters.

[75] 1 Cor 7:9.

[76] N. 16 of the declaration.

[77] Cf. Innocent IV, Ep. *Sub catholica professione,* March 3, 1254; DS 835; Pius II, Propos. dann. in his Ep. *Cum sit accepimus,* November 14, 1459, DS 1367; decrees of the Holy Office, November 24, 1665, DS 2045; March 2, 1679, DS 2148; Pius XI, *Casti connubii;* AAS 22 (1930): 558–59.

[78] Paul VI, apostolic exhortation *Quinque iam annis,* December 8, 1970; AAS 63 (1971): 102.

There are those who go as far as to affirm that mortal sin, which causes separation from God, only exists in the formal refusal directly opposed to God's call, or in that selfishness which completely and deliberately closes itself to love of neighbor. They say that it is only then that there comes into play the fundamental option, that is to say, the decision which totally commits the person and which is necessary if mortal sin is to exist (n. 10, par. 2).[79]

Certainly, human acts receive their radical goodness from their orientation to God as the last end; but experience confirms that this orientation can be lost—and frequently this is the case—not only by the desire to oppose oneself to God—something rather diabolical—but also through weakness, passion, selfishness, pride. "A person therefore sins mortally not only when his action comes from direct contempt for love of God and neighbor, but also when he consciously and freely, for whatever reason, chooses something which is seriously disordered" (no. 10, par. 6).[80] Indeed, "according to Christian tradition and the Church's teaching, and as right reason also recognizes, the moral order of sexuality involves such high values of human life that every direct violation of this order is objectively serious" (no. 10, par. 6).[81]

■ Certainly, passion often enters into sins in the sexual domain, and the responsibility of the subject can be diminished; but this of itself does not exclude grave sin, even if the sin is not one of malice.[82] In every case, one must make a judgment in conscience, aware that the final judgment belongs to God and that pastors "must exercise patience and goodness; but they are not allowed to render God's commandments null, nor to reduce unreasonably people's responsibility" (no. 10, par. 9). Naturally, this is valid with respect to contraception. Its intrinsically immoral character signifies that man cannot abandon himself to it without destroying his own humanity. It does not,

[79] On the matter of the fundamental option, see Ramón García de Haro and Ignacio Celaya, *La moral cristiana* (Madrid: Rialp, 1975), pp. 34ff. See also Joseph Boyle, Jr., "Freedom, the Human Person, and Human Action", in *Principles of Catholic Moral Life,* ed. William E. May (Chicago: Franciscan Herald Press, 1980), pp. 237–68.

[80] This teaching has been recently stressed by John Paul II in his apostolic exhortation *Reconciliatio et poenitentia,* December 1, 1984, no. 17.

[81] After referring readers to the documents cited in its nn. 17 and 19, the declaration cites other teachings of the Magisterium on this matter: Decree of the Holy Office, March 18, 1666, DS 2060; Paul VI, *Humanae vitae,* nos. 13 and 14; AAS 60 (1968): 489–96. See no. 24 of the declaration.

[82] Thus St. Thomas notes that many mortal sins, particularly adultery and murder, are committed under the impulse of passion. See *Summa theologiae,* I–II, q. 77, a. 8.

however, mean that at times one ought not to recognize that weakness diminishes its wickedness; even less does it mean that the Church ignores the real difficulties that spouses can often encounter. The Church never compromises with sin, but she understands the sinner quite well. She has no difficulty in pardoning a person of the same sin, even if committed many times in the same day. She does not demean anyone who has sinned, but welcomes him, encourages him, helps him. As a Mother, she only wants spouses to avoid ruining their own love and family by giving up the struggle against a way of acting that will destroy them. Moreover, the Church does not regard the wickedness of contraception as equal to that of other sins even more grievous and degrading—adultery and abortion, for instance. But she knows that, unfortunately, spouses who abandon themselves to contraception can be seriously tempted to abort; she therefore warns them to avoid this danger.

The virtue of chastity not only requires one to avoid specific acts, but also to keep one's heart pure and generous either in the state of marriage or in that of celibacy. Moreover, in the Christian, this purity is enlarged and supremely demanded by the inhabitation of the Holy Spirit, as the apostle reminds us (1 Cor 6:15 and 18–20). In reality, the virtue of chastity frees man from the selfishness of the flesh and makes him generous in his relations to God and to other men. However, in this life, this liberation is never perfect, because concupiscence is not suppressed. Thus it requires a continual ascetic struggle, particularly necessary today because of the selfishness that is so dominant (nos. 11–12). Thus the declaration reminds us of the remedies to be used.

Means always recommended by the Church for living a life of chastity

Specifically, these means are: "discipline of the senses and the mind, watchfulness and prudence in avoiding occasions of sin, the observance of modesty; moderation in recreation, wholesome pursuits, assiduous prayer and frequent reception of the Sacraments of Penance and the Eucharist. Young people especially should earnestly foster devotion to the Immaculate Mother of God" (no. 12, par. 4). Moreover, there is an obligation for all, bishops, priests, and laity, citizens and social authorities, to create an environment conducive to chastity (no. 13).

B. *Other teachings on conjugal morality*

The principal means of assuring a good moral married life are: a faithful and positive presentation of Catholic doctrine, recourse to grace, ascetic commitment, adequate pastoral help.

Today it is thought that, at the beginning of the 17th century, the distinction between moral, dogmatic, and spiritual theology became exaggerated.[83] This gave rise to pastoral activities without content and some doctrinal studies deprived of any real interest for the Church and her mission.[84] In any event, both in the Magisterium and in the Fathers of the Church, these aspects—moral, dogmatic, and spiritual theology—are always united. The Pope of *Humanae vitae* insists upon some of the consequences this entails for the presentation of the doctrine on marriage.

The gravity of the questions raised today make ever more necessary *a presentation of doctrine that is able to strengthen the convictions of the faithful; that is, a faithful, positive, and encouraging presentation of doctrine.* The first condition is "a clear and courageous preaching" totally faithful to the Magisterium.[85] This is an idea, one can say, that Paul VI repeated every time that he had to speak to people responsible for providing formation to the engaged: "You are charged with the task of bearing a witness that is totally faithful to the thought of the Magisterium."[86] Not having acted in this way is the cause of the fact that

[83] For the history of this dissociation see Ramón García de Haro, "Dogmatica y moral en la obra teologica de Santo Tomas", *Escritos el Vedat* 12 (1982): 97–143, esp. 98–113.

[84] The same has happened in modern exegesis, as Ignace de la Potterie observes: "We cannot deny that one can begin to speak of a crisis in exegesis. There is a growing awareness, even in the Protestant world, that the historical-critical school of exegesis does not satisfy the needs of the believing person today. This way of interpreting Scripture is incapable of helping men discover the rich depths, spiritual and doctrinal, of God's message. This excessive interest in technique and this slavery to the letter is not what the Church, theology and the faithful have need of. Without doubt, there is a positive value in such criticism; the biblical scholar can derive great profit from it; but one cannot remain there: one must study and plumb the depths of Scripture in the spirit of the Fathers" (cited by A. Gonzalez Moreno, *Scripta Theologica* 11, no. 1 [1979]: 361).

[85] Paul VI, Address to the Teams of Our Lady, September 22, 1976, in *Insegnamenti di Paolo VI*, 14 (1976), p. 734; *Enchiridion Familiae*, 3.2170.

[86] Paul VI, Address to the Committee of the Family; *Insegnamenti di Paolo VI* 15 (1977), p. 1012; *Enchiridion Familiae*, 3.2191–93.

today the majority of couples are in need of help. They are overwhelmed first by distrust and by doubt, then by fear and discouragement, and finally they abandon the most noble values of marriage. And often they find themselves in this condition because those who ought to have been their teachers have put these values into doubt, have reduced their theological dimensions, or have deemed as utopian, antiquated, inaccessible, and useless the most important requirements of marriage and of the family.[87]

In addition to being faithful to the Magisterium, teaching, if it is to be encouraging, must have the following characteristics:

■ *It must be positive and show the grandeur of an ideal.* This is a matter of experience: certainly, it is not enough to know the good in order to do it, but a knowledge that is truly alive easily leads one to become enthusiastic, inasmuch as the good is more conformed to our nature and aspirations: the ideal gives birth to love, and love gives birth to generosity. Therefore, in discussing *Humanae vitae* with the faithful, the Pope took note that the encyclical indeed excludes contraception, "but that it is above all the positive presentation of conjugal morality as directed to its mission of love and of fertility 'in an integral vision of man and of his vocation, not only natural and earthly, but above all supernatural and eternal'."[88] Similarly, one of his addresses to the Teams of Our Lady is devoted to insisting on the ideal of the family as the path and "school of holiness": "You have been called to holiness, according to the teaching of the Church as solemnly reaffirmed by the Council.[89] It is up to you to attain it in the proper way, within and by means of your family life."[90,91] It is the Church who teaches this, and it would be a "tragedy for our time" if this were to be neglected.

It must reassure spouses that the Christian ideal of marriage can be attained with the help of grace. "The sacrament of marriage, permanent fountain of grace" is the title of another of his addresses to the Teams of Our Lady. The realization of an ideal requires sacrifice, demands that one go the way of the cross; otherwise it would not be Christian. But this can be done with the help of grace: "The cross cannot be lacking

---

[87] Paul VI, Address to the Teams of Our Lady, September 22, 1976, in *Insegnamenti di Paolo VI* 14 (1976), p. 735; *Enchiridion Familiae*, 3.2172.

[88] Paul VI, Address of July 31, 1968, AAS 60 (1968): 527; *Enchiridion Familiae*, 3.1940.

[89] Cf. *Lumen gentium*, no. 11.

[90] Cf. ibid., no. 41.

[91] Paul VI, Address to the Teams of Our Lady, May 4, 1970; *Insegnamenti di Paolo VI* 8 (1970), p. 425; *Enchiridion Familiae*, 3.1992.

in the communion of conjugal love, as it cannot be absent from any manifestation of true love. It would be vain and dangerous to want a marriage that does not carry for anyone the sign of the cross, whether by means of psychical sufferings or of moral or spiritual sorrows. You have the task of witnessing that grace, the power and fidelity of God give the energies needed to carry the cross. The sacrament is a permanent source of grace, which accompanies spouses their whole life long."[92]

Finally, *instruction must make the spouses understand that fidelity to the plans of God fulfills their deepest desires for happiness.* It is necessary that spouses be convinced that "by living the sacrament of marriage, they walk 'with a generous and unquenchable love'[93] to that holiness to which they are called by grace,[94] seen not as an arbitrary need but as the work of love of a Father who wills your full perfection and the total happiness of your children."[95]

Moreover, the actual situation requires that spouses learn that the grandeur of their ideal and the happiness that it will bring them will not be understood by everyone. But this cannot be a matter of surprise, since the Lord himself promised his apostles that they, who had "given up home, brothers or sisters, mother or father, children or property, [would] receive in this present age a hundred times as many homes, brothers, sisters, mothers, children and property—and persecution besides—and in the age to come everlasting life" (Mk 10:30). The Holy Father says:

Do not let yourselves be brought down by the temptations, the difficulties, the tests that rise up on the road, without fear of going, if necessary, against the current regarding what is thought and said in a world whose attitudes have been paganized. St. Paul already noted: "Do not let yourselves be conformed to this world, but be transformed by the renewal of your mind.[96]"[97]

Finally, it is necessary that *priests know how to experience God's mercy for souls, without compromise—which would be a sign of cowardice or of lack*

[92] Paul VI, Address to the Teams of Our Lady, September 22, 1976; *Insegnamenti di Paolo VI* 14 (1976), pp. 733 and 737; *Enchiridion Familiae*, 3.2172.

[93] Cf. *Lumen gentium*, no. 41.

[94] Cf. Mt 5:48; 1 Th 4:3; Eph 1:4.

[95] Paul VI, Address to the Teams of Our Lady, May 4, 1970; *Insegnamenti di Paolo VI* 8 (1970), pp. 431–32; *Enchiridion Familiae*, 3.2004–5.

[96] Rom 12:2.

[97] Address to the Teams of Our Lady, May 4, 1970; *Insegnamenti di Paolo VI* 8 (1970), p. 432; *Enchiridion Familiae*, 3.2005.

of interest — in a way that the spouses do not become discouraged by their falls, but rather encouraging them to take up once more their struggle with humility. This idea is developed with particular attention in his Address to the Teams of Our Lady of May 4, 1970 (nos. 13–17). We will note the more fundamental passages. The fullness of the ideal is not attained without struggle. The work of the priest

> is a work of liberation, whose fruit is the true freedom of the children of God; their conscience asks to be in its turn respected, educated and formed, in a climate of trust and not of distress; divine laws are presented to their conscience not with an inhuman coldness of an abstract objectivity, but in their proper mission, which is to guide the couple along their path...; in such a way that they are not seen as hindrances but are recognized as being the great help that they are.

Nonetheless, even if doctrine is presented pastorally in this way, there can come a time when either the husband or the wife

> discovers that he or she is as it were unable to respect — in its integrity — the moral law; and this in such a fundamental terrain that it arouses in him or her a reaction of discomfort. And then comes the decisive moment, in which the Christian, instead of abandoning himself to a sterile and destructive revolt, approaches — in humility — to the disturbing discovery of being a man before God, a sinner faced with the love of Christ the Savior.

With this experience as a point of departure, all the marvels of the work of grace in the soul are progressively discovered. One knows that grace is not merited, but one receives it with joy and gratitude; one has the peace of God, which exceeds all understanding (Phil 4:7). Without being free of discouragements, nor of efforts, nor of sufferings "which at times only the thought of participating in the passion of Christ helps to support,[98] the spouses understand that the demands of the moral life — of which the Church reminds them — are not intolerable laws but a gift of God for helping them to arrive, even in their weakness, to the riches of a fully human and Christian love."[99]

---

[98] Cf. Col 1:24.

[99] Address to the Teams of Our Lady, May 4, 1970; *Insegnamenti di Paolo VI* 8 (1970), pp. 432–35; *Enchiridion Familiae*, 3.2005–7.

C. *Teachings on marriage cases and on the indissolubility of marriage*

Two problems preoccupied the Pope: an excessive delay in processing marriage cases and erroneous interpretations of the role of conjugal love in marriage and of rights within the Church, which tended to weaken the firmness of the marital bond, in the resolution of marriage cases.

There are three principal documents of relevance here: the motu proprio *Causas matrimoniales* of March 28, 1971,[100] and two addresses to the Roman Rota, that of January 28, 1971, and that of February 9, 1976.[101]

In his motu proprio, the Holy Father stresses the importance of a correct development of the judicial function in order to let the holiness of marriage shine forth. As a foundation for proper activity, judiciaries ought to have in mind two points: to consider as their valued fruit *the promotion of everything that "tends to secure the firmness of the bond"* and at the same time *to avoid unnecessary delays,* the source of not a few inconveniences for the spouses and their children. With this in view, he gives norms concerning the constitution of the tribunals, for appeals, and for particular concrete cases.

> ■ The document begins by recalling that "marriage cases among the baptized, *iure proprio,* pertain to ecclesiastical judges, whereas cases concerning the merely civil effects of marriage belong to the civil magistrate, unless a particular norm establishes that these cases, if they are incidental and accessory, can be known and resolved by an ecclesiastical judge."

The Address to the Sacred Roman Rota of January 28, 1971, is intended to point out the *importance of law in the Church and, in particular, the importance of the Church's judicial power over marriage.* An erroneous critical mentality about the "canonical functions of the ecclesiastical society" had been created: from it came the opinion of an indiscriminate freedom, of an autonomous pluralism, and an accusation of "juridicism levelled against the tradition and the normative practice of the hierarchy" (no. 1, par. 5). Faced with this error, he

---

[100] AAS 63 (1971): 441–46.

[101] Found, respectively, in *Insegnamenti di Paolo VI* 9 (1971), pp. 59–67 (*Enchiridion Familiae,* 3.2019–20) and 14 (1976), pp. 96–101 (*Enchiridion Familiae,* 3.2155–60).

makes it clear that "authority . . . is not opposed to the pouring out of the Spirit in the People of God, but rather is its vehicle and custodian"; and this authority was invested in Peter and the apostles by Christ himself (cf. Mt 16:18–19; 18:18, 28:18–19; Lk 10:16; Jn 20:23, 21:16–17, etc.) (no. 1, par. 6). The judiciary power is so bound to that of lawgiving and governing that "if the authority did not have judiciary capacity it would be socially inane, giving rise to arbitrariness, to despotism, and to violence" (no. 2). This power must be exercised with charity, but without weakness; let the words with which St. Paul

> judges and condemns a Christian of Corinth guilty of incest be kept in mind.[102] It suffices to read the Second Epistle to the Corinthians and the Epistle to the Galatians, which was written immediately afterward, to understand how the Apostle of the Gentiles, that inspired singer of charity,[103] exercised the power that he felt had been given him by Christ (no. 3).[104]

> ■ The Pope insists, moreover, on guarantees that derive from a "sound juridical formalism", always keeping in mind preoccupation for the salvation of souls (no. 4). Not to forget this is efficacious in helping to solve the difficulties that today some often raise in an artificial way with respect to ecclesiastical justice.

Another real problem, one particularly alive, is faced in his address of February 9, 1976. *The importance given by the Council to love in marriage cannot serve as an excuse for creating new causes for nullity: the loss of love in marriage does not annul it.* The Pope says: "In no way can that notion of conjugal love be admitted, which would lead to relinquishing or diminishing the force and meaning of that well known principle: *the consent of the parties makes the marriage.*"[105] Here, he continues, we are dealing with a fundamental principle of canonical and theological science, received by them by way of Tradition, and as such confirmed by the Magisterium.[106] This is also, as we stressed in the previous

---

[102] 1 Cor 5.
[103] Cf. 1 Cor 13.
[104] AAS 63 (1971): 441ff.
[105] Address to the Roman Rota, February 9, 1976; *Insegnamenti di Paolo VI* 14 (1976), p. 99; *Enchiridion Familiae*, 3.2158: "Nullo modo talem coniugalis amoris notionem admittere posse, quae perducat ad relinquendam vel imminuendam vim et significationem pernoti illius principii: *matrimonium facit partium consensus.*"
[106] Cf. Mt 19:5–6; DS 643, 1497, 1813, 3701, 3713.

chapter, the teaching of *Gaudium et spes*.[107] This in no way means a diminishing of the dignity of conjugal love, because its values are not only juridical. Even supposing that conjugal love has no relevance juridically, it is always necessary so that marriage "can be perfected according to that full form of its perfection, which it is able to attain by its own nature."[108]

> ■ The new *Code of Canon Law* (1983) does not change the teaching on the causes of nullity, but more explicitly recognizes the role of love in its norms (cf. cans. 1055 and 1095). The difficulties that up until that time had blocked such recognition derive from an imprecise idea of a right, identified too much with a purely positive and directly coercive norm, when in truth—at least when we are talking about a "natural right"—what is at stake is a right of the person, owed to the person by reason of the natural law and in justice. And there can be no doubt that spouses owe each other conjugal love, not only by reason of charity but also by reason of justice. The fact that a way of acting cannot, in practice, be required coercively, with juridical sanctions for grave infractions, in no way lessens the juridical obligation to act in this way. Thus, not a few of the obligations proper to spouses and to the family have this characteristic (e.g., mutual help and fidelity).

We must not forget that consent consists in the acceptance of the conjugal community—a community of life and love—that has been created by God: it is not consent itself that gives structure to the content of marriage. Therefore, the same goes for marriage as for indissolubility: unless it has been explicitly excluded—and such exclusion, which it is difficult to imagine happening, would render consent null—love belongs to marriage in a constitutive way, even when those who contract marriage do not think about it (as when they are ignorant of the indissoluble character of the bond).

D. *Mixed marriages*

Mixed marriages are those "celebrated between a Catholic party and a non-Catholic party, whether baptized or not". The Church

---

[107] Vatican Council II, *Gaudium et spes*, no. 48.

[108] Address to the Roman Rota, February 9, 1976; *Insegnamenti di Paolo VI* 14 (1976), p. 100: "Perfici potest secundum plenam illam perfectionis formam, quam suapte natura assequi valet."

tolerates these marriages under the following conditions: dispensations, promises, and instructions given to the spouses, and she defines their juridical and liturgical form.

In his motu proprio on this subject of March 31, 1970,[109] Paul VI gave opportune norms for these situations in our age, along with a detailed exposition and reconfirmation of the traditional doctrine. We will first set forth the principles and then specific provisions.

The real conditions of life (an increasing pluralism and social mobility) have multiplied the occasions for contracting mixed marriages. This kind of marriage, the fruit of the diversity of religions and of division among Christians, does not ordinarily favor unity between the spouses; indeed, it creates difficulties for unity, for spouses and for children. Therefore, *"the Church, conscious of her duties, dissuades the faithful from contracting mixed marriages."*[110] Notwithstanding this, however, taking into account the truth that man has a natural right to marry, and always with the admonishment that the faithful take the necessary cautions in order to secure the requirements of the divine law, the Church *tolerates their existence.*

■ The Motu proprio lists some of the inconveniences of mixed marriages, which have repercussions on the unity between the spouses, on their personal faith, and on the education of their children. These are: an absence of agreement on such basic matters as the recognition of the *sacramental character* of marriage, of some of the *moral principles* concerning marriage and family, of the *ends and properties* of marriage, and, finally, of the competence that the Church has over marriage.[111] There is, in addition, the threat of indifferentism.

These difficulties are not so great in marriages with Eastern Orthodox Christians because of their greater communion with the Catholic Church;[112] for marriages of this kind there is already a discipline helped by the decrees of Vatican Council II.[113]

As far as *the canonical discipline of mixed marriages goes, it is advisable, in light of the wide range fo situations, that this not be uniform, but that it*

[109] AAS 62 (1970): 257ff.; *Enchiridion Familiae*, 3.1980ff.

[110] Ibid., 258, par. 2; *Enchiridion Familiae*, 3.1980.

[111] Ibid., 259; *Enchiridion Familiae*, 3.1980.

[112] Congregation for the Doctrine of the Faith, *Lettera ai Vescovi della Chiesa Cattolica su Alcuni aspetti della Chiesa intesa come communione*, May 28, 1992, no. 17.

[113] Cf. the conciliar decree *Unitatis redintegratio*, Nov. 21, 1964, no. 3, and also the decree *Crescens matrimoniorum* of February 22, 1967, given by the Sacred Congregation for the Eastern Churches.

nonetheless always maintain the divine law, i.e., the order established by Christ for salvation. Specifically, the faith of the Catholic spouse must be protected adequately, inasmuch as no one has the right to put himself into a condition where there is *the danger of losing the Faith.* Moreover, it is necessary to make sure that the Catholic spouse will take care that *the children are brought up in the Catholic Faith.* Both these matters can be secured in different ways. Moreover, there can be different canonical and liturgical forms for such marriages.[114]

In the light of these principles the document proceeds to establish a specific regime for mixed marriages. Its principal points are the following: (a) The marriage between baptized persons, one of whom is Catholic and the other not, is not *licit* without the appropriate dispensation of the Ordinary; on the other hand, marriage with a non-Christian party without such dispensation is *invalid* (norms 1–2); the dispensation is given in cases in which there is a just cause (no. 3). (b) To obtain the dispensation, the Catholic party must show a disposition to protect himself from *dangers to the Faith;* he must also give a sincere promise to do as much as he can to fulfill his *grave obligation* to educate his children as Catholics (no. 4). *The non-Catholic party must be informed* of both these promises (no. 5). Episcopal conferences will decide about the opportuneness of also asking for written guarantees or about giving these promises before witnesses (no. 7). (c) Moreover, both parties must be informed of the ends and essential properties of marriage, which they cannot repudiate (no. 6). (d) For *the canonical form* of such marriages, the norms up to now in force are still valid (with the particularities envisioned for Eastern Christians); in each case, the bishop can dispense from the canonical form (nos. 8–10). With respect to the *liturgical form,* this should conform to the norms established by the episcopal conferences; these, however, cannot authorize any rite with the active participation of a non-Catholic minister, not even as an *a posteriori* celebration (nos. 11–13). (e) Finally, there must be special pastoral care for these marriages (no. 14); on the other hand, the previously established canonical penalties are abrogated (no. 15).[115]

---

[114] AAS 62 (1970): 259; *Enchiridion Familiae,* 3.1980.
[115] Ibid., 260–63.

The *Declaration on Procured Abortion*

Although the evil of abortion occurs more frequently outside marriage than within it, it is also found in marriage; therefore, it has traditionally been treated in connection with marital morality. Faced with the increase of such a grave crime and with the growing legalization of this crime by civil legislatures, the Church published a new and detailed declaration of condemnation of this crime, dated November 18, 1974, issued by the Sacred Congregation for the Doctrine of the Faith.[116]

Regarding abortion, the document notes that "it is not a question of opposing one opinion to another, but *of transmitting to the faithful a constant teaching of the supreme Magisterium,* which teaches moral norms in the light of faith. It is therefore clear that *this declaration necessarily entails a grave obligation for Christian consciences*" (no. 4). That is, it deals with a definitive teaching of the ordinary and universal Magisterium, a teaching that is, therefore, infallible (cf. *Lumen gentium,* no. 25). In what follows, the declaration examines the foundations in Scripture, in Tradition, and in the Magisterium, that show that this teaching of the Church "has not changed and is unchangeable" (nos. 5–7). Then it adds that this doctrine is true for all men insofar as it is accessible to the light of reason (nos. 8–13). The document then responds to objections posed most frequently today (nos. 14–18) and concludes by clarifying the relationship between morality and law, as well as the obligation to do what can be done to see that this fundamental right of the person is recognized in all civil legislation.

[116] AAS 66 (1974): 730–47. The text of this document is given in *Enchiridion Familiae,* 3.2071–94.

Chapter Eight

THE MAGISTERIUM OF JOHN PAUL II ON THE FAMILY AND THE APOSTOLIC EXHORTATION *FAMILIARIS CONSORTIO*

In his apostolic exhortation *Familiaris consortio,* the present Pope has written, "The future of the world and of the Church passes through the family."[1] This conviction is at the basis of his constant attention to the well-being of the family from the very beginning of his pontificate. This conviction culminated in the publication of *Familiaris consortio,* which John Paul II has himself defined as "a *summa* of the teaching of the Church on the life, the tasks, the responsibilities, and the mission of marriage and of the family in the world today".[2] This *summa* will be the first object of our analysis. The remainder of his abundant magisterial teaching on marriage and family can be divided into three groups of documents: the catecheses in his Wednesday audiences (which were published in one large volume in Italian and in four volumes in English);[3] second, his *catecheses on the family in his apostolic journeys to*

---

[1] Apostolic exhortation *Familiaris consortio,* November 22, 1981, no. 75. For the rest of this chapter this document will be cited in the text as FC, leaving other citations for the footnotes. The document is found in *Enchiridion Familiae: Textos del Magisterio Pontificio y Conciliar sobre el Matrimonio y la Familia (Siglos I a XX),* ed. Augusto Sarmiento and Javier Escrivá-Ivars, vol. 4 (Madrid: Ediciones Rialp, 1992), pp. 3201–72.

[2] Address of December 22, 1981, in which the Pope presented his new apostolic exhortation; *Enchiridion Familiae,* 4.3415ff.

[3] The Italian volume is entitled *Uomo e donna lo creò (Catechesi sull'amore umano)* (Rome: Città Nuova Editrice/Libreria Editrice Vaticana, 1985). The four English-language volumes are: *The Original Unity of Man and Woman (Catechesis on the Book of Genesis)* (Boston: St. Paul Editions, 1981); *Blessed Are the Pure of Heart (Catechesis on the Sermon on the Mount and Writings of St. Paul)* (Boston: St. Paul Editions, 1983); *Reflections on "Humanae vitae": Conjugal Morality and Spirituality* (Boston: St. Paul Editions, 1984); and *The Theology of Marriage and Celibacy* (Boston: St. Paul Editions, 1986).

America, Africa, Asia, and Europe, as well as in his visits to the parishes of the diocese of Rome;[4] and finally the allocutions, homilies, and addresses held in Rome, on the occasion of visits of various associations, congresses, and institutions that are concerned with the family.[5]

I. The Occasion, Importance, and General Scheme of *Familiaris Consortio*

The apostolic exhortation *Familiaris consortio* came to birth on the occasion of the Fifth Synod of Bishops, celebrated at Rome in 1980. The Holy Father notes that in this document he gathers together the propositions of the synod, taking also into account the suggestions formulated during its meetings.[6] The great *importance* of the document is evident in two factors: the fact that it is a document of the Supreme Pontiff which, "gathering together the proposals and the experiences of the Episcopate of five continents", is also "an authentic expression of the collegiality of the Church";[7] and the fact that it contains a summary of all the doctrines of the Church — a *summa* — in which "the clear teaching of Vatican Council II on marriage and the family is deepened and amplified."[8]

As far as its scheme is concerned, the exhortation is divided into an introduction and four parts. The introduction and the first part, entitled "Bright Spots and Shadows for the Family Today", contain both an analysis of the current situation and the setting forth anew of the most important moral principles for giving an adequate solution to the problems of our day. "The Plan of God for Marriage and the Family" is the title of the second part, which treats of the notion of marriage, its

---

[4] We will make mention of these at the end of the chapter. A selection of these discourses and homilies, together with those from the following group, can be found in Juan Pablo II, *A las familias*, under the editorship of T. López, 4th ed. (Pamplona: Eunsa, 1982). These addresses and homilies, along with those referred to in n. 3, are also found in vols. 4 and 5 of *Enchiridion Familiae*. References to pertinent volumes and pages of this excellent source will be given when material from these sources is cited in this chapter.

[5] See the preceding note.

[6] Address of December 22, 1981, no. 7; *Enchiridion Familiae*, 4.3416. Cf. *Familiaris consortio*, no. 2.

[7] Address of December 22, no. 7; *Enchiridion Familiae*, 4.3416–17.

[8] Ibid.; *Enchiridion Familiae*, 4.3417–18.

fundamental structure, and its origin in the conjugal covenant. The third part studies what marriage and the family must become according to the divine plan inscribed in them; in fact, it has the title "The Role of the Christian Family". The fourth and last part is called "Pastoral Care of the Family: Stages, Structures, Agents, and Situations", and gives explicit attention to situations of greater difficulty.[9]

2. A Detailed Commentary on the Content of *Familiaris Consortio*

The purpose of the exhortation is set forth in the introduction as follows: the Church, "knowing that marriage and the family constitute one of the most precious of human values . . . once again feels the pressing need to proclaim the Gospel, that is the 'good news' ", concerning these realities "at a moment of history in which the family is the object of numerous forces that seek to destroy it or in some way to deform it", as a result of which "the Church perceives in a more urgent and compelling way her mission of proclaiming to all people the plan of God for marriage and the family, ensuring their full vitality and human and Christian development" (FC, nos. 1–3).

A. *First part: bright spots and shadows for the family today*

This is concerned with giving a description of current reality, but a description not limited to brute facts but rather one strengthened by the Faith. In order to do this, the exhortation investigates the principles that allow one to make a judgment.

This is somewhat novel. It is not usual, in this kind of document, to be concerned with the principles of morality but rather to throw light on some specific questions. It was, however, opportune to introduce this matter in order to address properly the characteristics of the real

---

[9] For a bibliography, see *La "Familiaris consortio"* (Vatican City: Libreria Editrice Vaticano, 1982); "L'Esortazione apostolica *Familiaris consortio* commentata da teologi di varie nazioni", *Divinitas* 26.3 (1982): 247–76; A. Sarmiento, *A missão da Familia Crista* (*Commentarios a Exortacao Apostolica Familiaris consortio*) (Braga: Ed. Theologica, 1985); Michael Wrenn, ed., *Pope John Paul II and the Family* (Chicago: Franciscan Herald Press, 1983).

situation facing us. We will therefore, comment on this feature of the exhortation.

1. *The real situation of man: history as an event of freedom*

"History is not simply a fixed progression towards what is better, but rather an event of freedom, and even a struggle between freedoms that are in mutual conflict, that is . . . a conflict between two loves: the love of God to the point of disregarding self, and the love of self to the point of disregarding God" (FC, no. 6, par. 6).

It is necessary to understand the real situation facing man if we are to order it in a Christian way. "Since God's plan for marriage and the family touches man and woman in the concreteness of their daily existence in specific social and cultural situations", to know this reality is "an inescapable requirement of the work of evangelization" (FC, no. 4, pars. 1 and 2). But all that is human can not be known simply by counting and measuring; precisely because man is free, what happens in history does not have an unambiguous meaning. Events have different value according to their own matrix: "The situation in which the family finds itself presents positive and negative aspects: the first are a sign of the salvation of Christ operating in the world; the second, a sign of the refusal that man gives to the love of God" (FC, no. 6, par. 1).

■ We find ourselves faced with an important theological clarification of the "signs of the times",[10] which have been, and not rarely, interpreted as a slavery to the world and in an evolutionary way that in effect denies the role of human freedom. If, on the other hand, the true significance of human freedom is recognized, it is evident that the "signs of the times" can signify either a positive response of man to God's action or his refusal to accept God's love. Therefore, "only an education for love rooted in faith can lead to the capacity of interpreting the 'signs of the times' which are the historical expression of this twofold love", i.e., the love of God to the point of disregarding self, and the love of self to the point of disregarding God (FC, no. 6, par. 7).
FC thus provides in effect twofold "signs of the times", some positive, others negative:

[10] Cf. Vatican Council II, *Gaudium et spes,* December 7, 1965, no. 4.

On the one hand, in fact, there is a more lively awareness of personal freedom and greater attention to the quality of interpersonal relationships in marriage, to promoting the dignity of women, etc. . . . On the other hand, however, signs are not lacking of a disturbing degradation of some fundamental values: a mistaken theoretical and practical concept of the independence of the spouses in relation to each other; serious misconceptions regarding the relationship of authority between parents and children; the concrete difficulties that the family itself experiences in the transmission of values; the growing number of divorces; the scourge of abortion; the ever more frequent recourse to sterilization; the appearance of a truly contraceptive mentality (FC, no. 6, par. 2).

We can understand man only in his real situation as a creature called by God to enjoy intimacy with him, and then fallen and redeemed by Christ, i.e., only within the perspective of a biblical anthropology. Whatever concerns man must be seen within this perspective. The exhortation reminds us of this from its very beginning: "Willed by God in the very act of creation,[11] marriage and family are inwardly ordained to fulfillment in Christ[12] and have need of His graces in order to be healed from the wounds of sin[13] and restored to their 'beginning,'[14] that is, to full understanding and the full realization of God's plan" (FC, no. 3, par. 3). Man, free and responsible for his own destiny, is wounded by sin and, without grace, cannot succeed in acting in a truly human way, at least consistently. Therefore, it can not be surprising to discover that there are negative "signs of the times" and backward steps. To deny this is the equivalent to denying the very nature of human freedom, which is a created freedom and not a kind of autonomous power without any content. This implies that "at the root of these negative phenomena there frequently lies a corruption of the idea and the experience of freedom, conceived not as a capacity for realizing the truth of God's plan for marriage and the family, but as an autonomous power of self-affirmation, often against others, for one's own selfish well-being" (FC, no. 6, par 3).[15]

[11] Cf. Gen 1–2.

[12] Cf. Eph 5.

[13] Cf. Vatican Council II, *Gaudium et spes*, no. 47; John Paul II, letter *Appropinquat iam Synodus* 1 (August 15, 1980); AAS 72 (1980): 791.

[14] Cf. Mt 19:4.

[15] On this matter see Ramón García de Haro, "La libertad creada, manifestación de la omnipotencia divina", in *Atti dell'VIII Congresso Tomistico Internazionale*, vol. VI (1982), pp. 45–72.

2. The discernment of faith, a condition for salvation

In this situation, "the discernment affected by the Church becomes the offering of an orientation in order that the entire truth and the full dignity of marriage and the family may be preserved and realized" (FC, no. 5, par. 1).

As a fruit of the disorder introduced by sin, men are not infrequently presented with "ideas and solutions which are very appealing but which obscure in varying degrees the truth and the dignity of the human person". The presentation of these ideas and solutions, moreover, is supported by powerful means of social communication, "which subtly endanger freedom and the capacity for objective judgment" (no. 4, par. 3). Only faith renders one able to discern rightly, because grace heals man's intelligence and corrects his wounded will.

The power of the Church is rooted in her knowledge and in her unquenchable love for the truth, far above the fallible opinions of men. "Following Christ, the Church seeks the truth, which is not always the same as the majority opinion. She listens to conscience and not to power" (FC, no. 5, par. 2).

■ Not only is the preaching of pastors important for this discernment, but also the life of all the faithful, since, in many specific issues, they have as their proper mission the task of incarnating in time the truth of the gospel, inasmuch as they are called by God to illumine and order temporal realities according to the plan of God the Creator and Redeemer (FC, no. 5, par. 2).

The most significant consequence of this is that *"the education of the moral conscience, which makes every human being capable of judging and of discerning the proper ways to achieve self-realization according to his or her original truth, thus becomes a pressing requirement that cannot be renounced"* (no. 8, par. 5). Disturbed by false doctrines and even more so by the spread of erroneous practices, men often feel that fundamental values are obscured, to the point that—and this even happens among the faithful—they raise false problems and accept degrading solutions. Not infrequently, this happens in the name of progress and of science, which are denatured and used in ways contrary to their original meaning. Only the return to contemplation of God's plan and the destiny of man can save the world from its present state of decadence. This is the theme of the primacy of ethics over technique.

> It becomes necessary, therefore, on the part of all, to recover an awareness of the primacy of moral values, which are the values of the human person as such. The great task that has to be faced today for the renewal of society is that of recapturing the ultimate meaning of life and its fundamental values. Only an awareness of the primacy of these values enables man to use the immense possibilities given him by science in such a way as to bring about the true advancement of the human person in his or her whole truth, in his or her freedom and dignity. Science is called to ally itself with wisdom (FC, no. 8, par. 3).

3. The divine pedagogy: graduality and conversion

In addition to pointing to the truth that saves, the Church notes that "to the injustice originating from sin—which has profoundly penetrated the structures of today's world", it is necessary to "set ourselves in opposition through a conversion of mind and heart", which implies a dynamic and gradual process of growth in union with Christ (no. 9).

[handwritten margin note: problems in world]

We cannot conceal the difficulties and doubts that arose during the Synod of Bishops on the Family, precisely in confronting the full practicability of the teaching of the Church. The Fathers often emphasized the existing divergence between the Christian ideal and the real state of social morals found in different countries. Thus there was talk of a "graduality of the law" as a practical and merciful solution: that is, of the opportunity of an accommodation "that would make Christian life possible for men and women who, otherwise, would find themselves either deprived of the sacraments or, discouraged by having to keep requirements that they find incomprehensible and inhuman". But the Holy Father thought necessary "a reversal of notions in order to exclude every 'graduality of the law.' The law can only be recognized, willed, and loved in its entirety by the believer; in truth, it makes the will of God known and expresses His wisdom."[16]

The "law of graduality", which FC opposes to the "graduality of the law" (cf. nos. 9 and 24), is the expression of that pedagogy which is shown in the

---

[16] Jean-Marie Lustiger, "Gradualité et conversion. En marge de l'Exhortation Apostolique *Familiaris consortio*", *L'Osservatore Romano* (February 16, 1982): 33.

path that God makes his people travel, a path for the disciples who follow Christ. That is, it expresses the historical and real way in which grace grows in the life of men and of societies, by means of a "dynamic process . . . which advances gradually with the progressive integration of the gifts of God and the demands of His definitive and absolute love in the entire personal and social life of man"; and, therefore, "an educational growth process is necessary, in order that individual believers, families and peoples, even civilization itself, by beginning from what they have already received of the mystery of Christ, may patiently be led forward, arriving at a richer understanding and a fuller integration of this mystery in their lives" (FC, no. 9, par. 2).

Two elements are to be noted. On the one hand, the law of graduality implies in no way *any compromises,* since from the beginning it demands "an interior detachment from every evil and an adherence to good in its fullness" (FC, no. 9, par. 2); it does not allow any reduced or gradual adherence to the divine law, which is the sign of the love and wisdom of God (FC, no. 34, par. 4): opposed to every kind of surrender, it is a manifestation of confidence in the action of God and in the possibilities of man. On the other hand, this law inaugurates a *divine pedagogy,* which does not correspond to any human criteria but surpasses them. In fact, it does not come from any dynamic of human powers but rather from God's gift, whose generosity and love arouse love in man: "The divine pedagogy consists in nothing else than the history of a conception in which the divine fatherhood and, in it, man himself as the son of God who is born to a new and original life are revealed at the same time."[17] Paradoxically, this can begin with the failure of man, conscious of his own sins, which the law makes known to him: "In effect, the key that opens or closes access to the following of Christ is in the very transformation of the apostles who, by following Him, experience their own fragility, their own incapacity to understand, their own blindness, and, at the price of His passion and resurrection, ultimately accept the gift of the Holy Spirit and faith."[18]

■ Because it is inspired by this divine pedagogy, FC is a cry of hope, which does not dissimulate but rather is born in the midst of an awareness of the difficulties human persons face today. But this presupposes a clear-cut repudiation of the pedagogy, *pelagian* in its depths, of

[17] Ibid., 41.
[18] Ibid., 49.

compromise, of rationalism, of evolutionism. The following observation makes this clear: "The idea of an evolution which tends towards an ever greater perfection and which attributes imperfection to the beginning comes from a philosophical *a priori* which has been the characteristic, since the nineteenth century, of both biblical criticism and ethnology and the sciences related to them: the history of religion, the history of culture, etc. This *a priori* cannot hold up, least of all in theology. A more rigorous reading of the [biblical] text, purified of these philosophical presuppositions, will be better able to receive the results of a critical study which sheds light on the difference of cultural situations but which, at the same time, affirms that, theologically, the totality of the content is given from the very beginning. Salvation history consists neither in the generation of the absolute spirit nor in the genesis of the truth of law. History consists in the liberation of the spirit of man and in his redemption, so that he can come to a full possession of what, *from the very beginning,* God's mercy, which is given to man, wills to give to him without reserve."[19]

B. *Second part: the plan of God for marriage and the family*

After these premises—on the knowledge, grandeur, and power of God's plan and on the way in which man comes to know and love it or, on the contrary, commits the absurd error of obscuring it—FC analyzes in detail the divine plan, in order to discover the essence and truth of marriage and the family. It is the shortest (nos. 11–16), but also the richest, section of the exhortation. We will summarize it in two points: a) the understanding of marriage in FC and b) the community of marriage and the conjugal covenant.

1. *The notion of marriage in* Familiaris consortio

Marriage is a community of persons, brought to life by love and at the service of life. Christ raised marriage to a sacrament and established it as a way of holiness.

In reality, between the second part of the exhortation, which is concerned with the very being of the community of marriage,

---

[19] Ibid., 37.

and the third, which is concerned with its dynamic, there is an intimate unity, since there is a deep correlation between being and acting: the authentic dynamism of family life flows from the truth of its being. This unity will emerge, therefore, in our treatment. Specifically, we will reserve for the commentary on the third part the more practical matters; here, on the other hand, we will set forth the notion of marriage that emerges from the whole body of the document.

The principal novelty of FC in this respect, as we will see immediately, is in the profundity with which it succeeds in showing how the various goods and properties of marriage *flow from the very reality of the person and of his innate vocation to love.* [20] This allows it to deepen the personalist concept of conjugal love, already shown to be so fertile in *Gaudium et spes,* and to extend its developments to the good of procreation, making ever more evident its unbreakable bond with love. Moreover, the rooting of the person in the image of the God who is Love gives to the traditional teaching of the Church on marriage an incomparable attractiveness. [21]

■ We will examine under this personalist perspective the three elements defining the notion of marriage that have already been identified in this work: the first two, i.e., the community of persons vivified by love and at the service of life, pertain to it as a created reality; the third is proper to it by reason of its elevation to a sacrament by Christ. However, we want to emphasize here that the enrichment of the vision of the person as an image of the God of love—and therefore of the person's fulfillment only through the sincere gift of self, i.e., in the very truth of every love worthy of the person—likewise enriches all the concepts concerning the institution of marriage. The idea of love as the life-giving principle of the conjugal and family community will be seen expressed in ways never before adopted; the way in which the openness to new life is deepened in the very nature of conjugal love seen in its origins—i.e., in divine love, always a gift—also becomes enriched by this new perspective. One also understands how the insti-

---

[20] John Paul II has deepened and developed the notion of the person at the heart of FC in his encyclical *Dominum et vivificantem,* May 30, 1986, no. 59, and in his apostolic letter *Mulieris dignitatem,* August 15, 1988, nos. 7, 18, and 29.

[21] On this matter see Ramón García de Haro, "El matrimonio, comunidad de amor, al servicio de la vida. Estudio sobre la noción de matrimonio en la Exhortación *Familiaris consortio*", in "L'Esortazione apostolica *Familiaris consortio* commentata", pp. 332–49, especially pp. 332–38.

tution of marriage—and the properties of unity and of indissolubility—spring from the very nature of the covenant of conjugal love. Finally, the whole analysis of the tasks of the Christian family, understood as the development of the essential dynamism of love, is completed by new shades of meaning. In sum, we find ourselves at the portals of a new and greatly enriched and deepened understanding of the whole Christian truth about marriage and the family.

Marriage is a community of persons, whose life-giving principle is conjugal love. Marriage appears, both to the eyes of faith and to simple human experience, as a community of persons. In the beginning, it is the communion between a man and a woman, the parents, which then extends itself to the children, the fruit of their love. But it is evident that not every communion between a man and a woman is a marriage, even if they generate children: what specifies the community of marriage, in addition to its destination to the generation and education of children, is conjugal love, that is, that kind of faithful and exclusive love that unites the spouses according to their truth as images of God. FC insists on this:

> God created man in His own image and likeness:[22] calling him to existence *through love,* He called him at the same time *to love.* God is love[23] and in Himself He lives a mystery of personal loving communion. Creating the human race in His own image and continually keeping it in being, God inscribed in the humanity of man and woman the vocation, and thus the responsibility, of love and communion. Love is therefore the fundamental and innate vocation of every human being (FC, no. 11, pars. 1 and 2).

Revelation, FC continues, clarifies that this vocation is authentically fulfilled, in its integrity, only in marriage and in virginity (FC, no. 11, par. 4): in virginity, by means of a direct giving of oneself to God; in marriage, by means of a unique form in which the self-giving between a man and a woman can be realized "in a truly human way": "The only 'place' where this self-giving in its whole truth is made possible is marriage, the covenant of conjugal love freely and consciously chosen, whereby man and woman accept the intimate community of life and love willed by God Himself"[24] (FC, no. 11, pars. 5 and 7).

[22] Cf. Gen 1:26ff.
[23] 1 Jn 4:8.
[24] Cf. *Gaudium et spes,* no. 48.

One can therefore understand how conjugal love in its unity and exclusivity—the sign of the authenticity of the relationship between the man and the woman that they have fully and definitively established with one another—is the *life-giving power* of the family: "Love is the principle and power of communion. . . . *Without love the family cannot live, grow and perfect itself as a community of persons*" (FC, no. 18, title and par. 2). Indeed, from its first nucleus—the community between the spouses—the family is "established and vivified by love": "By virtue of the covenant of married life, the man and the woman 'are no longer two but one flesh'25 and they are called to grow continually in their communion through day-to-day fidelity to their marriage promise of total mutual self-giving" (FC, no. 19, par. 1). Moreover, this love between the spouses, which reaches its culmination in the giving of life to children (cf. FC, nos. 14, 28, etc.), extends itself as the exemplary principle of the whole family community: "The self-giving that inspires the love of husband and wife for each other is the model and norm for the self-giving that must be practiced in the relationships between brothers and sisters and the different generations living together in the family" (FC, no. 37, par. 2).

> ■ The profundity with which the document describes the origin and dynamism of conjugal love is striking. First of all, its character as a *powerful force* is highlighted: "The family possesses and still continues to release formidable energies capable of taking man out of his anonymity, keeping him conscious of his personal dignity, and actively placing him, in his uniqueness and unrepeatability, within the fabric of society" (FC, no. 43, par. 5). Its concern is with an energy deposited in—inscribed in—man, with the power of a *natural inclination,* which flows from man's very being as one made to the image of God: an innate vocation, which continuously impels man from within, as an "interior and constant dynamism". Indeed, "man cannot live without love. He remains a being that is incomprehensible for himself, his life is senseless, if love is not revealed to him, if he does not encounter love, if he does not experience it and make it his own, if he does not participate intimately in it" (FC, no. 18, par. 2).
>
> This love, which is already "a profoundly human demand", is then *assumed by Christ,* who "purifies it and elevates it, leading it to perfection through the sacrament of marriage", in order to establish "a new communion of love that is the living and real image of that unique unity which makes of the Church the indivisible Mystical Body of the

25 Mt 19:6; cf. Gen 2:24.

Lord Jesus" (FC, no. 19, par. 2). Love, that power and life-giving principle of the community of persons established by marriage, is therefore a capacity and an inclination, an active power, which the spouses receive as a gift of nature and of grace; a gift which, made to a spiritual and free creature, becomes a vocation. This consists in a capacity which, at the same time, is a responsibility of recognizing the gift and of freely actualizing it. For this, it is both possible and necessary to awaken in "the modern Christian family [which] is often tempted to be discouraged and is distressed at the growth of its difficulties . . . reasons for confidence in itself, in the riches that it possesses by nature and grace" (FC, no. 86, par. 9), and in "the love between husband and wife and between the members of the family—a love lived out in all its extraordinary richness of values and demands: totality, oneness, fidelity, and fruitfulness" (FC, no. 50, par. 3).

The end of this personal community of love is service to life. A community of persons is specified, as we have already said, not only by the bonds and relationships that unite its members, but also by the purpose pursued, which, in large measure, determines the characteristics of their union. FC thus expresses itself on this matter: "According to the plan of God, marriage is the foundation of the wider community of the family, since the very institution of marriage and conjugal love are ordained to the procreation and education of children, in whom they find their crowning" (FC, no. 14, par. 1). The love of God for man, made in his image, has so disposed things that human life is born and grows under the protection of the community of love which is the family; this alone is able to give that welcome which is, for children, the first sign of God's love, and for the parents the enlargement of their conjugal vocation with that of parenthood: "When they become parents, spouses receive from God the gift of a new responsibility. Their parental love is called to become for the children the visible sign of the very love of God, 'from whom every family in heaven and on earth is named'[26]" (FC, no. 14, par. 4). Thus, the very dynamism of conjugal love, the life-giving principle of the community of marriage, tends of itself to the gift of life.

With the creation of man and woman in His own image and likeness, God crowns and brings to perfection the work of His hands: He calls them to a special sharing in His love and in His power as Creator and

[26] Eph 3:15.

Father, through their free and responsible cooperation in transmitting the gift of human life: "God blessed them, and God said to them, 'Be fruitful and multiply, and fill the earth and subdue it.' "[27] Thus the fundamental task of the family is to serve life, to actualize in history the original blessing of the Creator—that of transmitting by procreation the divine image from person to person (FC, no. 28, pars. 1 and 2).

As did *Gaudium et spes,* so too FC insists on the fact that the ordination to life is not a characteristic only of the institution of marriage but also of conjugal love itself (cf. FC, no. 14, par. 1); thus, it indicates that it is the sign of its authenticity (FC, no. 28, par. 3).

■ FC takes a new step in the deepening of Catholic doctrine on this matter; it shows, in vigorous language, that the tendency to give life is the deepest inclination of true love, its essential truth: "In its most profound reality, love is essentially a gift: and conjugal love, while leading spouses to the reciprocal 'knowledge' which makes them 'one flesh'[28] does not end up with the couple, because it makes them capable of the greatest possible gift, the gift by which they become cooperators with God for giving life to a new human person. Thus the couple, while giving themselves to one another, give not just themselves but also the reality of children, who are a living reflection of their love, a permanent sign of conjugal unity and a living and inseparable synthesis of their being a father and a mother" (FC, no. 14, par. 2).

As the text just cited bears witness, FC puts not only conjugal love but also procreation in a personalist context. It is precisely for this reason that contraception is the very negation the truth of conjugal love as a personal reality: "The innate language that expresses the total self-giving of husband and wife is overlaid, through contraception, by an objectively contradictory language, namely, that of not giving oneself totally to the other. This leads not only to a positive refusal to be open to life but also to a falsification of the inner truth of conjugal love, which is called upon to give itself in personal totality" (FC, no. 32, par. 4).[29]

---

[27] Gen 1:28.

[28] Cf. Gen 2:24.

[29] This is a recurrent theme in the teachings of John Paul II: "In the act which expresses their conjugal love, spouses are called to make *of themselves* a gift for one another: nothing that constitutes their *personal being* can be excluded from this gift. . . . The contraceptive act introduces a substantial limitation within this reciprocal gift and expresses an objective refusal to give the *whole* of one's femininity or masculinity to the other. In a word,

We must note that the inclination of love to serve life is not only biological but spiritual, rooted more in the spirit than in the flesh. Thus, when procreation is not possible (because of factors not within the control of the spouses), it takes other forms and in many and diverse ways "can be for the spouses the occasion for other important services to the life of the human person, for example, adoption, various forms of educational work, and assistance to other families and to poor or handicapped children" (FC, no. 14, par. 4).

The community of marriage and conjugal love reach their proper perfection in Christ who, by means of the sacrament, makes them sharers in his own love and makes of marriage a true road to holiness.[30] Christ on the Cross is the fullness of the revelation of God's love for man; the marriage of Christians then becomes a sign of and a participation in the New Covenant,

> sanctioned in the blood of Christ. The Spirit which the Lord pours forth gives a new heart, and renders man and woman capable of loving one another as Christ has loved us. Conjugal love reaches that fullness to which it is interiorly ordained, conjugal charity, which is the proper and specific way in which the spouses participate in and are called to live the very charity of Christ who gave Himself on the Cross (FC, no. 13, par. 3).

By virtue of the sacrament, the "normal characteristics of all natural conjugal love", which we have just examined here—unity and exclusivity, fidelity, the ordination to fertility—take on "a new significance which not only purifies and strengthens them, but raises them to the extent of making them the expression of specifically Christian values" (FC, no. 13, par. 9). Thus marriage becomes a way of true holiness. FC repeats this time and time again: "In God's plan, all husbands and wives are called in marriage to holiness" (FC, no. 34, par. 4); "Christian spouses and parents are included in the universal call to sanctity. For them this call is specified by the sacrament they have celebrated and is carried out concretely in the realities proper to their conjugal and family life" (FC, no. 56, par. 3).

■ It is important to emphasize the precisions made by the exhortation. On the one hand, the sacramental condition of marriage is a *requirement*

---

contraception contradicts *the truth* of conjugal love" (Address of September 17, 1983, no. 2; *Enchiridion Familiae,* 5.3940–41).

[30] On the richness of the doctrine on the sacramentality of marriage, seen in the Tradition of the more recent documents of the Magisterium, see Peter J. Elliot, *What God Has Joined: The Sacramentality of Marriage* (New York: Alba House, 1990).

for every baptized person, inseparable from the baptismal character: "Indeed, by means of baptism, man and woman are definitively placed within the new and eternal covenant, in the spousal covenant of Christ with the Church. And it is because of this indestructible insertion that the intimate community of conjugal life and love, founded by the Creator,[31] is elevated and assumed into the spousal charity of Christ, sustained and enriched by His redeeming power" (FC, no. 13, par. 6).

On the other hand, FC clarifies the *relationship between the vocation of marriage and the vocation to virginity.* Calling to mind the Tradition of the Fathers of the Church up to Vatican II, FC first of all insists on the complementarity between these two gifts: "Marriage and virginity or celibacy are two ways of expressing and living the one mystery of the covenant of God with His people. When marriage is not esteemed, neither can consecrated virginity or celibacy exist; when human sexuality is not regarded as a great value given by the Creator, the renunciation of it for the sake of the Kingdom of Heaven loses its meaning" (FC, no. 16, par. 1).

Evidently, the complementarity is manifold: because both represent, although in different ways, the mystery of the covenant of God's love; because they entail the same requirement of fidelity; because they are ordered, each in its own way, to fertility; in fact, virginity is the root of a new form of fatherhood and motherhood: "The celibate person becomes spiritually fruitful, the father and mother of many, cooperating in the realization of the family according to God's plan" (no. 16, par. 6).[32] This, however, does not imply a forgetfulness of the superiority of the charism to virginity, which "the Church, throughout her history, has always defended" (FC, no. 16, par. 5), but rather emphasizes the sense of service and the radical grandeur that marriage also possesses.

Finally, with deep humanity, the exhortation teaches that the value of virginity is also experienced by those who "for reasons independent of their own will, have been unable to marry, and have then accepted their situation in a spirit of service" (FC, no. 16, par. 8).

2. *The community of marriage and the conjugal covenant*

Marriage comes to be in the "covenant of conjugal love freely and consciously chosen, whereby man and woman accept the

---

[31] Cf. Vatican Council II, *Gaudium et spes,* no. 48.

[32] On this see Josef Ratzinger, "Matrimonio e famiglia nel piano di Dio", in *La "Familiaris consortio",* pp. 86ff.

intimate community of life and love willed by God Himself"
for the transmission and increase of human life (FC, no. 11,
par. 7).

Just as did Vatican II, so too FC does not use the word "contract" to
designate the act of freedom and of love which stands at the origin of
marriage, but rather that of the "conjugal *covenant*", because it is a term
more apt for expressing the reality of the will that founds a stable
community, made in likeness to those alliances of faithful love that
God established with men. The conjugal *covenant* is not an agreement
configured to the type of community designed by God, but is rather
one that *welcomes* this community: it makes it come to be, but it does
not determine its content.

FC emphasizes, on the other hand, the unity between love and the
institution of marriage: "*The institution of marriage is not an undue
interference by society or authority,* nor the extrinsic imposition of a form.
Rather it is *an interior requirement* of the covenant of conjugal love
which is publicly affirmed as unique and exclusive, in order to live in
complete fidelity to the plan of God" (FC, no. 11, par. 7). Both the very
nature of this conjugal gift and the good of the children demand this.
In fact, sexuality "is realized in a truly human way only if it is an
integral part of the love by which a man and a woman commit
themselves totally to one another until death. The total physical self-
giving would be a lie if it were not the sign and fruit of a total personal
self-giving" (FC, no. 11, par. 5) (note that the conjugal covenant is seen
as an act of love, of the love that founds the marriage). This totality
and indissolubility are also demanded by the nature of "responsible
fertility. This fertility is directed to the generation of a human being,
and so by its nature it surpasses the purely biological order and
involves a whole series of personal values. For the harmonious growth
of these values a persevering and unified contribution by both parents
is necessary" (FC, no. 11, par. 6).

■ Therefore, the phenomena of "free love" and of rejecting marriage
are nothing else than a degradation of true human love: the negation
of its truth. It is worth noting that precisely because of the *personalist*
concept of conjugal love and of marriage that has been given such a
prominent position, the requirement that the *conjugal covenant be
indissoluble and public* appears with new intelligiblity and power. Here

we return in another way to the development of the personalism of the Council that characterizes the whole of *Familiaris consortio*.[33]

C. *Third part: the role of the Christian family*

With vigor and inspired realism, the Pope begins this part with the following invocation: "Family, become what you are!" (FC, no. 17). The role that "God calls the family to perform in history derives from what the family is: its role represents the dynamic and existential development of what it is. Each family finds within itself a summons that cannot be ignored, and that specifies both its dignity and its responsibility" (FC, no. 17, par. 1). The family must, in practice, become precisely what it is already by creation and by the work of redemption; and this gives us reason, unassailable by doubt, for hope.[34]

The family is essentially a "living reflection of and a real sharing in God's love for humanity and the love of Christ the Lord for the Church His bride". Therefore, all its tasks are and must be interpreted as an expression and actualization of this kind of love (FC, no. 17, par. 2). Specifically, FC lists four major roles of the family: 1) the development of a community of persons, 2) service to life (to its transmission and education); and, by means of this, 3) participation in the development of society and 4) participation in the mission of the Church (FC, no. 17, par. 4).

1. *The formation of a community of persons*

Conjugal love, that power and inspiring dynamism of the conjugal and family community, has as its first task the development of that community, in its concrete characteristics of

---

[33] This fact ought not to be surprising if one thinks of the interventions of Karol Wojtyla during the Council and of the vigor with which he always stressed this matter. Cf. A. Scola, "Il compito della Chiesa. Gli interventi di Karol Wojtyla al Concilio Ecumenico Vaticano II", in *Avvenimento e Tradizione* (*Questioni di Ecclesiologia*) (Milan: Edizioni Universitarie Jaca Book, 1987), pp. 149ff.

[34] Thus Eduoard Gagnon was able to call his commentary on this part of the exhortation, "La Chiesa colloca la sua speranza nella famiglia cristiana", in *La "Familiaris consortio"*, pp. 111ff.

unity and indissolubility and according to the specific responsibilities of its different members.

God has willed that human life be transmitted and grow in the bosom of the community of persons constituted by the family, which has its origin in marriage. Therefore, the first task of the family, demanded by its very end, is "a constant effort to develop an authentic community of persons" (FC, no. 18, par. 1).

■ Like *Gaudium et spes,* FC takes as its scheme that of the *goods of marriage,* but it nonetheless enlarges and perfects this scheme. In fact, the *good of fidelity* or of mutual union is seen from a more complete perspective, as the formation of a community of persons. When it is concerned with the *bonum prolis,* it describes this as service to life. It introduces, moreover, the consideration of the goods that derive from the very nature of marriage for the whole human community, as a participation in the development of society. The *bonum sacramenti* is also seen in a much enlarged vision: without doubt as the Christian perfection of marriage, but also, precisely by reason of this, as the origin of its participation in the mission of the Church.

The first condition for the development of the community of persons that is marriage is respect for its characteristics of unity and indissolubility (FC, nos. 19–20). The community of marriage cannot grow save by respecting God's plan, inscribed by the Creator in the heart of man and woman and perfected by Christ in the sacrament of marriage. The nucleus of the family community is the conjugal community, born from the covenant of conjugal love and destined to grow as a communion by means of daily fidelity to the total reciprocal gift (FC, no. 19, par. 1). Unity is therefore a profoundly human demand, which Christ assumes and perfects with the sacrament, in the image of his indivisible union with the Church (FC, no. 19, par. 2). But the conjugal community is characterized also by its indissolubility, rooted in the requirements of a mutual total gift and of the good of the children and perfected by the gift of the absolutely faithful love of Christ for his Church (FC, no. 20, pars. 1–3).

■ By means of their faithful love—the exhortation has no doubt in proclaiming—Christian spouses give a precious witness to "the unfailing fidelity with which God and Jesus Christ love each and every human being" (FC, no. 20, par. 6). Those spouses who, abandoned by the other, remain faithful to their obligations give special witness to this fidelity, a witness of which the world today has such need (ibid.).

The community of marriage is destined to open itself to the full community of the family, in which all members, "each according to his or her own gift, have the grace and responsibility of building, day by day, the communion of persons, making the family 'a school of deeper humanity'[35]" (FC, no. 21, par. 4; nos. 21–27). The building up of this community is an attractive task, but not an easy one, because "family communion can only be preserved and perfected through a great spirit of sacrifice" (FC, no. 21, par. 6). In fact, "there is no family that does not know how selfishness, discord, tension and conflict violently attack and at times mortally wound its own communion" (FC, no. 21, par. 6). But, in order to carry out its role, the family can count on love's own movement, for love naturally animates the relationships among the different members of the family and "constitutes the interior strength that shapes and animates the family communion and community" (FC, no. 21, par. 2). Moreover, "participation in the sacrament of Reconciliation and in the banquet of the one body of Christ offers to the Christian family the grace and the responsibility of overcoming every division and of moving toward the fullness of communion willed by God" (FC, no. 21, par. 6).

In what follows, the exhortation seeks to set forth the mission of the different members of the family, who find in love the "source and the constant impetus for welcoming, respecting, and promoting each one of its members in his or her lofty dignity as a person, that is, as a living image of God" (FC, no. 22, par. 1):

a. First of all, the exhortation describes *the task of the woman,* as mother, spouse, and daughter. The point of departure is her "equal dignity and responsibility with men" (FC, no. 22, par. 2); the defense of this dignity can be called a true title of honor for the Church throughout the centuries, always faithful to the revealed teaching that "in Christ Jesus . . . there is neither male nor female, for you are one in Christ Jesus."[36] Within this perspective, FC then shows, in confronting a vulgar but very widespread error, that the promotion of the dignity of women would be false were it to compromise her specific role

---

[35] Vatican Council II, *Gaudium et spes,* no. 52.
[36] Gal 3:26, 28.

within the family: "*The true advancement of women requires that clear recognition be given to the value of their maternal and family role*, by comparison with all other public roles and all other professions" (FC, no. 23, par. 2).[37] In particular, this means that "wives and mothers are *not in practice compelled* to work outside the home, and that their families can live and prosper in a dignified way even when they themselves devote their full time to their own family" (FC, no. 23, par. 4).

■ In order to overcome the modern incomprehension that has arisen over this truth, the Holy Father singles out two pillars on which to build; on the one hand, as the synod had already taught, there is need to build a *renewed theology of work*, which might bring to light the meaning and radical dignity of every kind of human work, and therefore of that of the woman in the domestic hearth. In fact, many discriminations and current prejudices depend on a failure to comprehend the authentic meaning of the dignity of work (FC, no. 23, par. 3). The following words well express the matter: "It is well to remember that the dignity of work is based on Love. Man's great privilege is to be able to love and to transcend what is fleeting and ephemeral. He can love other creatures, pronounce an 'I' and a 'you' which are full of meaning. And he can love God, who opens heaven's gates to us, makes us members of his family, and allows us also to talk to him in friendship, face to face. That is why a man ought not to limit himself to material production. Work is born of love; it is a manifestation of love and is directed to love. We see the hand of God, not only in the wonders of nature, but also in our experience of work and effort. Work thus becomes prayer and thanksgiving, because we know we are placed on earth by God, that we are loved by him and made heirs to his promises."[38]

The other pillar is in overcoming preconceptions about the dignity of women that claim to repudiate all her proper characteristics, a gift of the Creator. Dignity "does not mean for women a renunciation of their femininity or an imitation of the male role, but the fullness of true feminine humanity which should be expressed

---

[37] On this matter, also developed by John Paul II's encyclical *Laborem exercens*, September 14, 1981, no. 19, see R. Ryan, "La formazione di una comunità di persone", in *La "Familiaris consortio"*, pp. 136ff. See also William E. May, "Marriage and the Complementarity of Man and Woman", *Anthropotes* 8 (June 1992): 41–60.

[38] Blessed Josemaría Escrivá, Homily of March 19, 1963, "In Joseph's Workshop", in *Christ Is Passing By* (New Rochelle, N.Y.: Scepter Press, 1974), no. 48, p. 75.

in their activity, whether in the family or outside of it" (FC, no. 23, par. 7).[39]

b. Next, FC insists on the fact that "efforts must be made *to restore socially the conviction that the place and task of the father in and for the family is of unique and irreplaceable importance*" (FC, no. 25, par. 4). The love for his wife, now become a mother, and his love and devotion to his children are the normal way for understanding and fulfilling his own duties. The community of the family is lacking something if either the mother's or the father's presence is missing.

c. Third, FC treats of the *rights and duties of children.* It insists on saying that these rights are more urgent, the "smaller the child is and the more it is need of everything, when it is sick, suffering, or handicapped" (FC, no. 26, par. 1): he then lists their range: "acceptance, love, esteem, many-sided and united material, emotional, educational, and spiritual concern" (FC, no. 26, par. 4). He then teaches that attention to this matter is a *sign of true humanity, as it is of the Christian meaning of the family:* "Concern for the child, even before birth, from the first moment of conception and then throughout the years of infancy and youth, is the primary and fundamental test of the relationship of one human being to another" (FC, no. 26, par. 3) and "a distinctive, essential characteristic" of Christian families (FC, no. 26, par. 4).

■ Like all members of the family, children have, along with rights, duties: the responsibility to participate actively in the family community: "By means of love, respect and obedience towards their parents, children offer their specific and irreplaceable contribution to the construction of an authentically human and Christian family" (FC, no. 21, par. 5).

d. Finally, the exhortation does not forget the role and task of *the elderly* within the family. It is necessary that "the pastoral activity of the Church help everyone to discover and to make good use of the role of the elderly within the civil and ecclesial community, in particular within the family": continuity in the transmission of values, their charism of wisdom and comprehension, etc. (FC, no. 27).

---

[39] This important teaching has been developed in John Paul II's *Mulieris dignitatem,* no. 17ff.; *Enchiridion Familiae,* 5.4844ff.

2. *Service to life.* The exhortation, contemplating the nature of this service, develops it in two aspects: the transmission of life (nos. 22–35) and education (nos. 36–41).

I. "The fundamental task of the family is to serve life, to actualize in history the original blessing of the Creator—that of transmitting by procreation the divine image from person to person" (FC, no. 28, par. 2).

By saying this, FC reproposes, one more time, "the Church's teaching and norm, always old yet always new" (FC, no. 20, par. 2). Conjugal love is ordained by God for the transmission of the immense gift of life. And FC does this in a very solemn way: it expresses it not as some helpful consideration but as a radical and perennial demand, rooted both in the most ancient patrimony of Tradition and in the recent declarations of the last Council.

> In continuity with the living tradition of the ecclesial communion throughout history, the recent Second Vatican Council and the magisterium of my predecessor Paul VI, expressed above all in the Encyclical *Humanae vitae,* have handed on to our times a truly prophetic proclamation, which reaffirms and reproposes with clarity the Church's teaching [on love and life] (FC, no. 29, par. 2).

Precisely because service to life is its fundamental task, an openness to life becomes the condition of true conjugal love and a sign of its authenticity. "Love between husband and wife must be fully human, exclusive, and open to new life" (FC, no. 29, par. 3); "fecundity is the fruit and sign of conjugal love, the living testimony of the full reciprocal self-giving of the spouses" (FC, no. 28, par. 3). This is a doctrine that today some have difficulty comprehending, but this only makes it "more urgent and irreplaceable" to proclaim it, in order to promote "the true good of men and women" (FC, no. 30, par. 1).

> ■ The exhortation then spends time describing the aspects of the modern situation and mentality, which give rise to contemporary difficulties: technological knowledge and progress, which arouse in some an anxiousness about the future; a consumer mentality that makes some incapable of understanding the spiritual richness of a new life; a certain panic derived from some ecological and futuristic studies that are not always balanced, to the point that they create an antilife

mentality. At their root "is the absence in people's hearts of God, whose love alone is stronger than all the world's fears and can conquer them" (FC, no. 30, par. 2).

Confronted by the harm that a mentality of this kind can do, the Church pronounces her "yes" to life. "Against the pessimism and selfishness which cast a shadow over the world, the Church stands for life: in each human life she sees the splendor of that 'Yes,' that 'Amen,' who is Christ Himself.[40] To the 'No' which assails and afflicts the world, she replies with this living 'Yes,' thus defending the human person and the world from all who plot against and harm life" (FC, no. 30, par. 4). As a result, she condemns every act directly aimed at limiting the freedom of spouses in begetting children, particularly programs of contraception, sterilization, and procured abortion, at times imposed as wicked conditions for receiving necessary economic help (FC, no. 30, par. 6).[41]

This service to life entails respect for the teaching of the Church on the regulation of fertility, a doctrine that needs to be made known and loved so that it can help all to live. To achieve this end, the Holy Father extends "a pressing invitation to theologians, asking them to unite their efforts in order to collaborate with the hierarchical Magisterium and to commit themselves to the task of illustrating ever more clearly the biblical foundations, the ethical grounds and the personalistic reasons behind this doctrine" in order "to render this teaching of the Church on this fundamental question truly accessible to all people of good will" (FC, no. 31, par. 3). He is concerned, in fact, with a critical point, that demands a "united effort by theologians in this regard, inspired by a convinced adherence to the Magisterium, which is the one authentic guide for the People of God", because "doubt or error in the field of marriage or the family involves obscuring to a serious extent the integral truth about the human person in a cultural situation that is already so confused and contradictory" (FC, no. 31, par. 4). In the following, he points to the pivotal truths on which to build this doctrinal and formative work:

a. *Its basic contents* are those already *established by Vatican II and Humanae vitae;* specifically, "there can be no true contradiction between

---

[40] Cf. 2 Cor 1:19; Rev 3:14.

[41] The condemnation of this abuse is explicitly taken up in the *Charter of the Rights of the Family,* October 22, 1983, art. 3b.

the divine law on transmitting life and that on fostering authentic married love" (FC, no. 33, par. 4); one must begin with an *integral vision of man,* one that recognizes that moral rectitude "does not depend solely on sincere intentions or on an evaluation of motives. It must be determined by *objective standards . . . based on the nature of the human person and his or her acts"* (FC, no. 31, par. 2). The first and unrenounceable consequence is that *man cannot break on his own initiative* "the insepa-rable connection, willed by God . . . between the unitive meaning and the procreative meaning of the conjugal act" (FC, no. 32, par. 3). From all this, one can understand the radical *"difference, both anthropological and moral,* between contraception and recourse to the rhythm of the cycle" (FC, no. 32, par. 6).

■ *Familiaris consortio,* therefore, does not forget, as some have thought, the twofold element, internal and external, of morality, that is, together with the object, the intention and the motives or causes that make it right; these are expressly mentioned by it together with the objective criteria of the completed act. Thus, in considering the moral journey of the spouses, FC provides, as we will see, very useful indications of this element. But FC is above all attentive to the criterion of the object of the moral act, to which it relates the most important question of *intrinsic evil.* There is a serious reason for doing this: the campaign, promoted by various authors, of claiming a moral equivalence between contraception and recourse to infertile periods.[42]

FC therefore affirms, as we have seen, that in contraception spouses act as *arbiters* of the divine plan; in having just recourse to the infertile periods, on the other hand, they can act as its *ministers.* Contraception is a falsification of love: "The innate language that expresses the total reciprocal self-giving of husband and wife is overlaid, through contraception, by an objectively contradictory language, namely, that of not giving oneself totally to the other. This leads not only to a positive refusal to be open to life but also to a falsification

[42] Thus, for example, one author writes: "Speaking from the moral point of view, between the different methods—absolutely excluding abortive ones and, in most cases, also sterilizing ones—there do not seem to be special reasons for reproving some as more grave and undignified than others. The inconveniences of each method are relative to each couple and ought to be investigated medically to show which is less damaging" (B. Forcano, *Nueva etica sexual,* 2nd ed. [Madrid: Ed. Paulinas, 1981], p. 186). Likewise, B. Haering, *Ethics of Manipulation* (New York: Seabury, 1975), pp. 92–96; Louis Janssens, "Morale conjugale et progestegenes", *Ephemerides Theologicae Lovanienses* 39 (1963): 809–24; Anthony Kosnik et al., *Human Sexuality: New Directions in American Catholic Thought* (New York: Paulist Press, 1977), pp. 114, 293, 295.

of the inner truth of conjugal love, which is called upon to give itself in personal totality" (FC, no. 32, par. 4). It is therefore necessary to understand well what the *natural regulation of fertilities signifies:* it is not a merely biological question, but primarily an ethical one.

"The morally proper regulation of fertility is also called 'the *natural* regulation of fertility,' which can be explained as conformity to the 'natural law.' By 'natural law' we understand here the *order of nature* in the area of procreation, insofar as this is understood by right reason: that order is the expression of the plan of the Creator for man. And it is precisely this that the Encyclical, together with the whole Christian tradition, both doctrinal and practical, emphasizes in a special way: the virtuous character of the attitude which is expressed in the 'natural' regulation of fertility is determined *not only* by fidelity to an impersonal 'natural law' *but also to the Creator-person,* the source and Lord of the order which is made manifest in that law. From this point of view, the *reduction to a merely biological regularity,* detached from the order of nature, i.e., from the 'Creator's plan,' debases the authentic thought of the encyclical *Humanae vitae.* The document, certainly, presupposes that *biological regularity,* and it thus exhorts competent persons to study it and to apply it in an ever more profound way, but it always understands this regularity *as the expression of 'the order of nature,'* i.e., *of the providential plan of the Creator,* in whose faithful execution the true good of the persons consists."[43]

As the Pope said on another occasion, in reality the so-called natural methods are concerned with a scientific question; they *are methods of determining fertility;*[44] but "this knowledge and the methods connected with it can be used for purposes which are morally illicit. It is on this point that the meeting with ethics and theology must take place. . . . Philosophical and theological ethics takes up *scientific knowledge* in such a way that this latter *becomes the path* whereby the freedom of the human person achieves responsible procreation."[45] In fact, one cannot forget "that truth known through science can be *used* by human freedom for purposes that are opposed to man's good — the good that

[43] John Paul II, Address of November 14, 1984; *Enchiridion Familiae,* 4.4224–29. Cf. D. Tettamanzi, *Un'enciclica profetica (L'Humanae vitae vent'anni dopo)* (Milan: Ancora, 1988), pp. 102ff.

[44] The task of science in this matter is very precise: "Knowledge of the fertile and infertile periods of the woman and the discovery of those *methods of determining it,* which make possible a certainty in discerning them" (Address of June 8, 1984, no. 3; *Enchiridion Familiae,* 5.4117).

[45] Ibid.; *Enchiridion Familiae,* 5.4117–18.

ethics knows."[46] Therefore, it is necessary to contrast, as has been said already, contraception with conjugal chastity rather than to contrast natural and artificial methods, for one of the manifestations of conjugal chastity is precisely periodic continence for just reasons.[47] More recently, the Holy Father has noted the need for just causes in order to have recourse to periodic continence: "The Church recognizes that there can be objective motives for limiting or spacing births, but she insists, in accord with *Humanae vitae,* that couples must have *serious reasons* in order licitly to refrain from the use of marriage during fertile days and to make use of it during infertile periods in order to express their love and to safeguard their mutual fidelity" (cf. ibid., no. 16).[48]

b. In adhering to these fundamental themes, and therefore by avoiding emptying the perennial norms established by God of any meaning, *the Church acts as Mother and Teacher,* i.e., she speaks the truth with and for love.

As Teacher, she never tires of proclaiming the moral norm that must guide the responsible transmission of life. . . . As Mother, the Church is close to the many married couples who find themselves in difficulty over this important point of the moral life. . . . But it is the one and the same Church that is both Teacher and Mother. And so the Church never ceases to exhort and encourage all to resolve whatever conjugal difficulties may arise without ever falsifying or compromising the truth (FC, no. 33, pars. 2–4).

Only the truth, in fact, saves. Therefore, *"to diminish in no way the saving teaching of Christ constitutes an eminent form of charity for souls"* (ibid.). On the other hand, the Church is concerned to make the value of this moral norm comprehensible; she helps one to make progress in its fulfillment, and she struggles *to create all the conditions necessary in*

[46] Ibid., no. 2; *Enchiridion Familiae,* 5.4117.

[47] Cf. Ramón García de Haro, "Orientamenti teologici per l'insegnamento della dottrina cattolica sulla procreazione responsabile", a paper given at the "Congresso Internazionale de Filosofia e Teologia della procreazione responsabile", Rome, June 1984, reported in *Studi cattolici* 336 (1989): 101–19; García de Haro, *La actualidad de la "Humanae vitae"* (Madrid: Epalsa, 1984), pp. 18ff.

[48] John Paul II, Address to the Participants in the International Meeting on the Theme "The Natural Regulation of Fertility: The Authentic Alternative", December 11, 1992, *L'Osservatore Romano* (December 12, 1992).

order to let it be understood and to be lived; specifically, she calls to mind the necessity of stirring up the virtues of "persistence and patience, humility and strength of mind, filial trust in God and in His grace, and frequent recourse to prayer and to the sacraments of the Eucharist and of Reconciliation" (FC, no. 33, par. 6). Also necessary as a condition for achieving this goal are "knowledge of the bodily aspect and the body's rhythms of fertility" and, above all, "the absolute necessity for the virtue of chastity and for permanent education in it" (FC, no. 33, par. 7).

■ We must emphasize the description that is made of this virtue: "In the Christian view, chastity by no means signifies rejection of human sexuality or lack of esteem for it; rather it signifies spiritual energy capable of defending love from the perils of selfishness and aggressiveness, and able to advance it towards its full realization" (FC, no. 33, par. 7). It is perhaps opportune here to clarify the malice proper to contraception. In truth, contraception is a *moral disorder against the virtue of chastity which, properly speaking, only spouses can commit:* that is, the use of marriage, depriving the conjugal act of its procreative capacity[49] and rejecting, consequently, their collaboration with God in giving life

[49] Consequently, the right formulation of the negative norm that prohibits contraception, insofar as it is *intrinsically evil,* is the following: "Do not close the marital act to the transmission of life", or "Do not deprive the conjugal act of its natural procreative power", expressions many times adopted by the Magisterium; or, in a positive formulation: "Every marital act ought to remain open to life." But to contradict this norm, that is, to deprive the act of its procreative capacity in order to enjoy the sexual pleasure without "risks" of procreation is neither an act of homicide nor does it require a homicidal intention, just as neither masturbation nor union with a prostitute are acts of this kind. It is an act against the virtue of chastity, and more concretely against the conjugal love for which chastity is an indispensable requirement, since chastity is the only power that protects this love from selfishness and aggressiveness. [Translator's note: I disagree with the author regarding the malice of contraception. I believe that contraception is not, of itself, a sexual act, but an act related to a sexual act and that its malice is that of a contralife will. It is not, indeed, an act of homicide, but it is an antilife act, since its precise point is to impede the beginning of the new human life that could begin if something were not done prior to, during, or subsequent to a freely chosen sexual act through which one reasonably believes new human life could be given (cf. Paul VI, *Humanae vitae,* July 25, 1968, no. 14). Contraception, indeed, is also contrary to the virtue of chastity. Married couples who contracept, by doing so, make their sexual act *to be* not an act of true marital union, but one that mocks and simulates their one-flesh unity. But fornicators can contracept just as married people can, and it is wrong for them to do so. When they contracept, they commit *two* evils: fornication and contraception. Traditionally in the Church, contraception has been likened to homicide, a kind of anticipated homicide. On this matter, see Germain Grisez, Joseph Boyle, Jr., John Finnis, and William E. May, " 'Every Marital Act Ought To Be Open to New Life': Toward a Clearer Understanding", *Thomist* 52, no. 3 (1988): 365–426.]

to a new human person and thereby denying the very meaning of their conjugal union, reducing in practice the act of mutual self-giving to an act of mutual masturbation. Therefore, properly speaking a contracepted act between persons who are not united in marriage is not contraception but, according to the cases, adultery, fornication, etc., or, if done by persons of the same sex, it constitutes an act of homosexuality. All these acts are sins against chastity even more serious than the contraception of spouses, and the use in them of contraceptive means does not diminish their malice to contraception but, to the contrary, aggravates it: that is, it joins the malice of contraception to the malice proper to these respective acts—adultery, fornication, etc.—inasmuch as the privation of its eventual procreative capacity facilitates the commission of these disorders and increases the progressive irresponsibility of committing them. But the fact of being contracepted does not transform adultery into contraception; and without doubt, both in the mind of the laity and in that of the Church, the malice of adultery is worse than the malice of contraception by spouses.[50] Now, why do we affirm that the contraceptive act does not have in and of itself a homicidal intention? *Surely it does not.* It is evident that very many women, in using contraceptives, above all when there are serious reasons for spacing births, do not have the least homicidal intention and are disposed to receive with love, or at least with resignation, the child who might eventually be conceived despite their precautions. But, one must not forget that *the contraceptive mentality or the generalization of contraceptive practices leads to abortion.*[51] The clearest proof of this is *the growing spread of abortifacient contraceptives,* which have terribly demoralizing consequences because those who use them— even Christian spouses—end up not wanting to be informed of the fact that they are not only contracepting but willingly risking abortion.

Here it is necessary to denounce clearly the grave moral responsibility of those who produce and sell contraceptive-abortifacient pills or other methods having the same nature. Like those who produce and

---

[50] On this matter, see Ramón García de Haro, "Fondamenti antropologici ed etici della procreazione umana", *Rivista Rosminiana di filosofia e di cultura* 83 (1989), in particular pp. 160–64. [Translator's note: I agree that adultery is a greater evil than contraception. I believe that adulterers and fornicators who contracept commit two sins: adultery and contraception or fornication and contraception.]

[51] "It is even necessary to add that the widespread acceptance of the practice of contraception through artificial means also leads to abortion, for the two deeds are situated, surely at different levels, on the same line of fear of a child, of a refusal of life, of a lack of respect for the act or the fruit of the union as this is willed for the man and the woman by the Creator of nature. Those who study these matters in depth know this well, contrary to what some kinds of reasonings and some currents of opinion would want us to believe" (John Paul II, Address to CLER and FIDAF, November 3, 1979, no. 9; *Enchiridion Familiae*, 3.2421–29).

sell and consume drugs, the producers and sellers of contraceptive-abortifacient pills and their like are guilty of the fact that, in an ever increasing number, so many women in difficult situations repeatedly commit the most serious crime of abortion, actually instilling thereby in themselves a mentality through which they end up aborting with the most absurd lightheadedness. To clarify the very serious responsibility not only of those who use contraceptive-abortifacient means but also—and perhaps even more—the responsibility of those who produce and sell these products, might help keep far from this terrible crime persons who, although not well-educated in ethics, nonetheless have a modicum of moral sensibility. Moreover, clarifying this matter is one way of stopping the banalization of abortion that, disgracefully, is ever increasing. It should be obligatory for civil law at least always to make it evident, in the medical directions accompanying pharmaceutical products, whether a pill is simply contraceptive or, on the other hand, both contraceptive and abortifacient. The contemporary failure to distinguish among these methods is perhaps one of the most demoralizing factors in the family life of Western society today.

c. *All spouses are called to live the fullness of the divine law,* and to it they must be led. Although it is proper for man to proceed gradually along the road in his way towards his own sanctification—to the extent that we can speak of a "law of graduality"—the "graduality of the law" is *not* admissible,

as if there were different degrees or forms of precept in God's law for different individuals and situations. In God's plan, all husbands and wives are called in marriage to holiness, and this lofty vocation is fulfilled to the extent that the human person is able to respond to God's command with serene confidence in God's grace and in his or her own will[52] (FC, no. 34, par. 4).

■ The exhortation highlights, with respect to this matter, the following truths already many times insisted on by the Magisterium: "*The moral order . . . cannot be something that harms man, something impersonal.* On the contrary, by responding to the deepest demands of the human being created by God, it places itself at the service of that person's full humanity with the delicate and binding love whereby God

---

[52] John Paul II, Homily at the Conclusion of the Sixth Synod of Bishops (October 25, 1980), no. 8; AAS 72 (1980): 1083; *Enchiridion Familiae,* 4.2885ff.

Himself inspires, sustains, and guides every creature towards its happiness" (FC, no. 34, par. 2).

In growing in the good proper to his being in history, man must not forget that *"without the Cross [Christian life] cannot reach the Resurrection."* Therefore, it is not possible to remove sacrifice from family life; indeed, it must be accepted from the heart (FC, no. 34, par. 3). Finally, growth—in fallen man—is never separated from the awareness of one's own weakness and from the admission of one's own sins, i.e., from that "awareness of sin" that leads one to the sacrament of reconciliation (FC, no. 34, par. 4).

Relying on these bases, spouses—who are the ones to make the judgment—not arbitrarily but as ministers of God's will (FC, no. 30, par. 6; no. 32, par. 4)—will consider what their own responsible parenthood demands: whether to have many children or to postpone for a time, or even indefinitely, a new birth (as *Humanae vitae* says, no. 10). With regard to this, FC insists that what is necessary for a right judgment, even more than the description and evaluation of the different circumstances—itself something not easily done and, in every case, the responsibility of the spouses—is the cultivation of the proper internal dispositions: the greatness of the gift of life (FC, no. 14, pars. 1–3; no. 28, pars. 1–3, etc.), the joy at raising up new human lives (no. 6, par. 4; no. 30, pars. 2–4, etc.), the goodness and generosity of the divine plan, the need to love the cross, the humility that helps one recognize and to drive out selfishness (no. 34), the practice of chastity (no. 33), frequenting the sacraments (no. 57ff.), etc. If confessors and pastors take into account that, in some cases, spouses allow their consciences to become lax—frequently the result of their environment—they must seek to give them, prudently and lovingly, a growing formation that will let them acquire an attentive and sensible conscience, by enlivening the dispositions mentioned above and, in particular, by relying on the generosity and faithfulness of God.

FC adds, moreover, a final counsel, of particular worth today. To help the faithful and to avoid anxiety and the deformation of conscience, of unique importance is the "unity of moral and pastoral judgment by priests", a unity based on the obedience due to the Magisterium (cf. FC, no. 34, par. 5, and no. 31).

II. Service to life includes the education of children, since, by cooperating with God in generating a new human person, the

parents "take on the task of helping that person effectively to live a fully human life" (FC, no. 36, par. 1).

The exhortation reminds us that the right and duty of parents regarding the education of their children is *essential and primary,* and therefore nonsubstitutable and inalienable. And it posits, as the founding element or inspiring principle of this right and duty, fatherly and motherly love, which finds "fulfillment in the task of education as it completes and perfects its service of life", while enriching those values— goodness, service, disinterestedness, the spirit of sacrifice—that are the characteristic fruit of that love (FC, no. 36, pars. 2–3).

With respect to the content of the educative work of the parents, FC lists the following: (a) the formation in values, especially, a "correct *attitude of freedom with regard to material goods,* by adopting a simple and austere life style and being fully convinced that 'man is more precious for what he is than for what he has'[53]" (FC, no. 37, par. 1); (b) helping the children learn to enrich themselves with the different virtues and particularly, in the selfish and violent world of today, with a sense of true justice and even more of true *love* (FC, no. 37, par. 2); and (c) finally, recourse to a *proper sexual education,* nourished by the *virtue of chastity* (FC, no. 37, par. 3).

> ■ No document has spoken with such clarity on this matter: sexual education, "which is a basic right and duty of parents, *must always be carried out under their attentive guidance,* whether at home or in educational centers chosen and controlled by them" (FC, no. 37, par. 4). The essential nucleus of this formation is the virtue of chastity, which leads to the gift of oneself, whose supreme expression is virginity; therefore, it implies *knowledge of and respect for* the "*moral norms* as the necessary and highly valuable guarantee for responsible growth in human sexuality" (FC, no. 37, par. 6). For this reason, "the Church is firmly opposed to an often widespread form of imparting sex information dissociated from moral principles. That would merely be an introduction to the experience of pleasure and a stimulus leading to the loss of serenity—while still in the years of innocence—by opening the way to vice" (FC, no. 37, par. 7).

The educative mission of the parents finds a new and specific source in the sacrament of marriage, through which they care for the development of

---

[53] Vatican Council II, *Gaudium et spes,* no. 35.

their children, not only as persons but also as children of God, by becoming "the first heralds of the Gospel for their children". The exhortation insists on two points. First, by educating their children in the Faith, the parents "become fully parents, in that they are begetters not only of bodily life but also of the life that through the Spirit's renewal flows from the Cross and Resurrection" (FC, no. 39, par. 4). Second, this work is above all developed—we are dealing with something that occurs frequently in the different aspects of the parents' mission[54]—by means of "family life itself", which "becomes an itinerary of faith and in some way a Christian initiation and a school of following Christ" (no. 39, par. 3).

■ Relative to this mission of the parents, the synod Fathers had hoped for—and the exhortation echoes this hope—the preparation of an adequate text for a *catechism for the family,* clear and brief, in such form as to make it easily understood by all (FC, no. 39, par. 5).

Finally, FC reminds us that *the family, although it is the first community for educating children, is not the last; its work of education extends to serving life in many ways* (nos. 40–41). This therefore requires collaboration between the different forces of education: the family, the Church, the state—for their mutual enrichment, but always with the obligation of recognizing that "the right of parents to choose an education in conformity with their religious faith must be absolutely guaranteed" (FC, no. 40, par. 3). State and Church, therefore, have the obligation to give to all families the helps possible to fulfill their mission; on their part, "parents must commit themselves totally to a cordial and active relationship with the teachers and school authorities" (FC, no. 40, pars. 4 and 5). If ideologies contrary to the Faith are promoted within the school, families must "join with other families, if possible through family associations, and with all its strength and with wisdom help the young not to depart from the faith" (FC, no. 40, par. 6).

■ Although the generation and education of children are the most immediate and nonsubstitutable of the services to life proper to the family, one must not forget that "every act of true love towards a human person bears witness to and perfects the spiritual fecundity of the family, since it is an act of obedience to the deep inner dynamism of love as self-giving to others" (FC, no. 41, par. 2). Prospects in this regard are inexhaustible, to the point that FC does not hesitate to say

[54] Cf. *Familiaris consortio,* nos. 20, 21, 23, 35, 36, 43, 50, 51, 52, 53, 55, 59, and elsewhere.

that "with families and through them, the Lord Jesus continues to 'have compassion' on the multitudes" (no. 41, par. 6).

3. Participation in the development of society

"The family is by nature and vocation open to other families and to society, and undertakes its social role" (FC, no. 42, par. 3). The rights and duties that derive from this are examined.

The social task is not something added to its being, but is above all carried out by the family's being what it is:

> The family has vital and organic links with society, since it is its foundation and nourishes it continually through its service to life; it is from the family that citizens come to birth and it is within the family that they find the first school of the social virtues that are the animating principle of the existence and development of society itself (FC, no. 42, par. 2).

Therefore, the *"first and fundamental contribution"* of the family to society is *"the very experience of communion and sharing that should characterize the family's daily life"*. Thus, solely by becoming what it must be, the family is already the first and most efficacious school of sociality, precisely through the spontaneous gratuity of the relationships among its members, which takes place through their cordial welcoming of each other, their disinterested disponibility, their generous service, their deep solidarity (FC, no. 43, pars. 1–3). The family possesses and releases, in an incomparably fertile way proper to itself, formidable energies for healing and giving form to an authentic social life, full of humanity.

Moreover, the family contributes to the good of society *by means of works of social service, especially by means of hospitality, whether material or spiritual:* i.e., by opening "the door of one's home and still more of one's heart to the pleas of one's brothers and sisters" (FC, no. 44, pars. 2–4). The exhortation insists on the originality of this contribution by the family, with which it is especially endowed, particularly with respect to giving assistance to those related to it. The family renders this service in a more human—and surely less costly—way than the state. Consequently, to restore to the family its own tasks would contribute no little to the resolution of the problem of unemployment, by taking care that a just family wage would not oblige the wife to work outside the home out of financial necessity, as is often the case.

Finally, *society and the state must serve the family: they must make it possible for it to obtain the helps of which it has need,* without trying to absorb its competencies. Thus, society and the state have a grave obligation to practice the principle of subsidiarity, by soliciting the greatest possible responsible initiative from the family. In order to fulfill this demand of good social order, the exhortation insists on two points: (a) families *must not passively be confident that they will in fact be helped because of their indispensable role.* History shows, on the contrary, that this often does not happen. They must therefore "be the first to take steps to see that the laws and institutions of the State not only do not offend but support and positively defend the rights and duties of families". It is appropriate that they become "protagonists" of "family politics", and "assume responsibility for transforming society" (FC, no. 44, par. 5); (b) moreover, *the rights of the family must be recognized clearly and in a formal way.* To secure this end, FC—here echoing a proposal made during the synod—expresses the hope that soon there would be a *charter of the rights of the family,* for which the Holy See proposed to prepare a draft.[55] FC, in what follows, provides a list of the most important rights: the right to found a family and to exercise proper responsibility in the transmission of life; the right to demand protection of the intimacy of conjugal life and of the stability of the marriage bond; the right to educate one's own children according to one's own beliefs; and finally, different rights of an economic-social kind relative to housing, security, public morality, the right to associate, etc. (no. 46).[56]

■ Baptism, by which one receives Christian life, deepens these rights and duties, provides them with a new title, and enriches them in their intimate content (FC, no. 47). Moreover, we cannot forget that Vatican Council II clearly stated, as one of the principal missions of the laity, that *they should see to it that the law of God become incarnated into the structures of the earthly city.*[57] This is especially true with respect to the

[55] This *Charter of the Rights of the Family* was in fact published on October 22, 1983.

[56] On this see A. Rodriguez, "La Carta dei diritti della famiglia", *Divus Thomas* 84 (1981): 330–41.

[57] See Vatican Council II, *Lumen gentium,* November 21, 1964, nos. 31 and 36; Vatican Council II, *Gaudium et spes,* no. 43; decree *Apostolicam actuositatem,* November 18, 1965, nos. 2 and 7.

duty to recognize, socially and juridically, the identity of the family and its rights. It is therefore quite urgent to react in the face of the situation today, when there is a juridical-social failure to protect the truth of the family, the root of every efficacious defense of the individual human person who, by means of the family, reaches out more efficaciously to other persons, becoming capable of overcoming difficulties otherwise insurmountable. Governments, citizens, and the international community are ever more becoming convinced of the fact that the survival of modern society and of the values of Western civilization depends on the well-being of the family.[58] The phenomena accompanying the abandonment of the family, indeed, phenomena at the root of its abandonment, make this matter most urgent. (a) There are, first of all, the *antifamily ideologies,* quite widespread, whose propaganda often affects persons who are not aware of them. This is shown by unfounded demographic fears and the approval that the contraceptive mentality enjoys; an ill-conceived feminism and the widespread refusal of the wonderful value of motherhood; the materialistic and pornographic hedonism diffused by the mass media; social permissivism regarding the acceptance of de facto or provisional "marriages", which unjustly are now becoming regarded as equivalent to families founded on marriage; the increasing number of couples who use contraceptive-

---

[58] Quite significant are the conclusions of the 22nd Session of the Conference of European Ministers in Charge of Family Matters on Family Policy and Decentralization, held at Lucerne, October 15–17, 1991 (see *Final Communication,* MMF–XXII [91] 5, final, Strasbourg, October 18, 1991, nos. 31, 39, 44): "The ministers agree that they must recognize that the end of the decentralization of family policy can be nothing else than to permit families to decide for themselves the views and conditions of life—i.e., school, living arrangements, the role of the mother in the home, etc.—which are best adapted to the family's development. Moreover, family policies ought to extend and amplify the family's responsibility and room for maneuvering, creating conditions favorable for those who are directly concerned with the needs of the members of their own families and coming to the help of those families which, on the other hand, encounter problems of such gravity that they are not able to cope with them by themselves" (*Final Communication,* no. 31). A bit later, at no. 39, the ministers called attention to the importance of the help that ought to be given to private initiatives; and finally, they emphasized that "in the new Europe which is being formed, all the positive forces of society must work together, along with families themselves", in the promotion of a climate favorable to the family (ibid., no. 44). Some of the declarations made by the ministers during the development of the conference were even more explicit: "We must create a world favorable to the family" (the French minister); "We must bind ourselves to removing the many obstacles and difficulties which up to this time we have placed in the way of the family's development" (the English minister); "We must move from a policy of assistance which protects only individuals to one which protects the family" (the minister from The Netherlands); "The center of every social policy must be the family" (the Portuguese representative), etc.

abortifacient methods, etc. (b) Moreover, there is the *legislative failure* in caring for the family founded on marriage. This legislative failure is manifested in many ways: not only has *divorce* been legalized, but there is not even the acceptance of an optional alternative of a civil, but indissoluble marriage, something amounting to an unjust discrimination with respect to Christians, made by states that boast of being lawful and frequently with Catholic majorities. Even more incomprehensible is the fact that *abortion has been subsidized by the state;* the state has likewise been of help in almost unbelievable abuses in the field of genetics (*in vitro* fertilization, surrogate motherhood, experimentation on embryos and fetuses procured through deliberate abortion, underhanded commerce in aborted embryos and fetuses), without any serious and efficacious effort on the part of public authority to suppress these abuses. Moreover, there is the incipient legalization of euthanasia and no effort is seriously being made to combat pornography. Finally, there has been the failure of *fiscal* legislation in confronting family matters; little or no assistance is provided to families to allow married women to care for their own families or to assist large families, so needed today yet so few in number.

Faced with this situation, *it is the family itself that must become the protagonist in defense of its own rights,* without deluding itself that others will do this: "Families must grow in their awareness of being *protagonists* of the so-called *family policy* and take upon themselves the responsibility of transforming society. Otherwise they will be the first victims of those evils which they simply viewed with indifference. The call of Vatican Council II to overcome the ethics of individualism has, therefore, value also for the family as such" (FC, no. 44, par. 5).[59]

But they must *take on these responsibilities with optimism,* because the family can do much: it possesses *formidable energies* (FC, no. 43, par. 5).[60] In addition, politicians today are calling on *private initiative* more and more, and this, when it is put into effect, *is shown to be active and effective.*[61] The obligation on the part of the family *to give all its force to movements and associations of families* is therefore both possible and

[59] *Enchiridion Familiae,* 4.3285–86.

[60] *Enchiridion Familiae,* 4.3285.

[61] The Holy Father, addressing the leaders of the prolife movement, thus said: "I thank you for your enthusiasm, your availability, and your generosity. There is in you a disinterested and gratuitous force which proceeds from spiritual values. You have the freedom to act without ideological presuppositions and bureaucratic burdens. The very nature of the cause for whose sake you labor is what makes you so generous: service to human life, even when it is hidden in the mystery of its conception" (John Paul II, Address of November 15, 1991, no. 1; *Insegnamenti di Giovanni Paolo II* 14.3 [Vatican City: Typis Polyglottis Vaticanis, 1991]).

morally incumbent. These movements and associations are meant to play an ever more important role in defining family policies: *the goal of their objectives is clear,* the realization of the *Charter of the Rights of the Family.*[62]

At the conclusion of these considerations—which have summarized the problems opened up with regard to the family in the contemporary state—we can sketch some fundamental points for serious and creative action on the part of believers in their cultural and sociopolitical action in defense of the family, within the changed political-social conditions of our day, following the collapse of the conception of Church-state relationships that prevailed during the so-called epoch of Christendom.[63] These can be regarded in some way, so to speak, as the central core of the teachings of the Magisterium after the crisis due to the laicization of the state—with the passing of time and the efforts to find solutions under the guidance of the Magisterium, in particular that of Vatican Council II. We can initially point them out in the following way:

a. First of all, there is an urgent need to find the means *to protect the family founded upon marriage insofar as it is founded on marriage* by means of the following: a) the defense of *the unity and stability of the family,* with an effort to put limits to the plague of divorce: for example, by better controlling the rigor of the processes leading to divorce and the nullification of marriages and to foster efficient and preventive measures designed to succeed in reconciling marital conflicts; to recognize the right of persons to contract a marriage that is civilly indissoluble, not obliging all to contract a marriage necessarily subject to divorce;[64] b) the defense of the values of *motherhood* and *fatherhood* (for example, by recognizing the right of the married woman with children under 15 years of age or handicapped or caring for the elderly to a reduced workday with appropriate compensation) and of *large families,* a most important source of social well-being.

b. The *right of parents to educate their children according to their own faith and according to basic ethical values* must be recognized.[65] This means not only the right to attend public schools or to promote others but

---

[62] *Charter of the Rights of the Family,* presented by the Holy See to all persons, institutions, and authorities interested in the mission of the family in the world today, October 22, 1983.

[63] On this see above, chapter 2, section 2.

[64] On this, see A. De Fuenmayor, *El derecho a contraer matrimonio civilmente indisoluble* (*El llamado divorcio opcional*) (Madrid: Ed. Acción Familiar, 1991).

[65] Here we note that the Holy Father in FC has emphasized three of these values: "a just freedom with respect to material goods . . . convinced that *man is of greater value because of who he is than what he has*"; the meaning not only of justice but of *authentic love,* and, finally, the value of *an education to chastity,* "the right and duty of parents, which must always be carried out under their solicitous guidance" (FC, no. 37; *Enchiridion Familiae,* 4.3272–73).

that the latter must also be subsidized equally by public monies, at least *by recognizing the right of parents to a discount concerning the expenses concerning their children's school*—at all level of education, including university education.

c. There should be established a policy of *economic protection of the family as such,* giving the rights and means to the family itself to care for itself—not only indirectly by means of governmental agencies such as social security administrations, which must be subsidized, but also by assisting in other basic social functions such as care of the children, of the elderly, etc. A policy of this kind must also be shown in assistance to families for the children and other persons in their care, in helping with housing, particularly for the first home and for housing fit for large families, and in tax policies favorable to the family.

d. There is also need to take concrete measures in order that the Recommendations of the Conference on the Population of Mexico might be respected. These absolutely proscribed *abortion as a method of birth control.* Undoubtedly, abortion is an instance in which irreparable damage is inflicted on a defenseless victim, with the approval of public authority. Therefore, laws on abortion are highly demoralizing and, as many contemporary philosophers and jurists have shown, constitute the beginning of the dismantling of a lawful democratic state.[66]

4. *Participation in the life and mission of the Church*

The Christian family shares in the saving mission of the Church, with an original and characteristic task, linked to its very nature. Because of this, the family can be called the domestic Church, a living image of the very mystery of the Spouse of Christ.

As was the case with society, so too intimate relationships bind the family to the Church. But in a certain way—FC puts this into relief from the very beginning—the vital currents are here in an inverse direction: while the family is the vital foundation of society, it is the Church, on the other hand, who generates, educates, and builds up Christian families as a Mother. She does this by proclaiming the Word of God, which reveals to the family its true identity, and by means of the celebration of the sacraments, which enrich it with power, in such

---

[66] See M. Schooyans, *L'enjeu politique de l'avortement,* 2nd. ed. (Brussels: Oeil, 1992); V. Possenti, *La società liberali al bivio* (Perugia: Marietti, 1991).

a way that charity is the soul that guides it (FC, no. 49, par. 2). In addition to this, the exhortation insists from beginning to end on the fact that the family fulfills its most important mission by "placing itself, in what it is and what it does as an 'intimate community of life and love,' at the service of the Church and society" (no. 50, par. 1). *Realizing itself as such,* and not by any task superimposed upon it, the family acquits its most essential and efficacious ecclesial mission.

> ■ With respect to the content of this mission, FC uses the scheme of participation in the *threefold mission of Christ as prophet, priest, and king.* It thus presents the family under the threefold aspect of being a *believing and evangelizing community, a community in dialogue with God, and a community at the service of mankind.*

The Christian family participates in the prophetic mission of Christ and of the Church, "by welcoming and announcing the word of God" (FC, no. 51, par. 1). Therefore, what is first and foremost demanded of Christian spouses and parents is the obedience of faith (Rom 16:26), because "only in faith can they discover and admire with joyful gratitude the dignity to which God has deigned to raise marriage and the family, making them a sign and meeting place of the loving covenant between God and man, between Jesus Christ and His bride, the Church" (FC, no. 51, par. 2). If the original power of the family is love, Christian spouses discover that their love is a sign and real participation in the love of God and in his redemptive power. This faith, which works through charity, is called to grow and incarnate itself "in and through the events, problems, difficulties and circumstances of everyday life. God comes to them, revealing and presenting the concrete 'demands' of their sharing in the love of Christ for His Church in the particular family, social, and ecclesial situation in which they find themselves" (FC, no. 51, par. 5).

Faith thus heard and experienced in love makes the Christian family a fire that sheds its light on many other families (cf. FC, no. 52, par. 1). The exhortation stresses that this apostolic mission of the family flows from what the family itself is and that it is exercised through fidelity to its own proper being as a community of life and love: the "apostolic mission of the family is rooted in Baptism and receives from the grace of the sacrament of marriage new strength to transmit the faith, to sanctify and transform our present society according to God's plan" (no. 52, par. 2). It is the development of the dynamism of baptism, in accord with the further configuration to Christ that comes from the vocation to marriage and from appropriate sacramental grace. Therefore, it is an apostolic work that must exercise itself and assume all "the characteristics of family life itself, which should be interwoven with love, simplicity, practicality, and daily witness" (FC, no. 53, par. 1).

■ FC then indicates two characteristics of the apostolate of the family. On the one hand, it is exercised above all among its own members, by helping them to live fully their Christian vocation. Thus the family becomes "the *primary and most excellent seedbed of vocations* to a life of consecration to the kingdom of God" (FC, no. 53, par. 2). The formation of children is the most fertile apostolate of the parents, and, as every apostolate, it is never exempt from the cross. But, this apostolate, begun with the family nucleus, at last bears witness to Christ "to the end of the earth" (Acts 1:8), by preaching the Gospel to all creation (Mt 16:15) (FC, no. 54).

The family exercises its proper priestly task "through the daily realities of married and family life", through which "the Christian family is called to be sanctified and to sanctify the ecclesial community and the world" (FC, no. 55, par. 3). FC reproposes and develops this fundamental doctrine of Vatican II, teaching how this call is specified in the ordinary realities of conjugal and family life, whose roots are nourished by the grace of the sacrament: "Christian spouses and parents are included in the universal call to sanctity. For them this call is specified by the sacrament they have celebrated and is carried out concretely in the realities proper to their conjugal and family life" (no. 56, par. 3). This is particularly suggestive, as has already been said, with respect to family prayer, in which the family learns to interpret family life itself, in all its circumstances,

as a call from God and as a filial response to His call. Joys and sorrows, hopes and disappointments, births and birthday celebrations, wedding anniversaries of the parents, departures, separations and home-comings, important and far-reaching decisions, the death of those who are dear, etc. — all of these mark God's loving intervention in the family's history. They should be seen as suitable moments for thanksgiving, for petition, for trusting abandonment of the family into the hands of their common Father in heaven (FC, no. 59, par. 3).

By being faithful to its vocation, the family not only sanctifies itself, but becomes a source of sanctity for the world. Since this entails human fullness, the family also contributes to the social good in its temporal aspects of promoting what is human, in such a way that, without the need of proposing this directly as a purpose, it renews the world: "The fruitfulness of the Christian family in its specific service to human advancement, which of itself cannot but lead to the transformation of the world, derives from its living union with Christ" (FC, no. 62, par. 3).

■ The exhortation lingers over the *sacramental foundation* of the sanctity demanded of spouses, which makes this possible despite difficulties. Concretely, "just as husbands and wives received from the sacrament the gift and responsibility of translating into daily life the sanctification bestowed on them, so the same sacrament confers on them the grace and the moral obligation of transforming their whole lives into a 'spiritual sacrifice'[67]" (FC, no. 56, par. 5). Just as love is the proper power of the family and participation in Christ's love is what defines the Christian family, so the Eucharist is the living fountain of marriage:

The Eucharist is the very source of Christian marriage. The Eucharistic Sacrifice, in fact, represents Christ's covenant of love with the Church, sealed with His blood on the Cross.... The Eucharist is a fountain of charity. In the Eucharistic gift of charity the Christian family finds the foundation and soul of its "communion" and its "mission" (FC, no. 57, par. 2).

The conjugal communion and its whole dynamic are also rooted in the sacrament of penance, in which "the married couple and the other members of the family are led to an encounter with God, who is 'rich in mercy,'[68] who bestows on them His love which is more powerful than sin,[69] and who reconstructs and brings to perfection the marriage covenant and the family communion" (FC, no. 58, par. 3).

Finally, the family exercises its kingly task by putting itself at the service of men, as Christ did and as he asks his disciples to do (FC, no. 63, par. 4). Taking up again the teachings of the Council, FC reminds us that this service properly pertains to the laity in a specific way, by sanctifying temporal structures, so that these might be "delivered out of their slavery to corruption and into the freedom of the glory of the children of God (cf. Rom 8:21)"[70] (no. 63, par. 4). In fact, the first and most

[67] Cf. 1 Pet 2:5; Vatican Council II, *Lumen gentium,* no. 34.
[68] Eph 2:4.
[69] John Paul II, encyclical *Dives in misericordia,* November 30, 1980, no. 13.
[70] Vatican Council II, *Lumen gentium,* no. 36.

important service to men consists in freeing them from this slavery, in a way that will help them become capable of living as children of God. The Christian family succeeds in doing this because its dynamic surrenders interiorly to the law of love:

> In continuity with Baptism ... marriage sets forth anew the evangelical law of love, and with the gift of the Spirit engraves it more profoundly on the hearts of Christian husbands and wives. Their love, purified and saved, is a fruit of the Spirit acting in the hearts of believers and constituting, at the same time, the fundamental commandment of their moral life to be lived in responsible freedom (FC, no. 63, par. 3).

> ■ Since, by God's will, the dynamic of love is proper to the whole of family life, more spontaneously in it than in any other institution, one can understand the influence of the family not only in its impact on society but also in its relationships within the Christian community: "Thanks to love within the family, the Church can and ought to take on a more homelike or family dimension, developing a more human and fraternal style of relationships" (FC, no. 64, par. 2).

D. Fourth part: pastoral care of the family

The fourth part is divided into four major sections, which treat respectively of the times, structures, agents, and situations encountered in the pastoral care of the family. The first three sections provide the general principles that must regulate the pastoral care of the family. We will divide them in two in our treatment: general principles and particular situations.[71]

1. General principles

The purpose of pastoral care is to help couples in their growth toward the "model of a family which the Creator intended from 'the beginning' and which Christ has renewed with His redeeming grace" (FC, no. 65, par. 4). This is realized through a constant catechesis that can form consciences in fidelity to the Magisterium.

[71] Cf. D. Tettamanzi, *L'Esortazione sulla Famiglia "Familiaris consortio"* (*Sussidi pastorali e liturgici*) (Milan: Massimo, 1982); Tettamanzi, *La famiglia, via della Chiesa* (Milan: Massimo, 1987).

This is a matter of fundamental significance, because "the future of the world and of the Church passes through the family" (FC, no. 75). Current conditions make it ever more urgent, circumstances in which—because of the changes that have taken place as well as because of different negative phenomena—many "not only lose sight of the correct hierarchy of values but, since they no longer have certain criteria of behavior, they do not know how to face and deal with the new difficulties" (FC, no. 66, par. 1).

> ■ The exhortation insists on three complementary points. First of all, speaking of the times in which we live, it insists on the necessity that a pastoral approach be a profound work of catechesis, since knowledge of the truth is the first support for authentic freedom. Second, in treating of structures, it emphasizes that we must come to a deeper grasp of the truth, in such a way that it leads to a *formation of consciences,* because otherwise the truth is not personalized and does not become a source of life. Finally, in referring to the agents of pastoral ministry, it reminds us that all this work cannot efficaciously be developed save by a deep *fidelity to the Magisterium* — otherwise it would not be a service to truth.

Therefore, *the pastoral care of the family is nothing else than a constant work of catechesis, which begins with the theme of preparing for marriage, continues in its celebration, and later throughout the whole life of the spouses.* With respect to preparation, FC distinguishes a "remote preparation", which begins in infancy and must show "that marriage is a true vocation and mission, without excluding the possibility of the total gift of self to God in the vocation to the priestly or religious life" (no. 66, par. 4); a "proximate preparation", directed to "a more specific preparation for the sacraments, as it were, a rediscovery of them" (no. 66, par. 5), and finally, an "immediate preparation", aimed at discovering the richnesses of marriage, and which "must always be set forth and put into practice in such a way that omitting it is not an impediment to the celebration of the marriage" (no. 66, par. 9).

The catechesis ought to be developed also in the *celebration of marriage,* inasmuch as this is an expression of the essentially ecclesial and sacramental nature of the conjugal covenant between the baptized, in a way that nourishes the dispositions of those who are getting married and, particularly, their faith (FC, nos. 67–68). Finally, catechesis ought to accompany the spouses *after the marriage,* by helping them discover and live always more and more their new vocation and mission, especially "that they may accept their children and love them as a gift received from the Lord of life and joyfully accept the task of serving them in their human and Christian growth" (FC, no. 69, par. 3).

> ■ With respect to the celebration of marriage, FC makes it clear—in confronting some erroneous opinions—that, even though it is an occasion when the spouses ought to be helped in growing in the Faith, nevertheless, one ought not to introduce practical inquiries that would lead people astray, rashly judging the faith of those wishing to contract marriage, and that would delay the celebration without cause. We cannot forget that those getting married, by virtue of their baptism, are already inserted into the spousal covenant of Christ with the Church and therefore into the plan of God for Christian marriage. Only if they show "that they reject *explicitly and formally* what the Church intends to do when the marriage of baptized persons is celebrated" can and ought the pastor not admit them to the sacrament, after having done everything possible to get them to change their dispositions (FC, no. 68, pars. 3–7).

The structures for the pastoral care of the family are the ecclesial community (in particular, the parish), the family itself, and associations of families; these must take care that the teaching of the Church on marriage penetrates consciences and becomes manifest in works of charity (FC, nos. 70–72). The whole pastoral work of catechesis must be directed to this end: that consciences be rightly formed "according to Christian values and not according to the standards of public opinion" (FC, no. 72, par. 2) and that "works of charity" be inspired (cf. no. 71, par. 2, and no. 71, par. 1). As is logical, in addition to the normal structures of the Church, one ought to count on families themselves: on their witness of a married life as they have experienced it and on their peculiar capacity to develop works of charity, both material and spiritual. Families, to the end of helping themselves in their task, are able—and often are obliged—to have recourse to different forms of solidarity adapted to specific cases.

> ■ Among the structures, the Holy Father also lists centers devoted to studies and teaching on the family. In fact, to spread the teaching of the Church with authority and sureness, and in an opportune way in this historical moment, there is need to deepen the doctrine itself. To

stimulate centers of this kind, the Pope established at Rome the higher institute for studies on marriage and family (FC, no. 70, par. 3).

Finally, FC emphasizes that *the work of pastoral agents—bishops and priests, religious, lay specialists, etc.—will be efficacious precisely to the extent that they faithfully adhere to the Magisterium.* Only if their teachings and counsels, as in general all their actions, are in full harmony with the Magisterium of the Church, will they give help to the people of God, because then it will form a right sense of the Faith and know how to apply it to concrete life. The Holy Father insists that

> the proximate and obligatory norm in the teaching of the faith—also concerning family matters—belongs to the hierarchical Magisterium. Clearly defined relationships between theologians, experts in family matters, and the Magisterium are of no little assistance for the correct understanding of the faith and for promoting—within the boundaries of the faith—legitimate pluralism (FC, no. 73, par. 5).

> ■ All those who work together in the pastoral care of the family ought also to take into account the fact that "all that [they] succeed in doing to support the family is destined to have an effectiveness that goes beyond its own sphere and reaches other people too and has an effect on society", because "the future of the world and of the Church passes through the family" (FC, no. 75).

2. *Pastoral care of the family in difficult situations*

A generous and intelligent pastoral commitment is required to help all those who find themselves—whether through their own fault or not—in difficult situations. FC insists that there be a commitment to eliminate the deepest causes of these difficult situations and on specific pastoral measures for each case.

FC proceeds in its analysis of families finding themselves in difficulties by first taking up situations caused by external circumstances (the families of migrant workers, uprooted families, those with handicapped children, families of alcoholics, families that are victims of unjust discrimination, families ideologically divided, etc.); it then treats especially of mixed marriages; and finally, it concerns itself with irregular situations: trial marriages, "free" unions, divorces.

With regard to *families with difficulties that are above all external, above and beyond helping solve their problems, there is need to help them discover, in the midst of their trials, an invitation to deepen their love,* to "understand and live *the lofty aspects of the spirituality of marriage and the family,* aspects which take their inspiration from the value of Christ's Cross and Resurrection, the source of sanctification and profound happiness in daily life, in the light of the great eschatological realities of eternal life" (FC, no. 77, par. 7).

Concerning *mixed marriages,* FC reminds us of the need for vigilance in order to carry out the *"obligations that faith imposes on the Catholic party* with regard to the free exercise of the faith and the consequent obligation to ensure, as far as is possible, the Baptism and upbringing of the children in the Catholic faith"[72] (no. 78, par. 3). In addition, it notes that it is important to help the Catholic spouse see that this situation must be a *stimulus for growing in faith and in love,* so that he may be able to help the other party, with total respect for his freedom, by giving a good example.

   ■ In pastoral care, it is most important that, in the preparation for this type of marriage, *"every reasonable effort must be made* to ensure a proper understanding of Catholic teaching on the qualities and obligations of marriage, and also to ensure that pressures and obstacles [to the conscientious religious beliefs of either party] will not occur." Moreover, all possible help must be given to the Catholic party that he may mature in the Faith, thus becoming a credible witness "through his or her own life and through the quality of love shown to the other spouse and to the children" (FC, no. 78, par. 6).

With regard to irregular situations (trial marriages, "free" unions, divorced persons who have remarried, etc.) FC denounces the falsification of love that these entail; and it insists on the need of helping persons involved in situations of this kind with true love, but without making any compromises, which would only aggravate their condition. The language of the document is clear. It declares, with respect to trial marriages, that reason alone "leads one to see that they are unacceptable, by showing the unconvincing nature of carrying out an 'experiment' with human beings, whose dignity demands that they should be always and solely the term of a self-giving love without limitations of time or of any other

[72] Cf. Paul VI, motu proprio, *Matrimonia mixta,* March 31, 1970, nos. 4–5; AAS 62 (1970): 257ff.; cf. John Paul II, Address to the Participants at the Plenary Session of the Secretariat of Christian Union, November 13, 1981; *Enchiridion Familiae,* 4.3188–89.

circumstance" (no. 80, par. 1). Concerning so-called "free" unions, it emphasizes the "grave consequences", religious and moral ("the loss of the religious sense of marriage seen in the light of the covenant of God with His people; deprivation of the grace of the sacrament; grave scandal") as well as social ("the destruction of the concept of the family; the weakening of the sense of fidelity, also towards society; possible psychological damage to the children; the strengthening of selfishness") (FC, no. 81, par. 3). Speaking of divorced persons who have remarried, FC speaks of this situation as "an evil that, like the others, is affecting more and more Catholics as well" (no. 84, par. 1).

Clearness in denouncing evil does not and must not mean lack of charity and understanding. Thus, the Church reaches out to couples in this sad situation, advising her pastors to "make tactful and respectful contact with the couples concerned, enlighten them patiently, correct them charitably and show them the witness of Christian family life in such a way as to smooth the path for them to regularize their situation" (FC, no. 81, par. 4). However, so long as the irregularity continues, the individuals concerned *cannot be admitted to the sacraments;* this holds true, as should be obvious, not only for those who simply live together outside marriage but for all irregular unions, e.g., Catholics who have been united only in a civil ceremony (FC, no. 82, par. 2), divorced Catholics who have remarried (no. 84, par. 4f.).

■ FC dwells particularly on this last point because it was the subject of long debates during the synod. While exhorting the divorced who have remarried to go to Mass, continue their prayers, etc., nevertheless the "Church reaffirms her practice, which is based on Sacred Scripture, of not admitting to Eucharistic Communion divorced persons who have remarried" (FC, no. 84, par. 4). In truth, they exclude themselves, since they put themselves in objective contradiction to the union of love between Christ and the Church; moreover, if the Church were to admit them, the faithful would be induced to think erroneously about the indissolubility of marriage. For the same reasons, the Church absolutely forbids pastors to provide any kind of ceremony whatsoever for divorced persons who remarry (FC, no. 84, par. 6). The exhortation, naturally, distinguishes carefully the case of those who do not cause this kind of situation but are rather its victims, while remaining faithful to their marriage vows. The exhortation thus takes pains to praise "their example of fidelity and Christian consistency", which "takes on particular value as a witness before the world and the Church" (no. 83, par. 3).

The exhortation concludes by reaffirming that "the future of humanity passes by way of the family", inviting all to collaborate cordially and courageously with the family, and reminding all that the Holy Family is the "prototype and example for all Christian families" (no. 86).

3. Other Teachings of John Paul II on Marriage and Family

Throughout the years of his pontificate, John Paul II has issued hundreds of documents — homilies, addresses, etc. — that are concerned in whole or in part with the family. This vast work springs from a deep conviction: the world will be renewed through the reconstruction of the family. Faced with the threats that weigh heavily upon society, it is necessary to restore the family. The Holy Father, therefore, has made this one of his basic commitments; he himself confirmed this in his Address to the Cardinals in 1980:

> It is necessary to restore the value of the family, the holiness of marriage, the intangibility of human life. I will never tire of carrying out what I consider a nondeferable mission, deriving benefit from the trips, meetings, audiences, personal messages, institutions, associations, consultations which are concerned with the future of the family, and which make it the object of their study and action.[73]

The very wealth of documents and unceasing insistence on the same ideas — made amidst a wide range of occasions — suggests that it would be better to set forth the principal themes on which the Pope dwells rather than attempt a commentary on individual documents. We will preface our presentation of these themes with some general remarks on the characteristics of this magisterial activity of John Paul II and on the occasions in which it took place, making the most of this to provide a list that, while not exhaustive, is eloquent enough.

---

[73] Address to the Cardinals and Prelates of the Roman Curia, December 22, 1980, in *Insegnamenti di Giovanni Paolo II*, 3.2 (1980), p. 1774; in *Enchiridion Familiae*, 3.2990.

A. *Characteristics of and major occasions for these teachings*

Without question here we deal with documents of diverse style and literary genre, just as the public to which they are directed is quite diverse. The teaching is set forth with power and with a peculiar originality, which seems linked to a constant and always more probing contemplation of reality. New aspects of the truth appear not as the result of a deductive process, but rather as the fruit of a searching meditation on human life, seen on the divine plane insofar as it is the gift of the Lord and Redeemer of man.

A like loving contemplation, illumined by faith, is at the source of that wisdom which goes beyond science and allows one to discover profoundly illuminating expressions; formulations that then can be recalled easily, as slogans, at the moment of choosing or judging, and that in truth are "powerful ideas" that move and help people in their living. In reality, they are "divine lights", which, once heard, are distributed *ex abundantia cordis* to others. We have seen different examples of these ideas in *Familiaris consortio,* and we will continue to see them in this section: expressions such as "the Church stands on the side of life", "human life has a family structure", "God is not a solitude but a family", or "love is the natural vocation of man", give light that does not easily fade away.

Moreover, this way of contemplating reality allows the use of the contributions of modern thought, and even if these come at times from authors who have freed themselves of Christian Tradition, their use does not remain mired in the conditions of the origin of these contributions. In fact, lucid attention to reality, in its fullness and totality, allows the use of every crumb of truth, wherever found, without need of connecting it to the "system" in which it arose or in which it developed, provided that the truth is reconnected with its original source, which is reality itself. On the other hand, when the truth is considered as a system, it is difficult to use others' expressions without becoming imbued with the substance of their system.

We can draw up the following list of documents issued by the Holy Father up to the present and the events with which they are connected:

1. The *catecheses in the general audiences held on Wednesdays* (from 1979 to 1984), which, as we have seen, constitute an organic picture of

his doctrine and have been published together, in Italian, under the title *Uomo e donna lo creò* (*Catechesi sull'amore umano*).[74] In these, the Holy Father treats of marriage and the family in the perspective of an "adequate" anthropology—i.e., one that teaches us revelation and coincides with our deepest experiences—where man appears as the one who is created by God in a supernatural state of justice, fallen into sin, redeemed by Christ, and destined to rise up at the end of time.

■ With this catechesis, the Holy Father wants to shed light, from the very first, on the work of the synod on the family: "The cycle of reflections we are beginning today ... has also, among other things, the purpose *of accompanying, from afar, so to speak, the work of preparation for the Synod,* not touching its subject directly, however, but turning our attention to the deep roots from which this subject springs",[75] i.e., the truth about man—the truth about human love and about the family. This cycle of reflections, an accompaniment to the synod, was continued up to the end of the synod and closed with an authentic and profound interpretation of *Humanae vitae,* intended as a response to questions about marriage and procreation that the encyclical aroused and were definitively at the root of the synod's work.[76] Here we cannot treat the content of this catechesis, which is so profound that it can only be taken up adequately in other studies.

2. In connection with the synod, there is another group of addresses, held in order to prepare for, develop, and promulgate *Familiaris consortio,* the principal fruit of the synod. Specifically, this group includes: Address to the Secretary General of the Synod, December 23, 1980;[77] letter *Appropinquat iam Synodus* to the Bishops, Priests, and Faithful of the Whole Church, August 15, 1980, on the approaching Synod;[78] Homily at the Opening of the Synod, September 26, 1980;[79] Homily and Address on the "Day of the Family", October 12, 1980;[80] Address Address at the Conclusion of the Sixth Synod of Bishops;[81] and

[74] As was mentioned in n. 3 of this chapter, these audience addresses have been published in four volumes in English. See n. 3 for their titles.
[75] John Paul II, General Audience, September 5, 1979, in *Original Unity of Man and Woman,* p. 19.
[76] Cf. John Paul II, *Reflections on "Humanae vitae".*
[77] *Insegnamenti di Giovanni Paolo II,* 3.1 (1980), pp. 472–76.
[78] Ibid., 3.2, pp. 388–91; *Enchiridion Familiae,* 3.2755–59.
[79] Ibid., 3.2, pp. 734–38; *Enchiridion Familiae,* 3.2815–22.
[80] Ibid., 3.2, pp. 842–52; *Enchiridion Familiae,* 3.2838–47.
[81] Ibid., 3.2, pp. 965–72; *Enchiridion Familiae,* 3.2885–93.

finally, Address to the Cardinals, December 22, 1981, after the publication of *Familiaris consortio.*[82]

3. There is a third group, particularly important, consisting of the *catecheses given during his apostolic journeys:* Homily at Puebla, January 28, 1979;[83] Homily at the Mass for Workers in the Airport of Nowy Targ, June 8, 1979;[84] Homily at the Mass for Laypeople and Families, Limerick, October 1, 1979;[85] Address to the United Nations, October 2, 1979;[86] Homily at the Mass on the Capitol Mall of Washington, D.C., October 7, 1979;[87] Address at Turin, April 13, 1980;[88] Homily at the Mass for Families, Kinshasa, May 3, 1980;[89] Homily in Uhuru Park, Nairobi, May 7, 1980;[90] Homily at the Mass for Families in the Aterro do Flamingo, Rio de Janeiro, July 1, 1980;[91] Homily at Velletri, September 7, 1980;[92] Homily at the Mass for Families at the "Butzweiler Hof" Stadium of Cologne, November 15, 1980;[93] Homily at the Mass for Families in the Airport of Lhung, Cebu, February 19, 1981;[94] Homily at the Mass in Terni, March 19, 1981;[95] Homily at the Mass for Families at Onitsha, February 13, 1982;[96] Homily at the Mass for Families in the Shrine of Sameiro, May 15, 1982;[97] Homily at the Mass for Families at York, May 31, 1982;[98] Homily at the Mass for Families, Madrid, November 2, 1982;[99] the Meeting with Families, March 5, 1983;[100] Homily for Spouses at St. Peter's, October 9, 1983;[101] Homily at the Mass for Families at Quidi Vidi Lake, September 12,

---

[82] Ibid., 4.2 (1981), pp. 1215–16; *Enchiridion Familiae,* 4.3415–19.

[83] Ibid., 2.1 (1979), pp. 254–58; *Enchiridion Familiae,* 3.2272–74.

[84] Ibid., 2.1, pp. 1488–91; *Enchiridion Familiae,* 3.2324–26.

[85] Ibid., 2.2, pp. 496–503; *Enchiridion Familiae,* 3.2364–70.

[86] Ibid., 2.2, pp. 522ff.

[87] Ibid., 2.2, pp. 699–704; *Enchiridion Familiae,* 3.2378–87.

[88] Ibid., 3.1 (1980), pp. 913–14; *Enchiridion Familiae,* 3.2612–15.

[89] Ibid., 3.1, pp. 1075–81; *Enchiridion Familiae,* 3.2646–57.

[90] Ibid., 3.1, pp. 1197–1202; *Enchiridion Familiae,* 3.2659–61.

[91] Ibid., 3.2, pp. 11–17; *Enchiridion Familiae,* 3.2717–26.

[92] Ibid., 3.2, pp. 557–61; *Enchiridion Familiae,* 3.2786–88.

[93] Ibid., 3.2, pp. 1188–95; *Enchiridion Familiae,* 3.2946–53.

[94] Ibid., 4.1 (1981), pp. 409–15; *Enchiridion Familiae,* 4.3049–57.

[95] Ibid., 4.1, pp. 714–21; *Enchiridion Familiae,* 4.3070–74.

[96] Ibid., 5.1 (1982), pp. 379–84; *Enchiridion Familiae,* 4.3480–85.

[97] Ibid., 5.2, pp. 1706–16; *Enchiridion Familiae,* 4.3560–75.

[98] Ibid., 5.2, pp. 2007–12; *Enchiridion Familiae,* 4.3577–84.

[99] Ibid., 5.3, pp. 1072–79; *Enchiridion Familiae,* 4.3753–60.

[100] Ibid., 6.1 (1983), pp. 579–84; *Enchiridion Familiae,* 5.3895–99.

[101] Ibid., 6.2, pp. 731–36; *Enchiridion Familiae,* 5.3960–67.

1984;[102] Homily at the Mass for Families at Caracas, January 27, 1985;[103] Homily at the Mass for Families at the Park of Miraflores, January 31, 1985;[104] Homily at the Mass for Families at Maastricht, May 4,1985;[105] and Address at Lucca, September 23, 1989.[106]

4. There is also a large group of homilies devoted to the family, in whole or in part, given during his *pastoral visits to the parishes of Rome:* for example, those to the Parish of St. Francis Xavier, October 30, 1978;[107] to the Church of the Most Holy Name of Jesus, December 31, 1978;[108] to the Parish of St. Joseph, March 18, 1979;[109] to the Church of St. Bonaventure at the Spaccata Tower, April 1, 1979;[110] to the Parents of the Alumni of the Major Seminary of Rome, March 20, 1983;[111] etc.

5. There are also many addresses to *institutions and associations concerned with the family:* Address to the Third International Congress of the Family, October 30, 1978, on the responsibility of the family in human and Christian education;[112] Address to the Participants in the European Congress of the Pro-Life Movement, on the defense of human life, February 26, 1979;[113] Address to Family Collaborators, in the Tenth Assembly of the Italian Association API–COLF (Associazione Professionale Italiana Collaboratrici Familiari), on the dignity of the woman and on her mission, April 29, 1979;[114] Address to the Participants at the Congress on the Pastoral Care of the Family, on the family as a reference point for integrally promoting man, May 5, 1979;[115] Address to the International Congress of the Teams of Our Lady, on the spirituality of the family that ought to be based on the

[102] Ibid., 7.2 (1984), pp. 468–73; *Enchiridion Familiae,* 5.4190–92.

[103] Ibid., 8.1 (1985), pp. 188–94; *Enchiridion Familiae,* 5.4247–50.

[104] Ibid., 8.1, pp. 305–11; *Enchiridion Familiae,* 5.4251–56.

[105] Ibid., 8.1, pp. 1336–42.

[106] Ibid., 12.2 (1989), pp. 611–15. Addresses of John Paul II on marriage and the family after 1988 are not found in *Enchiridion Familiae,* which includes documents only up to the end of 1988.

[107] Ibid., 1 (1978), pp. 274–78.

[108] Ibid., 1, pp. 455–58; *Enchiridion Familiae,* 3.2249–52.

[109] Ibid., 2.1 (1979), pp. 677–82; *Enchiridion Familiae,* 3.2291–95.

[110] Ibid., 2.1, pp. 767–71; *Enchiridion Familiae,* 3.2295–97.

[111] Ibid., 5.1 (1983), pp. 770–73; *Enchiridion Familiae,* 5.3903–8.

[112] Ibid., 1 (1978), pp. 80–82; *Enchiridion Familiae,* 3.2234–37.

[113] Ibid., 2.1 (1979), pp. 467–69; *Enchiridion Familiae,* 3.2280–82.

[114] Ibid., 2.1, pp. 1018–23; *Enchiridion Familiae,* 3.2303–12.

[115] Ibid., 2.1, pp. 1056–58; *Enchiridion Familiae,* 3.2312–16.

gospel, September 17, 1979;[116] Address to CLER (Centre de Liaison des Equipes de Recherche) and FIDAF (Federation Internationale d'Action Familiale), on marriage as an actuation of the Covenant;[117] Address to the Congress of Midwives, January 26, 1980;[118] Address to the Participants in the Fifth International Congress of the Family, November 8, 1980;[119] Address to the International Congress of Africa and Europe for the Family, on the inviolability of life and the holiness of marriage, January 15, 1981;[120] Address to the World Congress on the Family, organized by the "New Families" of the Focolari Movement, on the vocation of spouses to the interior truth of love, May 3, 1981;[121] Address to the Center of Studies and Investigation into the Natural Regulation of Fertility of the University of the Sacred Heart, July 3, 1982;[122] Address to the Teams of Our Lady, September 23, 1982;[123] Address to the Participants in a Symposium on the Pastoral Care of the Family in Europe, November 26, 1982;[124] Address to the Participants in the Congress of the Pro-Life Movement, December 3, 1982;[125] Address to the Participants of the First Plenary Session of the Pontifical Council for the Family, May 30, 1983;[126] Address to the Priest Participants at a Seminar of Study on "Responsible Parenthood", September 17, 1983;[127] Address to the Participants to the Seventh International Congress on the Family, November 7, 1983;[128] Address to the Participants in a Course on Responsible Parenthood, March 1, 1984;[129] Working Meeting with the Roman Clergy on the Pastoral Care of the Family, March 22, 1984;[130] Homily on the Occasion of the Jubilee of Families, March 25, 1984;[131] Address at

[116] Ibid., 2.2, pp. 320–23; *Enchiridion Familiae,* 3.2343–46.
[117] Ibid., 2.2, pp. 1030–35; *Enchiridion Familiae,* 3.2421–31.
[118] Ibid., 3.1 (1980), pp. 191–95; *Enchiridion Familiae,* 3.2521–28.
[119] Ibid., 3.2, pp. 1083–87; *Enchiridion Familiae,* 3.2922–28.
[120] Ibid., 4.1 (1981), pp. 80–85; *Enchiridion Familiae,* 4.3009–16.
[121] Ibid., 4.1, pp. 1092–1101; *Enchiridion Familiae,* 4.3122–33.
[122] Ibid., 5.3 (1982), pp. 5–8; *Enchiridion Familiae,* 4.3599–3604.
[123] Ibid., 5.3, pp. 540–50; *Enchiridion Familiae,* 4.3699–3715.
[124] Ibid., 5.3, pp. 1456–60; *Enchiridion Familiae,* 4.3776–83.
[125] Ibid., 5.3, pp. 1509–13; *Enchiridion Familiae,* 4.3792–94.
[126] Ibid., 6.1 (1983), 1405–10; *Enchiridion Familiae,* 5.3918–25.
[127] Ibid., 6.2, pp. 561–64; *Enchiridion Familiae,* 5.3939–44.
[128] Ibid., 6.2, pp. 1007–11; *Enchiridion Familiae,* 5.3981–86.
[129] Ibid., 7.1 (1984), pp. 580–84; *Enchiridion Familiae,* 5.4032–38.
[130] Ibid., 7.1, pp. 730–34; *Enchiridion Familiae,* 5.4038–44.
[131] Ibid., 7.1, pp. 766–72; *Enchiridion Familiae,* 5.4044–54.

the Meeting with the Families of the Entire World in the "Aula, Paul VI", March 25, 1984;[132] Address at the Meeting with the Families of the Schoenstatt Movement, April 27, 1984;[133] Address to the Plenary Session of the Pontifical Council for the Family, May 26, 1984;[134] Address to the Participants in Two Congresses on Marriage and Family: Responsible Parenthood Requires Dialogue between Science, Faith, and Theology, June 8, 1984;[135] Address to the Symposium of the Center of Studies and Research for the Natural Regulation of Fertility, June 5, 1987;[136] Address to the Participants in the Fourth International Congress of Africa and Europe for the Family, March 14, 1988;[137] Address to the Second International Congress of Moral Theology, "*Humanae vitae:* 20 Years Later", November 28, 1988;[138] etc.

6. Finally, the Pope frequently provides a *catechesis on the family in his addresses to cardinals and bishops, to bishops making their "ad limina" visits or to agencies of the Curia.* Thus, for instance: Homily to the Conference of Italian Bishops, May 15, 1979;[139] Allocution to the Bishops of the United States, October 5, 1979;[140] Address to the Bishops of Argentina, October 28, 1979;[141] Address to a Group of Venezuelan Bishops on Their *ad Limina* Visit, November 15, 1979;[142] Address to the Judges and Officials of the Ecclesiastical Tribunals, December 13, 1979;[143] Address to Cardinals and Prelates of the Roman Curia, December 22, 1979;[144] Address to the Seventeenth General Assembly of Italian Bishops, May 29, 1980;[145] Address to the Cardinals and Prelates of the Roman Curia, December 22, 1980;[146] Address to the Tribunal

[132] Ibid., 7.1, pp. 781–86; *Enchiridion Familiae,* 5.4055–63.

[133] Ibid., 7.1, pp. 1130–32; *Enchiridion Familiae,* 5.4073–75.

[134] Ibid., 7.1, pp. 1501–4; *Enchiridion Familiae,* 5.4086–93.

[135] Ibid., 7.1, pp. 1637–42; *Enchiridion Familiae,* 5.4116–22.

[136] *Enchiridion Familiae,* 5.4682–86.

[137] *Enchiridion Familiae,* 5.4753–57.

[138] In *"Humanae vitae": 20 anni dopo (Atti del II Congresso Internazionale di Teologia Morale (Roma 9–12 novembre 1988)* (Milan: Edizioni Ares, 1989), pp. 7–12 (Italian text), pp. 13–18 (English text); *Enchiridion Familiae,* 5.4919–30.

[139] *Insegnamenti di Giovanni Paolo,* 2.1 (1979), pp. 1128–29; *Enchiridion Familiae,* 3.2318–19.

[140] Ibid., 2.2, pp. 629ff.; *Enchiridion Familiae,* 3.2375–78.

[141] Ibid., 2.2, pp. 979–83; *Enchiridion Familiae,* 3.2410–14.

[142] Ibid., 2.2, pp. 1172–74; *Enchiridion Familiae,* 3.2449–51.

[143] Ibid., 2.2, pp. 1393–95; *Enchiridion Familiae,* 3.2475–76.

[144] Ibid., 2.2, pp. 1492–93; *Enchiridion Familiae,* 3.2484–87.

[145] Ibid., 3.1 (1980), pp. 1509–12; *Enchiridion Familiae,* 3.2682–87.

[146] Ibid., 3.2, pp. 1773–74; *Enchiridion Familiae,* 3.2988–90.

of the Sacred Roman Rota, January 24, 1981;[147] Address to the Diplomatic Corps, January 16, 1982;[148] Address to the Members of the Tribune of the Sacred Roman Rota, May 28, 1982;[149] Address to the Pastors and Clergy of Rome, February 17, 1983;[150] Address to the Canadian Bishops on Their *ad Limina* Visit, April 28, 1983;[151] Address to a Group of Bishops of the United States on Their *ad Limina* Visit, September 24, 1983;[152] Address to the Dioceses of Ancona and Osimo, September 24, 1983;[153] Address to the Bishops of Mexico on Their *ad Limina* Visit, October 1, 1983;[154] Address to the Bishops of Panama on Their *ad Limina* Visit, November 17, 1983;[155] Address to the Bishops of Puerto Rico on Their *ad Limina* Visit, November 24, 1983;[156] Address to the Bishops of Colombia on Their *ad Limina* Visit, June 11, 1985;[157] etc.

B. *Some contents of particular relevance*

Now it seems useful to emphasize some specific aspects which, since they pertain to the central truths of the Magisterium on the family, which has already been frequently repeated, have particular nuances that help us understand these truths in their richness and to set them forth in a lively and attractive way. We will follow the usual order of an organic treatment of marriage: its intrinsic reality according to God's plan; what its being entails for right moral conduct (and the light that this sheds, at times, on morality in general); the spirituality of the family; the pastoral care of the family; the defense of the family.

1. *The continuity of the Magisterium on the family, a title of glory for the Church:* "With legitimate pride," the Holy Father said at Cebu in the

---

[147] Ibid., 4.1 (1981), pp. 148–55; *Enchiridion Familiae*, 4.3017–26.

[148] Ibid., 5.1 (1982), pp. 123–25; *Enchiridion Familiae*, 4.3437–45.

[149] Ibid., 5.1, pp. 243–49; *Enchiridion Familiae*, 4.3435–62.

[150] Ibid., 6.1 (1983), pp. 446–50; *Enchiridion Familiae*, 5.3890–92.

[151] Ibid., 6.1, pp. 1082–87; *Enchiridion Familiae*, 5.3909–15.

[152] Ibid., 6.2, pp. 617–24; *Enchiridion Familiae*, 5.3944–56.

[153] Ibid., 6.2, pp. 632–35.

[154] Ibid., 6.2, pp. 688–93; *Enchiridion Familiae*, 5.3957–60.

[155] Ibid., 6.2, pp. 1106–11; *Enchiridion Familiae*, 5.3996.

[156] Ibid., 6.2, pp. 1170–74; *Enchiridion Familiae*, 5.4015–16.

[157] Ibid., 8.1 (1985), pp. 1767–72; *Enchiridion Familiae*, 5.4282–85.

Philippines, "one can state that whatever the Church teaches today on marriage and the family has been her constant teaching in fidelity to Christ." And he summed up the principal matters:

> The Catholic Church has consistently taught—and I repeat here with the conviction that springs from my office as chief Pastor and Teacher—that *marriage was established by God;* that marriage is a covenant of love between one man and one woman; that the bond uniting husband and wife is by God's will indissoluble; that marriage between Christians is a sacrament symbolizing the union of Christ and his Church; and that marriage must be open to the transmission of human life.[158]

■ A similar teaching is set forth on different occasions, for example, in the address given on the occasion of the day of the family: this time within the perspective of an enumeration of the values proper to marriage: "These values are love, fidelity, mutual help, indissolubility, fertility in its full meaning, intimacy enriched by an openness to life, awareness of being the first and originating cell of society, etc."[159] Likewise, in an address given to the French bishops on March 28, 1992, he said: "I know that you have at heart the formation of Christian spouses in order to prepare engaged couples for marriage. Without forgetting the contribution of the human sciences, it is important to show that the meaning of the sacrament of marriage is based on Scripture, Tradition, and the Magisterium of the Church."[160]

2. *The greatest richness of man is the family:* "Over and above every intellectual or social activity, however exalted, man finds his full development, his integral realization, his nonsubstitutable richness in the family. Here, truly, more than in any other area of his life, *is man's destiny at stake."*[161] For this reason, in Brazil, he stressed that not giving to the family all the attention that it deserves, perhaps because other

[158] Homily at the Mass for Families in the Airport of Lhung, Cebu; *Insegnamenti di Giovanni Paolo II,* 4.1 (1981), p. 409; *Enchiridion Familiae,* 4.3048.

[159] Homily and Address on the "Day of the Family"; *Insegnamenti di Giovanni Paolo II,* 3.2 (1980), p. 856; *Enchiridion Familiae,* 3.2851.

[160] The text of this address has not yet been published in the *Insegnamenti di Giovanni Paolo II.* At the time of this writing, volumes in that series end with the volume for 1990, i.e., volume 13.2.

[161] Address to the Cardinals and Prelates of the Roman Curia, December 22, 1980; *Insegnamenti di Giovanni Paolo II,* 3.2 (1980), p. 1773; *Enchiridion Familiae,* 3.2988.

things seem more urgent, would be "an error which we will have reason to repent of in the future".162

■ Again, at Chihuahua, on May 10, 1990, he made it clear that "the greatness and the responsibility of the family consist in the fact that it is the *first community of life and love*, the first environment in which man can learn to love and to find himself loved, not only by other persons but also and above all by God. Thus it is your task, Christian parents, to form and treasure a hearth where the profound identity of your children can germinate and mature: *to be children of God*."163

He developed this in an address to the prolife movement on November 15, 1991, when he said: "After having been welcomed, the child must be educated, guarded, and fostered in his total development, in such a way that he will be able to attain to the human maturity obligatory for him. Man, in fact, cannot succeed in knowing truly who he is and will thus become for himself an insoluble mystery, unless he learns to love and know that he is loved. Therefore, what is required is a common commitment to a human ecology, that is, a commitment to create, with the help of all, an environment favorable to the person and to his development. . . . The first and nonsubstitutable structure for achieving this is certainly the family: in its bosom man has his first and most determining experiences and receives the first and most valid teachings regarding the truth and the good, and learns what it means to love and be loved."

3. *The grandeur of conjugal love is fragile, and only union with God can preserve it:* in an address made on the Day of the Family (October 12, 1980), recalling what had been said in the synod, the Holy Father commented:

A fact emerging from the various experiences presented is the awareness, which can be noted in the words of all, that authentic love is the key for solving all the problems, even the most dramatic. . . . The way out is always and only love: a love stronger than death. Human love, however, is fragile and in danger: explicitly or implicitly all people have recognized this. Love, in order to survive, must transcend itself.

---

162 Homily at the Mass for Families in the Aterro do Flamingo, Rio de Janeiro; *Insegnamenti di Giovanni Paolo II*, 3.2 (1980), p. 15; *Enchiridion Familiae*, 3.2722.
163 *Insegnamenti di Giovanni Paolo II*, 13.1 (1990), p. 1204.

Only a love that encounters God can avoid the risk of becoming lost along the way.[164]

■ He put these same ideas into the form of a prayer in an Address to the Polish Faithful on July 26, 1990: "Let us not cease praying for our Polish families, that they may be strong in God, even when every kind of human weakness accompanies them. Pray that our family be strong in God. That it be strong from the beginning, from its foundations, from the time of engagement. Pray that it be strong in its indissolubility, in its union, in its love, in its conjugal fidelity unto death. Pray that it be strong in the service of new human life, which is a great gift of God and demands great responsibility. In this area during recent times much has been wrecked, many things have been distorted. . . . There is need to reconstitute the economy. This is a matter of justice. It is the basis, the foundation of life and also of the family. But this is not enough. There is need at this time to reconstitute that other economy which is called the morality of the family. To reconstitute the love which is responsible for indissolubility and for the life conceived in the mother's womb."[165]

In his homily to families at Kinshasa, he insisted on the same idea, describing in this manner the way the love of spouses can become strong: "A union of hearts! The nuances which distinguish the love of husband and wife are many. Neither can demand to be loved in the same way in which he or she loves. It is most important, for each party, to give up secret reproaches that separate their hearts. . . . It is a sharing in common that brings unity, in joys and even more so in sufferings. But it is above all in their common love for their children where hearts must be united. A union of minds and wills! . . . Finally, the union of their souls reaches its culminating point when they are united to God! Each of the spouses must keep for himself or herself moments to be alone with God, 'heart to heart', at a time when the other spouse is not a primary preoccupation. This personal life of the soul with God, which is indispensable, far from excluding a sharing of the whole conjugal and family life in common, stimulates Christian spouses to search for God together, to discover together His will and to fulfill it with the light and the energies they have found in God himself."[166]

---

[164] Homily and Address on the "Day of the Family"; *Insegnamenti di Giovanni Paolo II, 3.2* (1980), p. 855; *Enchiridion Familiae,* 3.2851.

[165] *Insegnamenti di Giovanni Paolo II,* 13.2 (1990), pp. 153–54.

[166] Homily at the Mass for Families, Kinshasa; *Insegnamenti di Giovanni Paolo II,* 3.1 (1980), p. 1078; *Enchiridion Familiae,* 3.2651.

And the theme recurs: "Divine love penetrates that human love, giving it a new dimension: it renders it profound, pure, generous; it develops it towards fullness, nobility, spirituality; it also makes it ready for sacrifices and mortifications and at the same time gives it the way to produce peace and joy as its fruit."[167] "As Christians, [spouses] love one another with a human heart but at the same time, I want to say, they love one another with the heart of Christ and in the heart of Christ. . . . It is necessary to discover in the person loved the image of God impressed in him, if one wants there to be a love without end for him."[168]

4. *Fidelity and fruitfulness are the two signs of true love:* this is also a constant teaching. Two values are constitutive of true

conjugal love. The first of these is the value of the person which is expressed in absolute mutual fidelity until death: the fidelity of the husband to his wife and of the wife to her husband. A consequence of this affirmation of the value of the person, which is expressed in the reciprocal relation between husband and wife, must be respect also for the personal value of new life, that is, of the child, from the very first moment of his conception.[169]

He repeated this in other words at the airport of Lhung in Cebu, the Philippines:

By making them [our first parents] male and female, God established the complementarity of the sexes, for a man leaves his father and his mother in order to be joined to his wife in that union of love that permeates all levels of human existence. This union of love enables man and woman to grow together and to care properly for their children. The union that makes them one cannot be broken by any human authority; it is permanently at the service of the children and of the spouses themselves. Thus the love between a man and a woman in marriage is a love that is both faithful and fruitful.[170]

[167] Address to the World Congress on the Family; *Insegnamenti di Giovanni Paolo II,* 4.1 (1981), p. 1094; *Enchiridion Familiae,* 4.3122–23.

[168] *Insegnamenti di Giovanni Paolo II,* 12.1 (1989), 1089–90.

[169] Homily at the Church of the Most Holy Name of Jesus; *Insegnamenti di Giovanni Paolo II,* 1 (1978), p. 457; *Enchiridion Familiae,* 3.2251.

[170] Homily at the Mass for Families at the Airport of Lhung, Cebu; *Insegnamenti di Giovanni Paolo II,* 4.1 (1981), p. 412; *Enchiridion Familiae,* 4.3051.

And, in a challenging way, he said to the Teams of Our Lady: "You must not limit God's ambitions for you; how could love be sustained if it no longer reflects, by means of your fidelity and fertility, the holiness of its source?"[171]

■ Therefore, *fidelity is a manifestation of the dignity of man:* "The definitive character of fidelity in marriage, which many today do not seem to understand any longer, is an expression of the unconditioned dignity of man. One cannot live only by 'trial'; one cannot die only by 'trial'; and one cannot love only by 'trial,' by accepting a person only by 'trial' and only for a limited time."[172]

Therefore, in his address to the members of the Roman Rota on January 24, 1981, he showed that its first duty in defending man is to safeguard the unity of marriage, without falsifying indissolubility by means of "easy" concessions regarding the nullity of marriage. The Church, in antiquity, healed the family by succeeding in overcoming the mentality of divorce; she must now struggle to do the same. We must not forget that "every protection of the lawful family always favors the person; while onesided preoccupations in favor of the individual can end up by harming the human person himself, in addition to harming marriage and the family, which are the goods of both the person and society."[173] At Kinshasa, the Pope wanted to recall that "the monogamistic and personalist concept of the human couple, far from being a western attitude, is an absolutely original revelation, which bears with it God's seal, and which must be even more profoundly understood today."[174]

In addition, *true love is inseparable from an openness to the gift of life:* "God, in his eternal design, has united the fundamental duty of the family—which is the *gift of life* offered by the parents, by the husband and the wife, to their children, to each new child—to their *vocation to love,* to participate in that love that comes from God, because He Himself is

---

[171] Address to the Teams of Our Lady, September 23, 1982; *Insegnamenti di Giovanni Paolo II,* 5.3 (1982), p. 548; *Enchiridion Familiae,* 4.3712.

[172] Homily at the Mass for Families at the "Butzweiler Hof" Stadium of Cologne; *Insegnamenti di Giovanni Paolo II,* 3.2 (1980), p. 1192; *Enchiridion Familiae,* 3.2950.

[173] Address to the Tribunal of the Sacred Roman Rota, January 24, 1981; *Insegnamenti di Giovanni Paolo II,* 4.1 (1981), pp. 150–53; *Enchiridion Familiae,* 4.3025.

[174] Homily at the Mass for Families, Kinshasa; *Insegnamenti di Giovanni Paolo II* 3.1 (1980), p. 1076; *Enchiridion Familiae,* 3.2647–48.

love."[175] He repeated this at Velletri in the following words: the family "is the place of love and of life, thus the place where love generates life, since each of these realities could not be authentic if the one were not accompanied by the other".[176]

5. *The true meaning of responsible parenthood* is not separable from the practice of virtue, nor from the light that the spouses' call to holiness casts upon marriage. The Holy Father made this doctrine explicit in an address to the delegates of the "Centre de Liaison des Equipes de Recherche" (CLER) and of the "Federation Internationale d'Action Familiale" (FIDAF) on November 3, 1979. After having affirmed that the sacrament, as a participation in the love of Christ for the Church, demands the absolute fidelity of the spouses, he added:

> It is also from this perspective [of marriage as a sacrament participating in Christ's love for His Church] that *responsible parenthood* must be seen. In this area the spouses, the parents, are able to find a certain number of problems that cannot be solved without a deep love, which includes the power of continence. The two virtues, love and continence, require a common decision on the part of the spouses and their submission to the teaching of the Church.

He considers this matter from three different angles. One must not obscure the teaching of the Church, as this has been set forth by the Council and by *Humanae vitae*. One must "without ceasing direct oneself to the ideal of conjugal relations [set forth by the Council and *Humanae vitae*], relations that are chaste and respect the nature and finality of the conjugal act, and that in no way are based on a concession, more or less full, more or less recognized, to the principle and practice of contraceptive methods". Moreover, there are many elements for reflection, rooted in the natural order, that can help the spouses to form for themselves convictions that will encourage them to obey with joy. For example,

> Can we not see that man's nature must be subordinated to morality? Have we thought of the impact that this refusal of children, repeated unceasingly, can have on the psychology of the parents, who carry

---

[175] Homily and Address on the "Day of the Family", *Insegnamenti di Giovanni Paolo II*, 3.2 (1980), p. 844; *Enchiridion Familiae*, 3.2840.

[176] Homily at Velletri; *Insegnamenti di Giovanni Paolo II*, 3.2 (1980), p. 559; *Enchiridion Familiae*, 3.2787.

written within their nature the desire for children? And what can we think of an education of youth in sexuality, which would not put them on guard against the search for immediate pleasure and selfishness, dissociated from the responsibility of conjugal love and of procreation?

Finally, one finds entailed in the right understanding of responsible parenthood, in a very radical way, the defense of human life itself: in fact, "the widespread practice of contraception characteristic of artificial means leads to abortion, since both are situated—certainly at different levels—in the same line of fear of children, of a refusal of life, of a lack of respect for the act and fruit of the union between husband and wife such as it is willed by the Creator of nature."[177]

In addition to clarifying the value of responsible parenthood, the Holy Father has been concerned, on other occasions, to illustrate the meaning of the generosity that is its proper characteristic. In fact, "the great danger for family life, in the midst of any society whose idols are pleasure, comfort and independence, lies in the fact that people close their hearts and become selfish. The fear of making permanent commitments can change the mutual love of husband and wife into two loves of self—two loves existing side by side, until they end in separation." The choice of the number of children, therefore, must be inspired not by selfishness but by generosity:

> Reflecting upon this matter before God, with the graces drawn from the Sacrament, and guided by the teaching of the Church, parents will remind themselves that it is certainly less serious to deny their children certain comforts or material advantages than to deprive them of the presence of brothers and sisters, who could help them to grow in humanity and to realize the beauty of life at all its ages and in all its variety.[178]

He repeated this to the bishops of the United States on their *ad limina* visit: "The Church encourages couples to be generous and hopeful, to realize that parenthood is a privilege and that each child bears witness to the couple's own love for each other, to their generosity and to their openness to God. They must be encouraged to see the child as an enrichment of their marriage and a gift of God to themselves and to

---

[177] Address to the Delegates of CLER and FIDAF; *Insegnamenti di Giovanni Paolo II*, 2.2 (1979), pp. 1033–35; *Enchiridion Familiae*, 3.2426–29.

[178] Homily at the Mass on the Capitol Mall of Washington, D.C.; *Insegnamenti di Giovanni Paolo II*, 2.2 (1979), pp. 701–3; *Enchiridion Familiae*, 3.2381–82.

their other children."[179] He said the same thing quite concisely to some Irish bishops: "Marriage must include openness to the gift of children. Generous openness to accept children from God as the gift to their love is the mark of the Christian couple."[180]

Fatherhood and motherhood must always be seen in the context of "God's design for the family and for the creation of new life"; a design that one finds

> impressed not only on the human body but also on the human spirit. How sad it is to note that the spirit of so many men and women has drifted away from this divine plan! For so many men and women of our time new life is looked on as a threat and something to be feared; others, intoxicated with the technical possibilities offered by scientific progress, wish to manipulate the process of the transmission of life and, following only subjective criteria of personal satisfaction, are prepared even to destroy newly conceived life.

Therefore, the presentation of natural methods themselves must

> never be reduced to a question of presenting one or other biological method, much less to any watering down of the challenging call of the infinite God. . . . Your task is above all to lead the men and women of our time to that true communion of life, love and grace which is the rich ideal of Christian marriage, appreciating the essential inseparability of the unitive and procreative aspects of the conjugal act, [as *Humanae vitae*, which has become] a prophetic Encyclical, [taught].[181]

6. *The difficulties in understanding the truth do not come from truth itself, but from concupiscence:*

> You can be certain of this: when your teaching is faithful to the Magisterium of the Church, you are not teaching something that men and women are not able to understand. Even men and women of today. This teaching, which you make resonate in their ears, is *already* written in their hearts. . . . The *true* difficulty is that the heart of men and

---

[179] Address to a Group of Bishops of the United States on Their *ad Limina* Visit, September 24, 1983; *Insegnamenti di Giovanni Paolo II*, 6.2 (1983), p. 634; *Enchiridion Familiae*, 5.3948–49. See also the Address to the Mexican Bishops on Their *ad Limina* Visit, *Insegnamenti di Giovanni Paolo II*, 12.1 (1989), pp. 424–30.

[180] Homily at the Mass for Laypeople and Families, Limerick, *Insegnamenti di Giovanni Paolo II*, 2.2 (1979), p. 496; *Enchiridion Familiae*, 3.2366–67.

[181] Address to the International Congress of Africa and Europe for the Family, January 15, 1981; *Insegnamenti di Giovanni Paolo II*, 4.1 (1981), pp. 83–84; *Enchiridion Familiae*, 4.3014–15.

women is accustomed to concupiscence: and concupiscence inclines freedom to refuse consent to the true demands of conjugal love. It would be a very grave error to conclude from this that the norm taught by the Church is in itself only an "ideal" which must then be adapted, proportioned, graduated to what are called the concrete possibilities of man: according to "a weighing of the various goods in question." But what are the "concrete possibilities of man"? and *who is the man of whom this is said?* Of the man *dominated by concupiscence* or the man *redeemed by Christ?*[182]

■ One must, in fact, never forget "that it is the one and the same Spirit who enlightens the Pastors of the Church when they teach the doctrine of Christ, with the authority which is proper to them, and who inhabits the heart of spouses so that they may realize God's plan in their marriage."[183] This is definite: "The grace of the Holy Spirit makes possible for man what is impossible for him left only to his own resources. Therefore, it is necessary, in order to support spouses in their spiritual live, to invite them to have frequent recourse to the sacraments of Confession and the Eucharist so that they may constantly return and be unceasingly converted to the truth of their conjugal love."[184]

7. *When the life of the conceived human being is not respected, it no longer makes sense to speak of human dignity.* The Holy Father, on his journey in Spain, said: "It is never possible to legitimate the murder of an innocent person. To do so would threaten the very foundation of society. What sense would it make to speak of the dignity of man, of his fundamental rights, if the innocent is not protected and if, in addition, public or private services are provided to destroy defenseless human lives?"[185] He has spoken with the same vigor on this matter throughout the world.

---

[182] Address to the Participants in a Course on Responsible Parenthood, organized by the Center for Studies and Investigation into the Natural Regulation of Fertility of the University of the Sacred Heart and the John Paul II Institute for Studies on Marriage and Family; *Insegnamenti di Giovanni Paolo II,* 7.1 (1984), pp. 582–83; *Enchiridion Familiae,* 5.4032–33, 4035–36.

[183] Address to the Participants in a Symposium on the Pastoral Care of the Family in Europe; *Insegnamenti di Giovanni Paolo II,* 5.3 (1982), p. 1458; *Enchiridion Familiae,* 4.3777.

[184] Address to Priest Participants at a Seminar of Study on "Responsible Parenthood", organized by the Center of Studies and Investigation into the Regulation of Fertility of the University of the Sacred Heart and the John Paul II Institute for Studies on Marriage and Family; *Insegnamenti di Giovanni Paolo II,* 6.2 (1983), p. 564; *Enchiridion Familiae,* 5.3943.

[185] Homily at the Mass for Families, Madrid; *Insegnamenti di Giovanni Paolo II,* 5.3 (1982), no. 2, pars. 9 and 10; *Enchiridion Familiae,* 4.3755–56.

If one crushes man's right to life the moment in which he begins to be in the womb of his mother, one strikes indirectly at the entire moral order that serves to guarantee the inviolable goods of man. . . . The Church defends the right to life, not only for the sake of the majesty of the Creator who is the *first Giver* of this life, but also *for the sake of respecting the essential good of man,*

the Holy Father said in Poland at Nowy Targ.[186] Taking his starting point from another angle, he encouraged love of new life in a talk to young people in St. Peter's on January 3, 1979: "It is necessary to do everything possible in order that every human being, from the very beginning, from the moment of his conception, be wanted, waited for, seen as a particular value, unique and nonrepeatable"; the "yes" of the woman, at times accompanied by objective difficulties, "always implies an interior act of confidence in God and of trust in the new human being who must be born . . . ; we must never leave alone, especially if she is vacillating or doubtful, a woman who is preparing herself to bring a new human being to light, a new human being who will be for each one of us a new brother or sister."[187] He thus denounces the spread of a mentality opposed to life:

This antilife mentality, whatever be its intentions or preoccupations, is in itself and of itself inhuman and aberrant. The first duty for the whole society is to create a climate of welcoming life; this is a duty, within society, for each one according to his own responsibility; it is a duty for individual citizens, governors, legislators. A politics clearly in favor of life and of the dignity of woman, that collaborator with God in the gift of life.[188]

8. *Christian marriage will never be understood apart from the sacrament of marriage,* which "like all the sacraments is a disconcerting divine initiative in the heart of a human existence", as the Holy Father said in an address held on the occasion of the Day of the Family (October 12, 1980).[189] In fact, "what riches, what demands, what dynamism flow

---

[186] Homily at the Mass for Workers in the Airport of Nowy Targ; *Insegnamenti di Giovanni Paolo II,* 2.1 (1979), p. 1491; *Enchiridion Familiae,* 3.2325–26.

[187] Address to Young People in the Basilica of St. Peter, January 3, 1979; *Insegnamenti di Giovanni Paolo II,* 2.1 (1979), pp. 11 and 15; *Enchiridion Familiae,* 3.2261–62.

[188] Address to Pro-Life Movement, November 15, 1991.

[189] Homily and Address on the "Day of the Family", October 12, 1980; *Insegnamenti di*

from the sacrament when it is lived day by day in faith, in the image of the mutual gift of Christ and of His Church."[190] Therefore, it is necessary *to renew "the awareness of the sacrament* from which is born and on whose basis the Christian family is developed. We want *to awaken again the divine and at the same time human powers* which are found in it. We want, in a certain sense, to enter into the eternal plan of the Creator and Redeemer and to join, as He has joined, the mystery of life with the mystery of love; this", the Holy Father said at a Mass for families, "will be the work of the Synod."[191] Finally, we recall his constant insistence that spouses "believe in the power which this sacrament has to sanctify them" and to "overcome every difficulty".[192]

■ The Holy Father has given a rich description of sacramental grace: "Every sacrament implies a participation in the nuptial love of Christ for His Church. But in marriage the modality and the content of this participation are specific. The spouses participate in it insofar as they are spouses, two in one flesh, as a couple, to the point that the first and immediate effect of marriage ('res et sacramentum') is not supernatural grace itself but the Christian marriage bond, a communion of two persons typically Christian because it represents the mystery of the Incarnation and the mystery of His Covenant. And the content of the participation in Christ's life is specific: conjugal love entails a totality, where all the elements of the person enter in . . . ; it tends to a profoundly personal union which, above and beyond the union in one flesh, leads them to be of one heart and of one soul; it requires indissolubility and fidelity in the reciprocal and definitive gift of self, and it is open to fertility."[193]

The grace of marriage is efficacious: "also charism of spouses and parents, which is in you by means of the sacrament of marriage. Only

---

Giovanni Paolo II, 3.2 (1980), p. 858; *Enchiridion Familiae,* 3.2859.

[190] Address to the International Congress of the Teams of Our Lady, September 17, 1979; *Insegnamenti di Giovanni Paolo II,* 2.2 (1979), p. 321; *Enchiridion Familiae,* 3.2344.

[191] Homily and Address for the "Day of the Family"; *Insegnamenti di Giovanni Paolo II,* 3.2 (1980), pp. 845–46; *Enchiridion Familiae,* 3.2841–42.

[192] Cf. Homily at the Mass for Laypeople and Families, Limerick; *Insegnamenti di Giovanni Paolo II,* 2.2 (1979), p. 500; *Enchiridion Familiae,* 3.2364; Homily at the Mass for Families at the Airport of Lhung, Cebu; *Insegnamenti di Giovanni Paolo II,* 4.1 (1981), p. 413; *Enchiridion Familiae,* 4.3054–55.

[193] Address to the Delegates of the CLER and FIDAF; *Insegnamenti di Giovanni Paolo II,* 2.2 (1979), p. 1032; *Enchiridion Familiae,* 3.2425.

by relying on this, is full pardon possible; only by relying on this grace is your reconciliation and the resumption of your common journey possible. By means of the sacrament human love is renewed and revived and with it the identity and the authenticity of human promises. The charism of marriage is also the charism, the grace, and the gift of life."[194]

9. *Some matters relevant for fundamental moral.* In connection with his catechisis on marriage, the Holy Father has illustrated different truths, above all, respect for the divine law and the moral conscience. First of all, it seems worthwhile to record the following words on *conscience,* words that truly give light on the need to go out from an imperious subjectivism, which is the origin of not a few errors:

> God says to every man: "Welcome life conceived by your action! Don't let it be suppressed!" God speaks in this way with the voice of His commandments, with the voice of the Church. But He says this above all with *the voice of conscience.* The voice of human conscience. *This voice is unequivocal, notwithstanding how much is done to keep one from hearing it or suffocating it,* i.e., that man not hear this simple and clear voice of conscience.[195]

Also noteworthy are his teachings on the *divine law,* on its reality and on its role in man's life. In his Address to the Cardinals and Prelates of the Roman Curia of December 22, 1980, he said: "*God's law does not put man to death but exalts him,* and calls him to an extraordinary cooperation with Him in the mission and joy of responsible father-hood and motherhood."[196] And it succeeds in doing this because it does not work only from without but rather from within the human person; it guides him intelligently from without and fills him inwardly with divine power:

> "The law of God is perfect, it strengthens human minds . . . makes the simple man wise. The precepts of the Lord are just." The law of the Lord which must govern your conjugal and family life is the only way to true peace and joy. It is the school of true wisdom. . . . The Spirit writes in *your hearts* the law of God for marriage. It does not remain written only on the outside: in Sacred Scripture, in the documents of

---

[194] Homily at the Aeroclub of Maslow, June 3, 1991.
[195] Homily at the Mass in Terni; *Insegnamenti di Giovanni Paolo II,* 4.1 (1981), p. 720; *Enchiridion Familiae,* 4.3073.
[196] *Insegnamenti di Giovanni Paolo II,* 3.2 (1980), p. 1774; *Enchiridion Familiae,* 3.2989.

Tradition and of the Magisterium of the Church. It is written *within* you. This is the New and Eternal Covenant, of which the prophet spoke, which replaces the Old Covenant and gives once more its original splendor to the primitive Covenant with creative Wisdom, written in the humanity of every man and of every woman. *It is the Covenant of the Spirit, of which* St. Thomas says: "the new law is the very grace of the Holy Spirit" (*Summa Theologiae,* I–II, q. 109, a. 1).[197]

We cannot, finally, pass over the description of the law of charity in marriage, which the Holy Father made on the Day of the Family on October 12, 1980:

> The *love* that unites man and woman as spouses and parents is, at the same time, a *gift and a commandment.* Above all, the second reading for the liturgy of today says that love is a gift, the reading from the First Letter of John: "Love then consists in this: not that we have loved God, but that he has loved us and has sent his Son as an offering for our sins."[198] Therefore, love is thus a gift: "Love is of God; everyone who loves is begotten of God and has knowledge of God."[199] And, at the same time, love is a commandment; *it is the greatest of the commandments.* God gives it to man, and confides it to him as a task. He requires it of man. Christ responded to the question about the greatest of the commandments by saying: "You shall love. . . . "[200]

> This commandment is at the basis of the entire moral order. It is truly "the greatest". It is the key commandment. *To fulfill it* in the family means to respond to the gift of love which the spouses receive in the conjugal covenant: "if God has loved us so, we must have the same love for one another."[201] To fulfill the commandment of love means to carry out all the duties of the Christian family. In the end, everything comes down to this: fidelity and conjugal honesty, responsible parenthood and education. The "little Church", the domestic Church, signifies the family living in the spirit of the commandment of love, living its interior truth, its daily practice, its spiritual beauty and its power.

> The commandment of love has its own interior structure: "You shall love the Lord your God with your whole heart, your whole soul, your

---

[197] Homily at the Mass for Families, Madrid; *Insegnamenti di Giovanni Paolo II,* 5.3 (1982), p. 1077; *Enchiridion Familiae,* 4.3757–58.
[198] 1 Jn 4:10.
[199] 1 Jn 4:7.
[200] Mt 22:37.
[201] 1 Jn 4:11.

whole mind.... You shall love your neighbor as yourself."[202] *This structure of the commandment corresponds to the truth of love.* If God is loved above everything, then man also loves and is loved with all the fullness of love possible for him. If that inseparable structure, of which Christ's commandment speaks, is destroyed, then man's love will be severed from its most profound roots, it will lose its roots of fullness and of the truth which are essential for it.[203]

> ■ This is a passage truly rich in theological content, where we discover both the source of the divine law as an interior power—the gift of charity—the content proper to it, and the intimate structure of human love rooted in God (from whom man receives it as a gift), who guarantees its vitality.

10. The transcendence of *the vocation of the woman to motherhood and the grandeur of domestic work.* The Holy Father said in Ireland: "May Irish mothers, young women and girls not listen to those who tell them that working at a secular job, succeeding in a secular profession, is more important than the vocation of giving life and caring for this life as a mother."[204] The work of women in the domestic hearth

> is an *authentic professional work which merits to be recognized as such by society;* it is a work which demands in a wholly special way courage, responsibility, ingeniousness, and holiness. It is therefore necessary to help women become aware of this responsibility and of *all the gifts of femininity* which God has placed in them for the greater good of the family and of society.[205]

> Daily experience shows us that a family is ordinarily entrusted to a Christian wife, a family in which a living love of God abides, along with the practice of a sacramental life and of love towards the neighbor.[206]

And this refers not only to the work of the mother of the family, but also to that of *family collaborators,* whose work—in an address of March 29, 1979—the Holy Father justly and convincingly praised:

[202] Mt 22:37.

[203] Homily and Address on the "Day of the Family"; *Insegnamenti di Giovanni Paolo II,* 3.2 (1980), pp. 846–47; *Enchiridion Familiae,* 3.2843–44.

[204] Homily at the Mass for Laypeople and Families, Limerick; *Insegnamenti di Giovanni Paolo II,* 2.2 (1979), p. 500; *Enchiridion Familiae,* 3.2368.

[205] Address to the Participants in the Fifth International Congress of the Family; *Insegnamenti di Giovanni Paolo II,* 3.2 (1980), p. 1086; *Enchiridion Familiae,* 3.2927.

[206] Homily at Chihuahua; *Insegnamenti di Giovanni Paolo II,* 13.1 (1990), p. 1204.

Domestic work is an essential part of the good ordering of society and has an enormous influence on the collectivity; it demands a constant and total dedication, and therefore is a daily exercise in ascetics, which requires patience, self-control, perspicacity, creativity, a spirit of adaptation, courage in the face of the unexpected; it also contributes to producing income and riches, well-being and economic value. . . . It has a direct influence on the good development of the family. This is a great task, and might be said to be a mission, for which a preparation and adequate maturation are necessary in order to be competent in the various household activities, to order work reasonably, and to know the psychology of the family, to grasp the so-called "pedagogy of effort," which helps one better organize one's services and helps one exercise the necessary educational function.[207]

■ This is a work, moreover, that is particularly fitting for the talents of the woman who "has, generally speaking, a greater perspicacity and greater tact for knowing and solving the delicate problems of domestic and family life, the basis of the whole social life". But above all, a woman has greater generosity. The Holy Father encourages women to exercise this above all laws and legal duties: "No code prescribes that you smile! But you can give one; you can be the leaven of the goodness of the family."[208]

11. Regarding the *education of children,* among other things, the clarity with which he insisted, in a homily in Spain, on the role of public authority merits mention. He insisted that public authority "has a secondary task in this area and does not renounce its own rights when it regards itself at the service of the parents. On the contrary, this is precisely its grandeur: to defend and promote the free exercise of the educational rights [of parents]."[209] Also noteworthy is his strong condemnation of certain false, but widespread "pedagogies":

Responsible Christians and, especially, parents and the agents of the *mass-media* [must] . . . above all carry out their charge respecting the

[207] Address to Family Collaborators, in the Tenth Assembly of the Italian Association API–COLF; *Insegnamenti di Giovanni Paolo II,* 2.1 (1979), pp. 1021–22; *Enchiridion Familiae,* 3.2309–10.

[208] Ibid.; *Insegnamenti di Giovanni Paolo,* 2.1 (1979), pp. 1020–21; *Enchiridion Familiae,* 3.2308, 2311.

[209] Homily at the Mass for Families, Madrid; *Insegnamenti di Giovanni Paolo II,* 5.3 (1982), p. 1077; *Enchiridion Familiae,* 4.3756.

human growth of the child: the claim that they are maintaining toward him a position of "neutrality" and of letting him "discover himself" spontaneously conceals, under the appearance of respect for their personality, an attitude of dangerous disinterestedness.[210]

The educational activity of the family, in turn, touches the essential elements of the life of every person:

Families will put themselves at the service of life not only by welcoming it and by providing it with a continual education, but also by accepting the serious obligation, perhaps neglected at times, of helping adolescents and young people, above all, in grasping the vocational dimension of all existence, within the plan of God. . . . Parents will truly serve the life of their children, if they help them make a gift of their own existence, respecting their mature choices and fostering with joy every vocation, including the religious and priestly.[211]

■ It seems opportune here to recall some directions given about *sex education*. In its true sense, he said at Rio de Janeiro, it is necessary to promote "a full, serious, and deep education to true love, which is required far more than the much praised 'sex education'. A generous effort and courage are demanded for creating in society a fitting environment for realizing the Christian ideal, based on the values of unity, of fidelity, of indissolubility, of responsible fertility."[212] On another occasion, he emphasized that "the delicate responsibility for sex education belongs principally to the families, where an atmosphere of loving reverence will be conducive to a fully human and Christian understanding of the meaning of love and life."[213]

"The family must also be the environment in which young people are educated to the virtue of chastity. The family must be the first school of life for children, preparing them for personal responsibility in all its aspects, including those which concern matters of sexuality. The education to love, as a gift of oneself, is an indispensable premise for a clear and delicate sex education, which the parents are called upon to impart. God has willed that the gift of life should rise up from

[210] Message for the Thirteenth World Day of Social Communications, May 21, 1979; *Insegnamenti di Giovanni Paolo II*, 2.1 (1979), p. 1192.

[211] Address to the National Convention of Pastoral Care of the Family, April 28, 1990; *Insegnamenti di Giovanni Paolo II*, 13.1 (1990), p. 1056.

[212] Homily at the Mass for Families in the Aterro do Flamingo, Rio de Janeiro; *Insegnamenti di Giovanni Paolo II*, 3.2 (1980), p. 15; *Enchiridion Familiae*, 3.2723.

[213] Homily at the Mass for Families in the Airport of Lhung, Cebu; *Insegnamenti di Giovanni Paolo II*, 4.1 (1981), p. 415; *Enchiridion Familiae*, 4.3057.

this community of love which is marriage, and He wills that children know the nature of that gift in the climate of familial love."[214]

12. With respect to the *spirituality of the family and to the pastoral care of the family,* we will note the following. In the address, already many times noted, made on the occasion of the Day of the Family, the Pope put the essence of family spirituality in living the realities that are proper to it ("human love between the spouses and between parents and children, mutual understanding, pardon, mutual help and service, the education of children, work, joys and sufferings") under the influence of grace. In fact, "all these elements in Christian marriage are bound up with and as it were imbued with grace and the virtue of the sacrament and charity. *Therefore there is a specific form of living the Gospel within the framework of the family. To learn this and to actualize it is to live fully the spirituality of marriage and the family.*"[215] With respect to the pastoral care of the family, the Holy Father said to the clergy of Rome: "*The fundamental pastoral program* for the family is this: *to help the family to be itself,* to develop its own tasks, to discover its human and Christian identity, to discover its vocation."[216] Again, in a Homily to the Conference of Italian Bishops on May 15, 1979, he set forth *the two signs of an efficacious and intelligent pastoral program for the family; that it welcome life joyfully and that vocations flourish:* "When there is an efficacious and enlightened pastoral program for the family, just as it becomes normal that life is welcomed as a gift of God, so it is much easier for the voice of God to resound and for it to be heard more generously."[217] For the Pope, the family is also the place where one learns to pray, where prayer overflows into apostolic activity that is particularly efficacious:

Among the religious practices which the Church has at times recommended, I am pleased to note what Pope Paul VI has written about the family rosary: "It pleases us to think, and we sincerely hope for it, that when a meeting of the family becomes a time of prayer, the rosary may be its frequent and welcome expression" (*Marialis cultus,* 54; see *Familiaris consortio,* 61).[218]

---

[214] Homily at Chihuahua; *Insegnamenti di Giovanni Paolo II,* 13.1 (1990), p. 1207.

[215] Homily and Address on the "Day of the Family"; *Insegnamenti di Giovanni Paolo II,* 3.2 (1980), pp. 858–59; *Enchiridion Familiae,* 3.2859–60.

[216] Address to the Pastors and Clergy of Rome; *Insegnamenti di Giovanni Paolo II,* 6.1 (1983), p. 448; *Enchiridion Familiae,* 5.3891–92.

[217] *Insegnamenti di Giovanni Paolo II,* 2.1 (1979), p. 1128; *Enchiridion Familiae,* 3.2318.

[218] Address to the Bishops of the Philippines on Their *ad Limina* Visit, November 19, 1990; *Insegnamenti di Giovanni Paolo II,* 13.2 (1990), p. 1241.

Prayer changes us, and by doing so changes the world. The public and common prayer of the people of God is an essential function of the Church and is learned in the family. "Where two or three are gathered in my name," Jesus says, "there I am in their midst" (Matt. 18:20). When the members of the same family pray together, Jesus strengthens their union by His presence.[219]

The future of the Church passes by way of the family where the Gospel lives and is transmitted, because all Christian families must convert themselves into evangelizing forces for all other families. Above all, you, Christian fathers and mothers, together with your children, have the task of announcing with joy and firmness the "Good News" to the family, as the foundation of society and as the "domestic Church."[220]

Today we experience, in different countries of Europe and of the world, but of Europe above all, a crisis, a certain de-christianization of marriage and of the family. Much has been written about this, many analyses of human love have been given. All this is useful, but if we wish to change the climate, to change the reality of marriage and of the family of the modern world, this must be done through families, through marriage, through couples. Christian spouses can convert other spouses, other couples, other families, making them Christian. This form of the apostolate is providential and quite actual today. Naturally, the first step is to discover the divine plan of marriage, of the family, and this plan is most rich, stupendously so. This divine plan is also profoundly human, making our humanity, our human personality, and our being as men and women increase. All this increases because God is the Creator and if we find ourselves within His plan we find growth, we find progress, we find perfection. Now, when there are spouses who have found this divine plan and have been able to put it into practice in their own lives, then they can become apostles of other couples, of other families. And I wish this for you.[221]

13. We conclude with some words on the essentiality and the *dynamism of the family in social life,* pronounced by the Pope in his Homily at the Mass for Families at the "Butzweiler Hof" Stadium of Cologne on November 15, 1980:

---

[219] Homily in Ruanda, September 9, 1990; *Insegnamenti di Giovanni Paolo II,* 13.2 (1990), p. 552.

[220] Homily at Curacao, May 13, 1990; *Insegnamenti di Giovanni Paolo II,* 13.1 (1990), p. 1292.

[221] Address to the Parish of All Saints, March 3, 1991.

Marriage and the family are today more important than ever. They are the living cells for renewing society, fountains of energy for saying "yes" so that life can become more fully human, and a security net that brings strength and unity, emerging, as it were, from the depths of the sea. Let us not let this net be destroyed. The state and society invite their own ruin the moment they do not promote actively and protect the good of marriage and of the family.[222]

The family, therefore, has priority in every serious social action. "When the family is not able to carry out the duties which nature itself, and God the Creator, have entrusted to it, the forces of social organizations, and even of the Church, are in danger of being frustrated. . . . To sustain, foster, defend the family by means of adequate choices of political science, is to guarantee the very future of the nation."[223] And once more:

The more faithfully marriage is preserved and is allowed to bear fruit by reason of its sacramental grace, the more fully couples and families, and therefore society itself, will reflect the loving presence of God in their midst. . . . To give back to the family reasons for having confidence in itself, in its own riches of nature and of grace, in the mission that God has confided to it, is indeed a supreme form of love.[224]

■ This requires the collaboration of everyone, since its realization is not "optional", but essential for the very life of man in society. "The society that is wounded in its families does not have a future. For this reason the new Europe, which all of us long for, will do well to provide great care for the safety and promotion of this fundamental cell of society, in the light of its own true traditions, which are profoundly permeated with Christian values."[225] "We are all called to promote an environment favorable to the family, and, therefore, to motherhood and fatherhood, an environment where, increasingly, the optimal conditions can be found for bringing it about that the family can develop its own riches: fidelity, fecundity, the intimacy enriched

[222] *Insegnamenti di Giovanni Paolo II*, 3.2 (1980), pp. 1191–92; *Enchiridion Familiae*, 3.2948–49.

[223] Address at Lucca, September 23, 1989; *Insegnamenti di Giovanni Paolo II*, 12.2 (1989), p. 614.

[224] Address to the Bishops of the Philippines on Their *ad Limina* Visit, November 19, 1990; *Insegnamenti di Giovanni Paolo II*, 13.2 (1990), p. 1239.

[225] Address to the Second European Conference on Families, September 28, 1990; *Insegnamenti di Giovanni Paolo II*, 13.2 (1990), p. 759.

by an openness to others, etc. It is necessary that the family become the center of every social policy." [226]

" 'Honor your father and your mother.' In the Law of God, in the Decalogue, this commandment immediately follows the first three, which have to do with man's relationship to God. It is the first of the commandments which unite our relationship to God (the commandments of the first table of the law) with our relationship to men (the commandments of the second table, from the fourth to the tenth). This alone indicates already the key importance of the family. The commandment which obliges man to honor his parents, his father and his mother, assures the well being of the foundation of the human community. The family, in fact, is at the basis of every human community and of every society."[227]

[226] Address to the Pro-Life Movement, November 15, 1991.
[227] Homily at the Aeroclub of Maslow.

Chapter Nine

THE POSTCONCILIAR EPISCOPAL TEACHING ON MARRIAGE: GENERAL LINES OF THOUGHT

In chapter 1, we emphasized the Magisterium of the bishops as a form of the ordinary Magisterium, having value within the scope of their proper jurisdiction. The Council and the new Code of Canon Law are particularly concerned with this, clarifying some characteristics of this Magisterium. We will look briefly at these precisions and make reference to some documents of special interest for marriage and the family, above all some issued on the occasion of *Humanae vitae.*

1. The Unique Characteristics, Modality, and Scope of the Obligatory Nature of the Episcopal Magisterium

Although the Magisterium of the bishops is not of itself infallible, it is a manifestation of the authentic Magisterium of the Church, within the scope of its proper jurisdiction.

Vatican Council II, in addition to confirming the traditional doctrine on the Magisterium of the bishops, gives some indications on the modality of its exercise, particularly in its collegial form, within different territorial circumstances.[1] These indications, made more precise in the motu proprio *Ecclesiae sanctae* of August 6, 1966, have been definitively specified in the new Code of Canon Law promulgated

[1] In the Dogmatic Constitution *Lumen gentium* November 21, 1964 (no. 25) and in the decree *Christus Dominus,* October 28, 1965 (nos. 11–12 and 36–38).

by Pope John Paul II on January 25, 1983. We will give its most salient features in what follows.

> ■ Here we will not discuss the *solemn* Magisterium of the bishops (in an ecumenical council). And we note that their ordinary Magisterium becomes the ordinary and infallible Magisterium when, in communion with themselves and with the Roman Pontiff, they teach as definitive a doctrine pertaining to faith or to morals (cf. *Lumen gentium*, no. 25).

"The bishops in communion with the head and members of the college, whether as individuals or gathered in conferences of bishops or in particular councils, are authentic teachers and instructors of the faith for the faithful entrusted to their care."[2] This canon, in relationship with canons 381, 439 to 446, and 447 to 459, specifies what is said in number 25 of *Lumen gentium* and in the corresponding paragraphs of the decree *Christus Dominus*. At their base, one can note, with respect to the value and to the general characteristics of the Magisterium of the bishops, the following:

a. The principal concern is with the *simple ordinary (or authentic) Magisterium* that, although it does not directly bind in faith, demands a religious obedience (assent) (*obsequium religiosum*) of the mind and will (can. 753, at the end). In this, the Magisterium of the bishops is like the rest of the authentic Magisterium (cf. can. 752) and entails for the faithful the precise obligation of avoiding every doctrine contrary to it (cf. can. 750, at the end).

b. It is a Magisterium that *concretely binds the faithful entrusted to it.* In fact, the power of the bishop is "ordinary, proper, and immediate" (can. 381) with regard to the "portion of the People of God which is entrusted for pastoral care" to him (can. 369). For them, bishops are "teachers of doctrine, priests of sacred worship and ministers of governance" (can. 375). Canon 753 affirms this explicitly: "The faithful must adhere to the authentic teaching of their own bishops with a religious assent of soul [Cui authentico magisterio suorum Episcoporum christifideles religioso animi obsequio adhaerere tenentur]."

---

[2] CIC, can. 753. All translations of the Code of Canon Law are those found in *The Code of Canon Law: A Text and Commentary,* commissioned by the Canon Law Society of America, ed. James Coriden et al. (New York: Paulist Press, 1985).

■ Therefore, a bishop's teaching does not oblige *other faithful, unless it is a manifestation of the ordinary and universal Magisterium* (cf. *Lumen gentium,* no. 25). And, then, it obliges not as the Magisterium of a bishop, but as a teaching of the entire episcopal college in union with the Supreme Pontiff, when—even though dispersed throughout the world—the bishops proclaim a doctrine in a definitive way.

Therefore, both the decree *Christus Dominus* (no. 38) and the motu proprio *Ecclesiae sanctae* (no. 41, par. 5) are concerned with the transmission of experiences among the different episcopal conferences, as a useful exchange for each one to elaborate its own documents, etc. The acts of the Magisterium of the bishops are valid for the faithful who are not under their respective jurisdiction to the extent of their scientific and moral authority.

c. In order that the Magisterium of the bishops be authentic, it must be "in communion with the head and members of the College [*in communione cum Collegii capite et membris*]" (can. 753). Evidently, this entails that the bishop maintain ecclesiastical communion *stricto sensu,* that is, that he not be excommunicated; but even more is necessary. In fact, like every faithful Catholic, he must obey the Magisterium of the Supreme Pontiff. With due "reverence" and in an opportune way— therefore not publicly—he can, however, make known difficulties that he sees in the application of the Pontiff's directives (cf. can. 212, par. 1, and can. 3, par. 754).

■ If a bishop, either as an individual or when acting collegially within his own episcopal conference or particular council, should distance himself from the authentic Magisterium of the Supreme Pontiff, his teaching cannot any longer be considered as an authentic act of the Magisterium of the bishops, and, consequently, cannot oblige anyone of his own faithful (cf. *Lumen gentium,* no. 21, par. 2).

The bishops can exercise their Magisterium collegially, together with bishops of the same province or ecclesiastical region, in particular councils. Vatican II recommended this:

From the first centuries of the Church, bishops in charge of particular churches, moved by a spirit of fraternal charity and by love for the universal mission entrusted to the Apostles, have united their energies and their intentions to promote both the common good and the good of individual churches. Synods, provincial councils, and finally plenary councils were established for this purpose. . . . Now this sacred ecumenical Council desires that these venerable institutions of the synod and councils may flourish with renewed vigor (*Christus Dominus,* no. 36).

■ In reality, Vatican II promoted new synods and particular councils (provincial and plenary or regional) with pastoral rather than magisterial purposes in view: "So that provision might be more efficaciously and adequately made for the growth of faith and the maintenance of discipline in the various churches" (*Christus Dominus,* no. 36, par. 2). Similarly, the new code says: "A particular council sees to it that provision is made for the pastoral needs of the people of God in its own territory, and it possesses the power of governance, especially legislative power, so that with due regard always for the universal law of the Church it can decree what seems appropriate for increasing faith, organizing common pastoral activity, directing morals and preserving, promoting or protecting common ecclesiastical discipline" (can. 445).

However, as we have seen, the new Code is concerned explicitly with the Magisterium exercised by bishops in particular councils (can. 753). For its decrees—whether disciplinary or doctrinal—to become obligatory, their promulgation is required, with the prior approval of the Apostolic See (can. 446).

Moreover, bishops can exercise their Magisterium collegially by means of doctrinal declarations of episcopal conferences. Like particular councils and synods, conferences of bishops were not initially foreseen as magisterial sees, but as pastoral and apostolic: "An episcopal Conference is a kind of assembly in which the prelates of a particular nation or territory exercise jointly their pastoral office for better promoting the good which the Church offers to men; especially by those forms and methods of the apostolate which are fitting in the circumstances of our day" (*Christus Dominus,* no. 38, par. 1). This notwithstanding, especially after *Humanae vitae,* it frequently happened that episcopal conferences issued doctrinal declarations; and the new code has explicitly sanctioned this power—as we have seen (can. 753).

■ Regarding the nature of this power of episcopal conferences, one can note all that is involved. According to its divine institution, for the universal Church, every power resides originally in the Supreme Pontiff and, for particular churches, in the diocesan bishop. Episcopal conferences, therefore, are a form of ecclesiastical right. Their primary function is to promote *collegial* affection among bishops of a determinate territory, so that they can exercise their pastoral mission by helping one another in carrying out some of their obligations ("munera quaedam pastoralia coniunctim pro christifidelibus eius territorii exercentium" [can. 447]). They can make some decisions with obligating force for all the bishops within their region. In such cases, according to the opinion of some canonists, their "power is not original, but received from the Roman Pontiff in a way conformable to the technique of decentralization (they have this power, therefore, only in cases in which it has been granted to them by the Apostolic See, and their decisions must be recognized by it). This does not prevent this power from being, in juridical terms, ordinary and proper, nor does it prevent the acts proceeding from it from being attributed of necessity to them as to their source [for example, they do not require promulgation on the part of each individual bishop]."[3]

With respect to the *way in which episcopal conferences,* and therefore the respective individual bishops in a collegial mode, *exercise their Magisterium,* the new code contains no explicit determinations.

2. Declarations Emerging from the Conferences of Bishops on the Occasion of *Humanae Vitae*

As we have said, this has to do with a very salient case of the exercise of the postconciliar Magisterium of bishops, realized by means of the new form of conferences of bishops, one which was requested by the secretary of state. In fact, in the restless climate of the time, it was concerned with fostering by all possible means the understanding and wholehearted acceptance of the encyclical. Thus the conferences of bishops were asked to intervene, by giving "a courageous and decisive implementation" to the encyclical.

■ Another moment of significance for an exercise of this kind of the Magisterium of the bishops took place with the publication of *Familiaris consortio.* On that occasion, the bishops of Mozambique issued a joint pastoral letter on "The Christian family in the Church of Mozambique", in which they analyzed the positive and negative aspects of the African

[3] J. L. Gutierrez, "El Obispo diocesano y la conferencia episcopal", *Ius Canonicum* 21, no. 42 (1981): 507–42; text cited is at 542.

tradition in the light of the last synod and of the papal exhortation, making known the principal directions of the latter. The Conference of Bishops of New Zealand issued a pastoral letter on the topic of divorced persons who have remarried, insisting on the necessity of applying the doctrine freshly reaffirmed by *Familiaris consortio*. Finally, the pastoral declaration on marriage of the Colombian bishops ought to be noted. It emphasized the importance of the papal exhortation and in particular the call issued by the exhortation to awaken consciences at a time when often "civil laws are limited to legitimate behaviors that have acquired a certain diffusion, inevitably ending up by opening the way to legislation without an ethical content." In fact, "in a decisive hour for humanity, the word has always been 'defend the altar and the home' (*pro aris et focis*), no matter how much it costs."[4]

With respect to the declarations of the conferences of bishops concerning *Humanae vitae*, we will give first of all a global overview. Since a certain confusion on the subject was created by reason of some of their affirmations and some of the doctrinal discussions subsequent to them, in what follows we will discuss the pastoral attitude toward the faithful who have difficulties in accepting the teaching of the encyclical, in particular its crucial point (*punctum dolens*), i.e., the absolute condemnation of contraception.

A. *A global overview*

The 38 conferences of bishops that issued doctrinal declarations on *Humanae vitae*[5] show the full respect with which they accepted it; the great majority insist clearly on the religious assent due to it; only a small group, while defending its teaching, do not sufficiently clarify the way of overcoming doubts among the faithful.

It is necessary to recognize that, notwithstanding this general acceptance of the encyclical, some conferences showed this with words that are much less clear than would have been desirable, perhaps because of

---

[4] *L'Osservatore Romano* (September 5, 1982).

[5] A collection and comparative study of these documents is found in *Humanae Vitae and the Bishops: The Encyclical and the Statements of National Hierarchies*, ed. John Horgan (Shannon, Ireland: Irish University Press, 1972). See also *"Humanae vitae" e Magistero episcopale*, ed. L. Sandri (Bologna: Ed. Dehoniane, 1969).

a pastoral concern to avoid open dissent of some of their faithful. In fact, in some countries, part of the clergy and of the faithful had begun practices contradicting what *Humanae vitae* authoritatively confirmed regarding the intrinsic immorality of contraception. Thus, declarations were made, as theologians who have studied them in detail have shown, that at times were a bit vague or confused, which some authors presented as a true crisis between the Holy Father and the bishops.[6] But this is not precise. Rather, a careful study of the different declarations teaches something else. Specifically, according to the painstaking study of Marcelino Zalba,[7] the following is the true situation:

1. Within the ensemble of the declarations of conferences of bishops, *the following groups can be distinguished:* (a) a first group, the most numerous, which takes up the defense of the encyclical and *vigorously supports the whole teaching of the encyclical,* without minimizing the significance of the most difficult problems of the time: the absolute and unequivocal condemnation, obliging for all, of contraception, even chemical contraception; (b) a second group that *expresses with sufficient clarity its adhesion to the encyclical and gives pastoral directives* for its practical application to special situations, according to the traditional criteria of morality (for instance, with reference to the possibility of invincible ignorance; cases in which one can, provisionally, allow the penitent to remain in material sin, etc.); some theologians, however, interpreted these clarifications as examples of reticence; (c) a third group, less numerous, includes conferences treating the encyclical *briefly and within the context of a program appropriate for teaching,* but with a clear and full adhesion to the encyclical, and those that simply give their adhesion without further comments; and (d) finally, a fourth group—less numerous than one would be given to believe by the comments set forth at that time by the means of social communication—perhaps excessively concerned with the difficult situation of some of the faithful that would occur "by clearly defending the Encyclical in all its demands", proclaimed, at the same time—*in a way that could end*

---

[6] Thus, for instance, argued B. Haering, *Crisi intorno alla Humanae vitae* (Rome: Ed. Paoline, 1969), 140–49.

[7] M. Zalba, *Las conferencias episcopales ante la "Humanae vitae" (Presentación y comentario)* (Madrid: Ed. Cio, 1971). See also John Ford and Germain Grisez, "Contraception and the Infallibility of the Ordinary Magisterium", *Theological Studies* 39 (1978): 258–312. On pp. 308–12 Ford and Grisez offer a short, but exceptionally perceptive and helpful analysis of these statements by various episcopal conferences.

up in equivocations — as a way of balancing matters, the teaching on conscience as the proximate, although not arbitrary, norm of morality (frequently with some imprecisions);[8] this group insists on the possibility of error in the Magisterium when it does not speak *ex cathedra;* it perhaps widens excessively the scope and duration of invincible ignorance.[9]

2. Therefore, *from the point of view of adhesion to the teaching of "Humanae vitae", the great majority of the conferences of bishops explicitly accepts it in its integrity.* "It is necessary to recognize that an overwhelming majority (we have calculated roughly 1300 as opposed to 300–350)" of the bishops—those who belong to the first and second group, and a large part of the third—"have accepted and supported the Encyclical in all the integrity of its teaching." *The remainder accept it in a less formal way.*[10]

Therefore, *Humanae vitae* must be considered as an act of the ordinary Magisterium of the Roman Pontiff, of definitive value and the object of the morally unanimous consent of the whole body of bishops, thus becoming the ordinary and universal Magisterium. This is true, above all, as we have seen, after the Synod of Bishops of 1980, with the explicit confirmation of the Holy Father in *Familiaris consortio:*

> The Synod Fathers made the following declaration at their last assembly: "This Sacred Synod, gathered together with the Successor of Peter in the unity of faith, firmly holds what has been set forth in the Second Vatican Council (cf. *Gaudium et spes,* n. 50) and afterwards in the Encyclical *Humanae vitae,* particularly that love between husband and wife must be fully human, exclusive and open to life (*Humanae vitae,* n. 11; cf. 9 and 12)."[11]

And, in a note, he records the text of number 11 of the encyclical of Paul VI, where Paul affirms: "Ut quilibet matrimonii usus ad vitam humanam procreandam per se destinatus permaneat [it is necessary

---

[8] The notion of conscience as the *proximate,* and, at least after the contemporary debate, *imprecise norm* of morality is treated by Ramón García de Haro, "Il rapporto fra verità, autorita e coscienza", in *"Humanae vitae": 20 anni dopo (Atti del II Congresso Internazionale di Teologia Morale: Roma, 9–12 novembre 1988)* (Milan: Ed. Ares, 1989).

[9] Zalba, *Las conferencias episcopales,* pp. 185–87.

[10] Ibid., p. 192.

[11] Apostolic exhortation *Familiaris consortio,* November 22, 1981, no. 29, par. 3 and n. 83.

that each conjugal act remain ordered in itself to the procreating of human life]."[12]

■ Therefore, if initially the doubts of pastors were a sign of a teaching —although definitive because of the way it was expressed by the Holy Father—that did not yet pertain to the ordinary and universal Magisterium, today this is no longer possible. Actually, as the Holy Father has emphasized publicly and explicitly, questioning the teaching of *Humanae vitae* concerning contraception is an act *with truly grave and disintegrating consequences,* the obscuring of *a truth that cannot be questioned,* and "not a sign of 'pastoral understanding,' but rather *of a failure to understand the true good of persons"*.[13] To question the teaching of *Humanae vitae* today *"is equivalent to denying to God Himself the obedience of our intelligence.* It is equivalent to preferring the light of our own reason to that of God's Wisdom, *thereby falling into the obscurity of error* and ending up by damaging other fundamental principles of Christian doctrine.... These last twenty years have demonstrated this."[14]

Some considerations for the future

From a pastoral perspective, the experience of the interventions of the conferences of bishops in the case of *Humanae vitae* has not been as positive as we could have expected, perhaps because of the difficulties in relating the particular good of the dioceses, in situations at times critical, to the common good of the Church. Thus Zalba says:

The safeguarding of doctrinal and moral principles, in this case principally the holiness of marriage, where the honor of God and that of the authentic Magisterium of the Vicar of Christ for his Church come into play, is always more important than a particular good obtained at the price of compromises or of an ambiguity which endangers these values. We do not want to say that some pastoral approaches have

[12] Encyclical *Humanae vitae,* July 25, 1968, no. 11; AAS 60 (1968): 488.

[13] John Paul II, Address to the Participants in the Fourth International Congress of Africa and Europe for the Family, March 14, 1988, no. 3; *Enchiridion Familiae: Textos del Magisterio Pontificio y Conciliar sobre el Matrimonio y la Familia (Siglos I a XX),* ed. Augusto Sarmiento and Javier Escrivá-Ivars, vol. 5 (Madrid: Ediciones Rialp, 1992), p. 4755, no. 3.

[14] John Paul II, Address to the Second International Congress of Moral Theology, November 12, 1988, in *"Humanae vitae": 20 anni dopo,* p. 16 (English translation); in *Enchiridion Familiae,* 5.4922–33.

positively created this risk; but we are by no means sure that they have not done this.[15]

This can lead, he adds, to some reflections "perhaps of importance in the life of the Church",[16] in particular, on the necessity of insuring, in the exercise of collegiality, that "sollicitudo omnium ecclesiarum" which "contributes greatly to the good of the universal Church", permitting the bishops to carry out efficaciously their obligation of "promoting and defending the unity of faith and of common discipline for the whole Church" (*Lumen gentium*, no. 23, par. 2).

> ■ It seems that a like difficulty would be eliminated at its *roots* after the new code comes fully into force, if the requirement of the Apostolic See's *recognition* of the decrees—even doctrinal—of bishops' conferences is interpreted in a strict sense (cf. cans. 455, 456, and 753).[17]

B. *The problem of the faithful who are reluctant*

Different conferences are concerned with the pastoral care of the faithful who show that they do not accept the encyclical. Ordinarily, they recall traditional criteria; some, however, have been imprecise, as some authors have emphasized.

Specifically, it has been justly observed that some of the declarations of bishops' conferences, in one way or another, affirm that one can *easily, or almost frequently, find oneself in good faith with a conscience that cannot accept the encyclical.* They likewise affirm that pastors should respect these decisions of conscience, if made responsibly, even in the administration of the sacraments. Usually, the words of such declarations can also be understood rightly. But at times, ambiguities have resulted, and they have in fact created confusions. Moreover, even today they are used to manipulate consciences and to promote an attitude that challenges and contests the papal Magisterium.

[15] Zalba, *Las conferencias episcopales*, p. 191.

[16] Ibid., p. 187.

[17] On this see Josef Ratzinger, *The Ratzinger Report* (San Francisco: Ignatius Press, 1985), pp. 58ff.

■ Let us give some examples. Speaking of the difficulties some of the faithful can encounter in living the doctrine of *Humanae vitae,* it has been affirmed: "To the extent that such persons have made an effort to conform themselves to the directives proposed, but nonetheless without success, they can have the certainty that they are not deprived of grace inasmuch as they choose the way that seems best to them." Therefore, the judgment of these individuals would seem to prevail over that of the Magisterium.[18] In another place one reads: "Contraception can never be a good. It is always a disorder. But this disorder is not always culpable. It happens, in fact, that some spouses think that they find themselves faced with a true conflict of duties. No one is ignorant of the anguish in which these sincere spouses debate about the matter, especially when the observance of rhythms is not successful in giving them a sufficiently secure basis for regulating births. On the one hand, they are aware of the duty to respect the openness to life of every conjugal act; they feel at the same time the obligation to delay the birth of a new life, and they are not able to trust biological rhythms. On the other hand, they do not see, as far as they are concerned themselves, how to deny the physical expression of their love without the security of their union being endangered. With respect to this, let us simply call to mind the constant teaching of morality. When a person finds himself confronted with an alternative of obligations whose fulfillment, no matter what choice is made, cannot avoid an evil, the traditional wisdom recommended searching before God what would be the lesser evil in this case. The spouses make a choice on the basis of a common reflection, conducted with all the care demanded by the greatness of their conjugal vocation."

In this way, it seems that one forgets that, if the conflicts between different obligations of the divine law can appear real to consciences, they cannot however be really of this kind. Therefore, they can find their way out by means of a better formation of conscience, which must not be left only to them. The same declaration affirms that, when there is discord between the spouses on this matter—when one accepts the encyclical and the other does not—"each one should respect the conscience of the other, trying to enlighten it with tact and safeguarding always the truth of their love and the unity of the home." But in truth, it is only the spouse who accepts the Magisterium who can enlighten the other.[19]

---

[18] For examples, see Zalba, *Las conferencias episcopales,* pp. 115–16.
[19] On this see ibid., pp. 141–59.

One of the pastorals comments that many of the faithful welcome the encyclical from the heart and joyfully, only to say afterward that "others, on the contrary, who have no less concern for the perfection of Christian marriage, find themselves disappointed by the declaration of the Pope and do not see how they can apply it in practice." In the following paragraph, it adds: "No one must be allowed to put in doubt the content of the Encyclical, without having previously tried, with a full awareness of his own responsibility before God, to enter seriously and loyally into the reasonings and intentions of the Holy Father. But when a man, for grave and well thought out reasons, is not convinced by the arguments of the Encyclical, he has the right to have a different opinion from that which is presented in a non-infallible document. Let no one be treated as a bad Catholic solely because of this kind of dissent."[20]

Therefore, it seems that here is forgotten the truth that a teaching of the Magisterium binds not only and principally because of its reasoning, but also and primarily because of the assistance of the Holy Spirit and the divine authority with which it is invested, whether it teaches in an infallible way or not. When the matter is put this way, it would seem that one is attributing to the Magisterium the character of an "authoritative opinion", which individuals can consider like that of a theologian. All this leads to relativism and gives rise to a lack of clarity on the obligation of the faithful, many times emphasized — and on this precise issue — by *Gaudium et spes* (cf. nos. 50–51), of giving a religious assent of will and mind to the Magisterium.

Finally, another pastoral says that since we are not dealing with an *ex cathedra* declaration, one cannot exclude "the possibility that a Catholic Christian, basing himself on serious reasons, can believe himself not to be obligated." This statement risks causing confusions; in fact, even the authentic but noninfallible Magisterium binds in conscience, according to the tone of the statement and the mode of expression. Moreover, cases in which there can be — in these conditions — an inculpable error are very rare, whereas the declaration criticized here seems to allow for many such instances.[21]

Let us end with the following considerations, which belong to the traditional teaching of theology.

1. The fact that a *document is not infallible* does not mean that *it is an opinion,* nor may we forget that it can contain *particular affirmations that*

[20] See ibid., pp. 122–34.
[21] Cf. ibid., pp. 38–58.

have been previously qualified as irreformable or infallible. In the case of number 14 of *Humanae vitae,* the discussion concerned a teaching that, if it did not pertain to the ordinary and universal Magisterium—with respect to the use of the "pill"—at the time of its publication, is today at least to be held as such without any doubt and therefore is included within the infallibility described in number 25 of *Lumen gentium.*[22]

Moreover, even if it is granted that initially number 14 of *Humanae vitae* did not treat of a teaching infallibly proposed according to the criteria set forth in number 25 of *Lumen gentium,* one must keep in mind that *the formation of conscience cannot be made the equivalent, purely and simply, of the hypothesis of a doubt built on a noninfallible magisterial teaching,* similar to that which, in exceptional cases, a pastor or theologian can formulate. This is so, first of all, because the ordinary faithful usually lack the necessary competence that his doubt can be regarded as so based, but moreover and above all, because conscience directs concrete action, where a grave offense against God is at risk, while the doubt of a theologian or of a pastor is related to the possibility of continuing theoretical "investigations", always with the respect demanded by a religious submission of mind and will.

■ In fact, the way in which the Magisterium guides "theoretical" knowledge and "practical" knowledge is different. With regard to the first, the teaching characteristic of the authentic but noninfallible Magisterium determines the possibility of pursuing the study of the reasons that have been the basis of its judgment. In the second case, although the judgment of the Magisterium is not infallible, when we are concerned with an authentic teaching, its precept already rules conscience in an obligating way. In effect, this judgment makes the contrary hypothesis at least gravely doubtful; and Christian morality has always denied that a conscience suffering a positive doubt can authorize an action—and it is difficult to think that *Humanae vitae* does not give rise to such a positive grave doubt.[23] But not only Christianity but also pagan authors were convinced of this. Cicero said: "They prescribe well who forbid one to do something which they doubt might be the equivalent of an evil [Bene praecipiunt, qui vetant quidquam agere, quod dubitant aequum sit an iniquum]."[24]

---

[22] Cf. F. Ocáriz, "La nota teologica di sull'insegnamento dell'*Humanae vitae* sulla contraccezione", *Anthropotes* 3 (1988): 25–43.

[23] See, for instance, D. Pruemmer, *Manuale Theologiae Moralis,* 13th ed. (Fribourg-Barcelona-Rome: Herder, 1958) I, nos. 328–30.

[24] Cicero, *De officiis,* I, 9.

Therefore, in the formation of conscience the clear and explicit judgments of the Magisterium, even if not infallible, are binding. The Church repeatedly noted this during and after the Council, precisely while treating this matter (cf. *Gaudium et spes*, no. 50, par. 2; no. 51, par. 3; *Familiaris consortio*, no. 73, par. 5). As we have seen, the Polish bishops' conference noted that after the promulgation of *Humanae vitae* "it is difficult to speak, with respect to Catholics, of inculpable ignorance or error in good faith", with reference to the evil of contraception.[25] In practice, this kind of ignorance can be at stake only when someone does not know that the encyclical condemns contraception clearly, or when one judges—in good faith—that the Holy Father does not want to make his teaching binding.

It is paradoxical indeed that the affirmations of some theologians and priests have been able to create among the faithful, in certain cases, this erroneous but inculpable conscience. But it is difficult to keep this for a long time in good faith, because it is enough to reread *Humanae vitae* in order to see that it gives no grounds for doubts, if—as it ought to be—it is read in the presence of God.

2. Finally, *respect for the freedom of consciences must always avoid any misunderstanding that might lead to indifferentism or to skepticism with regard to the truth*. Certainly it is never required to impose truth by force; if a person without faith—otherwise the case would not be possible—judges in conscience that he cannot accept the Incarnation of God in Jesus Christ (the example is that of St. Thomas, when he speaks of an erroneous conscience),[26] one must respect him, while encouraging him to continue his search for truth. This, however, absolutely does not imply that pastors should find themselves constrained, should such a person ask them, to treat him as a Catholic or to admit him to the sacraments. Therefore, it is nonsense to say that pastors, in the administration of the sacraments, must respect the conscience of those faithful who do not accept the Magisterium of the Supreme Pontiff in the condemnation of contraception. To the contrary, they have the obligation, inside and outside the administration of the sacraments, to teach them and to correct them, with love, with understanding, but nonetheless with firmness. And if disobedience should become public,

[25] *Introduzione all'enciclica* to *Humanae Vitae* (Vatican City: Typis Polyglottis Vaticanis, 1969), p. 97. See above, chapter 7, nn. 30 and 42.

[26] *Summa theologiae*, I–II, q. 19, a. 5.

the sacraments can publicly be denied them; the common good and respect for the other faithful would demand this.

True pastoral solutions do not consist in making compromises with error, which degrades man, but in teaching the truth—which saves him—with love: "doing the truth in love", says St. Paul (Eph 4:15). Certainly, the weaknesses, difficulties, obscurities, doubts, and falls of each person must be understood. And, therefore, the truth must be spoken by having and showing understanding, by helping souls progressively to climb up, by steps; but without forgetting that only the truth saves, and that the law of graduality is totally opposed to the graduality of the law. It is necessary to have courage and humility to teach the truth with love, but without dissimulation, trusting in the fact that the action of grace will not be lacking.

Definitively, and in conclusion, in this way, with the same ideas with which we have begun these inquiries, to make men free is the exclusive privilege of the truth. The Magisterium, the continuation of the visible guidance of Christ our model, does not restrain human freedom; it shows God's zeal for it. In the divinization of man, the meaning and end of Christianity, it is God who takes the initiative for redeeming us from sin and for making us become children of God. As St. Thomas was pleased to repeat, following St. Paul, the children of God, rather than acting of themselves, *are led by the Spirit of God* [*Spiritu Dei aguntur*];[27] rather than by their own inclinations, they are moved by the inspiration of the Holy Spirit.[28] God brings them to works that oppose their appetites and surpass every human prudence: to act not according to the prudence of the flesh, but according to that of the Spirit (cf. Rom 8:6). What else can *Humanae vitae* be if not this? But God does not want to act within us without our cooperation. He asks men, giving them the grace to do it, to conduct themselves according to the prudence of the Spirit; and, at the same time, he informs them and urges them on in a visible way, so that they will agree to his demands. Sensible lights that externally illumine conscience prepare and accompany the intimate and liberating action of grace; this is the work of the Magisterium.

[27] Rom 8:14; cf. St. Thomas, *In Ep. ad Rom.,* cap. 8, lect. 3.

[28] St. Thomas, *In Ep. ad Gal.,* cap. 5, lect. 5; *In Ep. ad Rom.,* cap. 8, lect. 1; *In Ep. II ad Cor.,* cap. 3, lect. 3; *Contra Gentiles,* 4.22; *Summa theologiae,* II–II, q. 184, a. 4, ad 1, etc.

INDEX

abortion, intrinsically evil, 157, 202, 296f.

Ambrose, St., indissolubility of marriage, 72

Ancilli, E., call to holiness, 220

anthropology, need of sound, 42f.

Apostolicam actuositatem, apostolate of marriage and family, 280

Arcanum divinae sapientiae, Leo XIII's encyclical on marriage, 93ff.

Arricia draft of *Gaudium et spes,* 212f.

Athanasius, St., excellence of virginity, 229

Aubert, Jacques Marie, competence of Magisterium in morals, 27

Augustine, St., evil of contraception, 131; goods of marriage, 116, 118ff., 125f.; meaning of history, 45

Baldanza, G., *Casti connubii* and grace of sacramental marriage, 110, 123; correct interpretation of Vatican II on conjugal love, 249; doctrinal importance of Trent, 71; marriage as sacrament, 65; Trent and grace of sacramental marriage, 73

baptism, and sacramentality of marriage, 348

Bellarmine, St. Robert, inseparability between sacrament and contract, 88

Benedict XIV, marriage ordered to procreation and education of children, 199; power of Church over marriage, 90, 206

Benedict XV, contraception intrinsically evil, 203

Betti, U., assent due magisterial teachings, 50

Beyond Rhetoric, impact of divorce on children, 70

Bishops, Magisterium of 409ff.; see also Conferences of bishops

Bökmann, J., binding character of *Humanae vitae,* 305; contraception and infallibility, 133

Bonnet, P., relationship between conjugal love and institution of marriage, 240

Boyle, Joseph, contraception an anti-life act, 298, 360; critique of fundamental option theory, 320

Braga, Council of, marriage a vocation to holiness, 201

Caffarra, Carlo, conscience, 51; freedom and morality, 225; Magisterium and moral theology, 22f.; need of sound metaphysics, 42; *Persona humana,* 316; relationship between nature and grace in marriage, 67

Calvin, John, teaching on marriage, 67f.

canonical form, required by Trent, 75f.

Caprile, G., authority of Magisterium, 307

Cardona, Carlos, difference between "thinking" and "knowing", 35; genesis of scientist thinking, 23; human situation and faith, 22

Casti connubii, analysis of; 107–46; divine institution and sanctity of marriage, 110–18; errors concerning marriage, 129–39; goods of marriage, 118–29; historical genesis, 107–10; love as form of marriage, 253; remedies for marriage, 139–42; see also Pius XI

Catechism of the Council of Trent, contraception intrinsically wicked and anti-life, 131f., 202, 304; gravity of offenses against conjugal fidelity, 204; infallibility of ordinary Magisterium, 30ff; love as form of marriage, 253

Celaya, Ignacio, critique of dissent, 27; relationship between science and faith, 44

Chapelle, A., continuity and progress in Church teaching, 173

Charter of Rights of the Family, 367f., 370

Ciappi, L., authority of Magisterium, 305

Clark, Colin, myth of over-population, 288

Code of Canon Law (1917), ends of marriage, 200; marriage in, 95ff.; marriage and grace, 201

Code of Canon Law (1983), marriage in, 97

Conferences of bishops, authority of, 412ff.; *statements regarding Humanae vitae,* 413ff.

Conference of European Ministers in Charge of Family Matters, rights of families, 368

conjugal act, gift of self, 346f.

conjugal charity, perfects conjugal love, 123

conjugal love, in John Paul II, 341ff.; in Paul VI, 293ff.; in Pius XI, 115ff.; in Pius XII, 157ff.; in Vatican II, 234ff., 248ff.; intrinsically ordered to procreation and education of children, 115f., 157ff., 235ff., 256ff., 293ff., 345ff.; life-giving principle of marriage, 123, 234ff.; 344f.; never regarded as an end of marriage by Vatican II, 244ff.; never understood as secondary end of marriage, 200

conjugal morality, in John Paul II, 341ff., 350ff.; in Paul VI, 291ff., 322ff.; in Pius XI, 129ff.; in Pius XII, 152ff.; in Vatican II, 268ff.

contraception, anti-life, 131, 298, 304, 360; described by Pius XII, 297; described more fully by Paul VI, 296; gateway to abortion, 361; intrinsically and gravely immoral, 131ff., 157ff., 202, 276ff., 296ff., 355ff.; teaching of Church on, infallibly and irreformably proposed, 132ff., 420ff.

contraceptive mentality, analyzed, 287ff.

Costanzo, Joseph, authority of Magisterium, 306

Cottier, Georges, on contraceptive mentality, 287

Curran, Charles, logic of Majority opinion, 56; spurious attempts to defend dissent, 32ff.

Cyril of Alexandria, St., sacramentality of marriage, 68

Declaration on Procured Abortion, 331

De Fuenmayor, A., rights of family, 370

Dei verbum, role of Magisterium, 21

Delhaye, Philippe, authority of Magisterium, 305; beauty of bod-

Delhaye, Philippe (*Continued*) ily conjugal love, 241; continuity of Vatican II with Tradition, 221; failures of postconciliar theologians, 196, 222; harmony between conjugal love and procreation, 258; marriage as institution animated by conjugal love, 237; objective moral criteria, 261; situation of marriage today, 263; work of Vatican II, 195, 317

Delpini, F., indissolubility of marriage, 65

Destro, Robert, rights of family in education, 280

Dignitatis humanae, significance of, 83f.

dissent, critique of theological, 29ff.

Domenico of Flanders, theology's need of sound metaphysics, 42

Dominis, M. A. de, apostate bishop, views on marriage, 80

Doms, H., misunderstanding of ends of marriage, 234

education, family's responsibilities for, 179f., 184f., 280, 363ff.

Elliott, Peter, sacramentality of marriage, 347

Escrivá, Blessed Josemaría, apostolate of laity, 223; beauty of bodily conjugal love, 241; divinization of Christians, 226; holiness of marriage, 227f.; human longing for God, 47; man's vocation, 226; marriage a vocation to holiness, 232; presence of Christ in Christians, 224; responsible parenthood, 275; superiority of virginity over marriage, 73

Fagiolo, V., misunderstanding of Vatican II on role of conjugal love, 249

Faith, articles of, principles of theology, 39ff.

Familiaris consortio, detailed analysis of, 335–81; occasion, importance, and general scheme, 334f.; *see also* John Paul II

family, as community of persons demands unity and indissolubility of marriage, 351; domestic church, 278, 371ff.; forming a community of persons, 350ff.; need to defend itself, 369; principle and foundation of society, 205; participation in development of society, 366ff.; participation in life and mission of the Church, 371ff.; responsibilities in education, 179f., 184f., 280, 363ff.; rights of, 184ff., 205f., 367f., 368; service to life, 355ff.

father, role of, 354f.

Festorazzi, F., marriage and virginity, 73, 229

Finnis, John, contraception as antilife, 298, 360; moral absolutes, 56; moral methodology of Vatican II, 198; practicality of ethics, 36

Florence, Council, *Decree pro Armenis,* and marriage, 63; goods of marriage, 63f., 201; marriage, divine institution elevated by Christ to dignity of sacrament, 199; marriage, ordained to procreation and education of children, 199; marriage, a holy state of life, 201

Forcano, B., mistakenly identifies periodic abstinence with contraception, 357

Ford, John, contraception and infallibility, 133, 308

Fuchs, Joseph, dissenting views of, 27f.

Gagnon, Eduoard Cardinal, on *Familiaris consortio*, 350

García de Haro, Ramón, adultery and contraception, 361; competence of Magisterium in morality, 27; conscience, 52; continuity of Magisterium, 197; contraception outside marriage, 298; critique of dissent, 27; critique of fundamental option, 320; difference between contraception and periodic abstinence, 299; essential elements of moral action, 167; freedom and God's omnipotence, 337; infallibility of ordinary Magisterium, 314; injustice of artificial fecundation, 182; marital consent, 115; marriage and true personalism, 342; moral absolutes and infallibility, 50; obligation to assent to Magisterium, 28, 305; objective moral criteria, 261; periodic abstinence and chastity, 359; quest for happiness, 154; relationship between dogmatic and moral theology, 322; relationship between science and faith, 44; true personalism, 312; roots of laicist thought, 81; theology and the Magisterium, 20

Gaudium et spes, concept and nature of marriage, 264ff.; conjugal love, ordered to procreation and education of children, 235ff.; conjugal love and procreation, 256ff.; conjugal morality, 268ff.; duty to nourish conjugal love, 269ff.; contraception, 276ff.; end (procreation) and formal principle (conjugal love) of marriage, 245ff.; historical background, 211; holiness of marriage, 264ff.; inseparable connection between procreation and conjugal love, 256ff.; marriage and vocation to holiness, 215ff.; nature, properties, and ends of conjugal love, 241ff.; objective criteria for sexual acts, 318; role of conjugal love in structure of marriage, 234ff.; situation of marriage in contemporary world, 262ff.; *see also* Vatican Council II

Gil Hellín, Francisco, goods of marriage, 117, 126; history of *Gaudium et spes*, 214; Vatican II and goods of marriage, 119; proper place of conjugal love in structure of marriage according to *Gaudium et spes* 234–56, passim; Vatican II and goods of marriage, 119, 251ff.

goods of marriage, in *Casti connubii*, 118ff.; in Council of Florence, 63f., 201; in *Familiaris consortio*, 351f.; in Vatican II, 119f, 264ff.

Gregory XVI, contraception intrinsically evil, 202; need for grace, 292; power of Church over marriage, 206

Grisez, Germain, authority of Magisterium, 305; competence of Magisterium in morality, 27; conscience and Magisterium, 262; contraception an anti-life act, 298, 360; contraception and infallibility, 308; critique of dissent, 24, 33

Grygiel, Stanislaw, scientistic thinking, 23

Guenthor, A., Church and human needs, 233

Guerrero, P., misconception of call to holiness, 220

Gutierrez, J. L., Magisterium of bishops, 413

Haering, Bernard, dissenting views of, 57; mistakenly equates periodic abstinence with contraception, 357

Hera, A. de la, correct interpretation of Vatican II on conjugal love, 249; work of Pius XII, 147f.

Hervada, Javier, correct interpretation of Vatican II on conjugal love, 250; ends of marriage, 193; inseparability between contract and sacrament, 76; love as good of marriage, 118

Heylen, V., conjugal love, 270; holiness of marriage, 216; misinterpretation of Vatican II on ends of marriage, 272; responsible parenthood, 274, 275

Hildebrand, Dietrich von, authority of Magisterium, 306

historicity of human nature, 58f.

history, meaning of, 45, 336ff.

Horgan, John, conferences of bishops and Humanae vitae, 414

Humani generis, obligatory character of ordinary Magisterium, 29

Humanae vitae, appeals to previous Magisterium on evil of contraception, 304; competence of Magisterium, 292f.; confirms Pius XII's judgment on contraceptive character of chemical methods, 308; conjugal love, 293ff.; definition of contraception, 303f.; development of doctrine on contraception, 310; development of doctrine on periodic abstinence, 172f.; enduring importance and significance, 300ff.; historical context, 286ff.; issues confronting married couples, 288ff.; liceity of periodic abstinence for serious reasons, 298ff.; need for integral vision of man, 293f.; obligatory force, 300ff., 315; pastoral directives, 299ff.; responsible parenthood, 294f; summary of contents, 291–300; see also Paul VI

Illanes, José L., call to holiness, 220; nature of theology, 34

Innocent III, marriage and holiness, 201

Innocent XI, abortion intrinsically evil, 202

inseparability of contract and sacrament, 76ff.; 87ff.; 200f.

Instruction on Ecclesial Vocation of the Theologian (Donum veritatis), illegitimacy of dissent, 34; Magisterium and moral absolutes, 62

intrinsically evil acts, 54–62

Irenaeus, St., need of Magisterium, 21

Janssens, Louis, dissenting views, 57; mistakenly equates periodic abstinence and contraception, 357

Javierre, J. M., work of Paul VI, 283

Jellinek, M. S., impact of divorce on children, 70

John Chrysostom, St., family as domestic church, 280

John XXIII, competence of Magisterium, 292; condemnation of contraception, 304; marriage and vocations, 230; sacredness of human life, 295

John Paul II, anthropological and moral differences between contraception and periodic continence, 357ff.; charter of family rights, 367; Christ as one who reveals man to himself, 44f.; confirms condemnation of contraception, 307ff., 355ff.; contraception the gateway to abortion, 361; conjugal act as total gift, 346f.; conjugal love the life-giving principle of marriage, 344f.; conjugal love and procreation, 122; development of doctrine on conjugal morality, 174; difference between truth and opinion, 25; eucharist and divorced who have remarried, 73; family, participation in life and mission of Church, 371ff.; family, rights and responsibilities, 205, 363ff.; family, role in development of society, 366ff.; family, serves life, 355ff.; family life, holiness of, 228; fundamental option, 320; God's plan for marriage, 341ff.; history, meaning of, 45, 336ff.; indispensability of faith for theology, 36, 41; indissolubility, 72; infallibility of ordinary Magisterium, 314; innate vocation of person to love, 342f.; law of graduality vs. graduality of law, 339ff., 362; liberating role of truth, 20f.; Magisterium as proximate norm for theology, 41; marriage as covenant of love, 349ff.; marriage a vocation to holiness, 221, 347ff.; need for education of conscience, 338ff.; need for sound anthropology, 42; pastoral care of family, 375ff.; periodic abstinence as exercise of chastity, 358f.; proper development of doctrine, 196f.; relationship between philosophy and theology, 35, 37f., 43; role of father, 354f.; role of woman, 352ff.; soundness of St. Thomas' metaphysics, 42; teaching on marriage, 333–408; true freedom, 84ff.; see also *Familiaris consortio*; Wojtyla, Karol

Kant, Immanuel, denies procreation as end of marriage, 82

Kasun, Jacqueline, myth of overpopulation, 288

Keane, Eamonn, myth of overpopulation, 288

Kosnik, Anthony et al., mistakenly equate periodic abstinence and contraception, 357

Kozul, S. D., history of *Gaudium et spes*, 212

Laborem exercens, role of women, 353

"laicist" thought on marriage, 81f.

laity, responsibility of, 86; vocation to holiness, 209

Lambeth Conference, acceptance of contraception, 56

Lateran Council II, marriage and holiness, 201

Lateran Council IV, marriage and holiness, 201

law of graduality, vs. graduality of law, 339ff., 362

Lawler, Ronald, competence of Magisterium in morality, 27

Le Bras, G., Luther on marriage, 69; secularization of marriage, 79f.

Leo the Great, St., inseparability between contract and sacrament, 77

Leo XIII, abortion intrinsically evil, 202; contraception intrinsically evil, 203; family, foundation of society, 205; family, rights of, 205; inseparability of contract and sacrament, 88, 89; marriage, divine institution raised by Christ to dignity of sacrament, 199; marriage, ordained to procreation and education of children, 199; marriage, subject to divine laws, 202; marriage, a vocation to holiness, 201; mixed marriages, 92; power of Church over marriage, 90, 206; sacrament of marriage and grace, 201; teaching on marriage, 93ff.; see also *Arcanum divinae sapientiae*

Lio, Ermenigeldo, authority of Magisterium, 306; binding character of *Humanae vitae*, 304; conscience and Magisterium, 262; contraception and infallibility, 133; enduring significance of *Humanae vitae*, 301; work of Vatican II, 195

Lombardia, P., ends of marriage, 193

López, T., competence of Magisterium in morality, 27

Lumen gentium, Christian family a domestic church, 278f.; infallibility of ordinary Magisterium, 32, 314; marriage a vocation to holiness, 218; obligation to assent to Magisterium, nature of, 28, 32f.; superiority of virginity, 229; universal call to holiness, 216ff.; see also Vatican Council II

Lustiger, Jean-Marie Cardinal, Church and human needs, 233; graduality of law, 339ff.

Luther, Martin, views on marriage, 66ff.

Lyon, Second Council of, power of Church over marriage, 206

Mackin, Theodore, misinterpretation of Vatican II on ends of marriage, 272

Maggiolini, S., marriage and virginity, 229

Magisterium, guardian of truth of salvation, 44ff.; infallibility of ordinary, 29ff.; mission of, 20ff.; moral absolutes and, 62; obedience due, 48ff.; ordinary, of Pope and bishops, 29ff.; position on marriage at opening of Vatican Council II, 195ff.; principal errors concerning, 24ff.; prophetic mission of, 21ff.; proximate norm for theology, 41f.; theology and, 34ff.

Majdanski, K., marriage a vocation to holiness, 216, 227, 232

"Majority Opinion" of Papal Commission, and moral absolutes, 56

marital consent, an act of conjugal love, 114ff.; covenantal in character, 349f.; nature of, 113ff.

marriage, *Code of Canon Law (1917)*, 95ff., 220; *Code of Canon Law (1983)*, 97; in *Gaudium et spes*,

Marriage (*Continued*)
211–82; in John Paul II, 333–408;
in Leo XIII, 93ff.; in Magisterium
at opening of Vatican II, 195–210;
in Paul VI, 283–332; in Pius XI,
110–46; in Pius XII, 147–94; in
Trent, 69–77; overview of
Magisterial teaching on, 63–106;
in postconciliar teaching of
bishops, 409–20; in Vatican Council II, 211–82

Mateo Seco, L. F., St. Vincent of
Lerins, 37; superiority of virginity,
73

May, William E., complementarity
of male and female, 353;
conscience and Magisterium, 262;
contraception as anti-life act, 298,
306; critique of arguments denying moral absolutes, 57ff.; critique
of theological dissent, 33; difference between periodic abstinence
and contraception, 168, 299;
infallibility of ordinary
Magisterium, 30f.; logic of Majority Opinion, 56; moral absolutes,
56ff.; moral methodology of Vatican II, 198; principle of double
effect, 164

McCarthy, Donald, Magisterium and
morality, 22, 305

McGrath, M. G., history of *Gaudium
et spes,* 212

McCormick, Richard, dissenting
views of, 25f.

McInerny, Ralph, indispensability of
faith for theology, 41

metaphysics, and theology, 41f.

Miralles, Antonio, correct interpretation of Vatican II on conjugal
love, 250; God as author of
marriage, 266; love and marriage

in *Gaudium et spes,* 241, 246;
relationship between baptism and
marriage, 279; responsible
parenthood, 275

Molano, E., on H. Doms, 234

Montaigne, Michel, and divorce,
82

moral absolutes, 54–62

Moreira Neves, L., apostolic dynamism of Christian family, 180

Navarrete, U., Vatican Council II
and goods of marriage, 251

Newman, John Cardinal, need of
Magisterium, 33f.

Ocáriz, F., authority of Magisterium
in morals, 27, 306; contraception
and infallibility, 308, 421

O'Connell, Timothy, dissenting
views of, 26

Ordonez Marquez, J., work of Paul
VI, 283

Paul VI, Church a sign of contradiction, 24; competence of
Magisterium in morals, 27;
contraceptive character of
chemical methods, 272; correct
interpretation of Vatican Council II on conjugal love, 249;
marriage in teaching of, 291–332;
overview of pontificate, 283ff.;
pastoral directives, 323; principal
means of leading good married
life, 322ff.; see also *Humanae
vitae*

periodic continence, difference from
contraception, 357ff.; liceity of,
167ff.; 203

Persona humana, on sexual ethics,
315ff.

Pinckaers, Servais, ends of marriage in Aquinas, 193; happiness and morality, 154; moral knowledge, origin and nature of, 36, 38; need for faith, 48; principle of double effect, 164; proper moral method, 43, 44; theology and the Magisterium, 20

Pius VI, Church's authority over marriage, 74, 90, 206; inseparability of contract and sacrament, 88; nature of marriage, 199

Pius VII, contraception intrinsically evil, 202

Pius VIII, nature of marriage, 202

Pius IX, Church's authority over marriage, 91, 206, 292; inseparability of contract and sacrament, 88, 89; need for grace, 292

Pius X, St., Church's authority over marriage, 206, 292

Pius XI, abortion intrinsically evil, 202; Church's authority over marriage, 206, 292; contraception intrinsically evil, 56, 203f., 310; family, the foundation of society, 205; goods of marriage, 201ff.; gravity of offenses against conjugal fidelity, 204; inseparability of contract and sacrament, 89; marriage, teaching on, 107–46; see also *Casti connubii*

Pius XII, abortion intrinsically evil, 202; artificial fecundation immoral, 181f; conjugal love and procreation, 157–79; conjugal morality, 152–83; contraception intrinsically evil, 56, 157ff., 162ff.; 203, 304f., 310; contraceptive character of anovulant pills, 56, 272, 308; distinction between directly and indirectly intended, 164; gravity of offenses against conjugal fidelity, 204; family, the foundation of society, 205; family, role and rights of, 184ff.; licit use of infertile periods, 157ff., 165ff.; marriage in teaching of, 147–79; sex education, 179ff.; virginity, 190ff.;

Portillo, Alvaro del, Church and moral theology, 40

Possenti, V., task facing Church, 108

Potterie, Ignace de la, crisis in exegesis, 322

Rahner, Karl, dissent from *Humanae vitae,* 303; early recognition of infallibility of ordinary Magisterium, 30

Ratzinger, Joseph Cardinal, challenge of *Humanae vitae,* 24; continuity of Magisterium, 197; fidelity to Magisterium, 26, 28; indispensability of faith for theology, 41; marriage and virginity, 348; need for authority, 37

Redemptor hominis, Christ as the one who reveals man to himself, 44f.

Redondo, G., task facing Pius XI, 107f.

regalists, views of marriage, 79ff.

reformers, views on marriage, 66ff.

responsible parenthood, 273ff., 294f.

Rodriguez, A., rights of family, 209

Roman Rota, on ends of marriage, 192ff.

Ruether, Rosemary, dissenting views of, 26

Ryan, J., contraception in *Casti connubii,* 133

Ryan, R., forming a community of persons, 353

Sarmiento, A., on *Familiaris consortio*, 335

Sacra virginitas, 190ff.

Sancho, F., irregular marriage situations, 73

Schema receptum of *Gaudium et spes*, 212

Schillebeeckx, Edward, marriage as sacrament, 65

Schooyans, M., abortion and public policy, 371; task facing Church, 108

Scola, A., personalism of Karol Wojtyla, 350

sex education, 179ff.

Slovik, L. S., impact of divorce on children, 70

Smith, William B., authority of Magisterium, 305; critique of theology of dissent, 24, 32ff., 50

Soria, J. L., difference between contraception and periodic abstinence, 169; myth of overpopulation, 289

sterilization, intrinsically evil, 157, 202, 296f.

Stephen V., abortion intrinsically evil, 202

Tametsi, Tridentine decree on canonical form, 75f.

Tertullian, excellence of virginity, 229

Tettamanzi, Dionigi, authority of Magisterium, 306; background to *Humanae vitae*, 286; pastoral care of family, 375; significance of *Humanae vitae*, 301

textus denuo recognitus of *Gaudium et spes*, 212

textus recognitus of *Gaudium et spes*, 212

theology, anthropology and, 42; Magisterium and, 34ff.; metaphysics and, 42; science of faith, 34ff.

Theron, S., natural law in *Humanae vitae*, 295

Thomas Aquinas, St., conjugal love as good of marriage, 250; conscience, 51; ends of marriage, 193ff.; fidelity to Magisterium, 26; goods of marriage, 116f., 247; indispensability of faith for theology, 35, 39f.; Magisterium as proximate norm for theology, 41; moral absolutes, 61f.; need for guidance of Holy Spirit, 423; passion and mortal sin, 320; perfections of marriage, 253; requirements of virtue, 261

Thomasius, secular ideas on marriage and sexuality, 82

Toledo, First Council of, marriage and holiness, 201

totality, misuse of principle in Majority Opinion, 57f.

Trent, Council of, authority of Church over marriage, 206; decrees and canons on marriage, 69–77; marriage ordained to procreation and education of children, 199; sacrament of marriage and grace, 201; sanctity of marriage, 72

Vatican Council II, conditions for infallibility, 49ff.; conjugal love, duty to nourish, 269ff.; conjugal love, and procreation, inseparably connected, 256–62; conjugal love, role in structure of marriage, 234–56; conjugal morality, 268ff.; continuity with previous

Vatican Council II (*Continued*)
Magisterium, 196ff.; contraception
condemned, 56, 132, 276ff.;
goods of marriage, 119; legitimate
autonomy of earthly realities,
83f.; marriage, concept and nature
of, 264ff.; marriage, a vocation
to holiness, 202, 215ff.; moral
methodology, 198; objective
criteria for conjugal acts, 276ff.;
responsible parenthood, 273ff.;
rights of family, 205; stability of
human nature, 60; superiority of
virginity, 229; task assigned to,
207ff.; teaching on holiness of
marriage, novelty and importance
of, 219ff.; vocation of laity, 209;
see also *Gaudium et spes; Lumen
gentium; Apostolicam actuositatem*
*Vatican Instruction on Respect for
Human Life in Its Origin and on
the Dignity of Procreation (Donum
vitae)*, role of civil law, 86f.;
conjugal love and procreation,
294
Vermeersch, A., contraception in
Casti connubii, 133
Viladrich, J., conjugal consent and
marriage, 248; critique of Doms,
234

Vincent of Lerins, St., orthodox
doctrine, 195
virginity and marriage, 190ff., 201f.,
229f., 348
vocation, theological meaning of,
223ff.
Voltaire, attack on indissolubility,
82

Wojtyla, Karol, authority of
Magisterium, 306; difference
between contraception and
periodic abstinence, 167;
foundations of morality, 38;
freedom, 36; prophetic mission
of Magisterium, 22; significance
of *Humanae vitae*, 301; see also
John Paul II
woman, role of, 352f.
Wrenn, Michael, on *Familiaris
consortio*, 335

Zalba, Marcelino, authority of
Magisterium, 27, 305; critique of
Rahner, 303; statements of episco-
pal conferences on *Humanae vitae*,
415, 419
Zumaquero, J. M., rights of family
in education, 280
Zurich text of *Gaudium et spes*, 212